The San Francisco
Bay Area

MEL SCOTT

SECOND EDITION

The San Francisco Bay Area

A Metropolis in Perspective

UNIVERSITY OF CALIFORNIA PRESS
Berkeley   Los Angeles   London

University of California Press
Berkeley and Los Angeles, California

University of California Press, Ltd.
London, England

© 1959, 1985 by
The Regents of the University of California
Published 1959.   Second Edition 1985.

Library of Congress Cataloging in Publication Data

Scott, Mel, 1906–
The San Francisco Bay Area.

Bibliography: p.
Includes index.
1. Regional planning—California—San Francisco Bay
Area—History. 2. San Francisco Metropolitan Area—
History. I. Title.
HT393.C32S2465   1985   307.7′64′097946   84-24152
ISBN 0-520-05510-1
ISBN 0-520-05512-8 (pbk.)

Printed in the United States of America

1 2 3 4 5 6 7 8 9

To Gerrie

Contents

Preface

When the first edition of this book appeared in the fall of 1959, it had been preceded by many other histories of California and the cities and towns around San Francisco Bay, but none of these earlier volumes had focused sharply and exclusively on the physical growth and development of the nine counties bordering on the great estuarial system—the metropolitan region generally recognized as constituting the San Francisco Bay Area. The work was a pioneer effort to trace the influence of time and geography on the planning and replanning of cities and to delineate the emergence of an interdependent, closely linked metropolitan complex extending into the several valleys whose watercourses drain into the bay.

Published in a small edition, the book was out of print in a few years and unavailable to the public except in libraries. In time it disappeared from some of these institutions, to the frustration of many people who wished to make use of it. In recent years rare book dealers have advertised for copies at the request of patrons who have had some particular need for the work. I am therefore pleased that the University of California Press has decided to publish a second edition, as a historical document, with no changes in the original text but with an additional chapter summarizing developments of the past twenty-five years. All too rarely does an author have an opportunity to reflect on what he has previously written and to continue his historical account, lending further perspective to the perspective he had formerly deemed relatively broad.

Early in the 1970's one of the editors of the Press asked me to consider preparing a new edition of the book, but for numerous personal reasons I did not wish to undertake the work. Now, more than a decade later, I am indeed glad that I declined. Hindsight has shown that many important movements were then in midcourse, their outcomes uncertain; others had not yet gathered enough momentum to be clearly discernible as irreversible changes that would decisively affect the entire region. The conclusion is inescapable that one should not attempt to update history until a sufficient span of time has elasped—a generation, or approximately a quarter century.

Readers doubtless will note that there is some shift of emphasis in the new chapter, with less attention given to the evolving physical form of the metropolitan conurbation and more to the governmental agencies responsible for guiding the uses of land and the development of the transportation systems serving the various parts. The reason for this change in approach is that governments of all kinds—local, regional, state, and national—have become much more influential than they were in the 1950's, when the main text of the book was written. Moreover, several new regional agencies have appeared on the scene, each exercising a function not previously considered essential. The multiplication of agencies and programs reflects the growing complexity of metropolitan affairs, the increase in population, the advent of new technologies and new problems, and the greater public awareness of the need for regulation to protect valuable natural resources and scenic assets.

In the preface to the first edition I questioned whether the majority of residents of the Bay Area thought of the region as a single entity, as did some politicians and some outstanding business and professional leaders. And one of my reasons for wanting to write a history of the area was to disseminate knowledge of how it had become an interrelated community. "If history demonstrates anything," I wrote, "it demonstrates that great achievement, civic or national, is possible only when all elements of a society are conscious of a common heritage and enjoy the prospects of individual benefit in a future to which all contribute." I should like to think that in the past two and a half decades the number of residents who are capable of thinking regionally has tellingly increased, since freeways and transit systems enable people to travel more widely and since the decisions of regional agencies have a more direct bearing on their lives. Sectionalism persists, to be sure, but in such matters as the control of air and water pollution, transportation, the preservation of San Francisco Bay, and the long-term assurance of adequate water supplies, people more and more are obliged to take an areawide view. In such matters they must voice their concerns to regional boards, or at least to subregional agencies whose policies reflect consideration of the welfare of the metropolitan population. If the region has not yet been welded into a cohesive urban community, it is certainly a good deal less hampered by political boundary lines and geographic barriers than it was at the beginning of the 'sixties, as I have sought to show in the new final chapter.

Endeavoring to bring any history up to date is a bit like trying to take a photograph of a wriggling youngster. Something is going to be blurred. The significance of trends and events cannot be fully understood or even divined. So one hazards interpretations and indulges in tentative forecasts, knowing that time may reveal them to be partly or altogether erroneous. Some persons would say, furthermore, that a writer of history has no business making projections into the future, but should be content with illuminating the past. So dynamic is the San Francisco Bay Area, however, that the temptation to speculate on the next ten or fifteen years is irresistible. The new chapter therefore concludes with a few observations about the prospects of the region, based on consideration of certain developments that seem prophetic.

For readers who would like a view of the region not limited mainly to its physical organization, I should like to mention a collection of short essays recently issued by the Institute of Governmental Studies at the University of California, Berkeley (with which I was associated during most of the 1960's and to whose staff I am indebted for much assistance in producing the additional chapter). *Golden Gate Metropolis*, by Charles Wollenberg, does not pretend to be a comprehensive history of the Bay Area, even though it sweeps along from the period of Spanish settlement in lands occupied for centuries by Native Americans to the Gold Rush, the era of clipper ships, the coming of the railroads,

the violent earthquake of 1906, and on through the present century to the tumultuous 'sixties and the volatile activities of Silicon Valley in the 'seventies and early 'eighties. Wollenberg is fascinated, above all, by the individuals and groups who helped to make Bay Area history, and his essays are rich in human interest. The perspective throughout is regional, making the collection fortuitously complementary to this volume.

Many of the persons who aided me with my research in the 1950's and gave me valuable advice after reading preliminary drafts are no longer living and probably would not be known to most present-day readers, but a few colleagues at the University of California, Berkeley, to whom I expressed gratitude in my original preface are still deeply involved in regional activities and have been as generous as ever in helping me prepare a concise account of developments in recent decades. Victor Jones, professor emeritus of political science, not only lent me several of his own papers on regional governance but also suggested many other sources of information, read and criticized drafts, and acted as chief counsel and sparring partner. T. J. Kent, Jr., who was chairman of the Department of City and Regional Planning when I began work on this history in the early 'fifties and is now a professor emeritus, has offered detailed criticism of the new chapter and has provided welcome information about People for Open Space, on whose executive committee he serves. Corwin Mocine, also a professor emeritus of city and regional planning, reviewed the manuscript of the new chapter and gave suggestions based on his own extensive experience in the area.

My friends Eugene C. Lee and Stanley Scott, director and assistant director, respectively, of the Institute of Governmental Studies, permitted me to use their own and several student papers which provided information about the activities of important regional agencies. Scott, author of *Governing California's Coast* and editor of an Institute publication on coastal conservation, also answered questions about the programs of the state and regional coastal commissions.

I wish to thank Daniel Luten, formerly a lecturer in the Department of Geography on the Berkeley campus, for giving me the benefit of his specialized knowledge of the metropolitan region.

To Lawrence D. Dahms, executive director of the Metropolitan Transportation Commission, I am indebted for reviewing a draft of the section on the commission and for providing some details I needed. Dian Gillmar, information coordinator of the agency, made available many annual reports and copies of speeches by Mr. Dahms that were especially helpful to me. In addition, she lent me documents in the commission's library that I found useful.

Patricia R. Perry, coordinator of the Census Center of the

Association of Bay Area Governments, and Nora Juarbe, a member of the staff of the San Francisco Bay Area Council, readily responded to my requests for analyses of census data.

In preparing the section on regional parks, I made use of reports and data provided by Eugene Erba, program analyst of the California Department of Parks and Recreation; Linda L. Chew, development administrator of the East Bay Regional Park District; Charlotte MacDonald, public communications coordinator of the Midpeninsula Regional Open Space District; and Barbara Ott, a member of the staff of the Santa Clara County Planning Department. I thank them for their cooperation.

Brian Wilson, a member of the Save San Francisco Bay Association, generously consented to compile a summary of major permits issued by the Bay Conservation and Development Commission from 1974 to 1983.

Sonny M. Ismail, public relations representative of the Port of Oakland, provided information about the growth of the port in recent decades, together with photographs of port terminals. I appreciate his assistance.

I have drawn so liberally on a few works that I wish to express special indebtedness to the authors and to list their names and the titles of their studies here rather than in the bibliography: Deidre A. Heitman, *The Association of Bay Area Governments: A Critical Look at the Bay Area's Regional Planning Agency*, a University of California, Berkeley, senior honors thesis in a political science course offered by Professors Lee and Jones in 1982; John Martin Eells, *Local Agency Formation Commission Spheres of Influence: Effective Planning for the Urban Fringe?*, a University of Cali-

fornia, Berkeley, master's thesis in the Department of City and Regional Planning, issued in 1977 as Working Paper 77-3 by the Institute of Governmental Studies; David W. Jones, Jr., Robert Taggart, and Edith Dorosin, *The Metropolitan Transportation Commission: An Innovative Experiment in Incremental Planning; A Cautious Experiment in Regionalism*, Stanford Transportation Research Program, Stanford University, August, 1974.

The passage of time has not diminished my appreciation of the help Charles Richard Dunann gave me as my research assistant when I was writing this book in the 1950's. The handsome historical maps he prepared to illustrate the volume continue to be one of its best features.

Since Dorothy Huggins, who edited the first edition, is still enjoying life, I wish to thank her again for ironing out inconsistencies of style, punctuation, and capitalization and for insisting that I rewrite some awkward sentences. She was a most capable editor, paying meticulous attention to detail.

I hardly know how to thank James H. Clark, director of the University of California Press, and William J. McClung, editorial director, for their willingness to reissue this history with a new preface and an additional chapter. Their confidence that there is a new readership for the book has lightened the work of compressing the developments of the past twenty-five years into a limited number of pages. May their faith in the venture be well rewarded.

I especially appreciate the very capable editorial services of Sheila Levine and Mary Renaud, who guided this preface and the last chapter from manuscript to printed page.

MEL SCOTT

The San Francisco
Bay Area

CHAPTER ONE

Heritage

Imagine, if you can, the San Francisco Bay Area without the bay. Geologists tell us that there was a time, fifteen to twenty-five thousand years ago, when the vast area now occupied by the bay was a long coastal valley. To the northeast a deep canyon connected this valley with the Central Valley, and through this canyon, which is now Carquinez Strait, flowed a great trunk river, carrying the runoff of the entire interior of California.

As the mighty current emerged from the canyon, it swung westward toward the Marin hills, passed through the narrow part of the valley now submerged beneath the waters of San Pablo Strait, curved southward round a hill known today as Angel Island, and finally flowed through the precipitous walls of Golden Gate Canyon into the Pacific Ocean. The depth of this river may have been as much as thirty feet.

Somewhere near the hill that we call Angel Island another river joined this one. A smaller stream, it coursed through the southern part of the elongated valley, collecting the runoff from what is now the Santa Clara Valley and from the slopes and mountains that enclose the southern arm of present San Francisco Bay.

Exactly what caused the inundation of the long trough valley by the waters of the Pacific no one knows. Drowned valleys can be produced by depression or subsidence of the land. But a theory now rather widely accepted attributes the formation of San Francisco Bay to the rise of the ocean level from the melting of the great ice sheet of the last glacial period. As the waters crept through the gorge at the mouth of the trunk river, they gradually covered

not only the coastal valley but also a low area east of Carquinez Canyon, filled today by Suisun Bay. In all, more than four hundred and fifty square miles of valley lands disappeared beneath the invading flood.

How different the metropolitan scene would now be if the waters of the Pacific Ocean had remained outside the Golden Gate! The center of the valley, between Angel Island and Yerba Buena Island and about opposite the end of the abandoned Berkeley Pier, might be the heart of an enormous metropolis, discernible from the distant hills as a cluster of skyscrapers. And in the shadows of these tall buildings ships might be loading at docks along the trunk river. To the north, to the south, to the east, and to the west the metropolis would cover mile after square mile of the valley, its pattern of streets broken here and there by the hills we see as islands—Alcatraz, Angel, Yerba Buena, Brooks, and many smaller islands. But the mosaic of blocks and structures would be recognizably a single urban form. Even though it might be divided politically into many municipalities, as is the sprawling urban complex of the Los Angeles basin, its underlying physical unity would be apparent to the dullest eye.

Because a bay now fills the valley, many residents of the San Francisco Bay Area are scarcely aware that they live in what is essentially a single metropolis. The bay splits the urban pattern into several parts, and there is not one center but two: San Francisco on the west side of the bay and Oakland on the east side. Yet the cities, some eighty in all, are so interdependent, economically and socially, and the problems they face—air pollution, vanishing open space, bay pollution, inadequate transit, uncoördinated planning—are so pervasive that the oneness of the area cannot be denied. Smog respects no city and county boundaries, and the people in six of the nine counties bordering on the bay have already acknowledged that they must deal with it collectively. The air pollution control district they formed in 1955 does not yet include the three northern counties of the Bay Area (Sonoma, Napa, and Solano); but some political scientists regard this district, which has on its governing board representatives of both cities and counties, as the beginning of metropolitan government. Perhaps it is only a matter of time until population growth and mounting problems will force recognition of the actual regional city or regional metropolis. And when that time comes, undoubtedly the voters of the regional metropolis will devise some appropriate form of metropolitan government.

In the meantime, the cities only occasionally act in concert. The jealousies and rivalries of more than a century of urban growth and development in the San Francisco Bay Area plague them. The bay at times seems a sinister element, encouraging competition between ports, political bickering over the location of additional bridges, and endless arguments over whether industries discharging wastes into its waters are being properly regulated. Yet the bay is also a unifying force. The people who live around its shore are one in their pride in its universally attested magnificence. It is an incomparable harbor, a huge recreation area for fishermen and yachtsmen, the one great open space that will never be entirely lost to metropolitan dwellers, no matter how many tideland reclamation projects reduce the area of its surface.

The history of the regional metropolis encircling this great bay is a paradoxical one, in which, as in a kind of morality play, the forces of division struggle with the forces of unity. One can understand the present difficulties in solving area-wide problems only if he knows this complex history. One can take hope only if he sees what has already been accomplished. Physically the area is well on the way toward integration. The principal problems now are political, not technical. History is not lacking in suggestions for solving them. Even an account dealing primarily with the physical growth and development of the Bay Area, as this one does, must accord the prophets of metropolitan planning and metropolitan federation special notice, in the hope that their dreams will come true.

The First Inhabitants

The story of man's occupancy of this area begins, of course, with the Indians. Each of the various tribes living in what is now the San Francisco Bay Area had its roughly defined territory. The Costanoans inhabited the San Francisco Peninsula and most of present-day Santa Clara, Alameda, and Contra Costa counties. The Coast Miwok occupied the Marin Peninsula and the southern part of Sonoma County. The Pomo held the upper part of Sonoma County and the territory to the north. The Wappo regarded themselves as having proprietary rights to the Napa Valley. Solano and Yolo counties were the home of the southern Wintun. The Yokuts dwelt in eastern Contra Costa County and San Joaquin County. Natural barriers such as mountain ranges and the bay thus tended to define the areas belonging to each tribe, although the divisions of territory were not exactly what one might expect from a study of the topography. The pattern of Indian occupancy does suggest, however, that any human beings living in the Bay Area would be inclined to think of it as being composed of several divisions. And certainly the Europeans and Americans who none too gradually ousted the Indians after their thirty-five hundred years or more of occupancy did tend to think of it in this way, even though they recognized an over-all unity in the area.

Confused Explorers

The discoverers of San Francisco Bay, Don Gaspar de Portolá and his band of some sixty soldiers, priests, Christian Indians, muleteers, and servants, at first thought of their find as an immense estuary that blocked their way to the only Bay of San Francisco that they had heard of, the little bay near Point Reyes now known as Drakes Bay which had been given the name *Bahia de San Francisco* by the mariner Sebastian Rodríguez Cermeño in 1595. Joseph González Cabrera Bueno, pilot of one of the Manila galleons that annually made the perilous voyage from the Philippines to Acapulco, had described this small bay in some detail in a book on navigation published in Madrid in 1734, and this description the members of the Portolá expedition had with them.

The entire episode of discovery is one of confusion compounded by confusion. In the first place, Portolá and his followers were not trying to reach any Bay of San Francisco but to rediscover the port of Monterey, which the seventeenth-century adventurer Sebastian Vizcaíno had visited in 1602 and had extolled as a superlative haven—exactly the place for the richly laden Manila galleons to take on fresh water and supplies after months of beating across the north Pacific. For more than one hundred and sixty-five years Spain had not bothered to follow up Vizcaíno's explorations by colonizing Alta California or by making provision for a refreshing break

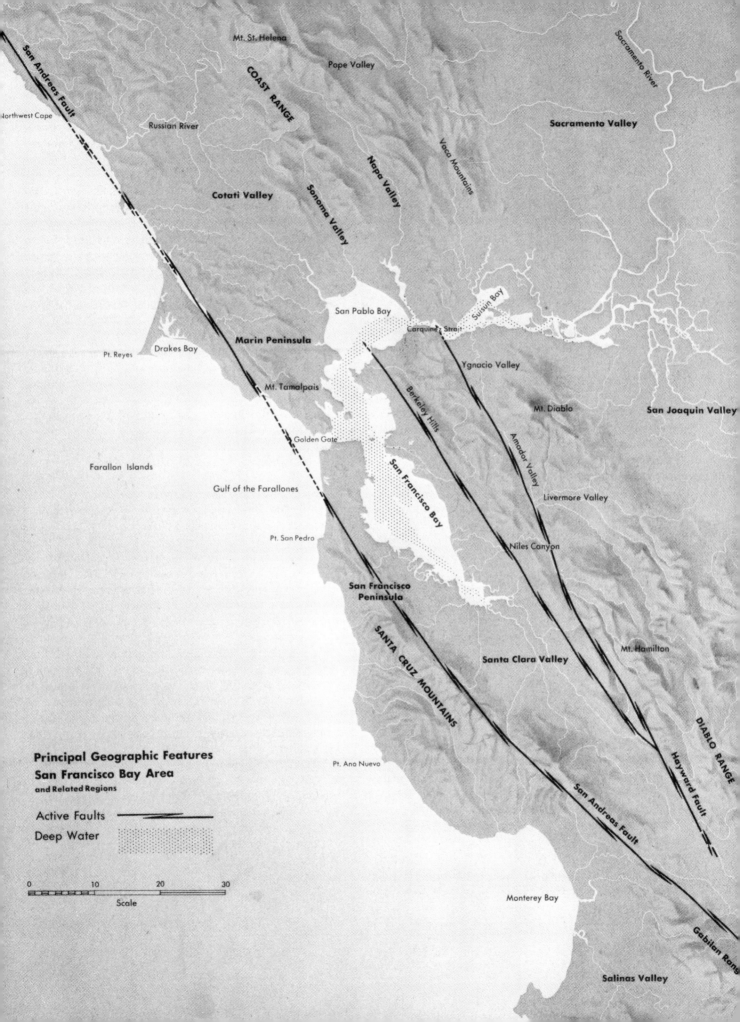

Northwest Cape

San Andreas Fault

Russian River

Mt. St. Helena

Pope Valley

COAST RANGE

Vaca Mountains

Sacramento River

Sacramento Valley

Cotati Valley

Sonoma Valley

Napa Valley

Pt. Reyes

Drakes Bay

Marin Peninsula

San Pablo Bay

Suisun Bay

Carquinez Strait

Ygnacio Valley

Mt. Tamalpais

Berkeley Hills

Mt. Diablo

San Joaquin Valley

Golden Gate

Farallon Islands

San Francisco Bay

Amador Valley

Gulf of the Farallones

Livermore Valley

Pt. San Pedro

Niles Canyon

San Francisco Peninsula

SANTA CRUZ MOUNTAINS

Santa Clara Valley

Mt. Hamilton

DIABLO RANGE

**Principal Geographic Features
San Francisco Bay Area**
and Related Regions

Pt. Ano Nuevo

Active Faults

Deep Water

San Andreas Fault

Hayward Fault

0   10   20   30

Scale

Monterey Bay

Gabilan Range

Salinas Valley

in the tedious journeys of the galleons at Monterey. But in 1769 uneasiness over possible Russian interest in this most remote of lands to which Spain claimed sovereignty moved Charles III to approve a program for its occupation. Marching wearily north from the first settlement at San Diego, Portolá and his followers reached Monterey Bay near the mouth of the Salinas River. Failing to recognize any of the landmarks mentioned in Vizcaíno's account of the area, the captain and his men pressed on up the coast, still searching for the long-lost port.

They were far up the San Francisco Peninsula when they found their progress arrested by the great bulk of Montara Mountain. Dispirited, half-starved, and soaked by an early rain, they decided to camp beside a creek near the base of the mountain. The next day, October 31, 1769, was fair, and the sea sparkled as they climbed a westward flank of the mountain to survey the coast ahead. To the west were several small islands. Forty miles to the north a long headland jutted into the sea. Not far from it rose some white cliffs. From the maps of Vizcaíno and from the description of Cabrera Bueno they at length recognized the headland as Point Reyes, the islands as the Farallones, and the flashing waters before them as the Gulf of the Farallones. They now knew that they had passed Monterey, but Portolá decided that he would not turn back without making a reconnaissance of Point Reyes and Cermeño's Bahía de San Francisco.

This is the little bay in which Francis Drake is believed to have reconditioned the *Golden Hind* in 1579 before sailing across the Pacific on his celebrated piratical voyage round the world. Thirty-seven years before Drake's visit, the explorer Juan Rodríguez Cabrillo, the first European to chart the coast of California, had noted the harbor but had been unable to land there because of a storm. He had sailed on southward past the Golden Gate without realizing that an enormous anchorage lay behind the hills. Cermeño, a Portuguese commissioned by the Viceroy of New Spain to make a search for safe ports on the California coast where the Manila galleons could allow their scurvy-ridden crews to recuperate, brought his *San Agustín* to anchor under the headland of Point Reyes sixteen years after Drake's sojourn on the coast. Cermeño's ship, carrying a fabulous cargo of silk, wax, porcelain, and spices, was totally wrecked by a sudden storm. Fortunately the crew had already put ashore a launch, more or less dismantled, on which they were working when the vessel foundered. In this craft, the *San Buenaventura*, they had intended to make careful explorations close to shore. Had they done so, they might have come upon the entrance to the great body of water now known as San Francisco Bay. But in their anxiety to

return to Mexico before the winter grew worse, they provisioned the launch as best they could, headed toward the Farallones, and made their way down the coast, having given the small bay in the lee of Point Reyes the name that was to confuse historians and later explorers, among them Portolá.

Discovery of the Bay

In the faint hope that a packet named the *San José*, dispatched from San Blas in Mexico with supplies for the Alta California colonists, might by some remote chance be awaiting him in this little harbor, Portolá ordered Sergeant José Francisco de Ortega and some scouts to proceed to Point Reyes and return within three days. They set out after Mass on Wednesday morning, November 1, following the coast.

Portolá remembered what the Visitor General of New Spain, José de Gálvez, had promised Father Junípero Serra when the two were discussing plans for the first three missions that the Franciscan was to establish in Alta California. In reply to Serra's hurt remonstrance that none of the three was to be named for St. Francis, Gálvez had remarked: "If St. Francis wants a mission, let him cause his port to be discovered, and it will be placed there."[1] Should Ortega reach the Bahía de San Francisco, Gálvez would have no choice but to authorize the president of the missions to build an establishment on its shore dedicated to Francis of Assisi.

The day after Ortega departed, some of the soldiers in the camp begged permission to go into the near-by mountains to hunt for deer. Returning after dark, they reported having seen from the crest of the Santa Cruz Mountains "an immense arm of the sea, or an estuary, which penetrated into the land as far as the eye could reach, extending to the southeast."[2]

Puzzled, Father Juan Crespi, one of the two priests in the expedition, consulted the description of the Bahía de San Francisco by Cabrera Bueno and concluded that the waters seen by the hunters must be the estuary mentioned as leading inland from the main bay under Point Reyes. There is such an inner bay, known today as Drakes Estero.

Toward evening on Friday, November 3, Ortega and his scouts returned to the base camp on San Pedro Creek, bringing some extraordinary news. They had found their route along the coast intercepted by an immense "estuary" that penetrated far inland and branched to the north and to the south. Indians they met in their march had signified, they thought, that there was a port or a ship at the head of the *estero*.

The band of hunters and Ortega's group had both

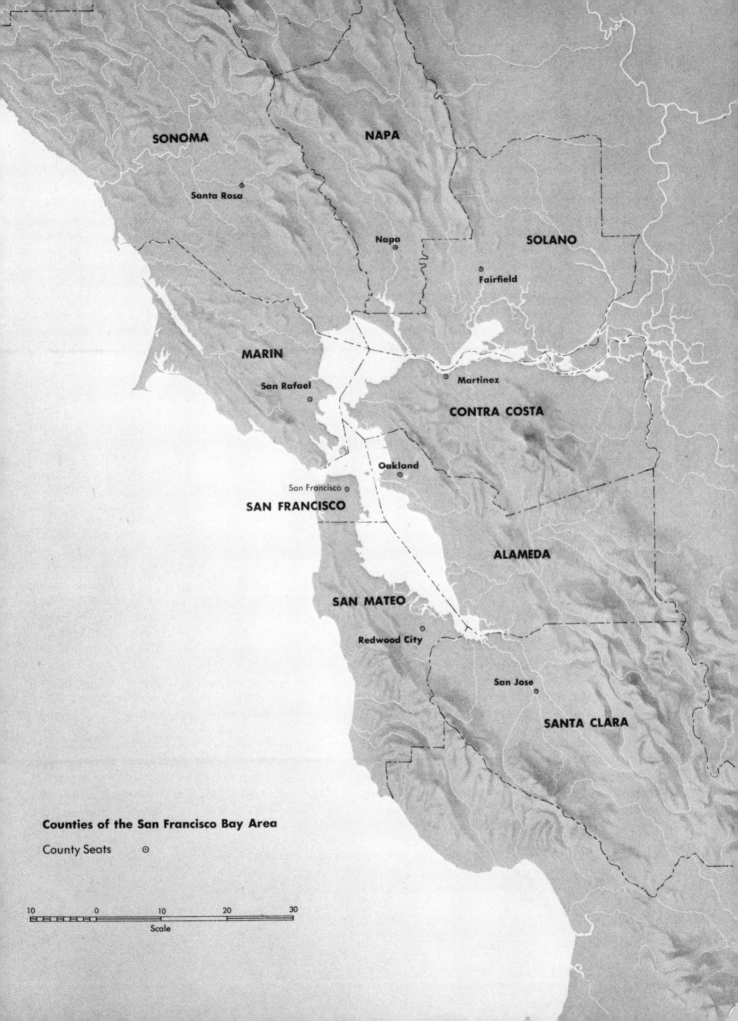

SONOMA

NAPA

SOLANO

Santa Rosa

Napa

Fairfield

MARIN

San Rafael

Martinez

CONTRA COSTA

Oakland

San Francisco

SAN FRANCISCO

ALAMEDA

SAN MATEO

Redwood City

San Jose

SANTA CLARA

Counties of the San Francisco Bay Area

County Seats   ⊙

10   0   10   20   30
Scale

discovered the greatest natural harbor on the Pacific Coast, but the import of the discovery entirely escaped them at the moment. The expedition was single-mindedly intent on reaching the bay near Point Reyes. This meant that they had to circumvent the *estero*.

Discouragement and Retreat

Portolá and the whole force crossed the mountains on the east, traveled southeastward through the San Andreas Valley, and on November 6 camped on San Francisquito Creek near the future site of Stanford University. The captain then began to doubt the wisdom of proceeding round the southern arm of the *estero* without knowing more about what to expect. He again sent out Ortega and his scouts, who turned the southern end of the bay and journeyed northward "eight or ten leagues" before being forced by hostile Indians to retrace their steps. Ortega's estimate that the *estero* "extended inland more than eighteen leagues"[3] (47.64 miles) indicates that he arrived at some point from which he could see the full length of the bay; but Portolá bitterly wrote in his diary that his scouts "had found nothing."[4]

The captain and his men had concluded, in their confusion, that Cabrera Bueno's description of the Bahia de San Francisco applied to the whole open Gulf of the Farallones and that the newly discovered great bay was the diminutive estuary today known as Drakes Estero. This misunderstanding was to continue for some years, until the unique nature of the new-found bay was realized and it ceased to be an *estero* and became instead the *Gran Puerto de San Francisco*, or San Francisco Bay.

The wanderers returned to San Diego, pausing en route at Monterey a second time without identifying it as the object of their search. Their unintended explorations north of that point had accomplished much more than Portolá appreciated. The expedition had raised the curtain on an area that within six or seven decades was increasingly to become the focus of the expansionist ambitions of the nation that was about to be formed on the east coast of America—the United States. An early consequence of the discovery of San Francisco Bay was to be the founding of a mission named for St. Francis and the establishment of a presidio, or military outpost. But since Portolá had not actually reached the supposed port of St. Francis, he left that task to others, thereby setting the stage for further discoveries.

Discovery of Interior Valleys

Young Pedro Fages, who succeeded Portolá as governor of Alta California, was the next to attempt to bypass San Francisco Bay on the east in order to reach Cermeño's Bahia de San Francisco. In the fall of 1770, some months after Monterey Bay had finally been rediscovered, Fages blazed a new trail to the San Francisco Bay Area through the Salinas and Santa Clara valleys. From the southern tip of the bay he made his way along the *contra costa*, or eastern side, through the sites of the present-day cities of Oakland, Berkeley, and Richmond. But when scouts who had been sent ahead reported that the *estero* continued indefinitely, he decided to turn back, for he feared to be too long away from Monterey and his regular responsibilities.

In the spring of 1772 Fages returned to the Bay Area with official instructions to explore the "Port of San Francisco"—that is, what is now called Drakes Bay—and look for a suitable site for a mission. Accompanied by Father Juan Crespi and a small company of soldiers, he again marched through the Salinas and Santa Clara valleys, along the route that was to become the regular line of travel between the provincial capital at Monterey and Bay Area settlements. As before, he proceeded up the eastern side of San Francisco Bay. He saw the Farallones through the Golden Gate from the slopes of the Berkeley Hills and continued northward along San Pablo Bay. Still following the shoreline, he swung eastward along Carquinez Strait and Suisin Bay until marshlands forced him inland to Willow Pass, in the hills between present-day Concord and Pittsburg. From the summit of the pass an amazing prospect greeted him and his companions—the vast interior valley of California and the snow-crowned Sierra far in the distance. Flowing into Suisun Bay from the east was the broad San Joaquin River, which Fages christened the *Rio Grande de San Francisco*. To the north he could also see the Sacramento River. In the vicinity of present-day Antioch, Fages concluded that there was no possibility of getting across or around the waters and marshes at the eastern end of Suisun Bay. He turned back, having discovered an inland domain so extensive and seemingly so remote that both Spain and Mexico were to leave it largely untouched during their years of rule in California.

On the return to Monterey the explorers opened another new route, later to be much used by gold seekers hurrying from Monterey and San Jose to Carquinez Strait and the river routes to the Mother Lode country. Moving southward, Fages and his men followed a series of valleys on the eastern side of the Berkeley Hills. They traversed in succession the Ygnacio, San Ramon, Livermore, and Sunol valleys until they came to Niles Canyon and marched west. As they passed through these warm, pleasant vales, Mount Diablo was on their left, a lonely peak only a little more than thirty-eight hundred feet high

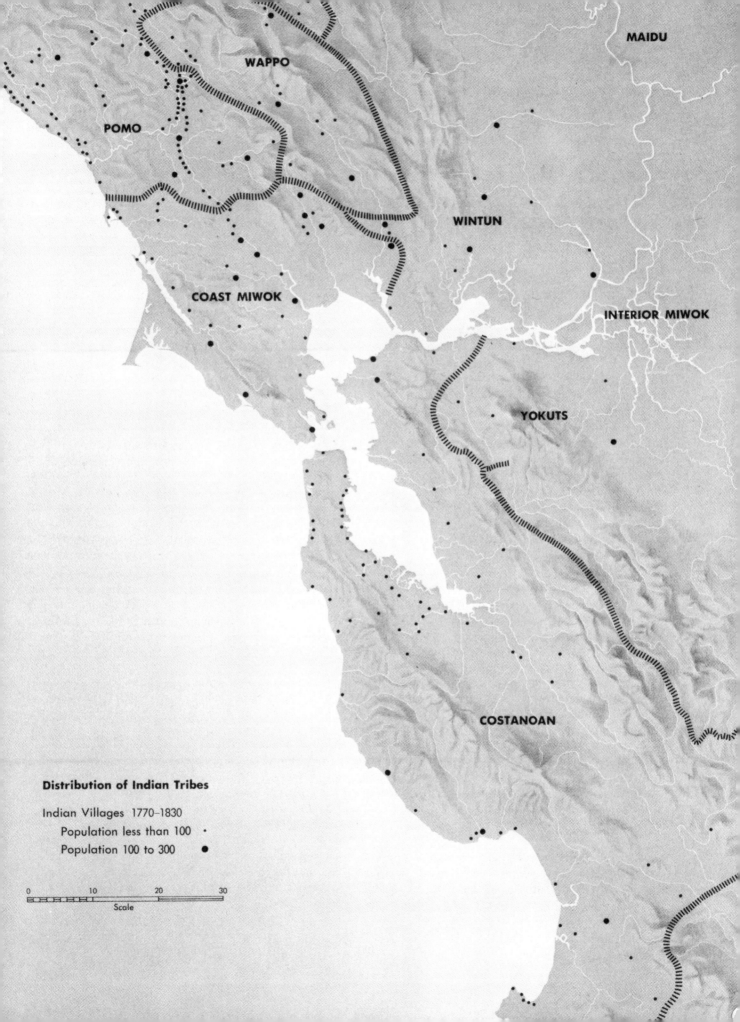

MAIDU

WAPPO

POMO

WINTUN

COAST MIWOK

INTERIOR MIWOK

YOKUTS

COSTANOAN

Distribution of Indian Tribes

Indian Villages 1770–1830

    Population less than 100 ·

    Population 100 to 300 ●

0   10   20   30

Scale

but with a majesty belying its actual height. From its summit the governor and his soldiers could have surveyed the entire Bay Area and the greater part of the Central Valley. Perhaps they wondered how much one could see from this serene landmark. But, homeward bound and eager to report their discoveries, they indulged in no side excursions. Emerging from Niles Canyon, they went southward past the future site of Mission San Jose on the gently rolling lands overlooking the southern shores of the bay, and then down the Santa Clara Valley again to Monterey.

Survey of the Bay

The Spanish colonists now began to appreciate that the so-called Estuary of San Francisco was indeed an extraordinary body of water. Yet it was not until 1775, when preparations were at last under way for the founding of San Francisco, that a detailed survey of the bay was undertaken—this time by boat. At twilight on August 5 of that year the first vessel ever to enter San Francisco Bay sailed slowly through the Golden Gate against the strong, outflowing tide. She was the supply ship *San Carlos*, under the command of Juan Manuel de Ayala, who had orders not only to take soundings and make observations throughout the bay but also to assist an overland party from Monterey in the construction of houses for settlers whom Juan Bautista de Anza, a frontier captain, was then gathering together on the west coast of what is now Mexico and in the outpost of Tubac, near the site of present-day Tucson.

Ayala himself was unable to participate in the exploration of the bay because he had been wounded in the foot by the accidental discharge of a double-barreled pistol. He entrusted the actual reconnaissance to José de Cañizares, first pilot, and to Juan Bautista Aguirre, second pilot. In the forty-four days that the *San Carlos* remained in the bay, anchored most of the time off Angel Island, Cañizares made three voyages in the ship's boat to the northern parts of the bay, exploring San Pablo Bay, Carquinez Strait, and Suisun Bay to the mouth of the San Joaquin River. Aguirre surveyed the southern arm of the bay. From information collected by the two, Cañizares prepared a report and a chart showing the great bay as a separate entity, in no way connected with the Bahia de San Francisco (Drakes Bay). Thus at last the importance of San Francisco Bay was recognized. In his report Cañizares said that it was "not one harbor, but many."[5]

Cañizares' map, known officially as Ayala's map, was somewhat vague about the northern shore of San Pablo Bay and left unanswered a question raised that year by the mariner Juan Francisco de la Bodega y Cuadra, who on his return from a voyage to northern waters had discovered Bodega Bay in what is now Sonoma County: Was this coastal bay in some way connected with San Francisco Bay? That it was not was proved the following year when Cañizares and others reëxamined San Pablo Bay and rowed up Petaluma Creek.

On September 18, 1775, Ayala in the *San Carlos* sailed back to Monterey, having seen nothing of the overland party that was to assist his crew in building houses for Anza's colonists. When, somewhat later, Father Francisco Palóu and others arrived from Monterey, they, too, were disappointed to find no one to aid them in preparing shelters for the prospective settlers. The work of creating a presidio and a mission at San Francisco remained for the colonists who were at the time more than eleven hundred miles away, about to begin their long trek across blazing deserts and high, cold mountains.

Colonists for San Francisco

The recruitment of settlers for San Francisco in the northern provinces of New Spain was part of an ambitious plan to open and maintain an overland supply route to Alta California from Sonora. The precarious condition of the establishments in the new province suggested that some means more dependable and faster than the two supply ships *San Carlos* and *San Antonio* should be found for transporting provisions to them. Time and again these vessels were long delayed on the dangerous voyage from San Blas, in what is now the Mexican state of Nayarit, while the colonists at San Diego, Monterey, San Antonio, San Luis Obispo, and San Gabriel all but starved. The newcomers had as yet made little progress in cultivating the soil, and the Indian neophytes at the missions had scarcely learned even the rudiments of farming. Practically everything required for subsistence had to be brought by sea. So difficult was the problem of sustaining the little settlements on the distant periphery of civilization that officials in New Spain more than once talked of abandoning the Alta California venture. But at the moment when the future of the province appeared blackest, Anza had come forth with a proposal to the viceroy, Antonio Bucareli, that he be commissioned to explore a route from the frontier in Sonora to Monterey. This hazardous route the hardy captain had opened in 1774, and over it he led the 240 colonists for San Francisco in the fall of 1775 and the winter of 1775–76.

The wayfarers arrived in Monterey on March 10, 1776, after a journey from Tubac of 130 days. They were the first and last large party to travel the overland route. The unenlightened policy of the commandant general of the frontier provinces, Teodoro de Croix, fanned the flames of resentment among the Indians of the Gila-Colorado region until the Yumas, roused to savage fury, massacred the Spaniards in two settlements on the west bank of the Colorado River in 1781 and exterminated the soldiers accompanying a party of colonists on their way to California. Thereafter the overland route to the coast remained closed except to small military groups. Upon his arrival in Monterey, Anza fully believed that he had started an immigration movement that would make Alta California more populous and prosperous, as well as permanently Spanish. Had it not been for the indifference and temporizing of one official, California might indeed have become deeply rooted in Latin culture—and perhaps it would have been a good deal more difficult for Americans later to incorporate into a republic with a predominantly Anglo-Saxon political and social heritage.

While the future residents of San Francisco remained at Monterey, Anza set off to select sites for the presidio and mission they were to build. His instructions from Viceroy Bucareli also bade him select a site somewhere else in the Bay Area for a second mission and explore further the Rio Grande de San Francisco that Fages had discovered. Anza was accompanied by ten soldiers and by Father Pedro Font and Lieutenant José Joaquín Moraga, who had made the arduous trek from Tubac with him. Among the soldiers was one who had journeyed with Fages to the Rio de San Francisco four years earlier, and another to whom the trip up the San Francisco Peninsula was familiar, for he had been over the same ground in 1774 when Father Palóu and Fernando de Rivera y Moncada, successor of Fages, were also prospecting for mission sites. This veteran of the reconnaissance of 1774 guided Anza to the tip of the peninsula by way of the San Andreas Valley, the west flank of the San Bruno Mountains, and Lake Merced. The march from Monterey took four days.

Sites for Presidio and Mission

The party camped on the banks of Mountain Lake, now on the southern edge of the San Francisco Presidio. After a day spent in intensive exploration of the terrain in the area, Anza was satisfied that the mesa "a gunshot away" from the lake was an excellent site for a fort settlement. From this high point "one sees a large part of the port and its islands, as far as the other side, the mouth of the harbor, and of the sea all that the sight can take in as far as beyond the farallones," Father Font wrote.[6] Anza's decision designating this area as a military reservation has never been reversed. Until airplanes and nuclear weapons were invented, it was one of the most strategic locations to be found in the San Francisco Bay Area.

On the third day of exploration, Anza, Font, and Moraga reached "a beautiful arroyo which, because it was Friday of Sorrows, we called the Arroyo de los Dolores."[7] A little stream emerging from the hills impressed Father Font as being adequate for irrigation and for operation of a small mill. To test the soil, Moraga planted a little maize and some chick-peas. All three agreed that here the mission of St. Francis should be built, near the head of a slope that stretched gently down to the little bay now known as Mission Bay. The site was about three miles from that chosen for the presidio.

Father Font and other priests thought that the Arroyo de San Mateo, farther down the peninsula, would be an appropriate site for the second mission planned by the viceroy; but as matters turned out, that mission was built on a site near Guadalupe Creek in the northern part of the Santa Clara Valley. As Anza and his cohorts rounded the southern end of the bay on their way to explore the Rio Grande de San Francisco, the soldier who had accompanied Rivera and Father Palóu in 1774 pointed out the location that had pleased them. Anza noted the advantages of the valley for settlement: the level terrain, the rich soil, and streams which would supply the needed water.

But the leader of the San Francisco colonists learned no more than Fages about the San Joaquin River. The tule marshes blocked his progress, and besides, Father Font convinced him, after much argument, that the Rio Grande was not a river at all, but a fresh-water sea. The excursion to the river was noteworthy chiefly because on the return trip to Monterey Anza crossed the Diablo Range from the east and emerged at the southern end of the Santa Clara Valley in the vicinity of Gilroy. No earlier expedition had traversed this route.

The territory north of the great bay remained for the most part *terra incognita*. The bay itself constituted a formidable barrier to exploration in this early period when not a single settlement had yet been established in the Bay Area. By contrast, the San Francisco Peninsula and the country on the east side of the bay were fairly well known. Various expeditions had blazed the principal routes in use today in these areas and had traversed the sites now occupied by the major cities of the region.

Time and Place

From time to time variously interested persons have contended that the logical place for a metropolitan center in the Bay Area would be on the east or mainland side of the bay, at the terminus of transcontinental railroads and at the ends of canyons and mountain passes affording direct access to the raw materials of a whole continent.

But the historical circumstances under which the Bay Area was settled and gained the impetus for its early development clearly explain why San Francisco, though surrounded on three sides by water, and though it has from time to time been crippled by earthquakes and fires, has continued as a metropolitan focal point despite the competition of other cities in the area, and despite the metropolitan dispersion of recent decades.

Between Spanish Alta California and the British colonies on the Atlantic seaboard lay a continental wilderness. The settlements on both sides faced outward across the seas rather than inland. For Alta California the resources of civilization were at the ends of the sea lanes, even though the colonists briefly had hopes of maintaining an overland route to New Spain. The sea lanes were to continue for a century or more to be the vital links with the sources from which flowed manufactured goods, books, music and art, many of the delicacies of the table, fashions, news of critical political developments, and, most important, the majority of newcomers who swelled the population. In the early days of Alta California the sea lanes extended chiefly to San Blas, and the Pacific was almost exclusively a Spanish ocean. But it did not long remain so. In the very year that San Francisco was founded, word reached Mexico City that the English were sending Captain James Cook to explore the Pacific, and of course Spain was already fearful of Russian designs on the west coast of North America. The sea was an open road to any ambitious nation. A sovereign power anxious to hold a newly discovered harbor large enough to accommodate all the fleets in the world would naturally establish a settlement at the entrance to that harbor; and as long as the sea remained the easiest and fastest means of importing and exporting goods, that port could reasonably be expected to attract trade, population, and economic and political influence more readily than other settlements less advantageously situated in relation to the sea. So it was with San Francisco, which for a century was not so much at the edge of a continent as it was at the edge of an immense ocean that was connected with all the other great seas of the world. The early growth—slow during Spanish and Mexican days, lightning-like during the gold rush, slow for a decade or more after that, then rapid again during the Nevada silver boom—gave the city the deep roots it needed to sustain itself and flourish at a later time when the sea was no longer so important as it had been.

Founding of San Francisco

The beginnings of the metropolis were crude but picturesque. Anza did not participate in the founding—he had departed for his outpost in Sonora some two months earlier. It was Moraga who conducted the colonists to their new home. The journey from Monterey consumed

Mission Dolores, San Francisco, in 1856. Drawing from Henry Miller's "Journal of a Sketching Tour of the California Missions." Courtesy of Bancroft Library, University of California.

all of ten days because the women and children had to rest often and the herds of cattle and horses and the mule train also moved slowly. On June 27, 1776, the colony at last reached the Laguna de los Dolores, where the mission was to be erected. The next day a shelter of branches was made, in which on the following day Fathers Palóu and Cambon celebrated the first Mass. Then ensued a long period of waiting for the supply ship *San Carlos*, which carried essential equipment and had among its crew skilled carpenters who were to assist in the construction of the presidio and the mission. It was August 18 before the vessel sailed through the Golden Gate, after spending almost two months at sea and being blown about so much that it had sailed more than two thousand miles just going from Monterey to San Francisco Bay. The settlers had not been idle during the long wait, however. They had cut supplies of logs with which to build the presidio and the mission, and they now set to work building the military establishment. When completed in the middle of September it included a chapel, a warehouse, and flat-roofed log houses for the soldiers. The temporary mission church, also of logs, was blessed on October 3 and was formally dedicated on October 9. San Francisco at last was on the map. The colonists celebrated the joyous event in typical early California style: they killed two beeves and held a barbecue.

One of the most interesting facts about the birth of this city is that it coincided with the proclamation of the Declaration of Independence and the birth of the United States of America. Mass was said in the rude shelter on the banks of the Laguna de los Dolores just five days before the Continental Congress formally adopted the great document penned by Thomas Jefferson. But all during the time that the settlement was being planned, restless and adventurous Americans were moving over the Allegheny Mountains into the Ohio Valley, initiating the westward migration that was to surge all the way to the Pacific and engulf the fringe of Spanish-speaking communities in California. Just seventy years after the new nation was founded three thousand miles from San Francisco Bay, that nation's flag flew over the Presidio of San Francisco.

Founding of Mission Santa Clara

In the month following the dedication of the mission at San Francisco the governor of the province, Rivera, again inspected the place on the Guadalupe River in the Santa Clara Valley that he and Father Palóu had favored in 1774 as a site for the second mission to be established in the San Francisco Bay Area. But it was January before he ordered Moraga, who was now *comandante* of the

Presidio in San Francisco, to proceed with the founding of Mission Santa Clara, dedicated to Clare of Assisi, founder of the Franciscan Order of Poor Clares.

Moraga, accompanied by Father Tomás de la Peña and some soldiers who were to assist in building the new ecclesiastical establishment, encamped on the banks of the Guadalupe on January 7, 1777, preparatory to selecting the exact spot for the mission. In a country rainless the greater part of the year, water to irrigate crops was a prime consideration. About eight miles up the river from the shore of the bay, the group discovered a little creek that emptied into the Guadalupe. The flow of this creek, they saw, could easily be diverted to irrigate the mission gardens. On the west bank of the river near the confluence of the two streams and just north of the present Bayshore Highway, the soldiers some days later cleared a plot of land for the mission building, not without certain misgivings that the site selected might be subject to flooding. As later events proved, their fears were well founded.

The Town of San José

Before long the priests and soldiers at the mission received an important visitor, Felipe de Neve, the new governor of the province. Rivera had been transferred to Loreto in Baja California as lieutenant governor, Monterey had become the capital of the two Californias, and now the new administrator was on his way to visit the port of San Francisco. He turned a sharp eye on the broad expanse of the Santa Clara Valley, because he was looking for a site for a new type of settlement, neither military nor ecclesiastical but primarily for the production of food and the propagation of more Spaniards to populate Alta California.

At the time he had assumed office, months earlier in Loreto, Neve had received instructions from the viceroy to establish agricultural settlements that would supply the missions and presidios with foodstuffs and perhaps eventually relieve the viceroyalty of the responsibility and expense of shipping provisions from San Blas. One such community Neve already had in mind, the future Los Angeles on the Rio de Porciuncula not far from Mission San Gabriel. Still another civil settlement, or *pueblo* (town), should be located in the Santa Clara Valley, he decided as he surveyed the virgin land through which the Guadalupe serpentined to the bay.

The Pueblo de San José came into being on November 29, 1777, with Moraga for the third time serving as a kind of colonial accoucheur. At the direction of Neve he assembled in the Presidio at San Francisco early in November the sixty-six hopeful souls who were to form the pioneer agricultural colony of the province: nine soldiers of "known agricultural skill" from the garrisons of Monterey and San Francisco and five *pobladores*, or settlers, together with their wives and children. At the head of this company Moraga marched to a place on the eastern bank of the Guadalupe roughly two miles from Mission Santa Clara and approximately a mile and a quarter north of the present center of San Jose.

To each of the settlers the *comandante* assigned provisionally a lot upon which to erect a dwelling, and a field large enough for the sowing of a fanega (approximately two bushels) of grain. Each man also received the necessary farming implements and two cows, a yoke of oxen, two horses, two beeves, two sheep, two goats, and a mule. The settlers were to pay for both goods and animals in products of the soil within five years. In addition, as an assurance of security during the possible tribulations of a new venture, the government granted each colonist a soldier's pay of ten dollars a month and daily rations for three years.

How wise Neve was in thus bolstering morale against discouragement and unforeseen miseries was soon demonstrated. Moraga, unhappily, had chosen a low-lying site for the town. In the spring of 1778, and again the following winter, the unruly Guadalupe inundated the fields of the settlers and flooded their houses, as well as the near-by mission. In the spring of 1779 the people of San José built new homes on higher ground, and in 1781 the mission fathers began construction of new buildings a little more than two miles south of their first establishment (at what is now the intersection of Campbell Avenue and Franklin Street in the city of Santa Clara).

Interdependent Settlements

Within a few years both settlements demonstrated the desirability of the Santa Clara Valley as an agricultural area. The produce and livestock of the San José residents was more than enough to supply their own needs and those of the presidios in Monterey and San Francisco. On a visit to Mission Santa Clara in 1792, George Vancouver, captain of the first foreign vessel to put in at San Francisco Bay, marveled at the abundant harvests of wheat, maize, peas, and beans, "which had been obtained with little labour and without manure."[8] In the mission gardens he noted peach, apricot, apple, pear, and fig trees flourishing—a sight prophetic of the thousands of acres of orchards eventually to be planted in the valley. Only in the cultivation of the grape did the Franciscans appear to have no success, owing perhaps, Vancouver thought, to "a want of knowledge in their culture" since the soil and the climate were "well adapted to most sorts of

fruit."[9] On the fertile plains surrounding the mission he observed black cattle "in large herds . . . in a sort of wild state."[10]

Although they were more than forty-five miles apart, the settlements at San Francisco and in the Santa Clara Valley enjoyed a close relationship from the very beginning. As the only establishments in the Bay Area, they naturally depended upon one another for social contacts. The visit of one of the fathers from Mission Santa Clara to Mission Dolores was an event; and the appearance of a foreigner such as Vancouver at Mission Santa Clara under an escort from the Presidio of San Francisco was an occasion calling for an exhibition of roping and slaughtering, a feast, and much other festivity. But it was the economic tie between San Francisco and the Santa Clara Valley that was particularly significant. The people in the settlements at the port needed foodstuffs from San José and Mission Santa Clara and could obtain them as they were needed. San Francisco was thus an outlet for the producers in the valley, whereas the valley itself was to become one of the chief sources of supply for the lusty young metropolis born of the gold rush. Indeed, the first important railroad in the Bay Area would be built chiefly as a means of transporting foodstuffs from the valley to markets in San Francisco. The early interdependence of San Francisco and the Santa Clara Valley was the basis for the metropolitan relationships that exist today.

Mission San José

After twenty years the ties binding together the first four little establishments in the Bay Area were lengthened to entwine a fifth—a new mission on the southeastern side of the bay. The original intention of mission authorities had been to select a site for this mission on the San Francisco Peninsula about midway between Mission Santa Clara and San Francisco; but since a large Indian population on the opposite side of the bay offered a more promising field for missionary endeavor, a site in what is now southern Alameda County was chosen. It was fifteen miles from Mission Santa Clara and twelve miles from the town of San José. Behind the site rose Mission Peak, and near by flowed the small stream now known as Mission Creek. The soil in the area was especially fertile. In only a few years Mission San José was to become one of the most prosperous establishments in the entire mission chain and was to be known far and wide for its grain, its fruits and wine, and its hides and tallow.

The founding took place on June 11, 1797, with Mass sung by Father President Fermín de Lasuén in a shelter of boughs. For the next ten years construction was under way. The neophytes made bricks from the clay at hand,

Mission San José in 1856. Drawing from Henry Miller's "Journal of a Sketching Tour of the California Missions." Courtesy of Bancroft Library.

but they carried redwood timbers for the church all the way from the hills overlooking the site of present-day Oakland—a distance of thirty miles. Years later, sweating crews of Americans were to cut down redwoods in the same groves to build the crude city of San Francisco.

A New Site for San José

The year 1797 also witnessed the removal of the Pueblo de San José to its third and final site, approximately a mile and a quarter south of the second. The Guadalupe River had overflowed its banks so many times that life was neither healthful nor comfortable in the location selected in 1779. The intersection of Market and West San Fernando streets in present-day San Jose marks the approximate center of the third town, from which almost half a century later the modern city began to develop.

Two years after the third start was made, Father Magin Catalá of Mission Santa Clara, with the help of Indian neophytes, began transforming the road that connected the mission and the town into a beautiful, willow-lined avenue. This road is today The Alameda, one of the principal east-west arteries of San Jose.

Communication among the five establishments in the Bay Area was entirely by land during the early period, although the bay offered an alternative means of travel. The failure of the Spaniards even to provide themselves with small boats that could be used for voyages on the bay greatly surprised G. H. von Langsdorff, the physician who accompanied Count Nikolai Rezanov on his famous visit to the Presidio of San Francisco in 1806 to obtain food for the starving Russian colony in Alaska. When Langsdorff and two companions sailed down the bay in a ship's boat to landing places near Missions San José and Santa Clara, he showed that water routes of communication could be established among the settlements and introduced the means of local travel that became common when foreign vessels in increasing numbers came into the bay.

Fort Ross, Russian Colony

The long isolation of Alta California from contact with people of other nations was swiftly ending, thanks to the presence along the California coast of swarms of sea otters. Langsdorff noted in his diary that San Francisco

Bay was "full" of these lustrous, brown-black creatures, which American ships under contract to the Russian American Fur Company of Alaska had been hunting on the islands off the coast and even on the forbidden mainland itself since 1803. The pursuit of the otter not only served to acquaint New England ship captains and their crews with a land that had more potentialities than the Spaniards seemed to be aware of, but it also aroused in the Russians a desire for a base on the California shore from which they could hunt independently of their American partners.

In the fall of 1811 the "Little Czar" of the Alaska colony, Alexander Baranov, finally took the step he had long contemplated. He sent an agent named Ivan Kuskoff to establish two permanent settlements north of the Golden Gate—a small one in Salmon Creek Valley six miles inland from Bodega Head, and a larger one at Fort Ross on the high bluffs twelve miles north of the mouth of the Russian River. The latter was dedicated in the spring of 1812. Baranov had decided that since intensified Spanish vigilance made clandestine hunting in San Francisco Bay and on the coast to the south well-nigh im-

possible, he would restrict his pursuit of the otter to the region north of the Spanish settlements. By avoiding conflict with the Spaniards, he hoped sooner or later to obtain a much-desired concession for hunting privileges in their territory. As for his relations with American ship captains, he now dispensed with the services of the Yankee ships and relied entirely upon his own vessels.

In an earlier period the Spaniards doubtless would have made a supreme effort to prevent colonization by the foreign power that they most feared. But New Spain was aflame with the revolution begun by the obscure parish priest Miguel Hidalgo in 1810, and the troops of the viceroy were engaged in battle after battle with the equally militant successor of Hidalgo, José María Morelos. The still loyal Spaniards in Alta California could expect no expeditionary force to arrive to dislodge the Russians, who continued to occupy the new outpost until 1841, when they voluntarily abandoned it because it was no longer useful to them either as a hunting base or as an agricultural colony. After 1810 no ships reached the province from San Blas with the usual supplies, mail, government decrees, and money to pay the presidio garri-

Fort Ross as Seen from the Hill. On the left is the sandy beach; on the right, the landing. Drawing from Historical Atlas Map of Sonoma County, 1877.

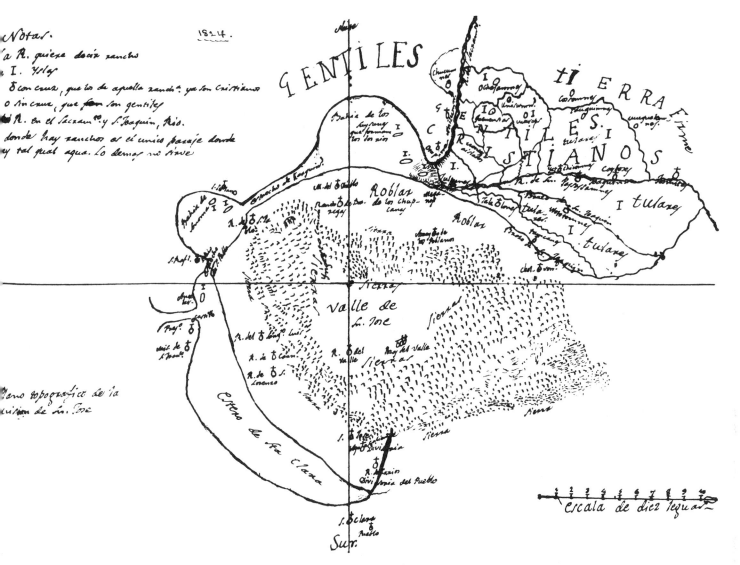

Map of the San Francisco Bay Area about 1824. Found among records of Mission San José. Photograph courtesy of Bancroft Library.

sons. Alta California, cut off from New Spain, was obliged to tolerate the planting of a Russian fort on soil claimed by Spain, however bitter acceptance of the situation might be.

Missions in the North Bay

The presence of this unwelcome foreign colony directed Spanish attention to the country north of San Francisco Bay and probably spurred expansion into that area. Gabriel Moraga, son of José Joaquín Moraga, at the direction of the provincial authorities, made three trips to Fort Ross and the Bodega settlement between 1812 and 1814 to learn what he could regarding Russian intentions and activities. These expeditions served to acquaint him with the trails and valleys of what are now Marin and Sonoma counties and to suggest possible sites for new settlements.

Moraga is believed to have recommended the site on the sheltered bay side of the Marin Peninsula for the auxiliary mission, or *asistencia*, of San Rafael, founded in 1817. This establishment, the nucleus of the present county seat of Marin County, was built as a kind of rancho sanatorium for the Indians of Mission Dolores, who for several years had been dying at an alarming rate from the ravages of venereal disease and from general weakening of their constitutions by the change from a roving, outdoor life to a confined, regulated existence within the mission compound. Transfer of a small number of the ailing neophytes to the sunnier, drier climate of San Rafael on an experimental basis a few months earlier had so improved their health that the decision was made to create a permanent establishment there. There was probably still another reason for founding this new Spanish settlement, and that was to bulwark Spain's claim to the inviting but little-known country north of San Francisco Bay with an actual establishment.

As the Russians showed no disposition to expand, provincial fears of their intentions gradually abated, and a good deal of stealthy trade developed between Bay Area settlements and Fort Ross. By the time the news that Mexico had won its independence from Spain reached Alta California, in 1822, the exchange between Russian traders and families living in the bay settlements was being carried on in the open, to the mutual satisfaction of both groups. The Russians had such exotic goods as laces, jewels, china, and silks to barter for hides and tallow, wheat, and pelts of deer, bears, and foxes trapped by the Indians.

San Francisco Solano, the last of the twenty-one California missions, came into being in the Sonoma Valley less as a barrier to Russian expansion than as a scheme to suppress both Mission Dolores and Mission San Rafael. With the apparent encouragement of Luis Ar-

güello, the first governor under the Mexican regime, young Father José Altimira, a newcomer to Mission Dolores, urged the first territorial *Diputación*, or legislative assembly, to transfer the "unhealthful" Mission Dolores to a locality north of San Rafael. The six legislators not only approved the proposed change, they also decreed that the establishment at San Rafael, which had recently been made independent of Mission Dolores, likewise should be consolidated with a new mission in the country of the Petalumas, or Canicaimos. Before Church authorities could act upon the protests of Father Juan Amorós of San Rafael, the audacious Father Altimira and a party of soldiers were tramping through the Petaluma, Sonoma, Napa, and Suisin valleys in quest of a site for the proposed mission. They settled on the valley known to the Indians as Sonoma, and on July 4, 1823, dedicated a site that recommended itself to them because of its fine climate, timber, stone, and water.

Great was the displeasure of the father president of the

Map of the Ranchos of Vicente and Domingo Peralta, about 1857. Note the intersection of Broadway, Fourteenth Street, and the County Road, now San Pablo Avenue, in Oakland. Photograph of map courtesy of Bancroft Library.

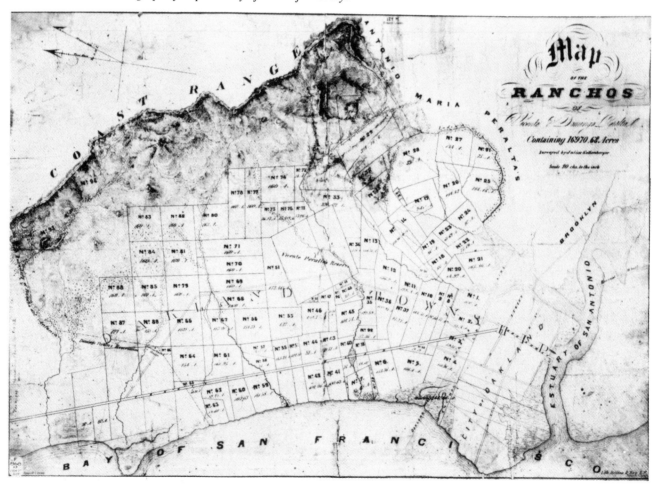

mission and the other fathers when they learned of the unauthorized actions of Father Altimira. Nevertheless, late in August, work began on a granary, irrigation ditch, corral, and other necessary structures at New San Francisco. At length the controversy precipitated by Father Altimira's unprecedented course ended in a compromise; he was appointed priest of the new mission, but neither Mission Dolores nor Mission San Rafael was abandoned.

Mexican Ranchos

Under the new Mexican regime there was a gradual increase in a type of landholding that was to cause endless complications for the energetic Americans when they gained possession of California. This was the rancho, of vast acreage, indefinite as to boundaries, held by a single family, and ideally suited to an economy producing chiefly hides and tallow for export, but highly frustrating to later-day American settlers bent on acquiring lands of their own, building homes, platting cities, and subdividing the valleys into family-sized farms and orchards. Only about thirty grants of land for ranchos were made in Alta California in the Spanish period, and relatively few in the first decade of Mexican rule. Most of the allocation of the rich valleys and tawny hills of coastal California to land-hungry Mexicans and to a few foreigners who had become Mexican citizens followed decrees of the Mexican Congress in 1833 and 1834 secularizing the missions and placing spiritual jurisdiction of the churches in the hands of parish priests. Many ranchos in the San Francisco Bay Area were created from lands formerly occupied and used by the missions, although thousands of acres in the area had never been used by these establishments. These vacant public lands, as well as the mission lands, were disposed of in accordance with a colonization law of 1824 and supplementary regulations of 1828. The law of 1824, intended to encourage permanent settlement in the more sparsely populated territories of the republic, such as Alta California, provided that Mexican nationals and

The Intersection of Broadway, Fourteenth Street, and San Pablo Avenue, Oakland, 1941. Aerial photograph courtesy of Mike Roberts.

foreigners wishing to settle in Mexican territory might petition for as much as eleven square leagues of land (approximately 48,700 acres), but not more. The law stipulated, however, that no person should receive more than one square league of irrigable land, four leagues of land dependent on rain, or six leagues of grazing land. Very few grants in the San Francisco Bay Area were of the maximum size allowed under the law; most of those in the Santa Clara Valley, for instance, contained from one to three square leagues, and only a few were as large as six or more leagues.

Don Luis Peralta, who had come to San Francisco as a boy of seventeen with the Anza expedition and had later served as a soldier in the Presidio garrison, acquired one of the most famous of the ranchos in the last years of Spanish control and the first years of Mexican rule. Known as Rancho San Antonio, his feudal holding stretched from San Leandro Creek in what is now central Alameda County northward to the Cerrito de San Antonio (little hill of St. Anthony), a landmark now surmounted by a mane of tall eucalyptus trees and commonly called Albany Hill. On the land later divided among his four sons now stand the cities of Oakland, Berkeley, Alameda, Piedmont, Emeryville, Albany, and San Leandro. The boundary separating the Peralta rancho from the Rancho San Pablo of the Castro family was eventually to become part of the boundary between Alameda and Contra Costa counties.

Yankee Trade and a New Town

Almost from the beginning of the Mexican period, rancho and mission became linked with an economic system that stretched all the way round the Horn to soap, candle, and shoe factories in Massachusetts, Rhode Island, Connecticut, and other Atlantic seaboard states. Republican Mexico reversed the centuries-old monopolistic trade policies of Spain and opened California ports to ships of all nations. Through the Golden Gate sailed Yankee vessels seeking chiefly hides for the New England leather industry. English and occasionally Peruvian and Russian ships also sought anchorage in the lee of the *Alta Loma* (high hill), as Telegraph Hill was then called; but for the most part the ships that entered San Francisco Bay were registered out of Boston, Providence, and other down-East ports.

From the San Francisco anchorage the crewmen set out in their launches to rancho and mission *embarcaderos*, or landing places, on sloughs and creeks around the bay, seeking "California bank notes," as hides were called because rancheros used them in lieu of currency to pay for goods bought from the ships. To the anchored vessels came schooners owned by the missions and built by the Indians according to plans drawn by the mission fathers. The bay thus served as a unifying element for the entire territory surrounding it, and the anchorage at San Francisco became the focus of commercial activity.

In 1834 the increase in the number of vessels trafficking in San Francisco Bay for hides and tallow suggested to Governor José Figueroa and the territorial *Diputación* the possibility of establishing a commercial town or trading post on Yerba Buena Cove (now the area between Montgomery Street and the Embarcadero in San Francisco), so called because the fragrant "good herb" (*Micromeria chamissonis*) was found growing on the surrounding slopes. The decision to center importing and exporting activities in the cove coincided with a three-part plan which contemplated the secularization of Mission Dolores, the shifting of the garrison of the Presidio to a new town to be developed in the Sonoma Valley as secularization of Mission San Francisco Solano was carried out, and recognition of the Presidio of San Francisco as a town, with an area of four square leagues of land (27 square miles), as provided by Spanish and Mexican law.

In a letter to Mariano Guadalupe Vallejo, *comandante* of the Presidio of San Francisco, the *Diputación* designated the boundaries of the new town as a line running from the south side of Rincon Point on the bay (Fourth and Berry streets) to the *Divisadero* (Lone Mountain) and thence to the south side of Point Lobos, on the ocean. These boundaries were to be cited years later by the City of San Francisco when it was growing rapidly and had to prove its title to lands needed for urban expansion, including the thousand or more acres embraced by Golden Gate Park.

In the protracted legal battle over the pueblo lands the city also was required to prove that the Presidio, which the *Diputación* recognized as a town, had actually functioned as a civil settlement. The *Diputación's* order in November, 1834, for the election of an *ayuntamiento*, or town council, was therefore extremely significant for the city that was to develop from the town of Yerba Buena. The territorial assembly included territory on both sides of the bay in the jurisdiction of the town. This action brought a protest to the governor from Antonio María Peralta and twenty-six other rancheros of the *contra costa*, who complained that "to be obliged to go to the port by land, we are under the necessity of traveling forty leagues, going and coming back; and to go by sea, we are exposed to the danger of being wrecked."[11] But His Excellency the Governor was not moved by the suggestion that the *contra costa* be included in the jurisdiction of the Pueblo de San José. The town council of Yerba Buena was duly elected in December, 1834, and was installed in January, 1835, with four rancheros of the East Bay among its nine members. The council was regularly renewed each year until 1839, when it was superseded by an alcalde, a kind of mayor and petty justice combined. Its existence during those four years was of crucial importance, however, in establishing San Francisco's claim to its pueblo lands.

The protest of the rancho owners of the East Bay against being obliged to participate in decisions affecting the new trading town bears early and eloquent testimony to the obstacles placed in the way of regional action by the great bay. Bridges, telephone and telegraph cables, radio, and television today have overcome the physical barrier, yet sectional feeling persists.

First Town Plans

William A. Richardson, an Englishman who had jumped ship and lived at the Presidio, became the first settler in the port village of Yerba Buena, which developed in the general area marked today by Portsmouth Square. Initially he carried on a small retail business with ships' crews and Indians, from a tent stretched over pine posts, and in 1837 he built his *Casa Grande*, a large adobe, on the one street in the town, the *Calle de la Fundación*. This street, shown on a "plan" of the townsite made by Richardson in 1835, ran at an angle to the beach and connected at the north with a road to the Presidio and at the south with a road to Mission Dolores. The government retained title to a strip of land about two hundred yards wide between the beach and the street.

By 1839 several lots in the town had been granted without regard to any street system, except for the Calle de la Fundacion, and it became necessary to establish some orderly arrangement of streets in the growing community. At the order of Alcalde Francisco de Haro, a Swiss newcomer named Jean Vioget devised a town plan to be used in granting additional lots. In preparing his plan, Vioget sought to include within near-rectangular blocks all the houses and fences already erected. In an area bounded by California Street, Montgomery Street, Pacific Avenue, and Grant Avenue—occupied today by part of Chinatown and part of the financial district—he indicated twelve blocks and parts of blocks more or less conforming to a rectilinear arrangement, though these were never actually laid out on the ground. No street names appear on extant copies of the Vioget map, but present-day San Franciscans can identify Kearny Street and Grant Avenue as the north-south streets and Jackson, Washington, Clay, and Sacramento streets as the east-west streets. Richardson's Calle de la Fundacion is shown intersecting at an angle the street now called Grant

Avenue. Vioget's north later proved to be eleven degrees too far east, and his north-south streets intersected the parallel east-west streets at two and one-half degrees from a right angle.

The most significant feature of the plan was its division of the townsite into more or less rectangular blocks. Vioget later testified that his original map included dotted lines indicating possible extensions of the streets, but he probably never thought of the town as expanding beyond the gently sloping land bordering the cove. He could hardly have foreseen that Yerba Buena would become a great city stretching far to the south, west, and north over steep hills and through valleys. The projection of his parallel streets up forbidding gradients and over crests to terrifying descents was the work of later surveyors, but he initiated the pattern that they elected to extend with total disregard for topography.

The Town of Sonoma

While the trading village was being established at the Port of St. Francis, the territorial government proceeded with its plan for a town at Mission San Francisco Solano in the Sonoma Valley. It also undertook to start small settlements on the sites of present-day Santa Rosa and Petaluma. But Indian hostility and trouble with settlers brought an end to both schemes. The order to Mariano Guadalupe Vallejo to found the pueblo that is now the town of Sonoma was dated June 23, 1835. All efforts were concentrated on making the new town a success.

Using a pocket compass, the young officer, with the assistance of William Richardson and Indian laborers, staked out a typical Spanish-Mexican town. A square, eight-acre plaza in the center of the town was surrounded by rectangular blocks. Extending southward from the plaza was an avenue 110 feet wide, which connected with a road to an *embarcadero* four miles away. In the block at the northeast corner of the plaza stood the mission, in which Vallejo and his family took up quarters, and on Battery Hill, just north of the pueblo, the *comandante* mounted cannon.

Sonoma in time became the trading center for the North Bay area. Some two hundred settlers lived within its jurisdiction by 1840.

In more than a century the plaza and the streets conceived by Vallejo have not changed, and though each generation has left its contribution of buildings in the town, Sonoma even now retains some of the unhurried atmosphere of its early days.

San José, though larger in population, was by contrast a straggling, formless community. In 1841, Nicholas ("Cheyenne") Dawson, of the Bidwell-Bartleson party, the first group of emigrants from the United States to reach the Mexican territory by the overland route, described San José as "a sleepy village of perhaps one hundred and fifty inhabitants, with no regular streets."[12] With one or two exceptions the houses were of adobe, "resembling unburnt brick kilns, with no floors, no chimneys, and with the openings for doors and windows closed by shutters instead of glass."[13] Dawson found "no farms around, but a few gardens; very few stores, and very little in them; no vehicles but carts, made entirely of wood; very little money, but plenty of hides and tallow."[14]

The End of Mexican Rule

The unprepossessing appearance of the few little towns and the run-down state of the missions and the presidios evoked the ill-concealed disdain of American immigrants who came overland in good-sized parties in 1843, 1844, and 1845. They referred contemptuously to the Mexican population as indolent "greasers" and waited for the day when the United States would take over the country. Some even dreamed of creating a new, independent nation on the Pacific Coast.

Official American interest in California dated from the declaration of the Monroe Doctrine, which, among other things, served notice on the Czar of Russia that he was not to use Fort Ross as a springboard for further colonization on the Pacific Coast. The first attempt of the United States actually to acquire territory on the Pacific was Andrew Jackson's offer of $3,500,000 to Mexico in 1835 for that part of California lying north of the thirty-eighth parallel. This proposed transfer of territory would have given the United States control of San Francisco Bay. Though Jackson's efforts were unsuccessful, the visit of Lieutenant Charles Wilkes, of the United States Navy, to the bay in 1841 as head of a scientific expedition plainly indicated to the Mexicans that the United States had not ceased to covet the magnificent harbor. And the abortive seizure of Monterey by Commodore Thomas Ap Catesby Jones, commander of the United States Pacific Squadron, in 1842 as a move to forestall a rumored British plan to occupy California, perhaps made unmistakably clear the ultimate fate of the territory. By the time James K. Polk, a resolute expansionist, moved into the White House in March, 1845, the annexation of California was one of the main items on the national agenda.

Polk wanted the transfer of California to the United States to take place without bloodshed; but his careful plans, implemented in California by Thomas Oliver Larkin, confidential agent of the State Department, were disrupted by the provocative maneuvers of Captain John Charles Frémont, by the Bear Flag revolt staged by Amer-

ican settlers in the North Bay area and the Sacramento Valley, and by the outbreak of war with Mexico. Even so, all the ports in California were occupied without opposition, including San Francisco, over which Captain John Montgomery, of the United States Navy, raised the American flag on July 9, 1846. It was mainly the arrogant behavior of the commander of the American occupation force in Los Angeles that touched off resistance by the native Californians and precipitated a series of engagements in southern California. As far as the San Francisco Bay Area was concerned, American control was effective months before the capitulation of the Californians in January, 1847.

Heritage from Spain and Mexico

The Spanish-Mexican population of the San Francisco Bay Area and the few score foreigners who more or less adopted their customs and religion upon settling among them bequeathed to the Americans a potentially rich area the resources of which had scarcely been touched, although the promise of things to come had been indicated.

The mission fathers, with the help of Indian neophytes, had amply demonstrated that the lands in the fertile valleys were suitable for growing various grains, fruits, and vegetables. And both the padres and the rancheros had shown that the entire country was suitable for stock raising, though little or no effort had been made to breed superior cattle.

The few valuable redwood forests of the area—on the Marin Peninsula, in the Russian River country, in the Santa Cruz Mountains on the San Francisco Peninsula, and in the Berkeley Hills—were known; some of them had been lumbered for many years, but to an insignificant extent.

In 1845 Andrés Castillero, a visitor from Mexico, while staying at Mission Santa Clara had discovered that mineral deposits which had been known to the Indians for centuries contained quicksilver. Soon the New Almaden Company was formed, and the New Almaden Mine became famous as one of the greatest quicksilver mines in the world.

The great bay was already famous around the world. Seamen from Latin America, from Europe, and from the United States had described its magnificence in waterfront taverns from Copenhagen to Valparaiso. Once the magic word "gold" was spoken, the sea lanes were filled with vessels bound for the celebrated harbor.

Nor was there lack of roads to lead the gold seekers to the "diggings," serve the stagecoaches, and much later provide the framework for a twentieth-century regional circulation system. These roads, often the merest ruts,

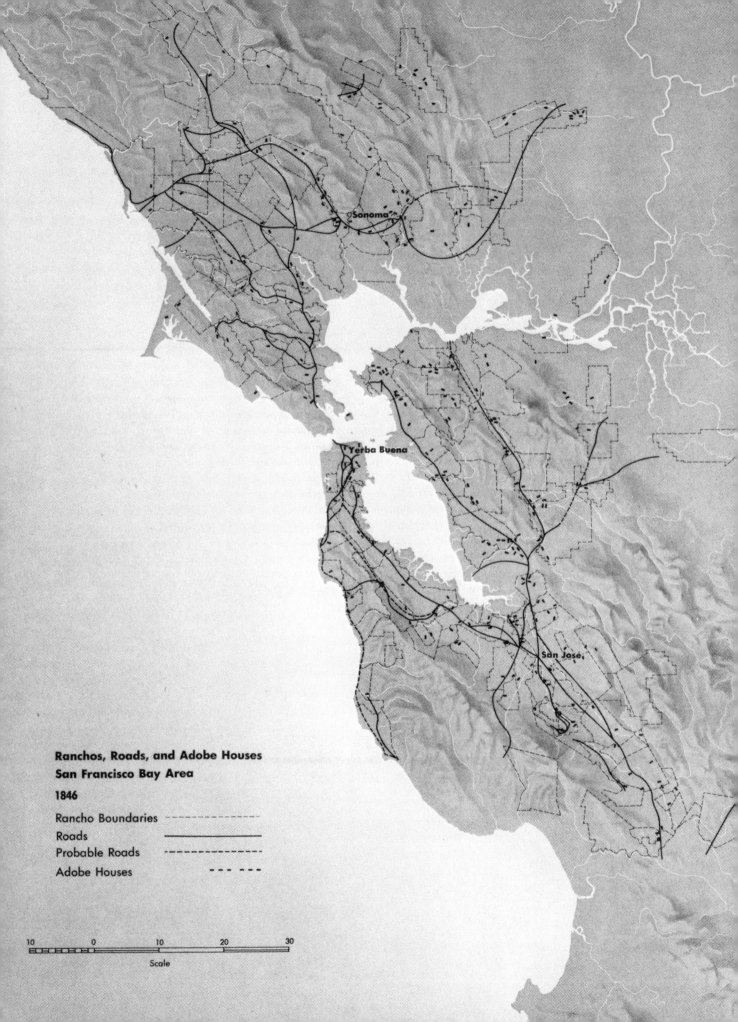

Ranchos, Roads, and Adobe Houses
San Francisco Bay Area

1846

Rancho Boundaries	----------
Roads	——————
Probable Roads	– – – – –
Adobe Houses	▬ ▬ ▬ ▬

Sonoma

Yerba Buena

San Jose

10   0   10   20   30

Scale

acknowledged the logic of topography. They avoided, wherever possible, steep grades, marshes, deep sand, and boulder-strewn washes. They threaded the valleys and the natural passes; they crossed the well-known fords in the streams that flowed from the hills to the bay. Where they were indirect, their very indirection was purposeful and was no irritation to those who traveled over them in ox carts or astride handsome mounts.

From Monterey a highroad ran to Mission San Juan Bautista and thence through the Santa Clara Valley to San José, following virtually the same route through the valley as Highway 101 today. A second road penetrated the valley from the west, coming from Santa Cruz through the mountains to the site of present-day Los Gatos and continuing to Santa Clara. The road from Santa Clara to Yerba Buena was that known today as El Camino Real, though in Spanish and Mexican times that term was used for any main road and did not denote this particular road as a "King's Highway" or "royal road." From San José a well-traveled route swung northeast to Mission San José and continued from there all the way to Ignacio Martinez' adobe on Pinole Creek. From Mission San José a traveler could reach the valleys east of the Berkeley Hills by going through Mission Pass or through Niles Canyon. At the eastern end of the pass one road led across the Livermore Valley and through the hills to the San Joaquin Valley and Sutter's Fort near the Sacramento River; another turned north through the Amador, San Ramon, and Ygnacio valleys to Carquinez Strait. In the North Bay area there were roads from Mission San Rafael to the grist mill of Stephen Smith at Bodega and from Smith's mill to the Cotati, Sonoma, and Napa valleys, to say nothing of many shorter roads.

All the main routes, with the exception of the one along the *contra costa*, are shown on the topographical sketch of "the gold and quicksilver district of California" that Lieutenant Edward Otho Cresap Ord prepared to accompany President Polk's message to Congress of December 5, 1848, announcing the discovery of gold in the newly acquired territory.

Seventy years of Spanish-Mexican occupation of the San Francisco Bay Area had set the stage for a drama that electrified the world. So swiftly did that drama unfold and so numerous and polyglot were the actors who crowded upon the scene that the easygoing folk who first held the spotlight were all but shoved aside; yet their culture has not completely vanished. Most of the names they gave the bays and promontories, the mountains, the rivers, the valleys, canyons, and settlements remain. Countless land titles throughout the area can be traced directly to rancho grants, and some rancho boundaries are perpetuated in the boundaries of counties, cities, and modern subdivisions. Most of the adobes of the pastoral age have crumbled, but some of the customs of those who built them have survived—the barbecue, the fiesta, the rodeo—and, though modernized and Anglicized, serve as reminders of the vanished dons, vaqueros, and padres. Traditions and legends have a vitality that defies time, and though it seems indisputable that the greatest heritage from the first white settlers of the Bay Area is the record of their heroic trek from northern Mexico under Anza and their pioneer struggles to make a home in exile, their contribution to the physical form of the vast metropolitan region of today must be acknowledged.

CHAPTER TWO

Mother of Cities

Residents of the town of Yerba Buena had scarcely become accustomed to seeing the Stars and Stripes fluttering from the staff in front of the customhouse on Portsmouth Plaza when, on July 31, 1846, the ship *Brooklyn* arrived with approximately two hundred Mormons under the leadership of Elder Samuel Brannan. The unheralded advent of these wayfarers more than doubled the population of the settlement, then estimated at 150.

Merchants and traders of the town were profoundly impressed by the arrival of this numerous company of Americans. True, they were sectarians who had been persecuted and were anxious to begin life anew in a far country; but other citizens of the United States would surely follow, now that their flag had been planted on the Pacific shore. The residents of Yerba Buena talked of its becoming a great city.

William Heath Davis, a shrewd American-born merchant who knew the bay and all coastal California as only a man who had spent years in the hide and tallow trade could know it, thought that there was reason to believe that wholly new towns could be established. He invited his old friend Don Vicente Peralta to dinner and offered him $5,000 in cash for a part of his rancho on the *contra costa*. On that part of the rancho known as the Encinal de Temescal, where the skyscrapers of downtown Oakland now rise, Davis proposed to lay out a town that would be a kind of Brooklyn to the metropolis a-borning on the San Francisco Peninsula—a picturesque retreat for overworked businessmen. It would include all the land

from the bay to what is now Lake Merritt and from the Estuary of San Antonio to the present Fifteenth Street. Davis outlined his plans to construct a wharf on the estuary and to inaugurate a ferryboat service between his new town and Yerba Buena.

Alas for the dream! After taking the matter "under advisement" for some days, Don Vicente refused to part with any of his acres. To no avail did Davis prophesy, correctly, that if the ranchero did not himself open a tract to legitimate settlement, eventually squatters would wrest his land from him, slaughter his cattle, and sell the meat in the port across the bay.

A Rival City

Unlike the land-loving Vicente Peralta, Mariano Guadalupe Vallejo was eager to increase the value of land in his Rancho Suscol by inviting settlement. He willingly deeded to his friends Thomas O. Larkin and Robert Semple, a participant in the Bear Flag Revolt, a townsite on the north side of Carquinez Strait. There, on deep water about midway between the Golden Gate and the vast interior valleys of California, promoters Larkin and Semple envisaged the rise of the great metropolis of the West Coast. In Semple's view, Yerba Buena, on its windy peninsula, was off the direct route of communication between Monterey, the territorial capital, and the huge, promising interior, in which John Sutter, at New Helvetia, was raising wheat and cattle. From Monterey, travelers could proceed by way of San Jose, Mission San Jose,

Mission Pass, and the warm valleys on the east side of the Berkeley Hills to a crossing at the strait. A city on the north side of this waterway could dominate the trade of all northern California, Semple asserted.

"Francisca" was the name chosen for the city-to-be, in honor of Vallejo's wife, María Francisca Felipa Benicia Carrillo Vallejo. Semple began advertising the prospective city under this name in the first newspaper in the territory, *The Californian*, which he and Walter Colton had begun to publish in Monterey.

So effectively did the former Kentuckian ballyhoo his and Larkin's dream city that the residents of Yerba Buena became alarmed, then idignant. A city with a name so closely resembling that of San Francisco Bay would easily become known throughout the world, cheating Yerba Buena of recognition. The first alcalde under the American regime, Lieutenant Washington Allen Bartlett of the United States Navy, decided to forestall the infringement. On January 23, 1847, he proclaimed that "San Francisco was the official name," of the first settlement, and he ordained that it should thereafter "be used in all official communications and public documents, or records appertaining to the town [of Yerba Buena]."[1]

Compelled to change the name of their projected city, Larkin and Semple substituted the fourth of Señora Vallejo's many names for the one originally chosen. The columns of *The Californian* on June 19, 1847, notified the world that Francisca had become Benicia City. To impress the villagers of San Francisco with the strength of his conviction that their town had no chance in competition with Benicia, Semple ostentatiously gave away a lot in San Francisco on the Fourth of July.

By September, Benicia was beginning to develop. Semple, on the site daily, showed lots to twenty or thirty visitors a day and made a good many sales. In fact, his success encouraged him to raise the price of lots from twenty to fifty dollars. San Franciscans were frankly troubled by this real-estate venture. Larkin, living in their midst, missed no opportunity to make them wonder if they ought not to invest in Benicia.

Surveys in San Francisco

Actually, San Francisco itself had been in a flurry of land speculation all summer and had little reason to be perturbed by the activities of Larkin and Semple. In anticipation of a rapid increase in population and a demand for additional lots, Alcalde Bartlett, at the urging of a citizens' committee, had ordered a survey made that enlarged the town on all sides, and then had acceded to pleas for the laying out and selling of lots on the mud flats of Yerba Buena Cove. This area, partly submerged except at low tide, was of immense potential value because eventually it was certain to be filled to deep water. Town officials favored the proposed sale as a means of obtaining funds to supply an inadequate treasury; speculators saw an opportunity to enrich themselves.

Both the general survey and the survey of the waterfront lots were made by a Dublin Irishman named Jasper O'Farrell, who had come to Yerba Buena in 1843. He is said to have tried to introduce streets adapted to the hilly terrain; but landowners would tolerate no deviation from the gridiron street system shown on Vioget's map of the town, because they considered this pattern most convenient for the subdivision of lots. O'Farrell therefore realigned the streets platted by his predecessor and extended them, even though continuance of the rigid rectilinear system would eventually necessitate cutting streets through dunes and lofty hills to the north, west, and south of the settled area. He used his own judgment concerning Market Street, however. That thoroughfare he surveyed as a diagonal artery 110 feet wide, following the direction of the old road to Mission Dolores. South of Market Street, O'Farrell laid out blocks at right angles to it and made them four times the size of those on the north side of the street, because he deemed small lots undesirable. Downtown San Francisco, consequently, consists of two different gridiron patterns spliced together at an acute angle at Market Street, with a series of triangular blocks and several dead-end intersections along the north side of the thoroughfare.

O'Farrell's survey, including the water lots, covered some eight hundred acres and extended approximately three-quarters of a mile from north to south and two miles from east to west. North of Market Street it included the area bounded by Post, Leavenworth, and Francisco streets and the waterfront. South of Market Street were four full blocks fronting on Fourth Street and eleven full blocks on Second Street.

Even though California had not yet become a part of the United States by treaty with Mexico, and no representative of either nation could give valid title to land, General Stephen W. Kearny, military governor of California, released the waterfront lots to the town and decreed that they should be sold at auction for the benefit of the community. More than half of the 450 parcels into which O'Farrell had divided the submerged area were snapped up in four days in late July, 1847. Beach lots measuring 45 by 137½ feet sold for as much as $600, while submerged lots of the same dimensions brought from $50 to $400. By contrast, lots 100 varas wide in the big blocks south of Market Street sold for only $29, including fees. (A vara was about 33 inches.)

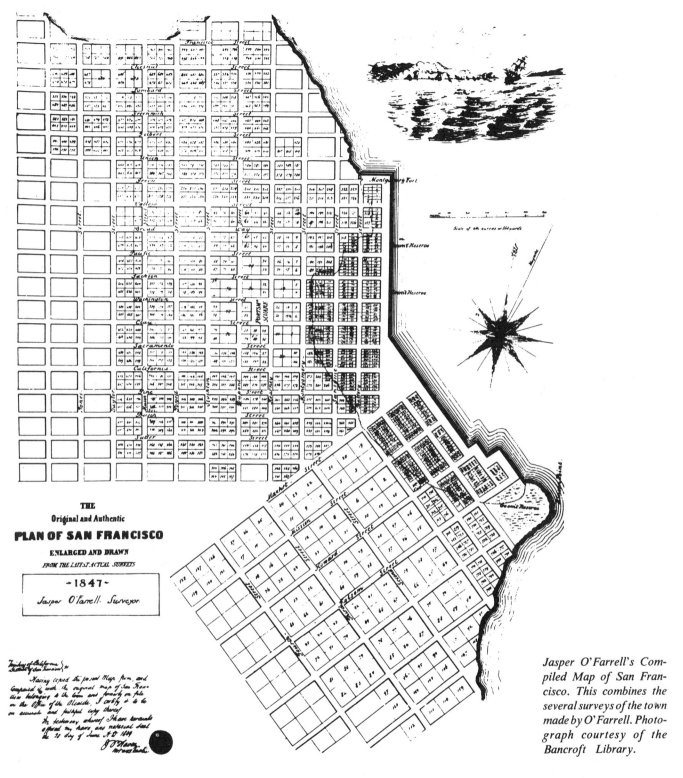

THE
Original and Authentic
PLAN OF SAN FRANCISCO
ENLARGED AND DRAWN
FROM THE LATEST ACTUAL SURVEYS

~1847~
Jasper O'Farrell. Surveyor.

Jasper O'Farrell's Compiled Map of San Francisco. This combines the several surveys of the town made by O'Farrell. Photograph courtesy of the Bancroft Library.

The population of San Francisco was then estimated at approximately 460, exclusive of Colonel Jonathan D. Stevenson's Seventh New York Volunteers, who had arrived on three transports in March. Although the prospects of the town impressed Army and Navy officers favorably and encouraged them in all manner of land speculation, William Tecumseh Sherman was one West Point man who would not invest in San Francisco real estate. The future hero of the march through Georgia "felt actually insulted" at being thought "such a fool as to pay money for property in such a horrid place as Yerba Buena."[2]

The Ubiquitous Gridiron

So far as land platting was concerned, the rival city of Benicia was no better than San Francisco. O'Farrell laid out that community, too, with a pattern as uncompromisingly rectangular as the one fastened upon San Francisco. His town survey contains not the slightest indication that the site on Carquinez Strait is characterized by gently rolling hills. With complete disregard of the irregularities of the shoreline, he platted the blocks into the offshore area. On paper Benicia is a mechanical arrangement of more than four hundred blocks divided uniformly into eight lots measuring 100 by 150 feet, with alleys 25 feet wide running lengthwise through the blocks. All streets are 85 feet wide, as Semple and Larkin had agreed they should be. The only concessions to urban amenity in this monotonous scheme for vending land are four public squares, each equal to two of the rectangular blocks, a centrally situated park four blocks in extent, and a cemetery of the same size, also occupying a focal position in the layout.

Gridiron platting was everywhere identified with urban order and progress under the new American regime in California. In San Jose, first one surveyor and then another imposed the rectitude of straight streets upon the meandering roadways of the old pueblo. In Sonoma, O'Farrell and an associate named J. M. Hudspeth augmented Vallejo's simple design for a plaza into a gridiron town plan, to the evident satisfaction of the American alcalde, Lilburn W. Boggs, an appointee of the military governor. And in the spring of 1848 when Nathan Coombs founded a fifth town in the Bay Area, it too was staked out according to a rectilinear plan.

This new town was called Napa, a name derived from an Indian word. Coombs, having received eighty acres from Nicolas Higuera in payment for work on the latter's new adobe house, decided to start a town at the confluence of the Napa River and Napa Creek. Since the river was navigable to this junction, the founder foresaw a good future for the community as the natural shipping point for farmers in the Napa Valley, which was even then fairly well settled by American and Spanish-Mexican families.

Before the first building in the town was completed, the owner heard momentous news that sent him flying to the foothills of the Sierra Nevada, there to be joined by most of the residents of San Francisco, San Jose, Sonoma, Benicia, Monterey, San Juan Bautista, and every other town and crossroads settlement in northern California.

Gold Fever

Rumors that gold had been found at Sutter's sawmill at Coloma and at Mormon Bar on the American River had been circulating since mid-February, 1848; but Californians remained skeptical until Samuel Brannan made a trip to the areas of discovery in April and May and returned to San Francisco with glittering particles of the precious metal. Then, seeing him dash up and down the streets shouting "Gold, gold, gold from the American River!," the Doubting Thomases believed.

By early summer, gold fever struck the populace of southern California and the northwestern provinces of Mexico. In late summer, fortune seekers from Hawaii joined the rush to the placers. By early fall, American settlers from the Willamette Valley in Oregon were invading the Mother Lode country. Still later came Chileans, Australians, and some Chinese. With shovel, pan, basket, and bowl, prospectors ranged from the eastern tributaries of the Sacramento River southward to the tributaries of the San Joaquin. They numbered not more than eight or ten thousand by the end of the year, however, and were but the vanguard of the hordes of gold-lusting migrants yet to come.

Winter rains and snows drove large numbers of miners from the placer regions to the bay towns, where they filled every available shelter to overflowing. Carpenters earning from $16 to $20 a day hastily clapped together more buildings in Benicia, which had had only fifteen or twenty structures before the stampede to the gold country began. San Francisco, a town of some two hundred buildings at the beginning of the summer, expanded on all sides as the prices of lots recently thought almost worthless soared fantastically. Speculators gladly paid $10,000 for certain choice corners. In San Jose, Sonoma, and Napa both substantial and flimsy structures augmented the supply of housing.

On December 5, 1848, President Polk spoke the word that dissolved the last lingering doubts entertained by Easterners concerning the fabulous stories of California that they had been reading in their newspapers since mid-September, or earlier. In a message to Congress based on communications from Larkin and Colonel Richard B. Mason, the Chief Executive proclaimed: "The accounts of the abundance of gold in that territory are of such an extraordinary character as would scarcely command belief were they not corroborated by the authentic reports of officers in the public service, who have visited the mineral district, and derived the facts which they detail from personal observation."[3]

The Great Migration

Not only were tens of thousands of more than usually energetic and adventurous Americans immediately impelled toward the sparsely settled territory that Mexico had formally ceded to the United States just nine days after the discovery of gold; thousands of impoverished or persecuted Europeans were also provided a haven where every man was as good as the next one and the capabilities of all were needed to develop a country practically untouched. Restless veterans of the war with Mexico, destitute survivors of the potato famine of 1846–1847 in Ireland, and libertarians who had defied autocracy in the revolutions of 1848 in France and central Europe alike responded to the sudden opportunity to begin life anew in El Dorado. Still later, in 1850, thousands of farmers uprooted by the Taiping rebellion in southeastern China embarked for the golden sanctuary. The nuggets in the stream beds were lodestars of hope to the distressed, beacon fires of temptation to the unscrupulous and the greedy.

Throughout 1849 and on into the next year and the next the great migration continued, by way of the steaming Isthmus of Panama, across Nicaragua, through the Strait of Magellan, and round Cape Horn, across the plains from Missouri, across the southern deserts, over the plateaus and through the bandit-infested barrancas of Mexico. Along the way thousands died of cholera and tropical diseases, of thirst, of hardship, privation, and exposure. Ships disappeared at sea and were never heard of again. But large numbers of the Argonauts reached their destination. Hubert Howe Bancroft, the historian, estimated that forty-two thousand emigrants came overland to California in 1849, of whom nine thousand were from Mexico.[4] The authors of *The Annals of San Francisco* placed the number of sea-borne arrivals at forty thousand,

San Francisco in 1849, as Seen from Broadway near Kearny Street. Long Wharf and the storeship Apollo are the most prominent features in Yerba Buena Cove. Happy Valley lies in the low sand hills south of the town. From an engraving in Gazlay's American Biography, 1861.

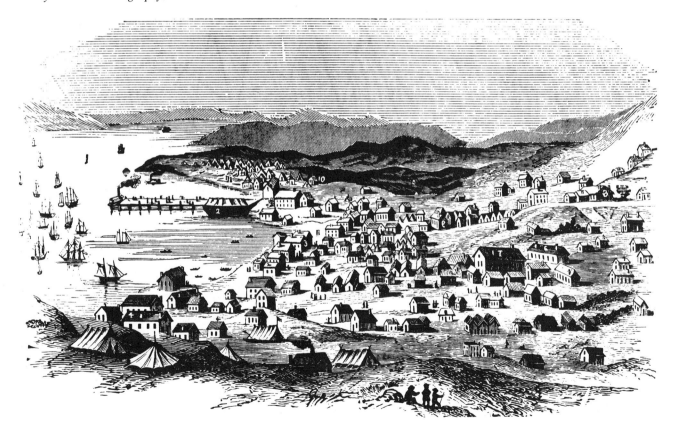

not including the three or four thousand seamen who deserted from hundreds of ships after reaching San Francisco Bay.[5]

Bay and River Routes

Overland parties headed directly for the mining regions. Probably two-thirds or more of the passengers of incoming ships struck out for the gold fields as soon as they could procure horses and wagons or buy passage on sloops and steamboats destined for Sacramento or Stockton. The water route to the interior was by far the easier, since roads were little more than ruts and the land journey from San Francisco involved a long, slow trip down the Peninsula and round the southern arm of the bay or an equally roundabout peregrination through the North Bay country, after a crossing to Sausalito or Mission San Rafael.

The bay in 1849 and 1850 was the equivalent of a network of highways and rail lines. Together with the Sacramento and San Joaquin rivers, it afforded easy access to the mines, and it united all the surrounding country with the port at San Francisco. With few exceptions the towns established in the Bay Area just before the gold rush and during it were situated on the bay or on navigable sloughs and creeks tributary to it—Benicia, Napa, New York of the Pacific (now Pittsburg), Martinez, Alviso, Vallejo, San Antonio, Clinton, Mezesville (Redwood City), San Rafael (as a platted town), Antioch, Suisun, Union City, Petaluma, Oakland, and Alameda. Communities in the fertile valleys represented a secondary ring of settlement, which developed as the gold fever abated and tired or disillusioned miners realized that the common soil held for the ordinary man riches at least as great as those in the gravel of the Mother Lode country.

San Francisco Waterfront

San Francisco, the metropolis suddenly brought into being by the gold rush, virtually rose from the bay, or at least in part on the bay, for the immediate endeavor of her residents, aside from devising temporary shelter for the hordes of newcomers, was to extend wharves into the bay and then begin the process of filling Yerba Buena Cove to deep water. Nature favored the city by making the western side of the bay deep and the eastern or continental side shallow. But the motley parade of steamers, brigs, whalers, colliers, barks, schooners, and bottoms of every sort that swept in through the Golden Gate in the spring and summer of 1849 had to drop anchor at arm's length from the bustling shore, and passengers and cargoes had to be lightered across the mud flats to the waterfront on Montgomery Street.

The most impressive of the piers built to eliminate this inconvenient and bothersome little journey was Central Wharf, or Long Wharf, in a location now marked by Commercial Street. It extended two thousand feet into the bay, to a point where the water was deep enough to permit Pacific Mail steamers to lie alongside. So profitable was this wharf to the men who financed it that other groups quickly followed their example. Before long the shore of the cove was spiked with piers. Sacramento, Clay, Washington, California, and other streets grew bayward on pilings. Many smaller piers, some built by the municipality, also sprang up between the longer ones.

On both sides of the wharves arose a ramshackle assortment of buildings perched on piles—commission houses, groceries, saloons, cheap-John shops, and mock auction rooms. Plank walks laid on piles linked the wharves, and here and there a crosswalk enclosed an unseaworthy hulk that had been converted into a warehouse, store, hotel, or office. By 1850 more than a thousand people were living on these old ships and in the buildings constructed on piles. Along the crosswalks, as along the wharves, merchants and shipping companies constructed more warehouses and shops resting on piles, little realizing that these built-up crosswalks would become, in the not distant future, the cross streets of the lower business district, such as Sansome, Battery, and Drum streets. The port of entry to El Dorado thus presented to the arriving voyager the appearance of a rickety Venice, hemmed in by a forest of masts.

Cities on the Strait

More than the desire to make a fortune in wharf charges spurred the businessmen of San Francisco to action along the waterfront. Their chronic fear that Benicia, a city on deep water, might really become the metropolis of which Larkin and Semple had dreamed was kept alive by the interest of the Army and Navy in Benicia. General Persifer Smith, who relieved Colonel Mason in the territorial command, established a general depot for his division there and made no secret of his hearty dislike for San Francisco. It was, he informed the Adjutant General in Washington, D.C., "in no way fitted for military or commercial purposes; there is no harbor, a bad landing place, bad water, no supplies of provisions, and inclement climate, and it is cut off from the rest of the country except by a long circuit around the southern extremity of the bay."[6] Benicia, on the other hand, appealed to the general as a place "open to the whole country in the rear and accessible without difficulty to ships of the largest class."[7] It was also "above the influence of . . . fogs."

Others shared the general's opinion that the country in

the vicinity of Carquinez Strait had the advantage of superior geographical location. Colonel William M. Smith, agent for Ignacio Martinez, owner of the huge Rancho El Pinole, determined to give Larkin and Semple some near-by competition by building a town directly opposite Benicia on the south side of the strait. There, at the terminus of the road coming up from San Jose through the San Ramon and Ygnacio valleys, Smith had a surveyor divide 120 acres into blocks and lots. The town was named Martinez, after the ranchero on whose land it stood. Lots sold readily, and houses and two or three stores began to rise almost immediately.

Speculative Ventures

A less successful promotional effort was that of Colonel Jonathan D. Stevenson, late of the New York Volunteers, who engaged William T. Sherman and some of his cohorts to lay out New York of the Pacific on Suisun Bay near the mouth of the San Joaquin River. The city languished for many decades as one of the abortive ventures of the gold rush era, though time was to prove Sherman wrong in the statement made in his memoirs that " 'New York of the Pacific' never came to anything."[8] Eventually, after various changes of name, it became Pittsburg, today a thriving industrial city.

At the extreme southern end of San Francisco Bay still another get-rich-quick town appeared in the winter of 1849–50. Jacob D. Hoppe and other leading residents of San Jose obtained a tract of land not far from the old *embarcadero* of Mission Santa Clara on the lower Guadalupe River and employed Chester S. Lyman to lay out the city of Alviso. To stir up interest in what they hoped would become the port for the Santa Clara Valley, they talked of a canal to San Jose. Lots went on sale at $600, and the city founders braced themselves for a rush of business.

They were disappointed. At the end of two years Alviso had two hotels, several stores, a tavern, a blacksmith shop, and a handful of dwellings. Thereafter the sound of the hammer was heard only occasionally in the town. The price of lots tobogganed. For two decades or more there was, however, a considerable movement of grain, fruits, and vegetables from the docks of Alviso to San Francisco. Then the town sank into a lethargy from which it has never roused itself. It was the victim of progress, in the form of a railroad on the Peninsula.

Agitation for the railroad began the very winter that Alviso was founded, and it continued, off an on, for more than a decade, through various unsuccessful attempts to finance the enterprise, until the line was finally started in the 'sixties.

Growth of San Francisco

In the meantime, in San Francisco the unceasing arrival of voyagers and the winter retreat of miners from the gold fields to the city stimulated an orgy of land speculation that made the promotional activities of the founders of Benicia, Martinez, New York of the Pacific, and Alviso appear trivial. Few lots were sold in the city's first suburb, the Potrero Nuevo, laid out by Dr. John Townsend and Cornelius de Boom on the south bank of Mission Bay in 1849; but the failure of the Potrero Nuevo as a subdivision was due more to its then seemingly remote and inaccessible location than to any lack of market for real estate. In the city proper the firm of Finley, Johnson and Company sold for $300,000 property that had cost them only $23,000 the year before. A lot on Portsmouth Square, bought in the spring for $6,000, sold in the fall for $45,000. The lot which Semple had given away two years earlier to demonstrate his faith in Benicia now commanded a small fortune.

Because the last of the lots surveyed in 1847 by Jasper O'Farrell had been sold early in 1849, the town council in October ordered William Eddy, the city surveyor, to survey additional lands as far west as Leavenworth and Eighth streets, in the vicinity of the present Civic Center. More than three thousand lots in this newly platted area were sold by January, 1850. Together they contained nearly two square miles of territory, exclusive of streets.

The built-up area of the city extended from Clark's Point to the Rincon, overflowed through the little gap known as the *portezuela*, between the hills at Pacific and Jones streets, and surged west over the sand hills far beyond the original confines of the village of Yerba Buena. Tents spread around the base of Telegraph Hill toward the north. South of Market Street, in an area protected by high sand hills and supplied by a good spring of water, more tents, perhaps a thousand, stood side by side. This was "Happy Valley," which became anything but happy as torrential rains descended during the winter of 1849–50. Here, at approximately the present intersection of First and Mission streets, Peter and James Donahue, pioneer industrialists, established a small foundry to produce picks and shovels for miners, and here began to develop the city's first manufacturing district. Still farther south, near what is now Howard Street, was "Pleasant Valley."

Approximately twenty thousand people inhabited this city of tents, shanties, and flimsy houses with walls covered by muslin in lieu of plaster. It had sprung up with weedlike rapidity, to the utter amazement of miners who had left it in the early spring when it was a town of perhaps two thousand residents.

First State Legislature

Many of the inhabitants of this boom town considered themselves merely temporary residents of California. When their luck ran out or the going got tough, they would leave. But there was another class, in Sacramento, Stockton, and other towns as well as in San Francisco, who had come to stay. The men of this class were eager to assume civic responsibilities and to establish demo-cratic self-government in place of the military authority that was proving inadequate to protect life and property in California's fast-growing communities.

This better element was represented by the men who began convening at San Jose on December 15, 1849, as members of California's first state legislature under Amer-ican rule. Their coming together in the temporary state capital was irregular, to say the least, but so had been an earlier gathering in Monterey at which a state consti-tution had been drafted. The people of California had ratified the constitution and had elected a civil governor, lieutenant governor, state legislators, and two representa-tives to Congress; and now the lawmakers of the auda-cious, self-created commonwealth were going to organize a state government even though Congress had not yet admitted California to the Union. Both Missouri and Michigan had done the same thing before admission, setting a precedent for California.

Once the lawmakers had overcome the initial difficulties of an unfinished state house (originally planned as a hotel) and the lack of such essential equipment as paper, pens, ink, and writing desks, or even the funds with which to purchase these articles, they elected John C. Frémont and William M. Gwin to the United States Senate, drafted civil and criminal codes, created tax and judicial struc-tures, and provided for the organization of counties, cities, and towns.

The senate committee on county boundaries at first suggested creation of eighteen counties, but the legislators finally agreed upon a total of twenty-seven, seven of which bordered on San Francisco Bay: San Francisco, Santa Clara, Contra Costa, Marin, Sonoma, Solano, and Napa. Both Sonoma and Napa counties extended considerably farther north than they do today, and Sonoma County had only a short coastline, compared with its present rather long boundary on the Pacific. San Francisco County included most of what is now San Mateo County. Contra Costa County and Santa Clara County each in-cluded parts of what is now Alameda County. Since no accurate surveys of the state had yet been made and the legislature lacked reliable maps, the boundaries of So-noma, Napa, and Solano counties were left indefinite, subject to more precise delineation at a later time.

County seats designated by the legislature were: San Francisco, for the county of that name; San Jose, for Santa Clara County; Martinez, for Contra Costa County; San Rafael, for Marin County; Sonoma, for the county of that name; Benicia, for Solano County; and Napa, for the county of that name.

Among the first cities incorporated as self-governing municipalities were four in the Bay Area—San Francisco, San Jose, Benicia, and Sonoma.

The New City of Vallejo

Toward the close of the session, the legislature turned its attention to the subject of the permanent location of the state capital. Various citizens of San Jose offered tracts of land for a capitol and other public structures. The municipal authorities of Monterey offered Colton Hall, in which the state constitution had been drafted, and all the land needed for public buildings. San Francisco was willing to contribute such buildings and grounds as the legislature might select, providing the whole did not cost more than $100,000. Senator Mariano G. Vallejo, of Sonoma, topped all these propositions in a "memorial" in which he offered, if the legislature would establish the capital on land which he owned "upon the straits of Carquinez and Napa river," to lay out a city to be called "Eureka or such other name as the legislature might suggest."[9] Further, he proposed to give to the state, as soon as the legislature accepted his offer, 156 acres for building sites and a total of $370,000 in grants for specific purposes, including $125,000 for a capitol.

The permanent location for the capital proved to be a controversial issue that the legislature decided to side-step, preferring to schedule an election in which the people of the state should choose among the cities com-peting for the honor. The voters, not being politicians, found the choice easy: they enthusiastically endorsed Vallejo's offer.

At the time the senator from Sonoma presented his memorial, the site of what was to become not Eureka but the city of Vallejo was marked by two small sheet-iron buildings, one of them called, somewhat pretentiously, the Union House. Here travelers to and from the mines found lodging. On this site Vallejo and his associates laid out a town of rectangular blocks south of present Georgia Street. Several interested persons were induced to erect buildings in 1850, but the town was far from being equipped to function as the seat of government when the lawmakers assembled there in 1851. After a few days they adjourned to San Jose, which was still the legal capital since no act had been passed changing the location.

Anticipating that the city of Vallejo would be ready to accommodate them properly a year later, the legislators on February 4, 1851, enacted a measure making the new city the permanent seat of government. But in 1852 they were to be disappointed in Senator Vallejo's ability to produce the statehouse that he had promised. In 1853 the legislators shifted the capital to Benicia, and in 1854 to Sacramento.

Señor Vallejo lacked business experience of a type that could rally his associates to support his magnificent project. The city that he had envisaged as a state capital owed its growth to the Navy Yard established on Mare Island in 1854 and to its selection somewhat later as the bay terminus of a railroad to the Sacramento Valley. Both in its unique origin and in its development under the stimulus of military activity it differed from other Bay Area towns, the majority of which owed their existence directly or indirectly to the mushroom growth of San Francisco.

Mother of Cities

The city on the Peninsula was literally a metropolis, a mother of cities. Although it grew from about twenty thousand in the winter of 1849–50 to not more than fifty thousand in the winter of 1854–55 (when the boom ushered in by the gold rush collapsed), San Francisco was of sufficient size, in an almost totally undeveloped country, to stimulate the birth and growth of settlements throughout the territory surrounding the bay. The people of this port city at first were dependent upon distant sources for practically everything they ate, wore, slept on, rode in, read, and bought and sold. Alternately, the wharves in Yerba Buena Cove were glutted with imports or were almost empty, depending upon whether several ships arrived within a few days of one another or a week or more went by without the arrival of a single large cargo. With an entire urban population thus at the mercy of unreliable sources of supply and deprived of many of the more delectable articles of the table, such as fresh fruits and vegetables, opportunities were wide open for men who had not succumbed to the lure of gold to start farms, to set up sawmills or grist mills, to manufacture salt from the waters of the bay, to build sloops and schooners for the transportation of lumber and farm produce, to develop toll roads, and to engage in every type of enterprise that would aid in supplying the market. At the landing places around the bay, from which raw materials and foodstuffs were shipped to the city, there were opportunities for still other men to lay out towns and sell real estate. The development of a good-sized port city in a few short years not surprisingly brought into being a whole complex of towns that were socially and economically linked to it.

Two of the basic needs, food and shelter, provided the stimulus for most of the villages and towns formed in this nascent period of the metropolitan region. The ranchos, particularly those in southern California, supplied the ever-expanding demand for beef; hunters of wild game provided a small part of the fresh meat consumed; and ships brought in nearly everything else required for sustenance during the first two or three years of the gold rush. But little shelter could have been provided if the hastily improvised city had had to depend on remote sources for lumber. A few precut houses were shipped all the way from Massachusetts, but it was the primeval redwood forests of the San Francisco Bay Area that supplied most of the boards, two-by-fours, and shingles needed for building shanties, hotels, and gambling houses in San Francisco. The first nonspeculative communities spawned by the metropolis were small lumber settlements, most of them only temporary. One or two that survived the period of ruthless exploitation of the ancient redwood groves did so because they enjoyed additional locational advantages. The assault on the virgin stands of timber was so unrelenting that by the end of the 1850's most of the early lumber settlements were surrounded by stumps and devastation. Six terrible fires in San Francisco between December 24, 1849, and May 4, 1851, also contributed to the exhaustion of the forests. The timber operators moved ever farther from the scene of their first endeavors—northward from the Marin Peninsula into the Russian River country, and over the mountains from the bay side of the San Francisco Peninsula into the more inaccessible canyons on the coastal side.

Lumber Towns

A hamlet on Redwood Slough, some twenty miles south of San Francisco on the bay side of the Peninsula, was one of the few settlements associated with lumber operations to achieve permanence. In 1853, when fifteen sawmills were going full blast in the Cañada de Raymundo, a few miles inland, the little settlement on the slough boasted wharves, stores, and boat works in which lumber schooners were built. Schooners piled high with milled lumber twisted down the slough to the bay, and logs were rafted on the ebb tide up the bay to San Francisco. What more natural than that S. M. Mezes, an attorney who had received a large tract of land in Rancho de las Pulgas from the Argüello family in payment for his work in protecting their title from squatters and other encroachers, should conceive the idea, in 1854, of laying out a typical gridiron town near the landing place? A busy *embarcadero* invariably suggested the possibility of attracting trade and permanent settlers. Mezesville, now Redwood City, had the further advantage of being at the junction of El Camino Real with a road from the lumbering area, the site of the present city of Woodside. Before another decade the town would also be a railroad stop.

The village of San Antonio, on upper San Antonio Creek, as the Oakland Estuary was then called, owed its existence in part to lumbering operations in the hills above the present Fruitvale section of Oakland, but other developments also contributed to its prosperity. Even before 1851, when James Larue built the wharf and store that became the nucleus of the village, the *embarcadero* of San Antonio was a busy place. Three sawmills were operating in the redwoods on the hills above the landing by the end of 1850, and lumber was being shipped from the landing to San Francisco. Captain Thomas Gray's propeller steamer *Kangaroo* began making semiweekly trips from the city to the *embarcadero* that same year, inaugurating the first transbay ferry service. Stages first ran to Stockton and to San Jose from the landing about the same time. Miners, too, set out on horseback from the *embarcadero* for the gold country, taking a route through Niles Canyon and Livermore Valley. San Antonio thus sprang up at a break in transportation routes and had not only lumber shipping but also travel to encourage its development. It was one of two small communities that were the progenitors of East Oakland. The other was Clinton, a promotional venture on the east side of the slough that has since become Lake Merritt. Both towns later merged to form Brooklyn, which in turn was absorbed by Oakland in 1872.

Pressure on the Ranchos

The collective appetite of the rapidly growing city near the Golden Gate was a much more potent force in spurring the formation of new settlements than was the need for shelter. Relatively few men could engage in the lumber operations, because, for one thing, the forests grew only in certain areas. But since all the valleys that drained into the bay offered good land for farming, as soon as the novelty of placer mining wore off or the vicissitudes of mining became discouraging, many of those who had been farmers elsewhere naturally turned to the soil to make a living.

At first the California rancho system tended to be a deterrent to widespread settlement. Would-be agriculturists found some of the choicest acres in the possession of Mexican rancheros. When the rancheros refused to sell, as they often did, the land-hungry Americans had the choice of moving on, becoming squatters, or resorting to legal trickery to get possession of the land. For years,

relations between the earlier Californians and the newcomers were marked by struggles on the ranchos and in the courts. Presumably the rancho system was protected by a clear-cut provision of the Treaty of Guadalupe Hidalgo stating that the United States would recognize "legitimate titles to every description of property, personal and real, existing in the ceded territories" formerly belonging to Mexico. But a Congress not unsympathetic to the desires of Americans who were eager to obtain land enacted a measure in 1851 that required all holders of land grants to establish the validity of their titles, thereby encouraging a certain amount of squatting on the ranchos of families whose grants were suspected of being fraudulent, though squatting of course was not confined to dubious grants. Some of the old families whose records were in good order had as much trouble with squatters as landholders who had grabbed large tracts in highly irregular fashion in the last days of the Mexican regime. Protracted legal battles, in which the rancheros sought to establish the validity of their titles, however, probably did more to break up the coveted grants than did the invasions of squatters. Many rancheros were forced into bankruptcy by the cost of defending their titles; some forfeited their grants because they were unable to bear the cost of presenting their claims; and still others, lacking cash, paid their attorneys with huge tracts of land. Thus the rancho system gradually yielded to the pressure of the newcomers, and acres once given over exclusively to cattle raising passed into the hands of men who sowed grain, set out fruit orchards, and planted potatoes, cabbages, and other vegetables.

Shipping Points

Just as some of the lumber shipping points became permanent towns, so did many of the produce shipping points. Antioch (originally Smith's Landing), Union City, Petaluma, and Suisun all developed at landings from which small craft transported agricultural products to San Francisco; and all four served as trading centers for the fertile agricultural areas in which the products were grown. Smith's Landing, renamed for the Biblical city by a group of pious folk who settled there in 1850 at the invitation of the Reverend J. H. Smith, was at the mouth of the San Joaquin River. Union City, founded in 1851 by J. M. Horner, occupied a site at the junction of Alameda Creek with a navigable slough and took its name from a small steamer called *The Union*, used by Horner to transport the vegetables and flour of his friends and neighbors to "the city." Petaluma, sixteen miles upstream on meandering Petaluma Creek, was surveyed as a town in January, 1852, and soon flourished as a shipping outlet for not only the Cotati Valley but also for settlements as far away as Mendocino County. The town of Suisun, at the head of Suisun Slough in Solano County, was laid out in 1854, after the landing first used by Captain Josiah Wing for the loading of wild grain had become a shipping point for farmers in the vicinity.

A platted town at the *embarcadero* of San Rafael in Marin County preceded several of these agricultural outlets but is in the same general category of subregional shipping and trade centers. The export of firewood and beef from the ranchos in the vicinity of the old mission settlement encouraged speculators by the name of Myers and McCullough to lay out a town in blocks three hundred feet square in 1850.

Interior towns that developed as population fanned out into the valleys around the bay were Vacaville, in Solano County, Santa Rosa, in the upper Cotati Valley, and San Jose and Santa Clara, in the Santa Clara Valley. The discovery of artesian water in San Jose and its vicinity early in 1854 immediately stimulated many new agricultural ventures and brought about further growth of both San Jose and Santa Clara. The latter town also had the distinction of being the seat of one of the first institutions of higher learning in the Bay Area, the College of Santa Clara, opened in 1851 in the dilapidated buildings of the old Mission Santa Clara.

The significant thing about most of the towns at the water's edge and in the valleys was that they were marked off into blocks and lots only after various kinds of economic activity indicated that an urban community on the site might enjoy some degree of permanence. Some of the towns, such as Antioch and Suisun, were slow in achieving importance, and one, Union City, later faded away as the near-by towns of New Haven and Alvarado developed; but the majority rested on solid if not spectacular economic foundations. The appearance of the promoter and the surveyor tended to confirm the geographical and economic advantages of the fledgling settlements.

East Bay Towns

At least two towns, Oakland and Alameda, differed from the others in origin. Neither started as an agricultural outlet, as a meeting point of transportation routes, or as a trading post. Both were akin to Benicia in that they were launched by men who were more interested in selling real estate and making money than in anything else.

From the day that William Heath Davis dreamed of laying out a town on the rancho of Vicente Peralta, the Encinal de Temescal seems to have been destined for some kind of speculative venture. Its very location directly opposite San Francisco made it especially tempting to land merchandizers. Next to attempt a town-planning scheme on the site now occupied by Oakland was Colonel Henry S. Fitch, a real-estate auctioneer, who persuaded Don Vicente to agree to sell him 2,400 acres for $8,000 if Fitch could raise that amount within fifteen days. But the colonel's deal fell through when his backer discovered a stranger living on the land and became fearful that the purchasers would be unable to get clear title to the property. The city that Fitch was unable to start by legitimate means a less scrupulous trio had no difficulty in launching by "all the devious ways of chicanery."[10] Oakland is the classic example of the shady real-estate operation, brought off at a time when rancho owners seemed rather helpless in the face of trespassers, squatters, and conniving attorneys.

In the summer of 1850, Horace W. Carpentier, a recent graduate of Columbia College in New York (now Columbia University), Edson Adams, a Yankee trader, and Alexander Moon, a much older man with a varied career, deliberately squatted on Vicente Peralta's land, each grabbing 160 acres. When Don Vicente, accompanied by forty of his vaqueros and a deputy sheriff with a writ of ejectment, sought to oust them, either Moon or Adams won the day by calm and conciliatory talk and protestations of innocence of any intention to deprive the ranchero of his land. But the three partners did not depart. Some time later, backed by a gang of Americans, they returned the call, at Peralta's own home, and "persuaded" him to grant them a lease, presumably with the promise that if his claim should be upheld by the United States Land Commission, they would leave peaceably. Having thus bullied Peralta, they proceeded to employ Julius Kellersberger to map a townsite, so that they could get on with their plan to sell lots on land that belonged to Peralta.

The surveyor drew up a typical gridiron platting scheme for the area extending from First to Fourteenth streets and from a line 300 feet west of West Street to Oak Street. The blocks were uniformly 200 by 300 feet, and the streets were all 80 feet wide with the exception of Main Street (now Broadway), which was 110 feet wide. Kellersberger has been praised for the width of his streets; he also deserves credit for allocating seven blocks, or squares, for parks. These are today the much-appreciated breathing spaces in the older part of Oakland.

In the meantime, Vicente Peralta received an honest offer for his land and in March, 1852, sold all the property south of what was known as the Encinal Line (roughly between what are now Eighteenth and Twentieth streets) to six men who were willing to pay him $10,000 for it. Among them was John C. Hays, who eventually acquired title to practically all the holdings of his associates. Far from deterring Carpentier and his unprincipled partners from proceeding with their scheme, the legitimate transaction merely spurred them to bolder acts. Carpentier obtained through his friend State Senator David C. Broderick the position of enrolling clerk of the senate and used the office to engineer the passage of a bill incorporating the town of Oakland. The act was signed by the governor on May 4, 1852, and became effective immediately.

Before the few souls living within the area of the town knew what was happening, the Carpentier-Adams-Moon triumvirate had set up a town government and put through an ordinance making Carpentier sole owner of the entire waterfront, comprising ten thousand acres of overflowed land, and giving him exclusive right to build wharves, piers, and docks for a period of thirty-seven years, with the privilege also of collecting wharfage and dockage. In return for this grant, Carpentier agreed to build three small wharves and a schoolhouse and to pay the town 2 per cent of the wharfage receipts. This, shorn of details, was the astonishing transaction that raised the

Julius Kellersberger's Map of Oakland, 1853

curtain on a bitter legal drama that was to continue until 1911, when at last Oakland regained the waterfront lost at its inception.

As for the conflicting claims of the Hays group and of Carpentier and his partners, these kept Oakland embroiled in disputes over land titles all through the 'fifties and 'sixties.

While Oakland was being conceived in iniquity and nurtured on corruption, W. W. Chipman, a lawyer and schoolteacher from Ohio, and Gideon Aughinbaugh, a Pennsylvania carpenter, laid out the town of Alameda at the eastern end of the oak-shaded peninsula known as the Encinal de San Antonio. The partners had purchased the entire *encinal* from Antonio Peralta at a time when the ever-active Colonel Fitch was dickering for a portion of it. By way of adjusting the breach of contract between Antonio and Fitch, Chipman and Aughinbaugh offered the colonel a minor interest in their new town, asked him to make the plan for it, and employed his auctioneering skill to dispose of lots. To lure prospective buyers from San Francisco, the promoters resorted to ballyhoo. They purchased two small ferryboats, the *Bonita* and the *Ranger*, and inaugurated their famed "watermelon excursions"—free boat trips and lunches, complete with watermelons and the perfervid oratory of Fitch.

A New County

One result of the growth of towns and farming settlements along the eastern side of the bay was a major change in political boundary lines in the Bay Area. The residents of Oakland, Alameda, Clinton, San Antonio, the unplatted community of Squatterville (on the site of present-day San Lorenzo), New Haven, and other small communities on the bay plain joined forces to create a new county, composed of parts of Contra Costa County and Santa Clara County. Henry C. Smith, who lived in New Haven and was Assemblyman for Santa Clara County, spearheaded the drive for the establishment of Alameda County. His petition to the state legislature pointed out, among other things, that Martinez, the county seat of Contra Costa County, was inconveniently situated to serve such towns as Oakland and Alameda, because it was at least twenty-five miles away and was separated from the bayside communities by a range of hills.

Horace Carpentier, Assemblyman for Contra Costa County, as well as owner of the Oakland waterfront and operator of the ferry service known as the Contra Costa Navigation Company, fought to make Oakland the seat of justice of this eighth Bay Area county; but for once he met his superior in political maneuvering. Smith, who is appropriately remembered as the "father of Alameda

County," succeeded in winning for New Haven, or Alvarado, the honor of being designated the first county seat.

Besides surveyed towns and unplatted but well-recognized little settlements, there appeared between 1849 and 1854 many roadside inns and crossroads taverns around which towns were later to develop. These mere beginnings of communities were found along the stage routes that linked the Bay Area towns. Between San Francisco and San Jose, Thorp's Place opened for business in 1849 at the site of present-day San Bruno, and in 1850 or 1851 the Angelo House was erected on the site of present Belmont, where a road leading to the San Andreas Valley joined El Camino Real. On the East Bay road between San Antonio and San Jose one of the first stage stations stood where the town of San Leandro later sprang up; and another, operated by William Hayward, marked the place where the town of Hayward was to develop.

Expanding Metropolis

The port metropolis toward which the people in all these wayside stops, rural settlements, bayside outlets, and valley towns looked for news of the distant world beyond the seas increased in population with each passing year. Its population was estimated at approximately thirty thousand at the end of 1851. In 1852 almost 77,000 newcomers arrived by ship—more than double the number who had disembarked the previous year; and only 23,000 homesick or disheartened people booked passage on departing vessels. As usual, thousands of the newcomers hurried on to the mines; yet the population of San Francisco rose to between 36,000 and 42,000.

The streets became more crowded; the wharves stretched farther into the bay, as if to welcome the pageant of ships; the sides of Telegraph Hill came tumbling down under the concussions of blasting powder and were dumped into the bay to create more land for buildings. Steam excavators cut Market Street through from Kearny to Battery Street, leveled the mound of sand that had obstructed Bush Street, and made way westward for California, Sacramento, and other streets. Horse-drawn carts dumped the sand into Yerba Buena Cove, and wagons on temporary rails also rolled to the water's edge with their freight of sand, until little by little the city pushed the bay many blocks from the original beach.

Between the post office at Kearny and Clay streets and Mission Dolores, a new omnibus line, the first regular transportation in the city, began operating on a thirty-minute schedule. This was the famous "Yellow Line," which charged a fare of fifty cents on week days and one dollar on Sundays. Just as the plank road to the Mission, when first completed, had proved a stimulus to real-estate

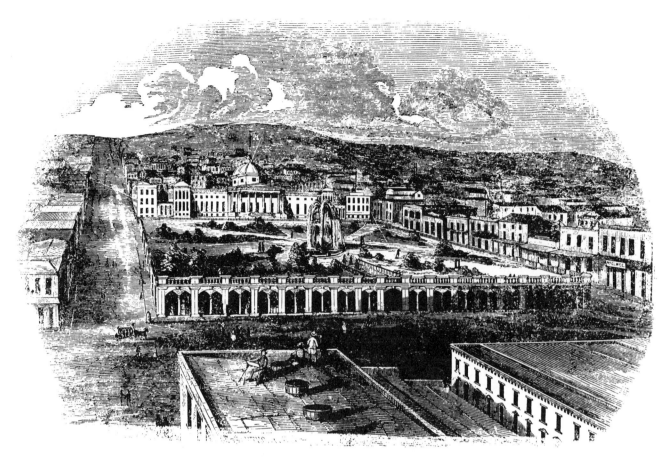

A Design by an Artist Named Stewart for the Improvement of Portsmouth Plaza, San Francisco, 1853. Estimated to cost $100,000, this proposed scheme was never carried out. Photograph courtesy of the San Francisco Public Library.

and building activities, so did the new omnibus line. The pattern of growth in San Francisco, westward and southward and up the slopes of many hills, was to be shaped largely by transit lines—and these would be extended not in response to any plan of development but, as in other American cities, wherever the opportunity for private gain appeared or the mere whim of a tycoon dictated.

Portents of Disaster

Immigration during 1853 was described as "spectacular"; yet there were signs that the boom days of the gold rush would sooner or later come to an end. A great many adventurers departed for Australia, said to be the scene of gold discoveries more promising than those in California. The weekly *Golden Era* observed in July that "our city is filling up with disappointed and disheartened miners, who say that a scarcity of gold and water in the diggings has made it necessary to seek employment in the city."[11]

Despite these portents, the wave of speculation that rose higher and higher with the arrival of each new ship-

load of immigrants surged to fantastic heights. On the day after Christmas, bidders outshouted one another in their frenzy to purchase 120 small water lots that were covered by water of an average depth of eight feet. Only at great expense could these lots be filled for building, but the bewitched purchasers eagerly paid a total of $1,193,500 to possess them.

Two months later, creeping paralysis attacked the real-estate market and unimproved town lots were "almost unsalable at any price."[12]

A dream of animated newcomers forever crowding down gangplanks into the port of gold had sustained the saturnalia of speculation. Now immigration unexpectedly fell off and the city found itself appallingly overbuilt. Of one thousand commercial buildings available, only three hundred were occupied in the middle of 1854. Rents dropped 20 to 30 per cent. Several real-estate firms went bankrupt.

With clothing, household furnishings, imported foods, and luxuries of all kinds the city also was oversupplied.

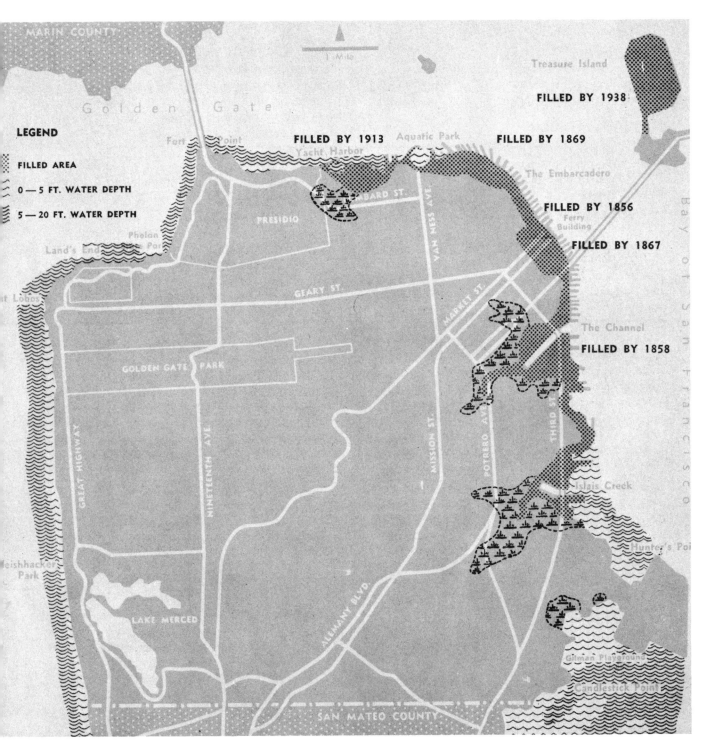

LEGEND

FILLED AREA

0 — 5 FT. WATER DEPTH

5 — 20 FT. WATER DEPTH

The Changing Shoreline of San Francisco

Now there were forced sales to ease the glutted market. Prices fell day by day. Business failures increased. Clerks lost their jobs and joined discouraged miners in a fruitless search for work.

As the depression grew steadily worse, forceclosures increased, the value of real estate diminished to half what it had been, and credit dried up. The once mercurial inhabitants of San Francisco were borne ineluctably toward the Black Friday of February 23, 1855, when the banking and express firm of Adams and Company failed to open its doors and general panic seized depositors and investors, bringing about the downfall of many banks and business houses and wiping out personal fortunes.

The Marvel of California

In a little more than eight years from the time of the American occupation San Francisco had been transformed from an obscure village to a world-famous city. To all Californians it was *the* city; for even San Jose, Stockton, Sacramento, and Marysville were hardly more than good-sized towns. From the new San Francisco Mint, opened in April, 1854, standardized coins flowed into the arteries of trade and finance, replacing the curious assortment of foreign coins, gold slugs, and pinches of gold dust previously used as money. In San Francisco's principal business streets the first gas lamps on the Pacific Coast lighted the way of the night reveler. The hills were "dotted with new cottages of all styles of architecture, ancient and modern,"[13] and at least one real-estate firm, that of the unctuous Henry Fitch, advertised that it could "transact business in the English, French, German, Spanish, and Italian languages."[14] San Francisco was the marvel of California, a city that the whole race of mankind had had a hand in fashioning—but it was, as yet, no breath-taking symbol of human brotherhood.

As Bancroft described it: "It was a straggling city . . . with its dumps and blotches of hills and hillocks, of bleak spots of vacancy and ugly cuts and raised lines. The architecture was no less patchy, for in the centre prison-like and graceful structures alternated, interspersed with frail wooden frames and zinc and corrugated iron walls, and occasionally the hull of some hauled-up vessel; while beyond rude cabins and ungainly superimposed stories of lodging-houses in neglected grounds varied with tasteful villas embowered in foliage, and curious houses perched high on square-cut mounds."[15]

The gridiron street pattern, perpetuated and extended through the surveys of O'Farrell and Eddy, involved the municipality and individual citizens in endless expenditures for the adjustment of street grades. "If the great thoroughfares had been adapted to the natural configuration of the tract of country upon which the city stands," the authors of the *Annals of San Francisco* pointed out, "there might have been some apparent irregularity in the plan, and some, perhaps some little ground available for building purposes lost, yet many millions of dollars would have been saved to the community at large, which, as matters stand, have already been unprofitably expended, while millions more must still be spent in overcoming the obstacles wilfully placed in the way by the originally defective plans," or, more precisely, by the "absurd mathematical notions" of Francisco de Haro and Vioget.[16]

CHAPTER THREE

The Plow, the Iron Horse, and New Towns

As thousands awakened from the gold rush dream of sudden wealth and began to regard California as something more than a Far Western treasure house stocked by an indiscreet nature especially for them to loot, they came soberly to the conclusion that the destiny of the area around San Francisco Bay lay principally in the development of agriculture, manufacturing, and transportation.

San Francisco, though shaken by the failure of two hundred firms in 1855, maintained its position as *the* commercial, financial, and shipping center of California. In addition, it became a center for the manufacture of the new and expensive mining machinery required to extract gold from the veins of quartz in which it was now chiefly to be found. Quartz mining, in fact, fathered a whole series of California industries, the plants of some of which formed the nuclei of new towns in the San Francisco Bay Area. But in the period 1855–1870, agricultural rather than manufacturing developments were of primary significance in shaping the future metropolitan region.

Farming and New Towns

The foundations for agricultural enterprises long associated with the various counties in the Bay Area were laid during the years of readjustment following the financial crisis of 1855. Louis Pellier introduced *la petite prune d'Agen* at San Jose in 1856–1857, giving Santa Clara County the fruit that was to make it famous throughout the world. Colonel Agoston Haraszthy, the Hungarian nobleman who later introduced 315 named varieties of wine grapes to California, settled in Sonoma in 1856, founded a horticultural society, and began importing vines from abroad. First to advocate the growing of grapes without irrigation, he wrote a treatise on the culture of the vine and the manufacture of wine that was published in 1858 by the state for gratuitous distribution. That same year Charles Krug started the Napa Valley wine industry, producing twelve hundred gallons of wine, on the John Patchet place near the city of Napa, by processes new to early residents. In the Point Reyes area of Marin County, three brothers named Steele and a number of other farmers in 1856 began developing the dairying interests for which the northern part of the county is well known. In Contra Costa County, which was to become a great wheat-producing area, many farmers in the 1850's followed the example set by Elam Brown, of Acalanes, in 1848 when he planted a rather large area to wheat and discovered that the yield was prodigious. By 1858 nearly seventeen thousand acres in the county were rippling with the golden grain.

A natural consequence of the accelerated development of farming was the establishment of new towns in the fertile valleys—Saint Helena in the upper Napa Valley; Sebastopol on the west side of the Cotati Valley, and Bloomfield on the road between the valley and Bodega Bay; Healdsburg on the main wagon road through the Russian River country to Mendocino County; Rio Vista on the Sacramento River in eastern Solano County; Fairfield on the same slough that served its near neighbor,

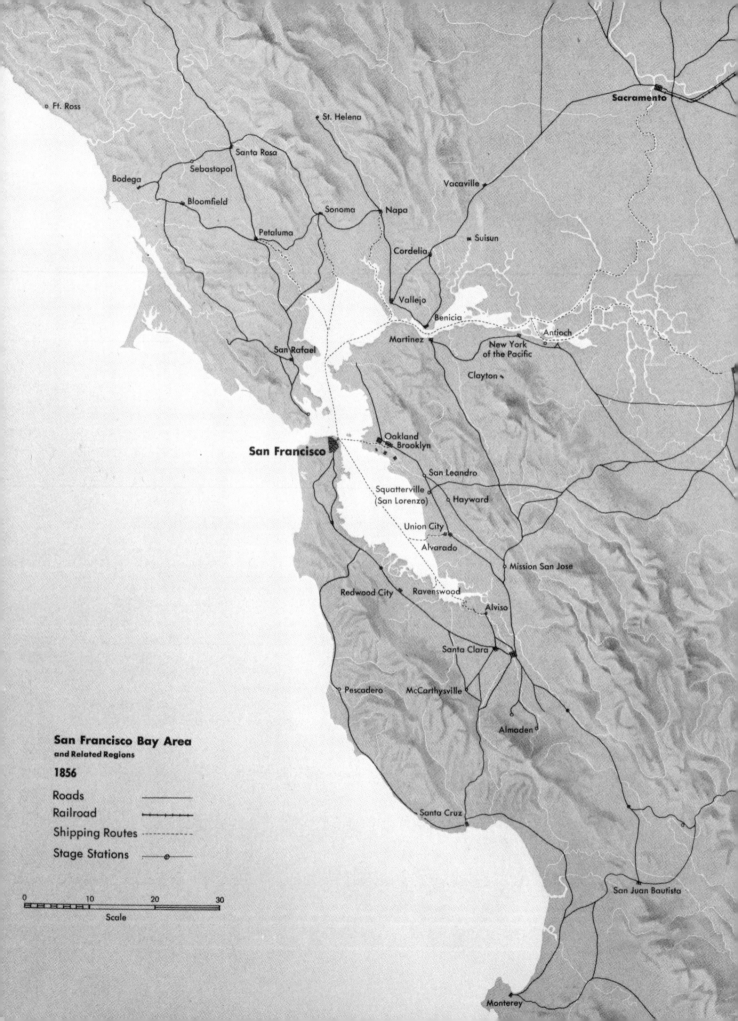

Ft. Ross

St. Helena

Santa Rosa

Sebastopol

Bodega

Bloomfield

Sonoma

Napa

Vacaville

Sacramento

Petaluma

Cordelia

Suisun

Vallejo

Benicia

Antioch

San Rafael

Martinez

New York
of the Pacific

Clayton

Oakland
Brooklyn

San Francisco

San Leandro

Squatterville
(San Lorenzo)

Hayward

Union City

Alvarado

Mission San Jose

Redwood City

Ravenswood

Alviso

Santa Clara

Pescadero

McCarthysville

Almaden

Santa Cruz

San Juan Bautista

Monterey

San Francisco Bay Area
and Related Regions

1856

Roads

Railroad

Shipping Routes

Stage Stations

0   10   20   30

Scale

Suisun; and Pacheco and Walnut Creek in the Ygnacio Valley of central Contra Costa County. In addition to these towns, all founded between 1855 and 1860, the town of Clayton was laid out at the foot of Mount Diablo in 1856 by Joel Clayton when the discovery of veins of coal on the northern slopes of the mountain gave promise of large-scale coal mining operations.

Two of this group of towns, Rio Vista and Pacheco, later proved to be subject to flooding. Rio Vista was removed to higher ground after the disastrous floods of the winter of 1861–62. Salvio and Fernando Pacheco and their friend Francisco Galindo started a new town in 1869 two miles east of Pacheco and named it Todos Santos (All Saints). Some Americans disrespectfully tagged it Drunken Indian, but others soon made amends by calling it Concord, by which name it is now known.

Fairfield got off to a good start, thanks to an ambitious founder, Captain R. H. Waterman. At a county-seat convention in 1858, the very year in which the town was platted, Waterman aggressively undertook to transfer the seat of justice from Benicia. His inducement to the voters to accept Fairfield as a county seat was an offer to deed to the county "a certain piece of land containing about sixteen acres, known upon the plat of the town of Fairfield as 'Union Park,'" and certain other properties.[1] In the battle of the ballots waged on September 2, 1858, the sometime state capital was further shorn of glory, and the county records were immediately moved to a temporary courthouse in Fairfield.

Industrial Growth

With few exceptions, industries in the San Francisco Bay Area in the 1850's developed *with* the towns and did not give rise to new communities. Perhaps one of the exceptions is in Contra Costa County where warehouses and a flour mill on Nueces (Walnut) Creek prompted the laying out of the town of Pacheco. Flour mills, however, were usually among the first structures erected in new towns, because in every county bordering on the bay the growing of grains was attempted. San Francisco, San Jose, and the larger communities each had several mills by the end of the 'fifties, some of which dated from the beginning of the gold rush.

Breweries, too, were established very early. One was in operation in San Francisco in 1850. Others were started in Oakland in 1852, in San Jose in 1853, and in other towns in subsequent years.

Wagon shops, blacksmith shops, saddle shops, small foundries, small planing mills, bakeries, soda works, confectionery shops, and similar establishments supplying home needs all helped to provide employment and stimu-late the growth of towns; but there was no appreciable manufacturing other than the production of mining machinery until the 'sixties, when the Civil War made importation difficult and Californians seized their opportunity to launch new industries.

The making of jellies from California fruit by Daniel Prevost in San Francisco in 1856 is worthy of note as marking the beginning of the fruit-processing industry, which would eventually account for the growth of many communities.

Road Building

A wider distribution of population and the gradual growth of towns stimulated not only an increase in staging and in transbay travel but extensive road building as well, particularly in the North Bay counties. The Napa County Board of Supervisors levied a tax in 1858 for the construction of a road from the city of Napa to the Russian River Valley by way of Knight's Valley, and for the construction of another road up the east side of Napa Creek to Clear Lake by way of Chiles Canyon. In Sonoma County a network of roads from Petaluma to other points in the county was authorized. Begun in 1859, these roads soon linked the shipping outlet on Petaluma Creek with Sonoma, San Rafael, Bodega, Two Rock Valley, and near-by Lakeville, on Petaluma Slough.

In Alameda County there were no less than thirteen road districts by 1858, with a road supervisor for each. Citizens of Oakland "felt more free and travelled more frequently" because the county board of supervisors the year before had paid Horace Carpentier $6,000 for his toll bridge across the arm of the estuary between Oakland and Brooklyn (the present Lake Merritt) and had abolished the restrictive charge.[2] Vicente Peralta added another footnote to county history when he petitioned the board in November, 1858, to have Telegraph Road, now one of the main thoroughfares between Oakland and Berkeley, extended around his property on Temescal Creek rather than through it. The request was denied, however, and Telegraph Avenue today runs straight as a ruler.

Improvements in local transit in the latter half of the 'fifties consisted chiefly of the establishment of several new omnibus lines in San Francisco and one between San Jose and Santa Clara in 1856. The new lines in San Francisco extended from the business district to Meiggs' Wharf in North Beach, to the Presidio, to Mission Dolores, and to Third and Townsend streets. Unfortunately, the competitive paralleling of routes tended to concentrate population unduly in certain areas, thereby preventing a distribution that would have contributed to a more open

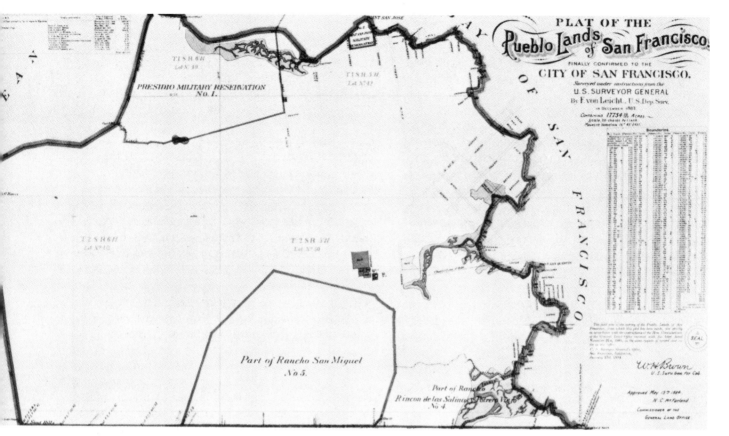

The Pueblo Lands of San Francisco as Surveyed in December, 1883. Of the 17,754.36 acres finally confirmed to the city as successor to the pueblo of Yerba Buena, all but approximately 4,000 were in federal or private ownership at the time of Judge Stephen J. Field's decision in 1864. The survey shows the shoreline of the bay as it was at the time of the American conquest in 1846. Filled lands beyond this shoreline were not included in the confirmation.

and more desirable type of urban development.

Expiration of the toll-collecting privilege on two plank roads to Mission Dolores and the construction of the San Bruno Turnpike from the mission to the site of present-day San Bruno in 1858 stimulated the movement of population toward the Mission Valley. The town of San Bruno developed around the San Bruno House on the turnpike.

Squatters and Land Titles

The influence of omnibus routes and toll-free roads in shaping the physical growth of the metropolis, though significant, was not so great as that of decisions reached in the political arena in the critical years following the end of the gold rush. Land commissioners, judges, squatters, venal local politicians, racketeers, reformers, and state legislators all had a hand in determining the manner in which the city developed. Two major problems faced the

city: the unsettled state of land titles, which retarded development of certain areas; and the corruption and extravagance of local officials at a time when the inhabitants were still suffering from the shock of the depression brought on by overspeculation.

In 1852 the City of San Francisco, as successor to the Pueblo of Yerba Buena, had filed a claim before the United States Land Commission for four square leagues of land, to which every pueblo was entitled under the laws of Spain and of Mexico. By this procedure the city sought not only to extend its corporate boundaries to the Pacific Ocean but also perhaps to get increased tax revenue from lands occupied by squatters. In December, 1854, the commission confirmed to the city all the land north of the so-called Vallejo Line, approved by the territorial *Diputación* in 1834 as the limits of the pueblo. This line, running from what is now known as Steamboat Point (Fourth and Berry streets) to the Divisadero (Lone

Mountain) and thence to the south side of Point Lobos, embraced only about three leagues of land instead of four. The city, therefore, appealed from the decision, asserting its claim to a larger quantity of land; while the United States government also appealed, on the ground that the city had no title to any land.

In the meantime, reasonably certain that its title to a good part of the lands within its 1851 charter limits would be upheld, the city sought to come to terms with the squatters. There were many of these in the unsurveyed area between Larkin and Johnson (Ninth) streets and the western boundary as established by the legislature in 1851 at Divisadero Street. Disputes between squatters, many of whom were hired representatives of some of San Francisco's wealthiest citizens, flared from time to time into open warfare and often resulted in bloodshed and loss of life. In the hope of putting an end to this violence by clarifying questions of ownership, the city enacted an ordinance giving title to those who had been in actual possession of lands west of Larkin and Johnson streets from January 1, 1855, to June 30, 1855. Titles to lands east of Larkin and Johnson streets obtained through grants made by the alcaldes, or municipal authorities, of the former pueblo likewise were recognized. But the ordinance provided that title to all disputed lands which were not actually held by bona fide property holders should be relinquished to the city.

As a plan for ending the disputes, the ordinance, signed by Mayor James Van Ness and cited as the Van Ness Ordinance, was for some years a failure, even after it was ratified by the state legislature in 1858. The squatter warfare continued, and it was not until the United States District Court, then the Circuit Court, and finally the Congress of the United States acted on the city's claim to the pueblo lands that the thorny issue of land titles was settled, in the 1860's.

The Van Ness Ordinance is important from the standpoint of city planning, however, because it determined the pattern of streets and public squares in the area known as the Western Addition. Actually, what is now called the Van Ness Ordinance was three separate ordinances—one dealing with land titles (No. 822), one with the reservation of lands for public purposes (No. 845), and one approving a map showing a plan for the area between Larkin and Johnson streets and the Divisadero (No. 846). This map, referred to as the Van Ness Map, extended the monotonous gridiron westward without regard to topography and designated certain areas as public squares: Jefferson Square, Alamo Square, Hamilton Square, and the so-called Hospital Lot, now in part Duboce Park. The width of Van Ness Avenue also was determined by this map.

The Ninth County

The Van Ness Ordinance affected only the citizens of San Francisco; but another enactment of this turbulent period, the Consolidation Act of 1856, which united the City of San Francisco and San Francisco County as a single political entity, affected residents of the San Francisco Peninsula as well. Originally San Francisco County extended southward to San Francisquito Creek, the present boundary between Santa Clara and San Mateo counties, and the city occupied only a small area on the northeast tip of the Peninsula. Through the years the criminal element and the big and little grafters had discovered that a system of dual authority, with one administration for the county and another for the city, was ideally suited for the protection of evildoers. Since corruption permeated both administrations, a malefactor could always find friends somewhere to connive with him in his shady operations and shield him from punishment. Popular indignation against the rampant abuses of local government eventually expressed itself in the second Vigilance uprising; but even before the murder of the crusading editor of the San Francisco *Bulletin*, James King of William, unleashed the thunderbolts, the tempest of reform was sweeping through the metropolis. Horace Hawes, San Francisco's representative in the state legislature, wrote and introduced a bill to restrict the area of the county, make the city and county boundaries coterminous, and establish a single governing body of twelve members, whose "powers were so carefully defined that they were almost nonexistent," as one historian remarked.[3] The bill was passed by the legislature and was approved by the governor on April 9, 1856, three weeks before the organization of the second Vigilance Committee.

Curiously, the title and enacting clause of the bill did not even mention that the measure provided for the creation of an entirely new county, San Mateo, the ninth and last of the Bay Area counties. Hawes apparently saw no way to consolidate the city and county governments of San Francisco without drastically reducing the size of the county. A story current at the time said that in order to get enough votes for his bill he was obliged to provide a haven for the crooked element—a new county. It is true that an undesirable element did try to organize San Mateo County, but fortunately the decent people of the area thwarted the attempt.

In working out his scheme for unification of city and county governments in San Francisco, Hawes had, of course, no example of a city embracing huge areas of farmland, as Los Angeles, for instance, did until fairly recently. A city in the 1850's was thought of as a compact,

Map of the City and County of San Francisco, 1861. Besides the areas surveyed by Jasper O'Farrell and William Eddy, the map shows three later additions to the city —the Potrero Nuevo, Horner's Addition, and the Western Addition. In the early 'sixties the city occupied some two thousand acres of the peninsula.

densely settled place. Hawes may have fancied himself daring, indeed, to propose sudden expansion of San Francisco to an area of forty-two square miles, or nearly twenty-seven thousand acres, for the city proper, even in 1860, occupied only two thousand acres. Within the new city limits were thousands of acres of pasture, cultivated farmland, and wildernesses of drifting sand.

The balloting in San Mateo County's first election was not without irregularities, as might have been predicted from the preëlection activities of the vicious element driven from San Francisco. Suspecting that there had been some padding of the returns, wary citizens challenged the votes in three precincts and succeeded in having them thrown out. The elimination of these votes denied the village of Belmont the honor of becoming the county seat and gave it to Redwood City. Afterward the State Supreme Court held that the entire election had been scheduled before the act creating the county went into effect, and a second election was therefore held in May, 1857. This second election did not, however, affect the location of the county seat.

Political developments also influenced the growth of a small community in Alameda County in 1856. The legislature passed a special act in February of that year authorizing the removal of the county seat from Alvarado to San Leandro, thus stimulating the growth of the latter town.

The Problem of Isolation

Like all the rest of California, the San Francisco Bay Area suffered increasingly from lack of rapid overland communication with the eastern United States and from lack of railroad transportation to the populous states east of the great deserts and mountains. Had San Francisco offices of certain important eastern banking institutions been able to communicate more readily with their home offices in early February, 1855, they might not have closed their doors and the city might not have been engulfed in financial panic. In the late 'fifties, when farms were beginning to produce abundantly, agriculturists realized that the problem of surpluses might be eased considerably if they could ship some of their products east by rail.

The possibility of a transcontinental railroad perennially engrossed the press, public speakers, and cracker-barrel philosophers; but all through the 'fifties the hopes of Bay Area residents and other northern Californians for a central route across the continent were alternately raised and dashed by the acrimonious debates in Congress between Southern and Northern senators over the location of the route and the parts to be played by the federal government and by private enterprise, respectively. The problem of overland communication was more readily solved—at first by the semiweekly Butterfield Stage, then by the Pony Express, and from 1861 on by the transcontinental telegraph. But not until the Civil War broke out and Congress became uneasy lest California support the Confederacy, or fall prey to foreign intervention, or become the nucleus of an independent Pacific republic was a railroad through the heart of the continent at last authorized—on July 1, 1862.

Rails on the Peninsula

More than a year before President Lincoln signed the Pacific Railroad Act, work had begun on a railroad between San Francisco and San Jose that prominent citizens of both communities hoped might become the last link in the transcontinental line. This was the railroad that farmers in the Santa Clara Valley had been talking about since 1849. The first and second companies organized to finance the line had taken the grandiose name The Pacific and Atlantic Rail Road Company and had proposed building eastward in some shining future. The third company modestly called itself The San Francisco and San Jose Rail Road Company; but it, too, failed to solve the problem of financing the project. The fourth company, formed in 1860, took the same name. It won the support of the state legislature and the press and was able to convince the voters of San Francisco, San Mateo, and Santa Clara counties that they should approve county subsidies for the railroad.

Ground was broken at San Francisquito Creek on the San Francisco Peninsula on May 1, 1861, for construction of the railroad, and by July grading of the route was well under way in both San Mateo and Santa Clara counties. The plan worked out in 1851 by William Lewis, the chief engineer, for a line running into San Francisco on a pile bridge east of the San Bruno Mountains had been abandoned in favor of a route west of the mountains and through the Mission Valley. With an eye on the county-aid elections, the officials of the line concluded that more San Franciscans would vote for financial assistance from the county if the railroad went through the more densely populated areas. Furthermore, the cost of construction through the Mission district would be less than along the bay shore.

No sooner was the railroad a certainty than large property owners along the route saw their opportunity to market land. Timothy Guy Phelps and some of his friends filed a map of a subdivision west of the County Road (El Camino Real) at Redwood City, convenient to the right of way of the new line. In September, 1862, C. B. Polhemus, one of the directors of the railroad, had William Lewis plat the town of San Mateo at the point where the right of way crossed San Mateo Creek. In the vicinity were the first of the great country estates for which the Peninsula was to be famous in the latter part of the century. In 1863 when the railroad was nearing completion between San Francisco and Mayfield, or what is now the southern part of Palo Alto, the Menlo Park Villa Association advertised five-acre "villa lots" in a tract of more than eight hundred acres. The name "Menlo Park" derived from Menlough on Lough Corrib, County Galway, Ireland, the former home of two brothers-in-law who had purchased a piece of Rancho de las Pulgas in 1854.

At ceremonies in San Jose on January 16, 1864, marking completion of the entire line, Judge Timothy Dame, president of the company, thrilled everyone by announcing that the Central Pacific Railroad had assigned to his company and to the Western Pacific Railroad (which is

San Francisco as Seen from Russian Hill, 1863. Reproduction courtesy of Bancroft Library.

not to be confused with the present-day railroad of the same name) the right to construct that section of the transcontinental railroad from San Francisco to Sacramento. As Dame was also president of the Western Pacific, which had been organized in 1862 to construct a railroad from San Jose to Sacramento via Stockton, the celebrants had little reason to doubt that the new line on the Peninsula would indeed become part of the great transcontinental railroad begun at Sacramento on February 22, 1863. But the distinction of being the last link in the great overland railroad was reserved by the fates for a four-mile local line that had been in operation in Oakland for some months.[4]

East Bay Railroads

The San Francisco and Oakland Ferry Railroad, extending from Seventh and Broadway in Oakland to the Oakland Wharf at Gibbon's Point, on the mud flats west of the city, was the first railroad completed in the Bay Area. Opened on September 2, 1863, it connected at Oakland Wharf with the transbay ferry *Contra Costa*. A year later it was extended across the arm of the estuary now known as Lake Merritt, and in 1865 it was linked with another small railroad known as the "Encinal Road."

The real name of this latter railroad was the San Francisco and Alameda Railroad. Built by Alfred A. Cohen, who participated in many Bay Area developments of the 'sixties, this line originally ran from High Street in Alameda to the Alameda Wharf, where passengers transferred to ferries to San Francisco. Cohen extended it southward to San Leandro in May, 1865, and to Hayward in August of that year. Although he was ambitious to join it at Niles Canyon with the Western Pacific Railroad, then building between San Jose and Stockton, he was unable to finance construction beyond Hayward. There the rails ended—until the day in 1869 when the "Big Four" of the Central Pacific (Leland Stanford, Charles Crocker, Collis P. Huntington, and Mark Hopkins) joined them to the transcontinental line and made Oakland rather than San Francisco the terminus.

Railroad Fever

The years preceding completion of the Pacific railroad were years of railroad fever in the San Francisco Bay Area. There was as much talk of stock subscriptions, county railroad bonds, public and private donations of land for depots, and of new subdivisions and new towns along railroad rights of way as there was of freeways,

fringe-area tract developments, and new shopping centers in the decade following World War II. At one time or another the residents of every major valley in the Bay Area furiously debated the merits of schemes for introducing the railroad to the local scene; and not a few of these schemes were successful. By the time the first overland train of the Central Pacific reached its destination, small engines with huge smokestacks were trailing plumes of black smoke up and down the Napa Valley and the Santa Clara Valley and between Vallejo and Sacramento, while a small railroad was under construction between San Rafael and Point San Quentin in Marin County. Voters in Contra Costa County had, however, decisively defeated a proposal that the county issue bonds for the construction of a railroad from Martinez to Danville, in the San Ramon Valley; and residents of the Cotati Valley had witnessed the failure of four successive companies that sought to finance a railroad in that area.

The Napa Valley Railroad, forty-one miles in length, extended from Soscol to Calistoga, where Samuel Brannan, treasurer of the line, had a hot springs resort which he hoped to make as fashionable as Saratoga in New York State. At Soscol the line connected with a ferry to San Francisco. The railroad provided Napa Valley farm-

ers with the kind of fast transportation that they needed, and it aided A. Y. Easterby, vice-president of the company, in marketing land in a new subdivision near Napa called Holly Oak Park. "This property is within two hours of San Francisco and is comparatively as near as Menlo Park," an advertisement of Easterby and Company proclaimed in 1869.[5]

The railroad through the Santa Clara Valley from San Jose to Gilroy, at the southern end of the valley, was constructed by the controlling interests of the San Francisco and San Jose Rail Road under a contract with a company chartered in 1865 as the Southern Pacific Railroad. Gilroy citizens who welcomed the iron horse with a brass band, shouts, and waving handkerchiefs believed that the railroad eventually would be extended down the state to a connection at the Colorado River with a railroad from Missouri. In anticipation of big things, they had voted to incorporate their town and to have the townsite surveyed some months before the first train actually pulled in.

The California Pacific, as the railroad from Vallejo to Sacramento was called, was linked with San Francisco by the ferryboat *New World*, which made the bay crossing in an hour and twenty minutes, bringing Vallejo as close to the metropolis in time as Redwood City on the San Francisco Peninsula and San Leandro in Alameda County. A branch of the line extended from Davis to Woodland, in Yolo County. Significantly, the first freight hauled over the tracks of the California Pacific was wheat, for the great wheat era of the state was beginning. The Starr Mills, erected at Vallejo in 1869 about the time the railroad was completed, were soon producing one thousand barrels of flour a day and shipping more than eighteen hundred tons monthly to Europe.

Like Alfred A. Cohen's railroads in the East Bay, the Napa Valley Railroad, and the California Pacific, the little line completed in March, 1870, between San Rafael and Point San Quentin also connected with a ferry providing service to San Francisco. And when Peter Donahue, founder of the famous Union Iron Works in San Francisco, built a railroad in the Cotati Valley to Santa Rosa, completed later that same year, its southern terminus at Donahue, eight miles below Petaluma on Petaluma Creek, likewise was beside a slip used by ferries plying to and from "the city."

In a single decade, then, combination rail and ferry services united the metropolis near the Golden Gate with almost the whole surrounding region and with an important section of the Central Valley as well, making towns from fifty to seventy-five or a hundred miles away fairly accessible.

San Franciscans were bitterly disappointed, however, that their city was not chosen as the terminus of the transcontinental railroad. "Almost sure" that the titans of the Central Pacific would build a railroad bridge across Dumbarton Strait near the lower end of the bay and bring their trains up the Peninsula to San Francisco, one real-estate firm had put on an intensive campaign in 1868 to sell villa lots of ten to twenty acres at Menlo Park and Fair Oaks (Atherton).[6] But any spurt that may have been given to the real-estate market in San Mateo County and San Francisco by talk of a railroad bridge to the Peninsula was quickly ended by the announcement of a major business deal in Oakland.

Oakland: Railroad Terminus

On March 31, 1868, Horace Carpentier, still sole possessor of the Oakland waterfront, deeded to a four-day-old corporation known as the Oakland Water-front Company almost the entire Oakland waterfront. The next day this company deeded five hundred acres to the Western Pacific Railroad, an affiliate of the Central Pacific, to be used for a terminal for the transcontinental line, with the stipulation that the railroad might select the land it wanted. In addition, the Oakland Water-front Company ceded to the railroad two strips of land, each not more than a hundred feet wide, for a right of way. In return for these grants, the Western Pacific agreed to complete its railroad from Niles into Oakland and to spend not less than $500,000 on terminal facilities within the next three years.

These swift developments climaxed a series of discussions that Carpentier had initiated with Leland Stanford. The Oakland Water-front Company was Carpentier's device for associating himself with the builders of the Central Pacific and benefiting by the potentially most profitable railroad venture in the West. Of the $5,000,000 worth of capital stock of the new company, Carpentier, as director, held 46 per cent, while his brother, Edward R. Carpentier, and Lloyd Tevis together held 9 per cent. Stanford, treasurer of the new company, owned 35 per cent, and attorney John B. Felton held 10 per cent. One share went to Dr. Samuel Merritt, Mayor of Oakland—and thereby hangs a tale.

The Waterfront "Compromise"

Although Oakland had struggled throughout its municipal history to regain the waterfront that Carpentier had grabbed in early days, the city now quickly arrived at a "compromise" with Carpentier. On the same day that the Oakland Water-front Company ceded land to the Western Pacific, it also regranted to the City of Oakland the parcel of land situated at the foot of Broadway—land also claimed by the San Francisco and Oakland Railway Company—and the arm of the Oakland Estuary known today as Lake Merritt. The Oakland City Council, for its part, ratified and confirmed the ordinances of 1852 and 1853 that had given Carpentier control of the waterfront. In other words, the city fathers, presumably on the urging of Dr. Merritt, released and abandoned all claims of the city to the waterfront and provided, by ordinance, that Carpentier should reconvey the waterfront properties in accordance with the terms of the contract between the Oakland Water-front Company, the Western Pacific, and other parties.

Although some scurrilous comment greeted this so-called "compromise," most Oakland residents were so jubilant over the selection of the city as the western terminus of the transcontinental railroad that they chose to overlook the "highly suspicious character" of the agreement. Generally, it was believed that real-estate values would increase and that Oakland's prospects for becoming a great commercial city were indeed roseate. Carpentier, formerly the "monster whose blighting influence had retarded the city's prosperity,"[7] now appeared to be a public benefactor.

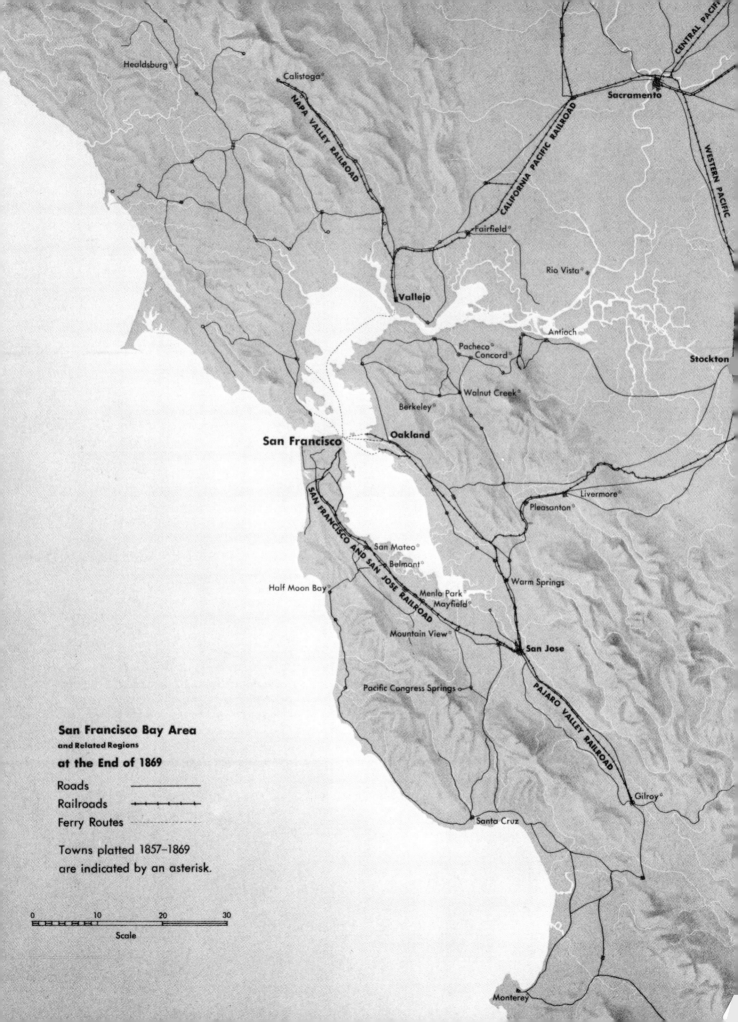

Healdsburg°

Calistoga°

NAPA VALLEY RAILROAD

CENTRAL PACIFIC

Sacramento

CALIFORNIA PACIFIC RAILROAD

WESTERN PACIFIC

Fairfield°

Rio Vista °*

Vallejo

Antioch°

Pacheco°
Concord°

Stockton

Berkeley°

Walnut Creek°

Oakland

San Francisco

Livermore°

Pleasanton°

SAN FRANCISCO AND SAN JOSE RAILROAD

San Mateo°

Belmont°

Half Moon Bay°

Menlo Park°
Mayfield°

Warm Springs

Mountain View°

San Jose

Pacific Congress Springs °

PAJARO VALLEY RAILROAD

Gilroy°

Santa Cruz

San Francisco Bay Area
and Related Regions

at the End of 1869

Roads ————————

Railroads ┼┼┼┼┼┼┼┼

Ferry Routes ------------

Towns platted 1857–1869
are indicated by an asterisk.

0   10   20   30
Scale

Monterey

First Overland Train

On September 6, 1869, the first overland train rolled through Niles Canyon and headed north toward Alameda, cheered by crowds at San Leandro and grade crossings en route. Although Oakland was to be the permanent terminus, this first train had as its destination Alameda Wharf, which it reached by way of the local line of the San Francisco and Alameda Railroad. On November 8 the main-line trains were routed to Oakland Wharf along the Seventh Street line of the Oakland-Alameda system that the Central Pacific had acquired from A. A. Cohen prior to the opening of the transcontinental line. In the following year, tracks were laid on First Street in Oakland for use of main-line trains, so that Seventh Street might be reserved exclusively for local service.

In the boom days before and after the arrival of the first overland train, real-estate activities rose to a high pitch and several new towns were platted. William M. Mendenhall, who owned a large tract near the village of Laddsville in the Livermore Valley, gave twenty acres to the Western Pacific for a depot and in July, 1869, laid out a new town named in honor of Robert Livermore, the pioneer settler in that part of Alameda County. Laddsville, which had grown up a few years earlier around the old Livermore house half a mile or more from the tracks, declined as the new town developed. Only six days after the opening of the railroad, the sale of lots started in the newly platted town of Pleasanton, at the place in the Livermore Valley formerly called Alisal. A year or more later the Central Pacific itself formed the Decoto Land Company, purchased 284 acres on the bay plain in southern Alameda County from Ezra Decoto and his brothers, and laid out the town of Decoto. The settlement, however, grew very slowly until recent decades.

Economic Expansion

Speeches and editorials on the completion of the transcontinental railroad hailed the end of California's isolation as the dawn of a new era of development in the state, but in reality the new era of economic expansion had begun about the time the "Big Four" broke ground at Sacramento for the Central Pacific. The discovery of the fabulous Comstock Lode in Nevada in 1859, the opening of copper mines in Arizona, and the decreased flow of manufactured goods from the East as a result of the Civil War all contributed to the establishment of new home industries and to the growth of many already in existence. In rapid succession appeared carriage-manufacturing enterprises, boot and shoe factories in San Francisco, tanneries throughout the Bay Area, woolen mills in San Francisco and San Jose, the Spreckels sugar refinery in San Francisco and a beet sugar refinery at the town of Alvarado in Alameda County, blasting powder plants in Marin and Contra Costa counties, and a large smelter erected by Thomas H. Selby, a hardware merchant, in the North Beach District of San Francisco. By the end of the 'sixties the new boot and shoe industry was manufacturing one-fourth of all the shoes sold on the Pacific Coast. Mining and railroad building created so great a demand for explosives that by 1870 California manufacturers were producing nine-tenths of the powder used west of the Rocky Mountains. As for Selby's smelter, in five years it was processing twice as much ore as the next largest reduction works in the United States, at Newark, New Jersey.

The increase in population in the nine counties bordering on San Francisco Bay reflected the swift economic upsurge. Total population in the area rose from 114,074 in 1860 to 265,808 in 1870—a gain of 133 per cent, compared with 47 per cent in the entire state. The census of 1870 showed that nearly half the people of California lived in the territory bordering on the bay. More than one-fourth lived in San Francisco alone, for the population of the metropolis nearly tripled in the ten-year period. Residents of the city had been disgruntled in 1860 because the census of that year reported no more than 56,835 inhabitants; but they were duly impressed by the figure of 149,473 in 1870, and the San Francisco *Evening Bulletin* boldly predicted on May 24, 1870, that in another ten years the city would have 300,000 inhabitants. J. Ross Brown, of Oakland, former United States Minister to China, was so optimistic that he thought it "safe to say" thay by 1880 San Francisco would be a metropolis of half a million souls.[8]

Urban Problems

Population growth in cities large and small created all kinds of problems and needs that enterprising men were quick to turn into opportunities. In those days, when municipal governments left such matters as the provision of adequate water supplies to private initiative, aggressive water companies began the search for sources of supply that would be more dependable and more ample than the wells, springs, and little local streams tapped in the 'fifties. Anthony Chabot went no farther than Temescal Creek, four miles from Oakland, to find a site where he could build a dam and create a storage reservoir to supply the growing number of water users in the East Bay city. But the Spring Valley Water Company of San Francisco reached out thirty-two miles to get an adequate supply for San Francisco. By flume it brought the waters of Pilarcitos Creek, in San Mateo County, to the metropolis, and later built a dam and created Pilarcitos Lake. In 1870 it constructed a second storage reservoir by building San Andreas Dam in the San Andreas Valley. Lobos Creek, Islais Creek, and springs on which the city had previously depended continued to supply some of its water needs, but these local sources were to become increasingly insignificant as the Spring Valley Company added more and more distant sources to its system.

Through Chabot and his associates, San Jose and Vallejo also acquired new sources of supply. The San Jose Water Company, headed by Chabot, obtained rights to the waters of Los Gatos Creek. The people of Vallejo in 1871 began using water from a reservoir known as Lake Chabot, three miles northeast of the city.

Progress in urban transit was as marked as that in water supply. In 1860 the horsecar made its appearance in San Francisco, and toward the end of the decade it became a feature of the local scene in San Jose and Vallejo, though its advent in the last-named city was premature. With only six thousand inhabitants, Vallejo was just not large enough to support a horsecar line. One by one the omnibus lines in San Francisco converted to the newer form of transportation; new transit companies were organized; and the city grew westward as horsecar lines were extended beyond Van Ness Avenue into the Hayes Valley and the Western Addition. The area at the foot of Twin Peaks also began to develop when a steam-dummy line of the Market Street Railroad was opened to Castro Street. Still another area opened to settlement was the Bay View district near Hunters Point, though the costly line to the Bay View racecourse was not profitable.

While private companies continued to influence the physical development of Bay Area communities through their control, under very limited regulation, of essential water supply and transit services, private speculative interests, operating under franchises, lost control over the port of San Francisco, and with them the City of San Francisco itself surrendered to the state the administration of its waterfront. The transfer of the port to a State Board of Harbor Commissioners in 1863 climaxed years of corruption and mismanagement in port affairs, during which city officials had used harbor revenues for the payment of old debts and for meeting current expenses, even though piers and wharves were disintegrating and filled land was constantly slipping into the bay and preventing ships from berthing and discharging their cargoes. Some wharves even operated without proper authorization and yielded no income to the city.

Within two years the new state board repaired several wharves, built a new one, did considerable dredging, and

employed an engineer to survey for a sea wall. By the end of 1869 the sea wall had been constructed along the old zigzag waterfront line on East Street from the foot of Mission Street to the foot of Pacific Street and on Front Street from Vallejo Street to Union Street.

New Wealth; Civic Poverty

San Francisco at the end of the 'sixties dominated an economic empire that stretched from the Pacific Coast to the Rockies. The financial heart of this empire was Montgomery Street, from which flowed the capital to finance new mines, orchards, large-scale grain farms, and countless other enterprises. In the early days of the Comstock Lode excitement the San Francisco Stock Exchange had been organized, and soon thereafter powerful banks, such as the Bank of California and the Wells Fargo Bank, had come into existence. The Bank of California, founded by William C. Ralson and Darius O. Mills in 1864, not only aided the "Big Four" in their struggle to finance the Central Pacific; it also invested in a wide variety of industrial and agricultural ventures, thanks mainly to the energy, daring, and imagination of Ralston, after whose name might well be written "the Magnificent," because he was indubitably the most spectacular member of a new, self-created aristocracy of wealth.

The rise of this new class signified that the West, or at least the area bordering on San Francisco Bay, was entering a new cultural and social phase. From the gold rush emerged comparatively few men of wealth: Thomas Larkin, Samuel Brannan, Peter Donahue, James Lick—a mere handful. The period marked by the opening of the Comstock Lode and the development of important new industrial enterprises and railroads produced the first of a rather numerous order of men of large fortune. Their ostentatious, not to say vulgar, spending habits; their cultivation of a taste for luxuries in dress, household furnishings, food, and carriages; their quests for rare plants with which to ornament their estates; and the efforts of their wives and daughters to establish an exclusive social set—all exerted a profound influence on public thinking. These men enjoyed a type of living popularly associated with older, more affluent, and more stratified societies, such as had developed in Paris, London, and even New York. In a way, their opulence raised San Francisco to a new level of urbanity and reflected the general improvement in material well-being.

Yet San Francisco by comparison with other world cities was sadly lacking in the physical attributes of metropolitan greatness. It had no large public parks, no splendid boulevards, no art museums and monumental civic buildings. Frederick Law Olmsted, the designer of New York's

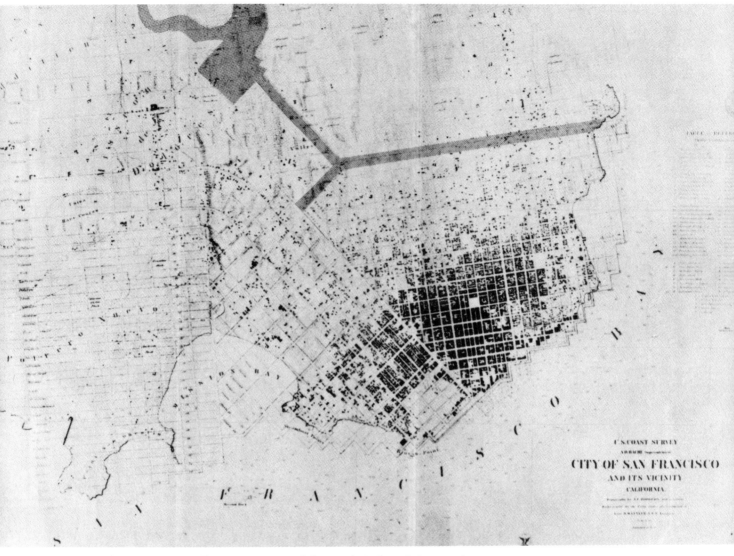

Map of San Francisco Showing Location of Proposed Park and Promenade.
Courtesy of Harvard University Library.

Central Park, observed in 1865 that the only open space San Francisco offered those who would go picnicking on a holiday was "a burial ground on a high elevation, scourged by the wind, laid out only with regard to the convenience of funerals, with no trees or turf, and with but stunted verdure of any kind, and this with difficulty kept alive."[9]

Agitation for a Park

Fortunately, about the time that San Franciscans became embarrassed by the shortcomings of their city, the opportunity to set aside land for an extensive park presented itself. Judge Stephen J. Field of the United States Circuit Court for the Northern District of California entered a decree on October 31, 1864, confirming the claim of the city "to a tract of land . . . embracing so much of the peninsula upon which the city is located as will contain an area equal to four square leagues as described in the petition [of the city],"[10] excepting lands previously reserved by the federal government or already privately owned, such as Rancho San Miguel and the Bernal rancho. These federal and private lands amounted to all but four thousand of the seventeen thousand acres affected by the decision. The decree stated that the confirmation of the residue of four thousand acres would be "in trust for the use and benefit of all the inhabitants."[11] Although this language of the court became the subject of precise judicial interpretation a few years later, most people immediately realized that it did not preclude the city from conveying title to individual citizens under some properly approved program. While various plans for disposal of the "outside lands" were being discussed, the San Francisco *Evening Bulletin* on September 8, 1865, published a lead editorial headed "The Need for a Great Park for San Francisco."

"To establish such an improvement to San Francisco at the present time would be an easy matter, but if it be left until our outside lands shall be divided and occupied, it will be a more difficult task, besides the cost of such an undertaking will be then very much increased," the newspaper urged. It suggested a park of three or four thousand acres "amongst the hills back of the city, south of Lone Mountain."

Talk of the desirability of creating a large park doubtless had been fairly widespread in leading circles for some time before this editorial appeared, for a letter written by Olmsted to his partner, Calvert Vaux, only three weeks later indicates that several prominent citizens, including the tireless Samuel Brannan, had already persuaded him to prepare plans for a park, on the assumption that the San Francisco Board of Supervisors could be induced to pay for his services.[12] Olmsted was then temporarily in the San Francisco Bay Area, doing preliminary work on plans for a new Berkeley campus of the College of California, predecessor of the University of California. For two years he had been manager of Frémont's mining estate in Mariposa County, but he was soon to leave for New York to resume work on Central Park.

The Olmsted Plan

The park plan for San Francisco that Olmsted was officially authorized to prepare after he had already set sail for the East was in some ways less ambitious than the proposals made by the press, in other ways far more imaginative and concerned with the long-term needs of the city. Olmsted projected the beginnings of a park system rather than a single park. At what is now Aquatic Park he planned a sea gate and parade ground. From this landing place for visiting dignitaries a depressed parkway, or promenade, was to run along the line of Van Ness Avenue to Eddy Street and there fork into two branches, one going to Market Street, the other to his main park in the general location of present-day Duboce Park. Though this recreation area, a pleasure ground of approximately one hundred and twenty acres, now seems unduly modest in view of Olmsted's recommendation that the contemplated park should be "conceived on a thoroughly liberal scale,"[13] his suggestion that the roads in the park would lend themselves to "indefinite extension"

throughout the western part of the city as parkways was very advanced for the times. Such costly features as the depressed parkway, which Olmsted thought necessary to afford pleasure seekers protection from the strong summer winds, probably doomed the plan to abandonment; yet this first great American landscape architect did make a contribution to the San Francisco of later generations. He succeeded in transmitting to Supervisors Monroe Ashbury, Charles H. Stanyan, and other officials his own deep conviction that the city should seize its now-or-never opportunity to create "a pleasure ground second to none in the world" and should plan it "with reference to the convenience not merely of the present population, or even of their immediate successors, but of many millions of people."[14]

Site for a Park

When, in 1866, Congress by special act terminated efforts of the federal government to upset Judge Field's confirmation of the city's title to the pueblo lands, and when, finally, the supervisors got down to the business of reaching agreement with land occupants and selecting reservations for public use, they displayed the kind of vision that Olmsted had hoped they would exhibit. Among the public areas recommended by a second Committee on Outside Lands was a park of more than one thousand acres.

San Francisco was not so fortunate, however, as to have its supervisors heed Olmsted's advice on the layout for streets in the unplanned section of the city. Instead of a system of streets ascending the hills diagonally, "in such a way as to secure sufficiently easy grades,"[15] the area west of Divisadero Street was committed to the same rigid gridiron pattern as the older areas.

The selection of the site for Golden Gate Park "was made in the face of bitter opposition," according to William Hammond Hall, the first park engineer. "It was generally believed and repeatedly urged by a good portion of the local press, that any attempt to build and maintain a Park on the dry sands and brush-covered hillocks which composed the site, would prove a costly failure," he wrote in 1886. "Powerful and winning pens, whose ink has within the past decade flowed in gratulation at the results attained and to be expected in Golden Gate Park, were within the ten years before busily engaged in denouncing the selection of the place for the purpose—declaring that no Park could be built there, and no verdure maintained, at any cost which the city could afford."[16]

"The Growth of Time"

The plan for the new campus of the College of California, the other important project that engaged Olmsted during

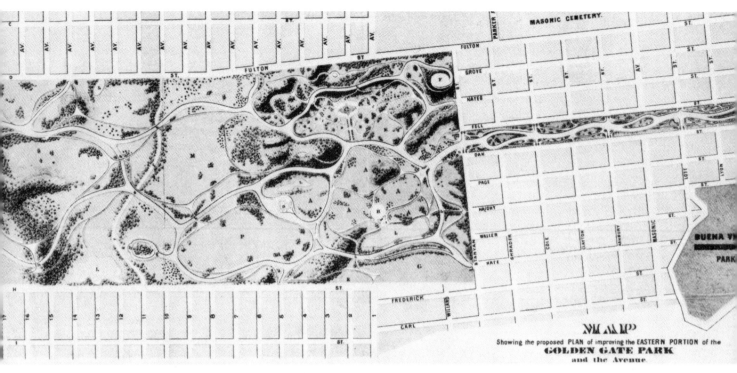

William Hammond Hall's Plan for the Development of the Eastern Part of Golden Gate Park and "the Avenue," Now Known as the Panhandle, 1870–1871. The eastern end of the park site included 270 acres of good arable land; the rest of the site was "a waste of drifting sand" that was reclaimed only after many years of patient labor.

his brief sojourn in the Bay Area in the summer of 1865, fared only a little better than his plan for parks in San Francisco. Aside from a main axis established by Olmsted "in the line of the Golden Gate,"[17] almost nothing about the campus of the university in Berkeley bears the imprint of his genius. The tenuous connection of the landscape architect with the private institution that was to be transformed into a state university is of minor significance beside the fact that in the late 'sixties the desire of certain farsighted leaders for an institution of higher learning supported by public funds was at last fulfilled. This, more than anything else, signified that California was indeed emerging from the pioneer stage.

The beginnings of this institution can be traced to conversations at Monterey in the spring of 1849 between Thomas O. Larkin and the Reverend Samuel H. Willey concerning the desirability of founding a college in California. The clergyman discovered that Larkin had a relative in Boston, the Reverend Doctor William M. Rogers, who was one of the overseers of Harvard University. At Larkin's suggestion the young divine wrote to Dr. Rogers, and in due time received a letter endorsing the idea that a college or university should be established, first of all, because California was too remote from the Atlantic seaboard to depend on eastern institutions for

higher education, and second, because the well-being of the people of California would depend, "as it has depended in New England, on the educated men of the country."[18] Dr. Rogers urged a "country location" for the proposed college and pointed out that since a university "must be the growth of time," the benefactors of the new institution should be content, at the outset, with "what will equal a New England high school."[19]

Thus encouraged, Dr. Willey sought the earliest opportunity to advance substantially the cause of higher education in California. It came to him when delegates to the first state constitutional convention assembled at Monterey in September, 1849. Although there was at that time "no near prospect of a youthful population to need a college,"[20] he found among the delegates a sufficient number who could appreciate the wisdom of laying the foundations for a state university. The constitution as finally drafted included a section contemplating the eventual establishment of a "university with such branches as the public convenience may demand, for the promotion of literature, the arts and sciences."[21]

A "Country Location"

Through the years the Reverend Dr. Willey never lost sight of this goal; and he remembered Dr. Rogers' advice about selecting a "country location" for any college that might in time become a university. When the Reverend Henry Durant, a Congregationalist, arrived in San Francisco in 1853 with the intention of founding a college, Dr. Willey was among those who helped him start the enterprise, and it was he who selected Oakland as a "country location" for the fledgling establishment, at first called the Contra Costa Academy. The academy had no sooner acquired an eight-acre site and received a charter as the nonsectarian College of California, however, than the trustees and faculty realized that it was in the heart of a growing business district and would have to be moved to a new location that genuinely qualified as "country."

The search for a suitably rural location included the entire Bay Area and finally ended with the selection, in 1858, of farm property some miles north of Oakland— "accessible and yet sufficiently removed from the disturbance of the city," Trustee Willey wrote nearly thirty years later.[22]

The fact that the trustees of the College of California had selected what is now Berkeley as the site for a new campus caused a board of directors for a proposed state agricultural and mechanic arts college to look favorably upon a near-by site in 1867. At this point, Governor F. F. Low, long a contributor to the impecunious College of California, suggested that a real university might be created if the state should contribute the money that would otherwise be used for the agricultural and mechanic arts college, and if the College of California should give for the purpose its new campus, its library, and its buildings in Oakland. Such, briefly, is the story of the genesis of the University of California and of the decision to build it on an East Bay site opposite the Golden Gate.

The Town of Berkeley

In the natural course of events a town would have grown up around the university. Samuel H. Willey was responsible for laying out the nucleus of one while the campus site still belonged to the College of California. Forced by the owner of the site to purchase more land than they could really afford or thought they needed, the trustees of the college were in a formidable financial predicament until the always resourceful Dr. Willey conceived the idea of paying for the property by the sale of lots in a homestead association, a new and popular method of marketing land on the installment plan. The trustees formed the College Homestead Association on September 1, 1864, made Dr. Willey the financial manager, and proceeded to lay out a gridiron pattern of streets on part of the college land and to divide the blocks into one-acre lots.

Two years later, the trustees learned how lacking in originality their town planning was. The plan for the campus completed by Olmsted in 1866 showed, in addition to a site for the college buildings, a well-defined and thoughtfully planned "Berkeley neighborhood" that was in sharp contrast to the rectilinear scheme of the homestead tract. Although the "neighborhood" proposal was never carried out, it deserves a brief description because it embodied several important principles of present-day planning for residential areas. No cross-town streets invaded Olmsted's Berkeley neighborhood of winding, tree-shaded roads. These roads were designed to serve no purpose "beyond the mere supplying of the wants of the neighborhood itself" and were intended to be safe and quiet.[23] The lots were grouped in five subareas around a central open space to be used as a recreation area and social gathering place. In planning smaller units within the neighborhood, Olmsted was more realistic than some twentieth-century planners who have failed to recognize the natural tendency of any residential population to break down into minor social groupings in which face-to-face relationships can be readily maintained. He anticipated by many decades the "modern" emphasis on close relationships between house and garden, suggesting that dwellings in the neighborhood should have "attractive open-air apartments, so formed that they can be often occupied for hours at a time, with convenience and ease in every respect, without the interruption of ordinary occupations or difficulty of conversation."[24]

Other Institutions

The 'sixties and the early years of the 'seventies saw the founding of other educational institutions and the growth of those established in the 'fifties, though none of these other institutions brought into existence new communities. The State Normal School, founded in San Francisco in 1862, was moved to Washington Square in San Jose by act of the legislature in 1870. Later the school became San Jose State College. Dr. and Mrs. Cyrus Taggart Mills, who had begun operating the Young Ladies Seminary at Benicia in 1865, sold their interest in this school in 1870, purchased a tract of 140 acres at the base of the San Leandro Hills about five miles from Oakland, and erected thereon a large building containing both dormitories and classrooms. Patterned after Mount Holyoke Seminary in Massachusetts, Mills Seminary—now Mills College—has become a leading women's college of the West. The University of the Pacific, which was called the California Wesleyan College when it was chartered in 1851 at Santa Clara, moved to a new campus about half way between

San Jose and Santa Clara in 1871. Property not required by the institution was sold by the trustees as the University Tract.

The increasing sophistication and affluence of certain elements of the Bay Area population also encouraged the development of health resorts and recreation places in the 'sixties. Brannan's spa at Calistoga has already been mentioned. Far more popular than this Napa Valley resort was Pacific Congress Springs, which Darius O. Mills, president of the Bank of California, and other capitalists opened in 1866 on Campbell Creek one mile from the town of Saratoga in Santa Clara County. The waters that bubbled from the ground on the upper reaches of Campbell Creek were thought to taste like those at Congress Springs in the eastern Saratoga. Wealthy San Franciscans also began to frequent San Rafael during summer months and to speak of it as a health resort. But city people who journeyed to the picturesque beaches near the new town of Half Moon Bay (established in 1863) in San Mateo County did so purely for fun and not to rid themselves of liver complaint.

At an earlier time the physical beauties of the San Francisco Bay Area no doubt were appreciated and mentioned with pleasure, but in the late 'sixties they were studied with a discriminating eye and for the first time were commercially exploited. The completion of the transcontinental railroad began to turn a small stream of promotional "literature" into a flood of guidebooks, brochures, and travel accounts extolling the area.

New County Boundaries

There was as yet, however, no reference in popular magazines or newspapers to a specific Bay Area composed of the nine counties now commonly regarded as political units in the metropolitan region; but it should be noted that in the 'sixties some revisions in county boundaries brought the area to approximately its present political configuration. These revisions might be classed as adjustments to the facts of geography. Napa County, expanded in 1852 to include half of Clear Lake and in 1855 to include the entire lake and the territory surrounding it, was reduced to about its present size in 1861 when Lake County was created. The new northern boundary more nearly coincided with the mountains enclosing the upper part of Napa Valley and recognized that the territory to the north constituted another physiographic area. An even more striking example of readjustment in accordance with topography was the detachment of the northern part of Santa Cruz County and its transfer by the state legislature to San Mateo County in 1868. Twice before, in 1861 and again in 1866, residents of the Pescadero area had sought this change, because they were forty miles north of the county seat of Santa Cruz County and were cut off by an intervening mountain range, whereas they were but twenty miles from Redwood City, the county seat of San Mateo County, and were served by daily stages to that town.

From time to time in later years minor changes were made, as in the realignment of the northern boundary of Sonoma County in 1917 to conform to the nearest United States survey lines. But for all practical purposes the counties bordering on San Francisco Bay achieved permanent boundaries within a little more than eighteen years after the first legislature organized the state into counties. No one would contend, though, that these political boundaries define a precise physiographic area.

CHAPTER FOUR

Urban Rivalries

Outside the San Francisco Bay Area the economic development of California had scarcely begun at the time the transcontinental railroad was completed. The upper Sacramento Valley, almost the entire San Joaquin Valley, the coastal valleys south of Monterey, and the timberlands of the northern coast all awaited further settlement and further exploitation of their natural resources. These huge areas of the state were, in effect, untapped economic provinces that would enrich and increase in prestige the cities that could establish transportation links and trade connections with them. They were the grand prizes in a new cycle of railroad building that began in 1870.

Two things appeared indispensable in the contest for the riches of these regions: direct access by rail and a deep-water port. San Francisco had a port but was cut off from the interior valleys by the bay. Oakland enjoyed the advantage of being the terminus of the overland railroad and could easily be linked to other areas of the state by branches of the main line, but Oakland had as yet no port facilities. Vallejo, smaller than either San Francisco or Oakland, had both a deep-water harbor and a railroad —the California Pacific—providing access to the lower Sacramento Valley. Extension of this road into other areas of the state and into other states could make Vallejo the rival of either San Francisco or Oakland, or of both.

Not the cities but the Big Four—Leland Stanford, Collis P. Huntington, Mark Hopkins, and Charles Crocker— actually held the trump cards in the game that started as soon as the transcontinental railroad was completed, though the fact did not immediately become clear. San Francisco, Oakland, and Vallejo found themselves contestants in a struggle in which each was handicapped in some way by its geographic situation. All three were also pawns in the hands of the owners of the Central Pacific.

Gloom in San Francisco

Only a few months after the first overland train completed its historic run, San Franciscans began to realize that the transcontinental rails were no unmixed blessing to their city. The Pacific railroad permitted eastern concerns, especially those in Chicago, to sell their products in areas theretofore served exclusively by the western metropolis. It carried East many products formerly shipped to the Atlantic seaboard from the wharves of San Francisco. Business at the port declined.

To make matters worse, production in the Nevada silver mines fell off because of floods, poor ventilation, and disastrous fires. And as always, depressed conditions were reflected in a slump in real estate in San Francisco.

Oakland, on the other hand, was enjoying a boom. "One only need take a walk or drive around and about Oakland, outside of the principal streets, to be perfectly astounded at the immense number of buildings in course of construction on every hand," the Oakland *Daily Transcript* reported on April 18, 1870. Scores of applicants for houses to rent were being turned away daily from real-estate offices, according to the newspaper.

So much gloom filled the spirits of certain business

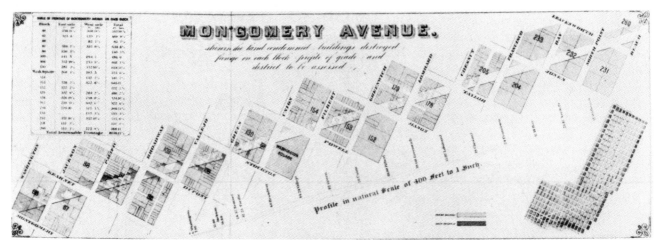

Plan for the Creation of Montgomery Avenue (Now Columbus Avenue). As presented in the San Francisco Municipal Reports for 1872–1873.

groups in San Francisco that the *Evening Bulletin* felt compelled to counteract "all the croaking one hears." "People talk of dull times, and compared to the days of high prices, when the interior consumed what the city imported or made and produced nothing but gold, the times are dull; judged by the standard of healthy business and progress they are not, and those who croak most now will be the most surprised five years hence at the rapid strides the city will have made," the newspaper editorialized on May 24, 1870.

The journal pointed to the "hundreds of modest dwellings" being constructed in areas that three or four years earlier had been "blank spaces." It cited improvements "of the most substantial and handsome character" in the thickly settled districts of the city: "The fine hotel on Market Street [William C. Ralston's Grand Hotel], the splendid book warehouse of Bancroft & Co.—the largest edifice of its kind west of New York—the elegant banking and store-houses on California, Sansome and Front streets, the numerous fine churches and school houses in progress, the new Mint, and the many handsome private residences, are among recent evidences of improved growth. Then the city is about to erect a City Hall at a point which five years ago was considered out of town, and is about to commence the work of laying out a great Park, stretching from its western charter line to the Ocean, which will be the signal for many private improvements in that direction. A magnificent new Avenue [now Columbus Avenue] is soon to be opened from the upper end of

Montgomery Street to North Beach, more than a mile through the built up portion of the city. Several new manufactures have been added to the city's industrial resources, and others will soon follow."

Struggle for a Terminus

In spite of such optimistic reassurances, many San Franciscans were troubled by the same sort of uneasiness that had taken possession of the fainthearted during the Benicia boom of earlier days. In increasing numbers they believed that somehow the metropolis must become the terminus of a transcontinental railroad, if not of the Central Pacific through its Western Pacific subsidiary, then of the Southern Pacific, originally chartered in 1865 to build southward from the Santa Clara Valley to a connection at the Colorado River with a railroad from the Mississippi Valley. Early in 1870 there were reports that Leland Stanford and his associates had consolidated this company, the San Francisco and San Jose Rail Road, and the extension between San Jose and Gilroy known as the Santa Clara and Pajaro Valley Railroad. If the line through the Santa Clara Valley were, indeed, to be built southward and then eastward, San Francisco possibly could become the terminus of a new southern transcontinental line; but the intentions of the Big Four were only to be guessed at. It was equally possible that the railroad being built down the San Joaquin Valley would be connected with a southern transcontinental line and would have its terminus in Oakland. For that matter, a southern transcontinental line routed through the Santa Clara Valley could just as easily be terminated at Oakland as at San Francisco. Nevertheless, the Big Four had the audacity to ask San Francisco to contribute a subsidy of $1,000,000 toward the building of a railroad southward from Gilroy, on the tacit understanding—but not the firm promise—that the terminus would be a thirty-acre site on Mission Bay granted by the state legislature in 1868.

The defeat of the subsidy by a narrow margin at an election in June, 1870, showed that a majority of San Franciscans either distrusted Stanford and his associates or were unconvinced that direct rail connections with the East and with remoter parts of the state were essential to the economic well-being of the city.

"The public saw a company of rich men, already the recipients of valuable subsidies, asking for more, but silent in their canvass as to their own purposes, and only 9,000 of our 25,000 voters were enough interested to go to the polls," the *Daily Evening Bulletin* pointed out on June 17, 1870. "This policy of coquetting with various towns, coaxing and threatening by turns, as if to get as much as possible from each, always holding in reserve an unavowed ulterior object, is hardly the best one to win confidence anywhere."

Ruin of a Grand Scheme

The election was scarcely over when San Franciscans became aware that there was still danger that Congress might enact a pending bill granting Yerba Buena Island to the Big Four for a terminal. The prospect of having transcontinental and San Joaquin Valley trains loading and unloading at docks on Yerba Buena Island, within sight of the waning port of San Francisco, was too much for citizens who were concerned about the shipping interests of the metropolis. Opposition to the proposal became vociferous; and the demand was renewed that San Francisco be made the western terminus of the transcontinental railroad. But the Big Four did not appear to be making a strenuous effort to secure passage of the pending bill. They were about to complete their famous Long Wharf at Oakland, extending two miles into the bay. The public outcry against the Yerba Buena Island proposal subsided, temporarily.

In the spring of 1871 San Francisco found itself threatened from another quarter—Vallejo. The California Pa-

Waterfront of the United States Navy Yard, Mare Island, 1870. The city of Vallejo appears in the distance. Photograph courtesy of Vallejo Chamber of Commerce.

cific Railroad Company, partly financed by British and German capital, bought the Petaluma Valley railroad of Peter Donahue and also the California Steam Navigation Company, which dominated commerce on the inland waterways of California. These additions to its system gave it complete control of all existing rail approaches to the bay from the north. But these mergers were merely the prelude to a grand scheme of the directors. They next announced plans for a line 950 miles in length from Woodland, on the Davisville-Marysville branch, to Christmas Lake in Oregon and thence to Salt Lake City.

"Vallejo will be an important railway center as well as a considerable shipping point," the San Francisco *Evening Bulletin* observed on May 22, 1871. And a few days later the San Francisco *News Letter* concluded that "so far as there is any rivalry between Vallejo and Oakland for commercial position, the latter may as well give up the contest."[1]

Oakland's lack of a harbor also led Lieutenant Colonel of Engineers B. S. Alexander to think that the Alameda County city was now out of the running in the struggle for dominance of the hinterland. Writing to General John B. Frisbie, vice-president of the California Pacific, he suggested: "...let there be a combination of the Central Pacific and California Pacific Railroads, which is highly probable at an early date, for the interests of both of these roads point in this direction, and then another combination with the China steamers, and Vallejo would be at once converted into the great railway centre of the State; the proposed great harbor at Oakland would probably never be excavated, and Vallejo from that time forward would contend with San Francisco alone for commercial supremacy."[2]

This was indeed a dazzling prospect for Vallejo, and Collis P. Huntington, Leland Stanford, and Mark Hopkins soon were in a position to fulfill the city's dream of becoming a great center, or to shatter it. Between July 13 and September 1, 1871, Huntington and his associates negotiated various contracts and agreements with the California Pacific that gave them undisputed control of this ambitious but financially weak railroad. They had watched with growing resentment the expansion of the California Pacific and had felt the pinch of competition from its operations, for its shorter route between San Francisco and Sacramento (87 miles) attracted more local passengers than their own circuitous line from Oakland via Stockton (137½ miles). To demonstrate that they meant to crush this potential rival, they had resorted to the well-worn stratagem of arranging to construct a branch from Sacramento paralleling its tracks. And so the directors of the debt-burdened California Pacific had

agreed to sell the greater part of their stock and to become parties to a series of involved transactions all greatly to the advantage of the Central Pacific.

Having gained control of the California Pacific, the titans of the Central Pacific were now masters of the railroad traffic of the entire San Francisco Bay Area and all northern California. And as if to leave no doubt of their monopoly, they immediately transferred the offices of the California Pacific from San Francisco to Sacramento, the seat of their railroad empire.

Panic in the Metropolis

In San Francisco many leading citizens were in a state of panic, clamoring for a railroad bridge to connect the metropolis with the Alameda shore. "San Francisco has quietly waited for the cars to bring themselves to her ships, until she finds the railroad transportation of the state, from the south, the east, and the north, fast concentrating on the eastern shore of the bay, and her ships passing themselves over to the cars," the *Daily Evening Bulletin* editorialized on October 26, 1871. "The fate of Venice awaits her if they are not brought back; and they can be brought back only by stretching the rails across the bay, and laying their ends upon our wharves."

The *Daily Morning Call*, which earlier had asserted that "Oakland is a part of San Francisco, so far as those influences are concerned which result from the aggregation of population and wealth,"[3] now reversed itself completely and acknowledged that "the necessity for some such medium of communication between San Francisco and Alameda shores of the Bay other than by vessel has long been felt and discussed by our citizens, but never with so much earnestness nor so much firm belief in its practicability as at the present time."[4]

The *Daily Alta California* alone opposed a transbay bridge as impracticable and urged San Francisco to save itself by providing superior harbor facilities and cheaper accommodations than any rival city could supply.

The Oakland *Daily Transcript* presented estimates by civil engineer George F. Allardt indicating that the cost of a low bridge five miles in length would be not less than $16,608,900. The "benefits" to San Francisco of such an expenditure, the Oakland newspaper predicted, would be an increase in the value of Alameda County property and "an exodus of families from San Francisco who object to steamboat travel," the continued exportation of grain from Oakland, and the refusal of the railroad companies to consider running through trains across a bridge because "open draws" would constantly disrupt schedules.[5]

"Nobody doubts that San Francisco must continue to be the metropolis of the Pacific Coast; and the shallow

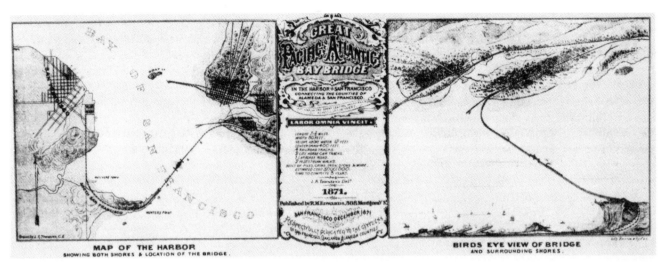

The Proposed Pacific and Atlantic Bay Bridge from Hunters Point to Alameda, 1871. Photograph courtesy of Wells Fargo Bank.

efforts of a few speculators to frighten San Franciscans into committing an outrage against themselves, and their posterity, is highly reprehensible," the *Transcript* scolded, concluding with the conciliatory thought that "Oakland is an invaluable adjunct to the commerce of San Francisco; and far-seeing San Franciscans are proud, not jealous, of Oakland."

But many San Franciscans *were* jealous of Oakland, and extremely apprehensive, especially when they learned that twenty-two members of the state legislature had forwarded a communication to Congress urging passage of the pending bill providing for establishment of a railroad terminal on Yerba Buena Island. In March, 1872, the San Francisco Chamber of Commerce sent a memorial to the President and Vice-President of the United States and to Congress attacking the proposed cession of part of the island; a citizens' meeting passed resolutions denouncing the grant; a committee visited the state legislature in an attempt to change the minds of the legislators; and finally, another committee hastened to Washington to request the President to veto the pending bill if Congress should pass it.

Futile Efforts

At this juncture San Francisco officials decided to attempt statesmanlike negotiations with the Big Four. The city offered to build a bridge across Dumbarton Strait in the southern arm of the bay, to construct a harbor belt line, and to fill in tidelands and grant a right of way to the Central Pacific if it would abandon all claim to Yerba Buena Island. The city insisted, however, that all rail-

roads should be permitted to use the bridge and should be granted occupancy of filled lands, and that no charge should be made for either privilege. The railroad magnates countered with a proposal that they would build the bridge and the harbor belt line, provided the people of the city would approve a subsidy of $2,500,000 and grant them a part of China Basin for commercial purposes. City officials were inclined to favor the proposed subsidy but reserved the right to confer upon any other company the privilege of laying track on land granted for a right of way, again insisting that any and all railroads should have the right to use the bridge. The arrogant monopolists then practically invited a mayoral veto of a supervisorial order for an election on the subsidy by demanding the option to shift the terminus from San Francisco if the growth of business elsewhere warranted a change. And a veto is exactly what they got from Mayor William Alvord, though it is doubtful that this perturbed them overmuch.

In the meantime, San Francisco capitalists toyed with two other railroad propositions—one to associate themselves with the Atlantic and Pacific Company (predecessor of the Atchison, Topeka, and Santa Fe Railway) in building a transcontinental railroad to San Francisco, the other to finance a railroad to connect with Thomas A. Scott's projected line from Fort Worth, Texas, to San Diego.

Both proposals were rejected in favor of a railroad to be built and owned entirely by California capitalists and to be known as the San Francisco and Colorado River Railroad Company. Like other ambitious railroad schemes of the times, this one depended upon approval by the voters of a large subsidy—$10,000,000. But long before the election on the subsidy could be held, a majority of San Francisco newspapers became suspicious of the directors of the new company and began attacking them as tricksters bent on obtaining the subsidy and then selling out to "Stanford & Company." On October 18, 1872, two weeks before the election, the directors announced in an advertisement in the *Daily Alta California* that they were abandoning, "for the present," all further efforts to obtain public aid. Thus virtually ended the movement to make San Francisco the terminus of an overland railroad.

New Developments

Once the local threat—if it were a threat—to their rapidly expanding railroad empire was eliminated, the Sacramento titans were free to concentrate on fighting Thomas Scott and on preventing entrance of the Union Pacific or the Northern Pacific into California from Oregon. In 1873 they built two branches of the Southern Pacific only far enough down the coast to block the approach of any rivals—one into the San Benito Valley to Tres Pinos, the other to Soledad in Monterey County. Their chief interest was in completing the line through the San Joaquin Valley and pushing their rails as rapidly as possible to the southeastern border of the state, acquiring large land grants from the federal government as they built. The only railroad in the Bay Area which the Big Four did not control was the Cotati Valley road built by Peter Donahue. They had added this to their holdings when they took over the California Pacific, but they later released it to Donahue to satisfy debts owed to him.

In January, 1873, the Board of United States Engineers for the Pacific Coast quieted San Francisco's fear that Yerba Buena Island would become the meeting place of rails and ships. The board suggested that a good harbor could be developed for Oakland in San Antonio Creek (now the Oakland Estuary) "for one-half the cost of a bridge from Oakland to Yerba Buena Island."[6] Congress authorized an investigation of the possibilities of dredging the shallow waters and, upon presentation of a report favoring the project, made the first of a series of appropriations for harbor improvements. For many years, however, the Long Wharf of the Big Four handled most of the cargo moving in and out of Oakland.

The port of San Francisco, meanwhile, was further improved, and its wharves again bustled with activity. Although it had become evident that the major railroad terminal of the Bay Area would be on the mainland side of the bay, San Francisco was no longer perturbed about the potential rivalry of Oakland. The metropolis was already so large that it attracted to itself, in spite of its peninsular location, the majority of newcomers and the lion's share of the new wealth of the state. Moreover, as time passed, San Franciscans observed that the Big Four themselves did little to build up Oakland but much to enhance the importance of the city by the Golden Gate.

A Torrent of Newcomers

An estimated seventy thousand people arrived in San Francisco by sea in 1873, compared with only twenty thousand in 1870. In 1874, eighty-five thousand disembarked at the metropolis, and although departures numbered in the thousands, the net inflow through the port brought smiles to the faces of those who had been lamenting its recent decline. Nothing like so many came by the overland train. Until 1873 the arrivals by train fluctuated between thirty and thirty-four thousand, then rose to forty-four thousand in 1873, and increased to fifty-six thousand in 1874. Not until 1875 did they approximate the number of arrivals by sea. In that year seventy-five thousand people made the long, tedious, dusty journey across the plains, the deserts, and the Sierra Nevada—and far more of them settled in San Francisco than in Oakland and other East Bay towns.[7]

The torrent of newcomers was impelled westward by financial panic in the East, by political convulsions in Europe, and by the strenuous efforts of the Big Four and the steamship companies to promote immigration. Stories of the big new bonanza that had been opened in the Comstock Lode at Virginia City in March, 1873, and of the stream of riches that was pouring into San Francisco from the mines also helped to increase the tide of immigration. Nor can one overlook, in seeking the causes of this new mass movement, the effect upon Easterners and Middle Western folk of the purple passages in letters penned by enthusiastic new arrivals in California.

Large numbers of Irish, Germans, and English, and a lesser number of French, Italians, Mexicans, Portuguese, and other foreign-born people swelled the influx into the state. Including the Chinese, the foreign-born accounted for two-thirds of the population increase in California during the 'seventies.[8] San Francisco, cosmopolitan from the time of the American occupation, became more than ever a city of many tongues, an international city in the true sense of the word. Not all the foreign-born came directly to California from other countries, however; a large proportion had lived for a time in Eastern or Midwestern states before moving to the Bay Area and other parts of the state. They were thus a part of the deep undercurrent of westward movement noted in American history even before the founding of the republic.

The Silver Boom

San Francisco, the great reception center for the influx of the 'seventies, became a city of shifting population, of new real-estate speculations, of feverish building activity. The old section around Portsmouth Plaza and the triangle bounded by Market, Kearny, and California streets became mainly commercial and lost population, while the section between California and Washington streets became more densely inhabited as people adopted the custom of living over shops. For three decades, or until the catastrophic earthquake and fire of 1906, the custom of living above commercial establishments was to be one of the characteristic features of San Francisco life, commented on by every visitor.

South of Market Street the growth of wholesale and industrial enterprises in the crowded Seventh Ward sent the fashionable scurrying from Rincon Hill and South Park to Stockton, Bush, Pine, Powell, and Mason streets, and to the southern slope of Russian Hill. Working-class families shifted westward along Mission, Howard, Folsom, and Harrison streets in the direction of Mission Dolores. In this South-of-Market area the congestion became so great that there was a demand for the creation of new streets parallel to Market Street in the large blocks created by Jasper O'Farrell in 1847.

The North Beach area, the lower slopes of Nob Hill, the area between Post and Market streets west of Kearny, and the homestead tracts and filled-in marshlands in the southern part of the city all attracted thousands of new inhabitants. Tracts west of Van Ness Avenue also vibrated with the sound of the hammer and saw as new dwellings rose.

In this westward and southward expansion of the city the horsecar lines played a major role. But it was not the picturesque and gaudy "bobtail" cars and bulbous "balloon" cars of the horsecar lines that excited San Franciscans in the period of the great silver boom; it was the cable car, the invention of Andrew S. Hallidie, a local manufacturer. A public demonstration of Hallidie's new

San Francisco in the late 1870's, with William C. Ralston's Palace Hotel in the distance. Photograph courtesy of Bancroft Library.

mode of transit on Clay Street between Kearny and Jones streets on the afternoon of August 2, 1873, presaged a boom in view lots and the conquest of once formidable barriers to city expansion, such as Nob Hill and Russian Hill. Steep grades that no horsecar line could surmount— grades resulting from the mechanical application of the gridiron street pattern to hilly terrain—were but an invitation to the smooth flight of the cable car; and wild was the scramble for hilltop lots and for cable franchises.

On the crest of Nob Hill arose grandiose residences that proclaimed the wealth and power of California's *nouveaux riches*, the railroad and mining kings. Among these ornate piles stood Leland Stanford's two-million-dollar show place, on the corner later occupied by the Stanford Court Apartments. In the fashion of the times, the house contained rooms in a variety of styles—Chinese, Pompeian, Italian, Indian, and plushy Victorian. Even more costly was the palace of Charles Crocker, which occupied the site on which Grace Cathedral now stands. But none could equal in vulgar pretentiousness the three-million-dollar gingerbread fantasy created by Mrs. Mark Hopkins on the property today occupied by the hotel that perpetuates her husband's name.

Of all these expressions of the ego of the self-made, only the brownstone mansion of James C. Flood, the sometime copartner with William S. O'Brien of the Auction Lunch Rooms, triumphed over the fire of 1906 and endures today, though its interior was gutted in the holocaust. As the exclusive Pacific Union Club, the old structure is a reminder of the kind of bonanza elegance that awed San Franciscans in the days when bartenders became millionaires almost overnight and chambermaids became mistresses of opulent households.

Leland Stanford headed the group that put into operation the historic California Street cable line, nowadays a delightful anachronism ding-donging up and down the slopes of Nob Hill and through a man-made canyon of the central business district. The immediate popularity of the new road forced the older Clay Street cable into a grim rivalry for the patronage of the social upper crust on the hill.

In the zestful mid-seventies tongues wagged not only over the splendor on "Nabob Hill" but also over the sumptuous Palace Hotel that the irrepressible William C. Ralston was building on Market and Montgomery streets. Himself the owner of a Belmont country house that was every bit as resplendent as the hilltop edifices, Ralston in 1874 set out to give San Francisco a hotel more luxurious than any other in America and twice as large as his earlier four-hundred-room Grand Hotel. If calculated in the inflated currency of the present, its cost would

be several times the $5,000,000 that the spectacular financier poured into it. Unfortunately, he did not live to hear the famous Palm Court echo to the clatter of four-in-hand teams hitched to shining landaus. He suffered financial reverses in 1875 and soon afterward was found dead in the waters off North Beach, perhaps a suicide.

Water Projects

Ralston was only one of the many who relished the bold and the colossal in the era when torrents of silver flowed from the Comstock. No project was too audacious to seem possible, not even a scheme of the Mount Gregory Water and Mining Company to conduct the waters of the Rubicon River, in El Dorado County, to San Francisco through 183 miles of iron pipes. San Francisco had visions of becoming a city of a million inhabitants; and whereas a few years earlier Professor George Davidson, of the United States Coast Survey, had derided Colonel A. W. Von Schmidt's scheme of tunneling five miles through the dividing ridge of the Sierra to bring the waters of Lake Tahoe to San Francisco, people were now willing to concede that it might be possible, though costly. In 1874 an official San Francisco Water Commission actually went to the Sierra to investigate the practicability of obtaining water from the lakes and streams near the sources of the Mokelumne River; but the following year the city turned from such distant sources and considered acquiring water rights on Calaveras Creek, a branch of Alameda Creek in northern Santa Clara and southern Alameda counties. The Spring Valley Water Company forestalled the move by purchasing riparian rights on Alameda Creek and its tributaries. A proposal to buy out the company failed at the polls, and San Francisco was content for almost a quarter of a century to let the private utility develop additional water resources on the San Francisco Peninsula and in southern Alameda County.

On the opposite side of the bay the Oakland *Daily Transcript* expressed the belief, however, that San Francisco sooner or later would have to build an aqueduct from the Sierra, and that it would be to Oakland's advantage to join in the project. Oakland, too, wrestled with the issue of municipal ownership of its water supply at this time and, like the metropolis, concluded that for the time being it might as well let private enterprise—Anthony Chabot and the Contra Costa Water Company—provide for its needs. However, the outgoing mayor of Oakland, Mack Webber, said in 1876 that if the city waited a few years the San Francisco supply would prove inadequate and Oakland could then join in building a great aqueduct from the Sierra to serve Sacramento, Stockton, Oakland, and San Francisco. Farsighted residents of the Bay Area

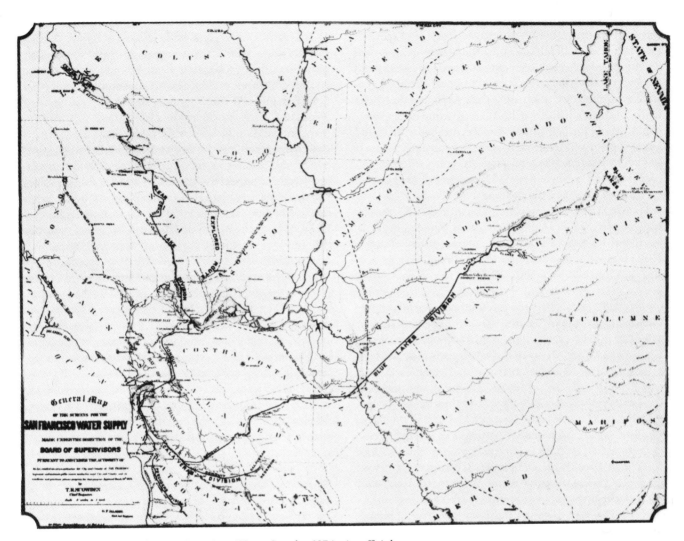

Map of the Surveys for the San Francisco Water Supply, 1874. An official water commission investigated Bay Area as well as distant sources of water supply. The proposed conduit marked "Blue Lakes Division" follows approximately the route of the present-day Mokelumne Aqueduct of the East Bay Municipal Utility District.

thus realized a long time ago that eventually the water deficiencies of the area would have to be met by importations from the streams that flow into the great Central Valley.

Speculation in Oakland

Chabot's new San Leandro Reservoir, impounding the waters of San Leandro Creek, added enough water to the supplies already in use to assure Oakland of an adequate supply for a good many years. The city was growing steadily, though not nearly so rapidly as some people had

expected when the transcontinental railroad was completed. In 1872 it had absorbed near-by Brooklyn and had annexed territory stretching as far north as present Thirty-sixth Street, thereby increasing its area from five to more than eleven square miles. It was linked with Alameda by the Webster Street drawbridge, and to the University of California campus at Berkeley by a "bobtail" horsecar line. Other lines, most of them built in 1875 and 1876, when there was much real-estate speculation and San Francisco capital was being invested in East Bay properties, extended to Temescal, Emeryville, West Oakland,

East Oakland, Mills Seminary, and Mountain View Cemetery, an extensive burial ground, designed by Frederick Law Olmsted, in the hills just north of the present city of Piedmont. Since many of these horsecar lines were built to open up new tracts rather than to serve already populated areas, the city toward the end of the decade tended to be overextended. Even in 1875, gas and water companies complained that they had been induced to spend large sums to provide service in areas only sparsely settled. In West Oakland, particularly, many whole blocks contained but a single house. Elsewhere houses built on speculation exceeded the demand.

Horace Carpentier, ever ambitious for the city that he had founded, advocated annexation of Berkeley to Oakland; but his proposal aroused the opposition of Judge J. W. Dwinelle, who declared that Oakland was in debt and that it would be well for Berkeley to keep out of her jaws. Berkeley succeeded in becoming a self-governing municipality in 1878, with its southern boundary five hundred feet south of Dwight Way. On the north the city extended to the county line, and in West Berkeley to Codornices Creek. Between the settlements near the University campus and the settlement of Ocean View, near San Pablo Road, lay vast fields. The total population in the built-up areas was only about two thousand.

Berkeley, Oakland, and Alameda had chiefly the status of "bedroom" communities during this period. Their attractiveness as places of residence for people who worked in San Francisco is indicated in part by the remarkable gain in transbay travel. Between 1873 and 1877 the number of passengers carried by ferryboats operating between San Francisco and Oakland more than doubled, increasing from 2,655,671 to 5,570,555.[9] The opening of a new ferry building at the foot of Market Street in San Francisco in September, 1875, facilitated the daily movement of commuters back and forth across the bay.

In passing, it should be noted that population gains and new construction did not contribute to the happiness of all the citizens of Oakland, because many of the beautiful oaks for which the city was named were sacrificed to "progress." "At almost every meeting of the Council there are petitions for the removal of trees, and if all these requests were complied with, Oakland would very soon be as windy and disagreeable as San Francisco," a citizen complained to the Oakland News as early as 1873.[10]

Politics and Rails

Another cause for discontent in Oakland was the domination of the Big Four, manifested by the defeat in the Oakland City Council of an attempt by a group of Oakland and Nevada capitalists to obtain a franchise for a railroad from Oakland to central and eastern Contra Costa County by way of Berkeley and a tunnel through the Berkeley Hills. The unequal struggle between the promoters of the Oakland, Berkeley, and Contra Costa Railroad Company and Charles Crocker, of the Big Four, occurred in 1876 some months before the monopolists completed their Southern Pacific line to Los Angeles through the San Joaquin Valley and made Oakland the Bay Area terminus. Immediately after the city council denied the backers of the little local road a franchise to lay tracks on Oakland streets, it submissively granted Crocker and his associates a franchise to build a new tentacle of the "octopus" that was tightening its hold on California. Known as the Northern Railroad, the new link ran from Oakland northward along the shoreline to Carquinez Strait and to Tracy in the San Joaquin Valley.

When the road was opened, in 1878, it provided a nearly level route from Oakland to the Valley and eliminated use by Southern Pacific trains of the more difficult route through Livermore Pass and Niles Canyon, with its heavy grades. At Port Costa, on Carquinez Strait, trains bound for Sacramento and points east and north made connection with the car-transfer steamer Solano. This train ferry, the largest of its kind in the world, began operating in 1879 and transported trains to Benicia, from whence they proceeded on a new cutoff to Suisin and the tracks formerly belonging to the California Pacific.

New Narrow-Gauge Line

No such tiger-like ferocity as was shown toward the capitalists who wanted to build the local railroad through the Berkeley Hills was displayed by the Big Four toward another railroad venture of the time, the South Pacific Coast Railroad. Yet this line, which stimulated the growth of Alameda, was potentially, at least, a competitor of the Southern Pacific and was eventually to become a property of the gigantic corporation formed by the Big Four.

The South Pacific Coast Railroad was an achievement of the ambitions of James G. Fair and James L. Flood, who had had the exhilarating experience of suddenly becoming Comstock millionaires. So pervasive was the talk of railroads in the ever-expanding, distance-conscious West that they, like other rich men with a desire to be known as empire builders, turned almost instinctively to a railroad scheme. They planned the South Pacific Coast Railroad as a narrow-gauge line that would run from the mainland side of San Francisco Bay to Santa Cruz and southward into the Salinas Valley. They thought of eventually extending it through the Coast Range and eastward to a connection with the Denver and Rio Grande Railroad, at that time a narrow-gauge line building westward.

Construction on the South Pacific Coast Railroad began at Dumbarton Point, in southern Alameda County, in May, 1876. From this location at the narrows in the southern arm of the bay the bonanza kings built their road to near-by Newark, a town founded in 1875 by the Newark Land Association and named for the manufacturing city in New Jersey. In the latter part of 1877, tracks were completed to San Jose via Alviso and Santa Clara. While construction was being pushed toward the village of Los Gatos, at the foot of the Santa Cruz Mountains, other crews were building southward from Alameda. Service between Alameda Point and Los Gatos (travel time: two and a half hours) was opened in June, 1878, and by 1880 the road had reached Santa Cruz. In 1881 it was extended to Oakland via the Webster Street Bridge. From Alameda Point a ferry service operated to San Francisco.

This narrow-gauge road triggered a real-estate boom in the southern and middle sections of Alameda, mainly because of the new rail-ferry service to San Francisco. As a commuter town, Alameda enjoyed an increase in population from 1,500 in 1870 to 5,700 in 1880. It was almost as large as Vallejo.

Metropolitan Hierarchy

A cloud hung over the city on Mare Island Strait. Vallejo was by-passed by through trains and had been hopelessly outdistanced by Oakland, its former rival. It had lost to Sacramento the railroad shops that the California Pacific once operated; it had failed in 1874 to wrest the county seat of Solano County from Fairfield; and it had reeled under an unexpected blow when the United States Navy drastically curtailed activities at Mare Island in the mid-seventies. The census of 1880 showed that its population had decreased to a little less than 6,000. Oakland, by contrast, had a population of 34,555 in 1880.

San Francisco, of course, overshadowed all other California cities, though its total population in 1880 (233,959) was considerably less than some of the forecasts made a decade earlier.

From the standpoint of metropolitan regional development, the 'seventies were significant for the accelerated growth of the East Bay and for the establishment of a San Francisco–Oakland axis in the Bay Area, with San Francisco as the major port and Oakland as the major railroad terminus. The population of Alameda County increased from 24,237 to approximately 63,000—a gain of 160 per cent. As the East Bay and San Francisco became more and more interdependent and began to complement each other's development, counties in the southern and northern sections of the Bay Area included relatively smaller proportions of the total population of the area. Santa Clara County gained less than 10,000 and slipped from second to third place among the counties in the area. Its residents numbered only a little more than 35,000 in 1880, compared with 26,246 ten years earlier. The four North Bay counties of Marin, Sonoma, Napa, and Solano together included only about 6,000 more inhabitants than Alameda County alone and among them had but 16.3 per cent of the total in the area, whereas ten years earlier nearly one-fifth of the population of the nine counties had lived in the North Bay. The proportion living in the two central counties of San Francisco and Alameda rose from 65 to 70 per cent, and for the next fifty years it remained about the same, though the percentage living in San Francisco declined steadily and the percentage living in Alameda County similarly increased. Not until the opening of transbay bridges and the construction of three-lane automobile highways throughout the Bay Area in the 1930's was the proportion concentrated in the two central counties to be reduced.

Outlying Counties

The growth that did take place in the North Bay was stimulated in large measure by the building of new railroads, the opening of new lumbering areas, and the further development of agriculture. Logging activities along the lower reaches of the Russian River in Sonoma County were fairly minor until Peter Donahue constructed a sixteen-mile branch of his San Francisco and North Pacific Railroad from Fulton to Guerneville in 1876, and the North Pacific Coast Railroad completed its narrow-gauge line to Duncan's Mills near the mouth of the river in 1877. The latter line had been opened between Sausalito and Tomales in 1875, providing an easy way for farmers in the coastal area of Marin County to ship their potatoes, butter, and oats to San Francisco; but its extension to the redwood forests of the Russian River had awaited the construction of a seventeen-hundred-foot tunnel through the mountains north of Tomales. On the line of the railroad in the San Geronimo–Nicasio Area of Marin County, three large new sawmills began operating; and in Sonoma County the towns of Valley Ford and Occidental made gains as local shipping points for agricultural products.

Not a little of the lumber produced around Guerneville was used for new structures in the thriving town of Santa Rosa, which increased in population during the 'seventies, while its rival, Petaluma, declined. (Santa Rosa in 1880: 3,616; Petaluma: 3,326.) Petaluma in that period gained an important new resident—a Canadian named Lyman C. Byce, who laid the foundations for the later fame of the city as a poultry and egg production center.

The Mill and Lumberyard of Heald and Guerne at Guerneville, Sonoma County.
From a lithograph in Historical Atlas Map of Sonoma County, 1877.

Besides building a branch of his San Francisco and North Pacific Railroad to Guerneville, Peter Donahue in the 'seventies built a railroad in the Sonoma Valley (Sears Point to Sonoma) and extended his Petaluma–Cloverdale main line to San Rafael in Marin County. When he laid rails of the last-mentioned line to Point Tiburon in 1882, the tip of the Marin Peninsula had two railroad terminals only half an hour by ferry from San Francisco. But even with the improved communication between the metropolis and the North Bay, developments in the northern counties were to progress slowly for many decades.

At the southern end of the bay, in Santa Clara County, a shift in production from grains to fruit began in the 'seventies; a similar change did not take place to any considerable extent in other Bay Area counties until the 'eighties. By 1875, San Jose had two large canneries, forerunners of many other processing plants later established there. In other respects this oldest of civil settlements in

the Bay Area continued to be like Santa Rosa, Petaluma, and Napa, primarily a trading center and shipping point for an agricultural territory.

Dawn of the Electric Age

The introduction of a new invention especially associated, in the early days of its use, with urban living emphasized the difference in tempo between these outlying cities and San Francisco and Oakland. This technological wonder was the telephone. In February, 1878, the American Speaking Telephone Company began regular service in San Francisco with eighteen subscribers; and two months later the American District Telegraph Company installed the first switchboard for a telephone system in Oakland, serving a dozen or more subscribers.

At first the wires were strung over boards nailed to roofs, but it was not long before telephone poles and overhead wires became one more means of distinguishing a large city from a small one.

"The city," as San Francisco was always called, alos led the way in the use of a new source of illumination—electricity. The Reverend Father Joseph M. Neri, professor of physics and other sciences at St. Ignatius College, gave the populace their first experience with the new marvel when, using a French dynamo, he installed three large arc floodlights on the roof of the college to illuminate the 1876 Centennial Exposition parade on Market Street.

Three years later, George H. Roe organized the California Electric Light Company and built the first central generating station in the United States, at the rear of a small lot near the corner of Fourth and Market streets. When the original station was destroyed by fire the following year, Roe moved to a new location and resumed service.

Still unknown was the secret of long-distance transmission of electricity, the use of electric power in the operation of transit vehicles, and the use of electricity industrially. But the electric age had dawned, presaging great new developments in the Bay Area and California—new developments that would contribute to the industrial growth of a state lacking in significant coal resources and as yet unaware of the extent of its petroleum deposits.

Social Turmoil

The social turmoil of the late 'seventies demonstrated how urgently the state, and the bay counties in particular, needed expansion of manufacturing and diversification of agriculture. The discontented mobs who gathered on the sand lots opposite the San Francisco City Hall in 1877 and 1878 to hear the vituperative Irish demagogue Denis Kearney berate the monopolists and the Chinese found what every mob wants—scapegoats. But the Number One enemy of these idle, frustrated men was an economy still in the early stages of development. Not that the railroad titans, the grain kings, and the land barons who had encouraged heavy in-migration could escape culpability for

Poplar City. A subdivision "connecting the cities of San Jose and Santa Clara . . . with orchards on the rear of each lot and poplar trees enclosing each block." From a lithograph in Historical Atlas Map of Santa Clara County, 1876.

the social ills of the times. This fraternity had created a huge labor force before there were crops and factories enough to provide jobs for all, and they had retarded economic development by charging excessive freight rates, stifling competition, and demanding high prices for land. But California was not fully awakened to the potentialities of its soils and the opportunities for agricultural diversification; nor did the West yet offer extensive markets for manufactured products. California was the land of grain, and the fields gave employment to labor only during the summer. In winter thousands of those who had sweated in the sun joined bread lines. But with the development of orchards in the Santa Clara Valley and vineyards in the Napa and Sonoma valleys came a new era of increased employment, for vine and orchard crops required a greater number of hands the year round. And as employment in agriculture expanded and became more stable, the market for products manufactured in the Bay Area also grew.

In spite of the ups and downs of the decade—the depression in the opening years, the silver orgy of 1873-1875, the slump of 1876, the turbulence and near insurrection of 1877-1878, and the political clashes leading to the adoption of a new State Constitution in 1879—the Bay Area made great gains. By the end of the decade every county in the area enjoyed railroad facilities. In remoter sections of the state, towns that were not even on the map in 1870 looked to the metropolis for goods and services. To bay ports and bay cities they shipped their grain and wine, their wool and lumber and potatoes.

The Bay Area had begun to develop an oceanic hinterland and to attract through the Golden Gate the tramp steamers of the world, the Alaska whaling fleet, and lumber schooners from Oregon, Washington, and the northern California coast. In 1878 the Pacific Mail Line, having established regular sailings to Honolulu, became a medium for supplying the area with raw sugar, pineapples, coffee, and hides from the Hawaiian Islands. From the Orient came ships laden with wood oils, burlap, and tea, and from the South Seas vessels reeking of copra.

The decade of the 'seventies was the last in which the Bay Area was the unrivaled magnet for population migrating to California. Southern California was being discovered by adventurous Europeans, by eastern tourists who drifted south from the Bay Area, and by a few San Francisco and Nevada capitalists. Its most exciting years were just ahead. In the 'eighties the Southern Pacific and the Santa Fe would both complete transcontinental railroads to Los Angeles, thereby precipitating the "land rush" that was southern California's equivalent of the gold rush. The Bay Area, however, was yet to enjoy several decades of dominance in the affairs of California before it would share the privileges and responsibilities of leadership with another great metropolitan area.

CHAPTER FIVE

The Heyday of Enterprise

The 'eighties were years of sober, patient advance, free from the speculative madness, the shattering crashes, and the abject misery of the previous bizarre decade. Men no longer became millionaires overnight or found themselves reduced to poverty by a capricious turn of the wheel of fortune. Adolph Sutro sold out his holdings in Virginia City and invested his millions in San Francisco real estate, even though most of his friends regarded his purchases of acres of sand hills as sheer folly. Time was to prove that there was more money in the sand hills of the bay metropolis than in the tunneled and blasted mountains of Virginia City. The wealth of the 'eighties came only in part from the mines; the greater part of it came from the soils, the new factories, the new inventions designed to increase production, and from the railroad and shipping enterprises that facilitated the development of the state.

The most striking changes in the San Francisco Bay Area took place in the major valleys rather than in the cities. A great shift from the production of grain to the growing of fruit completely transformed the appearance of many rural areas, as a description of the Napa Valley in 1890 indicates: "Where there were wheat fields now are vineyards; where there were pasture fields now are thrifty orchards; where there stood barns for holding the grain and sheds for sheltering the stock now stand imposing wine cellars and fruit houses."[1] A contemporary newspaper account of the agricultural revolution in the valleys of Sonoma County revealed that the vine and the tree "entirely engrossed the attention of the farmers."[2] In almost every area served by adequate railroad transportation the big grain ranches were subdivided into small holdings. Long rows of young fruit trees were set out, and within a few years a rich green canopy shaded the earth that had formerly been mantled in gold. Even the largest nurseries were taxed to supply the demand for budded stock.

Some idea of the upsurge of interest in fruit production can be gained from the historian Bancroft's figures on shipments of fruit from California to eastern states. In 1871, the second year after the completion of the transcontinental railroad, less than 2,000,000 pounds of California fruit was marketed in the East. By 1888 the amount was almost 54,000,000 pounds. In 1872 a mere 182,090 pounds of canned fruit went East, but by 1888 the total shipped beyond the Sierra was more than 39,000,000 pounds. Between 1875 and 1888 the volume of California dried fruit sold in the eastern market increased from a little more than 500,000 to almost 20,000,000 pounds.[3]

In a kind of chicken-and-egg relationship, freight rates lowered as fruit shipments increased, and fruit orchards spread over a vaster acreage as rates fell. In 1889 the rate on canned fruit was ninety-four cents per hundred pounds, whereas a few years earlier it had been $3.51 per hundred pounds. Not that California farmers and canners were satisfied with these freight rates; the cry was for still lower rates. But the railroads at least responded in their grudging fashion to the demands of the new economy that was evolving.

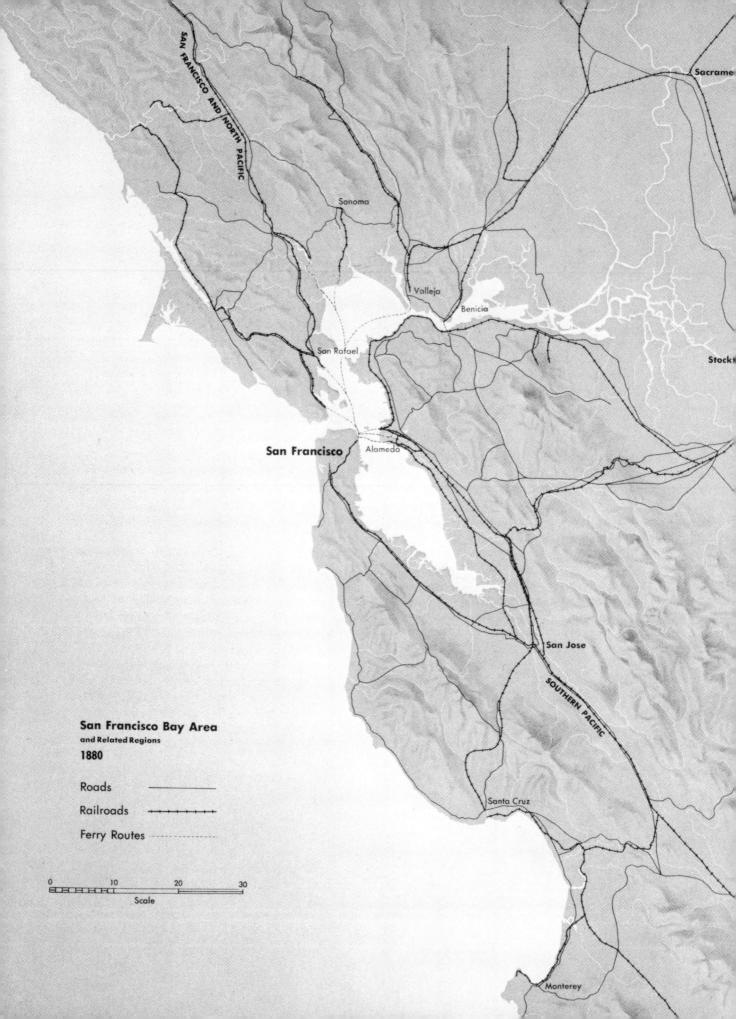

San Francisco Bay Area
and Related Regions
1880

Roads

Railroads

Ferry Routes

0   10   20   30
Scale

Sugar, Ships, and Pumps

In San Francisco, where perhaps four-fifths of the manufacturing enterprises of the state were concentrated, the most talked-about establishment in the industrial belt along the southern waterfront was the mammoth sugar refinery erected by Claus Spreckels at the foot of Twenty-third Street in 1883. Freighters from the Hawaiian Islands unloaded raw sugar at the refinery docks, and some five hundred employees converted it into the basic product upon which the operations of a growing number of fruit canneries depended.

Indicative of the transition of Bay Area agriculture from grains to fruit was the entrance of another steamship line into the Hawaiian trade. In the same year that the Spreckels refinery began operating, the Oceanic Steamship Company followed the Pacific Mail in the importation of raw sugar and other products of the Islands. By 1885 the Oceanic had linked San Francisco with Australia and New Zealand, thereby opening new fields for the exportation of manufactured products and providing new sources of raw materials.

Obscure at the time, yet related to the expansion of the Hawaiian sugar trade, to the building of the Spreckels refinery, and to the agricultural revolution, was John Bean's invention and manufacture of an orchard spray pump in the village of Los Gatos in 1883. By providing fruitgrowers with the means of combating insect pests, particularly San Jose scale, the retired inventor contributed to the remarkable increase in production that was one of the economic phenomena of the 'eighties and 'nineties. From his modest plant and several small canning-machinery factories developed the huge Food Machinery and Chemical Corporation, today a gigantic enterprise with headquarters in San Jose and branch plants throughout the United States.

The Grain Trade

In the great Central Valley of California the raising of wheat and other grains was still the chief agricultural activity. The magnitude of production was reflected in grain shipping at Port Costa and other ports along the northern shore of Contra Costa County. Founded by George W. McNear in 1879, just after the railroad was opened through the county, Port Costa quickly became the greatest grain port in the world. Immense warehouses, heaped with sacks of the hard, plump wheat of the San Joaquin Valley, lined the wharves for a mile or more, and it was no uncommon sight by 1884 to see within a single week as many as twenty-five tall-masted ships taking on cargo. By May, 1886, wheat poured into the waiting holds at the rate of one hundred carloads a day, while sometimes as many as five hundred carloads waited on the sidings. Barges and steamers also brought wheat to the docks. At Antioch, too, large numbers of ships loaded wheat, for eastern Contra Costa County was given over almost exclusively to the cultivation of that great staple.

Along the line of the railroad, villages began to develop at the stations of Brentwood and Byron, where warehouses were built to accommodate the rapidly increasing production. Stores sprang up, schools were organized, post offices opened for business.

The golden harvest flowed through Port Costa, Antioch, and even small landings in a veritable torrent throughout the 'eighties. Production hit a peak of 46,200,000 bushels in California in 1884, and land planted to wheat reached the climactic total of three million acres in 1888.[4] Thereafter plantings of wheat began to decline, although the yield remained above 30,000,000 bushels during the 'nineties, except in 1893–94 and 1897–98. The fairly rapid reduction in wheat acreage after 1900 has been attributed to exhaustion of soils in some areas; to the development of irrigation systems and the rise of intensive, diversified farming; and to the competition of new grain areas in the Mississippi Valley, in western Canada, and in Russia. Port Costa, nevertheless, handled an enormous amount of grain, including barley, each year until well after the turn of the century.

Iron and Steel Industry

The grain trade contributed in a curious fashion to the development of California industry. The grain ships arrived with cargoes of coal and coke, which supplied the energy for manufacturing in the days before hydroelectric power and petroleum; they also brought in tons of pig iron, scrap iron, and old steel rails. This raw material, unloaded from ships arriving at Oakland's Long Wharf to take on cargoes of wheat and barley, was indispensable to the growth of the iron and steel industry in the East Bay. The linkage with the major agricultural enterprises of the time was further strengthened by the production, by many of the iron and steel plants, of agricultural machinery, such as threshers, plows, pumps, and windmill equipment.

Most of the early iron and steel plants in Oakland were situated not far from the central business district, on First and Second streets west of Broadway, or on Market and Myrtle streets, just beyond the blocks laid out in 1853 by Kellersberger. An important exception was the Judson Manufacturing Company, which selected a nine-acre site with a frontage of twelve hundred feet on the Central Pacific tracks in what is now the industrial city of Emeryville. Slag and other refuse materials from the company's industrial operations served as fill for acres of near-by tidelands.

Foundries and similar enterprises were not confined to the Alameda County waterfront, however. In the new town of Crockett, founded in November, 1881, and named in honor of State Supreme Court Justice Joseph Bryant Crockett, rose the J. L. Heald Foundry. Until the plant was taken over in the late 'nineties by the California Hawaiian Sugar Refinery, it produced boilers, stationary and movable engines, threshing machines, separators, grape crushers, roller-crushing barley mills, and other agricultural machinery. On the opposite side of Carquinez Strait, at Benicia, the Benicia Agricultural Works likewise turned out a steady flow of agricultural implements that were shipped to many parts of the world, including Australia, New Zealand, South America, China, and Japan.

Industrial Dispersion

The industrial dispersion that has been so much discussed in the San Francisco Bay Area in recent years actually began in the 'eighties when smelting and explosives plants moved from San Francisco to western Contra Costa County. However, the first explosives plant in this area, the Vulcan Powder Works, was originally a Nevada rather than a San Francisco concern. It was established near Stege, in what is now Richmond, in 1878. The Giant Powder Company of San Francisco followed in 1880,

giving the name "Giant" to a site on a peninsula that juts into San Pablo Bay north of Richmond. The next year the California Powder Works, predecessor of the Hercules Powder Company, erected buildings in a series of ravines on a tract on San Pablo Bay, in order to safeguard the surrounding area. In 1882 several smaller plants began to cluster around the Vulcan plant at Stege.

The powder, dynamite, and nitroglycerine produced in these Contra Costa plants blasted away the ore-bearing strata in western mines, leveled hills and mountains that blocked the paths of railroad engineers, cleared boulders from new roads, and did hundreds of earth-moving jobs for companies that were building bridges, tunnels, and embankments throughout the West. The volume of explosives manufactured was, indeed, a fair measure of the physical development taking place in California and in near-by states and territories.

Closely allied to these explosives plants were the smelter and the cartridge factory of the Selby Smelting and Lead Company at Selby, on San Pablo Bay. By 1884 the smelter built at Black Point (Fort Mason) in San Francisco by Thomas Selby in 1865 had so greatly extended operations that Prentiss Selby, who became general manager upon the death of his father, was compelled to purchase a larger site in a more suitable location. He therefore selected a waterfront site in Contra Costa County far enough from any city to escape complaints about air pollution. Operations began at the new smelter

Artist's Drawing of the Refinery of the Pacific Coast Oil Company at Alameda Point, 1898. Photograph courtesy of Standard Oil Company of California.

REFINERY AT ALAMEDA POINT.

in 1885, and production soon reached a volume of $30,000 in gold and thirty thousand ounces of silver a day. The following year the cartridge factory was erected. This factory and the powder manufacturing plants near by coöperated with the Benicia Arsenal in developing newer and more powerful shells, which were tested at a proving ground at the arsenal.

In addition to the iron and steel plants, explosives plants, and the Selby smelter, one other East Bay manufacturing enterprise of the 'eighties was significant. At Woodstock, near Alameda Point, the Pacific Coast Oil Company, organized by San Francisco interests, began operating one of the first oil refineries in California in 1880, manufacturing chiefly kerosene from crude petroleum shipped by rail from Pico Canyon near Los Angeles and by tankers from Ventura. Small amounts of petroleum also were obtained from Moody Gulch, near Los Gatos, and from Sargent, in southern Santa Clara County. When the Standard Oil Company absorbed the Pacific Coast Oil Company in a merger in 1890, about the time that drilling began in the southern San Joaquin Valley oil fields, the eventual construction of a pipe line northward through the Valley to a larger refinery at some point on the eastern shore of the bay perhaps became inevitable. At any rate, the little refinery at Alameda Point may be regarded as a forerunner of the huge Standard Oil Company refinery in Richmond.

The Grip of Monopoly

This thriving Bay Area, resourceful in the organization of manufacturing enterprises related to the needs and opportunities of the times and far ahead of other areas in California in the development of a diversified agriculture, was the focal point of the far-flung railroad empire that the Big Four had begun building in the 'sixties. By the end of 1887 the driving ambition of Stanford, Huntington, and Crocker (Mark Hopkins had died in 1878) had made it possible for a San Franciscan to cross the bay to Oakland and entrain for Portland, Oregon, for Salt Lake City or Chicago, or for New Orleans. The "Sunset Route" to the great cotton port near the mouth of the Mississippi had been opened in February, 1883; and Charles Crocker had driven the "last spike" in the railroad to the Columbia River at Ashland, Oregon, on December 18, 1887. Yet the Southern Pacific system, then consisting of fifty-five hundred miles of track, was still in the formative stages and would eventually be three times as large.

Monopolistic, politically powerful, dedicated to a policy of charging all that the traffic would bear, the Southern Pacific took its toll of Bay Area enterprise and steadily increased the number of its enemies, among whom were civic leaders of great wealth and influence. Their opposition eventually was to crystallize into a scheme for a competitive railroad, but through the 'eighties Huntington and his associates continued to tighten their hold on the Bay Area. They absorbed Senator Fair's South Pacific Coast Railroad in 1887, thereby eliminating another potential rival. Since their purchase included the narrow-gauge railroad's ferryboat service on San Francisco Bay, all transbay interurban service came under single management—or in other words, monopoly control. Toward the end of the decade, the titans also extended their tracks from Napa Junction, on the original California Pacific route, to Santa Rosa by way of the Sonoma and Guilicos valleys. And in 1891 they completed another branch line, the connection that the farmers in the Ygnacio and San Ramon valleys of Contra Costa County had long sought to make with the main line along the shore of Suisun Bay.

Except for the new branch to Santa Rosa, the northwestern part of the Bay Area remained without a railroad operated by the Southern Pacific. In 1889 Peter Donahue built the main line of his San Francisco and North Pacific Railroad northward through the Russian River Valley from Cloverdale to Ukiah, in Mendocino County. Three years later he connected Santa Rosa with the apple country around Sebastopol by a branch road and also extended the Guerneville branch farther down the Russian River to Monte Rio, in the coast-redwood country. Ten years earlier he had pushed the little Sonoma Valley Railroad a few miles farther north of Sonoma to Glen Ellen, thereby providing an outlet for the vineyards and wineries of that historic area.

A railroad was as essential in those days for the exploitation of natural resources as highways and trucks are today—as was demonstrated by the extension of the North Pacific Coast Railroad from the Russian River to Cazadero. Until the rails were thrust six miles farther into the timber country to the lumber town on Austin Creek, logging and milling did not amount to much. They took a sudden spurt when the railroad came.

With the establishment of these additional branches and extensions, the rail network in the Bay Area had reached a stage of development in harmony with the potentialities of the metropolitan region. Practically every part of the area that could supply a railroad with regular freight shipments had been tapped by one. The Southern Pacific monopolized the areas with the greatest resources and the largest concentrations of population. The smaller, local roads served the least accessible and least populated areas and would later be among the first to feel the pinch of competition from trucks and buses.

California Street as Seen from Dupont Street (Now Grant Avenue), San Francisco, 1885.

Transit in San Francisco

The Southern Pacific, known simply as "the railroad," also had a tremendous influence on the growth of the city of San Francisco through its control of the Market Street Railroad. Beginning in 1883, Leland Stanford converted this transit system to a cable system at a cost of $1,750,000, thereby making possible faster travel and encouraging families to live farther from the central business district. The main line on Market Steets from the Ferry terminus to Twenty-eighth and Valencia streets contributed to the development of the outer Mission District, while the Haight Street and McAllister Street branches, particularly, stimulated the growth of the area at the eastern end of Golden Gate Park, two miles from the City Hall.

By the mid-eighties that pleasure ground was exciting great admiration and putting to shame all those early critics who had scoffed at the possibility of transforming sandy wastes into garden spots. Property in the vicinity of Stanyan Street, the eastern boundary of the park, was worth $25 to $50 a front foot in the early 'eighties but by 1891 was "in active demand at $125 to $250 a front foot."[5]

A meandering Hayes Valley branch of the Market Street Railroad and cable lines on Geary, California, and Sacramento streets all contributed to settlement of the Western Addition, particularly after 1885, when the wealthier citizens of San Francisco migrated west of Van Ness Avenue to vantage points from which they could enjoy views of the Golden Gate, the lyric silhouette of Mount Tamalpais, and the islands and inlets in the northern part of the bay.

Little development took place in the sandy open spaces now known as the Richmond and Sunset districts of the city, even though a steam line ran out California Street and around Land's End to the Cliff House after 1887 and another steam line operated to the ocean beach along the southern boundary of Golden Gate Park. The amusement places at the beach seemed a long way off in those days and were frequented chiefly on Sundays and holidays.

The most famous and the most enduring of San Francisco cable lines began operation in 1885. The Powell Street Cable, which then as now ran from Powell and Market streets up over Nob Hill and the eastern slope of Russian Hill to Taylor and Bay streets, made the North Beach district more accessible from the downtown area and aided development of the picturesque quarter later known as "Little Italy."

In 1891 the city hailed the last of the major cable installations, the Hyde Street cross-town line of the California Street Railroad, which traversed Russian Hill.

Connecting the business district and the southern part of the city were several lines of the Omnibus Railroad. One that terminated at Potrero Avenue and Twenty-second Street connected with a horsecar line to South San Francisco. Together the two lines contributed during the 'nineties to the development of that suburb as a meat-packing and manufacturing center.

Congestion in Chinatown

Even though rail lines spanned the entire peninsula, San Francisco in the late 'eighties remained a compact metropolis, confined mainly to the northeast quadrant of the city-county. Business and residential properties were indiscriminately mixed, not only in the heart of the city, but also in the areas surrounding the central core. Congestion had early become characteristic of San Francisco and was nowhere more appalling than in Chinatown, a twelve-block ghetto bounded by Kearny, California, Stockton, and Broadway, with Dupont Street (Grant Avenue) serving as its "Main Street."

A fascinating map of the Chinese quarter in the *Municipal Reports* for 1884–85 shows street-floor occupancy of every building and designates by various hues all the gambling houses, opium resorts, joss houses, Chinese houses of prostitution, and white houses of prostitution. This is probably the most accurate land-use map of a section of San Francisco that has survived from the days before the great conflagration of 1906.

A special committee of the board of supervisors "found that the rule is for two persons to each 'bunk,' and relays of sleepers through the day in many, if not most instances, but women and children seem also to be stowed away in every available nook and corner, without reference to any special accommodation being provided for them. Taking therefore, the total number of 'bunks' and multiplying that total by two, must be at least a safe minimum estimate of the population in these twelve blocks, with every probability favoring the conclusion that an addition of perhaps twenty per cent would not more than cover the real number of Chinese inhabiting that locality."[6] On this basis the committee's "lowest possible estimate" of the population in Chinatown was 30,360—a density of 200 to 300 persons per acre.[7]

The Ferry Building, San Francisco, 1886. Photograph courtesy of Southern Pacific News Bureau and Oakland Tribune.

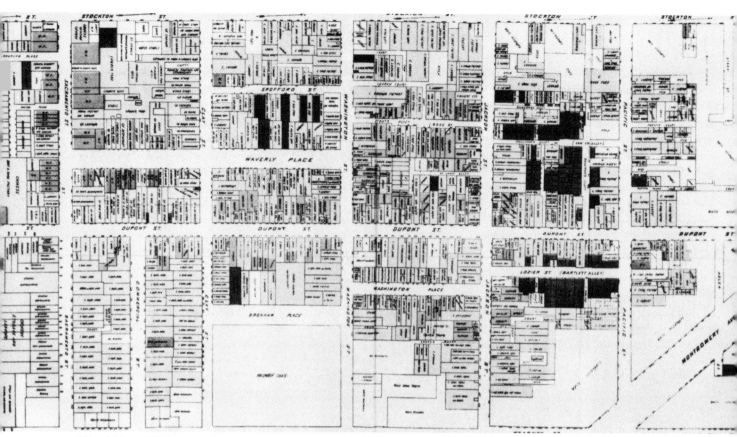

Official Map of Chinatown, San Francisco. The lighter grays show gambling houses, opium resorts, joss houses, and general Chinese occupancy; the darker grays show Chinese houses of prostitution and white houses of prostitution. From the San Francisco Municipal Reports for 1884–1885.

Seeking to fix responsibility for the slum conditions of Chinatown, the committee directed its attention especially to the owner of property in the quarter: "He has had no special reason to regret the occupation of his premises by Chinese in so far as the rate of revenue derived therefrom is concerned, for that revenue, if your Committee are credibly informed, has been materially larger than could have been obtained from any other class of tenants. . . . The property-owner in Chinatown must be made to feel his responsibility in this matter before Chinatown can ever be brought to a level with common public decency."[8]

The committee recommended, among other things, restricting the number of inhabitants in any given block in the city, but did not say how this might be accomplished. It might have learned a thing or two from the New York Tenement House Commission of 1884, the first citizens' commission appointed to investigate housing conditions in that city. On the recommendation of the New York body an act was passed in 1885 regulating the height of dwellings in the eastern city in relation to the width of the street on which they fronted. This was an early step toward restricting the volume of a building and thereby

limiting the number of occupants. From such legislation in time evolved modern zoning ordinances, which regulate population density by controlling the height and bulk of structures and, in some cities, by establishing a fixed ratio between lot area and floor area. In 1885, San Francisco had, however, nothing better than a so-called "Cubic Air Ordinance" to assure a minimum of breathing space to slum dwellers, and this law the Special Committee on the Condition of the Chinese Quarter found "constantly violated."[9]

Beginnings of Control

The incomprehensible and persecuted Chinese were contributors, albeit against their will, to the enlargement of the concept of the police power, the legal basis of all zoning controls. The laundries that the celestials opened in various neighborhoods of the city came to be regarded as public nuisances because the proprietors dumped dirty water into the street, because fires frequently broke out in these establishments, and because groups of Chinese gamblers congregated in them. In the interest of public health, safety, and morals, the board of supervisors in

1885 passed an ordinance excluding laundries from residential areas. Laundry operators Yick Wo and Soon Hing attacked the legality of the ordinance, charging discrimination; but in tests before the California State Supreme Court and the United States Supreme Court the city won noteworthy victories.

"With the decisions in these cases as precedent, other California cities, as well as cities in other states, proceeded to enact ordinances restricting other objectionable businesses," one authority writes. "Within a few years it had become generally recognized that it was within the police power of municipalities to protect residential areas from invasion by such disagreeable businesses as the manufacture of bricks, maintenance of a livery stable, operation of a dairy, stone-crusher, machine shop, or carpet-beating establishment, slaughter of animals, billboards, and a number of other such uses."[10]

Inherent in these early ordinances excluding the most obviously incompatible activities from residential areas was, then, the cardinal principle of zoning—the separation of inharmonious uses of the land and the grouping of establishments carrying on similar activities into special zones or districts. Little by little, as cities struggled with the problem of space for increasing populations and for rapidly growing industries and commercial establishments, they learned to build a new structure of public control over the utilization of land upon the judicial language of the Yick Wo and Soon Hing decisions.

First Apartment Houses

San Francisco in the 'eighties and early 'nineties was on the way to becoming one of the most densely populated cities in the United States. Chinatown may have been the most glaring example of overcrowding, but it was not to remain the only thickly settled area. Multiple residences, in the form of flats or apartment houses, made their appearance about 1884, as an article in the San Francisco *Chronicle* in 1887 reveals:

"One architect, who is agent for some foreign property-owners, tried an experiment about three years ago in the erection of a large flat building three stories in height, with four sets of apartments on each floor, so that the building accommodated twelve families under its roof. At the time of its erection the Chronicle fully described the building and commended the idea to capitalists as one which would return a good percentage on the investment. The history of the experiment has fully justified the investment, and the recommendation given to it by this paper. The flats were at once rented to a class of prompt-paying tenants at $16 and $18 a month. Not one of them has ever been vacant more than a day, and the rents have

been advanced to $18 and $20 a month. The building, from the day it was finished to the present time, has given a net income of 12 per cent on the cost. In the Eastern cities the owner who realizes 5 per cent net on real estate considers himself lucky, and the owner of the building spoken of is now having the plans made for three more of the same class. The architect and agent of the owner says that fifty such buildings would be equally profitable, and he is surprised that more of them have not been erected by capitalists seeking a profitable investment."[11]

Perhaps the unsung architect undertook a one-man crusade to open the eyes of moneyed gentlemen to the possibilities of more intensive use of the land. A return of 12 per cent on the investment must surely have been a powerful argument for constructing a dozen dwellings where ordinarily only one or two would be erected. At any rate, by 1890 San Francisco had nearly 900 structures containing accommodations for three or more families. By the end of the 'nineties it had more than 3,300 such buildings, and there had been an actual decrease in the number of single-family residences, from 43,418 in 1890 to 42,255 in 1900.[12] Around the central business district and as far out as Van Ness Avenue, new apartment houses offered families the dubious privilege of living in layers, one above the other.

First Skyscraper

In the downtown area, publisher Michael H. de Young introduced the architectural form now most characteristic of American central business districts from coast to coast —the towering, steel-frame office building, or skyscraper. This structural type, exemplified by the ten-story Chronicle Building at Market and Kearny streets, was an importation from Chicago; and the architects selected by de Young to design the new home of his newspaper were leading members of the "Chicago school," Daniel Hudson Burnham and John Root.

Wiseacres shook their heads over the proposal to erect such a tall building in a city known to suffer serious earthquakes occasionally. De Young, however, had faith in the ability of his architects to design a structure that would defy the most severe temblors—a faith that was rewarded at the time of the upheaval of 1906. Other skyscrapers appeared in the 'nineties, though there was no sudden change in the skyline of San Francisco. Not until the disaster of 1906 demonstrated the resistance of steel-frame construction to violent movements of the earth did the skyscraper become popular in San Francisco.

Nowadays it is ironical that Burnham, the designer of the Chronicle Building, the Mills Building, the Merchant's Exchange, and other early San Francisco skyscrapers, should be remembered hardly at all for structures like these and should be thought of principally as the creator of a "City Beautiful" plan that was almost wholly ignored in the hasty rebuilding of the city after the catastrophe of 1906. Perhaps it is even more ironical that he helped set the pattern for a concentrated commercial center which was the very opposite of the expansive baroque city contemplated in his plan of 1905 for the Association for the Improvement and Adornment of San Francisco. Paris and Washington, D.C., provided the inspiration for that plan, but Burnham through his endeavors of the 'eighties and 'nineties had already assisted in fixing upon American cities a character wholly unlike that of the Paris of Baron Haussmann and the Washington of L'Enfant.

Cosmopolitan Metropolis

At the time the soaring Chronicle Building was a novelty, San Francisco was still addicted to flamboyancy in architecture—in commercial buildings as well as in dwellings. The admiration of a *Chronicle* writer for some detached villas constructed by the firm of Roundtree Brothers at Page and Baker streets, a few blocks from Golden Gate Park, indicates the taste of the times:

"Viewed from the sidewalk, which like the steps and stone coping around the lot, is of artificial stone, it will be noticed at a glance that the style of architecture is a clever admixture of the colonial and the Queen Anne, with more than a suggestion of Eastlake thrown in. There are big gables and rounded bays, fancy shingling and stucco work, small turrets and look-outs, and the combination is pretty without being too pretentious . . ."[13]

The city in its entirety by then had gained that indefinable, cosmopolitan quality which endears it to travelers and reminds even its own residents of the cities of the whole world. Justin McCarthy, a writer and leader of the Home Rule Party in Britain, epitomized it in his novel *Lady Judith:*

"Convert the hills of Rome into dust heaps and plant them around the harbor of Queenstown; crowd on their sides a city made up indiscriminately of the Strand, Broadway, Wapping, Donnybrook, Hongkong, Denver, Vera Cruz, and Hamburg and you may create in your mind's eye something like an adequate picture of San Francisco.

"It is a city where houses seem indeed to have been literally built on sand; a city climbing up the sides of sandhills, overlooked and girt and crowned by sandhills; a city the color of dust and ashes; a summerless, winterless city, where men and women have no season of change in the substance of garments; where you may wear furs if you like them in July or in December."[14]

Oakland: "City of Homes"

The transbay city of Oakland presented an extreme contrast to the picturesque melange that was San Francisco. Although there were industrial developments along the Estuary and in West Oakland, the East Bay city impressed a newspaperman in June, 1887, as being "essentially a city of homes." There was, he wrote, "an appearance of comfort and quiet elegance about the residences which reminds one of some of the older cities of New England. Nearly all the houses are built on lots sufficiently large to give room for a garden, and great care is shown in the cultivation of rare and beautiful flowers."[15]

According to this anonymous scribe, Oakland, or at least that part of it lying between Lake Merritt and the bay, had had for several years "a reputation of being unhealthy on account of the defective sewerage, which caused a great deal of sickness in the shape of diphtheria and low malarial fever." But the San Francisco journalist was happy to report that "all that has been remedied by the construction of a main sewer running from the lake to the bay near Sixteenth Street." Twice a day, at each low tide, floodgates at the head of the sewer were opened and a flood of fresh water from Lake Merritt rushed through, carrying "all the foul, disease-breeding materials which usually find a lodgment in city sewers" into the bay beyond the low-water mark.[16] From there the tides presumably swept the raw sewage out through the Golden Gate, though actually, as population and industries increased, the tides proved more and more inefficient as disposal agents. Even in the 'eighties, then, Oakland and other cities around the bay were contributing to the growth of a pollution problem that would someday assume alarming proportions and nauseate everyone who came within smelling distance of the tidal flats.

Lake Merritt was far from being the effective flushing basin that it was represented to be. Engineer George F. Allardt found in 1889 that streams tributary to the lake had deposited 403,000 cubic yards of solid material in it since he first took soundings in 1871. A condition was building up that played into the hands of those who advocated converting the lands bordering the lake into a park. Before long it would be imperative to dredge the lake, and what would be more logical than to fill in the shallows along the shore and reclaim them for public use?

In the early 'eighties, petitions and memorials gave impetus to the park movement, and by 1885 an improvement plan estimated to cost $186,000 was put forth. No money was actually appropriated until 1888, when the city council authorized the expenditure of $20,000 to

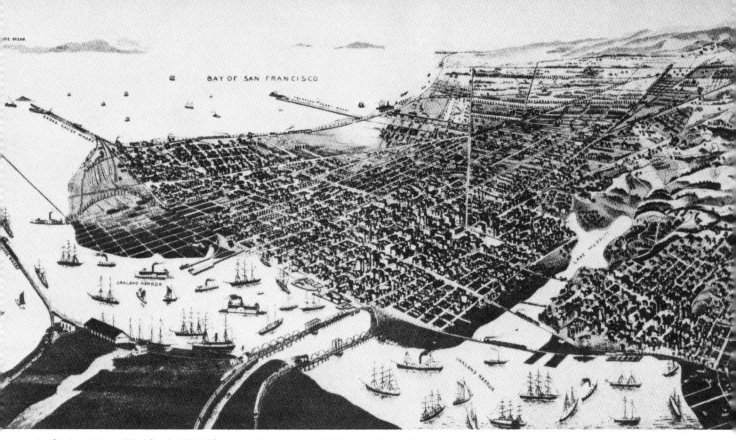

A Bird's Eye View of Oakland, 1893. Photograph courtesy of Oakland Public Library.

begin work on a boulevard on the east side of the lake. As yet, the majority of citizens cared little whether the lake silted up or not, and were apathetic about the agitation for a park.

Those who wanted some beauty in their environment and had the money to buy view lots built houses not within sight of the lake but in north Oakland and in Piedmont, both of which became accessible by cable lines in 1890. Piedmont, especially, attracted well-to-do families who could afford to construct houses costing $15,000 to $25,000—large sums in those days.

Boom in San Jose

Besides San Francisco, Oakland, and Alameda, the only other city in the whole Bay Area that made appreciable population gains in the 'eighties was San Jose. Toward the end of the decade it benefited unexpectedly from the collapse of the real-estate boom that Los Angeles experienced after the completion of the Santa Fe Railroad. As easterners who were singularly unimpressed by southern California drifted north to investigate the immensely productive Santa Clara Valley, land sales in the San Jose Area hit a peak of $2,000,000 a day in August, 1887. The following year the San Jose Board of Trade became so aggressive as to open an office in Los Angeles, to en-

courage those who were disheartened by the real-estate fiasco in the southern part of the state to move to the Santa Clara Valley. Civic leaders subscribed funds to build a huge tourist hotel to be called the Vendome; put over bond issues for a new city hall, park improvements, sewers, bridges, and other public works; and even talked about making Alviso a deep-water port. Several new banks and building and loan companies opened for business. By 1891, promoters were attempting to sell lots in a dream city called New Chicago, in the sloughs north of Alviso, and in other developments called New Bethlehem and Hacienda Park. The last-named was a gridiron plat on top of a mountain near the New Almaden Mine.

The San Jose area was too well established to be affected by these swindle schemes, which were as bad as any attempted in Los Angeles County when the Santa Fe and Southern Pacific were carrying on their rate war and were luring Middle Westerners by the thousands to southern California. The enterprising residents of San Jose and the surrounding area went steadily ahead, expanding fruit acreage, organizing new canneries, and building new educational institutions, public buildings, and farm-to-market roads; but the population increase in San Jose itself in the 'nineties was less than 3,500, compared with approximately 5,500 in the previous decade.

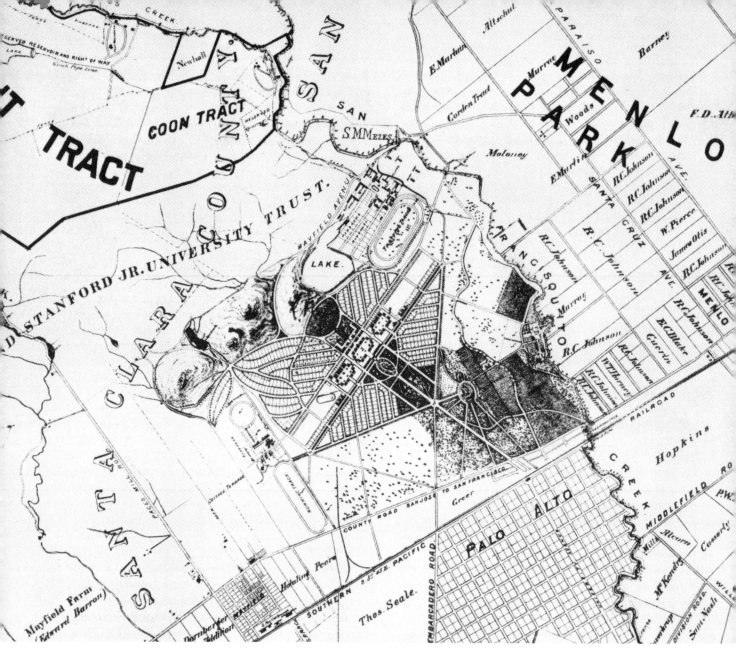

*Stanford University, the Town of Palo Alto, and Neighboring Estates in the Late
1890's. From an advertisement for ranch property ordered sold by Mrs. Leland Stanford after her husband's death. Photograph courtesy of Palo Alto Public Library.*

Stanford University

While San Jose was exhilarated by an unforseseen boom,
a development began to take shape on the San Francisco
Peninsula that revealed the aggressive Leland Stanford
in a new light. The man who had been a partner in the
creation of a railroad empire, who had reorganized transit
operations in San Francisco, and who had succeeded in
being elected to the United States Senate in 1885, now
appeared in the twin roles of bereaved father and co-
founder, with his wife, of a great new university. In 1884
his only son, sixteen-year-old Leland Stanford, Jr., had
died in Florence, Italy. As a memorial to him, the parents
conceived the idea of transforming the Stanford stock
farm on San Francisquito Creek in northern Santa Clara
County into the campus of a major institution of higher
education.

That Stanford's grief for the loss of his heir should be channeled into the building of a university is understandable. Two years before the death of the boy, the father had received an interim appointment as a regent of the University of California and had looked forward to learning at first hand about the administration of a great university. But when a hostile legislature, with a Democratic majority, had indicated that it would not confirm the appointment, Stanford had withdrawn his name. The new university was not only a memorial to a dead son but an opportunity for Stanford to demonstrate his ability to organize an educational enterprise.

Although privately endowed, Stanford University was similar in some respects to the public university in Berkeley. Like the University of California in its early years, it had a "country location." It, too, brought into being a new city—Palo Alto. Timothy Hopkins, the foster son of Mark Hopkins, planned the town, which was at first called University Park but was finally named for the ancient redwood tree that is still its most conspicuous landmark. And Frederick Law Olmsted prepared a plan for the Stanford campus, as he had the plan for the new campus of the College of California, the institution which became the University of California.

Whereas Olmsted's plan for the Berkeley campus was all but abandoned, his plan for the Stanford campus was in most respects followed. Olmsted's first idea for a group of buildings situated on a commanding site in the foothills of the Santa Cruz Mountains was, however, overruled by the Stanfords in favor of the plain at the foot of the hills, because young Stanford had roamed on horseback over that part of the stock farm and because the level site would be less expensive to develop. The buildings, as designed by the Boston firm of Shepley, Rutan, and Collidge in the Richardsonian Romanesque style then fashionable, formed a series of quadrangles connected by arcades. In planning the grounds, Olmsted attempted for the first time to utilize plants especially adapted to the long dry season in California.

Contrary to the opinion of the New York *Mail and Express* that "there is about as much need for a new university in California as for an asylum of decayed sea captains in Switzerland,"[17] Stanford University enrolled 465 students when it was opened in October, 1891. Neighboring Palo Alto, where some of the students and professors lived, grew rapidly and became an incorporated city in 1894, with an estimated population of 1,003.

Slow Growth of the Peninsula

From Palo Alto to San Francisco the Southern Pacific traversed a long, narrow bay plain which, all during the 'nineties and for at least two decades thereafter, was given over almost entirely to large estates and farms. The few towns along the route—Menlo Park, Redwood City, San Mateo, and South San Francisco (laid out in 1891)—remained small, and efforts to promote new communities met with little or no success. Only a few trains a day served the Peninsula, and fares were high in comparison with commutation rates on the transbay ferries. Wellesley Park, a new subdivision in Redwood City distinguished by handsome, curvilinear streets and a small elliptical park, attracted a few buyers, because it was a project of the Bohemian Club of San Francisco. The subdivision of property and sale of lots in the vicinity of San Mateo increased the population enough to bring about incorporation of the community in 1894. But San Carlos, a little north of Redwood City, for many years failed to develop, much to the disappointment of the promoters who planned it—a syndicate of men associated with the Southern Pacific. Likewise, a subdivision opened in 1889 on the Darius O. Mills estate was a business failure until after the San Francisco fire of 1906. Burlingame, too, was little more than a post office and a few houses until 1901, when a business district began to develop. South San Francisco, conceived by G. F. Swift, the founder of Swift and Company, as a new industrial community, also got off to a bad start, because San Francisco butchers opposed the removal of meat-packing plants to the new town. Until the late 'nineties Swift's Western Meat Packing Company was the only establishment of any consequence in the industrial tract west of the old San Bruno Toll Road; then W. P. Fuller and Company built a paint factory there, and after the turn of the century various steel companies erected plants in the town.

Even Marin County, separated from San Francisco by water, grew more rapidly than San Mateo County during the 'nineties and had a larger population in 1900. A good many of the new residents in the North Bay county were former city dwellers who took advantage of the improved commuting service established about 1894. Until then, Marin residents had been unable to reach "the city" before seven o'clock in the morning, or to return home after late performances at the theaters, because the ferryboats ran only during certain daylight hours. Upon the inauguration of more convenient service, Sausalito, Tiburon, Belvedere, the new town of Mill Valley, Ross Valley, and San Rafael all attracted families known as "San Francisco Marin County residents." The census of 1900 reported a population of 15,702 in Marin County, compared with 12,094 in San Mateo County. So many cemeteries were established in the Colma Valley, just beyond the San Francisco city-county boundary line, in the late 'eighties and the 'nineties that the increase in the number of the dead in San Mateo County far exceeded that of the living; the population gain of the county in the entire decade of the 'nineties was only a little more than two thousand.

Electric Railways

The East Bay in the meantime saw the successful introduction of a new form of local transportation that soon began to disperse population from the central cities and to accelerate the growth of peripheral areas and suburbs. The electric railway, antedating the automobile by only a few years, was one of a series of modern technological advances that set in motion the creeping urbanism which is today obliterating the intervening open spaces between communities and robbing municipalities of physical identity. The new agent of dispersal had made a brief, ignominious appearance on a line between San Jose and Santa Clara in 1888. Failure of an underground third rail to function properly had forced the operators to revert quickly to horsecar service. In 1891 the overhead trolleys of the Oakland and Berkeley Rapid Transit Company demonstrated conclusively, however, that the electric railway was a practicable means of locomotion far superior to the most respected form of transit then in use, the cable car. Wisely, the promoters of the new line between the two East Bay cities had taken the precaution of studying at first hand the successful operations of a Seattle electric railway. When they inaugurated service via Grove Street and Center Street, Berkeley, to the west gate of the University of California on May 12, 1891, they expected their venture to prosper. And indeed it did, in a curious fashion at first. The novelty of traveling twelve miles an hour by trolley attracted large numbers of patrons who were not going shopping or to work, but who believed that electricity would in some mysterious way alleviate their rheumatism. Others were curious to see whether their watches would be stopped by the magnetism generated in the motors.

History records no miraculous cures from trolley rides; nor were any watches stopped, so far as is known. Rather, the new form of transit had the effect of accelerating urban life. Because they could travel to work faster than before, many people moved to places somewhat farther from their shops and offices. The electric railway was a much more potent agent of expansion than the horsecar had been in the mid-seventies. The lines dependent upon the muscular energy of the horse had radiated from downtown Oakland to areas generally only three or four miles distant. The electric railway suddenly made accessible

territories six to twelve miles away. An elongated urban community that stretched in two directions, to the north and to the southeast, began to take shape along the level lands bordering on the bay. The hilly barrier on the east, of course, forced this trend of development. Laid down along the historic routes of travel, the electric railway systems invaded the areas previously served only by the less convenient steam railroad and steam dummy. And like the promoters of the earlier horse railways, the promoters of the new electric lines were usually interested in profiting from sales of real estate and were willing to operate their transit lines at a loss, provided sales of land were sufficiently remunerative.

The builders of the Oakland, San Leandro, and Haywards Electric Railway, which was incorporated just ten days after the Oakland and Berkeley Transit Company (later the Oakland Consolidated Street Railway Company) began operations, were heavily involved in real-estate and construction activities in the area through which the line ran. Starting in August, 1892, the road rendered service from the southeast limits of Hayward through San Leandro to East Oakland, and soon afterward effected an entrance into downtown Oakland by acquiring the franchise of the Twenty-third Avenue Electric Railway.

"Most of us have large property interests along the line of our road," A. L. Stone, one of the principal stockholders of the Oakland, San Leandro and Haywards Electric Railway, candidly told an Oakland *Daily Evening Tribune* reporter prior to the opening of the road. "Our original purpose in building the road is to improve our property and give it increased value . . ."[18]

In this respect the road succeeded. Entire farms along the route of the new line were subdivided and sold at large profits. The population of San Leandro increased considerably; but the operation of the road itself was "essentially unprofitable."

Conversion of Horsecar Lines

The Oakland Railroad Company, a Southern Pacific affiliate operating a combination horsecar and steam-dummy service to north Oakland along Telegraph Avenue, met so much competition from the parallel electric lines on Grove Street and Shattuck Avenue that it was forced to convert to the newer and faster form of transit in 1893. It thereupon gave great impetus to the settlement of the northern part of Oakland.

In 1893 the transportation companies hastened to transform the antiquated horsecar lines into electric railways. By the beginning of 1894 the East Bay boasted nearly sixty miles of electric and cable railways. Indeed, during this early phase of electric transit, Oakland and near-by communities had one of the most extensive electric railway systems in the entire United States. But the over-all picture was one of irrationality, waste, and exploitation, as one student of this period has pointed out: "Very considerable physical inconvenience resulted from the fact that on Broadway in Oakland there were at one time six sets of tracks for a short distance. Duplicating power plants were built. Service was rendered on tracks of three different gauges. Equipment and personnel were not adapted to permit interchange of service. The fare structures were such that travel was handicapped by that fact alone. All of these conditions definitely limited the quality of service . . ."[19]

San Francisco was served by a transit network as irrational and planless as the one in Oakland, but it included only one electric railway—the so-called Joost line built in 1891 from Steuart and Market streets through the South-of-Market and Mission districts to the site of present-day Daly City, just beyond the San Mateo County boundary. The metropolis clung to the horsecar and the cable car. Only five traction companies remained independent of a consolidation effected by the Southern Pacific in 1893; yet unification of control brought no major realignments of the old zigzag, corkscrew, and parallel routes that had developed in the course of the years.

Grandiose Scheme

The Southern Pacific firmly monopolized transbay ferry services, which connected in the East Bay with the railroad company's "poky" local steam trains serving Alameda, Oakland, and Berkeley. There were, however, two men in Oakland who planned to challenge this monopoly —and so contribute to further growth of communities on the east side of the bay. For several years the unbridled imaginations of Francis Marion Smith, the borax king, and Frank C. Havens, a promoter and land speculator, had been gestating a grandiose scheme for buying up undeveloped East Bay land, consolidating street railways, and extending new lines into vacant tracts. By establishing fast transbay ferry services to connect with the transit lines and by operating picnic grounds, amusement parks, and hotels at the ends of the transit lines, they hoped to assure heavy patronage. In 1893, Smith carried out part of the scheme by gaining control of four East Bay transit lines. The following year he took a further step toward realizing his dream when he got possession of the California and Nevada Railroad, an old narrow-gauge line that ran from Fortieth and San Pablo streets in Oakland to Orinda by way of Berkeley and the canyon worn through the Berkeley Hills by San Pablo Creek. He an-

Francis Marion Smith, Founder of the Key Route Electric Railway. Photograph courtesy of Oakland Tribune.

nounced plans to lay broad-gauge double tracks on a section of the line between Oakland and Berkeley, to extend a mole two and a half miles into the bay from the foot of Fortieth Street (or Yerba Buena Avenue), and to run fast electric trains from Berkeley to a ferry terminus at the end of the mole. There passengers would transfer to twin-screw, steel boats for an eleven-minute crossing to San Francisco. Although East Bay residents showed great interest in Smith's proposal to reduce the travel time between Berkeley and San Francisco from fifty-five to twenty-six minutes, the total scheme was too ambitious even for a man reputed to be worth $30,000,000, and nine years elapsed before the Southern Pacific found itself in competition with a superior interurban service.

In the meantime, Smith and Havens formed the celebrated Realty Syndicate and launched a grand-scale speculation in transit, real estate, and utilities. Late in 1897 the company assumed full control of the street railways in which Smith earlier had acquired interests. In 1898 the organization acquired four other companies and consolidated all its transit lines under the name Oakland Transit Company, popularly known as the "Syndicate Railways." By the end of that year the system included approximately ninety-eight miles of street railways, many of which penetrated tracts then being subdivided by the two "empire builders." In fact, the aggressive sales campaigns to sell off properties on the higher levels of ground between Mills College and North Berkeley and in other parts of the East Bay fully exploited the novelty and importance of the growing electric-railway system.

All this subdivision activity and railway building was to have significant political consequences later, as an election on June 24, 1897, demonstrated. On that date several areas between Oakland and Berkeley voted to become part of Oakland. The improved transit service between the two cities had been a major factor in influencing the residents of the unincorporated tracts known as Golden Gate, Temescal, Linda Vista, Peralta, and West Piedmont to favor annexation. Oakland by this election expanded from 11.3 square miles to 16.61 square miles and embraced all the territory within which its initial industrial development had taken place. But the city was to grow much larger through annexation of numerous subdivisions that Smith and Havens were marketing.

"Greater Oakland" Movement

Smith and Havens were also active in the "Greater Oakland" movement that paved the way for civic improvements authorized during the next decade. Initiated about 1896 by several industrial, social, and neighborhood-improvement groups, the movement at first focused attention on the need for a large hotel, an intercepting sewer, the opening of streets to the waterfront, and a major park.

Of all these proposed improvements, the park project appears to have received the most serious consideration. Committees of the City Council, the Board of Trade, the Merchants' Exchange, and the real-estate fraternity inspected proposed park sites near Mills College, in Indian Gulch (northeast of Lake Merritt), on the heights above Piedmont, near Mountain View Cemetery, in Dimond Canyon at the head of Fruitvale Avenue, and in the vicinity of Lake Merritt. In addition, the Realty Syndicate

offered to sell land in any of the areas where it owned property. The prices asked for the various tracts ranged from $100,000 for 476 acres above Piedmont to $360,000 for 280 acres in Indian Gulch.

The choice finally fell upon 62 acres in the Adams Tract on the north shore of Lake Merritt, and a bond issue of $290,000 for acquisition and development of the property was submitted to the electorate in October, 1898. As in an election held in 1892, the park bonds failed to receive the necessary two-thirds approval, though a majority of voters favored the proposition. "In a few years this land, which has been rejected both at $500 per acre and $3,870, will be worth not less than $20,000 per acre, and then the voters who killed the proposition . . . will be looked upon as being almost as blind as those who prevented the city acquiring a park in 1868," the Oakland *Enquirer* commented on October 31, 1898. But the newspaper was mistaken when it concluded that the city had probably "lost its last opportunity to create a park on the shores of the lake." A progressive element in Oakland was showing increased determination to convert the shores of the lake into a park, though this element was destined to receive several more setbacks before overcoming the resistance of a backward minority.

Struggle for the Waterfront

Harbor development during this period of civic frustration consisted mainly of dredging by the federal government, in accordance with an improvement plan approved by Congress in the 'seventies. By 1898 the work contemplated under this scheme was practically completed, at a total expenditure of approximately $2,000,000. Oakland had gained more than a deeper channel, however; the dredging operations had given it a new waterfront, as a State Supreme Court decision of 1897 confirmed.

Unwittingly the Oakland Water-front Company, the Southern Pacific subsidiary that monopolized the frontage on the estuary, prepared the way for a legal revelation. In 1893 it brought suit against a private property holder to quiet title to a parcel of waterfront land between Alice and Webster streets. To the company's surprise, the Superior Court held that the original grant of the waterfront to Horace Carpentier in 1852 was void because it was against public policy.

The startling decision encouraged the city of Oakland to go to court in 1895 to quiet title. Again the verdict of the court was the same: the waterfront grant of 1852 was void because it was not in the public interest.

The Southern Pacific of course appealed the ruling. As successor to the Oakland Water-front Company it brought the matter before the State Supreme Court, only to suffer a still greater defeat. Although Chief Justice Beatty shared the view of the lower court that the original grant was utterly void, he pronounced the so-called compromise of 1868 a valid regranting of the waterfront to the Southern Pacific interests in exchange for a few feet of waterfront property at the foot of Franklin Street. But to the consternation of the railroad, the justice declared that it owned land extending only to the low-tide line of 1852— a line that by 1897 was six hundred to a thousand feet inside the new waterfront line created by dumping detritus from the bottom of the estuary into shallow water near the shore.

The decision foreshadowed the eventual materialization of the Port of Oakland, though Oakland for some years took no steps to develop a port. The city received no applications for privileges of building wharves; the citizens were apathetic toward harbor development; and the Southern Pacific, far from regarding the State Supreme Court decision as the final word, was resolved to employ further legal or political maneuvers to retain its privileges.

A Stifling Combination

Oakland's struggle to free itself from the grip of the powerful railroad had a counterpart in the battle of San Francisco to win some measure of economic independence from the hated monopoly. Even before the unemployed queued up in bread lines at the time of the panic of 1893, San Francisco shippers, merchants, and industrialists were complaining loudly that an economic blight had fallen upon the metropolis. The growth of its trade and its general prosperity were being stifled, they charged, by an unholy conspiracy of the Southern Pacific and the Pacific Mail Steamship Company to throttle competition in transportation and to maintain freight rates at a standard of "all the traffic will bear."[20] In their efforts to deal the combination a crippling blow, the commercial groups not only brought about the entrance of the rival Atchison, Topeka and Santa Fe Railway into the Bay Area; they also gave impetus to the development of the new terminal city of Richmond, in Contra Costa County.

"The rates charged by the Pacific Mail and the railroads on tea from Yokohama to Salt Lake City, Denver, and Missouri River points are 2¾ cents a pound, while from Yokohama to the same points via the Northern Pacific or Union Pacific lines of steamers or sailing vessels the rate is only 1⅛ cents a pound," the San Francisco *Daily Morning Call* pointed out in 1892 in one of a series of articles later reissued under the title "Fettered Commerce." "San Francisco merchants are actually importing tea for customers in Salt Lake City through Portland instead of through their own port."[21]

The newspaper also disclosed that "the rate on (Brazilian) coffee from New York to San Francisco is $1.35 a hundred pounds, while a rate of $1.30 a hundred pounds is charged to the San Francisco shipper of Guatemalan coffee, even though he desires to ship his coffee for no greater distance than that from San Francisco to Denver."[22]

To prevent steamship competition with their transcontinental lines, the Southern Pacific, Central Pacific, and other railroads had paid the Pacific Mail subsidies amounting to $14,550,000 in fourteen years, the *Call* declared, yet the Southern Pacific and Central Pacific were themselves recipients of government subsidies. A bitter cartoon in the newspaper depicted Uncle Sam bestowing a money bag marked "Government Subsidy" upon Collis P. Huntington and remarking, "I give you this money, Collis, to encourage you in extending our trade and advancing the interests of all the people." Huntington's reply is, "Thank you, Uncle, I will do the best I can— (aside) for myself."[23]

Most galling of all were the freight rates charged by the railroads on the movement of goods between San Francisco and San Joaquin Valley points. Rates for some commodities shipped from the port to Bakersfield were actually greater than those charged for goods transported from Liverpool to San Francisco via New Orleans.

San Francisco's indignation against the monopolists expressed itself in the formation of a Traffic Association having as its chief objective the construction of an independent railroad from San Francisco to Bakersfield. First broached in 1891, the project was not seriously recommended to the public until the summer of 1893. Because of the depression in that year, the raising of funds proved impracticable. In 1894, however, the scheme was revived, and the proposed road was named the San Francisco, Stockton, and San Joaquin Railroad. Again the Traffic Association encountered difficulty in inducing San Franciscans to buy shares of the $6,000,000 capital stock.

Birth of a Railroad

In January, 1895, the project suddenly gathered new impetus. Claus Spreckels, the sugar king, subscribed $50,000 at a meeting on January 22 at which speakers vied with one another in denouncing the Southern Pacific. The next day, Spreckels increased his subscription to $500,000. Two of his sons, John D. and Adolph Spreckels, each subscribed $100,000. Almost all the big names in San Francisco quickly responded to the campaign for funds. Nor was the metropolis alone in extending financial aid to the project. Oakland interests contributed $187,350; Stockton put up $125,000 in cash and gave land; and the people of San Jose, which was not even on the route of the proposed railroad, subscribed $65,000. By February 20, $2,248,000 had been raised. Five days later the new line was incorporated as the San Francisco and San Joaquin Valley Railway, popularly known as the Valley Road.

At the state capital friendly legislators introduced a bill to permit the new railroad to lease state property in San Francisco for a terminal. While the measure was running the gantlet of Southern Pacific opposition, the directors of the Valley Road selected a site at China Basin on the San Francisco waterfront and entered into negotiations with the State Board of Harbor Commissioners, pending authorization of a lease by the legislature. On March 26, 1895, the governor signed the bill granting the lease.

In the following month the directors of the new railroad company approved a plan that placed the road in the hands of a trust. According to the document creating the trust, the trustees agreed that the railroad should "not be leased to, nor consolidated with any company which may own, control, manage or operate any of the roads now existing in the San Joaquin Valley";[24] but nothing in the document prohibited the trustees from turning over the independent line to a major railroad not then existing in the valley, namely, the Santa Fe, which was eager to extend its tracks from southern California to the Bay Area. If the trustees had, indeed, secretly agreed to sell out to the Santa Fe when the new road was completed, they kept their intentions to themselves as they proceeded with construction of the line.

The survey for the road began at Stockton on April 18, 1895, and was completed by July 22. The rails reached Merced on Thanksgiving Day of that year but were not completed to Fresno until October 5, 1896. A regular freight and passenger service was then inaugurated between Fresno and San Francisco, with boats making the connection between San Francisco and Stockton. Two years later, Bakersfield became the southern terminus.

Vision of a City

In the meantime, Claus Spreckels and other directors concerned themselves with the problem of bringing the tracks into the Bay Area. Their first plan of routing the rails into Oakland through the Fruitvale hills was abandoned when Augustin S. Macdonald, a real-estate promoter with a vivid imagination, convinced them that Point Richmond, once a part of the vast Rancho San Pablo, was the logical place for a railroad terminal in the East Bay.

Macdonald is credited with being the "discoverer" of Richmond. In his own words, this is what happened when he drove out from Oakland one November morning in 1895 to hunt ducks in the marshes of San Pablo Creek:

"It was a perfectly beautiful morning, sun shining brightly and not a breath of wind, consequently no ducks flying, and after sitting five hours without a chance shot I concluded to quit, walk over the Potrero hill and explore the bay shore. On reaching the summit of the hills a magnificent view greeted my eyes. Mt. Tamalpais looming up at the right, Berkeley to the left and seemingly just across the way San Francisco, without a sign of life to disturb the quiet and peaceful scene. I wondered why such a delightful spot had been neglected, for either pleasure or profit, as not only its beauty, but its commercial possibilities appealed to me at once and I determined to investigate.

"The government map and surveys showed a depth of 65 feet of water, the only point on the east side of the bay shore where land and navigable deep water met. . . ."[25]

". . . I learned a saving of 12 miles could be made by the Southern Pacific company freight ferry from Pt. Richmond, direct to San Francisco. I presented these facts to C. P. Huntington, who thought favorably of the idea and prepared to look over the proposition, but he had . . . to hurriedly leave overnight.

"Not discouraged, however, as soon as the Santa Fe Railway company announced its intention of reaching San Francisco, I submitted my plans to that company. To avoid attracting attention Chief Engineer Storey, the head officials, and I went out on separate routes and carefully examined the waterfront, with the result that it was considered the most feasible, economical and practical site on the bay as a terminal and was adopted. . . .

"As soon as this question was definitely settled I knew that a great city must grow up there and the next thing was to find a proper location. The Potrero was rough and hilly while the immediate land adjacent was low, flat and swampy. Considering the situation, the choice tract was some 500 level acres belonging to Geo. H. Barrett, a pioneer settler.

"This we purchased and named the City of Richmond. The country was uninviting enough at the time, the lone habitation being the Barrett homestead which stood on Tenth Street just north of Macdonald Avenue. . . ."[26]

Actually, the officials whom Macdonald took to see Point Richmond represented the Valley Road, not the Santa Fe, and it was Robert W. Watt, vice-president of the Valley Road, who handed John Nicholl, an owner of property at the Point, a check for $80,000 on February 26, 1897, in payment for 57 acres of high land and some 100 acres of tideland. Claus Spreckels, like stockholders in many earlier railroad ventures in the San Francisco Bay Area, invested money in 250 acres near by, hoping that the rails would contribute to development of a town.

First Sale of Lots in the New City of Richmond, 1902. Photograph courtesy of Richmond Public Library.

Founding of Richmond

Not until 1899 did Macdonald carry out his own scheme for a town of Richmond. By that time negotiations between the financially pressed trustees of the Valley Road and the Santa Fe were under way, and two Santa Fe officials were among the quartet of capitalists who provided the funds with which the Oakland promoter purchased Barrett's 500-acre hay ranch.

Macdonald filed his "Map of the Town of Point Richmond" at the County Recorder's office in Martinez on June 3, 1899. The plat showed a prosaic arrangement of rectangular blocks, divided into five thousand business and residential lots. Boundaries of the tract were Barrett Avenue on the north, Twenty-third Street on the east, Ohio Street on the south, and Garrard Boulevard on the west.

The rails from Stockton did not enter Richmond until almost a year later, because the last section of the road, through northern Contra Costa County, presented difficult engineering problems. Chief Engineer W. B. Storey, who was later president of the Santa Fe, constructed ten

miles of earth fill across the tule lands in the northeastern part of the county and built five tunnels through the hills, including one 5,595 feet in length through Franklin Ridge and another just under a thousand feet through the Potrero hills to Ferry Point. Excavations for this last tunnel formed a level area of about three acres at the base of the promontory. From this spot a wharf extended 800 feet into the bay, to a point at which the water was twenty-four feet deep at low tide.

Having secured what amounted to half ownership in the Southern Pacific line between Bakersfield and Mojave, in Kern County, the Santa Fe brought its first through train from Chicago into Ferry Point on July 3, 1900. From there the passengers proceeded to San Francisco on a rebuilt ferryboat called the *Ocean Wave*. The long struggle of the transcontinental line for an outlet to San Francisco Bay was over. The merchants and shippers of San Francisco and the farmers of the San Joaquin Valley had succeeded in their effort to create competition for the Southern Pacific, though there were those who declared that not much had been achieved by transferring an independent line to another big railroad system.

Bay Counties Power Company Crossing of Carquinez Strait, 1901. The single span of the cables was 4,427 ft., with a clearance of 206 ft. above high water to allow for the passage of tall-sparred sailing ships. Photograph courtesy of Pacific Gas and Electric Company.

Horn of Plenty

The Valley railroad project emphasized the increasing interdependence of the regional community developing around the shores of San Francisco Bay and the great valley east of the Coast Range. As the twentieth century began to unfold, the vast interior of the state became the Bay Area's cornucopia, pouring forth oil to supply its refineries and surface its roads, hydroelectric power to light its homes and run the machinery in its factories, and canned and dried fruit for exportation in the vessels that docked at its ports.

In the very first year of the new century, Eugene de Sabla, Jr., and John Martin completed a high-voltage transmission line from the South Yuba River to Oakland, by way of Carquinez Strait. In thus bringing hydroelectric energy to the East Bay from a source 142 miles away, the two partners defeated the hopes of André Poniatowski, a Polish prince and brother-in-law of the San Francisco banker W. H. Crocker, of being the first to deliver power from the Sierra to the Bay Area. Poniatowski encountered

one obstacle after another in building a powerhouse on the Mokelumne River, northeast of Stockton, and was unable to complete a transmission line to San Francisco until 1902. His line, forty miles longer than that of his rivals, entered the Bay Area by way of southern Alameda County and Santa Clara County and served San Jose as well as San Francisco.

Though industry was somewhat slow in making use of hydroelectric power, the Bay Area at last had a readily available form of energy to compensate for its lack of coal resources. As the power field expanded, more and more factories installed machinery operated by electricity.

Farmers in the Santa Clara Valley hailed as a great boon the arrival of hydroelectric power for the operation of irrigation pumps, not foreseeing the effect of uncontrolled pumping on the underground water supply. And before long the artesian wells that had once been a common sight in the area began to disappear. In time the sons of those who had rejoiced at the sight of linesmen stringing wires through the orchard country were to inherit such problems as the depletion of ground water and the settling and flooding of land.

No less important to manufacturing establishments than the "white energy" that flowed through the long transmission lines from the canyons and gorges of the Sierra was the "black gold" that became available in large quantities in the oil fields of Kern County. After western railroads had begun to use crude petroleum in their locomotives as a substitute for soft coal, manufacturers recognized it as a new industrial fuel. Together with hydroelectric energy, it helped to free western industry from dependence on expensive imports of coal and served as the basis for the development of a broader economy in the Bay Area and California.

The state's increasing production of petroleum was of particular significance because it coincided with the advent of the automobile. Oakland residents saw their first "gasoline carriage" in 1897; and people in other Bay Area cities gawked at the new marvel at about the same time. In the edition of the San Francisco *Examiner* heralding the birth of the twentieth century a feature writer named Edward Murphy categorically predicted that the automobile would "disfranchise" the horse and completely invade "all our big cities within a very short time."[27] The construction by the Standard Oil Company of a 283-mile pipe line from oil fields in the Bakersfield Area to its new refinery at Richmond was therefore of major importance. Large quantities of the kind of liquid fuel required by the increasing number of "horseless carriages" were now assured. The Richmond refinery had the distinction of being the second largest in the world when the $13,000,000 pipe line from the southern end of the San Joaquin Valley was completed, early in 1903.

Regional Transportation

The new self-propelled vehicle created a demand for roads that were free from dust in summer and mud in winter. Crude petroleum sprinkled with sand or gravel provided the answer to the problem of devising a relatively smooth, "permanent" surface. Road oiling in the Bay Area began in 1901, when Contra Costa, Napa, and Solano counties, following the example set by Los Angeles County three years earlier, each oiled a few miles of roads. The following year Alameda and Santa Clara counties began oiling roads; and in 1903, Marin, San Mateo, and Sonoma counties made their first experiments with the new surfacing. By the time the State Department of Highways published a bulletin on oiled roads, in 1904, there were more than 470 miles of oiled roads in the Bay Area.

Ironically, the oiled road and the automobile would someday cause the downfall of the interurban electric railway, which at this time was the chief agent of population dispersal in the Bay Area. So many intercity railways were projected or built in the opening years of the twentieth century that the period might well be called the electric railway age, just as the 'sixties and 'seventies of the nineteenth century have been designated the railroad age. But the railroad was to last for many years; the electric railways were doomed almost from the start.

In Marin County the old North Pacific Coast Railroad voluntarily wound up its business in 1901 and reorganized as the North Shore Railroad. The new company laid standard-gauge track from Sausalito to Mill Valley and San Rafael during the winter of 1901–1902 and electrified the lines to these points, in order to provide better commuter service. Steam trains continued to operate on narrow-gauge tracks in other divisions of the system.

About the same time that the Marin County commuter lines were being converted from steam to electricity, Francis M. Smith, the Oakland traction magnate, conceived the idea of building an electric railway from Oakland to San Jose by way of Hayward, with branches to

The Richmond Refinery of the Standard Oil Company, 1902. Photograph courtesy of the Standard Oil Company of California.

The Richmond Refinery of the Standard Oil Company, 1958. Photograph courtesy of the Standard Oil Company of California.

Santa Clara, Saratoga, and Los Gatos. In furtherance of this scheme, his Oakland Transit Company early in 1902 absorbed the Oakland, San Leandro and Haywards Electric Railway, which was the one remaining independent transit company in the East Bay. But Smith found that before he could finance construction of tracks from Hayward to the Santa Clara Valley, he would have to develop a profitable network in the urban areas already heavily populated. He therefore concentrated his efforts on his

earlier plans to link Berkeley, Piedmont, and various districts of Oakland with San Francisco by rapid electric transit and fast ferry service.

On October 26, 1903, Smith opened the Berkeley line, which was an immediate success because his Key Route trains and ferries transported passengers from the university community to San Francisco in only thirty-six minutes, compared with fifty-eight minutes on commuter steam trains and ferries of the Southern Pacific. This gratifying popular venture was followed by unification and improvement of the Oakland electric railway system, construction of the Piedmont line, and plans for a line to Twenty-second and Broadway in Oakland—a program so ambitious that it exhausted Smith's credit for long-term borrowing long before he could carry out his projected line to San Jose.

Valley Network

Meanwhile, down in the Santa Clara Valley two San Jose men, J. W. Rea and F. S. Granger, preëmpted some of the electric-railway empire that Smith dreamed of. After some difficulties with financing, they succeeded in constructing an interurban line from San Jose to Los Gatos via Saratoga, with a branch to the popular Congress Springs resort. Opened in March, 1904, the railway was successful enough to encourage Rea and Granger to begin building a much shorter line from San Jose to Los Gatos via Campbell. But the threat of other companies to invade the Santa Clara Valley caused the St. Louis banking firm that was financing the two local operators to sell its control to the Southern Pacific. That company, after fighting

other interests, eventually developed an interurban railway network of sixty-eight miles in the Santa Clara Valley.

One of the objectives of the Southern Pacific appeared to be to block the southward extension of the old Joost line, San Francisco's first electric railway. Extended to San Mateo in January, 1903, this line was thought by many Peninsula and Santa Clara County residents to be the first link in an interurban rapid transit system that would run from San Francisco to San Jose. The future of the line depended not upon decisions made in the Bay Area, however, but upon the policies of the New York banking house of Brown Brothers, which in 1902 had purchased the entire capital stock of the Market Street Railway from Southern Pacific interests and had combined the Sutter Street road and the San Mateo line with the Market Street properties to form the United Railroads Company, later a potential rival of the Southern Pacific in the interurban field. Had the San Mateo line proved as effective as Smith's Key Route lines in the East Bay in stimulating suburban development, the New York investors might have considered building it farther down the Peninsula, but in this respect it was a disappointment.

The Key Route Mole, 1903. The mole extended from the foot of Fortieth Street in Oakland to a pier and ferry slip not far from Yerba Buena Island. The Oakland Army Base now occupies the tideland area to the left of the mole. Photograph courtesy of the Port of Oakland.

No electric railway line was ever to close the gap between San Mateo and Palo Alto, the northern point in the Santa Clara County electric-railway system of the Southern Pacific, just as no line was ever to join San Jose and Hayward on the eastern side of the bay.

Bit by bit an area-wide electric-railway network appeared, nevertheless, to be taking shape in the early years of this century; and barring various quirks of fate, such a network might have materialized. A northern segment of the potential system was the Petaluma and Santa Rosa Railway, which in 1904 inaugurated service on a line running from its own wharf on Petaluma Creek at Petaluma to the county seat and thence to Sebastopol, with branches to Forestville and Two Rock. Success of this line was to inspire a similar venture in the Napa Valley, which by 1911 was to see an electric railway extending from Vallejo to Calistoga by way of Napa and Saint Helena.

Smith and many other electric-railway men of the period had begun to think of the entire area round San Francisco Bay as a territory that could be linked together by fast transportation. They more than vaguely foresaw the possibility of a metropolitan region with many interdependent communities. The East Bay, rapidly developing as a group of interrelated cities served by an expanding electric-railway system, exemplified the kind of urban growth that could be expected in other parts of the Bay Area if time and distance were conquered by fast, convenient transit. Only to a degree, however, was transit to be an integrating influence in the development of the Bay Area. And not just by steady accretion of population along the transit lines were the smaller cities and outlying areas to grow in the years immediately ahead, but by sudden, forced absorption of thousands of families sent fleeing from a stricken metropolis. As the year 1904 began, the dominant city that was to contribute uniquely to the emergence of a recognizable metropolitan regional community could not have been more unaware of the tragic manner in which it was to nurture the growth of its satellites.

CHAPTER SIX

The Burnham Plan for San Francisco

San Francisco was enjoying one of the greatest booms in its history. Not since the bonanza days of the 'seventies had residents of the city seen so many new office buildings, hotels, stores, and palatial residences under construction. Real-estate men, particularly, were inclined to believe that the goddess of prosperity had decided to settle permanently in the metropolis by the Golden Gate. Wherever they looked they beheld evidence of her beneficence. Atop Nob Hill the massive Fairmont Hotel was taking shape. On the west side of Union Square the St. Francis Hotel was nearing completion. Word spread through the city that these hotels would rival the finest in New York, London, and Paris. At the corner of Market and Powell streets workmen were busy on the Flood Building, an office building containing six hundred rooms. Those in the know said that it would establish a new standard of elegance in business structures. Just west of the business district, between Mason and Leavenworth streets, rose dozens of newly completed apartment houses. Others were still under construction. South of Market Street still more apartment houses were being built. So rapid was the increase in population that every structure was filled as soon as it was completed, or even before workmen had finished painting the walls and installing fixtures.

Some real-estate men estimated that the population of the city must be at least four hundred and fifty thousand, although more conservative residents doubted this. Certainly there was an influx from all directions. Ships tying up at the piers along the waterfront brought foreigners by the thousands—Japanese, Italians, Portuguese, Austrians, Greeks, and Russians. From Canada, the Middle West, and from such eastern states as New York and Pennsylvania a Pullman and chair-car invasion was under way, stimulated by the railroads, the California Promotion Committee, and the California Fruit Growers Association. Overland trains also transported large groups of foreigners who had lived for a time in eastern cities or had proceeded immediately to California after landing in New York, Boston, or Baltimore.

A Bright Future

After the low level of economic activities during the 'nineties, the upswing in business was wonderfully stimulating. Building contracts were averaging about $15,000,000 a year, whereas they had totaled only $6,167,000 in 1901. Real-estate sales in both 1902 and 1903 had aggregated more than $47,000,000, compared with $18,500,000 in 1900. By every other index of economic conditions—bank clearings, exports, retail sales—San Francisco was enjoying flush times.

As far into the future as anyone could see, the prospects of the metropolis were excellent. Businessmen spoke of "the certainty of war between Russia and Japan" and predicted that San Francisco would profit by furnishing supplies to both belligerents, although they hastened to add that they did not wish ill to anyone. The entire Orient was awakening: not only was the island empire of Japan seeking new commercial ties; China, with its four hundred

Market Street below Montgomery Street, San Francisco, 1905. Photograph courtesy of Bancroft Library, University of California.

million inhabitants, was also stirring restlessly. Alert exporters could sense a groping of hands across the sea toward the good things that America produced.

In the Western Hemisphere the development on which all eyes were focused was the projected Panama Canal. Although the United States had not yet ratified a treaty with the new Republic of Panama, a United States commission was preparing to begin construction of the "big ditch." Reuben Brooks Hale, a leading San Francisco merchant, was so sure that the canal would be built that he wrote a letter to the directors of the Merchants' Association on January 12, 1904, proposing that the metropolis hold a world's exposition in 1915 to celebrate completion of the gigantic enterprise.[1] San Franciscans fully expected that their city, the major port on the Pacific Coast, would be the chief western beneficiary of the new waterway through the Isthmus of Panama. They smiled when they thought of the attempts of a potential rival, Los Angeles, to create a harbor in the mud flats of Wilmington and San Pedro. The Panama Canal could never mean to that aggressive and noisy community what it would mean to San Francisco, the possessor of a superb natural harbor.

Appeal to the Public-spirited

Allan Pollock, manager of the St. Francis Hotel, was not among those who scoffed at Los Angeles. Many of his fellow citizens, in their smugness, might consider San Francisco unusually prosperous and progressive; but he had seen with his own eyes the constructive things that Los Angeles was doing, and he felt that his townsmen deserved a jolt. "San Francisco has been asleep, while southern California, which offers nothing like the inducements we have within our grasp to lay before visitors, has taken possession of the tourists and the wealthy people from the East who come to California looking for homes," he declared in a newspaper interview. The Bay Area metropolis needed to realize that it had "little really attractive" to offer either tourists or its own residents—no art gallery or museum worthy of the name, no civic auditorium for conventions, no tree-lined boulevards.

Golden Gate Park, the ocean beach, the new hotels, the exhilarating climate, the hospitality of the people—these were merely foundations to build upon. The greater part of the city was ugly, the product of a "bare commercialism" that persisted in erecting wooden buildings "hideous in design and flimsy in finish—architectural shams of lumber and paint." As if he sensed impending tragedy, Pollock asserted that "such disgraceful kind of construction should be discouraged; this can perhaps best be done by extending the 'fire limits' over the entire municipality, and thus prevent the possibility of a general and widespread conflagration." The hotel manager called upon the public-spirited men of San Francisco to organize a committee to work for the welfare of the city, to render the community "beautiful and enticing as a place for tourists and for residence," and "to make San Francisco to Americans what Paris is to Europeans—the great city of pleasure!"[2]

O'Farrell Street, San Francisco, 1905. The tall building at the end of the street is the Call Building. Photograph courtesy of Bancroft Library.

A plea so fervently expressed necessarily aroused instant response. Dissatisfaction with conditions in San Francisco was more widespread than the California Promotion Committee, for instance, would have admitted. The San Francisco *Bulletin* pointed out that "since the Grand Opera House [at Fourth and Mission Streets] was built long ago and the antiquated Mechanics' Pavilion was erected by the Mechanics' Institute, practically nothing has been accomplished on a befitting scale in adding to the attractions of the city." Numerous prominent men joined with Pollock and the *Bulletin* in advocating the construction of a public auditorium and a new opera house. Newton J. Tharp, an architect, proposed lining Van Ness Avenue and other major thoroughfares with trees and incorporating them all into the park system. Andrea Sbarboro, president of the Italian-American Bank, suggested building a great boulevard around the waterfront from the bay to the ocean beach. E. A. Brugiere, identified by the newspapers as a "capitalist," hoped for "a school that shall be to music what our universities— Stanford and California—are to literature and science." Police Commissioner J. R. Howell listed the Golden Gate Park Panhandle extension among public improvements that he wished to see undertaken. M. L. Gerstle and several others who deplored the "jagged, homely street lines that exist throughout the city, even in the most desirable residence districts," urged municipal regulation to preserve uniform street lines and prevent buildings from occupying three or four feet of the public walks. Many citizens called for the elimination of overhead telephone, power, and light wires, the improvement of the streets— "the streets are disgraceful and could not be much worse" —and the establishment of proper grades for sidewalks. Going along lower Market Street, said Julian Sonntag, a real-estate agent, was like walking up hill and down dale. The sidewalks in many places were four feet above the street, in others half a foot below the curb.[3]

Phelan's Proposal for a City Plan

James Duval Phelan, the former mayor, whom *The Wasp* later described as a "clever lawyer and business man, bon vivant, liberal patron of the arts and cultured gentleman,"[4] took a much broader view of the city's needs. First in a general plan of improvement should be the project to secure an abundant supply of water from the Sierra, so that population growth would not be hindered. "Then the city, next in order and before it is too late, should have a plan prepared by a competent person or commission, as has been done recently for the city of Washington, D.C., and for Cleveland, Ohio. This plan would show what old streets should be widened or new

James Duval Phelan. Phelan was president of the Association for the Improvement and Adornment of San Francisco, 1904– 1909. Photograph courtesy of the late Noel Sullivan.

ones made; where public buildings should be located; where new roads should be laid out, as along the bay shore to the Cliff House, and as to the extension of the panhandle of Golden Gate Park, and once having a plan, we can build with confidence."[5]

In Phelan's opinion, San Francisco was at the turning point of its growth. Either it would be a great and beautiful city, where men and women of taste would desire to live, or a great and ugly and forbidding city, which people would shun. The time had come "to take occasion by the hand to lead the city in the right direction, or to suffer the city to wander aimlessly to an uncertain end."[6]

On January 12, 1904, Phelan and two of his friends, J. W. Byrne, president of the Pacific Union Club, and Willis Davis, president of the San Francisco Art Association, issued an invitation to selected leaders "to meet a committee of about twenty gentlemen" on January 15 at the Merchants' Exchange. "The object of the meeting is to formally discuss a plan for the improvement of San Francisco," the invitation stated. "The plan contemplates making San Francisco a more desirable city in which to live."[7]

The San Francisco *Bulletin* anticipated great results. "Hopes are high," it commented. "The committee seems to mean business, and men who mean business can do wonders in a short while. These men are accustomed to producing results. They have what is called executive ability; that is, the faculty of doing things while others are talking about doing them. It is time for every public-spirited citizen to come forward."[8]

When the *Bulletin* referred to undesignated "others" who merely talked, it meant the current occupant of the mayor's chair, Eugene E. Schmitz, who had been elected Phelan's successor in November, 1901, in the aftermath of the bitter strike of the waterfront unions against the Employers' Association. In that strike Phelan had incurred the enmity of the unions by using police to suppress picket-line violence. His replacement by Schmitz, the candidate of the Union Labor party, left the economically powerful and socially prominent group of which he was a member with almost no influence in city government, yet such was the faith of the group members in their ability to "get things done" that they rose enthusiastically to the challenge of a new civic cause. The Schmitz administration, they reassured one another, could not last long. Its corruption was becoming more apparent every day. A vigorous political campaign at the next election would sweep it from office and restore control to those who had vision and a desire to make San Francisco one of the great cities of America.

An Association to Promote a Plan

At the meeting on January 15 the group formed the Association for the Improvement and Adornment of San Francisco and unanimously elected Phelan its president. Numerous improvements already mentioned in the newspapers were discussed, including a road along the bay shore and also boulevard approaches to Golden Gate Park. Among the new proposals advanced were the extension of Market Street to the ocean and the building of a great outdoor amphitheater. Phelan, however, was convinced that all these separate proposals should be integrated into a single over-all program of development; he had already sounded out the famous Chicago architect Daniel Hudson Burnham concerning his willingness to prepare for San Francisco the kind of plan that he, Frederick Law

Olmsted, and Charles McKim had prepared for Washington, D.C., in 1901. Phelan indicated that Burnham would probably be willing to contribute his services to the association provided the members paid the expenses of assistants and draftsmen.

The first order of business, then, was a program of procedure. To formulate one, Phelan appointed an executive committee composed of W. G. Irwin, Allan Pollock, Herbert E. Law, William Greer Harrison, and a young man named F. W. Dohrmann, who twenty years later was to head the first metropolitan regional planning organization in the San Francisco Bay Area.

The committee decided at the outset that the membership of the association should be broadened to include every citizen who was genuinely interested in improving the city. It drew up an appeal for membership, stating the general and the specific objectives of the organization:

"The main objects of the Association are to promote in every practical way the beautifying of the streets, public buildings, parks, squares, and places of San Francisco; to bring to the attention of the officials and people of the city the best methods for instituting artistic municipal betterments; to stimulate the sentiment of civic pride in the improvement and care of private property; to suggest quasi-public enterprises and, in short, to make San Francisco a more agreeable city in which to live."[9]

A Formal Invitation

By April the Association for the Improvement and Adornment of San Francisco was ready to issue a formal invitation to Burnham to draft a plan for the city. The architect arrived from Chicago and was feted at a dinner in his honor at the St. Francis Hotel on May 4. He spoke eloquently about "the possibilities of enhancing the beauty of the city,"[10] inspiring in his hearers the same kind of excitement that he had aroused among the architects, landscape architects, painters, and sculptors who worked with him when he was chief of construction for the World's Columbian Exposition in Chicago in 1893. At the conclusion of his speech the board of directors of the association adopted a resolution inviting him to prepare a plan.

Two nights later the association held a conference at the Palace Hotel at which more than two hundred representatives of civic groups presented their ideas concerning the general improvement of the city. With great tact the architect spoke as one only slightly familiar with San Francisco, although in the preceding ten years he had made many trips to the city and had designed buildings for clients there.

"Whatever may be my ideas," he said, "I can accomplish little or nothing without the cooperation of the people of San Francisco. I have come here an outsider, and am not in touch with the conditions that exist here. It would require years, perhaps, for me alone to become well enough acquainted with the city to enable me to draft a great general scheme of improvement and adornment that would be a credit to San Francisco if carried into execution. I must have your help. I must be aided by the ideas of the people who have been here for years and who have given this subject their most careful thought and consideration. You know the needs and the possibilities of San Francisco. You must give me your sympathy, for only with it and your appreciation can the highest conception be attained. If San Francisco is to be made more beautiful in the near future, the work to be accomplished must originate from the people of the city. Your suggestions must start the general scheme in operation and must furnish the basis on which I must work."[11]

Probably there has never been a better statement of the importance and the necessity of citizen participation in city planning. Nor have many comprehensive, long-range plans been prepared with a greater fund of citizens' proposals than was available for the Burnham Plan. Spokesmen for the Outdoor Art League, the California Club, the Merchants' Association, numerous neighborhood improvement clubs, the Market Street Club, and other organizations and the magazines *Out West* and *California Municipalities* offered suggestions to Burnham. Most of the projects described had already been proposed by the members of the Association for the Improvement and Adornment of San Francisco, but nothing was lost by their being advocated by others throughout the city.

Not until September 22, 1904, was Burnham able to return to San Francisco to begin work on the plan. In the meantime, President Theodore Roosevelt's Secretary of War, William Howard Taft, had engaged him to prepare plans for Manila and for Baguio, the summer capital of the Philippines. Burnham's schedule included a stay in San Francisco to initiate work on the plan for the association headed by Phelan, then a trip to the Philippines, then further work on the plan for San Francisco upon his return.

Accompanying the architect was his talented young associate Edward H. Bennett, who was to do most of the actual work on the plan for San Francisco. Bennett was, in the words of Burnham, "a poet with his feet on the earth." Burnham, then fifty-seven and independently wealthy, resembled "a railway locomotive under full steam, holding the right of way,"[12] according to one of his contemporaries.

Awaiting the pair and their assistants was a studio

Daniel Hudson Burnham. *Photograph courtesy of the Art Institute of Chicago.*

bungalow that the association had built, at Burnham's request, on a spur of Twin Peaks, overlooking the entire city, more than one-third of which was then undeveloped. Burnham, the man of broad concepts, always sought some physical eminence from which to view the cities for which he made plans. While working on the plan for the national capital, he had studied the city from the heights of Arlington. Later, when he was preparing a plan for his own city, Chicago, he took up quarters on the top floor of the Railway Exchange. The "shanty" on Twin Peaks, as he designated the bungalow designed by the San Francisco architect Willis Polk, afforded him just the kind of aerie he required while formulating a plan that would be geographically comprehensive, embracing the total area of the City and County of San Francisco.

A Fifty-Year Plan

The Burnham Plan for San Francisco, presented to the board of supervisors on the afternoon of September 27, 1905, was nothing if not grand in conception; but Burnham had no intention that it should frighten citizens and officials by the scope of its proposals. As if anticipating the criticism of those to whom any comprehensive plan is unrealistic, he wrote in the report explaining the plan:

"A scheme of parks, streets and public grounds for a city, in order to be at once comprehensive and practical, should take into account the public purse of today and embrace those things that can be immediately carried into effect, but should in no wise limit itself to these. It should be designed not only for the present, but for all time to come.

"While prudence holds up a warning finger, we must not forget what San Francisco has become in fifty years and what it is still further destined to become. Population and wealth are rapidly increasing, culture is advancing. The city looks toward a sure future wherein it will possess in inhabitants and money many times what it has now. It follows that we must not found the scheme on what the city is, so much as on what it is to be. We must remember that a meager plan will fall short of perfect achievement, while a great one will yield large results, even if it is never fully realized.

"Our purpose, therefore, must be to stop at no line within the limits of practicability. Our scope must embrace the possibilities of development of the next fifty years."[13]

In his view of San Francisco as a young and still-expanding city, in his faith in its potentialities, and in his determination to visualize it as it could be, Burnham was as "modern" as any city planner alive today. One may question his belief that any community could be designed "for all time to come" or even for "the next fifty years," but one cannot disparage the wisdom of attempting to "embrace the possibilities of development." Moreover, since he was aware that many of the proposals embodied in the plan could only be carried out far in the future, if carried out at all, he was careful to point out that the plan was "general" in nature and that "it is not the province of a report of this kind to indicate the exact details very closely."[14] He recognized, therefore, the necessity for some flexibility in the use of the plan, even though he thought of the over-all scheme as having validity "for all time to come."

The Circulation System

No irresponsible dreamer, Burnham set himself the task of making a plan "which shall interfere as little as possible with the rectangular street system of the city."[15] This street system most San Franciscans frankly conceded to be irrational and wholly unsuited to the hilly terrain. But since large-scale alteration of the street pattern appeared to be out of the question, the Chicago architect and his assistants accepted it as a necessary limitation upon their endeavors and contented themselves with planning a system of thoroughfares intended to obviate the major difficulties of circulation within the metropolis. Present-day city planners have taken much the same attitude, although

Bird's-Eye Perspective of the Burnham Plan for San Francisco, 1905

the solutions they have proposed have of course differed greatly from those suggested by Burnham at a time when automobiles were few and the bay bridges were no more than figments of the imaginations of writers in the Sunday supplements.

In principle, at least, Burnham was close to present-day planners in his approach to the design of a circulation system for San Francisco. He recognized that the most efficient pattern of arteries for an urban area is a system resembling a spider web—a series of concentric rings intersected by diagonals radiating from a small central loop or "perimeter of distribution," as in Paris, Berlin, Vienna, Moscow, and London. Such a system permits rapid and easy movement throughout a city and its environs and is regarded by most contemporary city planners as the ideal.

Adaptation of this system to San Francisco obviously required modifications, because the city is surrounded on three sides by water and its topography is highly irregular.

Burnham saw that a small inner circuit or perimeter of distribution could be established at or near the geographical center and that radials could extend from this in all directions, like spokes of a wheel, to an outer or peripheral boulevard traversing, as far as possible, the waterfront. But intermediary circuit boulevards, if carried in a concentric form, would be impracticable because of the numerous hills. He proposed, however, to create an irregular inner chain more or less concentric to the inner circuit.

Civic Center in the Inner Circuit

In his plan this inner circuit enveloped a core area of civic structures—administrative, educational, and cultural —and commercial amusement places and shops of the finer order. The focal point was the intersection of Market Street and Van Ness Avenue, approximately the geographical center of San Francisco in 1905, for the city proper at that time was hemmed in by hills on the west

Plan for a Civic Center in San Francisco, 1899

Burnham's Plan for a Civic Center, Looking from the South Side of Market Street

and south. At this spot Burnham proposed to create a great semicircular *place*, with nine arteries converging upon it from all directions. An extension of the Park Panhandle, for instance, would be carried through the *place* in a direct line to the docks of the Pacific Mail Steamship Company, on the Outer Boulevard near Second and Berry streets, and an extension of Van Ness Avenue would be projected to the south. Eleventh Street would be carried across the *place* toward the northwest. This central open space might be the logical point at which to group major public buildings; but Burnham concluded that the time would come when the civic structures of San Francisco would be too numerous to arrange around this one *place*.

"The Civic Center will, therefore, develop around the center in the form of a number of sub-centers having for location the intersection of the radial arteries with the perimeter of distribution," he explained in his report. "At each of these intersections there should be a public *place*."[16]

The subcenters shown on his plan are the old City Hall, at Larkin and McAllister streets, a union railway station near Eleventh and Bryant streets, and an opera house near Fulton and Gough streets. On the radial arteries within the inner circuit Burnham envisaged schools, museums, academies, theaters, and luxury shops.

These central features of the plan would now be of little more than antiquarian interest had not Burnham's selection of the general area of Market Street and Van Ness Avenue as the location for a civic center tended to fix that area in the public mind as the proper place at which to create one. In the years following the great earthquake and fire of 1906, San Franciscans therefore were willing to accept his recommendation that the principal administrative and cultural structures of the city be grouped in this general vicinity, although the area finally chosen was three blocks north of Market Street and Van Ness Avenue.

Contribution to the Future

Burnham's concept of an inner circuit might appear to have been forgotten during the passage of time, but San Franciscans of today need only consider the new Central Freeway looping round the Civic Center on the west and the central business district on the south. The route corresponds in part to Burnham's inner circuit, although the freeway is more in the nature of a bypass than a distributor thoroughfare.

A glance at a map of present-day San Francisco will reveal that many segments of Burnham's peripheral circuit now actually exist, though not, to be sure, as parts of the thirty-mile-long Outer Boulevard that he designed.

A great, arclike Crosstown Freeway shown in the 1951 Trafficways Plan corresponds roughly to certain connecting drives through a semicircle of parks that Burnham proposed for the southeastern quadrant of San Francisco.[17]

The many diagonal routes suggested by Burnham to facilitate movement in the South of Market area, the financial district, and in the Mission, Bayview, Sunset, and Richmond districts have not reappeared in present-day plans. Even if it were desirable to provide some of these arteries, they could be developed only at enormous cost, because the city is now almost solidly built up. In Burnham's time the Richmond and Sunset districts were, however, almost vacant, as were some parts of the Mission and Bayview districts.

Ahead of His Time

Burnham's recommendations for one-way streets and for subways in the central business district were years in advance of the times, since one-way streets were not adopted in San Francisco, even on a piecemeal basis, until 1942, and since arguments regarding the desirability of subways still continue. Subways had, however, been proposed at the turn of the century.

Traffic engineers currently struggling with the problem of clotted traffic in downtown streets planned in horse-and-buggy days cannot but admire Burnham's prescient recommendation for "a complete system of traffic regulation," including not only the use of one-way streets but also the restriction or even the prohibition of heavy traffic on boulevards designed for fast communication.

In residential areas in the nearly level sections of the city, Burnham saw the possibility of eliminating some of the streets in the monotonous system of blocks and creating a chain of parklike squares "formed in a measure by the unused or misused back-yard areas." These park chains "would become public avenues of beautiful planting, in which one could walk with great comfort, and where children could play, free from danger of traffic," since the main traffic would be routed along the intermediary streets. Such a system, he pointed out, would provide well for children who seldom know any life except that upon the streets of the city and would be the natural approach or connecting link between the larger parks and playgrounds proposed in his plan.[18]

Burnham thus argued for a kind of superblock, employed by many present-day city planners, architects, and site planners in the design of large-scale public and private housing projects as well as in that of single-family residential developments. The generous-dimensioned superblock, permitting the grouping of dwellings round central open space and relegating traffic to the bordering streets, assures maximum amenity, safety, and freedom from noise. It conserves for play space, walks, and gardens, a substantial amount of land that otherwise would be wasted in minor streets.

Many San Franciscans unfamiliar with the Burnham Plan have contemplated the hollow centers of typical San Francisco blocks, with their rows of high board fences dividing the land into twenty-five-foot strips, and have devised similar schemes for pooling individually owned plots and forming socially useful space; but invariably these plans have collapsed under the opposition of those who would rather do as they please on a few square feet of land than share several thousand square feet with their neighbors.

Aside from his recommendations for the formation of superblocks which would be made possible by eliminating some minor streets, and for the provision of small parks and playgrounds distributed throughout the city according to the density of population in various sections, Burnham had little to say about the future development of residential areas. One looks in vain for any mention of a proposed distribution of population, for recommendations concerning the types of residential structures suitable for specific districts, for standards for sites for schools and shopping facilities, or for proposed locations of transit routes—all of great concern to present-day city planners. In that nascent period of city planning most city plans included little besides proposals for boulevards, parks, and a civic center. Though Burnham and his co-workers in San Francisco limited themselves chiefly to these features, they dealt with them imaginatively and in many instances displayed a great deal more foresight than their contemporaries could appreciate.

Plans for New Parks

Burnham was eminently practical in recognizing that San Francisco was deficient in recreation space, even though Golden Gate Park and several squares had been reserved at an earlier period. The Mission and Potrero districts, particularly, lacked parks and were distant from those which did exist. In the city as a whole there were approximately 286 persons for each acre of park, since the Park Board estimated the total park area to be between 1,300 and 1,400 acres and the city population to be perhaps 400,000. The average for "the most important cities of the United States" was, however, 206 persons for each park acre; and Boston had set a standard of 42 persons per park acre.[19] To bring San Francisco into line with other large cities, more parks would be required. And then there were future needs to be considered.

Burnham proposed to add to the park system numerous tracts which possessed a certain natural beauty but which were, in his opinion, ill adapted for private occupancy because of their steepness, their inaccessibility, or difficulties of drainage. The numerous hills then in a pristine state came, of course, within his definition of lands suitable for park development. These hills, indeed, were the unique feature of the site of San Francisco. So concerned was Burnham with their preservation and with the enhancement of their dramatic quality that he allotted an entire section of his report to a discussion of the general treatment of the hills.

"It may be stated in general that the tops of all high hills should be preserved in a state of nature, while their slopes below should be clothed with trees, not presenting a horizontal line where they leave off above, but a line adapted to the varying conditions of each case," Burnham wrote.[20]

He proposed circumscribing the base of each hill with a circuit road, developing contour roads on the slopes, and accenting places of interest with terraces commanding views of the city. Where contour roads ran through residential areas, he recommended reserving fifty to one hundred feet of land on the lower side, in order to retain in some degree the outlook over the city.

In those early years of the century it would have been possible to link numerous unspoiled hills in a great girdle of parks about the entire city; and this Burnham recommended doing. The park chain, as he outlined it, would start at Buena Vista Park near the Golden Gate Park Panhandle, extend across the Twin Peaks group and its continuation to the south, include Bernal Heights, and end at Potrero Heights. Significantly, he remarked: "In case of a great conflagration this system of parks and connecting parkways would form an effective barrier to its spread."[21]

A Great Park West of Twin Peaks

To the west of Twin Peaks Burnham's plan showed a vast park, two or three times the size of Golden Gate Park, extending southwest through Rancho San Miguel to Lake Merced, with an unbroken vista sweeping from an Athenaeum on the crest of the peaks down to the lake and the sea beyond.

The suggested treatment of the hills in the Twin Peaks area reveals the extent to which the planner of the "City Beautiful" era was inspired by the classic world of Greece and Rome. An amphitheater to the north of the peaks "would recall by its location the stadium in the hills at Delphi, which overlooks the Gulf of Corinth, and the theater of Dionysos, at the foot of the Acropolis." An Academy similar to the American Academy at Rome would have a little open-air theater "after the ancient Greek model." The courts, terraces, and colonnaded shelters of the Athenaeum would be arranged "after the manner of the great Poecile of the Villa Hadrian."[22]

In some circles it is the fashion nowadays to ridicule Burnham and the young architects who worked with him, for their deference to the majestic achievements of the ancient world and their admiration for the great designers of the Renaissance. The perspective drawings of Telegraph Hill, the view from the Athenaeum toward the sea, the drill ground from the heights of the Presidio, and the approach to Twin Peaks from Market Street are sneeringly described as "grandiose" rather than grand.

One may indeed criticize Burnham and his associates for following an aesthetic tradition foreign to America, for turning their backs on an emergent native architecture. But one cannot indict them for being genuinely inspired by the noblest architecture and site planning of the past, for grasping the aesthetic quality of the San Francisco hills, and for seeking to translate a passionate response to these natural forms into proposals of great breadth and scope, recapturing something of the spirit of Delphi and something of the more theatrical gardens and public places of Rome. Had some of these imposing projects been carried out, they would have been highly appropriate to San Francisco, a city with a dramatic history.

That the Burnham Plan presented extensive proposals

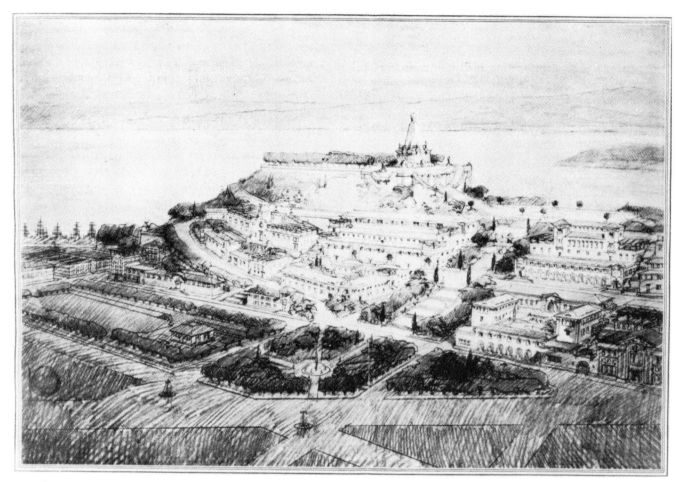

Burnham's "Suggested Architectural Treatment" of Telegraph Hill

for parks, boulevards, and a civic center and dealt only superficially with industrial, commercial, and waterfront areas did not seem strange to the businessmen who invited the Chicago architect to San Francisco. City planning in 1905 had the status of an art, and what was sought from Burnham was primarily a plan for the "adornment" of the city. Only secondarily were the members of the Association for the Improvement and Adornment of San Francisco interested in the plan as an instrument that could be used to facilitate the operations of manufacturers, retailers, shippers, and wholesalers. Today a group of business leaders would require that a long-range plan be based on a thorough analysis of the economic functions of the community and that it anticipate realistically the long-range physical needs of the business community. The brief discussion, in Burnham's report, of relationships within the working city and of the future development of the waterfront is more or less a gratuitous offering, incidental to an explanation of plans for the Outer Boulevard and for yacht harbors and piers for public recreation.

Suggested Controls

Just how his various recommendations for improving the city where to be implemented Burnham did not say. He advocated, "if necessary," an ordinance requiring public and semipublic institutions, such as churches and schools, to be set back from the sidewalk so as not to infringe upon "the rights of neighboring property."[23] But this was practically the only mention in his entire report of the use of local statutes to guide development. In recommending a uniform cornice height for buildings in the business district, he could not have been unaware of a Boston ordinance of 1904 restricting building heights; yet legal means to effect his recommendation were not offered.

Virtually the only concrete proposal for permanently influencing physical aspects of the city was a recommendation that an art commission be provided by charter amendment "to control all matters especially pertaining to civic art."[24] The list of matters that might properly come before the commission reveals, however, that Burnham was not thinking of a public agency that would be zealous in submitting advice on ways to carry out his plan. Rather, he had in mind an innocuous group who would busy themselves with approving or disapproving the designs of street lamps, postboxes, safety stations, electric signs, billboards, and street name plates. There was not at that time in the entire United States a single official city planning agency. The first one was established at Hartford, Connecticut, in 1907. If Burnham had proposed one for San Francisco in 1905, he would indeed have set a precedent.

The Chicago architect undoubtedly assumed that the Association for the Improvement and Adornment of San Francisco would be a continuing organization and that from time to time it would seize the opportunity to advocate a bond issue or an appropriation to carry out some specific proposal in his plan. He suggested that the first projects undertaken should be the extension of the Panhandle and the construction of the Outer Boulevard. "Once these are carried out," he wrote, "the whole civic life will be affected and the development of other parts of the plan will be hastened thereby."[25]

Presentation of the Plan

The banquet at the St. Francis Hotel celebrating the presentation of the plan to the city was outwardly all sweetness and light, but beneath the surface were political enmities that augured ill for the success of the plan. In the absence of James Phelan, who was vacationing in Paris, William Greer Harrison, vice-president of the association, served as toastmaster and spoke of the assembled officials, architects, and real-estate men as "neophytes in the temple of beauty, a temple within whose doors no discord could enter."[26] Mayor Eugene Schmitz, whose picture was just then appearing in the San Francisco *Bulletin* with the word "GRAFT" printed across the forehead, responded enthusiastically to the toast "The New San Francisco," after which the celebrants, all standing, drank to the health of Daniel Burnham. Probably every member of the association present hoped that in the coming municipal election the decorative Mr. Schmitz would be unseated by their fellow member, attorney John S. Partridge; but a clairvoyant might have told them that the mayor was not going to be turned out. And this was a circumstance that was to have peculiar bearing upon the fate of the ambitious plan that they were extolling.

How sincere some of the real-estate men attending the banquet were in their praise of the Burnham Plan is a matter for speculation. In an article written for the *Architectural Record* shortly before the disaster of April 18, 1906, but not published until the following June, a writer named Herbert Croly observed that at the very moment when the citizens were acclaiming the Burnham report, "that generally ignorant and obnoxious individual, the real estate speculator," was laying out new additions to the south "in the same bad old way."[27]

In order that San Franciscans might study the plan in all its details, the board of supervisors ordered Burnham's report printed as a municipal document. The appropriation for the purpose was $3,000, permitting the production of a volume replete with photographs of the city and with reproductions of the maps, perspective drawings, and plans prepared by Edward Bennett and his corps of artists and draftsmen.

In mid-April, 1906, bound copies of the report were delivered to the City Hall, and from the bungalow on Twin Peaks the handsome originals of the drawings and plans illustrated in the publication were brought for a public display. While the exhibition was being installed in the City Hall, a few copies of the report were released, chiefly to members of the Association for the Improvement and Adornment of San Francisco. The rest were never to be distributed.

Earthquake and Fire

At 5:13 on the morning of April 18 great rock masses along the San Andreas fault slipped, grated against each other, and settled into a new position almost instantaneously. From Upper Mattole in Humboldt County to San Juan in San Benito County, quick, sharp vibrations went out in all directions through the rocks and communicated themselves violently to the soft soils and sands of the valleys, to the made lands in downtown San Francisco, and to the sandy areas thereabouts.

The dome and most of the roof on the south and west wings of the pretentious, poorly constructed San Francisco City Hall spilled into the street. More than fifty miles away, in Santa Rosa, the dome of the Sonoma County Court House toppled onto the roof. At Point Reyes Station, near the head of Tomales Bay in Marin County, a train that was about to depart for San Francisco keeled over. At Agnew, a few miles north of San Jose, the State Insane Asylum collapsed, killing more than a hundred patients and eleven officials. At Stanford University the heavy spire of the chapel dropped through the roof. Some miles to the north, in San Mateo County, the pipe lines that conveyed water to San Francisco from Pilarcitos, Crystal Springs, and San Andreas reservoirs split apart, telescoped, or bent backwards at crazy angles, their precious contents wasting on the ground, while in the distant metropolis little serpents of smoke rose slowly in the still air.

In Oakland, Alameda, and Berkeley some chimneys fell, some walls tumbled, one church lost its tower, a small theater caved in, and some old, ramshackle buildings jostled together. But on the whole, damage was slight. Likewise in Richmond and Vallejo there was little physical evidence of the convulsive movement of the earth. In Petaluma and San Rafael, cities luckily situated on rocky —and therefore less yielding—ground, the destruction was minor. Almost all the towns on the San Francisco Peninsula suffered considerable damage but were able to function.

Toward all these places thousands of terrified residents of San Francisco began fleeing on that catastrophic Wednesday morning. All that day, all the next day, throughout Thursday night, and on into Friday the flames ravaged the city; but on Friday morning the east wind that had fanned the conflagration for almost twenty-four hours ceased and a strong wind from the west sprang up. It turned the fiery scourge toward Russian Hill and North Beach. There, finally, on Saturday morning, April 21, the straggling remnants of the fire sputtered their last as a heavy rain fell.

CHAPTER SEVEN

The New San Francisco

Where some twenty-eight thousand buildings had stood, now stretched a blackened wasteland of more than four square miles—512 blocks. The most historic part of San Francisco was ashes, rubble, contorted scraps of metal, and shattered walls. Above the debris rose only five or six habitable structures, the skeletons of half a dozen unfinished business blocks, and approximately thirty gutted but structurally sound steel-frame buildings, the harbingers of a new city.

The loss of property amounted to at least half a billion dollars. Exactly how great the loss of life was will never be known. Officially the toll was placed at 478; but scores, perhaps hundreds, were never accounted for.

In that part of the city which had escaped the holocaust approximately 175,000 persons congregated, a large proportion of whom looked to bread lines for their daily sustenance. Destitute families were encamped in Golden Gate Park, in the Presidio, in small parks, and on vacant lots. Many a house still standing harbored refugees from the disaster. The task of distributing food, clothing, and medical supplies among the dispossessed proceeded with remarkable smoothness, considering the enormous disruption of services occasioned by the earthquake and fire. As for the refugees themselves, they exhibited heroic courage and cheerfulness, sustained in the knowledge that humanity everywhere would help to relieve their suffering and to rebuild the devastated metropolis.

Refugees in Other Cities

In the cities about the bay thousands of refugees gratefully accepted shelter in private homes or camped in tents hastily erected in the parks by the municipal authorities. The Southern Pacific estimated that between 6 A.M. on the day of the earthquake and Sunday night, April 22, it provided free passage from the stricken city for 225,000 persons, some of whom left California altogether, and

Area Burned in the Great Fire of 1906

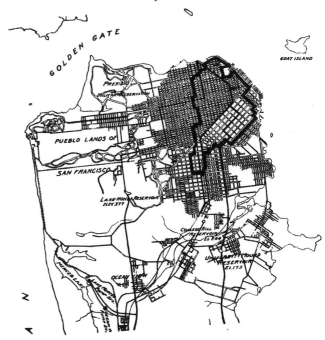

Ruins of the San Francisco City Hall, April 23, 1906. Photograph courtesy of Bancroft Library, University of California.

some of whom migrated to southern California and other parts of the state. Thousands of others fled on foot down the Peninsula or escaped by boat to Alameda County or Marin County.

In Oakland an estimated one hundred thousand refugees crowded into the homes of sympathetic citizens, filled every church in the city, and swelled to overflowing no less than twenty camps established in the city parks. Alameda made provision for ten thousand of the homeless, and Berkeley for fifteen thousand, not counting those who went directly to the homes of friends and relatives. In Richmond, John D. Rockefeller set up a special camp for the victims of the disaster. Vallejo officials estimated that their city cared for thirty thousand men, women, and children in the month following the catastrophe. Here, too, tent cities appeared in the parks, and citizens opened their homes to the refugees.

In Oakland, F. M. Smith and his associates sniffed the smoke of burning San Francisco as if it were the exhalation from an opium pipe—and conjured up "one of the most stupendous undertakings in the history of the advancement of Greater Oakland." They proposed merely to make Oakland "the greatest shipping point on the Pacific Coast." Their plan embraced "the construction of a double pier to the terminus of the Key Route Mole, the construction of a bulkhead from the Long Wharf of the Southern Pacific Company to the Key Route ferry slip, the filling of the five hundred acres lying between the two trestles, and the construction of a slip adjacent to the mole for the docking of the largest vessels that have ever entered San Francisco Bay."[1]

Wickham Havens, an Oakland realtor, bought space in the San Francisco papers to announce his desire to assist the burned-out residents: "To our friends, our clients, and all who may need our services in this hour we offer them freely. We want to help in this vast work of building up. We want to aid in the work of construction of a new metropolis of the Pacific on the East side of the bay."[2] The capitalization of the word "east" no doubt was deliberate.

Beginning of Rebuilding

Most San Franciscans had no thought of abandoning their city. "San Francisco will be rebuilt," the San Francisco *Bulletin* proclaimed while the embers still glowed. "At the supreme crisis in the history of the city her people have risen nobly to a situation which demands all that men and women could possess of courage, fortitude and hope. Plans for the greater, the new San Francisco, are rapidly taking shape, and out of the chaos of shattered buildings and broken fortunes, above the charred fragments of the once-proud metropolis will rise the new city by the western sea, the home of the strongest, bravest, and sturdiest people of their race."[3]

In homelier fashion a business sign on a newly erected stand expressed the spirit of the hour:

> We were at Howard, near 8th St.
> HONEST INJUN
> HERE'S WHAT'S LEFT OF US,
> 1 Shoestring, 1 Collar Button,
> 1 Necktie, 1 Pair Sox, 1 Pair Spex,
> and an INDOMITABLE WILL
> and the greatest of these
> is WILL—THE SPIRIT OF '06.[4]

The ruins of the city were not yet cool when some merchants set up shop on the very sites where they had done business before. They pulled from the debris assorted pieces of corrugated iron, bits of pipe, anything that would serve as building material. Undamaged sections of wall became supports for lean-tos. And in a surprisingly short time stocks of goods appeared in these temporary emporiums.

For the time being, Fillmore Street, in the population-swollen Western Addition, became the principal business street of San Francisco. Already a commercial artery in a small way, it now had the advantage of possessing one of the few undamaged car lines in the city, a service connecting with the Mission district. There was also a good deal of vacant frontage on the street. Every empty lot soon swarmed with workmen hammering together light frame structures to house the leading mercantile establishments of the city. Restaurants, theaters, saloons, and hotels opened alongside the stores, giving the streets the lively, tawdry aspects of the main stem of a frontier boom town. The "sights" of Fillmore Street became, indeed, so magnetic that within three months Oakland papers were complaining of the loss of business to this new gay way.

In Hayes Valley, on the southern edge of the Western Addition, another business district sprang up. Here the streets were well paved, the terrain was flat, and there were two car lines that could be restored to service before long. New homes as well as new stores went up rapidly, including dwellings on the alleys. Lot overcrowding, the curse of this section of the city, had its beginning then.

For the Western Addition as a whole the fire marked the start of a swift decline toward the status of a blighted area. This district was one of the few parts of San Francisco in which urban activities could be carried on with any semblance of normality. The clamor for dwelling space was so great that property owners quickly converted their homes into boardinghouses, even fitting up basements, attics, and storage rooms as bedrooms. Apartment houses, hastily enlarged, became commercial hotels. To meet the demand for commercial space, numerous householders raised their dwellings and built stores underneath them. Stores, restaurants, and workshops opened for business in basements. Industries, too, invaded the area, carrying on noisy and often dangerous operations next door to single-family homes or multifamily structures. Every condition that would make a modern city planner shudder was soon to be found in the Western Addition in exaggerated form: indiscriminate mixture of land uses, excessive density of population, substandard housing, traffic congestion.

Van Ness Avenue, the wide thoroughfare at which the flames had been checked, underwent a brisk transformation into a street of fashionable shops, past which the stylish paraded on Saturday afternoons as they once had on Kearny and Market streets.

In the undestroyed area of the Mission district a fever pitch of activity prevailed. New houses went up; many old ones were remodeled to accommodate more occupants, even though faulty room arrangements and bad lighting and ventilation resulted. The intersection of Mission and Twenty-second streets, a transfer point for the

Twin Peaks and Potrero districts, became the hub of a new retail center. Shopping areas also sprang up at Valencia and Sixteenth streets and at Twenty-ninth and Church streets.

In the outer Mission district, in the Richmond district between the Presidio and Golden Gate Park, and in other sparsely settled areas contractors and builders rushed construction of new houses. Thousands of workers who formerly had lived in the congested area south of Market Street and in the North Beach district rented or bought in the new tracts, and for the first time enjoyed private yards and adequate light and air.

A New Evil—Tenements

But civic leaders who had hoped that reconstruction would bring an improvement in housing were dismayed by the appearance of a new evil—the jerry-built tenement house. Ernest P. Bicknell, General Superintendent of the Chicago Bureau of Charities, warned San Franciscans that "the landlord does not build better unless he is forced to." Said he, "A handful of intelligent, thoroughgoing, enthusiastic people who are not easily discouraged will have to carry the burden if the city is to be saved from the danger of having built here tenements which would be a disgrace and a source of endless disease and trouble, and eventually of tremendous cost to the community in money."[5]

Despite the efforts of social workers, some members of the Commonwealth Club, and other public-spirited people to cope with the situation, the tenement-house problem became acute within six months. Probably at that time no combination of forces could have prevented the building of these rookeries, as Dr. Langley Porter, president of the San Francisco Housing Association, pointed out in 1911 in the first public report of the association: "The people wanted shelter, the workmen needed wages, the contractors in many cases had to rebuild shattered financial standing, and lot owners were anxious for the same reason to get the greatest possible income from their property. It was a time of turmoil and uncertainty. The bravest man was the one with faith enough to risk his money in building. The authorities, glad enough to encourage anyone to build, hardly enforced the mild provisions of the existing building laws. Merely that a building would not fall was all they asked. Thus tenements, not homes, were built."[6]

Unparalleled Opportunity

Hope for a better-planned city also faded as citizens of all classes raised their voices against anything that would delay reconstruction. When the fire was consuming block

after block, some people were well-nigh convinced that Providence was at work, effacing the mistakes of the past and providing an unparalleled opportunity for San Francisco to make a fresh start, utilizing the plan prepared by Burnham. But as the weeks passed and the work of rebuilding progressed, it became increasingly apparent that the city was not going to take advantage of the "clean slate" presented by the disaster.

On the very day of the earthquake, Ernest Graham sent a cable to Burnham, who was traveling in France, saying "Come at once!"[7] The architect boarded the liner *Deutschland* at Dover the next night and reached Chicago on May 1. From there he sent a telegram to Mayor Schmitz and the Committee for Reconstruction, announcing that he was on his way to San Francisco.

Before he arrived, city officials and civic leaders held preliminary meetings. At one of these James Phelan exclaimed, "This is a magnificent opportunity for beautifying San Francisco, and I believe that the property owners will gladly coöperate, now that their personal improvements have been swept away. I am sure the city will rise from its ashes greater, better, and more beautiful."[8]

At the same meeting, Benjamin Ide Wheeler, president of the University of California, spoke of "the glorious, gentle sweeps of the hills, offering themselves to contour gradients." Then he added, "I should like to see Nob Hill made into a park and that glorious view preserved for the people."[9]

The San Francisco *Chronicle* immediately sounded a note of caution: "There should be and must be some widening and straightening of streets. But we must not lose our heads. We may allow visions of the beautiful to dance before our eyes, but we must not permit them to control our actions." The newspaper warned, "If we expect to sell bonds we must give evidence of financial wisdom."[10]

The first full meeting of the Committee for Reconstruction or the Committee of Forty, as it was popularly known, began with an admonition from Mayor Schmitz on "the danger of outlining work on an extravagant scale."[11] The city, he said, was less able to reconstruct in accordance with the Burnham Plan than it had been a month before the fire. In his estimation one hundred million dollars would hardly pay the cost of erecting needed public buildings. If the Burnham Plan were adopted, the expense would be "an addition to this sum." He requested that suggestions from committee members be "practical, not theoretical."[12]

Stung by the implication that he, a former mayor, had been impractical in suggesting the extension of the Panhandle and the acquisition of land for boulevards, Phelan was on his feet at once, explaining how the Burnham proposals could be carried out without much cost to the taxpayers. By condemnation proceedings the city could acquire half a block on each side of the Panhandle and other boulevards for their entire length, use as much as necessary for right of way, and then sell the excess land at an advanced valuation based on the new public improvements. The increment would in most instances be sufficient to pay for the cost of the improvements. Lest his hearers consider this suggestion archsocialism, Phelan explained that Paris had employed this method in carrying out some of the plans for boulevards drawn up by Baron Haussmann under Napoleon III. In California, he pointed out, excess condemnation would have to be authorized by a special session of the state legislature.

Many of his hearers doubted that the state lawmakers would look with favor on any such grant of power; some questioned the constitutionality of the proposal. The use of tax funds or monies from the sale of municipal bonds, or both, therefore appeared inescapable. This was the hard reality that the press emphasized to the exclusion of all other considerations.

"Let us have a city beautiful but within our ability to pay," urged the San Francisco *Bulletin* in an editorial which undoubtedly strengthened the popular impression that many of the proposals in the Burnham Plan were purely for "show." "Much may be done without plunging the city in a debt that will impair our credit, or raise the rate of taxation to a point that will cripple business," the newspaper advised. It concluded that San Franciscans "without shrinking from the performance of duty, may leave some things for a future and more opulent generation to do in creating visions of the beautiful."[13]

Attacks on the plan brought from John Galen Howard, the official architect of the University of California and an advisory member of the Committee of Forty, the statement that the plan was "admirably conceived" and could be carried out, for the very sound reason that it was founded on "basic principles." Howard chose to stress the practical aspects of the plan—"the convenience involved in the arrangement, the provisions for taking care of traffic and for making each part of the city accessible."[14]

Proposed Improvements

Burnham's arrival fortified Phelan, Howard, Benjamin Ide Wheeler, Willis Polk, Rudolph Spreckels, John McLaren, and others who championed the plan. The Chicago "civic engineer," as some newspapers dubbed him, plunged into a series of daily conferences with various subcommittees, particularly the Subcommittee on Widen-

ing, Extending, and Grading Streets and Restoring Pavements; the Subcommittee on Parks, Reservoirs, and Boulevards; and the Subcommittee on Burnham Plans [sic], headed by Phelan. By May 21 the first-named subcommittee was ready to present to the full Committee of Forty the proposals that it had worked out with the other two subcommittees. Its report, recommending the very minimum of changes that it considered essential in the burned district, revealed how great had been the struggle with the formidable problem of financing the proposed improvements:

"Realizing the necessity for immediate yet conservative action which confronts us, and that in the present financial situation of the city, utility should be a more potent factor than mere beauty in the solving of the problems before us, yet recognizing that both of these important elements may be judiciously and advantageously combined, your committee has concluded to submit its several recommendations in the order of their apparent importance and of the ability of the city to carry them out without imposing too great a burden of taxation on the property owners of the city. To accomplish this end your committee has reached the determination that some of these recommendations should be executed and carried into effect immediately, some may well be deferred for a period of five years and some for longer, say ten years.

"In view of the fact that almost all of the lands through which the projected improvements are to run are now vacant and devoid of improvements, and therefore may be acquired more easily and economically now than at any other time, your committee has devised a plan which seems entirely feasible for securing the required lands at once, even though the projected improvements may not be fully accomplished for some time thereafter. This plan may be carried out without imposing any additional taxation on the property holders of the city by deferring payment until such time as by reason of increase in the amount of taxable property the same rate of taxation will produce the necessary revenue. Briefly, to accomplish this your committee recommends that the Board of Supervisors shall by ordinance declare the city's intention at or before five years from date of issuance. This will enable the city to acquire the lands necessary for the contemplated improvements during the five years without levying any tax therefor, and will at the same time enable the property owner whose land is to be acquired to accept bonds therefor, which bonds he will be able to dispose of at once or may carry as an investment. These bonds will undoubtedly be for a long term and will therefore be very desirable holdings. The improvement is a permanent one, which will enhance real estate values in all parts of the city; the amount of tax levied to meet them will be almost insignificant. The benefits of the added valuation accruing therefrom will increase a thousandfold as compared with the expenses required to produce them."[15]

Immediate improvements to be financed by bonds that would be repaid by provisions in the general tax levy were seventeen in all. They included proposals for widening to one hundred feet such important thoroughfares as Montgomery Avenue [Columbus Avenue], Golden Gate Avenue, and Pacific, Powell, and Pine streets. New contour streets were to encircle Nob Hill and Russian Hill, since few structures remained on either hill. Other proposals contemplated extending the Panhandle to Market Street and creating a number of diagonal routes, some of which had not appeared in the original Burnham Plan.

Improvements recommended for deferral for five years included the widening of Geary Street, the creation of a Panhandle continuation all the way to the waterfront, extensions of Potrero Avenue, and the widening and opening of Eleventh Street as an approach to the union station proposed by Burnham.

Triumph for Burnham

The unanimous adoption of the subcommittee report by the Committee of Forty was regarded as a triumph for Burnham and the stalwarts of the Association for the

SAN FRANCISCO CHRONICLE, WEDNESDAY, MAY 23, 1906.

NEW PLAN OF CITY ADOPTED BY THE CITIZENS' COMMITTEE

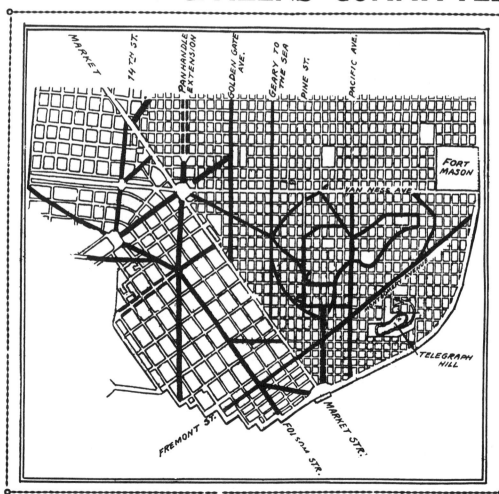

Plan Proposed by the Citizen's Committee for Reconstruction, May 21, 1906. "The heavy black lines show the widened streets, as well as the new diagonal streets which have not yet been named, and the winding streets by means of which easy access may be secured to Nob Hill," the San Francisco Chronicle explained.

Improvement and Adornment of San Francisco. But would the board of supervisors adopt it? Burnham himself attended the meeting at which the board considered the report and explained that the revised plan "had nothing to do with the proposed beautification of the city, but was designed simply to give quick and easy communication and to relieve the congestion of the downtown district." The proposed diagonal streets and the widening of existing streets were, he said, "absolutely necessary." One or two of the supervisors questioned the advisability of slicing blocks into "small triangles" by extending Montgomery Avenue to Market Street, but when the vote on political boss Abe Ruef's resolution for adoption of the plan was taken, all answered "aye."[16]

"The adoption of this plan makes it certain beyond all cavil or doubt that the men of San Francisco are in earnest in their determination to rebuild the city, and to rebuild it on a grander scale than before," Mayor Schmitz declared. "This means business. I am particularly glad that the committee disregarded the ornamental and confined itself to the practical in laying out this plan. Decoration can come later. But the main thing is that we can now get to work. Many prominent men have waited only for the settlement of the new street lines to put up splendid buildings. These will be completed within two years, and the city will stand rehabilitated within five years."[17]

Burnham returned to Chicago elated. The plans, he informed the people of that city, had been adopted "in their entirety." More optimistic than Mayor Schmitz, he prophesied that in a year's time it would not be easy to find a trace of the devastation left by the earthquake and fire. "San Francisco of the future will be the most beautiful city of the continent, with the possible exception of Washington," he rejoiced.[18]

Attack on Proposals

In the metropolis by the Golden Gate there was no premature exultation. The San Francisco *Chronicle* attacked the Committee of Forty for making "a serious blunder in proposing to place the ban of uncertainty for five years upon a large quantity of down-town property." It condemned the plans as being unworthy of consideration because they had not been brought forward "in a business fashion," with estimates of the probable cost of the improvements. "The crying need of San Francisco today is not more parks and boulevards; it is business," the newspaper asserted. "Unless we get back to work and effect a speedy restoration of old conditions, we shall find that we have more parks and wide streets than we can profitably use."[19]

At a meeting of the Down-Town Property Owners Association, M. H. de Young, publisher of the *Chronicle*, who had commissioned Burnham to design the first skyscraper in San Francisco, likened the situation of the California metropolis to that of London after the great fire of 1666, when Sir Christopher Wren evolved his celebrated plan for making over the English capital. The "practical men" of London, de Young told his audience, concluded that if an attempt were made to carry out Wren's project, business would be driven from London. They therefore determined to proceed with the rehabilitation of the city on the old lines, with the result that in five years London was rebuilt and the business of the city was left undisturbed. He urged the "practical men" of San Francisco to follow their example.[20]

The San Francisco *Bulletin*, which had always enthusiastically supported Phelan in his civic work, ran an editorial entitled "Wide Streets Are Wanted, but We Cannot Wait Long."

"Unless the property-owners, or at least the great majority of them, along a street which it is proposed to widen will consent to the improvement and donate to the public use a strip from the frontage of their lots, the project of widening that street may as well be abandoned. Unless the land is given freely it must be purchased, and there is no money available for the purchase. Should the owner be unwilling either to donate the land or sell it, the city must proceed by an action of condemnation, which the defendant landowner can prolong by various methods. There is no time for the slow processes of litigation. Landowners, eager to build, cannot hold back until the line of the street shall be determined by judgment of the Supreme Court. The city needs action, not litigation. Our energy must be spent in building, not in wrangling before juries."[21]

A few days later the same newspaper published another editorial, headed "Dreams and Schemes Must Not Retard Rebuilding," in which it mentioned that some of the proposed street widenings were encountering "violent opposition" from landowners. The *Bulletin* attributed some of the lag in rebuilding to the slowness of insurance companies in paying losses but said that much of the delay was due to "the uncertainty of the proposed widening of divers streets."[22]

On the opposite side of the bay the Oakland *Enquirer* observed, in commenting on Burnham's optimism about the new city-to-be: "It is to be hoped . . . that a year hence one will be able to find some trace of the Burnham plans in San Francisco, if the immediate necessities of the business situation do not mutilate them beyond all recognition."[23]

A New Threat to the Plans

Suddenly the plans were threatened from a new and un-expected quarter. The cunning Abe Ruef, seeing an opportunity to manipulate the street-widening projects to his own advantage, attempted to jam through the state legislature a proposed state constitutional amendment suspending certain provisions of the San Francisco City Charter for two years and conferring almost unrestrained powers upon the supervisors and mayor to acquire, sell, or exchange lands for streets, parks, boulevards, reservoirs, and other public purposes. Adroitly tucked in was a section granting the Ruef-managed supervisors wide authority to alter the terms of franchises for railroads, wires, pipe lines, and conduits. This dangerous measure, to the amazement, chagrin, and indignation of the Committee of Forty, was placed before the legislators as having the endorsement of that public-spirited body.

Without digging beneath the surface of Ruef's bare-faced grab for power, the *Chronicle* screamed that "if the committee of forty expects to retain public confidence as to the wisdom of any of its recommendations it must stop giving serious attention to such revolutionary and hysterical proposals as that submitted by the subcommittee of which Mr. Ruef is chairman, and which proposes to proceed by constitutional amendment to rip open the charter of this city and tear out of it [many of] its most salutary restrictions on the power of the Supervisors."[24]

Later, having ferreted out the facts, de Young's newspaper exposed Ruef's methods:

". . . As a matter of fact, there were very few members of the committee of forty who had anything to do with this constitutional amendment. It was drafted by Ruef himself and placed by him for indorsement to a subcommittee in San Francisco, which committee at Century Hall was composed of lawyers alone, and only part of the membership of the sub-committee was present at the meeting when Ruef's amendment was considered. Even had all of the sub-committee been in attendance, it would not have been a body that represented the people of San Francisco. The few lawyers who were present and who gave some attention to the proposition were friendly to Ruef, and while they did not like the scope of the measure, were content to put in it the few limitations which it now carries, and then they 'passed the buck' to the Legislature. The sub-committee report to the committee of forty was a long document, covering many subjects of legislation, and it was given formal approval without discussion when presented. Probably not more than half a dozen members of the committee of forty had read Ruef's measure attentively."[25]

This explanation came too late, however, to save the Committee of Forty from the fire of irate civic organizations. Their spokesmen, hastening to Sacramento to appear in opposition to the proposed amendment, berated Ruef and the Committee of Forty in the same breath. Matt I. Sullivan, representing the Mission Promotion Association, wanted the legislators to remember that "that charter was framed by as eminent a body of citizens as the Committee of Forty" and that its authors had "put in it provisions to protect the people against monopoly." Careful estimates, he asserted, showed that to carry out the committee's scheme of street alterations would subject all taxpayers of San Francisco to a bonded indebtedness of between $30,000,000 and $40,000,000—"solely for the benefit of rich property-owners north of Market Street."[26] Other opponents joined with him in suggesting that there was boodle in the proposition for Ruef and his friends. The crafty boss of the Schmitz Administration stubbornly defended his amendment, but, the *Bulletin* stated, "his talent for the plausible exposition of a sophistical argument was staggered by the job."[27] The legislature emasculated the menacing amendment and sent the spokesmen for the various associations home almost prayerfully grateful that San Francisco had escaped "a worse evil than earthquake and fire."[28]

The Committee of Forty, innocently but negligently entangled in Ruef's web for a brief period, now labored under a double burden. It fought not only the charge that it was impractical, idealistic, theoretical, visionary, and perhaps irresponsible, but also the suspicion, in some bitterly hostile quarters, that its members, or some of them at least, sought personal gain rather than the common good.

An Advisory Commission

Since matters were going from bad to worse, United States Senator Francis Griffith Newlands, of Nevada, one of the owners of the Palace Hotel property, pleaded at a meeting of the California Promotion Committee late in July for property owners to "get together, suggest improvements, compromise conflicting claims and interests and rehabilitate this great city." He suggested the establishment of a commission "with a man like Burnham at the head of it, that can advise the municipal authorities and property owners relative to combining beauty with utility in our new city."[29]

Senator Newlands seems to have recognized the need for something akin to the present-day city planning commission, though it is not clear whether he thought of his proposed commission as a permanent advisory group. At any rate, he deserves credit for having been the first, or at least one of the first, to understand that without a public agency specifically charged with the responsibility of recommending policies for the physical development of a city on the basis of a long-term plan that expresses community goals, there is little hope for substantial civic improvement or orderly growth.

The men who seized upon Newlands' suggestion were the leaders of the Association for the Improvement and Adornment of San Francisco—Phelan, Rudolph Spreckels and Thomas Magee. They joined in urging Mayor Schmitz to invite Burnham to return to San Francisco and supervise the rebuilding of the city in conformity with his plans.[30] But the mayor and his sworn political enemies, Phelan and Spreckels, could no longer maintain the pretense of collaborating in civic affairs. The hour of crisis—of civic prostration and acute human suffering—was over.

The Graft Investigation

A new kind of crisis was approaching, for the mayor and for Phelan and Spreckels. Schmitz perhaps knew that

Eugene Schmitz, Mayor of San Francisco, 1902–1907

Phelan and Spreckels had already agreed to finance an investigation of his administration; he may even have known that their friend Fremont Older, the crusading editor of the *Bulletin*, had obtained a promise from President Theodore Roosevelt that William J. Burns, a detective of the United States Secret Service, and Francis J. Heney, an attorney in charge of prosecuting timberland frauds in the Northwest, would be made available to conduct the investigation. Under the circumstances, it is not surprising that Burnham was not invited to head a new municipal commission, that no further thought was given to such a body, that the rebuilding of the city finally proceeded with hardly a change from the street pattern existing before the fire.

Burns and Heney arrived in San Francisco in October, a new grand jury was summoned in November, and soon thereafter Ruef and Schmitz were indicted for extortion. For the next three years San Francisco was in an uproar as the investigation spread from corrupt city officials to corrupt corporation executives who had paid bribes for privileges. Phelan and Spreckels, deeply involved in masterminding the investigation, had little time to think of anything but the hornet's nest they had stirred up by directing the prosecution toward an exposé of the leaders of San Francisco society and business. Around their heads flew accusations that they were "the despotic tyrants of the city," deciding who should and who should not go to jail and who should and who should not be mayor.[31]

Rapid Reconstruction

Notwithstanding the political storms that buffeted many financiers and large property holders, reconstruction progressed with a speed that astonished the world. The business community apparently did not question the desirability of rebuilding the financial and commercial center in exactly the same place as before. The location that Governor Figueroa and the territorial *Diputación* had selected in 1834 as the site for a commercial town was still the most desirable area in which to carry on the trade of the metropolis. Near by were the shipping facilities and the Ferry Building, which had escaped unharmed in the earthquake and fire. Transit lines, quickly restored to operation, converged upon this core area; to the south and west of it were level blocks in which there was room for commercial facilities to expand; and still standing, even though gutted, were the principal office structures of a big city. From the standpoint of accessibility to other important cities in the Bay Area the central business district of San Francisco was in the best possible location. Since no small part of the patronage of its stores, banks, and professional offices came by ferry from the East Bay,

Reconstruction in the Central Business District of San Francisco, 1907. Palace Hotel and Crocker Building, left; Wells Fargo Bank Building and Postal Telegraph Building, center; Mills Building and Merchants Exchange Building, right. Photograph by Frank Schwabacher, courtesy of Bancroft Library.

Marin County, Vallejo, and Napa, the hopes of some property owners that Fillmore Street and Van Ness Avenue might continue to be leading commercial thoroughfares were never well founded. Within three years practically every outstanding firm in the city had returned to San Francisco's highly centralized shopping district.

At first the lack of facilities for removal of debris handicapped the work of clearing building sites. But within a few weeks donkey engines were puffing in the streets, railroad tracks had been extended into the devastated area, and an army of men from the refugee camps was engaged in clearing bricks and piling them in neat stacks to be used in rebuilding. From all over California, work horses were shipped to San Francisco to haul dump wagons; and it has been estimated that not less than 15,000 were worked to exhaustion and carted off to the

boneyard in the first two years of reconstruction.[32] By July, 1906, 100 cars of debris were being removed daily, and by August, 125. Most of the refuse was dumped behind a new section of the sea wall at the foot of King and Townsend streets, just north of China Basin.

Rehabilitation of the large "fireproof" buildings that had been gutted but not structurally impaired began almost immediately. Among the major edifices restored were the Fairmont and St. Francis hotels, the Merchants' Exchange, the Union Trust Company Building, the Grant, Monadnock, Shreve, Wells Fargo, and Rialto buildings, and office buildings bearing the names of San Francisco millionaires—William Crocker, Claus Spreckels, James Flood, Darius O. Mills. Within three months, eighteen of these imposing structures were occupied in part, while work was progressing on others.

THE NEW SAN FRANCISCO 119

The construction of many substantial new buildings was delayed, however, by arguments over provisions of the proposed new building ordinance and over the proposed fire limits, within which no frame structures would be permitted. Debate in the sessions of the board of supervisors reached a crescendo when the use of reinforced concrete for tall structures was under consideration. Before the fire this type of construction had been prohibited except for floors. In the new building ordinance reinforced concrete was approved for buildings not exceeding 102 feet in height. Only steel-frame structures could be higher than that, and these were limited to a height equal to one and one-half times the width of the street.[33]

West of the main business district the fire limits agreed upon were bounded by Pine Street on the north, Van Ness Avenue on the west, Mission and Howard streets on the south, and the bay on the east. As soon as these were established, property owners on the north side of Pine Street erected large frame structures. On the south side of the street and in the entire area from Powell Street to Van Ness Avenue numerous sites remained vacant until as late as 1912, because of the costlier construction required.

Changes in the New City

Some types of enterprise shifted to new locations after the fire; others remained where they had been before. Wholesale houses, which formerly had been grouped near the waterfront north of Market Street, moved to new sites in the vicinity of Fourth and Townsend streets, in order to be near the railroad yards. This was a logical move, since the bulk of goods to be distributed no longer arrived by ship but by train. Produce merchants, however, elected to continue in business north of Market Street—a decision later regretted, for the area was too small and the location was inconvenient for incoming shipments.

The leaders of the Chinese population decided against transferring their activities to Oakland or to Hunters Point, as some people had hoped they would, and set about rebuilding on a more substantial scale in the blocks known as Chinatown. Unfortunately, some of the worst tenements in the city rose behind the colorful store fronts.

Several banks that previously had occupied buildings in the general area of California and Sansome streets reopened on Market Street, although most financial institutions returned to the time-honored location. Important retail stores deserted Kearny Street and the north side of Market Street for new quarters on Grant Avenue and on Stockton Street between Market and Post.

Few of the new buildings in the central business district provided living accommodations above shops, as had

great numbers before the fire. Socially prominent families who had formerly maintained elegant suites in the commercial area reëstablished themselves in fine houses on Pacific Heights and in the area west of Divisadero Street near the Presidio. Apartment houses and residential hotels made up a high proportion of the new construction in the blocks immediately surrounding the main business center. The southern slope of Nob Hill, especially, was covered with apartment houses. The trend toward this type of urban living had been noticeable before the fire; it now continued at an accelerated rate.

In the fourth month after the fire nearly 1,200 building permits were issued, for buildings to cost a total of $6,330,000, which was almost as much as the value of all construction in the year 1900. The value represented by permits for the year 1906 exceeded $39,000,000 and increased to $50,500,000 in 1907. Within three years 20,500 buildings were constructed, of which 19,000 were new frame structures. The whirlwind pace of building, once the question of payments from insurance companies was settled and the uncertainty about street layout was eliminated, provided employment for 40,000 building-trades workers, compared with less than half that number before the fire.[34]

Need for a City Hall

Conspicuously lacking among the thousands of new buildings was one for which city officials felt an urgent need—a city hall. With the exception of a wing temporarily retained and fitted up for the city treasurer, the auditor, and the registrar of voters, the ornate pile wrecked in 1906 had been razed and cleared away after numerous investigations revealed that rehabilitation would be impracticable and unwarrantedly expensive. Crowded conditions in the near-by Hall of Records, which had been repaired and retained in service, became more intolerable by the day.

Whether a new city hall should be built on the old site or on some other was the question uppermost in the minds of members of the board of supervisors when they decided to act upon the matter in April, 1909. To the satisfaction of Phelan and other members of the Association for the Improvement and Adornment of San Francisco, the supervisors sought the advice of the man whose comprehensive plan had been ignored during the reconstruction—Daniel Hudson Burnham. His presence in the city renewed hope that the plan of 1905 might be utilized in areas not yet entirely rebuilt and in areas still for the most part undeveloped.

At an informal reception of city officials in the mayor's office on April 14, 1909, Burnham seized the opportunity to advocate the creation of a civic center at the intersection of Market Street and Van Ness Avenue, as shown in a revision of his plan. The old triangular site at McAllister and Larkin streets was not only cut off from Market Street and, in his opinion, inconveniently located; it was inadequate to accommodate a group of public buildings and to provide a suitable setting for them. Enough property could now be acquired at a reasonably low cost, he pointed out, to create a large open space at Market Street and Van Ness Avenue and group around it a city hall, a courthouse, a library, a state building, a federal building, an auditorium, and other public edifices as needed. Moreover, the long-desired Park Panhandle extension could be brought down to this new center, and thus a beginning could be made on reorganizing the circulation system in accordance with the plan of 1905.

As to monetary considerations, Burnham contended, as he always had, that the expenditure of public funds for beauty would contribute to the prosperity of every citizen of San Francisco. An attractive city would draw visitors and hold them. Tourists and visitors had spent an estimated $500,000,000 in Paris the previous year, he said,

because Napoleon III had made the French capital so beautiful that no matter where people earned their money, they had to come to Paris to spend it. San Francisco would be false to itself and to its future to do less, the "planner of cities" maintained.[35]

James Phelan, with his customary eloquence, supported Burnham's recommendation for the purchase of a quadrilateral site bounded by Market, Franklin, Hayes, and Polk streets. Here, he urged, was the place to begin planning to make San Francisco an "ideal city."[36]

Civic Center Bond Issue

Five days later the supervisors voted to submit to the people a civic center bond issue of $8,480,000—$4,480,000 for land and $4,000,000 for a city hall. In the newspapers appeared a perspective drawing by Willis Polk, manager of Burnham's San Francisco office, showing a proposed civic center built in the style of the Place de la Concorde in Paris. Facing a semicircular plaza on Market Street between Eleventh and Twelfth streets were a city hall, a courthouse, and a library. Indicated on the south side of the plaza was a site for a union depot.

Willis Polk's Design for a Civic Center in San Francisco, 1909. Photograph courtesy of Bancroft Library.

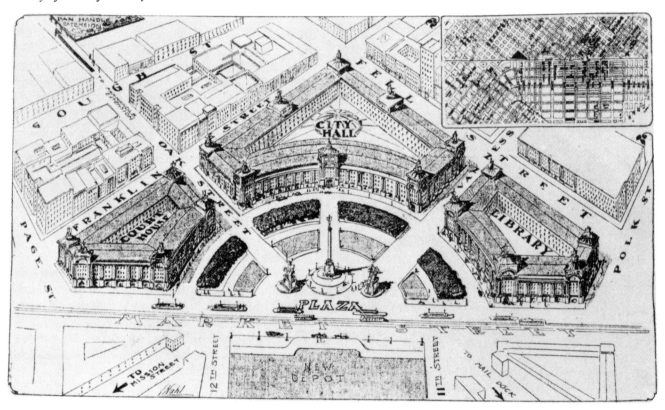

At the demand of residents in various sections of the city, the supervisors also voted to include on the ballot several other bond issues: $600,000 for a polytechnic high school, $160,000 for a detention home, $250,000 for a park on Telegraph Hill, $400,000 for a park in the Potrero district, $500,000 for an aquatic park on the northern waterfront, $25,000 for a park in the Bay View district, $90,000 for Glen Park, and $500,000 for three playgrounds in the southern part of the city. The interesting thing about the park and playground proposals was that every one of them had been included in the Burnham Plan of 1905; yet they were now being placed on the ballot not at Burnham's suggestion but at the insistence of conservative taxpayers.

Burnham was so heartened by the prospect of a civic center that immediately upon his return to Chicago he dispatched a characteristically enthusiastic telegram to Willis Polk:

"Not a day should be lost in beginning the campaign of education for the referendum. A complete and popular argument should be published for distribution.... Do everything in your power to help this cause. It is a precedent of great value to San Francisco and the whole country. If this improvement be determined upon it will attract attention to San Francisco from all quarters of the globe. It will stimulate real estate in and around the city. It will be the best thing ever done by an American city to make of itself a magnet attracting from every quarter those men and fortunes which bring lasting prosperity to a great commercial center.

"The San Francisco Report [of 1905] I should think ought to be revised and reprinted. Its wide distribution will be highly beneficial to those who are endeavoring to make a success of the work in San Francisco."[37]

In speeches before various organizations, the members of the Association for the Improvement and Adornment of San Francisco indicated that they, like Burnham, regarded the proposal for the civic center as a test of the possibility of reviving the great plan and carrying it out little by little. If the voters approved the civic center bonds, in time other features of the plan might be translated into reality.

"Too many of us are prone to look at such a plan as a whole, and all we can see is a hundred millions of dollars of cost and a hundred years to carry it out, and at first sight we condemn it," Thomas Magee observed in a talk to the Merchants' Association. "But the difficulty is in regarding it as a whole. All we hope to do in our generation is a small part. Posterity will do 90 per cent of the work. But now that our city is laid waste, and we can choose our location for our City Hall, and the City Hall

must be built somewhere, why not adopt the location recommended by the world's foremost architect in the planning and designing of the modern city beautiful and the modern city useful?"[38]

Editorial Debate

The San Francisco *Bulletin* reminded its readers of all the opportunities lost after the fire to widen streets and acquire parks and playgrounds "for the lowest prices." The opportunity to create a civic center, it said, presented a second chance "to commence the development of the city on the Burnham Plan." To reject the civic center proposal would be "tantamount to throwing the Burnham Plan in the waste basket forever."[39]

M. H. de Young attacked the civic center proposal as relentlessly as he had attacked Burnham's plans for the widening and extension of streets and the recommendations of the Committee of Forty in 1906. From the moment the supervisors contemplated a bond issue for a new city hall on a new site, his newspaper condemned the proposition as an extravagance that would endanger the financial capacity of the city and jeopardize the construction of the proposed Hetch Hetchy water system.

The San Francisco *Call* likewise at first objected to the issuance of bonds for a civic center on the ground that the indebtedness might hamper consummation of the water project, but it soon reached the conclusion that even with the addition of more than $11,000,000 in bonds for a civic center, technical high school, parks, and playgrounds, the city would still have an abundance of available credit reserved for waterworks. The *Call* "unhesitatingly" recommended the bonds to its readers. So did William Randolph Hearst's San Francisco *Examiner*, though not de Young's newspaper. Steadfast in its opposition, the *Chronicle* exhorted its readers at the eleventh hour: "Repair the streets. Rebuild the broken sewers. Provide schools for our children. Conserve the city's credit. VOTE DOWN THE CIVIC CENTRE."[40]

Counting of the ballots revealed the effectiveness of this vehement opposition. The voters authorized only the bonds for the polytechnic high school. The civic center bonds received a majority of votes but failed by 3,215 to receive the necessary two-thirds approval. The park and playground bonds also won the support of substantial majorities but failed of the required two-thirds approval. Most discouraging of all to the members of the Association for the Improvement and Adornment of San Francisco was the small turnout at the polls. Despite the "heat" generated during the campaign, only one-third of the registered voters went to the polls.

No doubt de Young was pleased when other newspapers gave him full credit for defeating the civic center, park, and playground bonds. The *Bulletin* went so far as to feature a letter branding him a "traitor to his city."[41]

James Phelan declared that the public had not been properly informed about the merits of the civic center proposal and announced that the Association for the Improvement and Adornment of San Francisco would raise $15,000 for a new campaign. The Board of Supervisors dampened his ardor by talking of building a new city hall on the old site, then lapsed into a state of prolonged indecision.

The utmost in civic zeal had been demanded of San Franciscans in rebuilding their city. To most of them the accomplishment seemed so prodigious that they were fairly indifferent to the lack of a suitable administrative center. Collective embarrassment over their failure to provide appropriate quarters for their municipal servants would seize them later, when the date for the opening of the Panama-Pacific International Exposition was approaching. Then, in a new burst of local pride, they would finance numerous public improvements. But now they wished to celebrate their labors of the past three years—years in which they had demonstrated that a city is its people, that community character and love of place and faith in the future can transcend the greatest calamity, that the spirit is unquenchable whatever befall the physical manifestations of the spirit—spires, domes, columns, façades, and monuments.

For five full days, from October 19 to 23, 1909, San Franciscans abandoned themselves to revelry. For historic propriety they announced that they were honoring the memory of the discoverer, Don Gaspar de Portolá, but obviously they were congratulating themselves on an amazing comeback. An estimated 480,000 visitors came to rejoice with them, to view parades and outdoor tableaux, to dance in the streets and throw confetti, to listen to school children singing in the public squares, to feast in the cosmopolitan cafés and hotels, to go aboard visiting Italian, Dutch, Japanese, German, British, and American warships in the harbor, and to gaze at the representatives of His Majesty the King of Spain, the Marquis of Villalobar, and at the Minister to the United States from the Netherlands, Jonkheer Dr. J. Loudon. This outpouring of joy, this first Portola Festival, proclaimed to all the world that San Francisco was again, in the words of Will Irwin, "the gayest, lightest hearted, most pleasure-loving city of the western continent"—"the bonny, merry city."[42]

CHAPTER EIGHT

Oakland—

The End of the Village Tradition

In the months just after the fire, Oakland manifested the mingled aggressiveness, pride, elation, insecurity, and nervousness of a bit player unexpectedly thrust into a stellar part. Having given shelter to thousands of refugees who had fled from the burning metropolis across the bay, Oakland quickly realized that much of San Francisco's loss might become her own permanent gain, provided she rose to the occasion. But was she prepared for the greater role to which she had suddenly been elevated? That was the troublesome question.

The formation on April 27, 1906, of the Oakland Clearing House, with eleven member banks, was cause for rejoicing, since the new institution would facilitate transaction of the greater volume of business that the city expected as a result of the establishment of the temporary offices of scores of San Francisco firms in the East Bay. But on the very same day, H. C. Capwell, a leading merchant, warned in a letter to the Oakland *Tribune* that the greed of landlords and property owners was jeopardizing the city's opportunity to become "the metropolis of this state."

"I have met representatives of all the large California and eastern wholesalers," wrote Capwell, "and to my great sorrow they had but one story to tell, viz: that the landlords and property owners had entered upon a policy of cinching them to such a point that they are already thoroughly disgusted with this side of the bay.

"For years we have been trying to lure the people of San Francisco to this side of the bay, and during the past

three years we have been to some extent successful. Now is our grand opportunity and we are throwing it away."[1]

Optimism and Problems

Ignoring such warnings, the Oakland Chamber of Commerce several weeks later held a quarterly meeting at which "the fact that Oakland is to be the metropolis of the West was accepted without cavil and the speakers dwelt at length upon the manner in which this consummation was to be most quickly attained." The secretary of the Chamber informed the membership that the staff had "furnished the postoffice department the names and present addresses of over three thousand former San Francisco business houses and professional men now located in Oakland," the Oakland *Times* reported.[2]

If anyone wanted evidence of the great increase in activity in the wholesale and industrial areas of the city, he had only to look at the streets. Heavy teaming was grinding the macadam surfaces to ruin, the *Times* reported on July 27. A million dollars would be required to put the streets in proper shape, the superintendents of streets estimated, adding that he had little hope of being given any such sum to do the job. "It is certain that they will be deplorable when the rains come," the newspaper declared.[3]

The next day the *Enquirer* noted with satisfaction that the city's trading center had moved northward beyond Fourteenth Street, but it feared that a large percentage of the refugee population would drift back to San Francisco unless there were "prompt and concerted effort to make Oakland more metropolitan, especially in the matter of lighting up the streets and supplying that variety of entertainment which is naturally to be found in a large city." The streets, said the *Enquirer*, were filled with "Stygian gloom."[4]

While the newspapers were fretting about the destruction of the surface of the streets and the lack of metropolitan entertainment in Oakland, the city suffered the very kind of blow to its hopes of becoming *the* metropolis of California that Capwell had feared. Early in August no less than two hundred of the refugee San Francisco business enterprises returned to the reviving city on the Peninsula; and the *Enquirer* bitterly accused "certain land owners" of having betrayed the city by raising rents and attempting to sell factory and warehouse sites for exorbitant prices.[5]

The *Enquirer* now expressed serious concern for the welfare of several industrial firms that had moved from San Francisco to a location in Oakland near the western end of the Tidal Canal. In the months just before and after the fire, these plants had selected the Oakland waterfront because it offered the advantage of transcontinental rail facilities of the Southern Pacific and would some day be served by the Western Pacific as well. Discussing the application of the Southern Pacific for a franchise for a harbor belt line, the newspaper admonished the city council not to grant such a franchise without demanding that it contain a provision to insure interconnection with the trackage of any other railroad that might enter Oakland, specifically, the contemplated line of the Western Pacific. The Southern Pacific, needless to say, had few friends in Oakland, because of its dogged efforts to monopolize the waterfront.

As winter approached, the *Enquirer* also noted that "there will be thousands of additional shoppers in Oakland and it is worthwhile to make a thorough and a systematic effort to put the streets, particularly in the business section of the city, in such condition that shopping in Oakland will be robbed of some of its terrors." What occasioned this suggestion was an unaccountable action of the street department: an order requiring the Oakland Traction Company to put the streets in proper condition along its tracks and to repair sinks and chuckholes in the downtown area before the rainy season. Expressing its surprise in an editorial headed "An Outbreak of Intelligence in the Street Department," the newspaper observed: "... Ordinarily it has been the custom of the street department to wait until the streets were miniature quagmires and a congeries of pools, slop, slush and slime

Looking North on Broadway, Oakland, about 1905. Photograph courtesy of Oakland Tribune.

Lower Broadway, Oakland, as Seen from the Top of the Union Savings Bank, about 1905. Photograph courtesy of Oakland Tribune.

so that it was with hazard to her apparel and health that a woman without a diving suit or rubber top boots attempted to navigate the chief thoroughfares of the city."[6]

Another sure sign that Oakland was rising to its new urban responsibilities was the approval by the voters of bond issues for construction of new schools and new outfall sewers.

While the votes on these improvements were gratifying, civic pride really reached new heights in September when the business leaders of the community announced that the building of a "magnificent modern hotel" was assured.[7] This hotel, which would occupy the entire block bounded by Harrison, Thirteenth, Alice, and Fourteenth

streets and was to be called Hotel Oakland, had so long been talked about that it had become a symbol of Oakland's commercial aspirations. When finished, the million-and-a-half-dollar edifice was certain to arouse the kind of expansive emotions that San Franciscans of the 'seventies experienced in contemplating Ralston's Palace Hotel. Merely the knowledge that it was going to be built gave Oakland businessmen the feeling that their city had "arrived."

The Robinson Plan

Lest the citizens develop smugness over all these accomplishments, the *Enquirer* reminded them that "one thing remains of vital importance to the future of the city, and that is provision for a comprehensive system of public parks, playgrounds and boulevards." Since the people of San Francisco were not sufficiently farseeing to seize their great opportunity to carry out the Burnham Plan, the newspaper pointed out, Oakland had a "splendid opportunity" to take the lead in city beautification.[8]

". . . In grasping for the immediate dollar, they [the men of San Francisco] are likely to sacrifice the future aesthetic beauty and attractiveness of the city. Herein lies Oakland's opportunity. THIS CITY HAS ARRIVED AT A TIME WHEN ITS COMMERCIAL EXPANSION IS ASSURED. NOW THE THING WHICH DEMANDS ATTENTION IS THE CREATION OF THOSE PUBLIC UTILITIES WHICH MAKE LIFE MORE FULL AND ENJOYABLE FOR THE CITIZEN. Charles Mulford Robinson, who has prepared plans for a more beautiful Oakland which ought to be immediately realized, says: 'A city should have a definite plan of development and every step should be made to count in the right direction. With changing conditions, it may be necessary to modify the plans from time to time in some particulars but the chief consideration is a general plan. The old costly, ineffective method of haphazard development is given over.' Oakland has a plan for its development and no time should be lost in proceeding to the creation of a more beautiful Oakland by the layout of boulevards, play grounds and parks."[9]

The Robinson Plan, ordered by the city council in 1905 and submitted to Mayor Frank K. Mott and the Oakland City Council soon after the San Francisco refugees swelled the population of the East Bay city, was by no means so impressive as the Burnham Plan, with its many perspective drawings, elevations, and detailed designs of parks and boulevards, and its large, over-all scheme for the peninsula metropolis. The "plan" conceived by Charles Mulford Robinson for Oakland was a short, printed report appraising existing conditions and recommending "what can be made out of Oakland, not how it might be made over."[10]. It contained seventeen recommendations in all, of which eight might be considered of major importance. Of these eight, almost none had the ring of novelty, for the more farsighted Oakland citizens had long dreamed of the possibilities that Robinson described; yet the report had the value of confirming progressive citizens in their good judgment regarding improvements that were desirable.

Robinson found Oakland a city with a superb natural setting and a climate that invited enjoyment of the outdoors. The residents had, however, no access to "their glorious waterfront on one of the most beautiful bays of the world" and no "inalienable right" to free pleasure grounds in the forested hills to the east. The combined acreage of all Oakland parks was only thirty-eight and one-half acres—"a pitiful showing" in comparison with other cities of similar size.[11]

Charles Mulford Robinson, Apostle of the "City Beautiful." Photograph courtesy of Blake McKelvey, City Historian of Rochester, N.Y.

A Natural Park Site

Viewing the city from the top of one of the few tall buildings in the business district, the Union Savings Bank, Robinson immediately noted the extraordinary possibilities of Lake Merritt and the canyon known as Indian Gulch (later Trestle Glen):

"From the top of the bank building, one overlooks a sea of houses that stretches far except in one direction. This is the northeast, where near at hand is Lake Merritt,

May Day Festival in Indian Gulch (Sometimes Called Sather Park), about 1914. By failing to acquire this natural park site, Oakland lost an opportunity to develop a superb recreation area.

bare bluffs on its eastern side, a little plot of oaks on the northern, while almost to its further end the hills stretch down in all their natural beauty, making a broad gore into the city, a natural park site, marvelously preserved from the builders' hands, and convenient of access."[12]

The city had acquired some land around the lake; it was negotiating for more and had begun construction of a boulevard round the east side of the lake. Robinson conceded that Lake Merritt Park would be "a most attractive and serviceable little park," but he pointed out that it would be altogether insufficient to satisfy the requirements of a rapidly growing community. He urged the people of Oakland to raise their sights and not only develop all the land around the lake but also create a really great park extending through Indian Gulch to and including Dimond Canyon, in the foothills east of the city.[13]. From East Oakland, Fourteenth Avenue could be developed as a handsome approach to Dimond Canyon, which was then a popular rendezvous for picnickers and hikers. Thus a loop drive from the heart of the city through canyons and around to East Oakland would be brought into being. Another loop drive, offering superb vistas of the East Bay cities and the bay rather than the closed vistas of the canyon drive, could be created from the head of Indian Gulch along the contours of the hills

to Piedmont Park and thence down Glen Echo Canyon to the north end of Lake Merritt. Oak-bordered Glen Echo Creek would become a park link, or parkway, similar to Boston's famous Fenway Park.

Robinson was well aware that the Sather Tract of some three hundred acres in Indian Gulch at one time had been proposed as a park but had been rejected as being too costly. "I know nothing about the reasonableness or otherwise of the proposed price, but I am sure that in not securing this land in some way or other there was a mistake," he wrote in his report. "It is so nearly a park now, thanks to the taste with which the road was laid out and to the preservation of the scenery's natural charm, that there will be need of very little expenditure beyond that required for the purchase of the land. And it will offer one of the most picturesque and romantic walks and drives that can be found near any large city of my acquaintance in this or other countries. Considering its availability—in convenience of access, in ease of grade, in opportunities for pleasant return by another route, in suitability of extent—I think, in fact, of no park drive of similar nature to which it is clearly second; and as an adequate municipal park system necessarily includes provision for driving and for . . . beautiful walks, I must urge the people of Oakland to obtain this property . . ."[14]

County Park System

Robinson's vision could not be restrained by the territorial limits of Oakland, however. As one acquainted with the great park systems of Europe and with the park systems of metropolitan Boston, Providence, Rhode Island, and Essex County, New Jersey, Robinson considered that he would be remiss in his work if he did not call attention to "the wisdom of cooperation, in the matter of park development at least, between the several communities that make up the greater Oakland."[15]

"Were such coöperation secured there would be no need to change in any respect the great park as I have sketched it. Topographical and social conditions would make it naturally the central feature of a county scheme, the latter mainly concerning itself hereafter with the opening of scenic drives into and along the hills, with the acquisition for the public's enjoyment of striking vantage points here and there, and with the broadening out into local parks for Berkeley and Alameda of the chain of public reservations."[16]

As an example of a development that could be included in a county park system Robinson suggested a parkway from Piedmont Heights to the Tunnel Road and down past the Claremont Hotel into Berkeley.

Certainly no other proposal that Robinson made was so important as his suggestion that a county park system was within the realm of possibility and would be of inestimable advantage to the cities of the East Bay. Unfortunately, there was at that time no leader in Alameda County with vision to match his own. But the idea did not lie buried in his report. Eight years later, Werner Hegemann, the German city planner who prepared a city plan for the municipalities of Oakland and Berkeley and the supervisors of Alameda County, resurrected the Robinson proposal and declared that "coöperation between the cities of the East side of San Francisco Bay can not be emphasized strongly enough."[17] Robinson's suggestion may have contributed to the movement for creation of the East Bay Regional Park District more than two decades later. Undoubtedly his idea was in some measure handed on from civic leader to civic leader for years.

Neighborhood Parks

Because Robinson was as aware as Burnham that one or two large parks or even a system of county parks could not satisfy all the legitimate park needs of a city, he saw the necessity of supplementing the proposed great park with neighborhood parks, some purely ornamental, others to be used for active recreation. Small children, he pointed out, could not "journey frequently at considerable distance" to reach a major park. And since a city ordinance prohibited boys from playing baseball in the streets, the city at least should provide proper play space in residential areas.[18] He urged the acquisition of the de Fremery property on Sixteenth Street, now one of the Oakland playgrounds. He proposed a waterside park near the western entrance to the Tidal Canal, because one Saturday morning he had found seventy-five to a hundred boys and girls playing on vacant land there.

This waterfront area, however, was already in the path of industrial development and was not long to be suitable as a residential section. Had Robinson begun his planning by assigning to the land in each part of the city its most appropriate long-range use, he might have designated the southern waterfront as a logical industrial area; but it would be idle to blame him for not doing something that probably would have been impossible at that early date. Government and business simply did not gather the many kinds of statistical data that now make possible the thorough analyses prepared by urban land economists and city planners. Nor were changes in technology and in ways of doing business so rapid that the study of trends and the projection of trends had become a primary activity of the business world and governmental agencies. Foresight on the part of the early-day city planner was a matter of human sympathies, the desire for improvement, and the wish to take advantage of obvious natural assets. It was not disciplined by the survey form and the punch card. Whatever Robinson's deficiencies, they were not deficiencies of the heart. And so he recognized the immediate need for a playground near the waterfront though he overlooked the long-run conflict between industrial and recreational uses.

His recommendation that the city build a platform, or "recreation pier," above the wharf at the foot of Broadway, so that the public could enjoy watching the shipping in the harbor, was a felicitous one with genuine long-range validity.[19] Any active waterfront evokes the romance of distant lands and attracts fascinated onlookers. The only trouble with Robinson was that he was a "piker" in foreseeing the recreational possibilities of the area that has now become Jack London Square. In his day this section of Oakland was drab but flourishing, but it later fell into decay. Happily it was redeveloped a few years ago, with colorful restaurants. Today patrons in these establishments view an unceasing parade of ships—and perhaps become pleasurably restless to hear the thunder of cataracts plunging into Norwegian fiords or the muffled boom of breakers rolling over coral reefs.

The "desolate and uninviting surroundings" of the Southern Pacific's Sixteenth Street station made so bad an impression upon Robinson that he proposed an imposing entrance parkway from the station to a civic center at Fourteenth Street and San Pablo Avenue. This parkway, three hundred feet wide, would be "comparable to the famously beautiful one from the railroad station at Milan," but Robinson's conception of the civic center toward which it would lead seems to have been restricted by an oppressive awareness of the high cost of land in the heart of Oakland. He suggested no magnificent group of buildings, permitted himself to "point out only the immediately necessary or advisable"—a curving street cut through the triangle formed by San Pablo Avenue, Seventeenth Street, and Telegraph Avenue, so as to link the City Hall with the Post Office.[20]

Municipal Rough Edges

Having formulated his major suggestions for the improvement of Oakland, Robinson offered some minor ones. These are interesting because they present a picture of a municipality with all the rough edges of an unregulated adolescence. Robinson commended the burial of wires on Broadway, "now happily in progress," and urged abolition of telegraph poles, regulation of advertising on and over sidewalks, and installation of handsome street lighting as far north as Seventeenth Street. He suggested substitution, throughout the city, of stone and concrete curbs for wooden curbs installed by the property owners themselves at their own expense. "The wooden curbs must go." To the neighborhood improvement clubs of the city he recommended the purchase and beautification of small triangular plots formed by irregular street platting. On residential streets he saw the need for the establishment of building lines beyond which no structure would be allowed to project, in order that an unobstructed view might be preserved for every householder. He advised the City Council to enact an ordinance banning the "double-decker" billboard and prohibiting the erection of large signs within one hundred feet of parks. He strongly recommended the establishment of two new municipal agencies: a special bureau, under the direction of a competent forester, to undertake uniform planting of street trees, and a park commission to develop and care for city parks. His report closed with a quotation from John Ruskin, that cultural divinity to whom all respectable lovers of beauty genuflected in the days of pyrography and portieres: "You may have thought that beauty was expensive. You are wrong. It is ugliness that costs."[21]

Frank K. Mott, Mayor of Oakland, 1905–1915. Photograph courtesy of Oakland Tribune.

Action on the Plan

Nowhere in the entire report was there any suggestion that a permanent agency was needed to continue the planning process, to advance first one proposal then another, and to revise the over-all scheme from time to time as circumstances demanded. Robinson, the consultant, had been asked for a plan, and a plan he had presented. His duty done, he departed, hoping that the people of the city would follow his advice. In his day the most that any architect, landscape architect, or engineer who practised as an itinerant city planner could hope for was that some of the citizens or officials would endeavor to carry out his plan; but he had no assurance that the plan would not be filed away and forgotten. No official planning group or technical staff remained at the scene of his labors to champion the plan, to remind the citizens that they had spent money for it and ought to make good use of it.

Fortunately for Robinson and for the people of Oakland, Mayor Frank Mott did intend to utilize the plan. He had been ardently in favor of parks before Robinson was engaged as a consultant. At Mott's suggestion the city council ordered the consultant's report published, in

The Northeast Side of Lake Merritt in the 'Nineties. The area to the left later became Lakeside Park. Photograph courtesy of Oakland Park Department.

order that citizens might study it. "Our problem is a very simple one," the mayor told the councilmen, "so simple, in fact, that it is difficult to suggest anything especially new. We all know about what should be done, but he [Robinson] has shown us how do to it."[22]

Mott spent the next several weeks in the East, visiting parks in New York, Boston, Kansas City, Washington, D.C., Cleveland, and Chicago, in order that he might "the more intelligently apply himself to the task of beautifying Oakland along the lines suggested by Charles Mulford Robinson."[23]

Upon his return, the Oakland *Enquirer* stated that Mott was "now more enthusiastic than ever over park improvements and boulevard developments as conducive to the happiness of a city's inhabitants." He signified that he would take steps immediately to further boulevard and park projects, including the extension of the boulevard along the east shore of Lake Merritt, the establishment of a park in West Oakland, the extension of Grand Avenue from the northeastern arm of Lake Merritt toward Piedmont, and the improvement of public squares long owned by the city but never properly developed. As for the lands around the lake, he said, "In my judgment the city should own all lands bordering on Lake Merritt."[24]

Thanks to Mott's vigorous leadership, the city council enacted an ordinance calling for a special election on January 14, 1907, on the question of issuing $992,000 in bonds for the purchase of parks. Of ten properties designated for acquisition, five bordered on Lake Merritt, including the tract now known as Willows Park, on the west side of the lake, some acreage in the area where the Municipal Auditorium later was built, a fine grove of trees on the eastern shore of the lake, and forty-five acres at Adams Point, now known as Lakeside Park. Here was a natural park containing a stand of the handsome old oaks from which the city took its name. The bonds were also to provide for the acquisition of the de Fremery property recommended by Robinson, for the extension of Bushrod Park in the northern section of Oakland, and for the purchase of small parcels in various residential sections of the city.

Robinson's Disappointment

In view of the vast park system that Robinson had urged the city to create, the proposed purchases were modest indeed. In an open letter "to the People of Oakland," the landscape architect, with no effort to conceal his disappointment, wrote from Rochester, New York: "If you vote for the purchase of these tracts, you may be sure that you will not be doing anything very big or very daring. You will be acting with exceeding conservatism, and doing about as little as you decently can do—for a city that does not want to appear, and to be, on the wane."[25]

Whether Robinson was justified in feeling somewhat scornful of the Oakland effort is debatable. For many years the voters had consistently defeated park proposals, or at least a backward minority of more than one-third had done so. Had the city council acceded to Mott's request for a bond issue of approximately one and a half million dollars, organized opposition might again have developed. But the council shrewdly asked the voters to approve a bond issue of just slightly less than a million dollars, and thereby probably mollified some of the regular opponents of bond issues, for Mott was able to an-nounce, four days before the special election, that he was "particularly jubilant" at hearing no "discordant note" in the campaign for "this great civic improvement."[26]

The Village Tradition Broken

On election day, "one of the stormiest and most dis-agreeable days of an unusually stormy and disagreeable winter,"[27] only 15 per cent of the registered voters ven-tured to the polls; but those who did enter the voting booths cast their ballots five to one for the bonds. The vote was 2,702 in favor of the bonds, 566 against. Only in one precinct in North Oakland was an effort made to defeat the proposal.

Citizens who had campaigned for park bonds in pre-vious elections and had known the heartaches of defeat now found belated consolation in the thought that their

Air View of Lake Merritt, 1914. The Civic Auditorium occupies a site at the southern end of the lake. To the right is the area once known as Indian Gulch. Photograph courtesy of Oakland Tribune.

labors probably had contributed to the education of the public. More than anything else, though, the sudden increase in population in Oakland, the sense of greater civic destiny, and the dramatic realization that the town had "to grow up" influenced the results at the polls. There was no denying the categorial imperative of abrupt change: Forward march!

The Oakland *Tribune* proclaimed that the citizens had "at last broken the bonds of conservatism and village tradition."[28] The Oakland *Enquirer* declared, "The new civic spirit of Oakland has asserted itself. At last Oakland has risen to its opportunity."[29]

Within the next two years the city bought the properties for which the voters had authorized bonds. Early in 1909 the city council appropriated $50,000 to dredge Lake Merritt and fill the marsh at the southern end of the lake. And in March of that year the people voted to amend the city charter to create the park commission that Robinson had proposed.

What the "civic adviser" called a "good beginning" had been made, and there was still a possibility that other parts of the great park system that he outlined would be developed. In this beginning the vision of the people of Oakland did not match his own, and it fell far short of that of earlier generations of San Franciscans, who were no more numerous than the people of Oakland when they decided to create Golden Gate Park. But Oakland had never known the gusto and romance and high living of San Francisco. For Oakland the decision to follow even a small part of Robinson's advice was a great step forward and probably was as much as could be expected from a people trying to cast off a "village tradition."

CHAPTER NINE

The Greater San Francisco Movement

For weeks before the census of 1910 was taken, San Francisco newspapers publicized the forthcoming enumeration, insisting that every man, woman, and child in the city must be counted. Editorials declared that the whole world would be waiting to see whether the metropolis stricken by earthquake and fire in 1906 had recouped its population losses and attracted additional thousands. Hopefully, the press predicted that the final count would credit San Francisco with a population of between 450,000 and 480,000. But the note of uncertainty was strong: the very prestige of the city, its hope of inducing businessmen and financiers to make further investments in new factories, office buildings, stores, and houses depended upon an official population figure substantially exceeding the 400,000 that the city was thought to have had at the time of the earthquake.

When the preliminary count of the Bureau of the Census indicated that the final figure would be considerably less than anticipated, San Franciscans felt disappointed but to some extent relieved. The city had at least made gains. The final count showed that the population had increased 22 per cent during the decade and San Francisco was now the home of 416,912 people.

What impressed city officials, civic leaders, and the press most was the growth of areas within a fifteen- or twenty-mile radius of San Francisco. Oakland was now a city of 150,174 residents and had experienced a population gain of 124 per cent. In those parts of the metropolitan district not included in the two principal cities

lived 119,787 people, nearly twice as many as in the same territories ten years earlier. The metropolitan district as defined by the Bureau of the Census embraced not only San Francisco and Oakland but Berkeley, Alameda, Richmond, and San Rafael, as well as some small towns and unincorporated areas.

A Name to be Coveted

The San Francisco press foresaw all parts of this metropolitan district naturally and inevitably gravitating toward the ultimate formation of a single municipality known as Greater San Francisco. Said the San Francisco *Chronicle* in a typical comment: "Probably during the next decade there will be a movement for a Greater San Francisco, one designed to bring in the present metropolitan area and to give the enlarged city a new one. For years the trend has been toward aggregation and away from segregation. Every man takes pride in being in a big town. All Cook County men are now proud of being Chicagoans. The once satisfied Brooklynite or Staten Islander likes to hail from New York. Here with us the name of San Francisco is sure to be coveted by the men across the bay and down the peninsula and by those on the near watershed of Marin County, and by that time the harbor, as well as San Francisco and Oakland, should have its busy subways."[1]

The author of this editorial was hardly unaware that there was already a "Greater San Francisco" movement, initiated quietly by the California Promotion Committee immediately after the disaster of 1906 and taken over in 1907 by a Greater San Francisco Association organized at the call of the San Francisco Chamber of Commerce. The model for Greater San Francisco was, of course, Greater New York, formed by the union of Manhattan, Brooklyn, and adjacent areas in a borough system of government in 1898. Greater San Francisco was to be an amalgamation of San Francisco, Colma, South San Francisco, the East Bay cities from Richmond to San Leandro, and the Marin County cities of Sausalito, Mill Valley, and San Rafael.

That a movement for a supermunicipality would wreck plans for a water system serving cities on both sides of the bay, and that it would antagonize Oakland officials and generate sectional bitterness which would long retard the economic development of the entire Bay Area, apparently did not occur to San Francisco leaders. Or if they did have some misgivings about the eventual success of the Greater San Francisco movement, they optimistically dismissed them. Plans for a great international exposition in 1914 or 1915 celebrating the completion of the Panama Canal aroused so much enthusiasm throughout the Bay Area that it was easy to believe in the possibility of a single municipality embracing populous communities in several counties.

Even the Oakland Chamber of Commerce, which was on guard against the Greater San Francisco movement, pledged its support to San Francisco when business leaders in New Orleans suddenly attempted to convince Congress that their city should be the scene of the official celebration marking the opening of the Panama Canal. In a telegram to Congressman Joseph R. Knowland the Oakland organization declared that it stood "ready to support a million-dollar bond issue by Alameda County, if required, in addition to the amount already subscribed."[2]

Heartened by the coöperation of the East Bay city, San Francisco fought New Orleans with every propaganda and lobbying device known, decisively defeated the southern city, and set to work preparing for the great exposition.

Slow-developing Peninsula

At a superficial glance, renascent San Francisco seemed carried forward on a wave of civic fervor, prosperity, and high hopes. Yet all was not well—or so some city officials and many businessmen thought. While the East Bay communities expanded rapidly and the crowds of commuters on the transbay ferryboats grew larger and larger, only a trickle of population moved into undeveloped areas on the San Francisco Peninsula.

In December, 1907, the Southern Pacific had opened its Bayshore Cutoff, thereby reducing the commuting time from towns on the bay side of San Mateo County. Promoters of the North Fair Oaks subdivision, just south of Redwood City, had advertised: "40 minutes from San Francisco—40 trains daily . . . No tedious and dangerous foggy or stormy ferry trips to make . . . Over 1400 lots sold since opening day. . . ."[3] But in 1910 most of the tract was vacant. South San Francisco and Burlingame, both incorporated in 1908, were still small towns. So was San Mateo, though it had annexed two near-by areas. Lomita Park, San Bruno, and other unincorporated areas within fairly close range of San Francisco had grown moderately; but renewed attempts to promote the town of San Carlos had failed. Hillsborough, hastily incorporated in April, 1910, to avoid becoming part of San Mateo or Burlingame, was a militant stronghold of country-estate owners, intent on maintaining an exclusive, semiurban environment characterized by roads without sidewalks and by very large lots. The entire county had a population of only 26,585, as compared with an only slightly greater total in the East Bay city of Alameda alone.

For the most part, the San Francisco Peninsula was the seat of the wealthy, though there were, to be sure, some middle-income families in the towns. One of the chief reasons why salaried people and families dependent on modest wages hesitated to live in this delightful area was the high cost of transportation. A North Berkeley commuter could reach his home for a 5-cent fare, whereas a commuter living the same time-distance down the Peninsula paid a one-way fare of 13 1/3 cents, in a period when that was the equivalent of 40 or 50 cents today.

Need for Rapid Transit

San Franciscans who wanted to see the Peninsula develop still hoped for an interurban electric line all the way to San Jose, such as the Southern Pacific had planned shortly before the earthquake. In January, 1906, the railroad had incorporated a subsidiary known as the Peninsular Railway and had announced that this company would build 204 miles of electric railways. "Lines are to be built from San Francisco to San Jose through Stanford University, Palo Alto, Redwood City, and San Mateo," advertisements informed the public. "Branches will extend to Los Gatos, Sempervirens Park, Alviso, Oakland, Alameda, Alum Rock Park [near San Jose] and Lick Observatory on Mt. Hamilton. The first lines constructed will be from San Jose to San Francisco and Oakland, one on each side of the bay. The main coast line of the Southern Pacific will be shortened by a cut-off from Mountain View and the trains for Los Angeles will go via Santa Cruz, while San Jose will be served by the new electric lines of the Peninsular Company."[4]

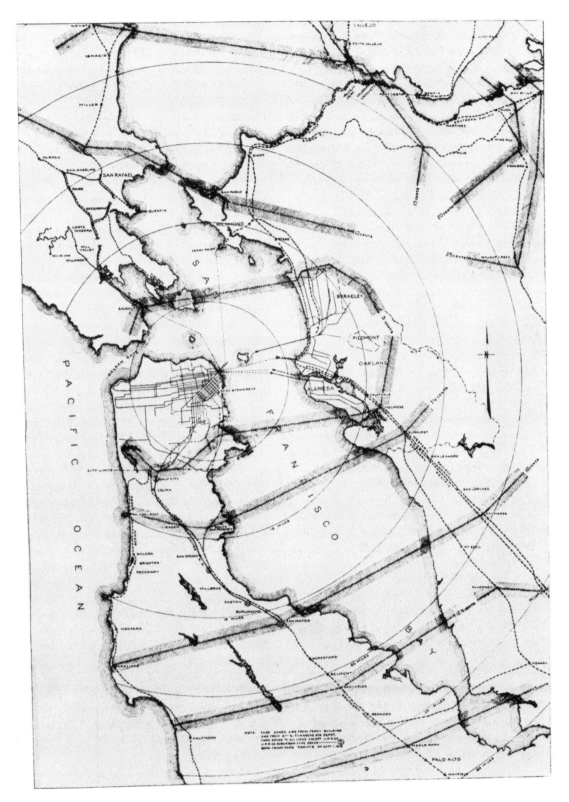

Fare Zone Map of San Francisco and Commuters' Districts, 1910–1912. Novato in Marin County and Menlo Park in San Mateo County mark the beginning of the 15-cent zone. Photograph courtesy of Bancroft Library, University of California.

Unluckily, in the summer of 1905 the Southern Pacific had faced a crisis which foredoomed these extensive plans. The Colorado River burst its banks, flooded the Imperial Valley, and inundated the main line of the railroad between Los Angeles and Yuma, Arizona. The battle with the flood was still going on in the summer of 1906 when the Southern Pacific started construction near Saratoga on a cutoff that was to extend from San Carlos to a point near Los Gatos. Presently the huge stock of rails for the construction of the cutoff had to be rushed to Yuma to build tracks to carry rock trains to crucial points along the rampaging Colorado. Engineers finally returned the river to its old channel in February, 1907, but the rails needed for the cutoff were gone.

In the following months a national depression forced the Southern Pacific to shelve—temporarily, company officials hoped—the plans for an area-wide transit system. The cutoff was completed only to Mayfield, near Palo Alto, and was not used by coast-line trains, which continued to run through San Jose rather than Los Gatos and Santa Cruz.

Gradually the Peninsular Railway became an interurban system with sixty-eight miles of track, linking San Jose with Palo Alto and both these cities with Los Gatos. San Franciscans interested in a low-fare electric line to the Santa Clara Valley wondered whether the Southern Pacific ever would be able to build northward from Palo Alto, or whether the United Railroads, the San Francisco transit organization, would extend its San Mateo line southward—or whether the two systems would come to some kind of agreement and combine forces to link San Francisco with cities south of San Mateo. Until there was fast, inexpensive transportation all the way down the Peninsula, San Franciscans looked for little population movement in that direction.

In San Francisco itself thousands of acres west of Twin Peaks were practically inaccessible, or could be reached only by a roundabout route. In the spring of 1910 the San Francisco *Chronicle* wrote of a Twin Peaks tunnel as "an improvement which should no longer be delayed."[5]

In the face of real-estate men's predictions of an influx of population from Europe as soon as the Panama Canal should be completed, the inability of San Francisco to offer ready access and low-cost fares to near-by residential areas began to assume all the aspects of a major predicament. One Italian pointed out that fares from Italy to San Francisco via the Panama Canal would be only seven dollars more than from Italy to New York and that "hundred of thousands" of immigrants would come to California direct from Europe.[6] Some worried citizens wondered whether San Francisco, bottled up on its peninsula, was going to become as overcrowded as the East Side of New York. Some downtown merchants speculated gloomily on the possibility that a large proportion of middle- and upper-income families would move to the East Bay and Marin County, where there was more room for homes, leaving San Francisco mainly to the poorer classes and immigrants.

Industrial Decline

The San Francisco Chamber of Commerce took as little comfort from the industrial situation as real-estate men did from the undeveloped state of areas beyond Twin Peaks and in San Mateo County. San Francisco in 1904 had been thirteenth among manufacturing cities of the United States, measured by value of product. By 1909 it had dropped to sixteenth place, and six of its fifteen leading industries had shown severe decreases in value of output since the Fire. Production in the men's clothing industry, for instance, had fallen off one-fourth, and in the paint and varnish industry nearly two-thirds. Substantial increases in production in several other industries did not offset the decrease in the actual number of manufacturing establishments, which had dwindled from 2,251 in 1904 to 1,796 in 1909—only a few more than in 1899.

William L. Gerstle, president of the San Francisco Chamber of Commerce in 1910, sought an explanation for the downward trend: "We have the harbor, the climate, transportation facilities, capital, and cheap fuel—in fact, everything requisite to a manufacturing city; but as against this the cost of manufacturing is so high that we cannot compete with neighboring communities. Everything is on a competitive basis excepting labor, and this is due to the fact that we have not had the courage in San Francisco to enforce the open shop principle which prevails in our competitive cities. . . . Unorganized labor has equal rights and the price of labor should be regulated like everything else by supply and demand. . . ."[7]

Others were not so willing to place the blame for the industrial decline of San Francisco on labor unions. The Fire had dealt many manufacturing concerns crippling blows. They had lost plants, markets, employees. Competitors elsewhere had been quick to take advantage of their distress. An even more patent reason for the industrial regression of San Francisco was the rise of the East Bay as a manufacturing area, as a party of chamber of commerce members discovered upon visiting Richmond in June, 1912:

"The visitors saw the great car shops at Pullman, the gigantic Standard Oil refinery, one of the largest in the world; the Enterprise foundry, the plant of the Western Pipe and Steel Company of California, started as a branch of a Los Angeles concern, and by sheer force of superior location now larger than the mother institution; the Pacific Porcelain Works . . . and other industrial concerns that have found cheap fuel, light and power, convenient transportation and other favorable conditions for locating on San Francisco Bay, and whose growth during the past five or six years has astonished their owners.

"From the top of a hill the visitors were shown the inland harbor running up toward the center of the town and the new industrial section that it will bring into use. H. C. Cutting, author of the inland harbor and lord of the lowlands about it, remarked: 'This growth means as much to San Francisco as though it took place within her own city limits, for financially it is all one. We grow together. An immense development is going to take place here, and San Francisco will always be the main office, the money reservoir where these industries will be financed.'"[8]

In effect, Cutting was telling the businessmen of San Francisco that the role of the metropolis in the economy of the Bay Area was changing. Although "the city" no doubt would always continue to carry on considerable manufacturing, in the long run its major functions would be those of an administrative, financial, commercial, and service center in the metropolitan region. This was a thought that the leaders of San Francisco were then somewhat reluctant to accept, though their preoccupation with the Greater San Francisco movement indicated that they already had gone far toward understanding certain social and economic metropolitan regional relationships. What forced them to resign themselves to the evolving status of San Francisco as primarily a commercial, financial, and service center was the aggressive, even chauvinistic, campaign of the Oakland Chamber of Commerce to build up the East Bay as a shipping, transportation, and manufacturing area.

Progress in Oakland

The Chamber of Commerce was not displeased to have a Visalia newspaper characterize Oakland as "the Los Angeles of the Bay section." It was flattered when the Stockton *Mail* declared that it was "not at all improbable that twenty years from now Oakland will be the chief city of the Pacific Coast." Its delight knew no bounds when Henri Halphen, secretary of the board of directors of the Compagnie Générale Trans-Atlantique, the great French steamship company, exclaimed after a tour of inspection on the east side of the bay, "I am convinced that the future of San Francisco lies in Oakland."[9]

If national advertising, drum beating, and exhortations to the citizens to accord their city perfervid loyalty could make a city great, the Oakland Chamber of Commerce

meant to make Oakland a metropolis second to none in the West. In the spring of 1910, when San Francisco was busy raising funds for the Panama-Pacific International Exposition, the Oakland Chamber was engaged in a costly publicity campaign. Double-page spreads appeared in the *Saturday Evening Post*. Display advertisements extolling Oakland as the most desirable location for West Coast manufacturing and distributing plants ran each week in daily papers in the South, Middle West, East, and Canada. Trade papers, house organs, and other media carried the Oakland story. At intervals of two weeks, letters of a sequential series went to five thousand selected manufacturers and others throughout the United States, describing Oakland as a potential supplier of goods to the Orient, Oakland as a transfer point for transcontinental freight destined for Pacific ports, Oakland as a strategically situated port with twenty-seven miles of waterfront where ship and railroad car meet, Oakland as a market for the great producing areas of the Pacific Slope, and Oakland as the gateway to the fertile interior valleys of California.

The city had made phenomenal gains as a manufacturing city between 1904 and 1909, data of the Bureau of the Census disclosed. Within that time the value of its manufactured products had risen almost 150 per cent, or more than $13,000,000, thanks in large part to the growth of the brewery, lumber, foundry and machineshop, bakery, printing and publishing, and canning and preserving industries. Value of the output of the canning and preserving industry alone had increased more than fifteenfold. The city boasted approximately 450 factories and was proud to point out that there were more than 130 in near-by Berkeley and Alameda. The Oakland Chamber of Commerce even wrote of new plants in Richmond as if they somehow were a credit to the initiative of Oakland enterprisers and officials.

The monthly *Bulletin* of the Chamber greeted each new development in the East Bay as heralding the growth of a tremendous new industry. For instance, in an account of the launching of the oil tanker *Coalinga*, the first steel ship to slide down the ways in an Oakland yard, the publication noted that the estuary was "as wide as the Clyde at the point at which the 'Mauretania' was launched,"[10] thus implying that Oakland sooner or later might become a rival of Glasgow as a shipbuilding center.

The announcement in the summer of 1910 that New York capitalists would spend $1,000,000 in the construction of electric lines in the San Joaquin Valley and that these lines would connect at Antioch with the Oakland and Antioch Railway, an interurban on which construction had begun at Bay Point (now Port Chicago) in February, 1909, immediately inspired the conclusion, in

OAKLAND OPPOSITE THE GOLDEN GATE
THE LOGICAL PORT AND INDUSTRIAL CENTER OF THE PACIFIC COAST

Cover of Promotional Booklet of the Oakland Chamber of Commerce, 1910.
Photograph courtesy of Bancroft Library.

capital letters: "This means that Oakland is to be the electric terminal city, the point from which will radiate roads to the great interior valleys of central California." The Chamber of Commerce thereupon began promoting plans for a central traction depot in the heart of Oakland, and it carried on agitation for such a depot for several years, though with less and less hope for actual consummation of the project.

The Western Pacific

The event which, above all others, sent Chamber of Commerce members, and Oakland residents generally, into ecstacies of rejoicing was the arrival of the first passenger train of the Western Pacific, on August 22, 1910. For this momentous occasion the Chamber organized a parade four miles long, the public schools declared a holiday, and business houses closed their doors. In the words of one newspaper reporter, the train came to a stop at the Third and Washington streets station amid "an acclaim riotous, unrestrained, and unrestrainable."[12]

The new line between Oakland and Salt Lake City, a distance of 923 miles, connected with the Denver and Rio Grande Railroad, giving the Bay Area a third transcontinental outlet. Like the early railroad of the same name, the twentieth-century Western Pacific entered the Bay Area via the Livermore Valley and Niles Canyon. Between Oakland and San Francisco it established its own ferry service, operating from a new Western Pacific Mole on the West Oakland waterfront.

The opening of this road merely whetted Oakland's appetite for additional railroad connections and for projects of all sorts that would extend its influence to surrounding areas. In the coastal counties of Mendocino and Humboldt the Southern Pacific and the Santa Fe jointly were building a railroad to link the Bay Area with Eureka, the largest city on the northern California coast. The new road, consolidating the North Shore Railroad of Marin County, the San Francisco and North Pacific, and three other short lines, started as the California Northwestern but was eventually to be known as the Northwestern Pacific. Watching progress on construction of this road through the Eel River Canyon in the northern forest country, the Oakland Chamber of Commerce decided in April, 1911, "it is time to start an active campaign for an upper bay cutoff from the Marin bay shore near Point San Pedro to Point San Pablo, linking Marin County shores with that of Alameda County, and giving the California Northwestern direct communication with Oakland."[13]

The Chamber also advocated ferry service across Carquinez Strait between Vallejo and Crockett because the service "would make the immense country to the north tributary to the east bay shore cities and afford a direct route for automobile travel which would attract thousands of visitors." The organization supported a proposal for extension of the Foothill Boulevard to Alum Rock Park, near San Jose. It urged direct service on the Santa Fe Railroad between Oakland and Antioch. And it supported a movement for a tunnel under the estuary between Oakland and Alameda.[14]

Of this project, which was not to be constructed until 1925-1927, the Oakland *Tribune* wrote:

"It is the next great improvement which Alameda County and the two cities most directly concerned . . . will have to tackle, to relieve the estuary of the obstructions to its navigation and its commerce centered in the two drawbridges crossing it at the foot of Webster and Harrison streets. These drawbridges are now maintained solely by the sufferance of the War Department and the intimation has been given by the United States engineer in charge (which is equivalent to a notice to quit) that the future improvement of the channel of Oakland harbor by the United States government for the benefit of commerce is largely dependent upon the removal of these obstructions to free use of the waterway. . . ."[15]

Showdown on the Waterfront

The maritime ambitions of Oakland came into focus with the advent of the Western Pacific, for the entrance of this railroad into the city brought to a head the long struggle between the city and the Southern Pacific over control of the waterfront. The last chapter of this historic fight began to unfold in 1906. When the City of Oakland, in that year, granted the Western Pacific a franchise and wharfing-out rights over an area a little more than a mile long and from six hundred to a thousand feet wide along the north jetty of the estuary, the Southern Pacific quickly sought an injunction in the United States District Court to restrain its new competitor from using the waterfront property, asserting that the City of Oakland had no right to grant wharfing-out franchises.

To the dismay and surprise of Oakland city officials and attorneys for the Western Pacific, the District Court in San Francisco pronounced in favor of the Southern Pacific, notwithstanding the State Supreme Court decision of 1897, holding that land just inside the new waterfront line created by the federal government's dredging operations belonged to the City of Oakland. The Western Pacific, however, was unwilling to accept the judgment of the District Court. Carrying the case to the United States Circuit Court on appeal, the railroad won a reversal of the District Court decision.

The sympathetic attitude of Oakland officials and citizens toward the new transcontinental railroad turned to wrath when the Western Pacific yielded to the desperate urgings of the Southern Pacific—still bent on controlling the waterfront—and coöperated with it in attempting to induce the state legislature to enact a bill creating a state harbor commission to administer the waterfront. Long used to having its way in state politics, even though it was then facing loss of political influence, the Southern Pacific assumed that control of the waterfront by a state agency would be preferable to control by city officials, whose memories of the railroad's defiant actions were all too vivid.

The new turn of events, far from saving the day for the Southern Pacific, served only to consolidate civic feeling and to send Oakland representatives hurrying to Sacramento to kill in the Assembly the Harbor Commission bill that had already passed the state senate.

The City of Oakland then faced a crucial choice: it could let the railroad company appeal the waterfront case to the United States Supreme Court, a procedure that might involve years of further litigation; or it could reach a settlement with the railroad. Mayor Frank Mott chose the latter alternative, met with Vice-President E. E. Calvin of the Southern Pacific, and arrived at a tentative agreement under which the railroad would accept the Appellate Court decision as final, would relinquish all claim to the waterfront, and would receive in return a fifty-year franchise on the property it was then using. The agreement also provided for removal of the railroad's Long Wharf by 1918, so that the city might have free access to the waterfront north of the Southern Pacific Mole.

While the negotiations between Mott and Calvin were under way, Oakland took still another step toward achieving its goal of becoming a major port. The annexation election of March, 1909, added 36.68 square miles to the city, including the once reluctant suburbs Fruitvale, Elmhurst, Melrose, Fitchburg, and Claremont and that part of the bay between the shore and the San Francisco boundary line. This tideland area included the Southern Pacific Mole, the Western Pacific Mole, and the Key Route Pier.

Later in the year the proposed settlement, or "compromise," with the Southern Pacific became the central issue of Mayor Mott's campaign for reëlection. In spite of charges by his opponents that the tentative agreement was a "sellout," the voters returned Mott to office with a substantial majority. On July 6, 1910, they ratified the settlement by passing a charter amendment reaffirming the city's right to control the waterfront; but it was not until November 8 of that year that the city council voted to grant the franchise upon which the agreement between

Mott and Calvin was based. A week after the granting of the franchise, Oakland citizens launched a municipal harbor-improvement program by voting $2,503,000 in bonds for a quay wall on the Estuary, a wharf in East Oakland, and a sea wall in the Key Route Basin and the "White Meat" district, between the Southern Pacific and Western Pacific piers.

Only one other matter required action before municipal control of the waterfront would be absolute. This was the transfer of title to the tidelands, vested in the state, to the city. The state legislature made the transfer in 1911, with the proviso that none of the waterfront should thereafter pass into private ownership.

Oakland, after fifty-eight years of controversy, finally was in possession of nearly two-thirds of its waterfront. The rest remained in the hands of private interests, from whom the city, as its needs required, purchased certain parcels.

The federal government, which had appropriated $1,000,000 in 1905 for dredging the inner harbor to a uniform depth of twenty feet, promised further coöperation in the improvement of the harbor soon after the citizens approved the charter amendment reaffirming municipal control over the waterfront. On July 25, 1910, the Secretary of War adopted a plan providing for a channel five hundred feet wide and thirty feet deep from the bay to the Tidal Basin, three hundred feet wide and twenty-five feet deep along the shore of the Tidal Basin, and eighteen feet deep in the center of the Tidal Basin. The estimated cost of the new program was $1,110,000.

The waterfront issue assumed overwhelming importance not only because of the basic dispute with the Southern Pacific but also because Oakland hoped to benefit, proportionately, as much as San Francisco from the opening of the Panama Canal. Even with the limited harbor facilities that Oakland had in 1910, its port handled approximately 30 per cent of the estimated total freight tonnage passing through the Golden Gate and nearly 20 per cent of the estimated total ship tonnage.[16] Civic leaders confidently believed that with the development of adequate docks, wharves, and warehouses, Oakland could attract an ever-increasing volume of shipping.

Bonds for Public Works

The driving force which enabled the city to triumph in the struggle over the waterfront, to look forward with San Francisco toward a solution of its water supply problem, and to lend support to a wide variety of private and semipublic endeavors to increase commerce and manufacturing found its best expression in efforts to improve the city for the people who lived in it. The old resistance to bond issues had crumbled in the 1907 election at which the voters approved $992,000 in bonds for parks. In the 1909 election the people not only voted $2,503,000 for harbor improvements but also voted $1,150,000 for a new City Hall, to be erected in the triangle at Fourteenth Street, San Pablo Avenue, and Broadway. A year and a half later, on May 16, 1911, they again authorized the expenditure of public funds for needed public buildings—$1,775,000 for elementary schools, $738,000 for high schools, and $500,000 for a civic auditorium to be erected at the south end of Lake Merritt.

President William Howard Taft laid the cornerstone of the Oakland City Hall on October 13, 1911, then departed for San Francisco to break ground for the Panama-Pacific International Exposition the same day. The City Hall was to be something new in civic architecture—a skyscraper, designed by the New York architectural firm of Palmer and Hornbostel. The limited site perhaps suggested the form of the building, though there was something peculiarly fitting about the selection of the skyscraper type for a city with the mercantile ambitions of Oakland.

The Hotel Oakland, already well advanced in construction as the City Hall began to rise, was in some ways an even more significant expression of community desires than the civic building. Financed by Oakland bankers and intended to be the East Bay equivalent of the Palace Hotel in San Francisco, the block-square Hotel Oakland was another indication that the city founded by Moon, Adams, and Carpentier had "thrown off the swaddling clothes of suburbanism and become distinctly urban," as a Santa Fe Railroad booklet observed in describing the growth of the city.[17] The Chamber of Commerce suggested that the city would soon have an opportunity to advertise: "Come to the Panama-Pacific International Exposition, and stop in Oakland."[18]

Rivalry and a Water Plan

In view of the heightened sense of community individualism evident in Oakland, San Francisco politicians and civic leaders might well have been cautious about spurring too vigorously their Greater San Francisco movement. East Bay spokesmen in the state legislature stubbornly fought approval of a proposed constitutional amendment providing for consolidation, and the Oakland Chamber of Commerce actively opposed the measure from the time it was first introduced, in 1910. Yet the San Francisco Chamber of Commerce, the Greater San Francisco Association, and other groups, not to mention the San Francisco press, fondly believed that cities within the metropolitan district could be induced to unite. The serious

interest of East Bay cities in joining with San Francisco in building an aqueduct from the headwaters of the Tuolumne River undoubtedly persuaded San Francisco groups that both sides of the bay had more in common than not, and that in time consolidation could be brought about.

Certainly, city officials in Oakland, Berkeley, and Alameda read every line of a long-awaited report on the metropolitan water supply that San Francisco hoped might be developed through a special district formed under the Metropolitan Water District Act of 1909. Soon after passage of this enabling legislation (which all the large cities of the Bay Area had urged the state legislature to enact), Secretary of the Interior Richard A. Ballinger had cited San Francisco to show cause why he should not revoke part of a permit issued by his predecessor in 1907 giving the city certain rights to the headwaters of the Tuolumne River. Ballinger was inclined to believe that San Francisco would never need to tap the waters of Hetch Hetchy Valley in Yosemite National Park and should be content with its primary rights to the comparatively small amount of water available from Lake Eleanor and Cherry Valley sources; but since city officials feared that revocation of secondary rights to sources in the Hetch Hetchy Valley would preclude the development of a water supply adequate for a metropolitan district, they had engaged John R. Freeman, an internationally known hydraulic engineer, to prepare a report demonstrating the need for all the water sources mentioned in the Garfield Permit of 1907. The City of Berkeley had assigned an engineer to assist Freeman, and the city council of Oakland had adopted a resolution in June, 1911, stating that the voters of Oakland would join with other Bay Area cities in providing for the joint use of the Hetch Hetchy water supply through formation of a metropolitan water district or through "any other practical method which may hereafter be agreed upon."[19]

Published in July, 1912, Freeman's report rejected a proposal made in 1901 for developing a supply of 60,000,000 gallons daily for San Francisco alone and boldly suggested a plan for supplying an entire metropolitan water district with 240,000,000 gallons daily from the Hetch Hetchy Valley through a first aqueduct, and eventually with 400,000,000 gallons daily by adding a second pipe line. The primary rights assigned in the Garfield Permit, Freeman stated, were "insufficient for present needs and for future conservation."[20]

In an introductory statement, the hydraulic engineer wrote: "For simplicity, in all of the following descriptions the word San Francisco has been used to indicate the group of cities of which that city is the commercial center,

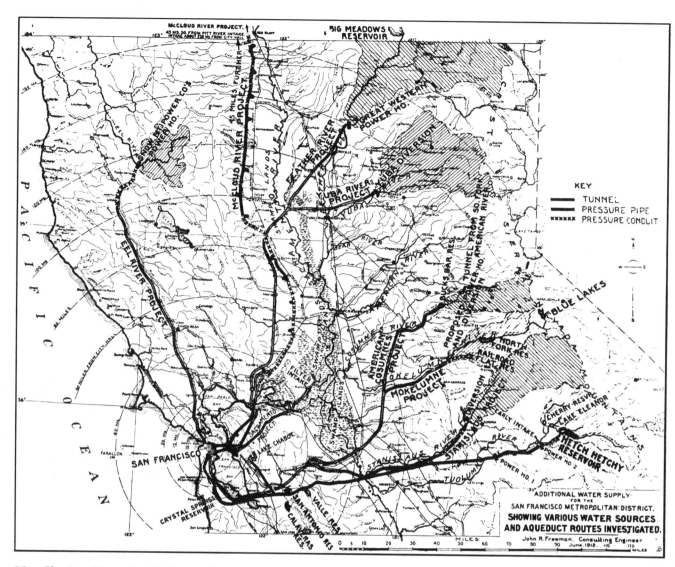

Map Showing Water Supply Sources Investigated by John R. Freeman, 1912.
Photograph courtesy of Bancroft Library.

comprising substantially all of the cities and smaller communities bordering upon the bay, from San Francisco around southerly, easterly, and northerly to Oakland, Berkeley and Richmond, some twenty-six municipalities, comprising thirty-seven separate communities in all. As will appear later, the matter of uniting more or less of these communities in closer municipal relations, possibly into a metropolitan water district, in some respects similar to that which supplies the Boston metropolitan district, is now being actively promoted, with practical certainty of ultimate success."[21]

A Population Forecast

Freeman predicted that the population of the district contemplated would "surely" be 2,000,000 within forty to fifty years, and that at some time near the end of the present century the population of "Greater San Francisco" would reach 3,000,000. He conceded, however, that there was a possibility that a population of 3,000,000 might be reached within half a century, depending upon "the wisdom and vigor with which San Franciscans seize their opportunity."[22] Time has shown that his more conservative prediction of a population of 2,000,000 within forty or fifty years was a reasonably good forecast, for San Francisco, San Mateo, Santa Clara, Alameda, and Contra Costa counties together had a population of more than 2,300,000 in 1950. A two-aqueduct system supplying 400,000,000 million gallons daily would be required when the urban population of the proposed water district reached 3,000,000, Freeman estimated.

The engineer based his prediction of rapid and continuous growth in the Bay Area on broader interchange of goods with the Orient and on increased trade with Europe and the eastern United States through the Panama Canal. He viewed the development of intensive farming in the Central Valley as contributing to this more extensive trade. Apparently by no means all civic leaders in the Bay Area shared the enthusiasm of chambers of commerce for industrial expansion, for Freeman remarked, "While thoughtful men have doubts about it being advantageous to the civic welfare to multiply a factory population here, the attractions of climate, food, and the high prevailing rate of wages and the zeal of steamship agents may bring it faster than desired." He himself was inclined to forecast only "some moderate increase in manufacturing." Significantly, he did not undervalue as a stimulus to growth "an awakening in civic pride and an apprecia-

tion of their remarkable opportunities throughout the communities of Greater San Francisco."[23]

Freeman proposed distribution of Hetch Hetchy water to Bay Area cities from an aqueduct terminal on the hills above Irvington, in southern Alameda County. From this point branch lines would extend southward to San Jose, westward across Dumbarton Strait to the Peninsula and San Francisco, and northward along the east side of the bay to a greatly enlarged Lake Chabot, near San Leandro, from whence water would be distributed to East Bay communities. An alternative route for the branch supplying San Francisco would be northward to Alameda and across the bay from Alameda Point to the Potrero district in San Francisco.[24]

The engineer recommended building the Hetch Hetchy Aqueduct full size in the beginning, for two main reasons. By actual diversion of the full appropriation, the water

Kolana Rock, Hetch Hetchy Valley, Before Construction of O'Shaughnessy Dam.
Photograph by Joseph N. LeConte, courtesy of Helen LeConte and Ansel Adams.

district would be making its water rights secure and placing them beyond all possibility of future adverse claims. Equally important, since tunnels through solid rock in rough, mountainous country could not be enlarged later, it would be necessary to construct them full size at the start. Los Angeles and New York, Freeman pointed out, were building their great aqueducts to full capacity, and Boston fifteen years earlier had designed its Wachusett Aqueduct to carry an augmented flow at some later time.

Errors of Judgment

The tremendous cost involved in the Hetch Hetchy project was, of course, one of the reasons why San Francisco was anxious for the participation of other communities in the undertaking. True, in 1910 the people of the city had voted $45,000,000 in bonds for construction of a complete water system; but that was before Freeman developed his plan for a system supplying a much greater quantity of water. In the appendix to his report was a letter from Leslie E. Burks, secretary of the Greater San Francisco Association, to Percy V. Long, City Attorney of San Francisco, stating that one of the objectives of the association was "the desire of procuring an adequate and inexhaustible supply of water for the communities about the bay, which San Francisco alone is not able to procure."[25]

That neighboring cities were genuinely interested in sharing the costs and benefits of the proposed system was indicated by resolutions included in the appendix. The city councils of San Jose, Palo Alto, Daly City, Oakland, and Berkeley had all officially gone on record as favoring the Hetch Hetchy Valley as a common source of water supply for the communities surrounding the bay. Four members of the Board of Trustees of Redwood City also had written to the city engineer of San Francisco expressing their personal belief that "ultimately a water supply at all adequate to meet the demands of the municipalities in and around San Francisco Bay, especially San Francisco, as well as our own city, will have to be obtained from the Sierra Nevada Mountains, and especially from Hetch Hetchy, which is the only source not now under adverse control."[26]

The numerous references throughout the Freeman report to "Greater San Francisco" and the inclusion of the letter of the secretary of the Greater San Francisco Association in the appendix to the report perhaps represented errors of judgment on the part of the author and San Francisco officials, since the movement for a metropolitan water district thus became identified with the political consolidation movement that was distasteful to the powerful Oakland Chamber of Commerce. San Francisco

groups, having met defeat in the state legislature in their attempts to obtain approval of a state constitutional amendment providing for consolidation, had resorted to circulation of an initiative petition to place the proposed amendment on the ballot at the general election in November, 1912. The amendment, as finally submitted, embodied changes suggested by an attorney representing the Oakland Chamber of Commerce; nevertheless, that organization viewed the measure as a bare-faced attempt to reduce Oakland to the status of a borough of imperialistic San Francisco. From the point of view of the Oakland Chamber, Burks' letter contained paragraphs that were offensive in the extreme:

"The sentiment for the consolidation is very strong in every locality, not excepting Oakland, which, because of the hostility of the political ring that has dominated Alameda County and Oakland for many years, appears to be hostile.

"The requisite number of signatures to the petition, which will place the constitutional amendment on the ballot, has been obtained without difficulty.

"As indicating the sentiment, I may instance the fact that less than two years ago the City of Alameda at a general city election adopted a proposition favoring consolidation with San Francisco by a majority of four hundred and forty-four out of a total vote of twenty-five hundred. Shortly afterwards, upon a proposal to annex Berkeley to Oakland, the voters of Berkeley, by a vote of six to one, defeated the proposal for the well-understood reason that they favored consolidation with San Francisco, but not with Oakland.

"The benefits expected to be derived from a consolidation will be a substantial reduction of taxes and the improvement of municipal affairs by giving those whose interests and business are in San Francisco, but who reside out of the limits of the city, participation in its affairs."[27]

Burks' belief that only a "political ring" in Oakland opposed consolidation, and his interpretation of the results of the election in which Oakland sought to effect an *Anschluss* with Berkeley, indicated the extent to which San Franciscans deceived themselves concerning East Bay sentiment about the Greater San Francisco movement. His letter, however, throws light on a technological development that was beginning to focus attention on the need for physical integration of the Bay Area through bridges and improved highways—the increasing use of the automobile. He stated that among the results expected to be obtained through consolidation were not only area-wide solution of the water supply problem but also "improved transportation facilities, which involve the construction of a bridge across the bay."[28] Motor-vehicle registration in California in 1912 was about ninety thousand, and already transbay ferries were having difficulty in handling automobile traffic at peak hours and on week ends. Moreover, the San Francisco Board of Supervisors had before it by this time an application of Allen C. Rush, of Los Angeles, for a franchise to construct a double-decked suspension bridge from Telegraph Hill to Yerba Buena Island and thence to Emeryville. Rush described the proposed bridge as being capable of carrying railroads, street-cars, automobiles, and horse-drawn vehicles.

However logical or worthy of consideration, arguments in favor of the proposed state constitutional amendment might be, in the East Bay they fell for the most part on deaf ears, especially after the Oakland Chamber of Commerce, the Alameda County League, the Oakland press, and the administration of Mayor Frank Mott joined forces to defeat it. The San Francisco Chamber of Commerce and the Greater San Francisco Association vainly sought to explain that under provisions of the amendment no community could be consolidated with any other unless a majority of each so voted, and that no county could be divided except with the consent of a majority of the voters of the entire county. Oakland opponents flatly branded the measure an annexation scheme and appealed to voters throughout the state to help them bury it under an avalanche of "No" votes.

Opposition to Unification

San Francisco discovered that though all parts of the state wished her success with the exposition, few areas looked favorably upon her efforts at metropolitan unification. The Pasadena *Star* sympathized with Oakland for resisting an effort "to drag it into the mire of San Francisco politics and despoil it of its individuality." The Sacramento *Union* observed that "San Francisco has pursued for many years a policy of belittling Oakland, yet wonders now why the big city across the bay should object to the submergence of its identity by consolidation." The Stockton *Independent* pointed out that "the political history of San Francisco will lend no strength to the campaign to make all the bay people members of one great municipal family."[29] The Burbank *Review* reflected the popular suspicion of bigness stemming from the trust-busting activities of Theodore Roosevelt and from the then current agitation for a federal income tax on huge incomes:

"We earnestly advise all our readers to vote against the annexation amendment. The tendency of the times for all large business bodies to absorb the smaller, thus creating trusts and big interests, is against the interests of the masses of the people, in fact is taking their life blood. . . . The attempt of big cities to absorb contiguous smaller cities and towns will also prove greatly detrimental to the advancement of the business interests of the outside communities and to all of their resident people."[30]

The Oakland Chamber of Commerce, only two years earlier the champion of a movement to annex Berkeley, saw nothing ironical in its own use of this last quotation as propaganda against the consolidation amendment.

Citing the Burks letter in the appendix of the Freeman report, the Oakland *Tribune* charged that the Greater San Francisco Association was organized as early as 1907 "for the express purpose of consolidating all of the bay cities and forming a single city and county government thereof to secure a water supply for San Francisco from Hetch-Hetchy and impose a share of the burden on the territory annexed."[31]

The newspaper said, further: "It has been later disclosed, since the filing of the initiative amendment, that Spring Valley [Water Company] is and has been also an active agent in promoting the plot, so as to saddle on the proposed new consolidated city and county its own system as an appendage to the Hetch-Hetchy scheme at a cost of $38,500,000, and that there are a multitude of other costly enterprises in which San Francisco alone is concerned but cannot provide . . . [except] through consolidation by appropriating the bonding resources of the populous communities annexed. . . ."[32]

Although it was true that eventually the Spring Valley properties would have to be purchased, by the City of San Francisco or by a metropolitan water district, it was equally true that a Greater San Francisco or a metropolitan water district also might have to purchase, at a cost of many millions, the extensive properties of the People's Water Company, the utility then serving fifteen communities in the East Bay. Moreover, the Oakland City Council had already appointed a municipal water commission to investigate the possibility of condemning the Oakland division of the People's Water Company.

The Oakland campaign against the consolidation amendment, however, had reached the point where emotion rather than cool analysis of the facts prevailed. The Oakland Chamber of Commerce had some "facts" of its own that it wished San Franciscans to consider. It resented the assertion that Oakland had been "built up by San Francisco's misfortune" and the charge that the majority of Oakland residents "lived off" San Francisco. The East Bay city had begun to grow rapidly before the earthquake and fire of 1906, the Chamber insisted, but its "real substantial and permanent development" dated from the successful outcome of the litigation over control of the waterfront. As for the irritating portrayal of Oakland as a bedroom of the metropolis, the Chamber offered these findings:

"Carefully compiled statistics show that no more than 18,000 people, living on the east or continental side of the bay, earn their living in San Francisco. 282,000 people living on the east side of the bay not only live here, but earn their living on this side or derive their income from sources outside of San Francisco."[33]

The real issue, so far as Oakland bankers, merchants, and businessmen were concerned, was the preservation of Oakland's identity. They feared that the opportunity for them to assert proprietary rights to the community prestige they were building would be jeopardized. In a front-page "Appeal to Voters" on the eve of the election, Mayor Frank K. Mott expressed exactly the sentiments of the men who financed the state-wide campaign against the "annexation scheme":

"The adoption of this amendment means: That the way will be opened for the disintegration of Oakland as an important municipality. It means that the way will be opened for the absorption of our city, the destruction of its splendid credit, the cessation of its independent activities, the stopping of every big project of public development, the wasting of years of thoughtful effort by its public-spirited citizens and, finally, its obliteration as an independent factor in the social, commercial, industrial and political upbuilding of its superb natural advantages.

"This amendment as proposed is to be the first step toward the wiping out of Oakland as a city. Its adoption will be followed by recurrent elections, producing a chaotic condition which can, in the very nature of things, result in nothing but stagnation of public and private development. Investors will keep aloof from the city so long as the confused conditions shall exist that will, beyond any question, follow in the train of the constant turmoil and agitation that annexation elections will cause....

"... Let us make this vote so overwhelming that it shall stand as a rebuke to this or any future attempt to take from us that which a fine civic patriotism has upbuilt."[34]

Defeat of the Amendment

So effective was the work of the Oakland groups fighting consolidation that on election day a majority of voters in every county except three cast ballots against the proposed constitutional amendment. Besides San Francisco itself, only San Mateo County and Marin County approved the measure. Marin County favored it two to one, San Mateo County two-and-a-half to one. Alameda County voters snowed it under: 16,919 votes for, 40,190 against. The state majority against the measure was some 60,000, out of 383,000 votes cast.

Former State Senator Frank W. Leavitt, secretary of the Alameda County League, an organization that had delivered some of the most telling blows against the initiative measure, pointed out that the votes of counties south of the Tehachapi Mountains made up only one-half the majority against the proposed amendment. "In other words," he gloated, "the vote in Northern California, outside of San Francisco, was sufficient to more than offset the 47,000 majority which San Francisco gave to the measure. That shows just how much influence in Northern California San Francisco wields when Oakland is opposing her on a platform of justice."[35]

A. A. Denison, secretary of the Oakland Chamber of Commerce, who had been particularly galled by the statement that Oakland and the East Bay cities "lived off" San Francisco, urged, "Now let us go to work and remove all grounds for this taunt in the future by demonstrating that Oakland is not an economic or political dependency, by making this a self-sufficient and self-sustaining city in every respect. Let us develop our wholesale and jobbing business, and our industrial life, so that we will be absolutely independent."[36]

In the metropolis across the bay there was much editorial licking of wounds. The San Francisco *Chronicle* found that "it was not in accord with justice that the people of the State have refused to so amend the Constitution as to permit the municipalities comprising the one city around San Francisco Bay to politically unite themselves for the management of common interests." The newspaper contended that the voters had gone to the polls without proper understanding of the proposed amendment. It concluded: "The greater city is here and it makes not the slightest difference except for advertising and sentimental purposes whether it be called San Francisco, Oakland, Berkeley, Alameda, Richmond, or San Mateo. It is one city and it has common purposes which cannot be properly dealt with except by a single political organization for these purposes."[37]

Rapid growth had indeed brought into being a vast urban community transcending city and county boundary lines and the dividing waters of the bay; and this extensive community undeniably did have certain problems that should become the concern of an area-wide government. But that this government should be a supermunicipality and nothing else was an indefensible argument. The *Chronicle* discounted the value of strong identification with a local environment and its human associations, including the ties between local politicians and their constituents. A vigorous democracy depends as much upon the participation of citizens in "home town" affairs as it does upon general concern over national issues. The newspaper dismissed the attachment to local institutions as mere "sentiment," but it did not address itself to the problem of building loyalty to the metropolitan region. It suggested no alternative to the supercity that the voters had emphatically rejected.[38]

Six years earlier, one perspicacious editorial writer had foreseen that political consolidation of the cities in the Bay Area would be distasteful and that a considerable degree of local autonomy would have to be preserved even if municipalities did unite for action on matters affecting all of them. The Oakland *Enquirer* had suggested formation of "a confederation of bay cities" to plan "a comprehensive scheme of development" and carry out projects of area-wide importance, among which would be a metropolitan water system.[39] But the proposal had aroused little interest and had been almost forgotten, though the idea of confederation was to receive renewed consideration from time to time as area-wide problems increased in intensity.

Proposed Unified Railway System and Distribution of Population, San Francisco, 1912. Photograph courtesy of Bancroft Library.

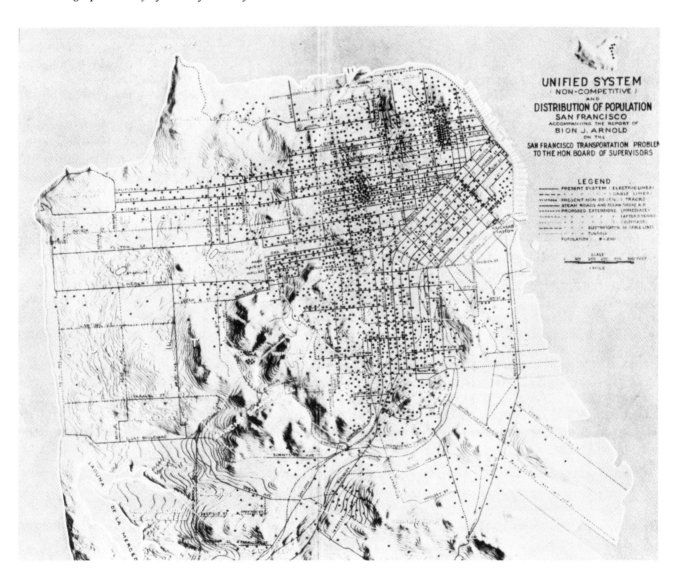

Bion Arnold's Proposal

In the heat of battle over the consolidation amendment hardly anyone noted a farsighted suggestion made by Bion Joseph Arnold, a Chicago consulting engineer and transit expert employed by the San Francisco Board of Supervisors to study the transportation facilities of the metropolis. In a report submitted just two months before the election, Arnold—without referring to the Greater San Francisco movement—urged San Francisco to "attempt to evolve, in conjunction with adjacent cities, some form of Metropolitan District Control by means of which the normal and adequate development of utilities and other enterprises vital to its life may be effected."[40] He specifically mentioned industries as being among the "other enterprises" that would come within the purview of a metropolitan district plan of control. Apparently he foresaw the need for long-range planning that would carefully relate manufacturing areas, transit, water and power lines, highways, and rail and shipping facilities throughout the metropolitan region, though he did not amplify his suggestion and it is difficult to know whether he thought a multiple-function special district or a metropolitan authority should do the planning—or whether cities should coöperate voluntarily in carrying out a plan prepared by some metropolitan regional planning agency.

When Arnold submitted his report there was not a single city planning commission in the San Francisco Bay Area; hence the idea of controlling development throughout the metropolitan area—an idea implicit in the conception of Greater San Francisco — was decidedly advanced. Arnold recommended that San Francisco create a city planning commission; and at a special election on December 10, 1912, the voters approved, among other ballot measures, a city charter amendment providing that the board of supervisors might by ordinance establish such a commission. But the close vote on the measure showed that public understanding of the need for even local planning was inadequate: the number of votes cast for the charter amendment was 33,819, the number against, 33,296. Since San Franciscans were almost evenly divided on the question of local planning, there was no great likelihood that Arnold's metropolitan-district plan of control would excite much comment, still

less provoke serious investigation of its possibilities. Six years had passed since Senator Newlands had proposed an advisory planning commission "headed by a man like Burnham," and San Franciscans were just accepting, by the narrowest of margins, the idea of forming a commission. Many more years were to pass before they and the residents of neighboring cities would know about city planning from actual experience and would be prepared to consider extending the planning function from the local community to the whole Bay Area.

To the metropolis that was chagrined by the blow to its hopes of organizing a complex of municipalities into a borough system, Arnold offered sage advice which, though it was given before the election, was especially pertinent after the ballots had been counted: "San Francisco . . . will always continue to be the business and social center [of the metropolitan district]; and instead of attempting to curtail trans-bay development, it should turn to the development of the immense acreage within its own borders and down the Peninsula. This will undoubtedly come through improved transportation and as a reflex of the Panama Canal, if the opportunities are taken advantage of."[41]

Arnold emphasized that "transportation must precede settlement of any territory." Any policy which attempted to reverse this process, he cautioned, would certainly lead to "utter failure to develop the resources of the city to the fullest extent."[42]

San Francisco had, indeed, a planning and development job to do within its own city-county boundaries, and to this work it now turned. But San Francisco was not a city without prestige and influence, set back on its heels by neighboring communities. Whether or not these communities recognized the fact, San Francisco had made a significant contribution to the growth and development of the Bay Area by advancing the important idea that major problems of the metropolitan region, such as water supply, transportation, and harbor development, should be solved on an area-wide basis. San Francisco advocated the unpopular method of political consolidation, but the rejection of this method by other communities did not kill the idea that there should be concerted action on problems common to the entire area. Today this idea has more champions than at any time since 1912.

CHAPTER TEN

The Panama Canal—
Stimulus to Planning

The fierce controversy over the consolidation amendment had engendered so much ill feeling that communities on both sides of the bay soon became conscious of the danger to the whole Bay Area of allowing rancorous division to continue. All expected to benefit economically from the opening of the Panama Canal; all foresaw the same need to plan for population growth and industrial expansion; and all had pledged themselves to make a success of the Panama-Pacific International Exposition. Repentant for the harsh things they had said about one another, the business leaders of the area began the year 1913 by exchanging olive branches.

The Oakland Chamber of Commerce invited William T. Sesnon, president of the San Francisco Chamber of Commerce, to speak at its housewarming banquet at the new Hotel Oakland on January 22. With peace pipe in hand, the honored guest might gave glossed over the recent unpleasantness with gracious platitudes; but he decided that the occasion demanded frankness and spoke accordingly: ". . . There is no good reason why two great cities like Oakland and San Francisco should not co-operate and work in harmony, situated as we are on the shores of the greatest harbor in the world, possessing unequalled shipping and manufacturing possibilities. But

the truth remains that we do not work in harmony. More or less jealousy seems to possess us; unkind things are said, with the result that both of us suffer and fail to get the full measure of benefit that is justly due us.

"It is all very well for us to sit here, to attend banquet after banquet, and tell each other what nice fellows we are. Unless we are willing to give and take, meet each other half way, our banquets and meetings count for naught. And what I say of San Francisco and Oakland applies to every section of the state. . . .

"Let tonight be the beginning of a new era. If you do this, I'll start the ball a-rolling by pledging the hearty support and cooperation of the San Francisco Chamber."[1]

Next morning the Oakland *Tribune* observed that the welcome given Sesnon "was an assurance that San Francisco has no enemies in Oakland and that she can count on the cooperation of the cities on this side of the bay in her efforts to make the Panama-Pacific Exposition the greatest thing of the kind the world has yet seen."[2]

The San Francisco Chamber of Commerce, making good on Sesnon's promises, invited delegates from other Bay Area cities to a conference called for the express purpose of doing away with petty jealousies and developing the type of metropolitan regional patriotism that would bring all the bay cities to consider themselves part of one great community. With the opening of the "Big Ditch" uppermost in their minds, prominent speakers discussed selective immigration and colonization, the establishment of a state immigration commission, the location of factories and industries, and proposals for attracting tourists. Mayor Frank Mott of Oakland "raised everyone to a high pitch of enthusiasm and local pride" with his speech on industrial expansion; and impromptu remarks of guests after the formal talks gave evidence of a pervasive one-for-all-and-all-for-one sentiment. An area-wide committee "to make plans and execute measures for the common good" was appointed.[3]

"If any bay community has ever had any small hatchet, even a toy one, out for any other bay community, it was decently and effectively buried," the San Francisco Chamber of Commerce *Journal* commented. "Everybody recognized the spirit of mutual helpfulness and the principle of co-operation. The following localities were represented: Alameda, Antioch, Benicia, Berkeley, Hayward, Martinez, Newark, Niles, Oakland, Palo Alto, Redwood City, Richmond, San Francisco, South San Francisco, San Jose, San Leandro, San Mateo, San Rafael, Santa Clara, Sausalito, Vallejo."[4]

Harbor Development

Having reëstablished amicable relations, the various communities about the bay proceeded, each in its own way, to prepare for the opening of the Panama Canal. None showed any interest in the formulation of a plan for over-all development and management of harbor facilities or in the organization of a harbor district including the metropolitan area around the bay, as proposed by Professor C. T. Wright of the University of California.[5] The prophecy of the Board of State Harbor Commissioners, who controlled the Port of San Francisco, that "the time will come, and it is not far off, when one State Harbor Commission shall have control and management of the entire Bay of San Francisco and perhaps of many of its tributary waters"[6] seemed to be no more than wishful thinking. Disregarding the board's warning that local control of bay ports inevitably meant "foolish cutting of rates, a practice leading surely to economic waste and chaotic conditions,"[7] San Jose, Vallejo, Richmond, Oakland, and other cities pursued completely independent harbor-development programs.

Aping Los Angeles, which had annexed a narrow strip of territory sixteen miles long in order to gain access to its harbor at San Pedro and Wilmington, San Jose annexed a strip of land two hundred feet wide and eleven miles long, from the northern city limits to the site of a proposed port near Alviso. The Port San Jose Committee of the San Jose Chamber of Commerce entertained visions of a municipal boulevard extending the full length of this strip, with a privately operated electric railway in the center connecting with docks, warehouses, and terminals at the port, but this ambitious scheme was never to come to fruition, although many attempts were made to revive it.

At the opposite end of the long bay the civic leaders of Vallejo discussed a proposal for reclaiming waterfront lands for industrial sites. The War Department planned to deepen the channel between that city and the Mare Island Navy Yard. If the city should construct a bulkhead, the mud pumped from the channel could be used to fill the tidelands, but first all private claims to the tidelands would have to give way to settlements in favor of the city. To this legal business City Attorney W. T. O'Donnell addressed himself while civic leaders made preparations for a campaign for a bond issue to finance the reclamation project.

The East Bay cities of Oakland, Berkeley, Emeryville, Albany, and Richmond had before them a grand scheme of waterfront development proposed by Lieutenant Colonel Thomas R. Rees, Division Officer of the Corps of Army Engineers. Primarily it was designed to overcome the major obstacle to use of the East Bay waterfront for shipping—the wide shoals or tidal flats that extended several miles from the shore. Rees suggested creating a large inner basin at Richmond just inside Point Potrero and Brooks Island, with an entrance channel six hundred feet wide extending inward past Point Richmond and Point Potrero to this dredged harbor. From the inner basin at Richmond a great channel would extend along the waterfronts of Albany, Berkeley, and Emeryville to the Southern Pacific Mole at Oakland. Three thousand acres of tidelands between the bulkhead lines and the shoreline would be reclaimed with dredged material, and a dike on the western side of the channel would also be constructed from it. Between Berkeley and Oakland the eastern side of the channel would be lined with piers.

Rees realized that the requirements of commerce and navigation at that time did not demand the extensive development he outlined. Consideration of his plan was justified, he believed, only by the probable requirements of the more distant future and by the existing demand for additional land, adjacent to deep water and suitable for industrial and warehouse sites and for railroad yards and terminals. He deemed that it would be "most unwise" for any one of the East Bay cities to undertake harbor improvements that did not conform to a comprehensive plan for the ultimate development of the entire bay

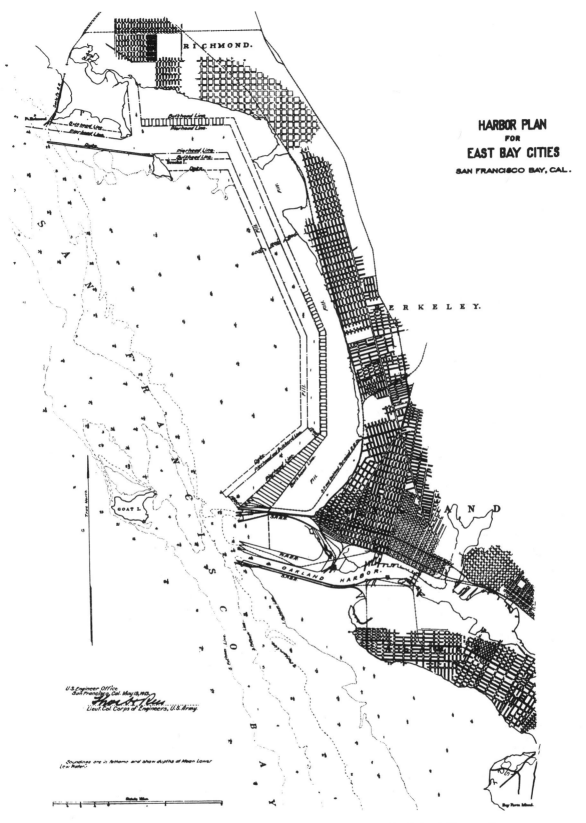

HARBOR PLAN
FOR
EAST BAY CITIES
SAN FRANCISCO BAY, CAL.

Plan for Unified Harbor Development in the East Bay, 1913. Colonel Thomas R. Rees proposed creation of "one continuous and unobstructed deep water frontage extending along the reclaimed shores from deep water at Oakland Estuary to deep water at Point Richmond."

frontage, because detached and nonrelated improvements would result and would involve greatly increased costs and diminished benefits to all. Coördinated projects, on the other hand, would give the East Bay cities "the finest harbor and the best harbor facilities in the world," he maintained.[8]

Dredging and construction of dikes and breakwaters would of course be undertaken by the federal government if Congress approved the plan and made the necessary appropriations. Projects carried out by the individual cities shoreward of the pierhead lines established by the government would complement the federal improvements.

Richmond Harbor

Richmond alone of the East Bay cities undertook harbor improvements related to the Rees Plan. P. A. Haviland, the San Francisco engineer whom the Richmond City Council had engaged in 1912 to formulate a long-range program of municipal harbor improvements, fully shared Rees' vision of the southern waterfront of the city as a major shipping and industrial area. Here, where Henry Cutting was dredging the canal now known as the Santa Fe Channel, were mud flats and sloughs that presented no more serious a challenge to engineers than the marshlands Los Angeles was then transforming into navigable ship channels, turning basins, and sites for warehouses and factories.

In his report on a program for harbor development Haviland proposed the construction of eleven deep-water piers along the entrance channel from Point Richmond to Point Potrero, a continuous bulkhead wharf round the projected northern arm of the inner basin, and twenty-one piers along the northern edge of this basin, where Liberty ships built by the Kaiser shipyards were to slide down the

The Richmond Waterfront as It Was During World War I. Looking toward the area in which the Santa Fe Channel, sites for industries, and the Inner Harbor were later developed. Photograph courtesy of Richmond Chamber of Commerce.

ways during World War II. To provide access to the piers along the entrance channel, he recommended construction of a tunnel and roadway through the Potrero hills, near the tunnel of the Santa Fe Railroad. The entire southern waterfront, Haviland said, should be served by a belt-line railroad and by a highway 150 feet wide. Further, the engineer urged the city to insure municipal control of land on the waterfront by acquiring the submerged areas that would be reclaimed by harbor dredging.

Even for a city many times the size of Richmond (the population was then approximately 10,000), the cost of the entire Haviland program—$18,500,000, or about $55,000,000 in present-day dollars—would have been burdensome. The Richmond City Council therefore took Haviland's advice and in 1913 began to develop the harbor in stages, starting with the tunnel through the Potrero hills and some limited wharf facilities near Point Richmond. Not until 1917 did Congress adopt a modified version of the Rees Plan for Richmond Harbor and appropriate the first funds for developing the entrance channel, the turning basin at Point Potrero, and a channel to Ellis Slough. Work on the large inner harbor was deferred until some date far in the future.

Oakland appeared to have dismissed the greater part of the Rees Plan without giving it proper study, for Oakland was drifting along without any discernible plan for the development of harbor facilities. Instead of concentrating on some well-conceived project that might benefit groups with various interests, it was expending the funds provided by its 1909 bond issue at various locations along the Estuary and in the Key Route Basin, now known as the Outer Harbor. In disregard of the Rees proposals, which contemplated eventual removal of the Key Route Pier and the creation of the southern entrance to the great Rees Channel directly through the Key Route Basin, the city had granted the Key Route a fifty-year franchise for its piers; and now the company was extending a solid fill into the fairway of the projected channel.

San Francisco interests, who might at the height of the Greater San Francisco movement have applauded any plea for area-wide harbor control and development, seem to have retreated from advocacy of single control and development and to have adopted a philosophical attitude which assumed that any development anywhere in the Bay Area would benefit the metropolis. An editorial in the San Francisco *Chronicle* of June 19, 1913, indicated the new mood of the leading city:

"The improvement of the tidelands which is projected at Vallejo, following the much greater enterprise contemplated between Richmond and Alameda, should serve to renew and increase our confidence in the future of the littoral of San Francisco bay. . . .

"But so long as the region about San Francisco bay prospers the financial center of the district will get its full share of prosperity. And the office buildings and the wholesale establishments and the multitude of minor industries which serve them will make business for the retailers. . . .

"When the man of affairs from the Eastern cities, or from Europe or Asia pays us a visit he does not think so much of San Francisco or Oakland or any other of the bay cities as he does of our magnificent bay. And if he thinks of founding an establishment here, he will look for the spot where he can get what he needs for the least money and will not care a rap in what political subdivision it lies. And that is a good way for all of us to think of it."

The Hetch Hetchy Grant

Although the Bay Area might grow and develop without political unification and without over-all harbor control, San Francisco officials—and East Bay officials as well—knew that the major urban areas could not grow beyond a certain point without an abundant, dependable water supply. The metropolis on the Peninsula had not given up hope of persuading other communities to join with it in creating a metropolitan water system. In 1913 it won the technical and legislative victories that put it in a position to offer them the prospect of an unceasing flow of water from the High Sierra to meet their increasing domestic and industrial needs.

On February 19, 1913, the Board of Army Engineers appointed to review evidence of San Francisco's need of Hetch Hetchy water reported to Secretary of the Interior Walter L. Fisher that this source of supply was not only the most readily available but also the cheapest and most economical. Heartened by the pronouncement of the board, the city decided to ask Congress for an outright grant of the use of public lands in Yosemite National Park, the Stanislaus National Forest, and other Sierra reserves rather than for a permit which might be subject to the whims of successive administrations in Washington. But to obtain the grant, the city had to overcome the opposition of irrigation and private utility interests and of the Sierra Club, an organization which feared the establishment of a dangerous precedent for encroaching on national parks quite as much as it dreaded the destruction of a valley almost as grand as Yosemite. Victory for the city came on December 19, 1913, when President Woodrow Wilson signed the Raker Act, granting San Francisco rights of way and the use of public lands for the construction of reservoirs, dams, conduits, and other structures necessary or incident to the development and use of water and power.

Congress recognized the interests of other Bay Area cities in Hetch Hetchy water by extending the provisions of the act to the "City and County of San Francisco and such other municipalities or . . . water districts as may, with the consent of the City and County of San Francisco or in accordance with the laws of the State of California, hereinafter participate in or succeed to the beneficial rights and privileges granted by this Act."

San Francisco ratified the Raker Act in the spring of 1914 and prepared to start construction on the Hetch Hetchy system immediately, as the act required. That San Francisco would be alone in the gigantic undertaking now began to appear almost certain. Dr. George C. Pardee, a former governor of California, had become president of a Municipal Water District League in the East Bay and was campaigning for a separate water district serving the cities of Oakland, Berkeley, Alameda, Albany, Emeryville, Piedmont, and San Leandro.

Troubles beset the East Bay leader, however. As the day drew near for an election on the proposed municipal water district, opponents harped on the suggestion that the appointive directors of the district might buy out the "mortgage-logged and piecemeal constructed distributing system" of the People's Water Company at a fancy price without a referendum by the people.[9] In vain Dr. Pardee pointed out that funds for purchase of the company's properties would have to be raised by bonds approved by two-thirds of the voters of the district and that under the enabling legislation the State Railroad Commission would have to fix the valuation of the properties. His cause was damaged when he was forced to admit that the law under which the district would be formed was "not a perfect law" and might encourage litigation.[10] Other proponents also acknowledged that the law was defective, but proposed to have it amended at the next session of the state legislature. The voters, consequently, were not enthusiastic about the proposed water district. On June 2, 1914, they cast 13,581 votes against it to 10,989 in its favor. For the most part, though, the East Bay electorate was indifferent. Of more than 84,000 registered voters, only 24,328 took the trouble to go to the polls.

San Francisco officials and those East Bay citizens who still favored a metropolitan water district again took hope, but they failed to understand the persistence of Dr. Pardee. Although he had suffered a defeat, he and his co-workers had not abandoned the goal of a separate publicly owned water system for the East Bay. Other in-fluential men in Oakland and Berkeley would continue to appeal to their fellow citizens to unite with San Francisco on the Hetch Hetchy development, but by the summer of 1914 there was only the most remote possibility that the East Bay would ever accept the suggestion.

Exposition and Civic Center

Political differences and a growing belief that the East Bay must avoid "entangling alliances" with San Francisco did not, however, diminish the interest of East Bay residents in the Panama-Pacific International Exposition and in the civic activity in San Francisco stimulated by it. The vitality displayed by this city which only a few years before had been shattered by earthquakes and gutted by fire evoked admiration even from Oakland and Alameda politicians who most feared its influence. Its citizens had an amazing capacity for rising to great occasions and throwing themselves wholeheartedly into undertakings which symbolized their faith in its future.

In 1911 the community leaders of San Francisco began to think of the exposition and a proposed civic center almost as twin enterprises. Even those who had formerly opposed the building of a new city hall and related public buildings agreed that it would be unthinkable for San Francisco to play host to the world without having suitable buildings in which to welcome visiting dignitaries and to use for other public functions. For a time during the summer of 1911 the directors of the exposition company contemplated planning a dispersed exposition that would build up the city generally and add the greatest possible number of permanent improvements. A special committee on selection of a site, advised by Willis Polk and other architects, recommended developing a yacht harbor, park, and aquarium at Harbor View (now the Marina), constructing a boulevard along the northern and western waterfronts from Telegraph Hill to the western end of Golden Gate Park, building an art gallery and various other structures at the eastern end of Golden Gate Park, and erecting a combination opera house and convention hall "at a civic center somewhere in the location of Van Ness Avenue and Market Street."[11] One of the arguments for this proposal was that it would give the city another opportunity to carry out some of the features of the neglected Burnham Plan, such as the Yacht Harbor, Outer Drive, and the Civic Center. But upon further consideration the exposition directors concluded that a concentration of buildings at Harbor View would assure exhibitors the mass attendance they desired. The directors did agree, however, that the exposition company should erect an auditorium in the civic center on a site provided

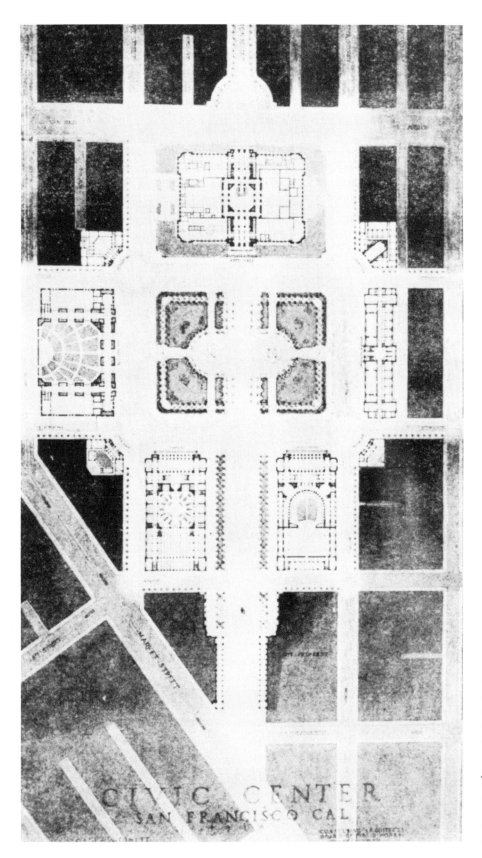

Plan for the San Francisco Civic Center, 1913. The City Hall, Civic Auditorium, and State Building are situated as shown in this scheme by architects John Galen Howard, Fred H. Meyer, and John Reid, Jr. The Public Library occupies the site suggested for an opera house. A twin structure proposed for the site on the opposite side of the mall has never been built. Photograph courtesy of Bancroft Library, University of California.

by the city. The prospect of a permanent building as a gift to the city served as a powerful incentive to city officials to come to a decision regarding the development of a civic center.

In planning this focal point of governmental activity the San Francisco Board of Supervisors sought the advice of a committee of distinguished architects, among whom were Edward H. Bennett, Willis Polk, and John Galen Howard, the official architect of the University of California. These three had always been equally ardent in championing the Burnham Plan; yet when the time came for them to submit a report to the public buildings committee of the board, they were at odds. Howard, W. B. Faville, Clarence R. Ward, and H. D. Connick recommended that the new city hall be built on the old site at Larkin and McAllister streets and that the other buildings of the civic center be grouped around it. Considerations of convenience, economy, and aesthetic possibilities supported the choice of this location, they asserted. Bennett and Polk, on the other hand, cited almost identical reasons in favor of their minority recommendation that the civic center be developed around the intersection of Market Street and Van Ness Avenue, which Burnham had approved in 1909.

Plans and suggestions submitted by more than fifty other architects to the public buildings committee of the board of supervisors tended to reinforce the choice of Howard and his majority group. The committee of the board therefore recommended on January 15, 1912, that lands for a civic center be purchased within the area bounded by Van Ness Avenue, Hayes Street, Market Street, and Golden Gate Avenue and that the new city hall be erected on the old site.

Aesthetic reasons for favoring the old site appeared to loom as large in the committee's thinking as practical ones, such as nearness to major commercial areas and avoidance of the necessity of rearranging streets. The old site offered "exceptional opportunities for vistas" of the city hall along Eighth Street and Fulton Street; it lent itself to "loftier and more monumental elevations"; and it offered a connection with the "best topographical route for an extension of the Park Panhandle to the Civic Center."[12] Mention of this perennially popular project indicated that the Burnham influence was still at work.

Because of the overwhelming sentiment in favor of the old site, the board of supervisors proceeded with plans for a civic center in the eighteen-block area recommended. It sought definite assurances from the exposition company that that organization would spend $1,000,000 to erect "a monumental auditorium" if the people voted to acquire a site in the civic center; it appointed John Galen Howard,

Fred H. Meyer, and John Reid, Jr., as consulting architects to advise on the procedure to be adopted to secure plans and specifications for the proposed city hall and civic center; and it scheduled a special election to authorize the issuance of bonds to acquire lands for the civic center and for construction of a city hall.

Approval of the $8,800,000 bond issue by a vote of ten to one on March 28, 1912, was followed the next day by a formal invitation to San Francisco architects to file their credentials by April 5 for a competition to be held to select an architectural firm to design the city hall. Competitions were then the favorite means of choosing architects for important public buildings. For this one the first prize was $25,000. Architects whose designs placed among the twenty "next best" were each to receive $1,000. The keen interest of the architectural profession in this contest was evidenced by requests from 110 individuals and firms for copies of the rules governing the competition.

On June 20, 1912, a jury composed of the mayor, one member of the board of public works, one member of the public buildings committee of the board of supervisors, the three consulting architects, and an architect selected by the competitors announced that plans submitted by the firm of John Bakewell and Arthur Brown, Jr., had been awarded the first prize.

From Plan to Reality

Commissioned on June 24, Bakewell and Brown set about designing a $3,500,000 edifice to be erected not on the old site at Larkin and McAllister streets but on a new site in the blocks bounded by Van Ness Avenue, and McAllister, Polk, and Grove streets. While the competition had been under way, the consulting architects had prepared two schemes for a civic center, one with the city hall on the old site, the other with the city hall on the Van Ness Avenue site and an opera house and public library on the site of the old city hall. Study of these two schemes by numerous civic organizations and by the local chapter of the American Institute of Architects had resulted in unanimous support of scheme "B," which would place the city hall on Van Ness Avenue. To make sure that opinions were carefully formed, the consulting architects had asked the civic groups and architects to consider specific points, such as the approach to the civic center, architectural effect, convenience of location, the position of a central plaza around which buildings would be grouped, the prevailing direction of the winds, and the relation of the buildings to the streetcar system. Fortified by the verdict of the civic organizations, the board of supervisors had voted fourteen to four to approve the scheme relocating the city hall.

Elevation Drawing of the San Francisco City Hall, Arthur Brown, Jr., and John Bakewell, Architects. Photograph courtesy of Bancroft Library.

Under this plan a new, broad avenue on the axis of Fulton Street was opened from Market Street to a five-acre central plaza with formal gardens. The City Hall and other major structures were built facing this open space. Leavenworth and Hyde streets were extended to Market Street through the site of the old city hall.

Of the first buildings erected in the Civic Center, only the Civic Auditorium was ready for use at the time the exposition opened, on February 20, 1915. The great convention hall, which the city's consulting architects had designed at the request of the exposition company, was the scene of a magnificent masked ball on the evening of January 9, 1915, when it was officially dedicated. The City Hall was not dedicated until the exposition was about to close, and not until March 1, 1916, did city employees actually move in. Construction of the Public Library did not begin until March, 1915, a month after the exposition opened. And the opera house that the San Francisco Musical Association was prepared to finance was not built—at least it was not built at that time and was never to be on the proposed site at Larkin and Grove streets.

Mayor James Rolph, Jr., and the wealthy men who had subscribed to the opera house fund reached an impasse when they asked for the privilege of bidding at public auction for permanent ownership of the boxes. The mayor denounced the request as "vicious and undemocratic" and vetoed the ordinance setting aside land for the opera house. Not until 1918 was another attempt made to raise funds for an opera house, and after a year that campaign was abandoned, far short of the goal of $2,000,000.

The Civic Center that came into being in accordance with the site plan prepared by Howard, Meyer, and Reid was in the tradition of L'Enfant, Baron Haussmann, and the World's Columbian Exposition at Chicago in 1893. It was in every respect the product of the "City Beautiful" movement and could be regarded as a partial fulfillment of the city plan prepared in 1905 by Burnham and Bennett, even though the arrangement of the buildings differed radically from that of the original plan. The City Hall, surmounted by a dome reminiscent of the one Michelangelo designed for St. Peter's, and the Civic Auditorium, with its low octagonal dome and classic façade, were truly monumental, as city officials, citizens, and the architects of the time wished them to be. So, too, was the Public Library designed by George W. Kelham. Italian Renaissance in style and adorned with heroic figures representing Art, Literature, Philosophy, Science, and Law, it was as frankly derivative as the other structures facing the huge plaza. These were buildings intended to glorify the city in much the same way that Renaissance cathedrals were intended to glorify the institution of the Church and baroque palaces the institution of monarchy. In a democracy holding the belief that government is the servant of the people there was something essentially false about them. As a group they overpower the citizen and reduce him to insignificance, whereas less pretentious structures arranged round a square bearing a closer relation to the architectural elements might communicate to the taxpayer and voter a sense of identification with local government. It is not the grand tradition that is out of place in San Francisco; rather it is the misconception of what the grand tradition is that seems alien. And yet there are those who pay high tribute to this Civic Center and honor the San Francisco of 1911–1916 for setting an example of large-scale, axial planning for other cities of the United States to follow in developing administrative centers. Christopher Tunnard, for instance, says that this group of monumental buildings may be regarded "as one of the very best civic complexes in the United States."[13] Certainly it is one of the most imposing.

Pleasure Domes

While this structure, of Ecole des Beaux-Arts inspiration, was taking shape, its impermanent sibling, the exposition, was born, lived briefly, and died, except for one superb architectural fantasy that San Franciscans cherished more than all the gray grandeur in the Civic Center—Bernard Maybeck's Palace of Fine Arts. This beautifully realized expression of a timeless melancholy won a popular reprieve from destruction at the close of the exposition and entered upon a perilous survival. Among older residents of the city it now evokes memories of a civic adventure

Palace of Fine Arts, Panama-Pacific International Exposition, 1915. As Architect Bernard R. Maybeck intended, this building gives the impression of "sadness modified by the feeling that beauty has a soothing influence."

that was one of the high points in the history of San Francisco.

To provide a site for the exposition, engineers completely transformed the waterfront area lying between Fort Mason and the Presidio. In 1911, when the exposition company decided that this section, then known as Harbor View, was most appropriate as a site for a world's fair with a maritime theme, a shallow cove indented the shoreline and a brackish lagoon extended into the Presidio between Baker and Lyon streets. Scattered about the adjacent bottom lands were more than four hundred structures, large and small, including a fifty-room apartment house, a gas reservoir, and the Fulton Engineering and Shipbuilding Works. All these buildings, the cove, and the lagoon disappeared as engineers prepared the 635-acre site for building operations. More than a hundred acres of submerged land curving along the shore within the Presidio reservation also were filled with dredged material. By February, 1913, land extending two and a half miles along the northern waterfront was ready for building operations. Included in the site were 18 acres of Fort Mason, 330 acres (eighty-one blocks) of Harbor View, and 287 acres of the Presidio.

Here, facing inward upon a series of connecting courts, rose eleven main palaces, constituting a related and particularly harmonious group of buildings. Their arrangement, based on a site plan developed by Edward Bennett, suggested a compact, walled city, somewhat oriental in character. The atmosphere of the East was further conveyed by low Byzantine domes, red tile roofs, and mellow, muted colors selected by Jules Guerin for the domes, portals, columns, walls, and architectural ornament. Except for the dominant Tower of Jewels, an architectural wedding cake shimmering with gems of purest glass, the architecture of the exposition eschewed the festive and frivolous and was of a generally high quality, though eclectic. Not only did such well-known San Francisco architects as George W. Kelham, Louis C. Mullgardt, Arthur Brown, Jr., Clarence R. Ward, Willis Polk, and William B. Faville participate in designing the various structures; Thomas Hastings, Henry Bacon, and the firm of McKim, Mead and White, all of New York, also received commissions from the exposition company. Polk was to have designed the Palace of Fine Arts but generously withdrew in favor of Maybeck when the latter, after conversations with Polk, was inspired to produce some sketches in charcoal and subdued colors depicting a loggia and dome rising from a lake, against a colonnade partly encircling it. These sketches, the exposition architects agreed, promised a building of surpassing beauty. Their expectations were more than fulfilled.

"The Palace of Fine Arts is so sublime, so majestic, and is the product of such imagination that it would have graced the age of Pericles," declared Dr. Van Noppen, Professor of Dutch Literature and Art at Columbia University. "For the first time have I seen color and form blended into perfection. It is not only the glory of San Francisco, but it ought to be the pride of all America. Nothing in any eastern city is at all comparable with it."[14]

Judgments equally rapturous emanated from art critics and humble laymen alike. Maybeck had, in his own words, sought to produce an effect of "sadness modified by the feeling that beauty has a soothing influence."[15] How well he succeeded! His palace touched the emotions of all who beheld it. It was the most talked about, the most photographed building of the entire exposition. In a world then engulfed in the flames of war the note of sadness perhaps was doubly meaningful, but this building was also eloquent of human values that endure. It had its place in an exposition dedicated to the future—an exposition bravely completed and opened on schedule even though many European countries had been forced to cancel plans to erect buildings in the area reserved for the states of the Union and for foreign governments.

"The spirit that made San Francisco dare to invite the world to an institution of international rejoicing in this year of international chaos is merely the expansion of the spirit in which San Francisco met her own calamity," Chester H. Rowell wrote in the *California Outlook* of April 24, 1915. "It is the finest spirit in the world. And the surest pledge that the human race is going to survive unscathed this year of catastrophe is the example which, on a small scale but before a world audience, San Francisco is now giving of the unwearying resilience of human nature. The world is only San Francisco's calamity writ large. As there are more to suffer it; so there are more to face it. What San Francisco is doing, the world can and will do."

The City Beneficial

World War I not only restricted the participation of foreign governments in the exposition; it limited the commercial use of the Panama Canal and reduced maritime trade, so that the West Coast did not benefit appreciably from the opening of the new intercoastal route until the early 'twenties. Before the outbreak of the war, however, Pacific Coast port cities, especially those in the Bay Area, were so sure of a new era of prosperity and population growth that they became seriously interested in city planning. So great, indeed, was the impetus given the city planning movement in California during 1913 and 1914 that it gathered momentum all during the war years and achieved the enactment of enabling legislation under which numerous cities established city planning commissions and adopted zoning ordinances intended to insure more orderly use of land.

In San Francisco the traditions of the "City Beautiful" movement remained strong, because the press and many prominent architects and public figures remembered the Burnham Plan and looked to it as an ideal; but in the East Bay the apostles of city planning accented a new note—the "City Beneficial" or the "City Practical." In a series of articles written for the Oakland *Tribune* in October, 1913, at the time the famous German city planner Werner Hegemann was invited to come to Oakland, Charles Henry Cheney, a California architect, pointed out that "modern city planning places small emphasis on the aesthetic and the beautiful, except that they may be productive of economical results, and lays particular stress upon practical and constructive ideas." Not that Cheney failed to recognize that Oakland needed "a proper civic center about which to group its buildings, a park system, a landscape study of the lay-out of a complete boulevard system, and particularly a study of the important matter of proper placing for future buildings of every kind that are at all monumental." But he wanted all this "as a part of a complete city planning study, which embraces also traffic and traffic arteries and the study of housing conditions and sanitation. . . ."[16]

Duncan McDuffie, a Berkeley developer who was one of the leaders of a state-wide movement to beautify cities by planting street trees, discovered that Hegemann, when invited "to tell Berkeley she ought to beautify herself," was a good deal less interested in looking at treeless residential streets than in "going down to the waterfront, walking the length of the municipal wharf, examining our outfall sewers, talking with manufacturers about shipping facilities, and with West Berkeley residents regarding rents and housing conditions." The German visitor, McDuffie soon saw, was "a planner, not only of cities good to look at, but of cities good to live in."[17] He represented a new conception of city planning, which the cities of the East Bay, at least, were then eager to embrace.

In 1912 Hegemann had been brought to the United States by the People's Institute of New York. Though a comparatively young man, he was already internationally renowned as secretary of the Committee for the Architectural Development of Greater Berlin and as general secretary of the City Planning Exhibitions of Berlin and Düsseldorf. As he traveled through the eastern states giving lectures and preparing city planning reports on New York, Philadelphia, Baltimore, Syracuse, and Rochester, his fame spread to the Middle West and the Far West. His advice was sought by Cleveland, by cities in the Mississippi Valley, by Denver, and then by Sacramento. From there he was invited to Oakland by the City Council. Soon after his arrival in Oakland, early in October, 1913, the Berkeley City Council, at the urging of Cheney and Professor Thomas H. Reed, of the Political Science Department of the University of California, engaged him "to inspect and report on conditions . . . and make recommendations."[18]

The Economic Basis

Hegemann, unlike the "City Beautiful" planners, approached the future circumspectly, asking himself some fundamental questions: What is a city? What are the reasons for its existence? On what does its future depend? Having posed these questions, he could not begin with plans for civic centers, parks, and boulevards. His starting point was the city economic, because he understood that a city is, above all, a place in which men pool their material resources, skills, and talents to make a living. It is a focus of production and distribution, and its opportunities for cultural advancement and civic achievement depend on the health of its economy. "The development of the wide area of a modern great city necessarily rests on the economic basis of commerce and industry," he began the first chapter of his *Report on a City Plan for the Municipalities of Oakland & Berkeley*. But he came swiftly to a conclusion that present-day economists would question: "The most efficient instrument of commerce and industry is a large harbor. The harbor binds together railroad and water transportation and produces at the place of exchange between land and water the ideal industrial site with the possibility of cheaply transforming, combining and distributing the transient goods. All large cities necessarily must have large harbors." And so he was convinced that "the future of the cities on the Bay and especially on the east side of San Francisco Bay, will depend on the development of a harbor."[19]

If subsequent economic developments have shown ports to be relatively less important in the economy of the Bay Area than they appeared to be at the time of the completion of the Panama Canal, Hegemann can hardly be blamed for failure to foresee conditions twenty, thirty, or forty years later. What he did see was that the East Bay cities had given "little forethought" to the development of one of the finest harbors on the Pacific Coast and that the opportunities for growth based on port development were great indeed. In his enthusiasm for harbor development he reflected the intense interest of Bay Area residents in building a new maritime trade with the Atlantic seaboard and Europe. That such trade, coupled with the

Pacific trade, would be the key to future prosperity of the West Coast, few people in the Bay Area then doubted. More significant than Hegemann's overemphasis on the importance of shipping in the future economy of the Bay Area was his appreciation of the city as an economic complex and his realization that city planning could contribute to the efficient functioning of the city. His was not the narrow, utilitarian approach that belittles the value of neighborhood amenities, stately public buildings, and effects that please the eye and uplift the spirit; he was aware that if city planning was to gain the popular support it deserved, it would have to stress those things which make the city more productive, more healthful, more convenient. "If civic art is the sublime flower that finally can be hoped for," he wrote, "the necessary roots, stems, and leaves must be found in the economic, social, hygienic and recreational life of the communities."[20]

As a first-class harbor seemed to him essential for the future growth and development of Oakland, he endorsed the Rees Plan for comprehensive development of the East Bay waterfront from Richmond to Oakland. On the west shore, rather than in the confined Inner Harbor formed by the estuary, Oakland would find the greatest possibilities for port expansion, he pointed out. But he deplored the city's having granted the Key Route a franchise that permitted it literally to "throw stones" across the entrance to the proposed deep-water channel along the East Bay waterfront. This franchise, he insisted, must somehow be revoked; and Oakland, Berkeley, and Richmond must unite in support of the Rees Plan. "Only a harbor that is large and that is growing larger each day can in the long run attract trade and wealth, and be the powerful instrument of civilization that attracts national activities," he contended.[21]

The Bay as the Harbor

Hegemann did not limit his study of harbor problems to the East Bay. He viewed separate and uncoördinated development of port facilities at various points around the bay as a mistake as great as that of the haphazard and disconnected method of providing harbor facilities in Oakland. "This regime [of administration of harbor facilities by different local bodies] has made comprehensive development impossible; it invites inefficient rivalry; it is a serious menace for the future and is against the fundamental rule of harbor organization," he wrote. "Somehow, and the sooner the better, the recommendable 'Hands Around the Harbor' movement must for the sake of higher efficiency lead to a uniform management of the Bay as a whole, a management of course, in which the East Bay interests are represented in a manner that cor-

responds to the superior strategic value of the East Bay section as a harbor to be."[22]

Had the distinguished German planner been alive in 1951 to read a report of the state senate's Fact-Finding Committee on San Francisco Bay Ports, he would have been interested in statements attributing some of the noticeable loss in the Pacific coastwise and intercoastal trades to lack of promotion of San Francisco Bay as a single harbor. "Much is being done by individual port and political units to make themselves competitive [with harbors elsewhere in the United States]. Very little is being done to make the *harbor* competitive. As some witnesses indicated, it is not necessarily the fault of the communities, ports, or terminals that this situation prevails; it is the result largely of the geographical aspects of the harbor area. The water of the harbor physically divides the units, whereas, from the point of view of the users of the harbor facilities, the water should unify every unit that borders on the Bay."[23] Although the committee recommended voluntary coöperation to make the harbor more competitive, rather than uniform management under a Bay Area port authority, its findings indicated that Hegemann was farseeing in warning of the dangers of failure to view San Francisco Bay as *the* harbor. Time may yet prove that he was wise to propose unified management of the harbor.

A Variety of Proposals

As was to be expected of a man who viewed city planning as a broad function capable of contributing to both the economic well-being and the livability of the community, Hegemann offered suggestions on everything from railroads and transit to parks and civic centers. He pointed out the desirability of consolidating the railroad traffic of the East Bay on two wide, grade-separated "railroad highways"—one to the north along the bay shore, the other to the east along the Oakland Inner Harbor. He noted that the suburban transit services of the East Bay had been planned mainly to provide connections with San Francisco and that transit from Oakland to other East Bay cities was intolerably slow and poorly routed. For proper growth of the East Bay he recommended extending rapid transit to all parts of the area and providing special transit highways, perhaps on elevated structures, between Oakland and Berkeley. To relieve the congestion caused by the convergence of radial streets in the heart of Oakland, he proposed creating a "delivery loop" capable of detouring as much traffic as possible around the center —a proposal so thoroughly sound that every planner who followed him within the next thirty-five years suggested something similar. Unusually appreciative of the vast social importance of decent, low-cost housing for workingmen and their families, Hegemann pinned his hopes for better housing less on municipal regulations advocated by the housing reformers of the time than on eventual rationalization of the building process, large-scale planning and construction, and lower interest rates on loans for the purchase of homes. Like the elder Olmsted and Charles Mulford Robinson, he recognized the possibilities of developing parks and scenic parkways along the creeks and canyons in the Berkeley Hills, including the beautiful Indian Gulch, or Sather Tract, northeast of Lake Merritt in Oakland. In addition to these, he proposed a Midway Plaisance or chain of parks and playgrounds through central Berkeley and an Island Park on the fill that would form the west side of the projected Rees Channel. Opportunity to develop the Midway Plaisance was lost within a few years by rapid building in the area designated, but something similar to the Island Park might be achieved in the future if Berkeley ever fills the thousands of acres of tidelands that belong to it. In his final chapter Hegemann suggested, among other things, a group of public buildings in the general area in which Oakland is slowly building an administrative and cultural center, near the southwestern end of Lake Merritt.

Campus Development

At the time Hegemann was in the East Bay, John Galen Howard published a revision of his plan of 1908 for the campus of the University of California. The revised scheme, relating numerous detached buildings to a broad, formal, east-west axis parallel to the axis proposed by the elder Olmsted in 1866, impressed the German planner as being a design for a development that would surpass any civic center in the state and even the capitol grounds in Sacramento. He had, however, grave doubts that the plan could be adhered to as the needs of the university changed, and he questioned whether, "in view of the menacing lack of space," it would be possible—and artistically desirable —"to try the difficult experiment of basing the final formal effect upon grouping of detached buildings." He was inclined to believe that a scheme which made provision for physically connecting buildings as additions were needed would produce a more satisfying campus in the long run, although he conceded that "the idea of having the buildings all detached is more worthy of California, where the climate makes every walk from one building to another a real delight."[24]

Howard's revised plan of 1914 was adopted by the Regents of the University as a basis for guiding the future building program and was, with occasional modifications, followed until the 'forties. In the period 1902–1914 Howard had arranged the Hearst Memorial Mining Building, the Charles Franklin Doe Library, Agriculture Hall, and other buildings for which he prepared plans, in relation to the axis shown in his 1908 and 1914 plans. Upon the passage, in November, 1914, of a state bond issue of $1,800,000 for new construction at the university, three new buildings—Wheeler Hall, Gilman Hall, and Hilgard Hall—were immediately begun, all placed in accordance with the revised plan. Thus the scheme of detached buildings related to an axis centering on the Golden Gate was well along toward realization soon after Hegemann wrote his report.

Planning Commissions

The German planner closed his report with a recommendation that the city councils of Oakland and Berkeley adopt ordinances providing for the appointment of city planning commissions at once. Indeed, he saw the need for planning bodies in all the East Bay cities, for frequent convocations of all the commissions, and for exchange of information among the "permanent secretaries" of the commissions. He did not, however, mention the need for metropolitan regional planning, or what Bion Arnold called "metropolitan district control," although a plea for such planning might have been expected from one who regarded San Francisco Bay as a single harbor. Hegemann tended, in the short time that he was in the Bay Area, to become a partisan of the East Bay. Nevertheless, he influenced the whole Bay Area by advocating the creation of planning commissions with "sufficient funds at their disposal not only to employ permanent secretaries but also outside expert advice on important issues in the solution of each of their particular problems." And he stated clearly what the individual communities needed: "a city-plan, very flexible in detail but firm in all matters of principle," which once having been worked out could be "safeguarded and made efficient by legislative acts, ordinances, funds, and daily practice."[25] In other words, the plan was not an end in itself but a guide for developing a better city. The process of carrying it out was as important as the plan itself.

Hegemann's report, though completed in 1914, was not published until 1915. By that time it was but one of many documents emphasizing the need for local planning bodies. San Francisco and Berkeley had already taken steps toward establishing official city planning commissions—the former by passing an ordinance authorizing the appointment of a city planning commission, the latter by creating a semiofficial body called the City Planning Committee. A permanent, official commission would have been established in Berkeley, however, if the city charter

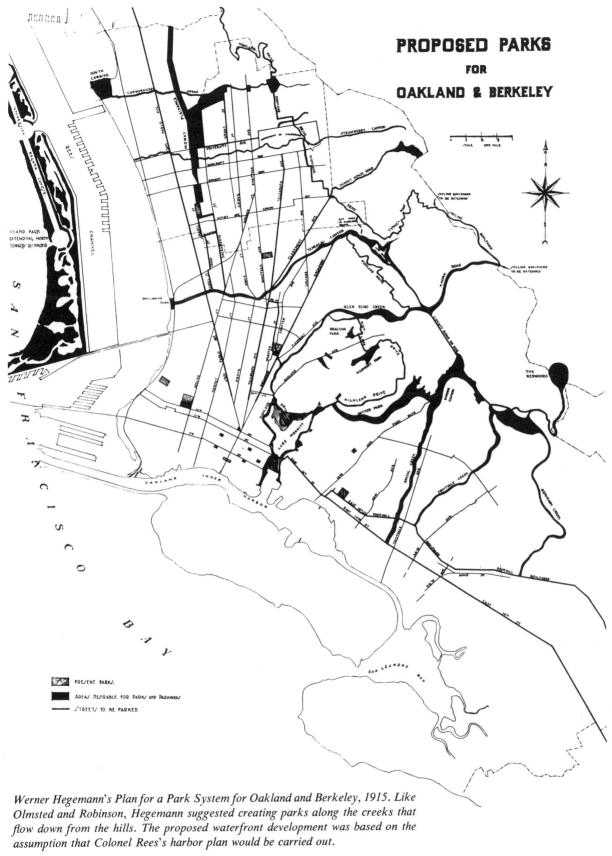

Werner Hegemann's Plan for a Park System for Oakland and Berkeley, 1915. Like Olmsted and Robinson, Hegemann suggested creating parks along the creeks that flow down from the hills. The proposed waterfront development was based on the assumption that Colonel Rees's harbor plan would be carried out.

had not provided for setting up a city planning organization to be called the Civic Art Commission. Since the term "civic art" was then in disrepute, the city council was unwilling to risk passing an ordinance establishing an official body with the title mentioned in the charter.

A Crusader for Planning

The major credit for new planning developments in the Bay Area belongs not so much to Hegemann as to Charles Henry Cheney, who seems almost to have used the German planner as an instrument for fulfilling his own burning desire to have city planning accepted as a new and permanent function of local government. Cheney was one of those able propagandists who appear in the vanguard of every important movement. After he was graduated in architecture from the University of California in 1905, he studied at the Ecole des Beaux-Arts in Paris, traveled extensively on the continent and in England, and lived in New York, learning everything he could about "the best city planning thought and development in this country."[26] When he returned to California in 1912, he was fired with zeal for the cause of city planning. He wrote articles on planning for newspapers, advocated the employment of Hegemann by Oakland and Berkeley, was prominently instrumental in bringing to Oakland and San Francisco a huge city planning exhibit prepared by the American City Bureau of New York, and was a prime mover in the organization of the city planning section of the Commonwealth Club.

Through the Commonwealth Club the young architect met Percy V. Long, San Francisco City Attorney, who became his steadfast partner in the crusade for city planning. Long at first thought that city planning was primarily a matter of aesthetics; but once Cheney convinced him that it was a "sensible and practical" means of effecting municipal economies and saving the taxpayers money, he plunged into the work of drafting enabling legislation for local planning and helped Cheney arrange a state-wide conference on city planning, to be held in Monterey, October 12–14, 1914.

Long enlisted the talents of the San Francisco Bay Area City Attorneys' Club in formulating the desired planning act. Cheney sent invitations to the conference to the city councilmen of every city in California, city engineers and city architects, chambers of commerce and other promotional organizations, city clubs and municipal leagues, improvement clubs, real-estate associations, societies of engineers and architects, the Commonwealth Club, and park, harbor, housing, industrial, and other commissions. In southern California he had active support for his and Long's organizing efforts from a number

Charles Henry Cheney, Crusader for City Planning. Photograph courtesy of Warren Cheney.

of men who had attended the national planning conferences held annually in the East ever since 1909.

The first California Conference on City Planning was neatly calculated to impress the state legislature with the widespread support for proposed planning legislation. It was held simultaneously with the seventeenth annual meeting of the League of California Municipalities, so that city officials attending sessions of the League might also participate in conference deliberations. Long, Cheney, and Gordon Whitnall, who was among the stalwarts of the planning movement in southern California, made many converts to their cause, and by the close of the conference had won overwhelming endorsement of the proposed planning law drafted by the city attorneys of the Bay Area.

The Local Planning Act

As passed by the legislature on May 21, 1915, the first city planning enabling act of the State of California differed only in minor details from the measure discussed at Monterey. It made physical planning permissive for cities rather than mandatory, because a mandatory provision would not have been in accord with the local home-rule provisions incorporated in the State Constitution. It authorized the legislative body of each municipality to create a nonpaid citizens' commission which, as an advisory body, would make recommendations to various officials, the legislative body, and even to private corporations and individuals concerning the future growth, development, and beautification of the municipality. To provide a basis for its recommendations, the commission was authorized "to prepare maps or plans" for the physical development of the city, including not only plans for streets, parks, public and private buildings, works, and grounds, but plans for sanitation, utilities, harbor, shipping, and transportation facilities. Thus this pioneer legislation extended the scope of city planning far beyond what it had been in the "City Beautiful" days. Further, the new law provided that the city council should refer plans of proposed subdivisions to the planning commission for report and recommendation before taking final action. The act also authorized the council to zone the city on the advice of the city planning commission, designating appropriate areas for residence, commerce, and industry.

Like all legislation in a new field, the act contained phraseology that was broad, vague, and ambiguous. It was, moreover, almost an open invitation to cities to undertake piecemeal planning, because it failed to indicate the interrelatedness and interdependence of the various plans mentioned. But its explicit authorization of physical planning ended permanently all controversies over whether cities could legally carry on city planning as a continuing, official function under the broad grants of power given them in the State Constitution.

Commissions in Action

San Bruno, in San Mateo County, is generally credited with being the first charterless California city to establish a city planning commission under the 1915 planning enabling act. Other cities in the Bay Area which promptly availed themselves of the authorization to create planning commissions were San Rafael and Martinez. Palo Alto and San Jose followed their example in 1916, Alameda in 1917, Richmond in 1918, and San Mateo in 1920.

After passage of the 1915 act the Berkeley City Council mustered sufficient courage to enact an ordinance establishing a city planning commission with the unpopular name Civic Art Commission, as the charter required. Duncan McDuffie, its president, undertook to allay the suspicion that this aesthetic designation aroused. In talks to citizens he sought to emphasize the broad approach of the commission to the planning function: "The commission must know all there is to know about Berkeley . . . before it can plan wisely."[27]

From his remarks a citizen might have gathered that the new commission intended to prepare a comprehensive plan showing what Berkeley could become if it made the most of its economic and cultural opportunities. But the Civic Art Commission actually had no funds for the preparation of such a plan. Moreover, though the members of the commission talked about broad-scale planning, their primary interest proved to be zoning, then being adopted as a practical means of safeguarding cities from the obvious chaos created by the invasion of apartment houses, stores, and even factories into single-family residential districts. The preparation of a zoning or districting ordinance was the first undertaking of the Civic Art Commission.

The measure it recommended to the Berkeley City Council in 1916 set up eight classifications of zones that could be established for particular areas upon petition of the owners of at least 25 per cent of the street frontage. Since more than 90 per cent of all the buildings in Berkeley were single-family residences, the primary purpose of the ordinance was to substitute municipal regulation for the deed restrictions imposed by private developers. These restrictions were expiring in some residential areas and had only a few years to run in other areas. Property owners, therefore, feared that the value of their homes would be destroyed by unwelcome flats and apartments or, worse still, by stores and small factories. The ordinance did provide, however, for two classifications of districts in which industry would be protected from the intrusion of residences—a most unusual feature at a time when residential areas were being accorded much protection and industrial districts were offered little or none.

Under this experimental legislation, which the city council adopted on March 28, 1916, Berkeley embarked upon a program of piecemeal zoning that preserved existing conditions. The whole practice of zoning was so novel that the planning commissioners and Cheney, their consultant, were of the opinion that an apartment house which happened to be in a single-family residential area would have to be zoned in a separate classification, instead of being included as a nonconforming use.

The Demand for Zoning

Four months after Berkeley adopted its ordinance providing for zoning by petition, New York City adopted the first comprehensive zoning ordinance in the United States, under which every block in the five boroughs of the city was placed in one of three classes of use districts: residential, commercial, and unrestricted (chiefly industrial). The ordinance also created five classes of districts limiting the height of buildings and five limiting the percentage of the lot that might be built upon. The example thus set by the largest municipality in the nation tended to focus the attention of cities throughout the country on problems of haphazard and unregulated development— overcrowding of the land, lack of air space and light between buildings, excessive density of population in tenement areas, and dangerous and unhealthful mixtures of machine shops, laundries, smoke-producing factories, and residential structures. Uncritical enthusiasts failed to note that the "model" New York ordinance was a fantastically unrealistic enactment which permitted enough building to house 77,000,000 people. To these new champions of zoning, this form of regulation was principally a device for preventing property losses. City assessors, particularly, viewed zoning as a type of fiscal salvation. "Improper development" in residential areas, they informed worried citizens, would considerably reduce assessed valuations and thereby cause the city to lose large sums of taxes, whereas zoning would assure the maintenance of the tax base. Zoning was a "must." To be without it was to invite individual and collective ruin.

In the spring of 1917 the city planning section of the Commonwealth Club sent a questionnaire to more than three hundred and fifty bankers, real-estate owners, and the city assessors of San Francisco and neighboring cities asking them to list examples of the intrusion of garages, stables, laundries, planing mills, undertaking parlors, and apartment houses in residential districts. On the basis of replies received, the section concluded that "many concrete instances clearly show the enormous cost of lack of regulation" and that "in San Francisco proper over one-half the total property, assessed for over three hundred million dollars, is . . . adversely affected for lack of a zone ordinance, such as Los Angeles, New York, Minneapolis and every other progressive city already has put into effect."[28]

Concern over zoning had now become so great throughout California that people interested in city planning gave little thought to anything else. Indeed, zoning *was* city planning to many city officials, real-estate men, and property owners. But there was much doubt whether the police power granted to cities by the State Constitution of 1879 was sufficient to permit them to enact valid zoning ordinances, and whether unchartered cities governed under the Municipal Corporations Act of 1883 legally could adopt zoning ordinances. The city planning enabling legislation of 1915 mentioned zoning as one of

the functions of city planning commissions but did not make clear the purpose or scope of zoning. Hence the California Conference on City Planning, the League of California Municipalities, the Commonwealth Club, and other organizations united in sponsoring enabling legislation authorizing cities to enact zoning regulations. The state legislature approved the proposed legislation in 1917.

The Zoning Enabling Act

The statute gave cities the explicit power to regulate private property by establishing zones or districts within which the use of property, the height of buildings, and the amount of open space could be controlled. In enacting zoning ordinances, city councils were to give reasonable consideration, among other things, to the direction of building development in accord with a "well considered plan"; but just what constituted "a well considered plan" the 1917 act did not state. Indeed, the act encouraged zoning with no reference to long-range planning by permitting cities which had no city planning commission to adopt zoning ordinances. Consequently, within the next two decades many cities adopted zoning regulations framed by city attorneys, city engineers, and others with little or no knowledge of the relationships between city planning and zoning. Instead of being used as a means of bringing about more appropriate and efficient uses of land, zoning often was an instrument for freezing existing uses, however undesirable these might be in some instances.

In San Francisco, which was still without a city planning commission even after the zoning enabling act went into effect on July 26, 1917, Mayor James Rolph, Jr., suddenly found himself under tremendous pressure to appoint planning commissioners. First, however, he demanded that the ordinance providing for the commission be revised. He notified the city planning section of the Commonwealth Club that he would name a committee of citizens to redraft the ordinance, and that if the revision met his approval, he would name the commissioners. Among the members of the committee he selected to revise the ordinance was Charles Cheney, the tireless and omnipresent Mr. City Planning.

By this time the agitation for a planning commission in San Francisco had shifted from arguments based on planning considerations to arguments based on the maintenance of property values through zoning. In 1915, when the Panama-Pacific International Exposition was in full swing, the San Francisco *Call*, the Downtown Association, the Home Industry League, the Rotary Club, and various architects, including Willis Polk, had all urged the appointment of a planning commission, so that the city might take steps to preserve as permanent improvements the Marina, the Palace of Fine Arts, the California Building, and certain other outstanding features of the exposition. Those interested in saving as much as possible of the exposition hoped that the formulation of detailed plans for the Marina and its vicinity would lead to preparation of a general plan that would show proposed improvements for all parts of the city. But a year or more after the exposition closed, the hue and cry for zoning drowned out pleas for a comprehensive plan. The Chamber of Commerce, the Real Estate Board, and other influential organizations wanted a city planning commission that would first of all prepare a zoning plan and a zoning ordinance.

And that is exactly what the commission appointed by Mayor Rolph on December 28, 1917, set about doing. It became almost exclusively concerned with a survey of the utilization of land in the city as a basis for determining various classes of zones rather than as the basis for preparing a flexible, over-all plan of the kind Hegemann would have recommended.

The Engineer as Planner

In the meantime, Michael M. O'Shaughnessy, the broad-gauge city engineer of San Francisco, continued to serve the community as a sort of city planner ex officio, as he had almost from the time he first became head of the engineering department. In the period 1912–1934 his name is associated with numerous public improvements that greatly influenced the course of physical development in the metropolis. Many of the projects carried out under his direction were, moreover, projects that had been suggested by Burnham, Bennett, Bion Arnold, and others who had a large vision of what San Francisco might become if its public officials, as representatives of the electorate, made certain farsighted policy decisions. O'Shaughnessy, although he was at times arrogant and inclined to impose his will upon others, understood that city development requires not only official action but also public participation, especially in the approval of bond issues, and the coöperation of private interests, particularly subdividers. He was tireless in his work with civic groups, with other city officials, with citizens and officials in neighboring cities and counties, and with state and federal agencies. His influence consequently extended beyond the sphere of his own department and made itself felt in matters affecting the entire Bay Area.

As one of the projectors of the Municipal Railway, O'Shaughnessy helped to develop areas of San Francisco which had long remained inaccessible—areas in which thousands of workers who lived in the East Bay might have made their homes had transportation been available.

These were the districts west of Twin Peaks, the Richmond and Marina districts, the remoter sections of North Beach, and the Mission district. Like Bion Arnold, O'Shaughnessy saw that new railway lines should be extended to these districts even though the lines might operate "in the red" for years. The primary purpose of a municipal public utility is to give service, he was fond of pointing out to critics who opposed the policy of using the "Muni" as a means of "developing the city's growth in well-ordered and predetermined directions."[29] With him as its ardent champion, this policy was consistently followed year in and year out, until the Municipal Railway was expanded from the initial, relatively short, Geary Street line in 1912 to sixty-three miles of single track in 1919. New houses sprang up by the hundreds in all the areas penetrated by the publicly owned transit facilities—the visible vindication of the policy of constructing extensions in advance of actual necessity.

Two important tunnel projects were involved in the program of railway expansion—the Stockton Street Tunnel, completed in December, 1914, and the Twin Peaks Tunnel, through which the Twin Peaks Tunnel Railway began operating on February 3, 1918. This latter bore was 11,750 feet long, fully a mile shorter than the tunnel proposed by one of the engineers employed by Bion Arnold. Since the project had to be financed by an assessment district, O'Shaughnessy had shortened the route of the tunnel, in order to reduce the cost from $7,000,000 to $4,000,000.

New Residential Tracts

The Twin Peaks Tunnel was vital to the development of residential tracts west of the hilly barrier in the geographical center of the city. Among these tracts were Westwood Park, Forest Hill, and St. Francis Wood, all on land once included in the San Miguel Rancho and later owned by Adolph Sutro. The developers, who purchased the raw land from the Sutro heirs in 1911 and put the tracts on the market in 1912, had difficulty attracting buyers at first, because of the inadequate transportation. Once the tunnel was completed, properties sold more readily, for the tracts were among the best planned in San Francisco.

Another project which aided the development of the area west of Twin Peaks was Portola Drive, a scenic route extending from St. Francis Circle to an extension of Market Street. In planning this highway through the pass between the peaks and Mount Davidson, O'Shaughnessy followed the general line of the old San Miguel Ocean House and Beach macadamized road, built in the 'sixties as a toll road to the popular Ocean House, an early-day equivalent of the modern roadhouse.

O'Shaughnessy was particularly interested in all the newer subdivisions opened in San Francisco before and during the exposition. At the annual convention of the League of California Municipalities in 1915 he quoted what Frederick C. Howe, an eastern city planner, had said about the city:

"I know of no city in America more keenly alive to its natural advantages than San Francisco. I spent several hours with the city engineer looking over St. Francis Wood, Ingleside Terraces, Forest Hill, West Clay Park, Seacliff, and other newly finished residence parks. I have seen nothing in America to equal these parks from the standpoint of brilliant suburban development."[30]

Howe was also impressed with the boulevard system which took shape rapidly between 1916 and 1920. Besides the Marina Boulevard, it included another unit that could be traced to Burnham's proposal for an Outer Drive, the road known as El Camino Del Mar, linking the Presidio with the Great Highway and the Esplanade along the Ocean Beach. Drives constructed by the federal government through the Presidio provided the necessary connections between the Marina and the Camino, on which some work had been done before the exposition opened. O'Shaughnessy also planned Sloat Boulevard, the southern boundary of the Sunset district, as a wide thoroughfare from the Great Highway to St. Francis Circle, the western terminus of Portola Drive. By the end of the decade, San Franciscans would take out-of-town visitors for a scenic automobile drive along the Marina and through the Presidio to Lobos Creek, thence through Lincoln Park to the Cliff House, down the Great Highway to the vicinity of Fort Funston and Lake Merced, eastward along Sloat Boulevard to St. Francis Circle, and then over Twin Peaks by way of Portola Drive, and down Market Street to the Civic Center.

The Metropolitan View

The city engineer would have been a backward San Francisco official if he had not taken as much interest in outlets to the Peninsula as he did in city thoroughfares. At the time the Twin Peaks Tunnel was bored, O'Shaughnessy observed that its construction would "also facilitate providing adequate means of transportation to the towns down the Peninsula, when adjacent communities see fit to become components of Greater San Francisco."[31] He recognized, though, that there was little public agitation for an interurban line from the tunnel to San Mateo County via Junipero Serra Boulevard, while there was some agitation for a Skyline Boulevard from San Fran-

cisco to Santa Cruz County and for a Bayshore Boulevard following the general route of the old San Bruno Road to a connection with El Camino Real near San Bruno. He was busy with plans for these two roads about the time the United States entered World War I.

To a man like O'Shaughnessy the eventual unification of San Francisco and San Mateo counties seemed logical and desirable. Though he recognized that the East Bay rejected consolidation with San Francisco, he still hoped, as late as 1918, that all the cities within the metropolitan area would unite in solving such common problems as water supply and transportation. Why not, he asked, form a single great public-utility district that would provide water, operate transit facilities, and perhaps perform other functions as well? Bion Arnold had seen the need for planning and developing essential utilities on a metropolitan basis. The city engineer liked the efficiency and the economy of the idea.

Looking across the bay, O'Shaughnessy saw the cities of Alameda County hard hit by a water crisis that he himself had predicted in 1916. In that year he had warned that the occurrence of two dry years in succession would cause a serious crisis in transbay urban areas. Now, in the summer of 1918, the East Bay cities were forced to prohibit the use of water for lawns and gardens. The East Bay Water Company, which had succeeded the People's Water Company as supplier of water to cities from Richmond to San Leandro, met the crisis by developing plans for a dam and reservoir on San Pablo Creek, behind the Berkeley Hills in Contra Costa County. Before this dam was completed in 1920, however, Oakland and Berkeley lost several important industries to the Los Angeles area, including a branch plant of the Goodyear Tire and Rubber Company, which could not be guaranteed a daily water supply sufficient for its needs. Nor did the new reservoir increase the supply enough to assure proper conditions for industrial growth.

Had San Francisco made great progress on the Hetch Hetchy project, the East Bay might by this time have been more interested in joining with it in forming a metropolitan water district; but disturbed financial conditions brought about by World War I had prevented the sale of some of the bonds authorized in 1910, and construction had proceeded at a snail's pace. Not until after the war was the city able to market approximately $7,000,000 in bonds and speed work on the Hetch Hetchy Dam. In the meantime, sentiment had been crystallizing in the East Bay for the formation of the type of municipal utility district advocated by Dr. George Pardee.

CHAPTER ELEVEN

Seeds of Metropolitan Regionalism

Although the Bay Area was politically unfederated, opposed to the idea of unified harbor development and management, and divided on the issue of a metropolitan water system, after 1912 it began to achieve, through the construction of state and county highways and the inauguration of additional ferry services, that greater measure of physical, economic, and social cohesion which interurban transit companies at one time gave promise of bringing about. These companies, reaching their peak of expansion about 1915, failed to provide the missing links that would have made it possible to journey from Santa Rosa to Sausalito, from San Francisco or Oakland to San Jose, from Oakland to Martinez, or from Benicia to Calistoga—or by electric railway and ferry through all the counties in the Bay Area. Yet certain vital gaps came near being filled; and the Oakland, Antioch and Eastern did link Oakland with Sacramento and other points in the great Central Valley in September, 1913.

Perhaps the greatest disappointment was expressed over the failure of the Southern Pacific to join San Francisco and San Jose by trolley and over the inability of F. M. ("Borax") Smith to extend the Key Route south of Hayward to the county seat of Santa Clara County. In 1913, in a final effort to carry out its projected line from San Francisco to San Jose, the Southern Pacific offered to include the trackage of the United Railroads between San Mateo and San Bruno in its San Francisco–San Jose route, leasing trackage rights. To this proposal the San Francisco traction company was by then agreeable, and eight new cars were ordered for the Southern Pacific's

subsidiary, the Peninsular Railway. Then came the outbreak of war, which meant the end of the through line. A scarcity of steel rails again prevented the building of the missing link between San Mateo and Los Altos, on the San Jose–Palo Alto line.

The bitter warfare between the Southern Pacific and the Key Route, which caused the former between 1908 and 1912 to build parallel lines within a few blocks of several Key Route lines, effectively checked F. M. Smith's last attempt to reach San Jose. In 1912, when he appeared to be ready to try for the third time to join Oakland and San Jose by electric railway, the Southern Pacific made plans to extend the Peninsular Railway to Oakland over the Dumbarton railroad bridge and the old South Pacific Coast Railroad route. Track was laid from Palo Alto to the bridge, while in Oakland a line was built from the downtown area to the Southern Pacific's Sixteenth Street depot. The upshot of these competitive maneuvers was a truce between the Southern Pacific and Smith whereby both agreed to refrain from connecting Oakland and San Jose by interurban. Actually, Smith's credit for large-scale, long-term borrowing was practically exhausted, and it is doubtful whether he could have completed the extension to San Jose if he had begun it.

First State Highways

Although private transit companies failed to bind together the metropolitan region with steel rails, the state and various counties succeeded in doing so with concrete roads, in response to the ever-increasing use of the private

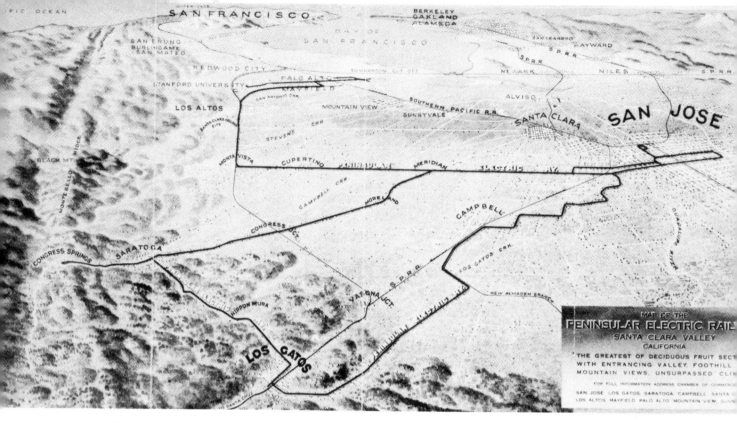

Pictorial Map of the Peninsular Electric Railway System, about 1915. Photograph courtesy of Palo Alto Public Library.

automobile, motorcycle, and truck. The state took the lead, inaugurating construction of a highway system corresponding in general with the plan formulated by the old Bureau of Highways in 1896. This system, for which the people of the state authorized $18,000,000 in bonds in 1910, was to include, in its final form, 3,052 miles of road. Its main features were two great highways, one running north and south through the Sacramento and San Joaquin valleys, the other traversing the western slope of the Coast Range from the Oregon border to Mexico. Both highways were planned to connect as many county seats as possible and to pass through the principal centers of population. Branch roads to county seats lying east and west of the two trunk highways were an integral part of the scheme. Sections of the system within the Bay Area nearly everywhere followed the historic lines of communication established during the Spanish-Mexican era.

Ground-breaking ceremonies for this far-flung system took place at South San Francisco, in San Mateo County, on August 7, 1912, and marked the beginning of the transformation of El Camino Real from a dusty county road to a two-lane state highway twenty-four feet wide, with an asphalt-on-concrete surface. By the end of 1915 El Camino Real had been paved from San Francisco to Gilroy, at the southern end of the Santa Clara Valley, and

an East Bay highway had been completed from Oakland to San Jose except for a stretch of a few miles between Niles and the Santa Clara County line. In other parts of the Bay Area there were small sections of concrete roadway: from Richmond to Pinole, from Benicia to Vacaville, from Livermore to the eastern boundary of Alameda County, and from the Marin County line to Willow Brook in Sonoma County.

The $18,000,000 voted for highway construction in the previous decade had by this time all been expended. Few, indeed, had thought that the funds would be sufficient to build even the modest state system projected in the State Highways Act of 1909, and Governor Hiram Johnson had commiserated the State Highway Commission for being expected to build for this amount a system that the best engineers in the county had estimated would cost from $35,000,000 to $50,000,000. The voters, however, were ready by 1916 to approve a second highway bond issue, providing $12,000,000 for completion of the original system and an additional $3,000,000 to be used in coöperation with counties for certain lateral roads, which, under the terms of the second bond act, were added to the state highway system. In the 1916 election, moreover, not a single county cast a plurality of votes against the bonds. The vote was four to one for good roads, whereas six years earlier the first bond issue had passed by a bare majority, fourteen counties being opposed to the state highway program.

Toward the close of the decade those parts of the state system that served the Bay Area constituted the framework of a metropolitan regional highway system. From Gilroy a motorist could travel north on the state system to San Jose, Oakland, and Martinez, cross Carquinez Strait by ferry to Benicia, and continue by way of Vacaville to Sacramento. Or he could travel from San Jose to San Francisco, cross by ferry to Sausalito, and enjoy the luxury of a paved surface all the way to Healdsburg, in northern Sonoma County, except for one small section south of Santa Rosa. A branch of the system extended eastward through Alameda County to the San Joaquin Valley, entirely paved except through Niles Canyon. In the North Bay an east-west lateral connected Petaluma, Napa, and Fairfield.

Bonds for County Roads

Counties in the Bay Area, as well as elsewhere, by this time were supplementing the state highway system with well-paved county roads. San Mateo County was the first in the Bay Area to meet the demand of its residents for improved highways by issuing county road bonds. Voters trooped to the polls on April 8, 1913, to approve $1,250,000 in bonds by a vote of four to one. With the funds provided by the bonds the county constructed an alternate route to El Camino Real, already a congested highway. The alternate road ran from San Bruno north along the shore of the bay through South San Francisco to the county line, following the route of the old San Bruno Road and, to a degree, the route of the modern Bayshore Freeway. Only slightly less important to the county than this road was the highway built along the coast from Colma to Pescadero and the Santa Cruz County line, paralleling

The Five O'Clock Rush in Richmond, 1916. Photograph courtesy of Richmond Public Library.

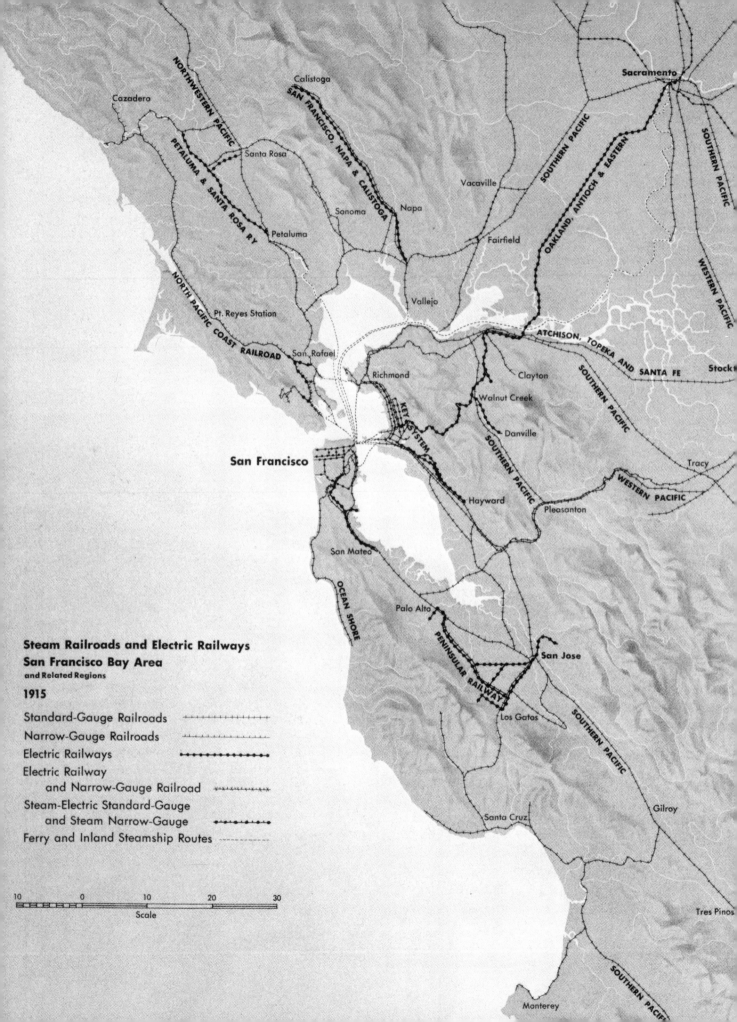

**Steam Railroads and Electric Railways
San Francisco Bay Area**
and Related Regions

1915

Standard-Gauge Railroads

Narrow-Gauge Railroads

Electric Railways

Electric Railway
    and Narrow-Gauge Railroad

Steam-Electric Standard-Gauge
    and Steam Narrow-Gauge

Ferry and Inland Steamship Routes

Scale
10   0   10   20   30

U.S. 40 near Vacaville in the Days of the First Paved Highways. Photograph courtesy of State Division of Highways.

the tracks of the Ocean Shore Railroad, which by 1920 was meeting so much truck, bus, and private automobile competition that it was obliged to appeal to the State Public Utilities Commission for permission to discontinue operations. From the coast highway to the bay side of the county ran two scenic lateral roads, one from Half Moon Bay to Belmont, the other from San Gregorio to Redwood City by way of La Honda, the heart of the old redwood logging area.

Though there were now better highways on the peninsula, San Mateo County did not attract many newcomers during this early period of highway construction. In the decade 1910–1920 its population increased only a little more than 10,000 and totaled 36,781 in 1920. On week ends San Franciscans invaded the county in their cars, but few families moved there. One explanation may be that new residential areas were opened for settlement within the metropolis itself. Interurban transit still was comparatively expensive, and automobile commuting, always costly, had not yet become the vogue. Furthermore, most towns in San Mateo County offered little opportunity for employment, and commercial and industrial activity during the war tended to be concentrated in major urban centers.

Other counties, finding that road building by direct tax was slow, attempted to follow the example of San Mateo County, but were not always successful. Sonoma County failed to approve road bonds in 1914. A Santa Clara

County citizens' committee worked hard for a $1,500,000 bond issue in the spring of 1917, only to see the electorate reject the measure by a vote of two to one.

In 1919, Sonoma County tried again and succeeded in putting over a $1,600,000 bond issue. In that same year, Napa County also voted $500,000 in road bonds and Contra Costa County $2,600,000. Sonoma County provided paved roads first in highly developed agricultural areas, then surfaced the roads to Russian River resorts, the favorite summer recreation spots of San Franciscans. With its bond funds Napa County built a highway twenty-seven miles long through the fertile Napa Valley. Contra Costa County, which had built only forty-eight miles of paved roads in five years by direct tax financing, planned a comprehensive county road system to connect at Martinez with the state highway. A first link in this county system was a highway originating at Stockton, in the San Joaquin Valley, and passing through Antioch, Pittsburg, and other points along Suisun Bay.

Coöperative Projects

A coöperative project financed and carried out by Marin, Sonoma, and Napa counties as a scenic route supplementing the state highways in the Bay Area was the road now known as the Black Point Cutoff, running from Napa across the marshes of southern Sonoma County to Ignacio, in Marin County. The three participating counties had hoped to have this road ready for the Panama-Pacific International Exposition, so that tourists might encircle the entire bay on paved roads; but difficulties in raising county funds postponed its completion until 1920.

Another coöperative project undertaken at the end of World War I was the Skyline Boulevard, from San Francisco along the crest of the Buri Buri Ridge in San Mateo County and on southward into Santa Clara and Santa Cruz counties. Under a law passed by the state legislature in 1917 to permit counties to associate themselves in a joint highway district, the four counties along the route of the boulevard formed Joint Highway District Number One and purchased rights of way for the scenic drive. Automobile clubs had carried on a publicity campaign for this mountain road for several years before it was included in 1919 among the highways to be financed by a third state highway bond issue, which, incidentally, was approved by a vote of seven to one and provided $40,000,000 for highway construction in California.

New Ferry Services

As the population of the Bay Area became more mobile, the water barriers which retarded communication—Sui-

The Automobile Ferry City of Richmond, *1915. Ferryboats plied between Castro Point and Point San Quentin until the opening of the Richmond–San Rafael Bridge in 1956. Photograph courtesy of Richmond Chamber of Commerce.*

sun Bay, Carquinez Strait, San Pablo Strait, the Golden Gate, and the great southern arm of the bay—presented increasingly serious problems. At one time or another, engineers, railroad tycoons, editorial writers, and plain citizens had proposed the building of bridges across every one of these bodies of water. The first wave of proposals came with the building of railroads. A second group accompanied the construction of electric railways. A third series of proposals very naturally burgeoned as motor vehicles multiplied on the highways in the counties around the bay. But additional ferries rather than costly bridges met the needs of the times.

As early as 1909 the communities of Martinez and Benicia, which had been out of direct communication by ferry ever since the late 'seventies, cited the increase in automobile travel as one reason for reëstablishing ferry service. Finally, on July 19, 1913, the long-sought service was inaugurated with the former Puget Sound steamer *City of Seattle.*

At the western end of Carquinez Strait another ferry service began operating about 1915 under the name Carquinez Ferry Company. The successor of this concern, the Rodeo-Vallejo Ferry Company, organized in 1918, later formed the American Toll Bridge Company, which obtained a franchise in 1922 to build a span across the strait. The wharf properties purchased by the Carquinez Ferry Company and taken over by the successor company were in time to become the bridgeheads of the first Carquinez Bridge.

In May, 1915, the Richmond–San Rafael Transportation Company started running automobile ferries between Point San Quenton in Marin County and Castro Point in Contra Costa County. Within two years the company was serving more than 265,000 passengers annually; yet financiers were not sufficiently impressed with the volume of traffic to finance a toll bridge designed by John G. Little, a San Francisco engineer. Moreover, the entrance of the United States into World War I halted projects requiring large amounts of steel. Little's proposal did, however, foreshadow the building of the span that was completed by the state in 1956.

A Board of United States Army Engineers held hearings on several plans for a crossing between San Francisco and Oakland in August, 1916, but rejected all of them as possibly interfering with military use of the harbor. The board recommended that consideration be given to a scheme that would combine a tunnel under the main part of the bay with a bridge over the eastern side. Soon after the Army engineers released their report, however, the declaration of war sidetracked further planning for a central crossing, and not until five years later did the

War Department schedule another hearing on the matter.

Although most people joked about proposals to span the Golden Gate, City Engineer O'Shaughnessy of San Francisco was among the few who believed that a bridge across the mile-wide entrance to the bay was within the realm of possibility. In due time he interested Joseph B. Strauss, the famous Chicago engineer, in developing plans for a bridge to cost "twenty-five to thirty million dollars at the most."[1] In 1919 Strauss presented what he considered feasible plans roughly within the cost limitation laid down by O'Shaughnessy and other San Francisco officials. And then the word battle over the bridge began, continuing almost until the time great piers began to rise above the surging tide, in the early 'thirties. Some engineers declared that the bridge would cost more than $100,000,000 to build; others said that it could not be built at all. To convince the skeptics, Strauss saw that he would have to undertake further studies.

Autos and Regional Parks

New concrete highways, automobile ferries, bus lines and bus depots, plans for bridges—these were only a few of the many evidences of a new period in history: the automobile age. On every hand there were others: corner service stations, garages, repair shops, automobile sales rooms, automobile supply stores, used-car lots, parking lots, huge new oil refineries and tank farms in Contra Costa County, additional oil pipe lines from the San Joaquin Valley to these refineries, docks for new fleets of oil tankers, resorts in previously inaccessible areas, new subdivisions beyond the limits of electric railway transportation, roadside commercial slums, and garish billboards in rural landscapes. The motor vehicle, truly, was not an unmixed blessing.

Its increasingly widespread use not only materially affected the physical environment and expanded the economy by stimulating new enterprises and creating new employment; it began to change patterns of living and forms of recreation. For many families the Sunday automobile trip gradually began to replace the Sunday afternoon promenade in the urban park or the visit to the amusement park. City dwellers took new interest in exploring the scenic areas that were either too distant or too difficult to reach before the private touring car came into use, and as this interest in the natural beauties of the Bay Area developed, there was a dawning realization that unless steps were taken to preserve outstanding wilderness areas, they might be destroyed if private owners were careless or commercial exploitation was misguided.

With the exception of Golden Gate Park in San Francisco, which had always attracted people from all parts of

First Chevrolets Manufactured in Oakland, 1916. The increasing popularity of the automobile contributed to agitation for construction of bridges across San Francisco Bay and the Golden Gate. Photograph courtesy of Oakland Tribune.

the Bay Area, there were only two publicly owned areas of metropolitan regional significance in the counties around the bay. Muir Woods, at the foot of Mount Tamalpais in Marin County, was a 425-acre national monument, presented to the federal government in 1908 by Congressman William Kent, who purchased the magnificent stand of coast redwoods (*Sequoia sempervirens*) to save it from destruction by a lumber company. The other public reserve of regional importance was Alum Rock Park, in Penitencia Canyon six miles east of San Jose. Once part of the pueblo lands originally belonging to the city of San Jose, it had become a municipal park in 1872 by authorization of the state legislature, which at that time exercised considerable control over presumably self-governing cities.

Both of these large scenic reserves might properly be incorporated in a metropolitan regional park system. Indeed, Stephen Child, a landscape architect employed by the city of San Jose in 1916 to prepare plans for the expansion and further development of Alum Rock Park, pointed out that this park was, "in fact, a 'Metropolitan Reservation' rather than an urban park and in its development should be treated as such."[2] He observed that the

state had begun building a comprehensive system of state highways and that parts of the system serving the Bay Area would make Alum Rock Park accessible to the residents of at least five counties. In the future it would be used not alone by the people of San Jose but "in increasing numbers" by the people of the metropolitan community surrounding the bay. Child believed, therefore, that the city of San Jose "would be entirely justified in urging upon your representatives at Sacramento the propriety of State aid,"[3] perhaps through establishment of a metropolitan district in which taxes for park purposes would be levied on the residents of many cities. "There is a precedent for this in the famous Metropolitan Park System of Boston," he pointed out.

The Metropolitan Park District of Boston, a state agency unfortunately removed from direct control of the people for whose benefit it was created by the Massachusetts State Legislature in 1893, was often cited as an example of the kind of special district that might be established in the Bay Area. In 1914 Professor Thomas H. Reed of the University of California had mentioned it in a lecture in which he urged the formation of three unified park systems in the Bay Area—one in the East

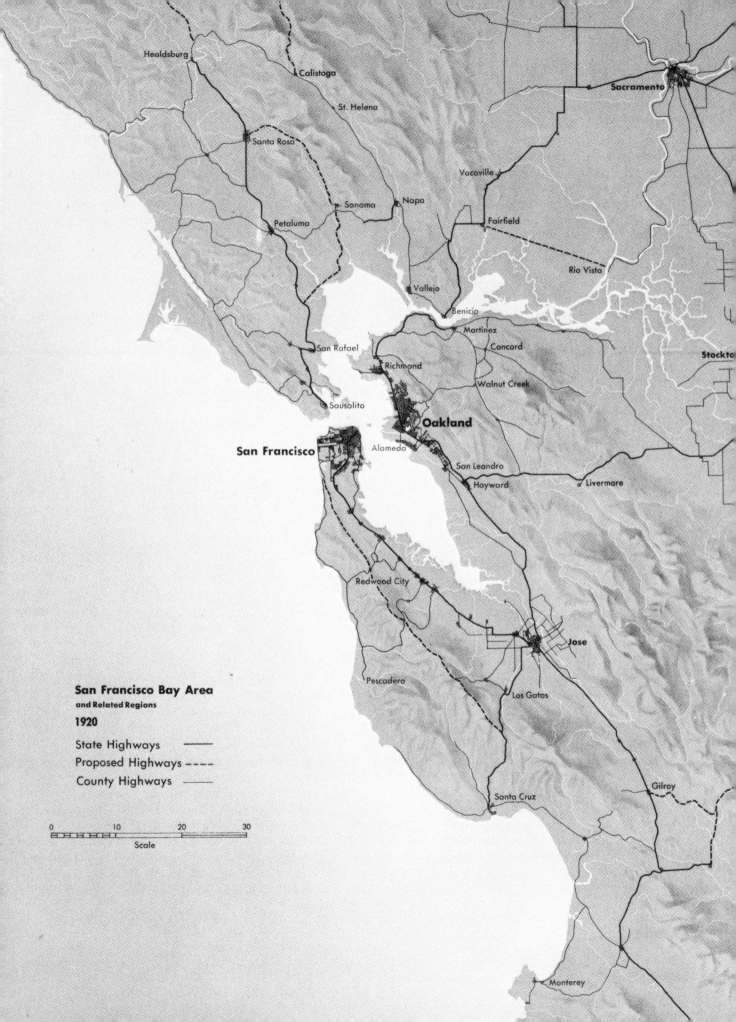

San Francisco Bay Area
and Related Regions

1920

State Highways ———
Proposed Highways ----
County Highways ———

0   10   20   30
Scale

Bay, one on the San Francisco Peninsula, and one in Marin County—all three of which might some day be combined to form a single area-wide system. But suggestions for a metropolitan regional park system aroused little response in the days of World War I. Automobile ownership was increasing rapidly but was not so widespread as to make every family potentially the supporters of a regional park movement. Nor were cities spreading at a rate that made the disappearance of open areas alarming.

What might be called "metropolitan thinking" did not become a force in the Bay Area until the 'twenties, when a new influx of population, a phenomenal increase in the number of automobiles, and the growing complexity of the problems of circulation, water supply, and bay development focused attention on the need for coöperative action.

Controversy over transbay transportation, for instance, tended to emphasize the interrelatedness of area-wide problems. How would a bridge, or bridges, across San Francisco Bay affect navigation and the expansion of harbor facilities? Should not there be a crossing between the East Bay and the North Bay at San Pablo Strait, and might it not be a barrier to the salt water that was making incursions into Suisun Bay? Might not the creation of a fresh-water lake in San Pablo Bay solve the water supply problems of the East Bay? These and a hundred other questions challenged the people of the whole Bay Area.

Problem of a Bay Crossing

By the fall of 1921, engineers had advanced thirteen different proposals for a bay crossing between the San Francisco Peninsula and Alameda County, including one proposal for a crossing near San Mateo and another for a crossing at Dumbarton Strait, thirty miles south of San Francisco. Great public interest attached to the plans of General George W. Goethals for a tube from the foot of Market Street to the Oakland Mole. Provided with two decks, the tube would accommodate vehicular traffic on the upper deck and trains on the lower. John G. Little, who had presented a tunnel plan at the 1916 hearing held by a Board of United States Army Engineers, suggested a combination tube and trestle, the tube section to be on the San Francisco side of the bay, where an unobstructed ship channel was imperative. J. Vipond Davies and Ralph Modjeski, employed by the San Francisco Bay Bridge Committee, likewise recommended a combination tunnel and bridge, extending from some point between Mission Rock and Potrero Point in San Francisco to a place on the Alameda County shore satisfactory to the naval authorities. Rear Admiral Joseph L. Jayne, commandant

of the Twelfth Naval District, made the familiar proposals that the Key Route trestle be extended to Yerba Buena Island, that a union ferry terminal be built on the island, and that a ferry be operated between the island and San Francisco until a tunnel could be constructed to replace the ferryboats. There were also two proposals for a high-level cantilever bridge, with 2,000-foot spans, from Telegraph Hill to Yerba Buena Island, and proposals for concrete viaducts from various locations south of Hunters Point to Alameda, Bay Farm Island, or the vicinity of San Leandro.

Present-day residents of the Bay Area will note that every location later suggested for a second mid-bay crossing was included among proposals for the first. John G. Little, moreover, based his plan on the assumption that many bridges would be required to accommodate future traffic.

Again the War Department felt compelled to schedule a public hearing on the problem of a bay crossing. The hearing was conducted on October 7, 1921, and on December 1, 1921, the Chief of Engineers of the United States Army announced the conditions that would govern the building of a bridge or tunnel or a combination of the two. No bridge of any kind north of Hunters Point would be approved, the Chief of Engineers stated, and no low bridge north of San Mateo. A tunnel crossing in any location, provided it was at least 50 feet below mean low water, would be approved. A combined bridge and tunnel at a location south of the proposed Alameda naval base site would be approved provided the tunnel was so placed as to leave the channel along the San Francisco side unobstructed to a depth of 50 feet at mean low water for a width of 3,000 feet. Finally, the War Department stated that not more than once crossing in any location north of San Mateo would be approved at that time.

Alternative Projects

The War Department's announcement met with varied responses. Some groups believed that through public pressure the Department could be induced to abandon its stand against a bridge north of Hunters Point. Others were inclined to accept the conditions stated by the Chief of Engineers and to concentrate on plans for a southern crossing. The Harbor Control Section of the Commonwealth Club thought that a bridge "somewhere south of San Mateo" would be "justified by the very considerable relief it would afford to traffic between San Francisco and other peninsular points and the east side of the bay and even to the East Bay cities themselves in emergencies." As for a crossing north of Hunters Point, the section concluded that "neither the present traffic nor the prospective traffic for the next twenty years, at least, justifies the cost of building such a structure as would be absolutely essential to avoid interference with the prospective and necessary expansion of the harbor."[4]

A. J. Dickie, editor of the *Pacific Marine Review*, assured the club that "the east shore terminal at Yerba Buena Island [as suggested by Rear Admiral Jayne] is the logical next step in the development of that ferry system which is now the finest in the world, but is yet not quite good enough for San Francisco Bay."[5] The ferries, he pointed out, had transported more than 49,000,000 passengers, nearly 800,000 automobiles, and approximately 2,000,000 tons of freight in 1921. By running a ten-minute schedule regularly from the foot of Market Street to Yerba Buena Island, it would be possible immediately to double the total capacity for San Francisco–Oakland traffic in passengers and more than double that for automobiles, Dickie contended.

C. E. Grunsky, former City Engineer of San Francisco, not only favored a mid-bay transit and ferry terminal; like the Big Four in the 1870's, he envisaged shipping operations at this point, and, like members of harbor improvement associations, he suggested leveling Yerba Buena Island and creating a man-made island on the shoals north of it, with deep-water harbor facilities alongside. Mainland freight trains could be routed over a viaduct from the end of the Key Route Mole to warehouses and piers on this artificial island, the visionary counterpart of present-day Treasure Island.

Proposed Salt-Water Barrier

Grunsky did not limit his interest in Bay Area transportation problems to the movement of people and goods between San Francisco and Oakland, however. He foresaw the need for the improvement of traffic between the East Bay and Marin County, as did John G. Little and many others. Grunsky pointed out that a crossing between Richmond and San Rafael might take the form of a vehicular roadway and a railroad right of way on top of a dam built to act as a barrier to salt water in Suisun Bay, as suggested by Captain C. S. Jarvis, of the Corps of Engineers of the United States Army, in a paper presented before the American Society of Civil Engineers in 1921.[6]

The possibility of constructing a dam to prevent saltwater encroachment into the upper bay and the delta region at the confluence of the Sacramento and San Joaquin rivers had been discussed periodically ever since the great drought of the mid-sixties, when the reduced flow of the rivers invited salt-water incursion. As Assistant State Engineer under William Hammond Hall, Grunsky had carried out an investigation in 1879–1880 to determine whether such a barrier at Carquinez Strait were needed but had reported adversely on the idea. In the years following that study many industries requiring large amounts of fresh water had been established on Carquinez Strait and Suisun Bay, and had at first taken their supply from these waters, then, as salinity increased, from wells. The California and Hawaii Sugar Refinery at Crockett for ten years employed barges to bring fresh water from many miles upstream on the Sacramento River. In 1920 it began obtaining water from a more convenient source, the Marin Municipal Water District, which delivered water to the barges at Point San Quentin. The plight of other industries became serious in 1918 and in 1920, two dry years during which reduced stream flow and overdraughts for irrigation in the Central Valley permitted the salt water of the bay to work its way far up into the delta region and to contaminate the underground basins in Contra Costa County that were a principal source of water supply for farmers, industries, and municipalities. These conditions, which occasioned a prolonged law suit (the Antioch suit) involving water users of the upper Sacramento Valley, the delta region, and Contra Costa County industrialists, prompted Captain Jarvis to revive the idea of converting San Pablo and Suisun bays into fresh-water lakes by building a dam across the narrows below San Pablo Bay.

Present-day residents of the Bay Area will recognize in the Jarvis proposal the genesis of one element of the controversial Reber Plan for converting the northern and southern arms of San Francisco Bay into fresh-water lakes. Because other drought years and renewed struggles between Central Valley agriculturists and Contra Costa County industrialists were to follow in the middle and late 'twenties, the subject of a salt-water barrier was to assume increasing importance in all discussions of harbor development, bay crossings, tideland reclamation, and industrial growth. Moreover, the barrier issue served to reëmphasize the close relation between the economic development of the Bay Area and that of the Central Valley. At the heart of the problem facing the farmers in the delta region and the manufacturing plants and municipalities in northern Contra Costa County lay the larger problem of the future use of the water resources of the vast territory drained by the Sacramento and San Joaquin rivers and their numerous tributaries. Indeed, the solution of this problem concerned the whole Bay Area just as much as it did the people of Contra Costa County.

Threat of Water Shortages

The water problem in another form troubled the East Bay communities of Oakland, Berkeley, Alameda, and Richmond. As population growth continued, it became increasingly certain that there would be water shortages unless action were taken to augment the supply available from local watersheds and wells. The Jarvis proposal for transforming San Pablo Bay into a fresh-water lake that could supply water for industrial use attracted considerable interest but hardly seemed a solution to the problem of impending water deficiency which the East Bay cities were trying to solve.

By 1922 these cities were at least equipped with legislation under which they could form a utility district. After a committee of officials from the principal East Bay cities had dissolved in 1920 because of disagreement on a plan for solving the common water supply problem, the mayor of Berkeley had appointed a committee to draft a bill to be presented at the next session of the state legislature. The result was the Municipal Utility District Act of 1921, providing for the creation of a utility district that would embrace parts of more than one county, and for the inclusion of unincorporated as well as incorporated territory. The way thus being paved for joint action by the East Bay communities, sentiment was rapidly crystallizing for formation of a district embracing most of the territory then served by the East Bay Water Company.

San Francisco nevertheless still hoped that the East Bay would participate in the construction of the Hetch Hetchy system and would share the costs and the benefits. Lake Eleanor Dam had been completed in 1918; one powerhouse of the gigantic development was in operation and work on another had begun; and construction of O'Shaughnessy Dam in the Hetch Hetchy Valley had been under way for more than two years. As Robert M. Searls, special counsel for the city, pointed out to prominent East Bay men attending a Commonwealth Club discussion, San Francisco was going to complete the Hetch Hetchy project with or without the aid of the communities on the opposite side of the bay, but "a water supply for the bay cities is something in which we should all share both the credit and the expense, and all develop in harmony."[7]

Warren Olney, ever the East Bay champion of area-wide coöperation, agreed. "There is but one thing for the East Bay communities to do," he said, "and that is to get together through some proper governmental organization, such as a water district, and unite with the city of San Francisco and go ahead with the development, so that all may be served from the common source."[8]

Edwin O. Edgerton, president of the East Bay Water Company, likewise conceded that it would be "vastly better" if a single water supply could be considered for San Francisco, the Peninsula, and the East Bay. Separate systems for the two sides of the bay would involve "undoubtedly a duplication of investment." But he saw no possibility of reaching accord on a single system. "The situation today," he said, "is that the communities are not together on this question, so that at the moment the East Bay Region must consider for itself what source of supply it will use."[9]

Further delay on the part of the East Bay communities in reaching agreement on a plan of action would be disastrous, Edgerton warned. "Our bay communities have become very ambitious to expand and grow, to attract industry, to persuade people to settle and build homes, to become large manufacturing and business communities, to emulate Los Angeles, if you please, and even to outdistance Los Angeles. I want to say to you that if the East Bay Region had the opportunity tomorrow to become as large as the city of Los Angeles, to have the industries that are now in the city of Los Angeles, and that are coming there at the rate of one industry a day, it could not be done. Why? Lack of an adequate future water supply. And yet every effort is made to expand and grow and attract industries, with no serious attention to the fundamental basis of the possibility of growth, which is water."

He summed up the situation bluntly: "The present supply of water in the East Bay Region is not sufficient for a period longer than ten years. Well before the end of that ten years there must be under way the construction of works to bring in a very substantial additional water supply."[10]

Formation of a Utility District

The warning, voiced by many leaders besides Edgerton, finally was heeded. On May 8, 1923, the voters of Oakland, Berkeley, Alameda, San Leandro, Emeryville, El Cerrito, Piedmont, and Richmond went to the polls to cast their ballots for or against the formation of the East Bay Municipal Utility District. In all the cities except Piedmont and Richmond the vote was favorable, but within a short time these two cities also joined the district.

The organization of the district did not preclude obtaining water from San Francisco's Hetch Hetchy system. When engineers of the East Bay Municipal Utility District began field surveys in July, 1924, to determine what source of water could best be drawn upon, they included the Hetch Hetchy project among sources to be investigated. Others were the Eel River, the Sacramento River, the American River, the McCloud River, and the Mokelumne River. In the end, though, a board of eminent engineers, composed of Chief Engineer Arthur P. Davis, William Mulholland, builder of the Los Angeles Aqueduct, and General George W. Goethals, recommended the Mokelumne River as the most promising and economic source of supply. The last hope that San Francisco and the East Bay would find a common solution to the water supply problem died in November, 1924, when the electorate of the East Bay Municipal Utility District approved a $39,000,000 bond issue for construction of an aqueduct from the Mokelumne River.

Ironically, this project was to be completed some years before the Hetch Hetchy system was in operation. Indeed, there was to be an emergency in San Francisco in 1930 during which the East Bay Municipal Utility District would supply the city across the bay with millions of gallons of water a day, in effect demonstrating the value of one big system.

Had San Francisco and the East Bay been able to reach agreement on a single water system, the coöperation between the two large urban areas in planning for the best use of water might have led, or at least could have led, to planning for a better distribution of population and industrial establishments, as had been suggested by Bion Arnold in 1912. Since water and transportation are essential for any form of urban development, they might well be used to influence and direct growth, though they have seldom been so used, because until recently communities have not prepared general plans that could be implemented through the construction of basic utilities. The projection of street-railway lines into the sparsely populated areas west of Twin Peaks in San Francisco is an example of official policy directed toward the settlement of territory that is "ripe" for development, though good physical planning in this instance did not precede the planning and construction of transit facilities. Today a municipality that is guided in its growth by a long-range, general plan can, if it owns and controls its water supply and its transit system, bring about the most desirable type of development in outlying areas. The failure of San Francisco and the East Bay to unite on a plan for providing the major concentrations of population in the Bay Area with a common water supply was a setback for coördinated metropolitan development. If these communities had formed a metropolitan water district with a board composed of representatives of the city councils of the various cities, they could have exercised a strong control over the whole pattern of urbanization in the Bay Area and could have regulated the "where and when" of subdivision activity and perhaps prevented the haphazard and wasteful expansion characteristic of the past decade. But this grand opportunity for guiding the growth of the Bay Area was lost when the East Bay formed a separate utility district with a board unrepresentative of the governing bodies of the municipalities which it serves. The utility district provided for in the act of 1921 is so divorced from other functions of government in the East Bay that it offers no more opportunity for planning and programing the development of outlying areas than would a private utility. It is an outstanding example of the independent special district that enormously complicates the problem of achieving coördination in the planning and development of a great metropolitan region.

Proposals for Rapid Transit

San Francisco in the early 'twenties really expected little coöperation from the East Bay on the water supply problem. Of greater importance to both sides of the bay was eventual accord on the matter of a bay crossing, but rapid solution of this problem did not appear possible. In the meantime, San Francisco needed outlets to the only land area to which she could gain ready access, the Peninsula.

The City Planning Section of the Commonwealth Club, reorganized in November, 1922, after several months of inactivity, scheduled several talks that reflected the interest of the metropolis in establishing closer relations with San Mateo County. Architect Willis Polk addressed the section on the subject "The San Francisco–San Mateo Regional Plan," and C. J. Rhodin, a consulting engineer, discussed rapid transit with particular reference to express service down the Peninsula.

"What a wonderful thing it would be for San Francisco," Rhodin exclaimed, "if there were a rapid transit system following, let us say, Howard Street, where you could take an express train that would run, without grade crossings, to San Mateo and other points south!"[11] But he estimated that a double-tracked system from San Francisco to San Jose would cost $30,000,000; and he doubted that it could operate profitably under the traffic densities then existing. Perhaps, he suggested, the Southern Pacific facilities could be adapted to rapid transit service.

San Francisco City Engineer O'Shaughnessy, speaking in the fall of 1923, pinned his hopes for rapid transit to the Peninsula on extension of the municipal railway system. "At the last election a charter amendment was carried, by which the city has the right to buy the railway lines in San Mateo County, connected with the Market Street Railway system, whenever we make up our minds to buy that system. . . . We have a road through the Twin Peaks Tunnel, 12,000 feet long, on a 3 per cent grade, double-tracked. It ends now in St. Francis Circle. We are building an extension from there about two miles long down to Ocean View. The right-of-way has been obtained, and that line will be finished inside of a year. From there down to San Mateo County is only half a mile, and the

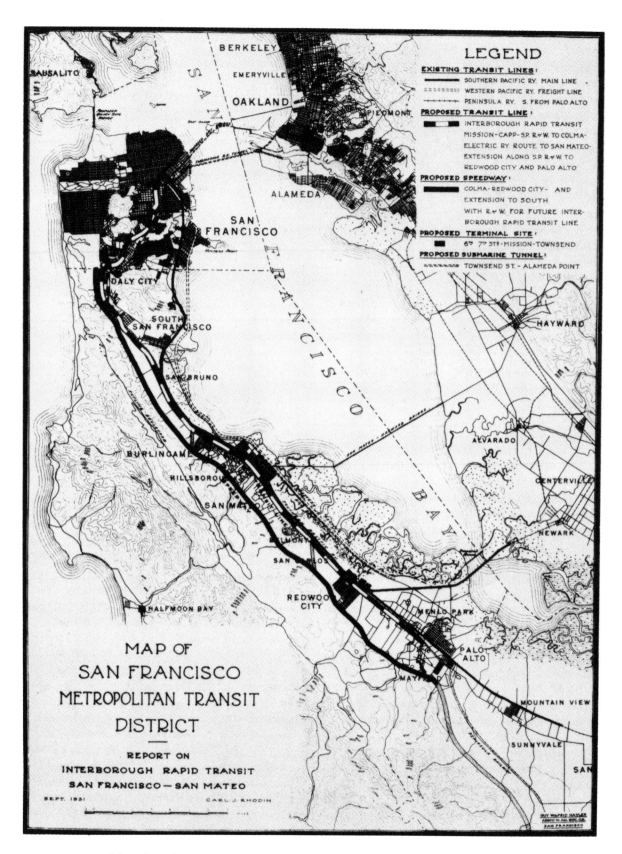

LEGEND

EXISTING TRANSIT LINES:

———————— SOUTHERN PACIFIC RY. MAIN LINE

∷∷∷∷∷∷∷∷ WESTERN PACIFIC RY. FREIGHT LINE

+—+—+—+— PENINSULA RY. S. FROM PALO ALTO

PROPOSED TRANSIT LINE:

▄▄▄□▄▄▄ INTERBOROUGH RAPID TRANSIT
MISSION-CAPP-S.P. R.∀W. TO COLMA-
ELECTRIC RY. ROUTE TO SAN MATEO-
EXTENSION ALONG S.P. R.∀W. TO
REDWOOD CITY AND PALO ALTO

PROPOSED SPEEDWAY:

▄▄▄▄▄▄ COLMA-REDWOOD CITY- AND
EXTENSION TO SOUTH
WITH R.∀W. FOR FUTURE INTER-
BOROUGH RAPID TRANSIT LINE.

PROPOSED TERMINAL SITE:

■■ 6TH 7TH STS-MISSION-TOWNSEND

PROPOSED SUBMARINE TUNNEL:

∷∷∷∷∷∷ TOWNSEND ST. - ALAMEDA POINT

MAP OF
SAN FRANCISCO
METROPOLITAN TRANSIT
DISTRICT
—
REPORT ON
INTERBOROUGH RAPID TRANSIT
SAN FRANCISCO — SAN MATEO

SEPT. 1931   CARL J. RHODIN

Map of Interborough Rapid Transit System Proposed by Carl J. Rhodin, 1931 natural gradient for a rapid transit line at a relatively moderate cost, not any thirty million or fifty million dollars, but four million or five million dollars. . . ."[12]

Not even that much money was available for a rapid transit system. To stimulate development west of Twin Peaks, the city had spent millions for tunnels and railway lines; but the new transit operations were not profitable, however essential they were for city growth. Under the circumstances, it was little wonder that the city did not embark on a program of interurban rapid transit.

New highways were to provide San Francisco with the outlets it needed. O'Shaughnessy told the City Planning Section of the near-completion of the Skyline Boulevard and of plans for the construction of the Bayshore Highway. The latter, to be built under state supervision with funds supplied by the City and County of San Francisco, was to run through Visitacion Valley to South San Francisco and thence along the marshy shore of the bay, bypassing the string of cities through which congested El Camino Real ran.

"We have hopes," O'Shaughnessy said, "that San Mateo, which has not been jealous of San Francisco, which has never broken a pledge they have made us for any coöperation, will join with us and form a Greater San Francisco, so that we can solve . . . the transportation problem, the water problem, and other problems."[13]

The Consolidation Movement

So far as the city engineer and a good many other San Franciscans were concerned, the Greater San Francisco movement was not dead; it had, of necessity, merely shriveled. It now aimed at amalgamating only San Mateo County, or at least the northern part of the county, with San Francisco.

In San Mateo County the Three Cities Chamber of Commerce, representing San Mateo, Burlingame, and Hillsborough, was the chief proponent of consolidation with the metropolis. This organization advanced a number of reasons for fostering union with the larger neighbor. Local limitations prevented most Peninsula cities from developing intensively or thoroughly, it contended. Further, the Peninsula was suffering from a lack of industrial development. Consolidation with San Francisco would open thousands of acres along the bay shore for factory sites. The Three Cities Chamber insisted, however, that San Francisco meet three major conditions if consolidation should be effected. It should establish and maintain the borough form of government for the consolidated territories; it should extend the municipal railway south to the town of Belmont; and it should establish and maintain an open port at San Mateo.[14]

San Mateo County opponents of consolidation saw in the movement another attempt of San Francisco to swallow all or part of their county. They doubted that the three basic conditions specified by the Three Cities Chamber of Commerce would be honored by San Francisco once consolidation was consummated. And they believed that San Francisco was advocating consolidation to achieve its own ends of acquiring a greater bonding capacity and more room for expansion.

From 1923 until 1932 the residents of both San Mateo County and San Francisco studied and debated every aspect of the proposed consolidation. Citizen groups, chambers of commerce, newspapers, the San Francisco Bureau of Governmental Research, the San Francisco Board of Supervisors, and the state legislature all became involved in the movement, which by 1928 had become a burning issue. "Consolidation, it can be concluded, failed of achievement in the 1928–1932 period largely because the opposition worked effectively, even with inferior tools, in concentrated areas where a single unfavorable election could defeat the whole effort," John Bollens has written.[15] Intermittent attempts to revive the movement were made between 1935 and 1957, but no later effort reached the intensity of that made in the late 'twenties.

Some elements who opposed consolidation suggested alternatives that would preserve the political identity of San Mateo County yet bring about improvements in governmental operations. Intercounty special districts, such as that formed to build the Skyline Boulevard, might be set up; a state agency of the sort commonly called a metropolitan district commission might be organized to perform specified functions, as in the Boston metropolitan area; or metropolitan regional planning might be initiated to facilitate coördination of the decisions of local governmental bodies with respect to physical developments affecting more than one of the political units of the Bay Area. All three suggestions were more advanced than any proposals made after the clash between Oakland and San Francisco over consolidation before World War I, because all three aimed at avoiding the bitterness generated by attempts at political unification.

Of the three alternatives, the suggestion that metropolitan regional planning be undertaken had perhaps the greatest appeal for public-spirited Bay Area residents at that time, because regional planning then had the attraction of novelty and seemed to meet the needs of large urban areas that were having difficulty in solving area-wide problems. In addition to New York, the cities of Chicago, Boston, Philadelphia, Baltimore, Cleveland, Buffalo, and Detroit all had private, unofficial regional planning organizations.

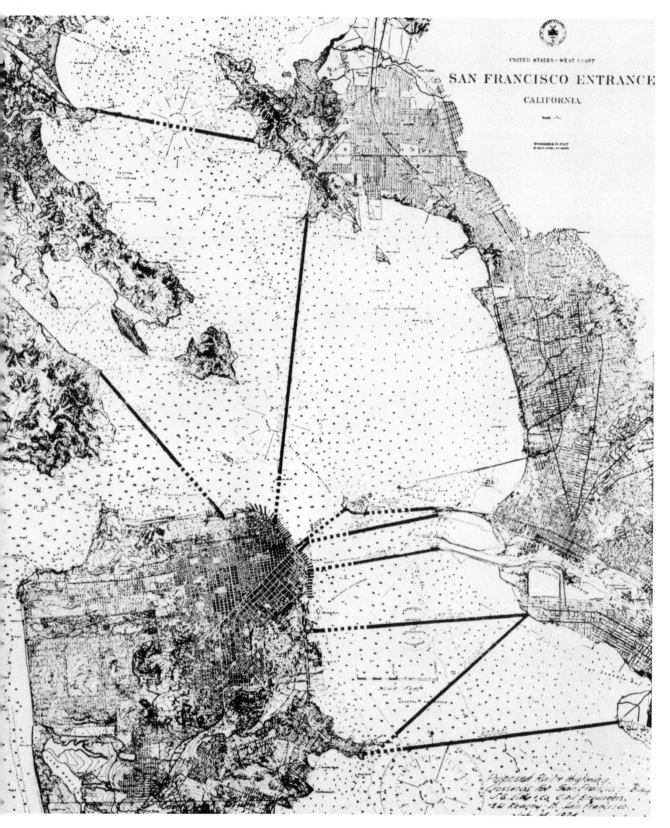

Proposed Rail and Highway Crossings for San Francisco Bay, 1924. The map shows bridge routes studied by J. G. Little and Co., Civil Engineers.

The Conjunction of Events

In the San Francisco Bay Area the members of the City Planning Section of the Commonwealth Club spearheaded the movement for a regional planning organization. And it is perhaps significant that their first important meeting on the subject of regional planning was held in September, 1923, about the time that the physical knitting together of the Bay Area began. The key figures in the San Francisco City Hall and leaders in the North Bay had recently revived the agitation for construction of a bridge across the Golden Gate, and the state legislature had just enacted permissive legislation under which a federation of counties, by forming a bridge and highway district, could construct the proposed mile-long span. In the spring of that year the American Toll Bridge Company had started construction of a high-level span across Carquinez Strait, thereby heralding the day when there would be uninterrupted automobile travel between the East Bay and the North Bay. In May the voters of Alameda County had approved a bond issue of $4,496,000 for the construction of a tube under the estuary between Alameda and Oak-

Proposed Bay Bridge from San Francisco to Alameda, 1925

land. A private company was preparing plans for an automobile toll bridge across Dumbarton Strait in the South Bay; and there was also talk of a toll bridge at San Mateo. Meanwhile, discussion of the need for a bridge or tube between San Francisco and the East Bay had prompted engineers to devise new schemes for a central crossing.

For information on metropolitan regional planning the Commonwealth Club turned to men who knew of the work initiated in the Greater New York area in 1921 by the Russell Sage Foundation. San Francisco City Engineer O'Shaughnessy explained that Mrs. Sage upon her death had left a large sum of money to be used for some unspecified metropolitan benefit. After careful deliberation, the board of trustees of the foundation had concluded that one of the most effective ways to use the funds would be to finance the preparation of a comprehensive plan for the future development of the metropolitan region of which New York City is the center. A Committee on a Regional Plan of New York and Its Environs was appointed; and under the chairmanship of Charles D. Norton, who had been the first chairman of the group which sponsored the Burnham Plan of Chicago, this committee selected a corps of outstanding city planners to undertake a complete physical, economic, and social survey of the metropolitan region as a basis for preparation of the comprehensive plan.

Los Angeles an Inspiration

Another metropolitan planning program that interested the Commonwealth Club was the then newly initiated program of the Los Angeles County Planning Commission, the first county planning agency in the United States. Fortunately, Los Angeles County had its own home-rule charter and could, without waiting for the enactment of state enabling legislation, establish a county planning agency to study problems that were of serious concern to municipalities throughout an extensive urban area. The county board of supervisors established the commission by ordinance in December, 1922; the members of the commission were appointed in January, 1923; and in June of that year the commission opened an office with a technical staff. Gordon Whitnall, who described the Los Angeles County agency to the Commonwealth Club in September, 1923, told how the Los Angeles City Planning Commission, of which he was then the head, had found a large part of its own program stalemated by municipal boundaries until the county commission was brought into being "to seek to interest the various municipalities and political subdivisions of the county in a joint effort to understand and solve the common problems of development confronting them and the county."[16] Among these

common problems, as enumerated in the ordinance establishing the county agency, the principal ones were flood control, unregulated residential development in unincorporated territory, the need for large park reservations and beaches for the use of people throughout the county, and the need for highways serving the entire county. Another problem, not specifically mentioned in the ordinance, was pollution of the underground water supply of cities at lower elevations by cities near the mountains, Whitnall pointed out.

All five of the county-wide conferences that led to the creation of the Los Angeles County Planning Commission were heralded as regional planning conferences; hence, although the county agency had no authority to plan for parts of the metropolitan region lying outside Los Angeles County, it came to be known popularly as a regional planning commission. It was, nevertheless, essentially a county planning agency and could not possibly serve as the model for an agency to facilitate coördination of planning in the San Francisco Bay Area, which was a much larger and vastly more complex area, physically, politically, and in every other respect. The Los Angeles County Planning Commission was, at best, an example of what was needed in each of the Bay Area counties before area-wide planning could be effective. Still, it was a source of inspiration to those who wanted metropolitan regional planning in the Bay Area.

A Proposed Organization

Not long after the meeting at which O'Shaughnessy and Whitnall spoke, the Commonwealth Club appointed a Subcommittee on a Regional Plan for the San Francisco Bay District, with Russell Van Nest Black as chairman. Under his leadership the subcommittee drew up a report proposing a semiofficial, permanent organization that would concern itself with "problems of water and food supply, sewerage, transportation, highways and bridges, port development, zoning, parks, and the conservation and development of natural resources" in a metropolitan region which would include all of Sonoma, Napa, Solano, Marin, Contra Costa, Alameda, San Francisco, and San Mateo counties and the northerly half of Santa Clara County.[17]

Black outlined a general program of procedure for the proposed organization which contemplated first of all a preliminary survey constituting "a general scanning of the district from a planning point of view." A report on this survey, he suggested, could be widely distributed to present the case for a regional plan and to gain financial support for "a much more exhaustive survey" on which to base the plan. "The plan itself . . . would determine the most economical use of the various portions of the entire district and then lay down a general system of highways, transportation, park and recreation facilities, regional zoning et cetera, taking into special consideration the regional phases of such problems as those of port and harbor development, water supply and sanitation."[18] Matters of "purely local concern" would be omitted from the plan.

To finance the preliminary survey and organizational effort, Black proposed that an initial fund of $5,000 to $8,000 be raised, and after that, enough additional funds to bring the total to $250,000, although he acknowledged that "much could be accomplished" with $100,000 or $150,000.[19]

The desirability of continuing the regional planning effort on a semiofficial basis was something about which Black evidently had doubts, as this statement testifies: "Much can be done with the plan through moral suasion coupled with a broad program of education and publicity and by providing mediating machinery for the cooperation of political units in solving common problems, but to be fully effective it may be found to be ultimately necessary to have the plan officially recognized. After the preliminary plans . . . have been completed and well published, it is possible that the work can be better handled through a special regional or metropolitan district, to be created by act of the legislature and directly administered by an official regional plan commission acting in conjunction with and elected within the membership of the preceding General Citizens Committee or Regional Plan Association."[20]

Choice of a Leader

To launch the regional planning movement, the City Planning Section of the Commonwealth Club arranged a one-day conference on regional planning on April 11, 1924. This was attended by approximately one hundred delegates from communities throughout the Bay Area. After hearing such noted city planners as George B. Ford, Edward M. Bassett, John Nolen, Flavel Shurtleff, and Harland Bartholomew, the delegates adopted a resolution favoring the creation of a regional planning association and authorizing Carl J. Rhodin, chairman of the City Planning Section, to appoint an organizing committee to devise a plan of procedure to be submitted to the conference at a later date.

The committee appointed by Rhodin held two meetings, then decided to enlarge its membership to include a number of particularly influential citizens of the Bay Area, among whom was Senator James Duval Phelan, who had served as the first chairman of the City Planning Section of the Commonwealth Club ten years earlier. Phelan became head of a small committee on organization and ways and means at a meeting on November 20, 1924. Other members of this group, besides Rhodin and Black, were Frank D. Stringham, Mayor of Berkeley, Marshal Hale, a San Francisco merchant, Fred E. Reed, an Oakland realtor, and George Roos.

The choice of Phelan as chairman of the ways and means committee was especially significant, because it was he who suggested that the problem of organizing the proposed regional planning association be placed in the hands of his old friend Frederick W. Dohrmann, Jr., who had been one of the original members of the earlier Association for the Improvement and Adornment of San Francisco. Thus the new regional planning movement was linked, in a very personal fashion, with the "City Beautiful" movement that had flourished in an earlier day.

Dohrmann belonged to that circle of wealthy, influential men with whom Senator Phelan had always associated. From his father, a pioneer merchant in San Francisco, Dohrmann had inherited interests in half a dozen enterprises in which the family name appeared and was a director in several other companies. Brought up in the tradition of service to the community, he had served continuously as a committeeman of the Community Chest from its inception, had been for several years a director of the San Francisco Chamber of Commerce, and was also a director of the Recreation Council. He was particularly proud of his membership on the San Francisco Board of Education and was reluctant, because of that civic responsibility, to undertake another which might interfere with it. But he had very early acquired an interest in the form and appearance of cities through the study of architecture in Europe for three years after his graduation from St. Ignatius College. The idea of developing a comprehensive plan for the entire San Francisco Bay Area so strongly appealed to the artist and the idealist in him that he could not refuse the invitation to undertake to organize the much-desired regional planning association. When he accepted this task in January, 1925, he probably did not realize that he had entered upon his greatest public service.

CHAPTER TWELVE

Fred Dohrmann and the
Regional Plan Association

Fred Dohrmann undertook the stupendous job of attempting to arouse a whole metropolitan region to the desirability of planning for orderly growth and development. Even in 1925, when the population of all nine counties surrounding the bay was less than a million and a half, the task of reaching public officials and civic leaders in more than fifty cities distributed throughout an area almost as large as the states of Connecticut and Delaware together must have seemed staggering. At first Dohrmann agreed to serve the cause of regional planning for only three months, during the organization period. But to himself he must have admitted that he would serve indefinitely, for scarcely three months had slipped by when he wrote Phelan a letter saying that he had "resolved to devote myself to this movement as much as it may require in the way of time and energy for anything up to the next eight or ten years."[1] He had enthusiasm and zeal, and so had Russell Black, whom the new Regional Plan Association of San Francisco Bay Counties employed for a few months as "planning engineer," and so had Mayor Stringham of Berkeley, and Carl Rhodin, and Percy V. Long, the attorney, and many others who undertook, in the early months of 1925, to present the challenge of regional planning to service clubs and chambers of commerce from Santa Rosa and Petaluma to San Jose and Los Gatos.

The Regional Plan Association "aimed not only to educate, but actually to devise in a technical sense solutions to the interrealted civic problems" of the Bay Area,

Dohrmann told the Public Spirit Club of Berkeley in one of the first talks that he made after assuming the presidency of the new organization.[2] He listed six problems which he said were regional in scope and could not be met except through the coöperation of two or more or perhaps all the cities and counties in the Bay Area. At the head of the list was "a unified plan for port and harbor development on all sides of San Francisco Bay, similar to that which has been made for New York Harbor." Next in order came "a coördinated system of highways and scenic boulevards and bridges," and related to it were "rapid transit connections between all parts of the bay district, with special attention to commuting facilities." A fourth objective of the association was to be public "acquisition and development of recreational areas and large park reservations while they are obtainable at a reasonable cost and in a fair state of preservation." A fifth was the removal of the growing menace of pollution of the bay by sewage and waste. Lastly, Dohrmann cited the need for "regional zoning for the determination of the areas best suited to home-building, to industry, and to agriculture, and to insure a convenient and proper relation between home areas and industrial sites." In other words, the Regional Plan Association contemplated a study that would produce, in essence, a long-range, comprehensive land-use plan for the Bay Area, showing how every part of the area might be appropriately developed.

Dohrmann explained that the association would strive to unify the various plans being prepared by the several

Fred Dohrmann, Jr., President of Regional Plan Association, 1925–1928. Photograph courtesy of Mrs. Dohrmann.

communities of the Bay Area and to become a clearing house for future plans and developments. And it would attempt to inform the public about planning, by issuing bulletins and press releases and holding frequent public meetings.

Mayor Stringham of Berkeley, who followed Dohrmann on the program, invited the audience to consider the long-term future: "Fifty years ago the bay region had a population of one hundred thousand. Today the same area has probably more than a million and a half. In fifty years it will likely exceed ten million. So we must think in large terms and face the human as well as the physical problems."[3] Even if his population prediction was something less than scientific, at least it had the merit of startling his hearers.

Way to a Civic Renaissance

In speeches before other groups, Dohrmann earnestly pleaded for "a real sense of cooperation" among communities of the Bay Area. "If a great ideal such as a better city and region is the promise of tomorrow," he told the Vallejo Rotary Club, "there is no reason why cooperation cannot be secured in lighting the way to a great civic renaissance. City planning has something more to it than the technical outlining of improvement schemes. In its essence it is a forward movement for better citizenship and for elevating the conditions of life which surround all who are making our civilization. Places are like people and must be surrounded by love in order to lift them to a level at which the citizens will do more than merely live and make a living. If nations can demand and secure the allegiance and self-sacrifice of countless multitudes to uphold their ideals, why should not cities, which are the birthplaces and homes of whole families, be equally honored and strengthened. Our regional planning movement first proposes to inform the peoples of the conditions that surround them, to educate them to the necessities, and to agitate for a solution of public problems. It can do this only by cooperation among those who think alike and who may be relied upon to educate the communities to think alike. Once this is accomplished, not only will the San Francisco Bay Area have entered upon a program of orderly development, but the whole standing and influence of the region will be enhanced."[4]

This speech, perhaps more than any other Dohrmann ever made, revealed his vision, his crusading idealism, his confidence—or rather, overconfidence—in the appeal of the idea of regional planning. The gains to be made through area-wide coöperation appeared so manifestly desirable that he could not doubt that once reasonable and intelligent men became familiar with the pertinent facts about regional problems, they would feel compelled to solve the problems through united effort. "You know, as I know," he once told the Commonwealth Club, "that when the public knows what the fact is, if that fact presupposes and demands . . . the accomplishment of something, *the public usually gets what it wants when it knows what it wants.*"[5] And so he thought of the Regional Plan Association as an organization that would tell the public "what we think would be the answers to their problems, and then help them to understand the answers, and then help them to get results." He had an abiding faith in the willingness of the public to act decisively when confronted with accurate information on any problem. "The public is not stupid," he was fond of saying; "it is only ignorant of the facts."[6]

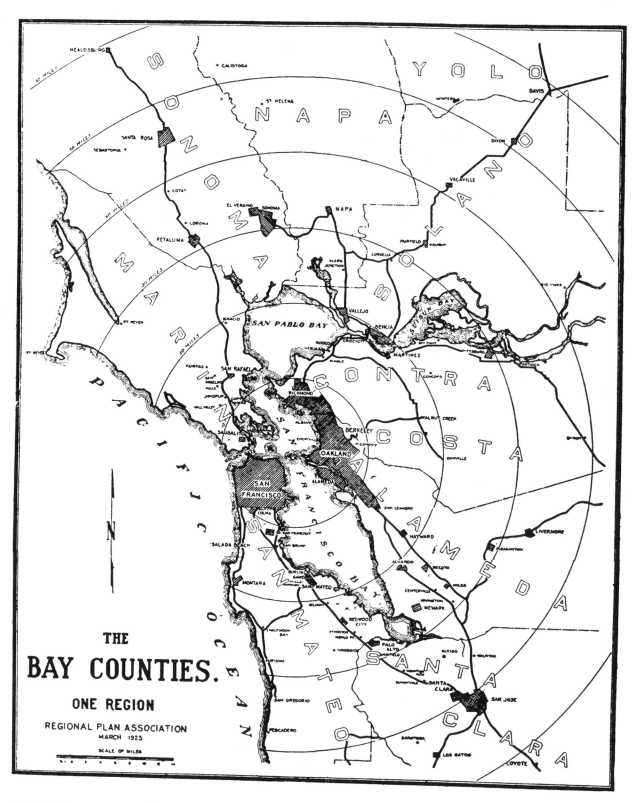

Map Used in Publications of the Regional Plan Association, 1925. The Association predicted that the San Francisco Bay Area would have 3,175,000 residents in 1950. The Bureau of the Census reported in 1950 that 2,681,322 persons were living in the nine counties of the area in April of that year.

In those early days of the new planning movement Dohrmann and his associates apparently brushed aside any misgivings that assailed them and refused to ask themselves: "Is this too great an undertaking? Can we possibly succeed in raising sufficient funds, in collecting sufficient data, in achieving sufficient publicity for our purposes?" Patience, perseverance, and performance would enable them to triumph over the ignorance, indifference, suspicion, and timidity of less inspired men, they evidently believed.

Building an Organization

Dohrmann spoke often before community organizations while the employees of the association gathered data on Bay Area problems and compiled lists of prospective members. Black concentrated mainly on obtaining information from city planning commissions, city engineers, county surveyors, chambers of commerce, and real-estate boards. Their replies indicated that Bay Area communities then were chiefly concerned about bridging the bay, improving streets and highways, and developing port facilities. City engineers almost invariably reported that local sewer systems discharged directly into the bay, and none of these officials appeared to question the desirability of this method of sewage disposal. Generally, the information supplied to the association was so sketchy as to be of little value, but its very inadequacy showed there was need of systematically collecting and analyzing data on physical, social, and economic conditions in the Bay Area.

A field representative named John F. Kennedy, who had previously been employed by the San Francisco Chamber of Commerce, called on prominent businessmen and industrialists to solicit memberships in the association. His efforts, though supplemented by telephone calls and personal letters from Dohrmann, unfortunately failed to yield the results anticipated. There was no rush to join the Regional Plan Association.

Dohrmann himself found that most of the men on whom he had counted for financial support—the kind of men described by journalists as "captains of industry" and "powers in the community"—were indifferent to his newly espoused cause. Of a dozen or more prominent manufacturers, financiers, real-estate men, and merchants to whom he addressed his first appeal for funds, only Marshal Hale and Phelan responded, each with $500. These two contributions merely equalled the amount Dohrmann had lent the association by way of "starting the ball a-rolling," as he said. Since the office rent, salaries, and operating expenses amounted to almost $1,000 a month, Dohrmann was soon subsidizing the association heavily from his own pocket; yet he showed no inclination to abandon his civic enterprise.

He concluded that in order to enlist active interest in the program of the Regional Plan Association, he should proceed at once to have the preliminary planning survey originally recommended by Black prepared by a well-known planning consultant. A report on the survey would give prospective members a clearer idea of the nature of regional planning and of the problems with which a general plan for the Bay Area would deal. He engaged as consultant Harland Bartholomew, of St. Louis, who had been one of the principal speakers at the Commonwealth Club conference on regional planning in April, 1924.

The Bartholomew Report

Bartholomew found that "the outstanding deficiency in the Bay Region" was "lack of unity in physical improvements and comprehensive planning."[7] Not mincing words, he singled out "psychological obstacles of local pride and prejudice" as the most serious difficulties to be faced. Lest communities mistake regional planning as a threat to their identities, however, he hastened to point out that this type of planning "need not deprive existing municipalities of local autonomy."[8] Such powers as a regional planning agency might exercise would necessarily be "distinctively regional in character" and would relate to problems which no local government could successfully cope with individually.

Bartholomew agreed that bay crossings by bridge or tube were of immediate necessity, but he observed: "The spectacular nature of the features of engineering design appear to have totally obscured the equally and perhaps more important questions of types of traffic accommodation and their influence upon present conditions and future growth. Will they result in accentuation of present congestion or effectually relieve it? The ultimate needs of the region in railroad connections, in rapid transit, in motor truck and passenger car traffic should be planned with care in advance of any hasty decision upon the location and type of bay crossings."[9]

If these statements had been written yesterday or last month, they could not be more pertinent to present-day discussions of additional bay crossings and problems of over-all development. Their logic is as sound today as it was more than thirty years ago.

Even in 1925 Bartholomew could point out that "the Bay Region requires rapid transit more than any other metropolitan community, because of the physical characteristics of the region."[10] Transportation planners have recognized, in the years since then, that no system of highways and freeways, however extensive, alone can solve the problem of moving masses of people swiftly, safely, and economically. Both a rapid transit system and a comprehensive trafficway system are needed.

The lack of united effort in the development of port facilities prompted the consultant to recommend "a general plan for development of the entire bay and waterfront." "It is not to be expected that any such plan would ever be carried out in its entirety, but if well done would give direction to growth and serve to effect economy and to prevent wasteful and needless local competitive undertakings."[11]

The poverty of the Bay Area in waterfront recreation areas was matched, Bartholomew found, by its poverty in other types of public reservations. "The Bay Region," he wrote, "is notably lacking in volume and distribution of recreational areas. The history of all great cities has been that unless generous provision of recreational space has been made early in the history of the city, the most suitable recreational areas either become absorbed or so increased in value that their acquisition becomes prohibitive. To serve the future population of this region there should be an enlargement of present public recreational spaces of several hundred per cent, and this will scarcely equal the average of other regions, such as Boston, New York and Chicago."[12]

He particularly recommended watershed areas as regional parks—a recommendation that had been made by Charles Keeler, Managing Director of the Berkeley Chamber of Commerce, in 1923 with the thought that the watershed lands of the East Bay Water Company in the Berkeley Hills would be suitable.

On the subject of water supply Bartholomew was brief, merely noting that the Marin Municipal Water District, the East Bay Municipal Utility District, and the Spring Valley Water Company together could serve but a small percentage of the total Bay Area and that "a regional plan must concern itself with the water needs of the ultimate population,"[13] which presumably would be spread over a vast territory.

The means Bartholomew suggested for improving the physical conditions obtaining in the Bay Area and for coördinating the planning activities of a multiplicity of governmental units was a vaguely described regional planning commission that would "make plans for the future development of the region" and "possibly" administer subdivision and zoning regulations in unincorporated territory throughout the nine-county area.[14] Bartholomew apparently was feeling his way in this proposal and intended that the Regional Plan Association should make a thorough study of the whole subject of enabling legislation, effective organization for planning,

and the knotty problem of financing area-wide planning.

Dohrmann and his associates, however, showed only mild interest in enabling legislation of any kind; whereas the League of California Municipalities, the California Real Estate Association, and various city planning commissions were then struggling for the enactment of legislation authorizing the establishment of planning agencies in counties not operating under freeholder charters. Without county planning, regional planning would be impossible, these organizations understood, but they faced at least two more years of campaigning for an act authorizing county planning, because Governor C. C. Young had failed to sign a county planning bill approved by the legislature at its 1925 session. Correspondence between Dohrmann and the groups interested in legislation that would broaden the scope of planning in California reveals that he and other members of the Regional Plan Association were aware of the struggle for an enabling statute, but they assumed an almost detached attitude toward the entire undertaking, mainly because of Dohrmann's own feeling that there was no urgency about establishing additional planning agencies. He said on more than one occasion that the governments of the cities and counties in the Bay Area would support regional planning only after a private organization had demonstrated its value— and he expected that the demonstration would take several years.

Struggle for Support

The Bartholomew Report, presented to the members of the Regional Plan Association at a dinner given by Dohrmann at the St. Francis Hotel on September 16, 1925, provided the association with the kind of "ammunition" its president believed was necessary for a successful membership campaign. With this document on hand, Dohrmann resolved to place the organization on a firm foundation by filing papers of incorporation, broadening the financial support, and enlarging the membership. Some months previously he had sought to enhance the prestige of the association by inducing Dr. Ray Lyman Wilbur, president of Stanford University, and Dr. David P. Barrows, a former president of the University of California, to serve with several others on the board of trustees of the organization. In selecting officers, he turned to those who had been advising him on legal and financial matters: Percy V. Long (vice-president), Mrs. Parker Maddux, a prominent clubwoman (vice-president), Randolph V. Whiting, an attorney (secretary), and Matthew A. Harris, a businessman (treasurer). But Dohrmann still needed the participation of the business leaders of San Francisco. Unless he could elicit more than vague expressions of good will and meaningless praise for the "wonderful work" he was doing, the association might be doomed.

He invited the financiers and outstanding executives of the city, eight or ten at a time, to meet with him at the offices of the Regional Plan Association, so that he could "show them . . . just what this association means to individuals in San Francisco and thereby sell to them the idea that each one of them should contribute $100.00 toward this cause."[15] Within three weeks, forty of the men who accepted his invitation contributed $100 each to the association; but it is doubtful whether many of them were deeply impressed with the desirability of regional planning, even though they assured him that they were. Probably for business and social reasons they could not refuse his personal appeal for funds; very likely, too, they had the feeling that their donations relieved them of further concern about a matter that seemed remote from their day-to-day affairs. Certainly, few of them thereafter participated in the activities of the association.

Dohrmann ardently believed, nevertheless, that he was building a genuine area-wide movement. "San Franciscans must realize," he wrote one prospective contributor, "that what is good for any of the counties and the places around the bay is also good for us here in San Francisco and vice versa; and that any legitimate and unselfish movement like this will surely rebound to the individual as well as the collective benefit of all residents."[16]

Resolutions and Questionnaires

Having replenished the exchequer of the Regional Plan Association somewhat, Dohrmann and his associates and staff began preparing for a membership solicitation throughout the nine counties of the Bay Area by requesting organizations that were familiar with the program of the association to adopt resolutions approving its purpose, scope, and activities. Organizations which endorsed the efforts of the association were chiefly the chambers of commerce before which its leaders had appeared in 1925 and the first six months of 1926. In some organizations all members voted on a resolution, in others only the board of directors. Just how valuable this type of support was would be difficult to judge. Much of it, surely, meant little more than the perfunctory praise offered Dohrmann by men who had no intention of joining him in his civic labors. Most organizations easily accept and quickly forget resolutions approving worthy causes.

The Regional Plan Association was a good deal less successful in inducing chambers of commerce and other associations to respond to a questionnaire seeking information on local industries, public utilities, housing, traffic, transportation, and community facilities. "The information asked for in your questionnaire is so voluminous and technical in nature as to make it impracticable for us to attempt to fill it out," the secretary-manager of the Oakland Chamber of Commerce complained in a rather typical reaction to the lengthy form distributed by the association. To answer all the questions in detail would require considerable research that the Oakland Chamber of Commerce was not prepared to undertake, he said; and then he added: "It seems to me that such a survey would have to be made by those who are promoting the Regional Plan Association, in which the Oakland Chamber of Commerce is not participating."[17]

The letter must have depressed Dohrmann, who had attempted more than a year earlier to persuade Joseph R. Knowland, publisher of the Oakland *Tribune*, to serve as vice-president of the Regional Plan Association and had been turned down. The organization simply had no effective support in Oakland. The leaders in that city were so preoccupied with its downtown congestion that area-wide problems, other than a transbay crossing, seemed beyond the realm of immediate concern. Oakland merchants, bankers, and terminal operators who formed the Major Highway and Traffic Committee of One Hundred did respect Dohrmann enough, however, to accept his recommendation that they employ Harland Bartholomew to prepare a major street plan for their city.

The Regional Plan Association never was able to form local advisory committees on various problems in every one of the Bay Area counties, although it endeavored all during 1926 and a good part of 1927 to perfect this type of organization. A board of twenty-seven regional representatives, including members from all nine counties, was the nearest it came to presenting even the appearance of area-wide participation. Outside San Francisco the most active members of the association came mainly from San Mateo, Marin, and Santa Clara counties, with a sprinkling of members from Napa, Contra Costa, and Alameda counties. Guy Wilfrid Hayler, who became planning engineer for the association in 1926, said that "it took a long time to get people on a selected list, because they were afraid of the domination of San Francisco."[18] In short, the very auspices under which the association came into being probably handicapped it from the beginning. It was suspect in many areas because most of its leaders were identified with the metropolis.

Regional Studies

In spite of the ever-present financial problem (which Dohrmann continued to meet by contributions from his own resources) and the difficulties of persuading promi-

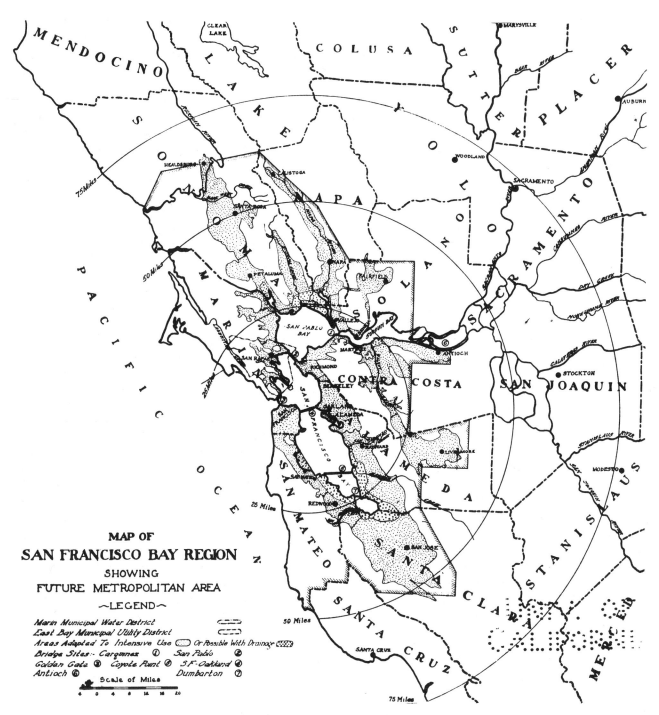

MAP OF
SAN FRANCISCO BAY REGION
SHOWING
FUTURE METROPOLITAN AREA

~LEGEND~

Marin Municipal Water District
East Bay Municipal Utility District
Areas Adapted To Intensive Use ⬭ Or Possible With Drainage ▨
Bridge Sites:· Carquinez ① San Pablo ②
Golden Gate ③ Coyote Point ④ SF-Oakland ⑤
Antioch ⑥ Dumbarton ⑦

Scale of Miles

Charles H. Lee's Map Showing the Future Metropolitan Area. In 1926 Lee forecast an "ultimate" population of 5,000,000 to 6,000,000 in the areas "adapted to intensive use" (shaded on the map). Photograph courtesy of Seismological Society of America.

nent men and women in various Bay Area communities to become members, the association did manage in 1926-1927 to make some progress on its announced program of developing a regional plan. Hayler prepared a series of maps depicting various types of existing regional development, such as highways, sanitation facilities, airfields, bridges, transportation, recreation, water supply, and zoning. On some of these maps, which technical divisions of the association used, Hayler indicated suggested regional improvements.

At no time, however, did the Regional Plan Association attempt the kind of projections made in a study published by Charles H. Lee, a San Francisco consulting engineer, in the *Bulletin* of the Seismological Society of America in June, 1926. Lee sought to determine the extent of the ultimate urban development in the Bay Area, not as a basis for the kind of city and metropolitan regional planning Dohrmann was promoting, but in order to outline "what might be done to reduce future hazards to life and property from earthquake and earthquake fires."[19] In particular, Lee was interested in the ultimate water supply requirements of this metropolitan region and in the kind of interconnected storage and water distribution facilities that would be effective in the event of a great distaster, such as occurred in 1906. His studies should have suggested much to the members of the Regional Plan Association, but they did not.

From a study of detailed topographic sheets of the United States Geological Survey and from personal knowledge and inspection of terrain, Lee roughly determined the uses to which the land in the entire territory surrounding San Francisco Bay might be put in the future. This would mean classification of areas according to their suitability for agriculture, industry, commerce, and urban and suburban residential development. Thus Lee arrived at a calculation of the amount of land useful for intensive occupation—876,000 acres, plus perhaps some 100,000 additional acres that might be reclaimed from marshes and tidelands. Of the 876,000 acres classified as "useful for intensive occupation," he designated 564,400 acres, or approximately 882 square miles, as useful for urban and suburban development.[20]

On the assumption that the ultimate population density would not exceed twice that in the San Francisco–Oakland metropolitan district in 1920, which averaged 3.2 persons per acre, Lee predicted a population in the metropolitan area of five to six millions, out of a state population of approximately seventeen millions.[21] From their knowledge of available water supplies, present-day analysts assume that California will have a population of sixty millions and the Bay Area several millions more than Lee

prognosticated; but in 1926 the forecast of an ultimate population of seventeen millions in the state must have seemed fantastic. The population of California in 1920 was only 3,426,861.

Population predictions aside, Lee made the kind of land use studies that are essential for any genuine regional planning. No one before him had attempted to show graphically the possible size and shape of the future urban complex in the Bay Area. Had the Regional Plan Association taken its cue from this engineer's studies, it might have made some progress toward the development of a regional plan. But for any single organization to carry out the kind of planning program Lee's approach suggested would have required a large staff, at least the $250,000 originally proposed by Russell Van Nest Black, and many years of patient labor. The Regional Plan Association had a skeleton staff, limited funds, and an unknown life expectancy. Inevitably, it pursued a piecemeal rather than a comprehensive approach to regional planning.

Detailed Studies

One of the detailed studies decided upon was an analysis of the difficulties of delivering produce from San Mateo and Santa Clara counties to the wholesale district in the general area of Clay and Davis streets in San Francisco, which thirty years later was to be declared a blighted area subject to redevelopment. Heavy traffic on El Camino Real and on city streets leading to the district delayed trucks coming from agricultural areas, thereby complicating the operations of commission houses and retarding the distribution of produce to markets throughout the city. Mapping of the routes used by produce trucks led to comprehensive mapping of highways in the entire Bay Area, then to study of the need for widening certain heavily traveled routes and for constructing additional routes. The Regional Plan Association hoped later to propose a system of circumferential roads, such as Bartholomew had suggested in his preliminary survey.

The study of wholesale produce delivery related to a problem that even in the 'twenties seemed serious and is now alarming to many Californians—the loss, through urban sprawl and "scatteration," of tens of thousands of acres of first-class agricultural land. "At the present time," Hayler wrote, "the wholesale produce delivered into San Francisco is coming more and more from remote points in San Mateo and Santa Clara counties, owing to land going out of cultivation in localities closer in. The East Bay situation may be said to be similar. This same condition has been found to exist in many other large cities in America where the situation has been investigated, and in every case it has played a great part in forcing up the cost of living in these particular cities."[22]

Although the Regional Plan Association pleaded for "earnest consideration" of the desirability of preserving land near cities for a variety of agricultural uses—truck gardening, fruit growing, poultry farming, and dairying, not even farmers at that time passed resolutions on the subject. Only within the past five or six years have agricultural associations attempted to save some areas from urbanization and to ponder the implications of withdrawal from cultivation of one fertile valley after another.

As settlement along the level lands bordering the bay increased, another problem grew worse: pollution of the waters of the bay. The Regional Plan Association studied the information it had gathered from cities and sanitary districts and found that there were more than fifty outfall sewers draining into the shallow waters along the eastern side of the bay between Richmond and San Leandro. "Much the same state of affairs exists from San Francisco southward on the peninsular side," Hayler pointed out.[23] Nevertheless, as new subdivisions opened and cities expanded, the number of outfall sewers polluting the bay increased. By 1927 the total was no les than 175.

To stimulate action on the pollution problem before it became truly menacing, the Regional Plan Association arranged a meeting in San Francisco in October, 1926, to which it invited representatives from municipalities and sanitary districts throughout the Bay Area. Sixty-five persons attended the meeting and heard officials of the United States Public Health Service, the State Board of Health, and local health departments recommend a survey of the problem. But when a special committee later estimated that a survey would cost $30,000 or more, interest in the pollution problem subsided. More than twenty years were to pass before Bay Area cities would make serious efforts to deal with the problem.

Dohrmann's personal interest in aviation as a new and important commercial activity caused the association to give a great deal of time and effort in 1926 and the early months of 1927 to a campaign for enabling legislation that would authorize the State Board of Harbor Commissioners to construct and operate a landing platform for commercial aviation over the waterfront piers in San Francisco. Although Governor C. C. Young signed the act drawn by the association, Dohrmann's dream of a landing platform a million feet square rising a hundred and fifty or two hundred feet above high-water mark never materialized. More commodious airports developed by San Francisco and Oakland in San Mateo County and on Bay Farm Island, respectively, answered the needs of the growing aviation industry.

A Conference in Oakland

In 1927, the last full year in which the Regional Plan Association was active, many city officials and all the city planners then employed in California joined forces to push through the state legislature an improved version of the local planning enabling legislation that had been pocket vetoed by the governor in 1925. That interest in this movement was widespread was indicated by the large attendance at a two-day conference on city planning arranged by Fred E. Reed, chairman of the City Plan Division of the California Real Estate Association and head of the City Planning Committee of the Oakland Real Estate Board. More than a thousand representatives of municipalities, county governments, the state legislature, chambers of commerce, women's clubs, and business organizations came to hear such prominent planners as John Nolen, Harland Bartholomew, Gordon Whitnall, Carol Aronovici, Hugh Pomeroy, Charles Cheney, and Stephen Child. Besides these speakers, heads of citizen groups, public health officers, managers of chambers of commerce, attorneys, real-estate men, and officials of the League of California Municipalities also spoke.

Asked to appear on the program, Dohrmann seized the occasion to make another plea for East Bay support and to explain the purpose of his organization. "I prefer to think of the waters of San Francisco Bay as uniting the various communities rather than dividing them, and on that account I consider that their common problems demand a common solution," he said. "The idea of planning the San Francisco Bay Area on a broad, comprehensive scale is one which should appeal to every community and to none more particularly than to Oakland and its sister communities." He assured his listeners that the Regional Plan Association had "no political aims or interests to serve for any one particular city or area" and that it would benefit each community in proportion to the coöperation given. Citing various features of the East Bay that might serve as inspiration for "a wide system of regional planning," he pointed out that "the one thing wanting is the striking of the popular imagination to what might be accomplished if the cities can only see with one eye."[24]

By way of "striking the popular imagination," Dohrmann pictured the Bay Area as "the home of an enormous population" in the future, but he warned that "we must not be led away by thinking that a great increase in population is the only thing necessary for progress." The great cities of the East, with their congested living conditions, their inadequate trading facilities, and their ever-increasing municipal costs, were paying the penalty for mistakenly equating population gains with "progress." In

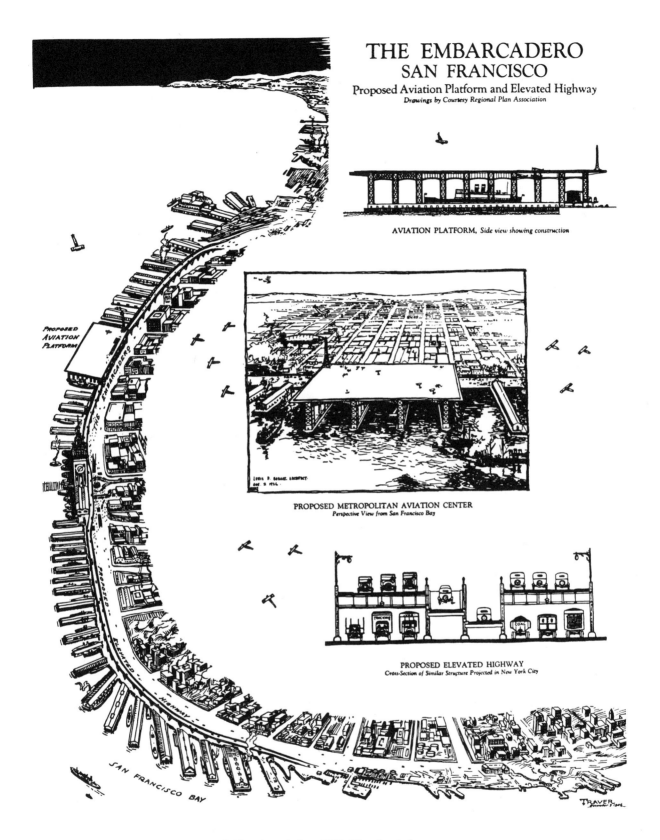

THE EMBARCADERO
SAN FRANCISCO
Proposed Aviation Platform and Elevated Highway
Drawings by Courtesy Regional Plan Association

AVIATION PLATFORM, *Side view showing construction*

PROPOSED METROPOLITAN AVIATION CENTER
Perspective View from San Francisco Bay

PROPOSED ELEVATED HIGHWAY
Cross-Section of Similar Structure Projected in New York City

Aviation Platform Proposed by the Regional Plan Association, 1927. The elevated highway shown in the drawings would have followed a route similar to that of the Embarcadero Freeway. Drawings by Louis P. Hobart, Architect.

the newer West "the grotesque menace of an ill-planned region" could be avoided by "concerted action" to utilize growth and development to the best advantage.[25]

Stephen Child, who spoke later in the session addressed by Dohrmann, was no less concerned than his friend with area-wide coöperation, but he was willing, as Dohrmann never was, to look beyond the preparation of a regional plan to the still more difficult process of making use of the plan. He chose to discuss the political problems involved in carrying out a comprehensive scheme for the future development of the Bay Area. In somewhat fanciful vein the landscape architect and consultant on city planning described a dream in which he awakened, like Rip Van Winkle, from a long sleep and discovered on the summit of Yerba Buena Island a temple-like structure that was the assembly hall of the Federation of the Boroughs of San Francisco Bay. Over the entrance was this inscription: "Dedicated to Unity of Purpose for the San Francisco Bay Region."[26]

Years before, he was informed by a knowing mentor who found him gazing at the beautiful white marble building, "a great deal of suspicion and narrow provincial municipalism" had produced so many "petty quarrels and jealousies" that the wiser and more farseeing men in the Bay Area began to realize that dissension was hurting everyone. They were in a mood to listen to a visitor from a far country who prophesied that the twentieth century would be the "century of the Pacific" and that millions of people would live in the Bay Area. Taking his words to heart, they saw that it behooved them to prepare for growth. Accordingly, after many months of discussion, they evolved a regional federation, since "it was evident that no real merger of all these communities into one single great city was either possible or needed."[27]

Each borough in the regional federation included "those communities whose important civic problems, such as drainage, sewage disposal, water supply, conservation, and the like, could best be solved by communal action." On the San Francisco Peninsula there were the boroughs of San Francisco, San Mateo, and Palo Alto; in the northern part of the Santa Clara Valley, the borough of Santa Clara, which included San Jose, Santa Clara, Saratoga, and several other communities; in the East Bay, the borough of Oakland, and so on. Each had a council, a borough manager, and all the officials required by a modern, efficient city government. In return for "a very considerable degree of liberty in regard to its own affairs," each borough recognized that it was the job of the federation "to undertake to solve those problems that no one borough could solve alone."[28]

This remarkable system of boroughs had all come about, according to the mentor, after Dohrmann's Regional Plan Association had prepared a preliminary regional plan and had "sold regional planning to the Bay District." "It was when it came to undertaking to put this plan into effect, however, that it was found necessary to establish this Federation of the Boroughs of San Francisco Bay..."[29] There was needed some over-all government that could authorize, finance, and construct projects of benefit to the entire metropolitan region or to subregions.

Still quoting his imaginary mentor, Child pictured the regional federation as having solved the area-wide water supply problem, as well as the problem of developing area-wide harbor facilities and a plan for utilizing every foot of bay shoreline, including sections for recreational use. Partly completed or under construction was "a splendidly effective system of main highways," following a well-considered scheme of the regional planners. The trackage of competing railroads had been consolidated wherever possible, a belt line had been built along the waterfront to serve industrial areas, and many grade crossings had been eliminated. The federation had also solved the problem of bridging the bay, "for this again was a problem far too big and too comprehensive for any one community."[30] Through the influence of the federation a metropolitan park commission had been appointed, which had included beautiful mountain canyons, watershed areas and their storage reservoirs, and scenic hilltops in a regional recreation system connected by a series of pleasure-ways in which there was a link named for each of the presidents of the United States from Washington to Coolidge.[31] In outlining this metropolitan park system, Child was expressing ideas he had cherished for more than ten years.

At the close of his talk, the main idea of which had been inspired by a federation organized in the Ruhr Valley a few years previously, Child asked his hearers, "Was it not something more substantial than a dream that I had, and is it not for us to bring it to earth, establish it upon firm foundation . . . , so that it may achieve its aims—unity of purpose for the San Francisco Bay Region?"[32]

Child was, of course, ahead of his time. Unfortunately, too, he was an elderly man, very deaf, and anything but a forceful speaker, though he did have a certain charm. His speech "fell flat," one delegate to the conference recalls.[33] The political realists of the day pinned their hopes for improvement of the Bay Area not on regional federation or some other form of metropolitan government but on a new local planning enabling act based on a model planning act prepared by the Advisory Committee on City Planning and Zoning of the United States Department of Commerce and on the planning act passed by the state of New York in 1926.

The Planning Act of 1927

The draft of the proposed California act not only provided for repeal of the city planning law of 1915 but also authorized for the first time county and regional planning in California. No proposed legislation providing for any form of metropolitan government to carry out area-wide plans accompanied it. The proponents of the legislation —the League of California Municipalities, the California Conference on City Planning, the California Real Estate Board, and the Commonwealth Club of California—had not faced that issue.

Besides providing for the organization of city, county, and regional planning commissions, the planning enabling act of 1927 authorized the preparation of a master plan for the area in which the city, county, or regional commission had jurisdiction, whereas the 1915 legislation had not embodied the concept of a single comprehensive plan. The new act stated: "The plan shall be made with the general purpose of guiding and accomplishing a coordinated, adjusted, and harmonious development of the municipality, or county, and its environs, which will, in accordance with present and future needs, best promote the amenities of life, health, safety, morals, order, convenience, prosperity and general welfare, as well as efficiency and economy in the process of development . . ."[34]

Seemingly the new legislation granted planning commissions powers broad enough to enable them to function effectively as advisory agencies to city and county governing bodies; yet many persons, including Governor Young, entertained doubts about this statute. It was expected to raise many new problems of city and county procedure and many new legal questions. As a condition of his approval the governor exacted a promise from the California Conference on City Planning that it would appoint a committee of representative citizens, versed in planning matters and in real-estate problems, to watch its operations and prepare any needed amendments in advance of the 1929 session of the state legislature.

The language of the act was vague concerning what constituted a region for planning purposes, and this vagueness tended to encourage small divisions within larger physiographic areas to form so-called regional planning commissions. The Palo Alto Chamber of Commerce, for instance, appointed a committee to make a field survey for a proposed "regional plan" for Palo Alto and its vicinity, but this movement progressed no further than the discussion stage. There was another misguided effort toward "regional planning" in southern San Mateo County, under the leadership of a group in Redwood City. Like the Palo Alto movement, this also died after a few committee meetings.

East Bay Association

So far as the Regional Plan Association of San Francisco Bay Counties was concerned, the most serious threat to genuine regional planning was the East Bay Regional Plan Association formed by Fred E. Reed, an Oakland realtor, in the spring of 1927. This organization, composed of citizens of Alameda and Contra Costa counties, petitioned the governor to designate the two East Bay counties a region for planning purposes, and although Governor Young did not act upon the petition, the East Bay organization succeeded in vitiating the efforts of Dohrmann's association to establish the concept of the nine counties bordering on the bay as a single geographical, economic, and social unit.

The East Bay Regional Plan Association busied itself at first chiefly with publicizing the streets and highways plan prepared by Harland Bartholomew for the Major Highway and Traffic Committee of One Hundred. This plan proposed the creation of a distributor loop around the central business district of Oakland, a superhighway along the East Bay waterfront from San Leandro to Richmond (similar to the route of the present freeway), parallel routes to relieve congestion on East Twelfth and East Fourteenth streets, several cross-town routes above Lake Merritt, and the widening and extension of the Skyline Boulevard in the Berkeley Hills.

Reed, who was named chairman of the newly formed Oakland City Planning Commission soon after presentation of the Bartholomew Plan, had written cordial letters to Dohrmann for many months preceding the formation of the East Bay Regional Plan Association; and the two continued to correspond politely even after the East Bay association was established. But the gentlemanly exchange of views did not alter the fact that for Dohrmann the attempt to keep alive his own Regional Plan Association had become a heartbreaking endeavor. In 1925 he had personally contributed $13,250 to the organization, in 1926 more than $10,000, and in 1927 nearly $14,000, not to mention hours and hours of time, his most earnest thought, and the very essence of his hopes and aspirations as a citizen of a metropolitan community not yet fully aware of the material and spiritual interdependence of its parts. Desperately resorting to his social position as a member of the merchant aristocracy of San Francisco, he had arranged a series of dinners at his own home, in 1927, to which he had invited the cream of San Francisco business executives, and, as before, he had wangled con-

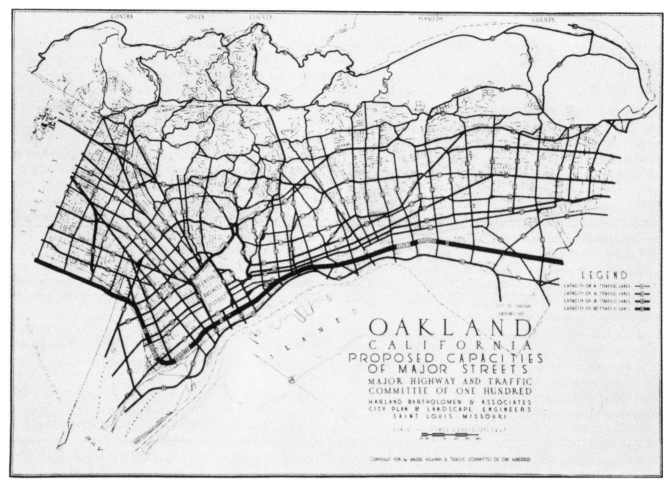

Harland Bartholomew's Plan for Major Streets in Oakland, 1927. The proposed superhighway along the waterfront foreshadowed the Eastshore Freeway built after World War II.

End of the Association

tributions from them that brought donations from other sources to $8,000. Yet he had not built an area-wide organization with a large and enthusiastic membership. In a letter to a political candidate who asked to appear before the Regional Plan Association, he disclosed that "the active members probably do not comprise more than ten."[35] This was all that the association amounted to after three years of steady effort, reams of publicity in newspapers and magazines, hundreds of speeches before other organizations, publication of several significant reports and a stream of factual bulletins, convocation of large groups to consider special problems of the Bay Area, and literally hundreds of letters from Dohrmann, Hayler, Black, Kennedy, Long, and others to prospective members, public officials, and inquiring citizens.

End of the Association

After futile efforts to raise money through the San Francisco Chamber of Commerce and through the Community Chest, Dohrmann and his fellow officers of the Regional Plan Association in April, 1928, discharged the staff, closed the office in the Phelan Building, and moved the records of the association to a vacant room adjoining the offices of an attorney member in the Foxcroft Building. In a memorandum headed "The Past, Present, and Future of the Regional Plan Association," Dohrmann avowed that the organization was "not going to die a full death," but was "going to try and hibernate for about a year."[36] He provided $125 a month for eight months to "enable the organization to keep itself before the eyes of the public," but after this fitful hibernation the Regional Plan Association slept the sleep of oblivion—or rather it became for Dohrmann a ghost that might some day return to life and achieve all that he had labored in vain to accomplish.

The president of the Regional Plan Association of San Francisco Bay Counties was one of those unsung civic heroes whose full contribution to the advancement of the metropolitan community can never be known. Somewhat aloof and humorless as a speaker, unexceptional as a thinker, and lacking the masterfulness that proclaims the genuine leader, he nevertheless made thousands of people aware that city planning and metropolitan regional planning are means of creating a better physical environment. He shared the typical businessman's distrust of politics and government and perhaps devoted too much effort to missionary work among his fellow businessmen when he should have been spending at least part of his time cultivating politicians and their cronies. He for the most part ignored the important job of helping to draft planning enabling legislation, and he regarded any consideration of political amalgamations or metropolitan federation as "controversial" and therefore taboo. But with all his limitations, he was far above the average in vision, in appreciation of the aesthetic qualities of his surroundings, and in devotion to the truly great ideal of metropolitan regional unity. He never regretted having spent thousands of dollars sustaining the Regional Plan Association; nor did he ever look upon his expenditure of time and effort as a fruitless sacrifice. He retained until his death in January, 1936, faith in the belief that at some time in the future other groups would prepare and carry out the regional plan of which he dreamed.

There is one indispensable ally that any new movement must have, and that is time. Time was not Dohrmann's companion in arms. Though he fought valiantly to establish the concept of the nine counties and nearly three score cities of the Bay Area as one community, he led a crusade for which the vast majority of people were unprepared. There were comparatively few city planning commissions and no county planning commissions in the Bay Area in the mid-twenties. The only county planning body appointed under the planning enabling legislation enacted in 1927 was in Santa Barbara County. The number of people in the Bay Area who had direct knowledge of the planning function through the operations of a local planning agency was relatively insignificant. Dohrmann publicized the role of planning and stimulated interest in forming local planning bodies, but he himself lacked the moral support that a substantial number of planning commissions might have given him. The absence of such support, together with other handicaps under which the Regional Plan Association labored, proved to be a fatal drag on the struggling regional planning movement.

Despite its brief and almost consumptive existence, the Regional Plan Association did provide a valuable legacy for later groups inspired by the ideal of area-wide coöperation. It succeeded in identifying almost all the major problems that affect the metropolitan region in its entirety, with the exception, of course, of the problem of air pollution, which is new since World War II. It emphasized that these problems are interrelated and should be attacked through a comprehensive, area-wide planning program, even though the association itself was unable to develop such a program. Through its very failure, the organization demonstrated that area-wide participation is essential to the success of a regional planning program and that local governments, especially, must support the program. It correctly conceived the functions of a regional planning agency to include conducting research, analyzing the data collected, serving as a clearing house for data on the area as a whole that would be needed by numerous local governmental agencies and private organizations, preparing an area-wide general plan in coöperation with local governments, and facilitating the coördination of local plans with the regional general plan. The greatest legacy of the association was, however, intangible: the inspiration it has afforded citizens and planning officials who desire development of the metropolitan region in accordance with a comprehensive, guiding plan.

CHAPTER THIRTEEN

Prosperity and Projects

In the 'twenties San Francisco enjoyed another of those periods of heady prosperity that have recurred at irregular intervals ever since it became a metropolis in the days of the gold rush. So congested were piers along the Embarcadero that many vessels seeking to discharge or take on cargo were diverted to Oakland or Richmond, which thus had the benefit of maritime commerce they had not expected. Within the decade the tonnage handled at the port of San Francisco doubled, and the value of the cargoes moving across its wharves soared in the year 1929 to the unprecedented figure of $1,613,100,000—twice that of cargoes handled at all the other ports in the Bay Area. San Francisco, the chief distribution center in the West, could boast in 1929 of almost half the wholesale trade of California, though southern California, growing more rapidly than the central and northern sections of the state, was soon to invade trade areas long monopolized by San Francisco. In retail trade, too, the city that was once "the miserable village of Yerba Buena" held an enviable position. In 1929 its stores rang up on their cash registers sales amounting to almost half of all those made in the nine counties bordering on the bay, although only two-fifths of the population of the Bay Area lived in San Francisco. And year after year that most sensitive barometer of economic conditions, the annual total of building permits, remained between fifty and sixty million dollars.

Structural steel workers precariously balanced on beams high above the streets reared a new skyline for the metropolis—a skyline that was to continue almost unchanged until after World War II. In 1926 and 1927 they fashioned the huge skeleton of the Russ Building, still the tallest and largest office building in San Francisco. Two blocks to the south on Montgomery Street rose the Hunter-Dulin Building, twenty-three stories high, with hundreds of offices for corporation executives and professional men. Near by, other massive structures, fifteen to twenty-two stories high, rose from piles driven into the sand and mud that once marked the edge of Yerba Buena Cove. And then there was the impressive edifice of the Pacific Telephone and Telegraph Company, twenty-six stories high, aloof on New Montgomery Street.

Suburban Growth

In this concentrated metropolis, "decentralization" only occasionally roused mild forebodings, yet growth in areas far beyond San Francisco's corporate limits had begun to accelerate. The challenge of the outlying shopping center, with its acres of parking space, was of course more than two decades in the future, but the kind of growth that was to give rise to the suburban shopping center was already evident in San Mateo County.

"The Peninsula has suddenly come into its own," the *California Real Estate Magazine* observed in June, 1927. "Where two years ago there were perhaps less than ten subdivision developments, there are now nearly one hundred in progress. Big profits have been made on lot resales and the developers of new lands are finding a ready market for their offerings."

Some of the large, old estates that had become islands of undeveloped acreage in the midst of small-lot developments finally were sold. One such was the 375-acre estate purchased by John Parrott in 1860 and named Baywood. Situated in the heart of the city of San Mateo, it had blocked development of the city to the west of El Camino Real ever since the time of the great earthquake and fire in San Francisco. The developers, who purchased it with the intention of dividing it into fifty-foot lots, reportedly paid a million dollars for it.

Real-estate groups would have been willing to pay similar sums for other large estates had the owners been willing to part with them, but the tradition of manor-house living died slowly in San Mateo County. For another two decades many big land holdings were to continue intact in the midst of subdivision plattings, thereby causing a peculiarly spotty pattern of urbanization unlike that of almost all other areas within a thirty-mile radius of San Francisco.

The growth of the Peninsula in the late 'twenties reflected the extensive adoption of the private automobile as a means of traveling to and from work and the desire of city dwellers for more space and more of the amenities of living. By 1930 the population of San Mateo County was twice as large as in 1920, and most of its 77,000 residents lived in towns and unincorporated areas on the bay side.

San Francisco itself added almost 128,000 new residents in the 1920's; but on the opposite side of the bay, in Alameda County, the same kind of low-density development that was occurring in San Mateo County absorbed an increase of more than 130,000. Growth of the small cities of Marin County that were within commuting range of San Francisco also reflected the search for more living space. San Jose, in the Santa Clara Valley, likewise continued to spread out in an uncrowded pattern. Agriculture in the surrounding area flourished, and the number of food-processing plants increased, providing many new jobs. Only the cities in the northern counties of Sonoma, Napa, and Solano failed to make noticeable population gains and to get used to the sight of surveyors laying out new blocks in fields and orchards beyond the existing residential districts.

Insecure Metropolis

The growth of San Francisco actually made it an insecure city, with a very real cause for worry. In the late 'twenties, when its population was approximately 600,000, it was still dependent upon the local water sources controlled by the Spring Valley Water Company, and it was using these almost to the maximum, with little or no margin of safety

in the event of a critical drought. True, work on the Hetch Hetchy project was progressing in the distant Sierra Nevada, but no one could say for certain how many years would pass before the melted snows of Yosemite would reach the Peninsula and the metropolis. Deep in the mud at the bottom of the southern arm of the bay lay a riveted steel pipe, five feet in diameter, that would form a section of the Hetch Hetchy Aqueduct and convey water under the navigable channel between Alameda County and the Peninsula; but still to be completed were a pipe line across the San Joaquin Valley and a twenty-five-mile tunnel through the Coast Range.

On May 1, 1928, the voters of San Francisco made reasonably sure, however, that when the waters from Hetch Hetchy Reservoir should come coursing through the long aqueduct, they would flow into storage reservoirs and a distributing system wholly owned by the City and County of San Francisco. On that date they approved by a vote of four to one a $41,000,000 bond issue for purchase of the properties of the Spring Valley Water Company. On four previous occasions, the last as recently as June 14, 1927, they had defeated bonds for acquisition of the private system. This time only one newspaper, the *Bulletin*, opposed the bonds.

After some difficulty in marketing the bond issue, the city took possession on March 3, 1930, of a private water system that had been developing for more than seventy years. It included 62,612 acres of reservoir and watershed lands in San Francisco, San Mateo, Santa Clara, and Alameda counties; four impounding reservoirs with a total capacity of sixty billion gallons; the Pleasanton well system at the lower end of Livermore Valley; the Sunol gravel beds in Alameda County, from which percolating water is drawn; main aqueducts totaling 111 miles; and a distributing system consisting of twenty reservoirs and tanks, 750 miles of pipes, and numerous pumping stations. The large landholdings acquired from the private utility now form valuable public open spaces in a more and more intensively developed metropolitan region.

Soon after San Francisco purchased the Spring Valley Water Company properties, the city faced the kind of severe water shortage that City Engineer O'Shaughnessy and others had long feared. The latest in a series of unusually dry seasons had reduced local water supplies throughout the Bay Area to a minimum. But fortunately for San Francisco, the East Bay Municipal Utility District was able to come to the rescue. In a six-month period in 1930 the city purchased twenty to thirty million gallons of water daily from the district, taking the supplementary supply from Lake Chabot and Upper San Leandro Reservoir in Alameda County and conveying it to the Peninsula

Pardee Dam and Reservoir, Chief Source of Water Supply for the East Bay.
Photograph courtesy of East Bay Municipal Utility District.

through pipes laid in the bed of Dumbarton Strait.

Mokelumne River Aqueduct

The East Bay, too, would have been in a desperate plight had not the East Bay Municipal Utility District completed the Pardee Dam on the Mokelumne River and built its ninety-eight-mile-long aqueduct in record time. The first contracts for construction of the aqueduct were awarded in September, 1925. In the summer of 1927 the construction of Pardee Dam was started. Two years later, on June 23, 1929, water from Lake Pardee flowed into San Pablo Reservoir, which supplied about one-third of the water used in the East Bay, and which at that time con-

tained only a few days' supply. Two other reservoirs, which also provided one-third of the supply, held only water enough to last a few weeks; and most of the wells in the East Bay had been pumped to capacity and were becoming saline. Large quantities of Mokelumne River water immediately were released to all the local storage basins, ending the menace of a shortage that had been threatening the East Bay for years.

Less than a year later, on May 4, 1930, Dr. George C. Pardee, president of the East Bay Municipal Utility District, looked out over the waters of the great mountain reservoir named in his honor, saw that it was filled for the first time, and said: "While other cities in California and on the Pacific Coast are concerned as to where their domestic water is coming from during the next few months we are sitting on top of the world with nearly five years' supply of the best water than can be secured. There has hardly been a time during the past ten years when there was not a possibility of a water shortage which would have crippled, if not ruined, these communities. We have seen the end of that. Our water problems are over."[1]

The threatened water shortages to which Dr. Pardee referred had frightened away many an eastern industrialist who had been looking for a site for a branch plant in the East Bay. Now that vexing problem had been conquered, but the price of victory was great. Not only had the East Bay Municipal Utility District contracted an enormous indebtedness in order to build Pardee Dam and the Mokelumne Aqueduct; it also had purchased, as a distributing system, the entire properties of the East Bay Water Company at a price of $33,752,000. This transaction brought the district's total investment to more than $72,000,000.

Water Problems in the Upper Bay

The northern part of Contra Costa County was in no such fortunate situation as the East Bay communities. Along the shores of San Pablo Bay, Carquinez Strait, and Suisun Bay stood large industrial plants that pumped water directly from the bay and had no other sources of supply sufficient for their needs. By 1929, a drought year, the amount of salt-water encroachment in Suisun Bay had become so alarming that these industries feared extensive damage to pipes and machinery. Teredo damage to pilings in company wharves already had cost millions to repair. Through the Industrial Water Users Association the major plants joined with the Salt Water Barrier Association in renewing the clamor for a barrier to protect the upper bay against salt-water intrusion and to conserve the fresh water brought down by the rivers.

Men who took a broad view of state water problems pointed out that a barrier unrelated to other water projects in central and northern California would not solve the industrial water supply problem of Contra Costa County. "The great expanding uses of water in the Sacramento and San Joaquin Valleys, unless they should be stopped, will, in a few years, increase the amount and frequency of deficiencies in summer flow in the river, such as occurred in 1924, so that there will be less and less water for the barrier to conserve as time goes on unless mountain storage is constructed," said Paul Bailey, an engineer who addressed the Commonwealth Club on November 21, 1929.[2]

The water problem of northern Contra Costa County was actually only a small part of a water problem of enormous scope, affecting the entire Central Valley of California. To solve this larger problem of providing more water for thousands of acres under irrigation in the great interior valleys, not only mountain storage was needed but also a gigantic revision of nature's arrangements. With no logic at all, nature supplies the Sacramento Valley, which has only one-third of the arable land of the five-hundred-mile-long Central Valley, with two-thirds of the rain and snow of northern California, while the San Joaquin Valley, with twice as much arable land as the upper valley, receives only half as much rain. Since 1921 the state legislature had been attempting to act on a bold scheme for correcting this imbalance—a scheme which,

Dr. George Pardee, Father of the East Bay Municipal Utility District. Photograph courtesy of Oakland Tribune.

as finally carried out, was incidentally to provide fresh water for agriculturists, industries, and municipalities from Antioch to Martinez. The daring plan, proposed in 1919 by Colonel Robert Bradford Marshall, chief hydrographer of the United States Geological Survey, envisaged, among other things, great storage reservoirs on the Sacramento River system and two large canals on each side of the Central Valley for transferring water from the Sacramento Valley to the San Joaquin Valley. In 1929 this grand design was in a fluid state, undergoing constant changes in the light of extensive research into all phases of the water problems of the state. Eventually it was to crystallize into the Central Valley Project, one part of which would be a canal to divert water from the delta at the confluence of the Sacramento and San Joaquin rivers to northern Contra Costa County. In the fall of 1929, however, the people of the county were pinning their hopes for fresh water on a salt-water barrier and were little concerned with the vast, long-range project evolving in the minds of certain state and federal officials.

Arguments presented by representatives of the Salt Water Barrier Association to the War Department's Board of Engineers for Rivers and Harbors concerning the necessity for federal contributions to the barrier scheme no doubt served to impress government officials with the importance of greater federal participation in solving California's water problems. Indirectly the Association thus helped to deepen federal interest in the grand plan that was to emerge as the Central Valley Project. Eleven years were to pass before the Contra Costa Canal, as one element of the project, provided water for industries along the shores of Suisun Bay.

New Supplies of Energy

Although people in the major urban communities and satellite industrial areas of the bay counties, when faced with possible shortages of water, concluded that they should resort to public ownership of water supply systems, they were content to leave in private hands the operation of utilities that were not in short supply. Long-established gas and electric companies expanded their facilities as population and industrial growth necessitated and continued to supply almost all the light, power, and heat required in the Bay Area.

The Pacific Gas and Electric Company became one of the largest private utilities in the nation and developed more and more extensive facilities for providing electric energy and natural gas to Bay Area communities, among hundreds served in central and northern California. In 1927 it took over the properties of the Sierra and San Francisco Power Company, the Western States Gas and Electric Company, and the Coast Valleys Gas and Electric Company. Then in 1930 it made the Great Western Power Company and two large San Joaquin Valley light and power corporations part of its system through stock purchase. These consolidations effected by the company gave the Bay Area the advantages of service from a vast, interconnected system transmitting and distributing energy from dozens of hydroelectric and steam plants.

Natural gas from Buttonwillow, in the San Joaquin Valley near Bakersfield, and from the Kettleman Hills, fifty miles north of Buttonwillow, first reached the Bay Area over a Pacific Gas and Electric Company transmission line in the summer of 1929. From the northern terminus of this main line at Milpitas, in northeastern Santa Clara County, two branch lines were constructed northward on the Peninsula to San Francisco and a third was laid along the eastern side of the bay to Oakland. The following year a second transmission line, owned jointly by the Standard Oil Company of California and the Pacific Gas and Electric Company, was laid through the San Joaquin Valley to San Pablo, just north of Richmond.

With these supplies of natural gas and electric power, supplemented by heavy fuel oils, coal from Utah, and minor fuels, the Bay Area by 1930 had energy more than sufficient to meet its needs. Actually, energy supply had not been a problem since about 1910, when industries were assured of adequate supplies of both electric energy and heavy fuel oils.

Regional Park Movement

In the process of buying out private water companies and placing the function of providing an adequate water supply in the hands of public agencies, the people of the larger urban communities of the Bay Area moved toward solution of still another metropolitan regional problem—the need for extensive natural areas that could be developed for picnicking, hiking, riding, overnight camping, nature study, and other leisure-time activities. Public acquisition of thousands of acres of watershed lands formerly owned by the Spring Valley Water Company and by the East Bay Water Company presented opportunities for the creation of regional parks and scenic drives only a short distance from centers of population. (The San Francisco Water Department, however, has never favored opening peninsular watershed areas for public recreation, because it fears that the water supply would thereby be polluted.)

The purchase of the holdings of the private water companies took place at a time when people throughout the state had become intensely interested in developing wilderness areas for public use. For several years a state park movement had been gathering momentum, stimulated to a considerable degree by a campaign to save the giant redwoods in the northern coastal counties. And California was not alone in its realization of the importance and value of recreation resources; since the early 'twenties many states had been acquiring state parks. In 1925 the California State Legislature had passed a state park bill, only to have it pocket vetoed by the governor. At the 1927 session the lawmakers tried again and this time succeeded in winning the governor's approval of three measures that initiated a state park system. One of the three acts created the Division of Parks in the Department of Natural Resources and established a State Park Commission to administer, protect, and develop a state park system. Another appropriated $15,000 for a state-wide survey to determine which lands were suitable and desirable for the ultimate development of a comprehensive and well-balanced state park system. And the third act provided that a proposal for a state park bond issue of $6,000,000 be submitted to the electorate at the general election in November, 1928.

The same session of the legislature also enacted a statute providing for the formation and management of local park, recreation, and parkway districts and a special bill providing for the creation and management of Mount Tamalpais State Park in Marin County. California at that time already had five state parks, although it had no state park system as such. The bill pertaining to Mount Tamalpais was an emergency measure, introduced at the urgent request of the Tamalpais Conservation Club soon after private real-estate interests announced that they intended to sell 550 acres on the south slope of the mountain. The legislation provided for a condemnation suit to fix the value of the land and appropriated $20,000 as the state's contribution toward its acquisition. The Tamalpais Conservation Club was aided in its fund raising by the Sierra Club, the California Camera Club, various hiking clubs, and several wealthy men. Together with the state's contribution, the $32,000 raised privately was sufficient to purchase 520 acres of the property. To this acreage Congressman William Kent added, only a few hours before his death, an area of 204 acres known as Steep Ravine. These parcels and other lands combined to produce a recreation preserve of 892 acres north and west of Muir Woods National Monument. Since the establishment of the park in 1930, additions have increased its size to more than 1,335 acres.

The state park survey conducted in 1928 by the distinguished landscape architect and city planner Frederick Law Olmsted, son of the great American whose name was practically synonymous with parks, served to make com-

munities from one end of California to the other aware of natural assets that had potential recreational value. More than 330 park projects were suggested to Olmsted and his staff as they progressed through the twelve survey districts into which they had divided the state. From this number, 171 projects were eliminated for various reasons, chief of which was that many of the areas proposed were unsuitable for state parks or were more of local than of state-wide value. Included in the 150 or more projects designated as desirable for state acquisition were several in the Bay Area: the coastal area from Bodega Bay to the mouth of the Russian River, 612 acres of redwood forests and open grazing land on the headwaters of Harrington Creek in San Mateo County, 5,000 to 6,000 acres on Mount Diablo in Contra Costa County, approximately 4,500 acres on Mount St. Helena in Napa County, additional lands at Fort Ross in Sonoma County, the M. G. Vallejo home at Sonoma, and the Petrified Forest in northeastern Sonoma County, five and a half miles from Calistoga. Not included among the proposed state parks were extensive undeveloped hill and woodland areas within easy reach of the major cities of the Bay Area, although advisory groups assisting the survey staff had come to appreciate the recreational possibilities of these areas, particularly the holdings of the private water companies.

The Olmsted report on the state park survey was not completed until after the general election of 1928 and was not available as a campaign document in the fight for the state park bonds. The electorate nevertheless approved the state park bonds by a vote of three to one, thereby indicating that many months of discussion about the survey and countless newspaper stories about hearings on proposed state parks had been good publicity for the bonds.

East Bay Park Organizations

Apparently the talk about state parks had also helped to create sentiment in the Bay Area for metropolitan regional parks; for the East Bay Municipal Utility District had no sooner reached agreement with the East Bay Water Company for purchase of its holdings, including some forty thousand acres in the Berkeley Hills, than park enthusiasts organized citizen groups to determine which parts of the surplus water district lands would be suitable for use as parks and to apprise the public of the opportunities for recreational use of the hills and canyons. Only a few weeks after the utility district and the water company came to terms in September, 1928, the East Bay Metropolitan Park Association, the Oakland Park League, and several other citizens' associations presented resolutions to the utility district which in effect asked that lands not needed by the district in the future be withheld from sale until public sentiment with respect to the development of parks could be ascertained.

The East Bay Metropolitan Park Association, with the assistance of Ansel Hall, of the National Park Service, then made a preliminary survey that showed the surplus lands to be admirably suited for recreation purposes. This initial investigation revealed, however, that a more detailed study was needed.

The Bureau of Public Administration of the University of California assumed responsibility for the comprehensive survey, using funds given for the purpose by the Kahn Foundation, established by Irving Kahn, an Oakland merchant. The bureau, headed by Dr. Samuel C. May, one of the leaders in the East Bay Metropolitan Park Association, engaged Ansel Hall and Olmsted to conduct the survey.

The report of the two consultants, dated December 1, 1930, disclosed that additional parks were indeed greatly needed in the East Bay. The urban area from San Leandro to Richmond, embracing 150 square miles and inhabited by 450,000 people, included only 900 acres in parks—less than 1 per cent of the total area, whereas recreation authorities agreed that 5 to 10 per cent of an urban community should be in recreational and open use. The obvious deficiency in parks and playgrounds could be overcome in part, the report showed, by developing 10,000 to 11,000 acres of the surplus watershed lands of the utility district as a chain of regional parks. The proposed park system would extend for nearly 22 miles through the hills from Richmond to San Leandro and would be easily accessible to all nine cities included in the utility district.

Need for a Park System

Olmsted and Hall were too well aware of the recreational needs of the entire Bay Area, however, to limit their study to consideration of the needs of the East Bay alone. The two consultants suggested that the proposed chain of parks in the Berkeley Hills might form an important link in a Bay Area park and parkway system that would extend from Richmond through the proposed East Bay parks to Hayward on the south, thence across the San Mateo Bridge (completed in 1929) to the Skyline Boulevard, thence northward through the watershed lands formerly owned by the Spring Valley Water Company, along the Great Highway to Golden Gate Park, thence to the Presidio and across the proposed Golden Gate Bridge to Sausalito and Muir Woods, Mount Tamalpais, and the

watershed lands of the Marin Municipal Water District, thence to San Anselmo and San Rafael, and from there over a proposed bridge across San Pablo Strait to Richmond. The metropolitan park system and the existing and proposed bridges would make possible a scenic circuit drive of 130 miles.

Here was vision of the kind needed to give the subregional plans for the East Bay truly metropolitan significance. Like Thomas Reed, Harland Bartholomew, and Stephen Child, the consulting team of Olmsted and Hall foresaw the time when a metropolitan regional system of parklike drives and public reservations would be invaluable in a highly urbanized environment. Though parks and playgrounds undeniably were needed, state parks alone or city parks and playgrounds in themselves could not serve the same ends as a metropolitan chain of large, unspoiled natural areas relatively close to the homes of the majority of city dwellers. If quick and easy escape to wooded canyons and scenic ridges was desirable for the urbanites of the East Bay in the year 1930, how much more desirable, not to say imperative, it would be for all the people of the Bay Area when the population was two or three times as great as it was in 1930 and the pressures of highly organized living were proportionately intensified! The leaders of the East Bay obviously intended to see that regional parks were established in their area, either under the East Bay Municipal Utility District or some special district. But who would take the initiative in acting upon the suggestion that a metropolitan park chain should be created?

Like all proposals of scope and imagination, this one would take a long time to carry out. The larger goal of developing an area-wide park system would be lost sight of again and again as individual cities and counties or special districts took piecemeal action to acquire available sites. There would be numerous unrelated acquisitions similar to those made by the Santa Clara County Board of Supervisors when it purchased the 400-acre Stevens Creek Park in 1924 and the 2,933-acre Mount Madonna Park in 1927. The board simply seized the opportunity to buy attractive holdings for presumably reasonable prices. Other governing bodies could be expected to act in much the same fashion until county planning and metropolitan regional planning became well established in the Bay Area and citizens agreed that a metropolitan park system should be created as part of a general scheme of development. Separate, piecemeal acquisitions of natural parks would not necessarily contribute toward the achievement of the most desirable type of regional park system, yet for many decades this seemed to be the way in which an ultimate area-wide system would take shape.

Hills of the Bay Area, Inspiration for the Creation of a Regional Park System.
Photograph courtesy of David Arbegast and Robert Tetlow.

The Connecting Links

As Olmsted indicated, a metropolitan park system in an area with as marked physical divisions as the San Francisco Bay Area would require several bridges as connecting links in a circuit drive uniting all the major regional parks. In 1930, when he outlined a system embracing five of the nine bay counties, only one of the bridges essential to the system had been built—the San Mateo Bridge, spanning the southern arm of the bay between the city of San Mateo and the Mount Eden–Hayward area. The Golden Gate Bridge was only in the preliminary engineering stage; and a proposal of the American Toll Bridge Company to build a $15,000,000 bridge from Richmond to San Rafael had been abandoned because estimated traffic volume was not great enough to interest investment

houses in lending funds for construction. The Bay Area had, however, entered a period of major achievement in overcoming the divisive influence of the great body of water that was its chief physical feature.

The first of the automobile crossings thrown across the continuous water barrier from Stockton to Alviso was the Antioch Bridge, five miles above the mouth of the San Joaquin River. This crossing had been in use since January 1, 1926. Built by the American Toll Bridge Company at a cost of $2,000,000, this comparatively narrow drawbridge—with a roadway of twenty-one feet—joined the Contra Costa shore with Sherman Island in the delta country of Sacramento County and shortened the distance between Oakland and Sacramento by many miles.

The first automobile bridge across the bay itself was the mile-long span built at Dumbarton Strait, in the

The Antioch Bridge, Connecting Contra Costa County with Sherman Island. Drawing from The Golden Link, publication of the Antioch Ledger, June, 1924.

southern part of the bay, by the Dumbarton Bridge Company, a group composed principally of San Francisco capitalists. This toll bridge, opened to traffic on January 15, 1927, saved a fifteen-mile journey round the lower end of the bay for motorists traveling between San Mateo County and southern Alameda County. It also provided for speedier communication between the Bay Area and the San Joaquin Valley. Glenn D. Willaman, secretary of the California Real Estate Association, hailed it as "the advance agent for the bridges that will connect the shores of the Golden Gate and bridge the gulf between the Oakland mainland and the San Francisco shore."3

A more appropriate candidate for the role of advance agent for the Golden Gate Bridge and the San Francisco–Oakland Bay Bridge was the Carquinez Bridge, which, completed four months after the Dumbarton Bridge, was jubilantly dedicated as "the world's highest bridge."4 Although some engineers had doubted that piers for a bridge could be constructed in the deep, swift waters of Carquinez Strait, the span carried a 30-foot roadway four-fifths of a mile across the swirling currents at a height of 314 feet. One hundred and thirty-five feet below mean low water level its piers rested firmly on the sandstone and blue clay that lay beneath 40 feet of silt. An engineering marvel of its day, the bridge evoked enormous pride in the thousands who attended the dedicatory ceremonies. The occasion wore the aspects of a national celebration: the Stars and Stripes were loosed over the

highest point of the steel towers by a telegraphic impulse transmitted by President Coolidge from the yacht *Mayflower* on the Potomac.

The year 1928 might have seen the dedication of a new drawbridge across the Oakland Estuary had not shipping interests waged a campaign to free this waterway of obstructions. The War Department agreed that a drawbridge would cause delays and be a hazard to navigation. A subway with a clearance of 40 feet below mean low water was therefore built from Harrison Street in Oakland to Webster Street in Alameda to replace the old Webster Street Bridge. The main part of this nearly mile-long subway is a tube 2,400 feet long and 32 feet in diameter, with two roadways for automobiles. Newspaper accounts of it made much of the fact that it was the first underwater vehicular tunnel in the world constructed entirely of reinforced concrete. Travelers between Oakland and Alameda were more inclined to appreciate the fact that the Posey Tube (named for its designer, George A. Posey) eliminated delays formerly caused by shipping movements.

A fourth toll bridge constructed in the Bay Area by private initiative was the seven-mile-long San Mateo Bridge, which, like the Dumbarton Bridge, was a low-level crossing with a vertical lift span above the main channel of navigation, to give passage for vessels bound for Alviso and other landings in the lower part of the bay. It, too, made possible an uninterrupted journey between the San Francisco Peninsula and the San Joaquin Valley.

Had the proposed Richmond–San Rafael Bridge been built by the American Toll Bridge Company, it would probably have been the last crossing undertaken by private enterprise in the Bay Area. By November, 1927, a majority of San Francisco voters had reached the conclusion, in a vote of policy, that a central crossing between Oakland and San Francisco should be publicly owned and operated. Sentiment in other communities also appeared to be veering toward public ownership of important bridges.

Central-Crossing Proposals

In 1926 the San Francisco Board of Supervisors had been besieged with applications by various private syndicates for franchises to build a central crossing. In an effort to arrive at some complete proposal that might be put before the War Department, which was still opposed to any bridge north of Hunters Point, the board held hearings from August 3 to October 26, 1926, on seventeen applications for franchises. Still later in the year four more proposals were advanced. So many different types of structures and so many promising locations for a bridge were suggested that the board could come to agreement on none. The harassed members finally asked four Bay Area educators—the presidents of California, Stanford, and Santa Clara universities and St. Mary's College—to prepare a list of qualified and disinterested bridge engineers from whom the Board of Public Works could choose three to collaborate with it in selecting a site and preparing preliminary plans.

The appointment of Robert Ridgway, Chief Engineer of the Board of Transportation of New York, Arthur N. Talbot, Professor of Engineering, retired, of the University of Illinois, and John D. Galloway, a consulting engineer of San Francisco, as a board to work with City Engineer M. M. O'Shaughnessy, marked a great forward step in the solution of the problem of a central crossing. Between the time of their appointment on March 23, 1927, and the completion of their report early in May, these experts studied not only bridge sites but traffic conditions, harbor developments, terminals, transit services on both sides of the bay, and the physical aspects of the bay. They selected a preferred location for the bridge, as well as two alternate sites. The preferred location was from Rincon Hill to the Alameda Mole; an alternate location was from Telegraph Hill to Yerba Buena Island and thence to San Pablo Avenue in Oakland by way of the Key Route Mole. Since the location actually chosen at a later time was a combination of these two, this board materially advanced the bridge project. It outlined three steps for the city to take: first, obtain permission from the War Department to build a bridge at the Rincon Hill–Alameda Mole site;

Carquinez Bridge, Dedicated in 1927 as "the World's Highest Bridge." Photograph courtesy of State Division of Highways.

second, explore this location by borings to determine foundation conditions; and third, prepare a proper design, make cost estimates, and carry out an economic study of the entire project.

Oakland was as much in favor of the Rincon Hill–Alameda Mole location as San Francisco was, because a bridge in that position would in no way interfere with long-range harbor projects planned by Oakland.

San Francisco sent a delegation to Washington to re-request a modification of the conditions laid down by the War Department in 1921 for the bridge, but in the meantime it attempted to anticipate another refusal of the department by seeking enactment of a bill in Congress that would authorize a bridge in the desired location. Senator Hiram Johnson won approval of the measure in the Senate. Congressman Richard Welch, meeting opposition in the House of Representatives, failed to secure passage of the bill.

Seemingly the bridge project was at an impasse. The year 1928 was, however, a presidential election year, and a California resident named Herbert Clark Hoover was talked about as a presidential possibility. The idea occurred to George T. Cameron, publisher of the San Francisco *Chronicle*, as he was en route to Kansas City as a delegate to the Republican National Convention, that if Hoover were nominated and elected, he might be willing, in coöperation with Governor C. C. Young of California, to name a commission to study and report on the feasibility of building the bridge. With a definitive report on the project in hand, the California representatives in Congress then would probably be able, with the support of the President, to overcome the opposition of the War Department and obtain Congressional approval of a bill authorizing a centrally located span.

As Cameron had hoped, Hoover won the Republican nomination and was elected President the following November. State and county officials were optimistic about the prospects of solving the bridge problem, but before approaching the new President they took steps to settle some important matters of public policy. Because the bridge project was by then of state-wide interest, a meeting of state and county officials was called to discuss future state policy with regard to construction, financing, and operation of toll bridges.

Creation of Toll Bridge Authority

As a result of this meeting the state legislature on May 7, 1929, passed a measure designating the governor, the lieutenant-governor, the director of the State Department of Public Works, the director of the State Department of Finance, and the chairman of the California Highway Commission as the California Toll Bridge Authority. The Authority was empowered to direct the State Department of Public Works to build and construct toll bridges and toll highway crossings and to arrange for financing through the sale of revenue bonds. The act declared that it was the policy of the state to acquire all toll bridges eventually; and it amended the existing law so as to vest in the State Department of Public Works the power to grant franchises for private toll bridges. Specifically, the act authorized the California Toll Bridge Authority to "lay out, acquire, and construct a highway crossing from the City of San Francisco to the County of Alameda." The legislation thus formally recognized as a state problem a matter that until then had been thought of mainly as a Bay Area problem.

Since the interest of the national government in the bridge project had been acknowledged from the time the first plans were presented, the central crossing, in reality, had been of more than local or state importance for more than twenty years. The great bay, one of the major harbors on the West Coast, was a national asset, and anything vitally affecting it as a harbor was automatically of national importance, from the standpoint of national defense and from the standpoint of peacetime trade.

The increasing emphasis on state and national interest in a central crossing may have indicated to the people of the Bay Area that as their problems became more difficult and more costly to solve, they would tend to rely more and more upon state and federal assistance—and perhaps would discover that sometimes their own legitimate interests were rudely subordinated to those of the state or national government. In the size of its population and in the scope of the problems that confronted it, the Bay Area had arrived at that stage of its development when it could no longer act independently in many matters. Its own cities and counties were increasingly interdependent, and all were becoming involved with state and federal agencies in solving problems of water supply, transportation, communication, sanitation, harbor development, recreation, and physical planning.

The appointment on September 25, 1929, by President Hoover and Governor Young of the Hoover-Young San Francisco Bay Bridge Commission marked the beginning of a new phase of greater federal participation in Bay Area affairs, well before the days of Franklin D. Roosevelt's New Deal. Thoroughly familiar with the bridge controversy and well aware of the urgency of expediting planning and construction of a central crossing, Hoover chose his close friend Mark L. Requa, a famous engineer, to head the group that was to investigate the engineering and financial feasibility of the bridge.

The commission reviewed all available data on the proposed bridge, visited suggested locations, and found, as had the Ridgway-Talbot-Galloway board, that before it could come to any final conclusions, it required preliminary borings, designs, and cost estimates, as well as estimates of traffic and potential toll revenues. The commission therefore requested the State Department of Public Works to provide the necessary information.

A Route for the Bridge

The borings revealed the existence of a ridge of submerged rock from Yerba Buena Island to Rincon Hill in San Francisco. On each side of this ridge, rock foundations lay at far greater depths. Obviously, a bridge at any other location than the submerged ridge would present more difficult engineering problems and would be more costly. In fact, it was estimated that a bridge could be built from Rincon Hill to Yerba Buena Island to Oakland for $23,000,000 less than the cheapest bridge from Rincon Hill to the Alameda Mole. Chairman Requa remarked as the commission opened public hearings on the proposed bridge that "the Almighty apparently has laid out this route for the bridge."[5]

Studies of transbay passenger and automobile traffic and forecasts of future travel also supported the selection of the Rincon Hill–Yerba Buena Island–Oakland location. Besides carrying interurban trains, the proposed double-decked bridge would divert four-fifths of the vehicular ferry traffic, investigations by the State Department of Public Works showed. The department foresaw a traffic volume of at least sixteen million cars a year; and it estimated that a structure costing approximately $72,000,000 could be paid for in less than twenty years.

A familiar question remained unanswered: Would the Army and Navy approve a bridge at this location?

At a private session of the commission on July 31, 1930, Rear Admiral W. H. Standley, Assistant Chief of Naval Operations, indicated that the military were softening. "No bridge north of Hunters Point is free from naval objections," he declared. ". . . Rincon Hill–Goat Island [Yerba Buena Island] is, however, the least objectionable. . . . It would not be a vital menace to naval operations."[6]

A few days later, Rear Admiral Luther E. Gregory, retired, one of the federal representatives on the commission, removed all doubt about the attitude of military authorities when he moved that the commission recommend a high-level bridge of four spans from Rincon Hill to Yerba Buena Island to the Oakland shore.

The commission had not been requested to consider the possibility of additional crossings in the future, but it foresaw a time when the San Francisco–Oakland crossing would be used to capacity. In its final report it remarked in passing that "location 5 [from the Hunters Point–Candlestick Point Area to Alameda] be considered for future bridge expansion when a crossing centrally located has become congested."[7] This was advice that was to be quoted frequently in the period 1947–1953, during controversy over a second crossing between San Francisco and Alameda County.

The struggle for the long-desired bay bridge was not over, but victory was in sight. In accordance with one of the recommendations of the Hoover-Young Commission, the California Toll Bridge Authority on November 6, 1930, authorized the construction of the bridge and the preparation of the necessary plans, specifications, and estimates of construction costs. No major difficulties in obtaining Congressional approval and War Department approval of the location and the construction plans were expected. The state legislature appeared ready to provide loans for additional surveys and engineering studies. Financing was still to be worked out, however; engineering problems of almost baffling complexity were yet to be surmounted; and the hazards of actual construction lay ahead. It appeared that the 'thirties would be well advanced before anyone traveled across the bay on a completed bridge.

Controversy over Golden Gate Bridge

Substantial progress had been made meanwhile toward construction of a bridge across the Golden Gate. Only brief consideration was ever given to the possibility that the bridge might be privately financed and constructed. By the spring of 1924, before any formal organization had been worked out to undertake the project, the City and County of San Francisco and Marin County jointly had applied to the War Department for authority to build the bridge in accordance with plans prepared by engineer Joseph B. Strauss. Surprisingly, military authorities raised no objection to a span across the entrance to San Francisco Bay. The War Department held a hearing on the application in San Francisco on May 16, 1924, and on December 20, 1924, Secretary of War John W. Weeks tentatively approved the project. Thereafter the organization of a bridge and highway district to finance and build the span was blocked for four years by litigation initiated by various local interests opposed to the project.

Besides ferry, railroad, and timber interests, the Golden Gate Bridge was opposed by those who feared that it would spoil the scenic beauty of the entrance to the bay, and by some engineers and geologists who doubted that it could be built at all. Some of the litigation which blocked the project was carried on by citizens who sincerely believed that the burden of financing the bridge should rest on all taxpayers of the state rather than on those within a special district composed of the counties that supposedly would benefit most from the project—San Francisco and the North Bay and northern coast counties. Those who favored utilizing the district form of organization as a means of constructing and operating the bridge contended, however, that a district could proceed more expeditiously than the state and that district bonds would bring a higher market price than those issued by the state. Lawsuits filed to block formation of a district under the Bridge and Highway District Act of 1923 prevented incorporation of the proposed district until December, 1928, when the counties of San Francisco, Marin, Sonoma, Napa, and Del Norte, and a part of Mendocino County finally succeeded in establishing the Golden Gate Bridge and Highway District. In the course of the protracted litigation, Humboldt County had joined the district, then later had withdrawn, as had a part of Mendocino County.

The formation of this superregional agency, with a board of directors appointed by the boards of supervisors of the member counties, took place only a few months before the state legislature enacted the California Toll Bridge Authority Act, which included a declaration that the state eventually should acquire all toll bridges. The adoption of that statute foreshadowed the eventual taking over by the state of the bridge then being planned by San Francisco and the group of northern counties. Logic could hardly support the proposition that the Golden Gate Bridge was less a bridge of state-wide importance than the San Francisco–Oakland Bay Bridge. No one attempted, even in the 'twenties, to argue that the Golden Gate Bridge was of interest only to residents of the Bay Area.

Preliminary Steps

The board of directors of the newly incorporated bridge and highway district immediately turned its attention to the selection of engineers for the proposed span. Joseph B. Strauss, as many had expected, was appointed chief engineer in August, 1929.

To provide funds for engineering expenses and preliminary organization, the board levied two taxes on the counties in the district, the first, of three cents per hundred dollars of assessed valuation, on July 24, 1929, and the second, of two cents, in July, 1930. These levies raised $467,367.75. No other taxes have ever been imposed upon the Golden Gate Bridge and Highway District.

The announcement of an election in November, 1930, to authorize a bond issue of $35,000,000 for the construction of the bridge precipitated a battle on a grand scale between those who wanted the bridge and those who still hoped to kill the project. Some opponents charged that a bridge of the required length would collapse of its own weight. Others advanced the idea that the foundations would lie over an earthquake fault and that heavy tremors would destroy the span. Andrew C. Lawson, professor of geology in the University of California, demolished this notion after conducting an exhaustive investigation of test borings covering all foundation areas. Still other opponents contended that the great costs of constructing the bridge would cause many taxpayers to lose their homes. Whispering campaigns were directed against the engineers and the financial operations of the district. Proponents accused the "ferry trust" of inciting the Pacific American Steamship Association and the Shipowners' Association of the Pacific Coast to issue propaganda against the bonds.

Notwithstanding the variety and intensity of the attacks, the bonds carried by a vote of more than three to one—145,057 in favor, 46,954 against.

The election was not the final showdown, as subsequent events would prove. Further litigation initiated by some of the opponents was to postpone the start of construction until January, 1933. But there was no longer any doubt that the people of the Golden Gate Bridge and Highway District meant to build a bridge across the entrance to the bay. Every delay had merely deepened their conviction that the bridge was necessary and that it could be built.

End of Ferries

When at last the mighty steel cables swung from pylon to pylon across the Golden Gate and across the waters separating San Francisco from Oakland, the ferryboats would soon disappear. But in 1930 forty-three of these boats, the largest number ever to operate in the bay, transported a total of forty-seven million passengers and more than six million vehicles from shore to shore. Each day, fifty to sixty thousand people crossed the bay between San Francisco and Alameda County; 25 per cent of them rode in automobiles, whereas five years earlier the overwhelming majority had used the Key System and the East Bay transit lines of the Southern Pacific. In a five-year period the number of transit passengers had declined more than five million—a portent of further losses in patronage on the interurban railways once the bay bridge was completed.

The year 1930 did not pass without demonstrating what

bridges would do to transbay ferries. Two of the most famous of all Bay Area ferryboats went out of service toward the end of the year. These were the Southern Pacific's huge car-transfer ferry steamers, the *Solano* and the *Contra Costa*, which for many years had carried freight cars and entire passenger trains across Carquinez Strait between Port Costa and Benicia. The construction of the 5,603-foot Martinez-Benicia railroad bridge, the longest and heaviest railroad bridge west of the Mississippi at that time, forced the retirement of the ferries from service. The $10,000,000 structure was begun in May, 1929, and opened to rail traffic on October 15, 1930. It was the second railroad bridge across the waters of the bay (the Dumbarton railroad bridge, completed in 1910, was the first) and the sixth span across the water barrier extending from Stockton to Alviso.

The Bayshore Highway

In the 'twenties the cities and counties sought other means besides bridges and tubes to improve travel and communication. In November, 1924, just before work on the toll bridge across Dumbarton Strait was started, Supervisor (later Congressman) Richard J. Welch of San Francisco pointed out that once this bridge was in use, congestion on El Camino Real, the only major highway on the Peninsula, would become intolerable unless the Bayshore Highway was built, as planned, all the way from San Francisco to San Jose.

At that time, work was in progress on a first section of five miles between South San Francisco and Burlingame, financed by a contribution of $500,000 from San Francisco. By 1928 this section had been surfaced and a large underpass had been built under the Southern Pacific main tracks at South San Francisco. Meanwhile the State Division of Highways had pushed the highway three miles farther south to San Mateo; but the road was of little use to city-bound motorists because a three-mile section within the city limits of San Francisco and a three-and-a-half-mile section between the city boundary and South San Francisco remained unfinished. The closing of the gap in February, 1929, gave San Francisco traffic a second major outlet, at least part of the way down the Peninsula. Immediate construction of the road as far south as Palo Alto and the Dumbarton crossing was scheduled. But public officials and civic groups in San Jose had hoped that the Division of Highways would complete the new highway all the way to their city in the 1929–1931 biennium, and when they found out that the state had budgeted funds only for extension of the highway to the Embarcadero Road in Palo Alto, they joined forces with San Francisco, San Mateo County, and Alameda County

groups to agitate for immediate construction of the fourteen-mile section between Palo Alto and San Jose. At a meeting in the San Francisco City Hall, representatives of four counties put "the heat" on State Highway Commissioner F. S. Moody, who politely but firmly told them that the Bayshore Highway "could not possibly be built as far as San Jose before the next biennium."[8]

In its day the Bayshore Highway set a new standard for highway construction. The right of way within the city of San Francisco was 125 feet and the paved roadway was 100 feet wide, providing for three lanes of traffic in both directions. Except in steep cuts and on fills, the roadway in San Mateo County also was 100 feet wide, but highway engineers had not yet come to the conclusion that on high-speed, heavy-traffic roads a center dividing strip is necessary to prevent head-on collisions. Lack of such a safety feature later earned for this once model highway the appellation "bloody Bayshore."

Barriers to East Bay Expansion

San Francisco prior to the opening of the Dumbarton and San Mateo bridges and the Bayshore Highway undoubtedly was one of the most bottled-up cities in the nation. But it was not the only community in the Bay Area that complained of physical barriers. When the East Bay Regional Planning Association held a meeting at the Hotel Oakland on March 1, 1928, to discuss the need for the construction of tunnels through the Berkeley Hills to suburban areas in Contra Costa County, more than a thousand persons, representing every district and community of Alameda and Contra Costa counties, attended. Three tunnels were proposed: the Broadway Low-Level Tunnel, a tunnel near Shepherd Canyon, and a tunnel piercing the hills at the end of Thirty-fifth Avenue in Oakland. The prospects of building all three projects were slight. Chief attention centered on a new tunnel at a considerably lower level than that of the old Broadway Tunnel, which had been opened in 1904.

Alameda and Contra Costa counties had already asked the State Highway Commission to build a low-level bore on the Broadway route, but their petition had been rejected. The mass meeting at the Hotel Oakland gave impetus to the formation by the two counties of a joint highway district, for the purpose of constructing the tunnel and widening the highway to Walnut Creek. Financial complications then developed that were to delay the beginning of construction until the spring of 1933. The Broadway Low-Level Tunnel was one more addition to a substantial list of major public works conceived in the booming 'twenties and hailed as a worthy means of providing employment during the Depression of the 'thirties.

A Modern Port for Oakland

The prosperous conditions and population increases that made people throughout the Bay Area impatient to overcome natural obstacles to movement also made the people of the East Bay eager to take advantage, from an economic standpoint, of the landlocked waters that hindered free circulation in the area. By the mid-twenties the residents of Oakland and Richmond were dissatisfied with the lagging pace of harbor development and were casting about for programs to accelerate the improvement of harbor facilities.

Until the late 'twenties, most of the harbor developments in the Oakland-Alameda area were undertaken by private operators, except for the further dredging of the estuary, which was done by the federal government. Fred D. Parr, a steamship executive, opened the Parr Terminal in 1920 on land leased from the City of Oakland at the Key Route Basin. He equipped the terminal with the most modern mechanical loading and unloading apparatus and induced the Southern Pacific to construct a new spur track to shipside. Vessels of several steamship lines began to make regular calls at the terminal; and Parr planned to expand the facilities. Then he became involved in a dispute with the city over terms of his lease. To force the city to reimburse him for improvements he had made at the waterfront, he filed a lawsuit. This he won, but his enthusiasm for expanding his operations at Oakland was dulled. When better opportunities presented themselves in Richmond, he was quick to grasp them. The harbor expansion undertaken at that city from 1927 onward can be credited in large measure to Parr, although studies by the engineering firm of Leeds and Nicholson had prepared the municipality for a program of port development. Oakland finally took over the Parr Terminal at the Key Route Basin and expanded it under a program formulated by a port commission created in 1926.

Another development in the Oakland outer harbor in the early 'twenties was the huge warehouse constructed by the Albers Brothers Milling Company. The wharf alongside this great storage facility became a Bay Area center for grain shipping.

Early in the decade, John L. Howard expanded the small terminal that he operated at the foot of Market Street on the estuary by adding a new wharf and new warehouses. The upswing in business prompted the construction of additional warehouses after 1925 for the storage of case goods, dried fruit, and manufactured articles. Like the Parr Terminal, the Howard Terminal attracted ocean-going vessels in increasing numbers. Copra, sulphur, lumber, coal, and other bulk commodities were unloaded there, and California canned and dried fruits were conspicuous among exports.

Under the management of the Lawrence Warehouse Company the municipally owned dock and warehouse at the foot of Grove Street in Oakland became a regular place of call for ships of several West Coast shipping lines.

In February, 1925, the Encinal Terminal opened in Alameda, not far from the basin in which the Alaska Packers berthed their picturesque fleet of sailing ships. The first unit of the new terminal, seven hundred feet long and two hundred feet wide, cost more than $1,000,000. Three other units, equally large, were added in quick succession, until the terminal had half a mile of berthing space.

Board of Port Commissioners

In spite of these gains in shipping facilities in both the outer and inner harbors, the majority of Oakland citizens believed that the port was greatly underdeveloped. In 1925 the presentation of a report by three nationally famous engineers recommending improvements in the outer and inner harbors was followed some months later by a special election at which the voters approved $9,600,000 in harbor bonds by a vote of more than eight to one. A year later, in 1926, the charter was amended to provide for a permanent Board of Port Commissioners, with control over the entire port area owned by the city. The real development of this East Bay port dates from the time the new board took office in February, 1927.

Between 1927 and 1930 the board added more than a mile of berthing space at the outer harbor, constructed new transit sheds that were equipped with devices for moving any kind of cargo, and dredged a channel to connect with the mile-long entrance channel dredged by the federal government. In the inner harbor the new agency completed the Grove Street Terminal and enlarged the Ninth Avenue docks. In all, the new transit sheds constructed at the various wharves provided more than fifteen acres of floor space. Oakland citizens began to feel that the potentialities of their port were at last being realized.

Economic and administrative developments likewise aided the growth of the Port of Oakland. In 1929 the railroads, under orders of the Railroad Commission, finally offered the same rates for the port area as for certain districts in San Francisco, thereby ending a discriminatory situation that had prevailed until then. That same year the Treasury Department greatly enhanced the prestige of the Port of Oakland by making it a full port of entry and establishing local customs service. Formerly shippers had complained of the inconvenience of dealing with the Custom House in San Francisco.

Perhaps the greatest boost to the port was the decision of Rosenberg Brothers, the largest dried-fruit packing concern in California, to ship at least fifty thousand tons of prunes and other dried fruit from Oakland annually. The company leased a site at the outer harbor on which the city erected a $400,000 warehouse. This soon became inadequate to accommodate the sorting, grading, processing, and packing operations carried on, and additional space was added. From the beginning, the company exported far more than the minimum specified in the contract with the city. The extensive Rosenberg operations at Oakland attracted other major food-exporting concerns to the port and led to the establishment of regular shipping schedules, which in turn brought still more business to the port.

Port Development at Richmond

In the meantime, the city of Richmond, like Oakland, was engaged in a program of harbor improvements, spurred on by an engineering report pointing out that the city had failed to take advantage of the opportunities which federal appropriations for harbor projects offered for industrial and shipping developments. Because the report recommended private rather than public operation of port facilities, the Richmond Chamber of Commerce invited Fred Parr to consider the possibility of assuming responsibility for control and management of the port. Having experienced difficulties in Oakland, Parr was in a receptive mood when approached by the Richmond organization in 1925. He outlined a program calling for dredging of harbor channels to a depth of thirty feet, filling of waterfront lands to create new industrial sites, provision of spur tracks and car storage yards by the Southern Pacific and Santa Fe railroads, the attraction of some nationally known industry to give impetus to industrial development, and the submission of a bond issue to the voters for the purpose of financing municipal improvements at the port. He himself proposed to acquire one hundred acres of waterfront land, establish the Parr-Richmond Terminal Corporation, and build a modern terminal facility jointly with the city.

This carefully detailed program kindled immediate enthusiasm for private management of port facilities and for municipal coöperation in developing the port. In 1926 the city leased its Terminal 1, in the outer harbor, to Parr, and at the same time it began building Terminal 2 in the inner harbor, with the intention of leasing this also to him. The following year the voters overwhelmingly approved a bond issue of $690,000 for harbor improvements. With funds provided by sale of the bonds, the local government contracted for dredging, filled waterfront areas, installed streets and sewers, and matched Parr's expenditures for the construction of Terminal 3, at the inner harbor. Put into operation in 1929, this major facility included a wharf with berthing frontage of 1,280 feet, a terminal building with nearly three acres of storage space, and an adjacent open storage area. To provide necessary rail service, the Santa Fe and Southern Pacific railroads extended trackage to the new terminal.

More than two years before the terminal was opened, Parr had carried out his design to attract a major industry to the inner harbor at Richmond. He vanquished South San Francisco in a contest for a branch assembly plant of the Ford Motor Company, even though that city could offer the company a site with hard-rock foundations and a waterfront location, while the site Parr suggested was then merely tidelands, into which thousands of piles would have to be driven. The Ford Company leased seventy acres from Parr and made plans to erect a $2,000,000 factory. This plant was not opened until 1931.

Other industries attracted to the Richmond waterfront by Parr soon after he became a power in the city were the Pacific Molasses Company, the Filice and Perrelli Cannery, and tank storage units of the Richfield Oil Corporation.

The vigor and determination with which this promoter, the Richmond Chamber of Commerce, terminal operators in Oakland and Alameda, the Board of Port Commissioners in Oakland, and various shippers combined to build up the East Bay ports did not escape San Francisco businessmen. The developments across the bay meant but one thing: that the Port of San Francisco, state operated, would have strong competition in the future. The East Bay was the terminus of transcontinental railroads, it had large waterfront sites to offer industries, it had by 1930 an adequate water supply, it was closer than San Francisco to the great agricultural areas of the state, and now it had up-to-date port facilities. Many San Franciscans feared that the ports on the *contra costa* would grow at the expense of the Port of San Francisco. And they were right, as a State Senate committee study revealed in 1951:

"In considering traffic at the Ports of Oakland and San Francisco, a steady increase in oceangoing tonnage from 1928 to the present was noted for Oakland, and, if military cargoes are included, a spectacular increase. No such tendency was noted for San Francisco. In fact, when the trade level of 1928–30 is taken for a basis of comparison, the trend of oceangoing tonnage handled at San Francisco appears to be downward."[9]

The port of San Francisco, nevertheless, is still the dominant port in the Bay Area if shipments of petroleum and its products are omitted from consideration.

Study for a Municipal Airport near China Basin, San Francisco, 1927. This proposed airport would have included 320 acres, of which 120 acres would have been land reclaimed from the bay. Drawing by C. H. Baldwin and M. Chappey.

Search for an Airport Site

Another kind of rivalry between San Francisco and the East Bay began to attract attention in the late 'twenties. This was in the comparatively new field of airport development. The unobstructed air space above the great bay soon appeared to be a commercial asset that had not previously been fully appreciated. The tidelands and certain level islands close to the shoreline took on new significance as potential airports. Not only municipalities and commercial airlines but also the Army and Navy initiated investigations to determine the best sites for landing fields.

Early in 1926 a decision of the United States Post Office Department to let its airmail contracts to private individuals started San Francisco on a search for an airport site. "The Board of Supervisors had better get busy and provide a place for the airmail to land," Colonel James E. Power, Postmaster of San Francisco, told Supervisor Milo Kent. "The government will not let the private companies land at the army base in Crissey Field [at the Presidio] and the alternate field at Concord [in Contra Costa County] is too far away."[10]

Supervisor Kent thereupon introduced a resolution calling for the appointment of a committee to obtain for San Francisco a site suitable for a "landing field." The resolution was adopted and Kent was named chairman of the committee.

After the members had satisfied themselves that there was no site in San Francisco itself suitable for an airport, they turned to a report prepared by the city engineer's office listing six possible sites in San Mateo County. These included property near the industrial area of South San Francisco, a part of the Mills Estate at San Bruno, small commercial airports at San Mateo and Millbrae, some property adjoining the Mills Estate, and a completely submerged site near San Mateo Point.

In the midst of discussion of these sites an attorney for persons who had recently purchased Bay Farm Island, just southeast of Alameda, offered to sell an eight-hundred acre site on the so-called island for $1,200,000. Numerous expert flyers testified that they favored Bay Farm Island because it was freer from obstacles and had less fog and better visibility than any other site offered.

Much impressed, the supervisors were giving serious consideration to the East Bay location when the San

Francisco Chamber of Commerce and Mayor James Rolph, Jr., emphatically declared that they believed an airport for San Francisco should be situated on the Peninsula. "It is at once apparent that the conveniences in transportation by motor over the new Bayshore Highway to the peninsula sites will enable the transport of the airport traffic at a minimum of handling risk and maximum of convenience," Louis E. Haas, assistant manager of the chamber, told the supervisors.[11] The mayor was certain that the Peninsula "will some day be part of San Francisco" and said that it would be a mistake "to give any thought to the putting of San Francisco's money in any other place than bears the name of San Francisco."[12] The

San Francisco governing body promptly cooled toward Bay Farm Island.

The Aerial Affairs Committee of the Chamber of Commerce then recommended that a temporary site be selected on the Peninsula, and that while it was in use, weather surveys be made at all possible sites to find the best location for a permanent airport. Guided by advice from the city engineer's office, the board decided in March, 1927, that the site known as Mills Field was the best place on which to conduct the experiment of operating a municipal airport. Ogden Mills, executor of the estate of his late father, was appealed to as a public-spirited citizen to permit San Francisco to lease a part of the family

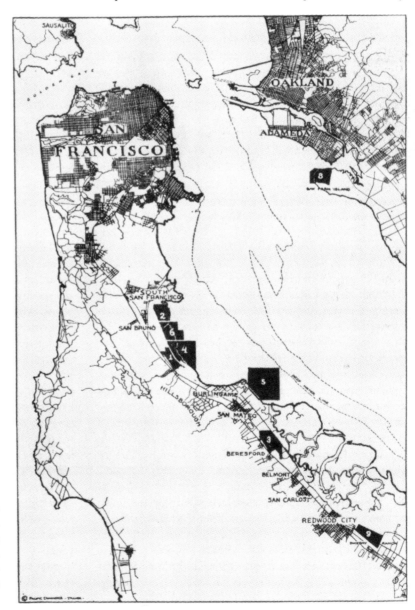

Sites Considered for a Municipal Airport for San Francisco, 1927. (1) Millbrae Airport; (2) South San Francisco Airport; (3) San Mateo Airport; (4) Millbrae Waterfront Airport; (5) San Mateo Point Airport; (6) San Bruno Airport; (7) The Marina; (8) Bay Farm Island; (9) Tweedy Ranch.

holdings at San Bruno for use as a temporary airport. This site, the city engineer's office had reported, was not near a high-powered transmission line, such as made hazardous a number of the other sites, and it was probably the northernmost site on the bayshore free from certain climatic drawbacks that made sites nearer San Francisco objectionable. In the meantime, the board proposed to conduct a series of observations, extending over a year, to get meteorological data on the entire Peninsula.

Mayor Rolph dedicated Mills Field, until then a pasture, as a municipal airport on May 7, 1927, shortly before a lanky youth named Charles A. Lindbergh made his epochal solo flight across the Atlantic and converted almost the entire nation into aviation enthusiasts.

Shoreline Airport for Oakland

Bay Farm Island, scorned by San Francisco, did not go begging as an airport site. No sooner had San Francisco turned it down than the Board of Port Commissioners of Oakland entered into negotiations to purchase 680 acres as a municipal airport for Oakland. By July a long runway was ready for use, and the Oakland Airport was selected as the take-off point for an air race to the Hawaiian Islands. The sponsor of the competition, James Dole, the pineapple king, offered a cash prize of $35,000 to the winner. Of thirty-five entrants in the long hop over the ocean, only two reached the Islands.

The public outcry over this tragic event was soon forgotten in the rush of fifty thousand people to greet "Lindy" upon his arrival at the Oakland Airport on September 17, 1927, in his monoplane, The Spirit of St. Louis.

Under the policies established by the Board of Port Commissioners, the Oakland Airport rapidly achieved a reputation as one of the best airports in the nation. By May, 1930, it had developed an operations area of 260 acres, 161,000 square feet of hangar space, a small hotel, and a restaurant. Five transport companies operated planes from it on regular schedules. Speedboats transported airline passengers between San Francisco and the airport. During the fiscal year 1929–30 the airport served 4,000 air transport passengers and 47,000 passengers on nonscheduled planes.

Controversy over Mills Field

Mills Field, unlike the Oakland Airport, seemed to be plagued by bad luck, even though Lindbergh had declared at the time of his visit that the field had the possibilities for becoming one of the world's most renowned air terminals. Boeing Air Transport, holder of an airmail contract, selected the field for its San Francisco base in October, 1927. On the day set for the official take-off of

the line's first airmail plane, the field was covered with fog. Boeing pilots became so strongly prejudiced against the field that the company left the airport a month later. In May, 1928, Western Air Express and Maddux Air Lines, operating up and down the Pacific Coast, both chose Mills Field for their Bay Area base of operations; but without explanation they moved to Oakland a short time later. Political bickering added to the unfavorable impression that many people seemed to have of the field.

Controversy over the field increased, even though the United States Weather Bureau recommended, on the basis of a meteorological survey conducted from July 1, 1927, to July 1, 1928, that the field be selected as the permanent location for the terminal airport for San Francisco. It had been found to be the closest to the metropolitan center in point of time and distance, and the freest from physical barriers, of any available site at which the topography was suitable and aerological conditions were safe, the bureau said. Nevertheless, enough voters remained skeptical about the field to defeat a $1,700,000 bond issue in November, 1928, for improvement and development of the facilities.

The following year a mishap suffered by Colonel Lindbergh caused Mills Field again to be held up to ridicule and contempt. As the flyer was taking off in the Patrician, the largest airplane (capacity: 32 passengers) that had ever been built up to that time, another plane appeared at the far end of the runway, ready to land. Wishing to afford the incoming plane all the room it needed, Lindbergh turned; his wide undercarriage, with its sharp tires, swept off the runway, cut through the one unfilled spot beside the runway, and sank into the blue mud. The accident was so minor that the plane, extricated by tractor, was air-borne five minutes later; but the damage to the reputation of the field was immense. Thousands of people concluded that Mills Field was a place where flyers ran the risk of getting stuck in the mud.

Officials operating the field waged an uphill fight to change public opinion. The publication of records showing that there were fewer hours of poor flying conditions at Mills Field than at any field or airdrome around the bay helped to dissipate the critical attitude. Maneuvers of hundreds of Army planes under the command of General William E. Gilmore, of the Air Corps, also aided in building optimism about the terminal.

The airport was still a political hot potato in 1930, however, when the three-year lease on the property expired and the San Francisco Board of Supervisors decided to open negotiations with Ogden Mills for purchase of the site. Mills was reluctant to sell, because he believed that the land had large potential value as a site for industrial development. It was August before the conferences begun in February terminated in an agreement under which San Francisco was to acquire 1,112.5 acres—the entire holdings of the Mills Estate between San Bruno and the deep water of the bay—for a total price of $1,050,000 through a ten-year purchase plan. Although 550 acres of the property lay west of the Bayshore Highway and could not be used for airport purposes, the supervisors gladly accepted Mills' terms, hoping eventually to sell this acreage as sites for aircraft industries.

In order to develop the airport properly and acquire adjoining subwater land that was needed, the board of supervisors decided to submit another bond issue to the voters. In spite of a carefully planned campaign in which almost all civic organizations and newspapers coöperated, the $4,000,000 bond issue failed, as had that of 1928, by only a few thousand votes.

Still, San Francisco at last had a municipal airport that it could call its own, and the majority of voters did favor development of this new public facility. Its future as a major air terminal seemed assured as more and more experts pronounced it the best available site in the Bay Area for a San Francisco airport. It was theoretically only twenty-two minutes from the heart of the city via the Bayshore Highway; there were no limitations to expansion as longer runways were required; and the southward movement of population on the Peninsula indicated that in the future the site would be convenient for an ever-increasing number of people.

"Nerve Center" of Defense

Some years before San Francisco and Oakland became interested in developing municipal airports, the Army and Navy had decided that there were three strategic areas, or "nerve centers," on the Pacific Coast in which additional military facilities should be concentrated—the region around Puget Sound, the San Francisco Bay Area, and the Los Angeles–San Diego area. Among the new installations to be built were, of course, air bases, including a base for dirigibles, though exact locations had not been determined for any of the bases.

In the fall of 1928 aviation enthusiasts in the San Francisco Junior Chamber of Commerce initiated a campaign to induce the Navy to decide on Sunnyvale, at the southern end of the bay, as the site for one of the bases. Nearly three years later, however, word reached the members that a Navy Airship Base Investigating Committee had recommended Camp Kearny, near San Diego, as the site for the West Coast dirigible base. Rather than see San Diego get a base without a fight, the San Francisco Chamber of Commerce joined the junior organization in

a move to force reconsideration of the entire question of possible Pacific Coast sites, no matter how many telegrams and letters had to be sent to northern and central California members of the House of Representatives requesting that they insist upon further investigations.

The investigating committee made a new survey of sites, inspecting ninety-seven in all, of which twenty-three were in the San Francisco Bay Area. In the end the choice was between Camp Kearny and Sunnyvale. Four members of the committee voted for Sunnyvale, one for Camp Kearny.

To make sure that there would be no reversal of this decision, the San Francisco Chamber of Commerce pledged itself to raise half a million dollars, purchase a thousand-acre site, and give it to the Navy. Fund raising was not easy in the year 1931; but by making the campaign a Bay Area affair, the chamber was able to fulfill its pledge within three months.

"We appealed to our neighbors—to San Jose, Oakland, Alameda, Berkeley, Palo Alto, San Mateo County cities, Marin County—all bay communities, corporations, and individuals," Leland Cutler, president of the San Francisco organization, told Admiral W. C. Cole, Commandant of the Twelfth Naval District, as he handed him the deed of gift of the Sunnyvale site on August 3, 1931. "Nobody failed us."[13]

No small part of the satisfaction of Bay Area leaders in this achievement was, some acknowledged, the defeat handed southern California. But the chief interest of businessmen in the new military establishment, aside from its importance for national defense, was in the sizable annual payroll that would be added to the Bay Area economy, and in the initial expenditures for construction of hangars, air strips, housing, and equipment. In the lean years of the early 'thirties nothing looked so substantial and desirable as a federal installation supported by all the taxpayers of the United States. Moreover, no one doubted that the whole Bay Area would benefit by the new base. The campaign for purchase of the Sunnyvale site was therefore a stimulating example of the way in which the business community of the Bay Area could reach agreement on a specific project for economic development. The success of the endeavor suggested that united action might be possible on other projects—and straightway the opportunity for a new demonstration of Bay Area coöperation presented itself.

A Gift to the Army

Having seen how effective the offer of a free site was in inducing the Navy to decide on Sunnyvale, the Marin County Board of Supervisors determined to make the

U.S.S. Macon *at Moffett Field, Sunnyvale, in the Early 1930's.
Official photograph, U.S. Navy.*

United States Army a gift of the Marin Meadows acreage that Assistant Secretary of War F. Trubee Davison had inspected in 1929 as the possible site for a bombing base. The only trouble was that the board's generosity exceeded the financial resources of the county. Although the supervisors had the enthusiastic support of Marin County taxpayers, they could afford to appropriate no more than $122,000 toward acquisition of the site, now known as Hamilton Field. This amount would make possible the purchase of 764 acres, whereas the Army needed an additional 163 acres. Public subscription of $53,000 appeared to be the answer to the problem. The board therefore agreed to spend tax monies only on condition that other Bay Area counties, civic organizations, and interested persons would contribute funds for the additional acreage.

Again the spirit of area-wide coöperation manifested itself. At a meeting called by the Downtown Association of San Francisco, the San Francisco Chamber of Commerce pledged itself to raise $12,500 and the Downtown Association and other civic organizations volunteered to contribute $14,000. The Oakland Chamber of Commerce made a pledge of $12,500. Citizens of Marin gave a guarantee of $14,000, but an appropriation by the Sonoma County Board of Supervisors of $5,000 toward purchase of the site reduced to $9,000 the amount that had to be raised among individual contributors in Marin County. In a little more than two months all the money required for the additional acreage was on hand.

"Amid cheers of a crowd that packed the Supervisors' chambers in San Rafael yesterday, the checks to purchase the land were handed over and the deed was transferred to the United States," the San Francisco *Chronicle* reported on March 18, 1932.

An initial Congressional appropriation of $1,412,117.87 in June of that year for development of the 927-acre site, followed in September, 1933, by a second appropriation of $3,462,184.41, brought the national investment in the new military establishment to almost $5,000,000.

In the meantime, the possibility that Alameda might be selected as the site for a second Navy air base in the Bay Area inspired still another demonstration of area-wide unity. Through the San Francisco Bay Industrial Committee, representing chambers of commerce in the area, cities in the nine counties agreed to support Alameda in its efforts to interest a Congressional subcommittee in the possibility of developing an aviation field at the western end of the city, where shoal areas could be filled and added to approximately one thousand acres of available land. A third time the one-for-all-and-all-for-one spirit proved its value. The subcommittee was favorably disposed toward the Alameda site. A more intensive survey by another committee in 1935 and an inspection by a Naval Board of Survey about the same time finally led to a decision to establish a naval air base in Alameda.

Underlying Unity

The addition of three new bases in an area which already had military establishments on both sides of the Golden Gate and at Mare Island and Benicia dramatized the fact that the federal government considered the whole Bay Area, in effect, one big base. But there were other ways in which the underlying unity of the area became increasingly evident. As bridges spanned the northern and southern arms of the bay and as public interest centered on the importance of constructing a bridge across the Golden Gate and a crossing from San Francisco to Oakland, it became clear that a long-deferred union of the several parts of the Bay Area was taking place. The growth of cities was shrinking the great bay, for the bridges were but highways across water from city to city, bringing the shores closer together. The cities themselves were reaching out beyond their corporate boundaries for access to areas of potential urban development, for regional parks, and for airports, as they had reached out earlier for all the near-by sources of water. This new penetration of the outlying areas was far different, however, from that older appropriation of what the cities needed; it was a profound demonstration that the cities functioned economically and socially as parts of a metropolitan complex and therefore could not be limited by mere lines of political jurisdiction. To meet the challenge of living in a metropolitan region, the residents of cities were prepared to resort to such governmental devices as special districts and state authorities. Yet they refused even to take seriously the advocates of metropolitan regional planning—and prophets of metropolitan government were scarcely to be heard. Expediently, project by project, the city councilmen and county supervisors and the voters who elected them were revising the physical environment they had inherited, making it in one sense smaller, by shortening its distances, and in another larger, by expanding its living space, and in every way more certainly a unit, by creating conditions that would eventually compel the cities to act together on matters of area-wide concern.

CHAPTER FOURTEEN

Progress in Troubled Times

The depression that created bread lines throughout the United States in the early 'thirties dealt especially harshly with the San Francisco Bay Area. "The slow recovery of major industries after 1932 was unexampled elsewhere in the state," the California State Planning Board observed in a report published in 1941.[1] Indeed, in 1939 the value added by manufacturing in the factories of the Bay Area was more than one hundred million dollars less than it had been in 1929. Wholesale and retail trade, too, suffered serious monetary declines, although employment in trade did expand slightly, toward the end of the decade.

A unique casualty of this period of human misery and economic regression was an industrial promotion program jointly sponsored by the San Francisco Chamber of Commerce and the Oakland Chamber of Commerce in 1931. Perhaps as a kind of defensive reaction to the intense competition from other Pacific Coast metropolitan areas, the two organizations issued a book with the cover title *San Francisco–Oakland Metropolitan Area: An Industrial Study*. The text and the charts in the book offered comparisons of the Seattle, Portland, San Francisco–Oakland, and Los Angeles areas as manufacturing and distribution centers, with emphasis on the special advantages of the Bay Area. The "apparently uninterruptible" tendency of the population of the United States to gravitate westward was cited as a chief reason for eastern manufacturers to "manufacture in the West for the western market."[2]

"It is not intended that there be any less individual effort to exploit the various sections around the bay than in the past but the new presentation of basic facts will unite all districts in a wholesome spirit of Bay Region unity," *San Francisco Business*, an official publication of the San Francisco Chamber of Commerce, declared hopefully. "This is how the outside investor is most favorably impressed."[3]

Without mentioning Los Angeles by name, the journal pointed out that "the most serious competitor . . . long ago learned the important lesson of the value of unified efforts."[4] The publication referred to the nine San Francisco Bay counties as "one economic unit" of 6,979 square miles and mentioned that the "progressive movement" for industrial promotion in the area actually had been conceived two years previously, in 1929.[5]

Unfortunately, this well-intentioned "selling campaign" was foredoomed. Each month the indices of economic activity in the nation fell lower and lower, and as they continued their downward course, other chambers of commerce in the Bay Area tightened their purse strings and declined to support the campaign with cash. By the fall of 1932 not even the most sanguine eastern industrialist was entertaining the notion of building a branch plant in the Bay Area. East of the Sierra it was no secret that some plants in the bay counties had shut down, that many others were operating with skeleton forces, and that any plant which had not to some degree trimmed the payroll was an exception.

Ill-starred though it was, this movement for area-wide industrial development did indicate that under favorable conditions some metropolitan regional coöperation might be achieved. Like many promotional efforts, it was not selective in its appeal to eastern manufacturers and it aimed to attract any industry, regardless of its labor relations record, its wage scales, or its operational efficiency, that might be thinking of expanding in the West. Entirely lacking were studies showing where certain types of industries might be established in the Bay Area to the greatest advantage of the industries themselves as well as to the greatest advantage of the area. In fact, little if any thought had been given to the relation between economic development and metropolitan physical development, but at least the ideal of coöperation among bay cities had been enunciated. In years to come this pioneer attempt at united effort would be remembered and cited as a precedent for further essays at advancing the economic fortunes of the entire area through a representative organization.

Progress Despite Depression

Regardless of economic strain, in the early 'thirties the people of the Bay Area did succeed in bringing to completion—or at least in materially advancing—some of the undertakings they had conceived and started in the prosperous 'twenties. On the night of October 15, 1932, for instance, an audience that was as fashionable as any that had assembled in 1926 or 1927 filled the sumptuous new War Memorial Opera House in the San Francisco Civic Center for the first performance in that now historic edifice, the birthplace, in 1945, of the United Nations. Begun in the late 'twenties, the gray granite structure at the time of its opening was the only municipal opera house in the entire United States. As the handsome gold curtain rose on the first act of Puccini's *La Tosca*, a burst of applause greeted the first words sung from the stage— *Ah! finalmente!* Finally, after more than a quarter of a century of being without an opera house, San Francisco had one; but it belonged not alone to San Francisco—it was a cultural institution claimed from the very beginning by the whole Bay Area. The audience that listened to Claudia Muzio, Alfredo Gandolfi, and Dion Borgioli sing the leading roles was composed of men and women from cities throughout the nine counties bordering on the bay, and from communities beyond the Bay Area, too.

At the time the acoustically superb opera house was being christened with song, San Franciscans showed that they could display just as much Old World fervor about the city's historic past, its scenic hills, and matters of urban aesthetics as they could about opera. With part of the money left to the city by the late Lillie Hitchcock Coit, who had been an honorary member of an early-day volunteer fire company known as Knickerbocker No. 5, the

San Francisco Park Commission proposed to erect a tower on Telegraph Hill to the memory of the volunteer fire fighters of the 'fifties and 'sixties. But many San Franciscans wanted no tower at all on Telegraph Hill, and just as many others particularly did not want the tower designed by Arthur Brown, Jr., the architect who had designed the War Memorial Opera House. Even at that date, the Palace of Fine Arts, sole remnant of the Panama-Pacific International Exposition of 1915, was beginning to crumble, and there were groups who urged that the Coit bequest be used to restore it rather than to build a tower. Several art groups protested that the massive shaft would "ruin" Telegraph Hill and spoil its silhouette.[6] A member of the San Francisco Board of Supervisors delighted the Federation of Artists when he declared that the proposed structure would look "like a chimney on a new incinerator."[7] Nevertheless, after all the protests had been heard, the Park Commission, with the approval of a bare majority of the Art Commission, built the tower as Brown had designed it. One hundred and seventy feet high and thirty feet in diameter at its base, it has become, since its dedication in October, 1933, an accepted landmark on the famous hill overlooking the Embarcadero. Only occasionally does some critic refer to it as "a Gargantuan milk bottle." If it were less conspicuous, if its design had not provoked a memorable controversy, if it were not associated with the name of an almost legendary character, it might go unmentioned in a volume dealing with the entire Bay Area; but the Coit Tower is symbolic of the kind of civic uproar that San Franciscans can create when their sense of beauty and their deeper feelings regarding the historic past are involved.

East Bay Regional Parks

On the opposite side of the bay a controversy just as bitter had broken out between the directors of the East Bay Municipal Utility District and citizens who in the late 'twenties had initiated the movement for development of regional parks in surplus watershed lands of the district. The East Bay Regional Park Association sought the coöperation of the directors of the utility district in persuading the state legislature to amend the Municipal Utility District Act of 1921 to enlarge the powers of the district to include park functions. But the chairman of the board of directors of the utility district unalterably opposed broadening the activities of the district, although this would have been the simplest way to provide for regional parks and would also have made easier the protection of the water system of the utility district. According to some reports, nothing more than a clash of personalities between the board chairman and certain advocates of regional parks was involved. It appears more likely, however, that the board chairman had a deep conviction that the utility district was, in effect, a business and should be managed as such, whereas a park division within the district would be, in his view, a "governmental agency" and would therefore be "sloppily run" and would cost more than it was worth.[8] The primary obligation of the utility district, he declared, was to reduce the bonded indebtedness of the district as fast as possible, not to increase its operating expenses. So strong was his opposition that he threatened to resign if the charter of the utility district were amended. His colleagues therefore adopted his inflexible attitude, despite the most cogent counterarguments that could be advanced by a Mayors' Provisional Regional Park Board appointed by the mayors of nine East Bay cities.

The only course left to the proponents of regional parks was to appeal to the state legislature to enact special enabling legislation authorizing the East Bay cities to create a park district. This the legislature did in 1933 with but one dissenting vote. The Regional Park District Act provided that two or more cities with contiguous territory, whether in one or more counties, might form a park district within the boundaries of an existing utility district. The Alameda County Board of Supervisors permitted seven cities—Alameda, Albany, Berkeley, Emeryville, Oakland, Piedmont, and San Leandro—to vote on a proposal to create the East Bay Regional Park District; but the supervisors of Contra Costa County refused to permit El Cerrito and Richmond to vote on the measure. The voters of the Alameda County cities approved the formation of the new district by a vote of 93,405 to 37,397 on November 6, 1934. Residents of the nonparticipating cities of El Cerrito and Richmond were thus assured the use of regional parks for which they would pay no taxes!

The park district made its first purchases of land in 1936, acquiring more than 2,200 acres in the Berkeley Hills, mostly on the eastern or Contra Costa County side. Sixty acres purchased from a private seller formed the nucleus of Redwood Regional Park, in the hills east of Oakland, where in early days the pioneers had cut timber to build houses in San Francisco, Oakland, and other Bay Area towns. Four parcels acquired from the East Bay Municipal Utility District provided Roundtop Regional Park, Lake Temescal Regional Park, and the greater part of Charles Lee Tilden Regional Park. Lake Temescal, above the Claremont district of Berkeley, which had been the first source of water for Oakland, was no longer needed for water supply.

Later in the decade, the park district expanded its holdings to some 4,250 acres, adding substantially to Tilden

Park and to Redwood Park. All but 249 acres of these later acquisitions were from the East Bay Municipal Utility District, which continued to own thousands of acres of watershed lands described by Olmsted and Hall as suitable for park development.

If the surplus watershed lands available for parks had all been in Alameda County, that county might have assumed the responsibility for park development, as some other Bay Area counties have done; but since the areas desirable for recreational use lay almost wholly in the neighboring county of Contra Costa, the people of the East Bay cities were obliged to entrust the park function to a district, although it need not have been an entirely new district. The creation of a separate East Bay Regional Park District unnecessarily complicated the governmental structure of the Bay Area and certainly effected no economies from an over-all standpoint. In the long run, the multiplication of special districts in a metropolitan region increases the difficulty of finding solutions to area-wide problems and carrying out metropolitan development projects.

State Parks

The State Park Commission created in 1927 also was active in the Bay Area during the 'thirties in providing publicly owned recreation areas, chiefly of the type that would be classified as regional—ocean beaches, mountain areas, and botanically important reservations. Thus the commission added to the recreation facilities of the metropolitan region several new areas similar to those owned by counties, the East Bay Regional Park District, the federal government (Muir Woods National Monument), and the state itself (Mount Tamalpais State Park). Outstanding among the areas developed for public use by the state were Mount Diablo State Park in Contra Costa County and the Sonoma Coast State Park, extending from the northern end of Bodega Bay to the mouth of the Russian River. Mount Diablo had been a scenic attraction ever since 1874, when a private toll road was built to the summit. After the two-thousand-acre park was dedicated on April 26, 1931, approximately fifty-five thousand people visited it in the next ten months. The Sonoma Coast State Park, eleven miles in length, includes sandy beaches and rocky cliffs entirely west of the coast road. Most of this park was acquired between 1931 and 1935, through various purchases.

Not well known to most Bay Area residents is another state park established in the 'thirties, the Kruse Rhododendron Reserve, on the northwest coast of Sonoma County, ten miles north of Fort Ross. The gift in 1933 of Edward Kruse, of San Francisco, the area is noteworthy for its beautiful growth of rhododendrons and its spectacular ocean frontage.

A transaction of special interest was the transfer of ownership, from Sonoma County to the State Park Commission, of the Armstrong Grove of redwoods, a stand of magnificent trees about two and a half miles north of the Russian River town of Guerneville. Colonel James B. Armstrong had wished to deed the grove to the state some years before his death in 1900, but since there was at that time no state agency to administer the property as a public recreation area, he was unable to make the gift. In 1917 his heirs aided in the purchase of the four hundred acres of *Sequoia sempervirens* by Sonoma County, which held the property as a county park until 1934, when the State Park Commission purchased it and began constructing trails, a water system for the convenience of campers, and an outdoor theater. This transfer of a county park to the state set a precedent for the acquisition by the state of other county parks, although the transaction involving the Armstrong Grove was unique, in that it would have become a state park decades earlier had the law permitted.

In addition to all these large acreages, the State Park Commission took title to an important historical monument in the Bay Area, the house built by General Mariano Guadalupe Vallejo at Sonoma soon after California entered the Union. The acquisition of the Victorian structure was in accordance with the policy of the State Park Commission of preserving significant historical buildings.

At no period prior to the 'thirties had the Bay Area gained so much public recreation space of regional importance as it did during that decade—more than seventy-seven hundred acres, excluding the Armstrong Grove, which was already in public ownership. Much of this acreage, such as the Sonoma Coast State Park and the Mount Diablo State Park, had, however, been used by the public while it was still in private hands. The acquisitions by the state, by the East Bay Regional Park District, and by a political subdivision not previously outstanding in recreation, San Mateo County, guaranteed that the people of the Bay Area would be able to enjoy large tracts of natural landscape permanently.

The San Mateo County park program was made possible by a new charter, adopted in 1932. A provision of the charter authorized the county supervisors to make annual appropriations to a Land Acquisition Fund, which was to be used to purchase sites designated on a master recreation plan. Under this pay-as-you-go procedure the county acquired several miles of coastal beaches between 1935 and 1940. Later it suggested that the State Park Commission also purchase some of the beaches included in the county-wide plan.

In 1937 a movement to "save the beaches" gained impetus in Marin County but did not become effective until after World War II.

Although much progress was made through state and local agencies in the 'thirties, regional recreation areas in the Bay Area were not well distributed. In Napa and Solano counties there were no large tracts set aside for permanent public use. Contra Costa County itself had done nothing to provide regional parks. Santa Clara County had no long-range park program, and the supervisors of Alameda County were content to let the East Bay Regional Park District meet the need for large-scale recreation areas. Yet the vast expansion of regional park acreage in the metropolitan area during the decade did make the public generally more aware of the opportunities for the creation of additional recreation reserves. Numerous sites then appraised by public-spirited citizens as being potential county or state parks have since passed into public ownership.

Water Problems

As in the field of regional recreation, the Bay Area made progress in the solution of its water supply problems through various subregional projects, one of which, the Contra Costa Canal, was part of the vast Central Valley Project begun in the 'thirties. The city-around-the-bay that was gradually developing was still so unconnected that most residents of the Bay Area identified themselves with this or that part of it and rarely considered the needs of the whole area. The annexation of new territories to the East Bay Municipal Utility District, the completion of the Hetch Hetchy Aqueduct by San Francisco, and the construction of the Contra Costa Canal all emphasized the growing dependence of the Bay Area upon a distant source of supply—the Sierra watershed. In the Santa Clara Valley the struggle to conserve local water supplies met with some success; but a major question remained unanswered: What would the valley do if population and industry greatly increased? Would not this section, like others in the Bay Area, have to import water?

Though the times were hard, San Francisco voters did not hesitate to vote additional bond issues to finance completion of the initial stages of the Hetch Hetchy project and to provide local distribution facilities. In May, 1932, they approved a $6,500,000 bond issue to complete construction of the tunnels through the Coast Range, one of which was twenty-five miles long and the other three and a half miles long. In June, 1933, the voters went to the polls again and authorized issuance of $12,095,000 of general obligation bonds to pay for a second pipe line across the bay and for other water system extensions. And five months later they voted still another bond issue of $3,500,000 to raise O'Shaughnessy Dam from its original height of 344.5 feet to 430 feet above bedrock, so that the storage capacity of Hetch Hetchy Reservoir might be increased from 67,000,000,000 gallons to 117,000,000,000 gallons.

Long before the dam was enlarged, however, the San Joaquin Pipe Line, the Coast Range tunnels, and new distribution system reservoirs and mains in San Francisco were completed. On October 24, 1934, the first Hetch Hetchy water flowed into the Crystal Springs Reservoir, thirteen miles south of San Francisco in San Mateo County, and thence through the distributing system to the metropolis. Twenty years had passed since construction of the Hetch Hetchy project was begun, and thirty-three years had gone by since Mayor James D. Phelan filed applications for permission to tap the headwaters of the Tuolumne River in Yosemite National Park. In that third of a century the people of San Francisco had approved a total of $89,600,000 in bonds for the project, to say nothing of more than $53,000,000 in bonds for new distribution facilities and for purchase of the properties of the Spring Valley Water Company. These huge investments assured them of an ample water supply for many years to come; but the future would require other large expenditures for a dam in the Cherry Valley, for a second pipe line across the San Joaquin Valley, and for additional tunnels through the Coast Range paralleling those already bored. The Hetch Hetchy water system in 1934 had been developed to produce less than half of its potential yield of 400,000,000 gallons daily; and although this partial development was then more than adequate to meet the needs of San Francisco and the Modesto and Turlock Irrigation districts (which had prior rights to the "natural flow" of the Tuolumne River), the time would come when it might not be sufficient, in a period of unusual drought, to avoid water shortages in a metropolis and in near-by cities that would become much more populous. San Francisco faced the job of eventually building the water system to the full capacity proposed by John R. Freeman in 1912.

The East Bay Municipal Utility District in the meantime extended its services to an ever-widening territory as one small water district after another sought a better water supply through annexation to the utility district. In 1931 the Lafayette, San Pablo, and Kensington areas in Contra Costa County and the Castro Valley in Alameda County became parts of the utility district. In 1932 and 1933 the Saranap and Fairview areas in Contra Costa County were annexed, and in 1933 and 1934 the Eden and Chabot districts in Alameda County. The inclusion of other areas followed, until by 1938 the utility district was serving a territory of 179 square miles and a population estimated at more than half a million.

Had a large city, such as Oakland, owned and controlled the Mokelumne River water supply, the jealous control of that supply might have stimulated a succession of urban consolidations and territorial annexations similar to those which preceded and followed the completion of the Owens River Aqueduct by the city of Los Angeles. But since no one city in the East Bay had undertaken to reach out to the Sierra without the help of its neighbors, and since a utility district had appeared to be the most satisfactory solution for all concerned, community identities were preserved and no supercity came into being.

The Contra Costa Canal

Industries situated between Martinez and Antioch on Suisun Bay had to wait until the summer of 1940 to get ample supplies of good water, because the solution of their water problems depended upon a grand plan of the state for impounding and redistributing the waters of the Sacramento and San Joaquin rivers—the Central Valley Project. The state legislature authorized the great development in 1933, but private utilities attacked the hydroelectric power provisions and forced the project to a state referendum on December 19, 1933. The voters upheld the project by a winning margin of 33,603 votes out of a total of 885,821 votes cast. State officials, who from the beginning had hoped for some federal contributions toward the project, made no particular effort to sell the $170,000,000 of revenue bonds authorized in the Central Valley Project Act and bent all their efforts toward getting the federal government to finance the project. To their very great satisfaction, President Franklin D. Roosevelt approved the project as a reclamation development on December 2, 1935. An initial allocation of $4,200,000 to the Bureau of Reclamation for field studies was followed by further appropriations in 1936, and by 1937 construction of various major features of the project (which in the meantime had been revised by the bureau) began. Among the first structures undertaken were Shasta Dam, spanning the Sacramento River at the northernmost tip of the Sacramento Valley; the Friant Dam, astride the San Joaquin River twenty miles northeast of Fresno; and the Contra Costa Canal, designed to bring fresh water from Rock Slough, a tributary of the San Joaquin River in the delta region in the eastern part of Contra Costa County, to the farms, cities, and industries in the northern area of the county.

Before the Contra Costa Canal could obtain federal financing and be included in the Central Valley Project, it was necessary for the people of northern Contra Costa

The Contra Costa Canal, with Mount Diablo in the Distance. Photograph courtesy of the United States Bureau of Reclamation.

County to organize their own water district. The election for the purpose of forming the Contra Costa County Water District was held on May 26, 1936. Active in campaigning for the district were many members of the Salt Water Barrier Association of the 'twenties, whose proposal for erecting a barrier to prevent salt-water incursion into Suisun Bay and the delta area had been abandoned when plans for the Central Valley Project cystallized.

Governor Frank F. Merriam participated in the groundbreaking ceremonies for the canal near Oakley on Sunday, November 7, 1937. Thirty-two months later, on July 10, 1940, the first water surged into a tidewater section of the canal and, raised by four pumping plants to an elevation of 135.6 feet, started on its forty-six-mile journey by gravity flow to a terminal reservoir near Martinez. In the following month the city of Pittsburg became the first city to use water from the Contra Costa Canal. The

Columbia Steel Company, at Pittsburg, was the first industry in the new water district to sign a contract for water from the $4,000,000 conduit. Twenty-two thousand acres of farmland in northern Contra Costa County before long also received water from the Canal for irrigation. The water problems that had plagued an important part of the county for two decades or more at last were solved.

Water-Conservation Plan

In another Bay Area county, Santa Clara, the years during which the people of Contra Costa County struggled to find a dependable source of fresh water were marked by a continuing effort to educate voters on the necessity for the flood storage dams, conduits, and percolation works first proposed by engineer Fred H. Tibbetts in 1921. In the eighteen years between 1915 and 1933 the groundwater level in the Santa Clara Valley had dropped 95 feet because of heavy pumping from more than two thousand wells, even in years of normal or above-normal rainfall. Pumping draft had risen by 1933 to an annual average of 134,000 acre-feet, but replenishment of the underground reservoir through infiltration was estimated to average only 70,000 acre-feet per year. Depletion therefore should have been some 64,000 acre-feet per year; it actually was about 40,000 acre-feet, according to engineering estimates. What had happened to account for the discrepancy of 24,000 acre-feet was that the formerly saturated dense blue clays underlying large parts of the north valley had been squeezed like a sponge when pumping lowered the water table and caused the heavy upper soils to press down upon them, compacting them and bringing about a settling of the entire central area of the valley.

This sinking of approximately two hundred square miles in the northern part of the Santa Clara Valley first came to light in 1920 when a survey by the United States Coast and Geodetic Survey revealed a slight change in the elevation of San Jose from the original 1912 survey. A new survey in 1932 disclosed that the central business district of the city was more than four feet lower than it had been in 1912—all because of the steady overdraft on the underground reservoir, the lessening of hydrostatic pressure on the blue clay subsoil, and the consequent compression of the clay. The storage capacity of the underground reservoir had been permanently reduced by about 500,000 acre-feet.

The lowering of the water table and the sinking of a large part of the valley created a whole complex of problems for the people of the valley, not all of which were immediately apparent. One thing agriculturists did know was that their costs for power to pump water from deeper levels increased, as well as their capital outlays for deepening wells and installing larger pumping equipment. Few of them realized, however, that the dewatering of the blue clay caused a reduction in the moisture content of the topsoil and required even more irrigation than before. Thus unwittingly they found themselves trapped by nature in a game that they were not likely to win, even by adopting a conservation program. The lowering of the water table, furthermore, invited salt-water intrusion into low-lying areas near San Francisco Bay. And the sinking of the land set the stage for a drama of floods and destruction in some season of unusual rainfall. Not that the low-lying plains of the Santa Clara Valley had escaped periodic inundation, but the area now subject to potential flooding had been greatly increased by the ground subsidence. Incalculable damage already had been caused to well casings, sewers, water mains, and other subsurface installations.

The first step toward carrying out a remedial program was taken in 1934, when the voters of the Santa Clara Valley Conservation District voted seven to one for bonds for a "well replenishment project," thereby reversing their seven-to-one rejection of a conservation plan submitted to them in 1931. The 1934 plan was based on the same principles as the Tibbetts plans of 1921 and 1931 but was more modest in cost. Instead of an estimated $6,000,000, it cost $2,683,000; but this sum proved to be $400,000 short of enough to complete the Coyote Dam, one of the most important projects in the plan. The voters authorized the extra funds in May, 1936.

"The dominant feature of this entire project and of the Coyote Reservoir, as well as of the other reservoirs, is the detention of flood water which would otherwise run to waste, and the gradual release of such flood water into natural streams at a rate so reduced that it will be entirely absorbed in the natural streambeds as released and passed into underground storage," Tibbetts explained.[9]

Measurements taken in 1931–1932 had shown that out of 155,000 acre-feet of runoff from the north valley watershed, only 45,000 acre-feet went into underground storage and 110,000 acre-feet went to waste in San Francisco Bay: 29 per cent was saved, 71 per cent was wasted.

The six retention reservoirs completed by the end of 1936 provided for storage of 49,000 acre-feet of runoff. Through gradual release of water into percolating canals and water-spreading beds, about 43,000 acre-feet was annually filtered to the underground reservoir. In March, 1938, Tibbetts was able to report that "from an all-time low in 1934 to January 1, 1938, the water table has risen more than 100 feet in places near the stream percolation works. In the main or central portion of the valley the average annual rise has been rather uniform. The total has been more than thirty feet, of which nearly one-half occurred during 1937. This was practically a normal year and the first year in which all the district's works were in use."[10]

Between 1937 and 1940 there was a cycle of wet winters, which enabled the retention reservoirs to make maximum contributions toward replenishing the subsurface water. But the people of the conservation district enjoyed only the illusion that they had improved conditions. Within the next ten years the water table was to recede even lower than in 1934. War, the growth of cities, shifts in agricultural production, and industrialization were all to intensify the problems created when early settlers began to upset nature's primal arrangements. The Santa Clara Valley sooner or later would be looking for external water supplies with which to augment its own local supplies.

From an over-all standpoint the San Francisco Bay

Area undoubtedly was more adequately supplied with water by the end of the 'thirties than it had been at any other time. But piecemeal solution of the area-wide problem of insufficient supply represented a long retreat from the unified approach of 1910, when for a time the city councils of San Jose, the East Bay cities, and some Peninsula communities were willing to consider joining with San Francisco in the Hetch Hetchy project. The various separate programs for obtaining water tended to perpetuate the habit of thinking narrowly about sectional problems and needs and to counteract the psychological good that may have come to the Bay Area from the San Francisco–Oakland industrial promotion program and the coöperative efforts on military air bases. Social and economic forces, however, in this geographically divided area, have always been acting to strengthen intercommunity ties; and action on one front no sooner fails than the struggle for area-wide coöperation opens anew on some other front. In the long run the idea of metropolitan regional unity perhaps makes some gains. Thus the diverse efforts to establish regional parks without relation to an over-all plan, to build subregional water systems and conservation works, and to attract industries to this or that locality were offset, to a degree, by a second attempt to promote metropolitan regional planning and by public works of importance to the entire Bay Area, such as the San Francisco–Oakland Bay Bridge and the Golden Gate Bridge.

Area-wide Planning—Second Try

The regional planning movement of the mid-thirties was peculiarly an outgrowth of the troubled times. In Washington, D.C., Franklin Delano Roosevelt's vigorous administration, supported by an anxious and coöperative Congress, was disbursing millions, nay billions, to feed the unemployed, put men to work, aid state and local governments, and stimulate the reopening of idle factories. The national capital and the regional offices of the federal relief and public works agencies became centers in which state and local officials and civic groups with job-creating projects to propose vied for favor. After the Works Progress Administration was started on May 6, 1935, every community that wanted a new highway, a new recreation building, a survey of its historical records, or a study of the adequacy of its school buildings turned to the WPA for assistance. The very possibility of getting WPA workers to staff a project suggested all manner of worthwhile activities that might not otherwise be undertaken.

To Hugh Pomeroy, who was consultant to several county planning commissions in the Bay Area, the new

work program looked like the means of getting some of the spade work of metropolitan regional planning done. Although thirty cities and five counties—Alameda, Contra Costa, San Francisco, Santa Clara, and San Mateo—had official planning commissions by 1935, not to mention an unofficial commission in Marin County, the value of city and county planning had barely been demonstrated in the Bay Area, because severe limitations of budget and personnel prevented commissions from doing any substantial amount of the data gathering that is a necessary first step in planning. Pomeroy, as a member of a WPA advisory committee for the coördination of professional and technical projects, believed that if some kind of regional planning organization were formed, the WPA might assign workers to it for field surveys and research projects.

At his suggestion the San Mateo County Planning Commission invited the other county planning commissions in the Bay Area, as well as the unofficial commission in Marin County and the Santa Cruz County Planning Commission, to join it in forming a so-called regional planning commission, which actually would be a voluntary association of planning commissions rather than the kind of elected commission required for a regional planning district organized under the planning enabling legislation approved by the state legislature in 1929. Santa Cruz County, of course, had not been included in the Bay Area as defined by the Regional Plan Association of the previous decade; nor has it in recent years been considered a part of the Bay Area. San Mateo County found the coöperation of Santa Cruz County necessary, however, on certain highway and recreation problems, and therefore sought its participation in the new regional planning effort. No doubt there also was something to be gained by bringing together as many citizen commissioners as possible in a period when planning commissions and professional planners were still struggling for recognition.

The letters of invitation to the seven-county conference held in August, 1935, stated that there were several problems of area-wide concern—old and familiar problems to anyone who had ever given any thought to regional development: "The highways in the counties surrounding San Francisco Bay should be developed as a coordinated network, in which adequately planned county highway systems will satisfactorily fit into the State Highway System. Roadside zoning is of similar inter-county interest, in that the traveler on a highway is not concerned with the location of county boundary lines but desires a safe and pleasant thoroughfare upon which to travel. The construction of the San Francisco–Oakland Bay Bridge and of the Golden Gate Bridge will more closely knit together the counties of the San Francisco Bay regional area and is requiring coordination of their transit and transportation plans. The major recreation facilities and potentialities of the region must be considered parts of a regional recreation system, not for the service of the individual counties within which the respective recreation areas may lie but for the use of the people of the entire region. Pollution by sewage of the waters of San Francisco Bay and the streams tributary to it constitutes a regional problem of interest to all the communities adjacent to the bay . . ."[11]

At the conference Pomeroy pointed out that in addition to coördination of their planning programs, the counties needed research on problems of regional concern, such as the distribution and densities of population, trends in the use of land, transportation requirements, and any number of other matters. A regional planning commission, he said, would be able to supervise several research projects.

The delegates signified their intention of forming such an organization, gave their blessing to an effort by Pomeroy to interest the WPA in providing research workers, and agreed to invite the counties of Sonoma, Napa, and Solano to participate in the proposed regional planning commission whenever those counties established their own planning commissions.

The California Works Progress Administration indicated that it would recognize the proposed regional planning commission as soon as it became a reality. L. Deming Tilton, director of the new California State Planning Board created as a division of the State Department of Finance, told Pomeroy that the state board would welcome suggestions from the commission-to-be and would sponsor projects it proposed.

Thus encouraged, the county planning commissions in the Bay Area organized the San Francisco Metropolitan Area Planning Commission in September, 1935, elected C. A. Buck, the chairman of the San Mateo County Planning Commission, to the presidency, and named Pomeroy secretary. But because this was only a voluntary association of planning commissioners and was without official status as an organization representing county governments in the Bay Area, negotiations for WPA assistance came to naught. Sadly the commissioners concluded that an effort would have to be made to strengthen planning in the various counties of the area before they could hope to succeed with regional planning.

A curious aspect of this short-lived regional planning venture was that cities other than San Francisco were given no opportunity to participate in it. San Francisco, of course, is legally both a city and a county, and on this occasion was represented as one of the bay counties. No regional planning organization could well omit the largest city of the Bay Area, regardless of the fact that it enjoyed the dual status of city and county combined. But Oakland, always sensitive about being accorded due recognition in the metropolitan scheme of things, was without representation except through the Alameda County Planning Commission, although this commission has no statutory authorization to carry on the planning function within the corporate boundaries of cities. Likewise, Berkeley, Richmond, San Jose, and many other cities were only indirectly represented.

Certainly, no organization that disregarded the cities, which collectively contained the preponderance of the regional population, could justifiably call itself a metropolitan regional planning commission. If the county commissioners had been able to keep the new regional organization functioning and had not sooner or later asked the cities to participate, there would eventually have been trouble. Because they failed to extend invitations to city planning commissions at the outset, they may have overlooked a source of strength that just possibly might have sustained the whole endeavor, even though the city planning commissions in the Bay Area in 1935 were, with a few exceptions, pitifully weak. This second attempt to establish a regional planning agency was a good example of how not to organize such an agency in an area embracing scores of municipalities.

Imminence of Change

In the mid-thirties many city councils in the San Francisco Bay Area were perhaps more aware of regional relationships than some of the county boards of supervisors. The rapid construction of the San Francisco–Oakland Bay Bridge and the Golden Gate Bridge brought ever closer the time when old patterns of trade and transportation in the area would be superseded by new ones. The crews of workmen who had been engaged since 1933 in fashioning the miracles of steel that were to link city with city were building change itself. Public works departments on both sides of the bay were constructing approaches to the bridges, and draftsmen were already at work on plans for a new transit terminal in San Francisco. As surely as the currents of traffic and the routes of transit lines shifted, the economic and social relationships of many communities would alter.

But how extensive and of what sort would the expected changes be? Who would be hurt by them and who benefited? San Franciscans knew that the Golden Gate Bridge would make possible ready access to the redwood canyons, scenic mountains, and beautiful beaches of Marin County; but would it cause their city to lose some population to the North Bay counties? Would it bring more shoppers from San Rafael and Petaluma and Santa Rosa to downtown San Francisco, or would trade follow migrating population? Some East Bay residents hoped that their side of the bay would attract San Francisco families who otherwise might move to San Mateo County, but the thought of bridge tolls raised doubts. Uncertainty marked the future—uncertainty that might have been dispelled somewhat if there had been a regional planning agency to investigate all the possible changes that might be effected by the two bridges and to present a general forecast of the new relationships that were likely to emerge.

Because there was no such agency, various specialists independently surveyed the future and made prognostications. None of the studies undertaken was based on a comprehensive analysis of all the factors that should have been taken into consideration; consequently, none was noteworthy for accuracy.

One of the earliest investigations was prompted by diverse opinions among Oakland businessmen concerning the effect the Bay Bridge would have on the economy of Oakland. Some were sure that upon the opening of the bridge, San Francisco would enjoy an increase in retail trade at the expense of Oakland; others were convinced that the East Bay would attract both population and trade from the larger city. The Residential Development Committee of the Oakland Chamber of Commerce therefore sponsored a study, by an advertising agency, of the effect the San Francisco–Oakland Bay Bridge would have on the population and on the retail trade of Oakland.

The report of the agency, issued in February, 1934, pointed out that similar bridges built in four eastern cities, Pittsburgh, Washington, D.C., Philadelphia, and New York, had all stimulated settlement in desirable outlying residential areas that became more accessible from the metropolitan center, regardless of the amount charged for bridge toll. For Oakland the agency predicted a minimum increase of approximately ninety thousand people in the decade, instead of "normal growth" of seventy thousand people, which it said might be expected if there were no bridge.[12]

This study was unusual in urging Oakland to prepare for a larger population by reserving sites for new schools, by extending transportation to suburban areas that would probably be developed, by improving zoning, and by taking steps to avoid speculation in land.

San Franciscans took comfort from the findings of a sample survey conducted by the San Francisco *Examiner* among housewives in fifty-one northern California com-

munities that would be within "four hours automobile driving time" of the city after the opening of the two big bridges. For retail stores and for hotels, restaurants, and garages the newspaper forecast a 50 to 60 per cent increase in patrons.[13] The survey, which was thought to be representative of the opinions of four hundred thousand families in the coastal area from Ukiah to Monterey, and in the Central Valley from Red Bluff to Fresno, presumably showed that approximately three-fourths of the families in communities outside the Bay Area believed San Francisco stores had advantages over those in their home communities, and that three-fifths of Bay Area families considered San Francisco stores generally superior to local establishments, particularly in the wide assortment of merchandise available.

The forecast included a veiled warning to San Francisco businessmen by predicting a 54 per cent increase in the use of automobiles by women shoppers. It indicated that there should be advance planning to provide more parking space for cars, but it placed no special emphasis on this point.

In answer to the puzzling question of how much population San Francisco might lose when the two great spans were completed, the forecast estimated that "about 6 per cent" of families in the city would depart.[14] On the basis of average family size in San Francisco in 1930, that would have meant a loss of more than thirty-four thousand people—the equivalent of the entire population of some of the state assembly districts in San Francisco in 1930. Had this happened, San Francisco would indeed have received some setbacks; but whatever outward movement of population the bridges did actually bring about was offset by in-migration; the 1940 census showed that population in San Francisco at least remained constant. The survey analysts were as wide of the mark as the advertising agency that predicted a decennial gain of ninety thousand for Oakland—the actual increase in that city was only eighteen thousand.

Stimulus of Fear

Fear that the population would decrease was, however, a powerful stimulus to action in official circles in San Francisco. As early as 1931, City Engineer M. M. O'Shaughnessy had written a report urging the development of a rapid transit system in San Francisco as one means of counteracting the attractions of reduced commuting time between the East Bay and San Francisco after the opening of the Bay Bridge. By 1934 the San Francisco Public Utilities Commission had begun work on the selection of a location for a terminal for transbay electric trains and had become fully aware of the danger to the metropolis of faster service to the East Bay. In its annual report for 1934–35 the commission stated:

"Studies of this problem [of selecting a location for the terminal] indicated the necessity for constructing rapid transit lines in San Francisco to offset the decrease in running time between San Francisco and the East Bay cities. The operation of suburban trains into San Francisco will cut the travel time by twelve minutes, and by bringing the terminal closer to the point of origin and destination of a larger number of commuters, the western part of San Francisco would be placed at a great disadvantage as it will require less time to cross the Bay via the Bridge than it will to reach a number of the desirable residence sections of the City by the present street car system. Also traffic congestion on Market Street has reached a point where street car operation during rush hours is so slow as to be detrimental to the best interests of the City."[15]

With an appropriation of $25,000 provided by the San Francisco Board of Supervisors in December, 1934, the Public Utilities Commission engaged Robert Ridgway, formerly Chief Engineer of the Board of Transportation in New York City, and Alfred Brahdy, Designing Engineer of the same agency, to review rapid transit studies already prepared by the commission and to make recommendations and estimate the cost of an initial rapid transit system. The two engineers, who had been responsible for most of the design and construction of New York subways costing $750,000,000, submitted a proposal on July 9, 1935, for a system of subways in which cars of connecting surface lines would operate until such time as the growth of population and the extension of the subway transportation system made it necessary to provide multiple-unit trains. Conditions in San Francisco, they said, did not yet warrant such extensive and costly subway systems as had been built in London, Paris, New York, and Philadelphia, in which multiple-unit trains operated entirely separated from surface lines.

The proposed system included three routes, all intended to provide faster service to the more distant residential areas of the city: a principal subway under the most heavily traveled portion of Market Street, with surface connections west of Van Ness Avenue to the Twin Peaks and Sunset tunnels; a branch from this main subway to the Mission district that might in time become a rapid transit route to the Peninsula; and a subway under Geary Street to Hamilton Square in the Western Addition. Cars of all three routes were to connect with the projected bridge terminal near Howard and Fremont streets.

Although this subway plan was spoken of as the Ridgway-Brahdy proposal, it was in reality the plan of the Public Utilities Commission, the two experts from New York merely having approved the plan after examining it in detail. The system recommended had evolved since 1931 from a proposal for a single subway under Market Street, with minor extensions into McAllister and O'Farrell streets.

Two features of the plan immediately aroused opposition: the estimated cost of $52,700,000 and the restriction of the subways to use by Municipal Railway lines only. Alarmed at the high cost, the members of the board of supervisors delayed approval of the plan. The failure of the plan to make any provision for the operation of the cars of the privately owned Market Street Railway in the subways brought protests from the company, from its organized employees, from some other unions, and from civic associations friendly to the company and its employees. Staunch proponents of municipal ownership of public utilities suggested that the first step toward improvement of transit in San Francisco should be the consolidation of transit services and the reorganization of routes and schedules.

Completion of the Bay Bridge

While debate on the proposed subway system raged, the San Francisco–Oakland Bay Bridge was completed and was opened to traffic, on November 12, 1936, six months ahead of the scheduled date of completion. For forty months the people of the Bay Area had been watching the great span take shape. During those months the nation had been making heroic efforts toward economic recovery. For the people of the Bay Area the finished bridge was something more than an aerial highway between two shores; it was a singular example of accomplishment in a period of hard struggle. The sight of the bridge towers standing against the cool sky, and of the long cables swinging in serene arcs between them, evoked emotions more intense than those that might have been felt if this gigantic structure had been completed in the prosperous 'twenties, when people tended to accept even sensational feats of engineering as foreordained achievements in the pattern of progress. When, on the day of the dedication ceremonies, Governor Frank F. Merriam with an acetylene torch burned asunder the heavy chain barrier across the bridge, he seemed to burn away the curtain of gloom that had hung over the Bay Area for years. "Cannons roared, bombs burst in air, sirens and whistles shrieked, and massed thousands of enthusiastic citizens at the east and west approaches of the great structure blasted the welkin with their cheers."[16] Fifteen squadrons of navy planes zoomed overhead, a marine parade of gaily decorated yachts and motor boats streamed under the bridge, and

The San Francisco–Oakland Bay Bridge as Seen from Yerba Buena Island. The Southern Pacific ferryboats shown in this view were the last to ply the bay. Photograph courtesy of State Division of Highways.

the United States battle fleet, anchored just south of the span, volleyed forth salutes.

"That this is the greatest bridge yet constructed in the world requires no repetition by me," former President Herbert Hoover declared. "Its construction also spans the whole advance in industrial civilization—our discoveries in science, our inventions, our increasing skill. It is the product of hundreds of years of cumulative knowledge."[17]

Earl Lee Kelley, Director of the State Department of Public Works, expressed what the bridge meant to the residents of the Bay Area. "The opening of this bridge is the first step in eliminating the isolation of San Francisco . . . It will bring the cities of the bay district into closer union . . ."[18]

As if to give immediate fulfillment to Kelley's prediction, approximately a million people traveled across the bridge in two hundred and fifty thousand automobiles, buses, and trucks in the first 108 hours of its operation as a state highway. Thousands of East Bay residents employed in San Francisco tried the novelty of driving to work, even though the toll was sixty-five cents during the

One of Joseph B. Strauss's Preliminary Designs for the Golden Gate Bridge. Perspective drawing published in Western City in March, 1930.

first three months after the bridge was completed. Then at 5 P.M. they dashed from their offices to garages and parking lots, raced home, and announced triumphantly, "I made it in twenty-two minutes tonight."

The majority of commuters, however, continued to make the daily journey back and forth across the bay by ferry, because the lower deck of the bridge was not yet equipped for interurban trains. Plans for the Bay Bridge Terminal had been completed early in 1936; but financing of the bridge railway, the terminal building, and the viaducts proved to be long and involved. Not until the summer of 1937 did construction on the $15,000,000 project get under way.

In the meantime more and more commuters formed car pools and stopped using the transbay services of the Key System and the Southern Pacific. Between 1936 and 1937 the number of transbay passengers carried by the Southern Pacific declined from 13,687,209 to 11,965,052.

The Key System experienced a similar decline in transbay passengers—from 12,334,743 to 10,749,307. For the two systems the total decrease in passenger trips was 3,307,593 during the first year the bridge was in operation, whereas both companies had enjoyed a slight increase in patronage between 1935 and 1936. The sharp drop in 1937 raised grave doubts whether the Bay Bridge Terminal would ever serve the large crowds for which it was designed.

Golden Gate Bridge

Six and a half months after the Bay Bridge was dedicated, the Golden Gate Bridge was completed. It had taken four years, four months, and twenty-two days to construct. As it was the largest and highest single-span suspension bridge built up to that time, it inspired millions of words of description in the newspapers of the world. Writers called it a "steel harp," "the bridge that sings," "the span of gold."[19] Its red towers, designed with four portal struts rather than conventional cross bracing, were more than three hundred feet higher than the Russ Building in the heart of the financial district of San Francisco. Its wire cables, each thirty-six and a half inches in diameter, were then the largest in the history of suspension-bridge construction; yet the concrete anchorage blocks to which they are attached are so huge that they could withstand twice the pull that the cables exert. But this "bridge that couldn't be built" is more than a feat of engineering; in an age in which architecture tends to become engineering, this span has the majesty and magic associated with the greatest architecture of all time. The two hundred thou-

sand pedestrians who swarmed across the bridge on May 27, 1937, the first day it was opened, responded not only to its colossal dimensions but also to its lyric beauty. By midafternoon they were walking across it at the rate of thirty thousand an hour. Automobile traffic was prohibited and they were free to gaze in awe at the soaring towers and the great sweep of the cables.

On the Marin County side of the Golden Gate the State Division of Highways had built an approach to the bridge that was one of the most costly stretches of highway in the Bay Area. Known as the Waldo Approach, this three-and-a-half-mile highway, with its thousand-foot

Air View of the Golden Gate Bridge, Looking Toward San Francisco. Photograph courtesy of State Division of Highways.

tunnel and heavy grading, cost more than $2,000,000. District Engineer John H. Skeggs pointed out that in the days when California was building highways with its first highway bond issue of $18,000,000, the money spent on the Waldo Approach would have built sixty miles of paved highway—the equivalent of the complete original Redwood Highway from Sausalito to Healdsburg. He probably would have been utterly incredulous if a prophet had then told him that within another sixteen years the state would schedule for construction a parallel duplicate of the Waldo Approach, tunnel and all, in order to provide for the heavy volume of traffic over this hazardous route.

The Waldo Approach bypassed the town of Sausalito, which immediately felt the effects of the opening of the bridge. As an increasing number of Marin County residents who were employed in San Francisco began driving to work, the daily ebb and flow of commuters through the Sausalito ferry terminal of the Northwestern Pacific Railroad steadily declined, until by 1939 the railroad was applying to the State Railroad Commission for permission to abandon its interurban service. The desired authorization was withheld, however, until motor coach service could be substituted. In the meantime, business fell off in the town, and the population decreased slightly. By 1940 Sausalito had 127 fewer residents than it had had in 1930, when its population was 3,667. Its historic importance as a land-water transfer point was lost altogether on February 28, 1941, when the interurban electric trains and ferry boats of the Northwestern Pacific made their last runs; but within another year the population rapidly increased as large numbers came to work in the wartime shipyard opened near Waldo Point on Richardson Bay. The renewed growth of Sausalito as a suburban residential outpost of San Francisco was to be a postwar development.

Other towns in Marin County within commuting distance of San Francisco made small population gains during the late 'thirties, thanks partly to the increased accessibility of the area. These communities included Mill Valley, Corte Madera, Larkspur, Kentfield, Ross, San Anselmo, and San Rafael, all on the warm bay side of the Marin Peninsula. In general, old residents of the county were not eager to have San Franciscans move into their domain. The proprietary lovers of "Marvelous Marin" winced at seeing the oaks and madrones cut down to make way for streets in new subdivisions. The farmers and timber operators farther north found the bridge a great convenience, but many an old family in Mill Valley and Ross and San Rafael regarded it as decidedly a mixed blessing for southern Marin County.

Greater Congestion in "the City"

In San Francisco an obvious result of the opening of the two huge bridges was greater traffic congestion, especially in the central business district. "In the past year Market Street congestion has increased very rapidly," the report of the Public Utilities Commission for the fiscal year 1936–37 observed. "This increase is in no small way due to additional automobile traffic which has been brought into San Francisco by the completion of the San Francisco–Oakland and Golden Gate Bridges."[20]

A report on a city-wide traffic survey conducted by WPA workers under the direction of Miller McClintock, a nationally known traffic consultant, pointed out that between 1914 and 1937 the number of registered motor vehicles in San Francisco had risen from only 12,000 to more than 160,000 and that completion of the San Francisco–Oakland Bay Bridge had brought into close communication with the metropolis a highly urbanized area in which there were approximately as many vehicles registered as there were in San Francisco itself.

McClintock discovered that "certain substantial volumes of traffic which are now forced through the central congested area are seeking destinations beyond this area."[21] The city therefore needed, in his opinion, routes bypassing the central area.

His recommendations for alleviating the many traffic problems of the city included a "basic cure" known as a "Limited Way Plan." Drawings in McClintock's report showed some of the proposed limited ways as elevated structures similar to the Westside Highway in New York City, others as semidepressed or fully depressed routes, and still others as trafficways at grade or on elevated earth fills with landscaped banks. In all, there were to be sixty-five miles of these divided, free-flow routes throughout the city, including an elevated limited way along the Embarcadero. All were designed for "an over-all operating average speed of 40 miles per hour, which is more than a 100 per cent increase over existing average experience."[22]

The cost of this early form of city-wide freeway system was set at $26,120,800, half the estimated cost of the subway plan proposed by the Public Utilities Commission. Like the subway plan, the Limited Way Plan was put forth as insurance against competition from the territories made accessible to San Franciscans by the new bridges. McClintock did not suggest means of financing the scheme but indicated that some of the burden might properly fall on the state, because the plan was "not only city-wide in its benefits but regional and state-wide as well."[23] It would assure swift passage through the city for

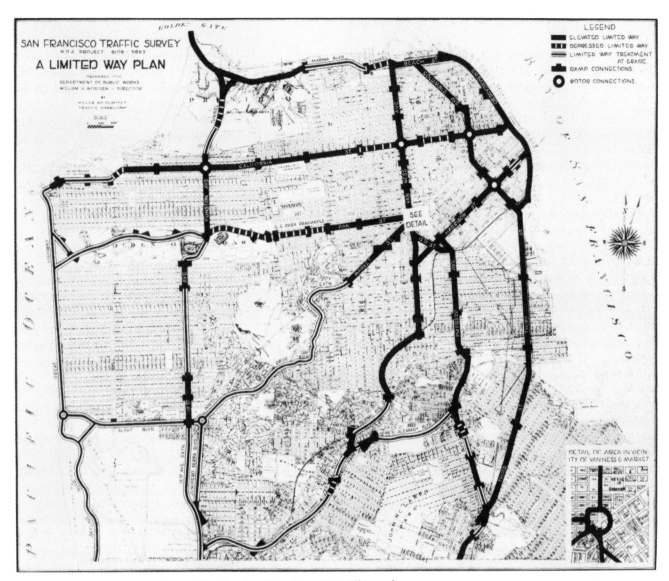

Miller McClintock's Limited Way Plan for San Francisco, 1937. This early proposal for a system of elevated, depressed, and surface freeways invites comparison with the system now being developed by the State Division of Highways.

motorists going from one part of the metropolitan region —or one part of the state—to another; it would provide easy access to the central business district; and it would reduce traffic congestion in that area.

The plan is of historic significance because it foreshadowed many of the freeways built after World War II. At the time it was proposed, however, it impressed local officials as being much too ambitious, especially since San Francisco was then facing an election on the subway plan recommended by the Public Utilities Commission in 1936.

Although the original cost of the subway plan had been shaved to $49,000,000, determined opposition of the privately owned Market Street Railway and of self-appointed transportation experts who had schemes of their own to champion brought defeat to the proposal. In November, 1937, only 68,834 voters cast ballots in favor of the plan; 95,246 voted against it. San Francisco was to make no real effort to improve transportation and traffic until after World War II.

Transbay Train Service

The transbay rail service that San Franciscans had both anticipated and worried about did not become available until January 15, 1939, the day after the Bay Bridge Terminal was dedicated, although motor coaches of the Key System had since 1937 been using the lower deck of the Bay bridge in transporting passengers from Richmond, East Oakland, and Hayward to the metropolis. When the interurban trains finally did begin rolling into the new terminal on Mission Street between First and Fremont streets, the day of the Ferry Building as the great reception center of San Francisco was over, even though some ferries continued to nose into its slips. Hordes of commuters no longer crowded lower Market Street, and retail business in the blocks below Fremont Street shrank to a fraction of what it had been.

The shift from ferry to bridge travel had other economic repercussions. Both the Key System and the Southern Pacific–Interurban Electric Railway incurred heavy expenses in adapting their trains to the grades on the bridge and to the new signal system, but neither company would convert its lines to the voltage of the other. Consequently, the California Toll Bridge Authority, after some delay, installed a dual voltage system on the bridge. In the meantime, so many thousands of commuters had taken to using their own automobiles that by the time transbay rail service could be inaugurated, the Southern Pacific–Interurban Electric Railway was doomed. It had been operating at a deficit for some years. In the first year of railway service over the bridge the number of passengers carried fell one-half million below the total transported in 1938. By 1940 the deficit had become so great that the railway filed an appeal to the State Railroad Commission to abandon all transbay rail service, and in the spring of 1941 the "big red cars" ceased to run.

The Key System, which had enjoyed an increase in patronage in 1939 and then had suffered a decline in 1940, now had the entire East Bay transit field to itself. It offered motor coach service on many of the routes formerly served by the Interurban and extended some rail lines. It also united all transit service, local and interurban, under single management and instituted the universal transfer system—an added convenience for the traveling public.

Notwithstanding all improvements in service, the number of transbay transit passengers declined. In four years the increased use of the automobile on the Bay Bridge had so far altered riding habits that less than two-fifths of all transbay trips were made by train; whereas before the bridge was opened, more than two-thirds of all transbay journeys had been by interurban service. The reduction in bridge tolls from fifty cents to thirty-five cents to twenty-five cents of course contributed greatly to the increasing popularity of commuting by automobile. And toll reductions also put out of business the Golden Gate Ferry between Berkeley and San Francisco, thereby diverting additional hundreds of vehicles a day to the bridge. The traveling public had, however, become more and more conscious of speed and time and more and more impatient with transit schedules, the walk to and from the train, and the wait at the station. Even though traffic jams and parking problems often negated the convenience of the private motor vehicle, people cherished the illusion that personal transportation had many advantages over public transit—and an illusion could be the undoing of transit companies that were unable or unwilling to adjust to the demand for faster, more comfortable, more convenient service.

On the eve of American participation in World War II the San Francisco Bay Area was even farther from achieving a metropolitan regional transit system than it had been at the time of World War I, when, with the construction of three or four missing links, at least five of the nine counties in the area might have been united by interurban railways. In Santa Clara County the once extensive Peninsular Railway had abandoned all its lines and had legally disincorporated in 1935. In Sonoma County the Southern Pacific had discontinued all passenger service on the Petaluma and Santa Rosa Electric Railway. The Golden Gate Bridge had doomed the rail-ferry service of the Northwestern Pacific in Marin County. The bus, steam train, and electric-railway services that did provide transportation were not coördinated. It was impossible to proceed in an unbroken journey from cities on the Peninsula to cities in the East Bay or Marin County, and it was equally impossible to go from Marin County to Oakland or Berkeley without interrupting the journey in San Francisco. New highways, the Golden Gate Bridge, and the San Francisco–Oakland Bay Bridge had brought about a physical unification of the Bay Area that had not been accompanied by any attempt to unify transit service. An opportunity had been neglected—but it was not permanently lost.

Disappearance of River Boats

New highways and the new bridges were fatal not only to two rail-transit systems and several automobile and passenger ferries but also to scores of barges and river boats. One by one they disappeared from the bay and its tributaries. Local shipping tonnage, trending steadily downward since 1925, dropped appreciably in 1937 as trucks began transporting agricultural and other bulk commodities formerly shipped from the interior of the state to metropolitan centers by inland waterways.

Several improvements in routes from the San Joaquin Valley to the East Bay and the San Francisco–Oakland Bay Bridge stimulated this increase in trucking. Nearly three years before the bridge was opened, the State Division of Highways widened to four lanes the Dublin Canyon route through the hills east of Hayward. In 1938 the division further improved this highway from Stockton and Tracy to Oakland by relocating the roadway through the Altamont Pass, east of the Livermore Valley, and making it a wide, divided highway. Transport from the interior by way of Contra Costa County increased in speed and convenience upon the opening of the Broadway Low-Level Tunnel through the Berkeley Hills in December, 1937. The tunnel and its highway connections were constructed as links in an eventual route from Stockton to Oakland that would be ten miles shorter than the route through Dublin Canyon. Almost two years later an eight-mile section of the Arnold Industrial Highway across the Diablo Valley (Franklin Canyon to Willow Pass) brought Richmond and the fertile Central Valley into closer communication.

Like the Waldo Tunnel on the Marin County approach to the Golden Gate Bridge, the Broadway Tunnel was to prove inadequate within fifteen years, but the decade of the 'thirties was a period when population experts foresaw a leveling off of population in the United States about 1970; and even optimistic Californians were not expecting such rapid population increases as had characterized the past growth of the state. Highway engineers doubtless thought that the tunnel would be able to handle traffic between the East Bay and the interior for at least two decades. Even if they had had some misgivings about their forecasts, however, they would hardly have dared to propose building a larger tunnel, for fear of being accused of extravagance. California highways were among the best in the nation, yet funds were entirely insufficient to meet needs. In 1938 John H. Skeggs, district engineer of the state highway division that included eight of the Bay Area counties (Solano County excluded) and Santa Cruz County, estimated that $67,409,200 would be required to bring the roads, bridges, and other structures of his district up to the standards of the time; yet the state legislature appropriated only $28,000,000 for the entire state highway program for the 1939–41 biennium.

This budget included no funds for freeways proposed in the late 'thirties. State highway engineers advocated construction of a Bayshore Freeway on the San Francisco Peninsula and a similar freeway on the east side of the bay between Oakland and San Jose, both routes to connect with the San Francisco–Oakland Bay Bridge. Neither freeway was undertaken until after World War II.

Bay Pollution Problem

Perhaps the most unexpected result of the opening of the Bay Bridge was a movement to stop pollution of the Oakland-Emeryville-Berkeley waterfront. Until the bridge was built, the western waterfront of Oakland was little more than the "back door" of the city. Passengers on Key System trains got a malodorous whiff from the tidal flats as they traveled along the Key System Mole to the ferry terminal near Yerba Buena Island. But aside from the momentary exposure to obnoxious gases, they had little personal acquaintance with the foul conditions created by the discharge of untreated sewage into the shoal waters on the east side of the bay. Only dock workers and employees of industrial plants near the harbor had to live with the evil smells emanating from offshore deposits of putrefying sewage sludge. When the Bay Bridge was completed and the western waterfront became, in effect, the "front door" of the East Bay, the stench from the mud flats quickly became a civic scandal—an affront to community pride and common decency. The press, chambers of commerce, and citizen groups began demanding action on conditions that had been troubling some city engineers for several years.

In the year after the opening of the bridge, noisy sessions in the council chambers of East Bay cities convinced councilmen that they were confronted with a problem that could not be solved satisfactorily through piecemeal programs initiated by individual municipalities. Along a twenty-mile shoreline between San Leandro Bay and the Standard Oil Refinery at Richmond approximately sixty outfall sewers were dumping raw sewage into the bay. In the vicinity of certain sewer outlets along the Oakland Inner Harbor great quantities of solid waste floated on the surface during the canning season and were transported by the current into the tidal canal connecting the harbor with San Leandro Bay. Faced with the necessity for coöperative action, the governing bodies of Alameda, Albany, El Cerrito, Emeryville, Piedmont, Richmond, and San Leandro responded with alacrity to an invitation from Mayor W. J. McCracken of Oakland to send representatives to a meeting in the Oakland Council Chamber to discuss plans for dealing with the common problem.

The outcome of this conference on November 3, 1937, was the formation of an East Bay Municipal Executives Association and the appointment of a committee of city engineers to prepare a preliminary report on sewage disposal. Submitted eight months later, the report recommended that the cities appropriate funds for a comprehensive survey of the sewage disposal problem by a board of consulting engineers.

As often happens, preparing the report seemed to make everyone feel that something had been accomplished. A year passed with almost no action on the chief recommendation of the report, and in the meantime San Leandro grew impatient with the dilatory tactics of other communities and began the construction of trunk sewers and sewage treatment works. Various groups began to fear that the opportunity for joint action by the cities would be lost. Again prodded by the public, city officials of seven cities—Alameda, Albany, Berkeley, Emeryville, Oakland, Piedmont, and Richmond—created an executive committee on June 21, 1940, to supervise the East Bay Cities Sewage Disposal Survey. Collectively the cities appropriated $57,000 for the survey and engaged Charles Gilman Hyde, Harold Farnsworth Gray, and A. M. Rawn as consulting engineers to conduct the investigation.

The consulting engineers reported that "foul conditions . . . have rendered the shores and shore waters hardly utilizable for recreational uses (boating, fishing, and the like); completely unsuitable for bathing; and a handicap to industrial development and shipping."[24] They perhaps minimized the seriousness of the problem by concluding that it was "one of aesthetics, primarily, rather than one definitely concerned with the public health, except perhaps indirectly."[25] But they made an important contribution toward eventual solution of the problem when they recommended that the construction and operation of sewage treatment plants and facilities for disposal of sewage be entrusted to the East Bay Municipal Utility District "for the reason that its administrative and engineering organization, with few additions to its technical staff, is exceedingly capable and well equipped to execute these functions."[26] This special district was indeed to become responsible for creating the facilities needed, but not until many years later.

Hyde and his associates completed their report only a few months before the Japanese attack on Pearl Harbor and the entrance of the United States into World War II. For some time thereafter the public gave no thought to the problem of bay pollution; then the wartime influx of population so aggravated the problem that it again came to the fore, though nothing could be done about it until hostilities ceased.

A New Island

The two great bridges that brought so many changes to the Bay Area were hardly begun before there was a movement for a celebration that would mark their completion. Gathering impetus, it quickly developed into a movement for an exposition on an international scale. A Bridge Celebration Founding Committee appointed by Mayor Angelo Rossi of San Francisco in October, 1933, was soon considering a problem familiar to every organization that has ever planned an exposition: the selection of a suitable site.

Of six possibilities—Golden Gate Park, the Presidio, China Basin, filled lands south of Hunters Point, the Lake Merced area, and the shoals north of Yerba Buena Island—the committee finally chose the shoal area because it was accessible from all parts of the Bay Area and it afforded an opportunity for an exposition of unique beauty. There was an even more compelling reason for the choice: the island created on the shoals could later become an airport for San Francisco.

Early in 1931 the San Francisco Junior Chamber of Commerce had become concerned about the need for additional runways to handle the growing volume of air traffic in the metropolitan region. Prodded by this organization, San Francisco officials persuaded the state legislature and the governor to approve a bill transferring title of the Yerba Buena shoals from the state to the City and County of San Francisco for development and use as an airport. Years might have passed before the shoals actually were filled, however, had not the Junior Chamber happily concluded that the way to speed reclamation of the shallow waters was to urge the use of the airport-to-be as an exposition site.

No sooner had an advisory planning committee appointed by the Bridge Celebration Founding Committee expressed the opinion that the mid-bay location would "guarantee freedom from sectional disputes and community jealousies" than the San Francisco Junior Chamber of Commerce discovered that "certain narrow interests" in San Francisco were fearful lest an exposition on the Yerba Buena shoals "bring a profit to Oakland at the expense of San Francisco." Again the specter of intercommunity rivalry! The leaders of the Junior Chamber steamed. "We believe that the time has come for San Francisco to throw off the yoke of provincialism and smug satisfaction and work in harmony with her sister cities in an effort to achieve her destined greatness, now threatened by the tremendous growth and enterprise of the cities of southern California," the young men advised those who would disrupt plans for the exposition.[27]

The "narrow interests" who muttered about Oakland were talked down, and the directors of the San Francisco Bay Exposition proceeded to make arrangements with the WPA and the United States Corps of Army Engineers for the creation of "Treasure Island." Barges dumped tons of rock into the bay to form the outline of a rectangle a mile and a quarter long and two-thirds of a mile wide; then dredges scooped thirty million cubic yards of sand and mud from near-by areas of the bay to fill the four hundred acres enclosed by the rock walls. Finally, engineers created a causeway connecting this man-made island with Yerba Buena Island.

Dignitaries and civic organizations participated in the dedication of the exposition site on November 21, 1937. Fourteen months later the Golden Gate International Exposition, a $50,000,000 wonderland dominated by a slim, octagonal Tower of the Sun, sparkled in the center of the bay. In the courts formed by the principal buildings were gardens, fountains, sculpture, and murals created by most of the well-known artists of the Bay Area. The architecture ranged from the romantically eclectic to the creatively modern, best exemplified in the Federal Building by the late Timothy Pflueger and the Yerba Buena Clubhouse by William Wurster. Several of the buildings were of permanent construction, designed for use as maintenance and operation buildings of an air terminal. The advisory planning committee appointed by the Bridge Celebration Founding Committee, however, had observed that "the shoals also lend themselves to development for Naval purposes,"[28] and it was to naval purposes that the man-created site was converted after the fountain ceased to play in the Enchanted Garden and the lights went out on the Towers of the East.

At first, occupancy by the Navy was considered temporary; but later this branch of the service took permanent possession of Treasure Island, thereby putting an end to the idea of a mid-bay air terminal.

Bridges and "Decentralization"

In 1940, when the exposition was in its second year, many San Franciscans began to wonder whether they really had any reason for celebrating the completion of the two mighty bridges. The decennial census returns tended to confirm some early predictions that the bridges would drain population from the metropolis, or at least arrest the development of the city. In the 1930's the city had gained only 142 residents, whereas every other county in the Bay Area had made gains in the thousands. The plight of San Francisco could not be attributed entirely to the bridges, of course, because improved highways on the Peninsula and in the East Bay, the establishment of additional industries in the East Bay, and many other developments had contributed to the growth of other areas; but the bridges had certainly played some part in denying the city the gains that various experts had predicted. At the beginning of the decade, the chairman of the City Planning Section of the Commonwealth Club had forecast a population of 760,000 in 1940;[29] and as late as 1937 Miller McClintock had "conservatively" estimated that the population would be 725,000 at the end of the decade.[30] Instead, the Bureau of the Census credited San Francisco with 634,536 residents, to the consternation of the local press and the Chamber of Commerce, who were sure that the federal agency must be wrong. What they did not recognize was that without

in-migration, the total population of San Francisco would have been approximately 8,000 less than in 1930, because deaths in the city had exceeded births during the decade, according to records of the California State Department of Health.

"Decentralization," a word with terrible connotations to numerous San Franciscans, was the term most often used to explain what had happened to San Francisco, but it was inaccurate and misleading. In the 'thirties, as in the 'twenties, much of the growth in the satellite fringe of the Bay Area was new, rather than a shift of population from central cities to the suburbs. What actual decentralization there was had a twofold character. Some families who had long lived in central areas moved to outlying cities and towns. Some other families who had come to the metropolis from other parts of California or from other states in the 'thirties had remained in San Francisco only a few years and then had joined the outward march to suburbia. San Francisco had thus served as a "reception center" in the Bay Area, and despite its poor showing in the 1940 census had continued to function as a magnet for new population in the metropolitan region.

Oakland, too, had experienced similar inward and outward flow of population, though it had more than held its own. An increase of 18,100 gave it a total population of 302,163.

The significant thing about the census returns for the East Bay was that they revealed greater relative gains in cities such as Albany, El Cerrito, Hayward, and San Leandro—all on the periphery of the built-up area in the East Bay—than in Oakland and Berkeley. As on the San Francisco Peninsula, population was shifting to small cities from established centers, and newcomers to the Bay Area were being attracted to them.

For the nine bay counties as a metropolitan unit the rate of growth during the 'thirties was the lowest since the American occupation—a mere 9.9 per cent, representing an increase of only 156,229 persons. By comparison, Los Angeles County gained 568,719 new residents and in 1940 had a total population exceeding that of the nine bay counties by more than 1,000,000. The figure for the Bay Area was 1,734,308, one-fourth of the population of the state of California, whereas Los Angeles County alone had more than two-fifths. In the latter area the discovery of a new oil field at Wilmington, the development of radio broadcasting in Hollywood, the rise of the aircraft industry, and the expansion of manufacturing plants utilizing new low-cost power from Hoover Dam all provided more employment and induced further in-migration. Since the Bay Area had nothing comparable to these varied developments, it did not attract large numbers of newcomers until World War II. And then they came in hordes, doubling and tripling the population of some cities.

CHAPTER FIFTEEN

Crisis in an Arsenal of Democracy

More than a year before the Japanese attack on Pearl Harbor brought the United States openly and precipitately into World War II, the San Francisco Bay Area had begun to shift from peacetime activities to "defense" production. The shipbuilding industry, which for the most part had been idle for twenty years, sprang to life as the United States Maritime Commission awarded huge contracts for cargo carriers and the Navy Department placed contracts for light cruisers, destroyers, and auxiliary craft. Skilled workers laid new keels in old shipways, rehabilitated long unused drydocks, made motors whine and sparks fly in machine shops that had been almost deserted for years. And in scores of related industries men worked round the clock to produce special materials and parts for ships. But the defense boom was not limited to shipbuilding. Plants throughout the Bay Area filled orders from the War and Navy departments for large quantities of denim working trousers, oilskin slickers, feather pillows, mattresses, flavorings, paraffin wax, trunk lockers, canned fruits and vegetables, laundry soap—a bewildering assortment of goods seldom thought of as "sinews of war." By the time the Japanese struck at Pearl Harbor a large proportion of Bay Area industry was operating on a wartime basis, expanding plant facilities, recruiting and training new workers, employing "expediters" to obtain critical materials, and curtailing production of many kinds of consumer goods.

For many years the shadow of war had been gathering over the Bay Area—if the development of military facilities could be taken as a sign of impending conflict. The selection of the western end of Alameda as the site for a naval air base in November, 1935, may have seemed at the time to be only remotely related to the Japanese fortification of distant islands of the Pacific. The negotiations of Navy Department officials with the Board of Port Commissioners of Oakland in the spring and summer of 1936 for 390 acres of tidelands in the Oakland Middle Harbor as a site for a supply depot certainly prompted no civilians to study the map of New Guinea or Guadalcanal. But when the Alameda Naval Air Station was commissioned, on November 1, 1940, a considerable segment of the local population realized that military men associated this and other Bay Area military installations with future campaigns in a Pacific Theater of War.

"Arsenal of Democracy"

The Bay Area had become by the summer of 1941 a major "arsenal of democracy." From Moffett Field at the lower end of San Francisco Bay to the Benicia Arsenal overlooking the waters of Suisun Bay, it was an enormous complex of military establishments, some dating from the early days of California statehood, some brand new. Army establishments included the Presidio, Letterman Hospital, and Forts Mason, Funston, Scott, and Miley in San Francisco; Fort McDowell on Angel Island; Hamilton Field and Forts Barry, Baker, and Cronkhite in Marin County; a new supply depot at the Oakland Outer Harbor; and the Benicia Arsenal. Even in the spring of 1941 approximately twenty thousand troops and a large complement of civilian employees were on duty in these

*The Kaiser Shipyards at Richmond During World War II. Photograph courtesy of
Kaiser Industries Corporation.*

various facilities. The Navy likewise had large numbers
of enlisted men and civilians at its establishments, which
included the new base on Treasure Island, the Hunters
Point and Mare Island navy yards, a naval radio station
in Marin County, Moffett Field, the new supply depot in
Oakland, the Alameda air base, and a naval station at
Tiburon, in Marin County. The labor force at Mare
Island alone was scheduled to number twenty-eight thousand by the end of 1941.

So important to the defense effort and the lend-lease
program of aid to Great Britain were the private shipyards that they were virtually in the category of military

installations. Among the first to be revitalized by the
armament program were the General Engineering and
Drydrock Corporation in San Francisco, the Bethlehem
and the Western Pipe and Steel Company yards in South
San Francisco, the Moore Drydock Company in Oakland,
and the Bethlehem Steel Company Shipbuilding Division
in Alameda. In January, 1941, the Todd-California Shipbuilding Company, of which Henry J. Kaiser was president, began constructing one of the largest yards of all,
on the southern waterfront of Richmond, where there
were acres of unoccupied land alongside deep water. The
company's first order was for thirty freighters for Great

Britain, to be built at a cost of $48,000,000—a mere starter in a program that was to keep expanding until four mammoth yards were in operation, one hundred thousand workers were employed, and ships by the hundreds were sliding down the ways, sometimes at the rate of one a day.

As the defense build-up accelerated and more manufacturing plants were drawn into it, the pattern of activities in the nine counties surrounding the bay gave striking evidence that despite city and county boundary lines and overlapping special districts, and despite the geographical division created by the bay itself, the thousands of square miles from Gilroy to Cloverdale and from the Pacific Ocean to the confluence of the Sacramento and San Joaquin rivers constituted in reality a single metropolitan region, marshaling its manpower, its machines, and its fertile farmlands for a single purpose. Some of the workers in the Mare Island Navy Yard lived as far away as San Mateo and Calistoga. Headquarters offices in San Francisco procured materials for plants in Pittsburg and Richmond. Troops from the Presidio in San Francisco maneuvered in Marin County. San Francisco contractors built demountable housing in Vallejo. Alameda shipyards obtained parts from plants in Richmond, Sunnyvale, and South San Francisco. Canneries in Santa Rosa, Santa Clara, and Oakland supplied fruits and vegetables for army and navy bases throughout the area. Every part of the nine-county area was dependent in various ways upon every other. Every part had something to contribute toward the war effort.

But this interdependent area was not organized to function with maximum efficiency, either under ordinary circumstances or during an emergency. In few of its widely distributed manufacturing districts did the factories form related industrial groups, in which certain plants supplied parts and materials needed by other units. Its highways were unduly taxed with the movements of trucks conveying semifabricated materials from plants in East Oakland or South San Francisco to Richmond, or from Pittsburg to Emeryville, because no organization representing the economic interests of the metropolitan community had ever studied the problem of industrial linkages and attempted to develop clusters of "homogeneous" industries. And since housing in the vicinity of the various shipyards was inadequate to meet the sudden demand, a new and heavy load of crosshaul traffic was thrown onto the already overburdened main routes. Even less well supplied with mass transit facilities than before the Golden Gate Bridge and the San Francisco–Oakland Bay Bridge were completed, the area was more dependent than ever upon private transportation—and would be in

great difficulty should rationing of gasoline and tires become necessary. None of its cities had completed even preliminary long-range, general plans to which they could turn for guidance in locating new housing projects, military installations, and factories; nor was there for the metropolitan community any kind of over-all plan that might help in solving emergency problems. In the development of new streets and highways, sewer lines and water mains, schools, and commercial areas, the cities and counties were certain to compound new mistakes with old ones, just as they had done in the years of depression, when an unemployment crisis forced them to act quickly in constructing public works.

Need for Area-wide Planning

"Defense activities concentrated in this area will require concerted thinking and action of us all," a speaker representing the State Council of Defense declared at a hearing called by the California State Planning Board on March 28, 1941, to consider establishment of a San Francisco Bay regional planning district. "Some regional agency to effectuate and assist such collaboration is imperative, to expedite defense undertakings, to help solve local problems arising from defense, and to assure the maximum ultimate benefit when a transition from warlike to peacetime pursuits is possible."[1]

Other speakers representing the press, the State Railroad Commission, the United States Public Roads Administration, the Pacific Gas and Electric Company, the State Bureau of Sanitary Engineering, the Home Builders' Institute, the United States Housing Authority, the Berkeley regional office of the National Resources Planning Board, and the old Regional Plan Association of the 'twenties all agreed that the numerous cities and nine counties surrounding the bay were in effect one metropolitan community and that they would benefit by regional planning, especially in a time of crisis. More than a hundred city and county officials and civic leaders of the Bay Area generally likewise accepted the idea that regional planning would be desirable. But the state law under which a planning region would be established proved to be a stumbling block to coöperation.

As amended in 1937, the Planning Act of California placed upon the State Planning Board the duty of dividing the state into regions for planning purposes. Since no areas of the state—except Los Angeles County, which had asked to have its planning body designated a regional planning commission ex officio—had made any clear-cut demand for the establishment of regional planning districts, the state board had taken no steps to carry out the mandate of the law. In 1941, however, certain members of the state legislature signified their interest in having it do so. Since the counties which touched upon San Francisco Bay seemed to have "enough problems in common to justify the establishment of a planning region," the state board decided to begin its districting of the state in the Bay Area.[2]

Attached to letters of invitation to the hearing in San Francisco were excerpts from the planning law pertaining to the duties of the board, to the appointment of regional planning commissions, and to the relationship of city and county planning commissions to a regional commission. These sections of the law contained certain phrases which the well-meaning members of the State Planning Board probably had not thought of as "dynamite"—phrases which were intended to provide for coördination among state, regional, county, and city planning bodies, but which aroused the suspicions of some city and county planning commissioners. One section of the act, for instance, stated that the State Planning Board "shall implant" upon the master plan of a region "those things which it considers pertinent," such as public improvements planned by state departments and by agencies of the federal government. Another section provided that city and county planning commissions "shall accept and embody in the respective master plans under their control the features and findings of the respective regional planning commissions in matters pertaining to the regional and state welfare." Did these provisions constitute a formula for state interference in local affairs? Did they mean that the state could "dictate" to cities and counties through a regional planning commission?

Opposition to a District

Representatives of Contra Costa County were particularly dubious about the proposed regional planning district. "Under this act you people [the State Planning Board] . . . have the right to implant your ideas on our own master plans [sic] for Contra Costa County," the district attorney of the county declared. "I think Contra Costa County feels, as do all bay counties, that one cohesive system of planning for the entire Bay Area would be a splendid thing. We are a little bit surprised, however, to be perfectly frank with you, to find that you have these powers. . . .

"We'd like to see you act as a group and make suggestions to us, but we don't like to feel that if we take a part in this thing, we have to take your suggestions."[3]

Somewhat in vain did officials of the state board attempt to explain that the intent of the authors of the planning act was simply to make sure that city and county planning commissions did not prepare plans in ignorance of state and federal plans. A member of the Contra Costa

County Board of Supervisors still objected to the "rather broad sentence" about implanting state plans on regional, county, and city plans.[4]

A member of the Santa Clara County Planning Commission expressed fear that the establishment of a regional planning district might be a step toward consolidation of counties. Not that he was necessarily opposed to county consolidation, but he disliked having it "forced by pressure from the state."[5]

A member of the San Jose City Planning Commission observed that the state law provided only for representation of counties on a regional planning commission and that cities were "left out in the cold."[6] Like other city planning commissioners present, he was well aware that the overwhelming majority of people in the Bay Area lived in municipalities, and he was not converted to the idea of regional planning by a county-dominated body when a member of the state legislature assured him that cities would have "indirect representation" through the counties.

Although many participants in the discussion endorsed the idea of regional planning and praised the State Planning Board for its desire to encourage over-all planning in the Bay Area, a good many of the city and county officials attending the hearing remained lukewarm about state designation of a regional planning district. L. Deming Tilton, administrative officer of the board, was frankly irked by what he termed "an effort . . . to develop and emphasize all the negative aspects of the planning act of California";[7] but what he and some members of the board interpreted as undue suspicion of the motives of the state body was to a degree a manifestation of the vigor of local democratic self-government. Again and again the local communities of the Bay Area have demonstrated their desire to maintain their identity, to make policies for themselves, and to be free from standardized and sometimes arbitrary programs imposed by the state and federal governments. In this desire to be as self-reliant as possible, local communities have, to be sure, occasionally displayed gross misunderstanding of beneficial policies formed by higher levels of government. To members of the State Planning Board the spokesman for some of the bay cities and counties appeared to be unreasonably skeptical of the proposal to create a regional planning district; but distrust of government-from-a-distance runs deep in the American mind, and impatience with this attitude rarely accomplishes anything. There were three good reasons why the response to the State Planning Board's proposal was somewhat negative. The cities and counties themselves had not initiated the move for a planning district; they had not had sufficient experience with planning to be sure of their own rights and responsbilities; and the state act did exclude cities from direct participation in regional planning. The members of the State Planning Board and its professional employees could not ignore these obvious facts. As soon as they faced them, they were able to formulate another approach to the problem of organizing the Bay Area for coöperative planning.

A "Voluntary" Organization

On December 8, 1941, the day after the surprise Japanese attack on Pearl Harbor, the State Planning Board suggested the formation of a temporary, advisory Regional Development Council "to investigate and report upon the resources and needs of the region and the benefits to be gained by a broader type of cooperative public planning."[8] Not only would the counties of the Bay Area be represented on this body by a member from each county board of supervisors and a member of each county planning commission; each city would also be represented either by its mayor or a member of its city council and by a member of its city planning commission. The State Planning Board stressed that participation in the proposed council would be "voluntary."

The board announced that it would seek nominations for the Regional Development Council and would call the members together for organization and election of officers. "The approval of a work program and subsequent management of its affairs will be the responsibility of the officers and members of the Council," the board stated, but it then went on to outline what it expected the new organization to do. It proposed the formation of three subregional councils, North Bay, East Bay, and Peninsula, to study major problems created by the war, as well as problems associated with postwar readjustment. It hoped that at the end of a trial period of one year the subregional councils would submit reports to the Regional Development Council, so that the council might evaluate the experience and accomplishments of the unofficial planning effort and prepare a final report for the State Planning Board. In this summary report the board expected to receive recommendations concerning "(1) the desirability of proceeding with a permanent, official San Francisco Bay Regional Planning District as provided by law, (2) boundaries of such district, if one be approved, and (3) changes in the Planning Act deemed necessary or desirable to facilitate regional planning."[9]

Without wishing to appear to be motivating a regional planning movement, the board still was in the awkward position of trying to provide the directional force for such a movement. Its new proposal showed, however, that it was endeavoring to apply the lessons learned from two

discouraging earlier hearings on the establishment of a regional planning district. In recognition of the important role of the cities in area-wide planning, the board now was anxious to accord each city, even the smallest, representation in the Regional Development Council. But the unincorporated area of a county was to have no more representation than, say, a city of five thousand population; and if even a fourth of the cities in the Bay Area participated in the new organization, they would completely dominate it, perhaps to the dissatisfaction of the members representing the counties. Truly, the issue of proper representation in a regional body was a thorny one.

When, on April 11, 1942, Charles O. Busick, Jr., vice-chairman of the California State Planning Board, called to order those who had assembled at the Claremont Hotel in Berkeley to organize the San Francisco Bay Regional Development Council, it was clear that metropolitan regional planning had little support. Only twenty-eight persons representing the cities and counties of the Bay Area attended, and few of these were city councilmen and county supervisors. The meeting was in the main a convocation of the "faithful"—the planning commissioners and staff members who could usually be counted on to assist in any effort toward area-wide planning. Such a beginning augured ill for the success of the council, for that body could accomplish nothing significant without the help of city councils and county boards of supervisors.

More Ships, More Guns!

The hopeful few who believed that ways could be found to overcome community rivalries, to exorcise suspicion of the State Planning Board, to revise the local planning enabling act, and to demonstrate the practicability of intercommunity coöperation in planning were like men carrying torches in a night of raging winds. As World War II spread ever wider, the cry for more tanks, more planes, more ships, more fighting men rose to a pitch of desperation. Get more labor, build more housing, blast away the bottlenecks, keep the machines running and the trains moving, never mind the future, plan for today— or there won't be any future for free peoples!

From the Ozarks, from the plantations of Louisiana, from the farmlands and small towns of Iowa, Minnesota, and Missouri, from all parts of the United States war workers poured into the Bay Area. Nearly half of them were young people between the ages of fifteen and thirty-four. Of those from the South, a large proportion were Negroes. Men who had never operated a rivet gun and women who had never handled an acetylene burner came in such numbers that by May, 1942, the population of the Bay Area was estimated to be one hundred and thirty thousand more than in April, 1940; but the newcomers were only the vanguard of an influx that was to swell the civilian population of the area at least half a million before the war ended.

Between June, 1941, and June, 1942, the number of wage earners employed in Bay Area industrial plants rose from 101,000 to 174,000. Six months later, in January, 1943, more than a quarter of a million production workers were employed in manufacturing establishments of the "San Francisco Bay industrial area," which included only five of the Bay Area counties—San Francisco, San Mateo, Alameda, Contra Costa, and Marin. By April, 1943, the number had risen to 269,700, of which 221,600 were in industries producing durable goods, chiefly the shipbuilding industry and allied industries.[10]

The Bay Area was now so overcrowded, its peacetime patterns of economic activities and daily living were so thoroughly disrupted, and its local governmental services were so strained—overwhelmed by the demands of populations which, in some localities, were three, four, or five times as great as in 1940—that it presented a picture of the greatest confusion. The situation was somewhat comparable to the sudden dispersion of population at the time of the great Fire in San Francisco in 1906, when communities in Marin County, San Mateo County, and in the East Bay from Hayward to Vallejo overnight found themselves responsible for the care of thousands of homeless refugees, many of whom never returned to San Francisco to live. San Francisco during World War II was not a city hit by disaster, and it did absorb new population almost to the saturation point; but because most of the plants engaged in war production were distributed over a wide area outside the metropolis, many of them also outside the Oakland-Alameda-Emeryville industrial complex, the war had the effect of sending waves of newcomers into outlying areas. This was largely a matter of geography—of the role nature had destined the Bay Area to play in a global war in which tanks, men, and supplies had to be transported across vast oceans. Shipyards had to be at deep water or on dredged channels providing ready access to deep water. Of the most advantageous locations for shipbuilding, four were on the fringes of the main urban areas: at Vallejo, Richmond, Sausalito, and South San Francisco, all small communities wholly unprepared at the beginning of the war for the hordes of war workers who descended upon them. Even in peacetime it would have been difficult to provide quickly thousands of new housing units in these less well developed territories, to expand transit services to serve them, to organize and accommodate new commercial, educational, recreational, and health services, to install sewers and build sewage treatment plants, and to recruit additional policemen, firemen, sanitarians, and garbage collectors. In wartime, with private building curtailed, with new transit equipment unavailable and existing equipment breaking down from overuse, with municipal employees being drafted or being lured to war industries by higher wages, conditions in the new population centers were practically chaotic. But the chaos in these war-swollen communities reflected the disorganization and lack of coördination in the entire metropolitan region. By the spring of 1943 the congestion and disorder had become so great as to threaten to delay proper prosecution of the war.

Congressional Investigation

In mid-April a subcommittee of the House Committee on Naval Affairs opened hearings in San Francisco for the purpose of learning just how bad the situation was and discovering, if possible, what Congress might do to improve matters. Startling testimony came from officials of the cities which had been more severely dislocated by the war effort than any others in the Bay Area—Vallejo and Richmond. Mayor John Stewart of Vallejo estimated that the population of Greater Vallejo was "close to" 100,000, two-thirds of whom lived outside the city limits. Three years earlier the population of Vallejo itself had been 20,027, and that of Vallejo Township outside the city limits had been 9,991, or a total of 30,018. At that time the Mare Island Navy Yard had employed less than 5,000 workers; now it employed 40,000, and would hire more workers if housing could be provided for them. Not only was practically every older dwelling, empty store, and dilapidated shack occupied; 25,000 people were living in new dormitories and temporary housing projects erected by the federal government. One project, Chabot Terrace, four miles north of Vallejo, consisted of three thousand units and was a city in itself; yet it had no public schools, even though applications for needed school buildings had been made at the time the project was first promoted. More than 4,000 people were living in private trailers, under conditions that were a constant source of worry to health authorities.

Far more serious than any complaints city and county officials made about inadequate finances and the difficulty of providing community facilities were the complaints of Navy Yard officials about the high rate of absenteeism, especially among workers who traveled excessive distances to and from work. Fourteen thousand of the men and women employed at Mare Island traveled three, four, or five hours a day to and from work. Navy buses, operated by the Pacific Greyhound Lines, brought them from points as far away as Healdsburg (sixty miles), Calistoga

Aerial View of Chabot Terrace, Housing Project for War Workers, Vallejo.
Photograph by Gardner, courtesy of Vallejo Chamber of Commerce.

(forty-one miles), Hayward (forty-one miles), Woodland (fifty-five miles), and South San Francisco (forty-four miles). Thousands of others rode to and from work in private automobiles, some of them traveling distances as great as those covered by the Navy buses. Twelve or thirteen hours of their day being consumed by work and travel, workers had little time for proper rest, family life, recreation, shopping, and community life—and rather than break under the strain, they took time off whenever they felt they had to. This costly but understandable absenteeism, together with the unceasing induction of skilled workers, taxed the administrative ability of Navy Yard officials to continue production on schedule.

Richmond, a War Casualty

Richmond, a city of 23,642 in 1940, had a population in April, 1943, variously estimated at 100,000 to 110,000. Exclusive of the four government-owned, Kaiser-operated

shipyards, the city boasted fifty-five major war industries, producing gasoline, jeeps, tanks, troop cars, munitions, and dozens of other essentials of war. Employment in the city had risen from less than 15,000 persons in January, 1941, to more than 130,000. Congressman E. V. M. Izac, Chairman of the investigating subcommittee, observed that if all the people working in Richmond were brought there with their families, the population of the city would be half a million.[11]

To provide housing for the newcomers, private contractors had built 4,557 houses, the Richmond Chamber of Commerce and local real-estate organizations had persuaded home owners to rent a total of 4,800 rooms, and the Richmond Housing Authority and the Maritime Commission had built 21,000 units. Dormitory accommodations for four thousand single men were planned. But in spite of all efforts to solve the housing problem, workers were sleeping in shifts in "hot beds," and in unincorporated areas outside the city limits they were living, as former sheriff John A. Miller said, "in trailers, tents, tin houses, cardboard shacks, glass houses, barns, garages, in automobiles, in theaters, or just in fenced off corners with the stars for a roof."[12]

Community facilities were totally inadequate. The chief of the fire department testified that there was no fire station within approximately a mile of any of the four shipyards; yet within that area were thousands of the wooden temporary housing units.[13] Schools designed to accommodate gradually expanding enrollments during the next ten years were operating double or even triple sessions, with sixty children to a classroom at every session. In local hospitals the patients were sleeping on floors and in hallways. Roads expected to last scores of years were disintegrating under the impact of heavy trucking. A city jail built to accommodate eight prisoners was intolerably overcrowded with thirty-five, and at times with as many as sixty. People stood in line to get into stores, because commercial facilities hadn't kept pace with the population increase. As at Vallejo, overloaded outfall sewers discharged raw sewage onto tidal flats close inshore, creating a potential health menace.

The transportation problem of Richmond workers was only a little less critical than that of workers in the Vallejo-Benicia area. Since shipyards and many other war industries were operating twenty-four hours a day, jammed buses, trains, and automobiles arrived and departed three times daily. The Maritime Commission had pressed into service large double-ended ferryboats, which operated from San Francisco direct to the shipyards, and harassed transportation officers of the Twelfth Naval District recommended that much more extensive use be made of water transportation. Basically the problem was a shortage of transportation equipment, both rail and bus, and the lack of a unified transit system serving the entire metropolitan region. The importation of old elevated-railway cars from New York and the inauguration of the Richmond Shipyard Railway along San Pablo Avenue from Fortieth Street in Oakland to Richmond some months after the subcommittee held its hearings afforded only partial relief of the transportation problem. Trains and buses were still overloaded, and many workers had to allow more than a reasonable length of time to get to work, because train after train, crammed from front to rear, might pass them by before they could get aboard one.

So spectacular was the impact of the war upon Richmond that many tended to overlook the fact that other communities in Contra Costa County also were struggling with manpower, housing, and transportation problems—and managing to set production records in spite of bottlenecks. The population of the county as a whole had risen

Temporary Housing for Shipyard Workers, Richmond. These structures, intended only for wartime use, were occupied for several years after the war and were finally vacated and torn down in 1956. Photograph courtesy of Housing Authority of the City of Richmond.

The Shipyard Railway, Oakland to Richmond, During World War II. This temporary line used old elevated-railway cars from New York City. Photograph courtesy of Richmond Public Library.

from one hundred thousand in 1940 to more than three hundred thousand by April, 1943. Industries of the county were producing 3.5 per cent of all the war products being manufactured in the nation. Three-fourths of all the powder manufactured on the Pacific Coast was being produced in Contra Costa County explosives plants; and seven-tenths of the chemicals being refined in the eleven western states were being processed in this one county. Industrial establishments in Antioch, Pittsburg, Crockett, Selby, Oleum, Rodeo, Hercules, Giant, Nitro, and other points along the county's sixty-eight-mile waterfront were operating like the shipyards on a three-shifts-per-day basis. At Port Chicago, the old lumber importing center founded in 1907 as Bay Point, a new Naval Ammunition Terminal was the shipping point for vast quantities of munitions manufactured in the county. Here, some months after the subcommittee held its hearings, occurred one of the worst home-front disasters of the war when two Liberty ships exploded, killing hundreds.

Marinship and Marin City

Suburban Marin County, which had never attracted a single major industry in its entire history, acquired one in a hurry in the spring of 1942. Near Waldo Point, on Richardson Bay—a location mentioned years earlier as the possible site for a naval base, the W. A. Bechtel Company, a Kaiser subsidiary, laid the first keel in its Marinship yard three months after construction of the yard began. By April, 1943, the working force was close to twenty thousand and the yard had one of the fastest-moving ship assembly lines in the country. In front of the ways, waiting to be lifted into position, were piled dozens of prefabricated sections of ships—bulkheads, ship sides, splinter shields for guns, and even afterpeaks, or stern sections.

Near by, to the west of the state highway, rose a brand new community for six thousand shipyard workers—Marin City. Although Marin County residents, who have generally been exceptionally appreciative of the scenic beauties of their environment, deplored the selection of one of their most beautiful meadows and the surrounding hills as the site for this war housing project, they conceded that it was outstanding among war born developments, both in site planning and in community facilities. It included seven hundred apartments in single-story, eight-family buildings and eight hundred units in demountable duplexes and single houses, all of redwood and all so carefully related to the contours of the irregular site as to create an aesthetically satisfying whole. In a horseshoe-shaped valley one mile north of the main development stood eleven dormitory buildings, accommodating twelve hundred men without families. In addition to its housing units and dormitories, the project had a nursery school for small children of working mothers, an elementary school, an auditorium designed to be used as a church on Sundays, playgrounds, a cafeteria and coffee shop, a library maintained by the county, and a post office. But it was some months before adequate shopping facilities were available. When completed, these included a meat market, grocery store, delicatessen, drugstore, shoe-repair shop, a laundry and dry cleaning establishment, a small variety store, a beauty parlor, a barber shop, and a candy store.

Congressman George J. Bates, of Massachusetts, a member of the subcommittee of the House Naval Affairs Committee, confirmed local opinion that this project was unusual when he said: "We have visited hundreds of war housing projects in the United States and we have seen none that so ideally meets the requirements of a community of war workers as does Marin City. Marin City and Dormitories have all the essentials that go into the makeup of a well rounded war housing project. Marin City furnishes sound housing at low cost and it builds up an active community life. It is the best administered and best organized war housing project that I have seen in our tour of the country."[14]

Dormitory Metropolis

Since South San Francisco shipyards were relatively close to San Francisco and the larger Peninsula communities, the problem of housing war workers did not assume the dramatic proportions that it did in Vallejo and Richmond, for instance. Several small temporary housing projects were built in the northern part of San Mateo County, but most war workers in South San Francisco shipyards and manufacturing plants utilized existing housing in near-by communities.

San Francisco became something of a dormitory metropolis in the war years, providing housing for thousands of workers employed in Oakland, Alameda, Richmond, Sausalito, and South San Francisco shipyards, as well as for military personnel stationed in the Bay Area temporarily or for the duration. The city was also a distraught host to thousands of war visitors—people who came to see someone in the armed services, to bid farewell to men leaving for combat overseas, or to welcome battle-weary soldiers and sailors returning from the Far Pacific. By the time the subcommittee under Congressman Izac arrived in the Bay Area, the population of the city had increased by more than ninety thousand people, and thousands more were expected to arrive every month.

Because of the acute shortage of critical building materials, the Housing Authority of the City and County of San Francisco had been obliged to defer construction of six permanent housing projects. As agent for the federal government, it was building temporary war housing, which required only about 20 per cent as much critical material per dwelling unit as did permanent housing. On the barren hills above Hunters Point and on the slopes around Candlestick Cove, near the San Mateo County boundary, building-trades workers were constructing fifteen hundred dormitory units and four thousand temporary family dwellings—an entirely new community to house some thirty-five thousand people, among whom would be the welders, shipfitters, and mechanics needed at the San Francisco Naval Shipyard at Hunters Point. The yard was then employing two thousand men, and officials expected to increase the working force to ten thousand within a year, and to twenty thousand within two years. Like the temporary housing at Richmond, Vallejo, and elsewhere in the Bay Area, all the units at Hunters Point presumably would be demolished at the end of the war, in accordance with the terms of the "Lanham Act," under which it was being constructed; but most of this housing—frankly substandard—was still in use many years after World War II because of housing shortages and the outbreak of war in Korea.

In San Francisco, as in other overcrowded cities, the National Housing Agency, under which thirteen federal housing agencies had been united in February, 1942, launched, with considerable fanfare, a conversion program intended to ease the critical housing shortage. The NHA estimated that five to ten thousand properties—houses, vacant stores, even warehouses—could be remodeled to increase the dwelling supply in San Francisco; but comparatively few property owners were willing to participate in the program. Housing experts such as Catherine Bauer warned that "the long-term ill effects of conversion may well over-balance the very small addition to the emergency housing supply."[15]

Problems in a Blighted Area

Some of the worst overcrowding in San Francisco occurred in the already deteriorated Western Addition. "Particularly is this true of the old Japanese district . . . into which the majority of our increased colored population has moved," Dr. J. C. Geiger, then Director of the San Francisco Department of Public Health, told the subcommittee of the House Naval Affairs Committee. "These people have occupied stores, rear porches, in fact practically any space available in this area. Occupancy consists of everything from single persons to married couples with four and five children. Some of the premises so occupied are lacking in proper light, ventilation, plumbing, and cubic area. Many of these units were previously considered substandard, and the individuals now occupying them have certainly not added to the desirability of the dwellings. Careless housekeeping and generally insanitary conditions prevail. The majority of the individuals housed in this section seem perfectly content with the accommodations and apparently are not interested in obtaining more desirable quarters. They do not seem to have any particular idea as to proper housing facilities nor do they seem interested in the dangers to health through improper ventilation of stoves, gas appliances, and other such household commodities. Careful survey of this area has been undertaken and a definite drive to relieve the congestion and improve housing conditions is well under way."[16]

In all fairness, the health officer might have pointed out that many of the families of whom he was speaking were from particularly poor rural sections of the South, had never lived in cities, were unfamiliar with gas stoves and heating appliances, had had little opportunity for education, and most of them were the products of a social system that resolutely kept them "in their place." Their escape from their former environment was in itself evidence that they desired more of life. In San Francisco they were like immigrants from another continent, squeezed together in an enclave which afforded them, if not decent housing, protection from a world that was really "foreign" to them.

By mid-November, 1943, seven months after the subcommittee hearings, the San Francisco Chamber of Commerce and twenty-nine other groups who were concerned with the housing crisis were determined to discourage any further in-migration. Through new construction, conversions, and the use of every available hotel room the shelter capacity of the city had been increased sufficiently to accommodate approximately 775,000 people, but there were thought to be 800,000 in the city. Many families were "doubling up" with other families. Two months earlier the War Housing Center had turned away 6,000 people who sought housing. For the first time in the history of the city numerous civic groups suggested holding no more conventions, sales promotion meetings, or other events which would attract mass attendance; visitors and sightseers definitely were not wanted.

East Bay Congestion

The city managers of Oakland, Alameda, and Berkeley all told the Congressional subcommittee of acute housing shortages in their cities. Charles R. Schwanenberg, City Manager of Oakland, estimated that his city needed nine thousand additional housing units, the lack of which was causing in-migrant war workers to leave the city.[17] City Manager Don McMillan of Alameda said that the twenty-five hundred units then being completed, the two thousand units scheduled to be built, and an additional two thousand about to be authorized would use almost all the available land in the city, but that the seven shipyards in the city would still be drawing the greater part of their labor force from other areas—men and women who would have to travel to work through the two-lane Posey Tube or across the three narrow bridges spanning the estuary.[18] An additional tube and improved transportation were the most pressing needs of Alameda, he pointed out. City Manager Chester C. Fisk of Berkeley reported that the wartime population influx had eliminated a 5.4 per cent vacancy ratio and had increased the population of the city by approximately twenty-two thousand. Fisk declared that he thought Berkeley should have more allocations and priorities necessary for building FHA housing, but that he was opposed to "a lot of barracks."[19]

All three city managers indicated by their testimony that they realized that some of the conditions with which they were attempting to deal in their particular cities were complicated by area-wide problems. Although thousands of units of temporary war housing were constructed in almost every city except Berkeley, the majority of workers could not find living quarters near their jobs. Consequently, interurban transit lines were so overloaded that McMillan, for one, feared "a complete disintegration of transportation facilities" unless drastic measures were taken to solve the problem of transportation.[20] Wartime conditions, in effect, were emphasizing the value to a metropolitan region of having a comprehensive transit system, just as they were emphasizing the desirability of housing workers, in peacetime as well as in wartime, close to their places of employment, so as to reduce movement and minimize the necessity for an excessive amount of costly rolling stock.

"The lack of adequate and properly coordinated transportation facilities in the San Francisco Bay area is undoubtedly the primary factor in the failure to obtain the highest degree of efficiency from the available labor supply," the subcommittee investigating the progress of the war effort in the Bay Area concluded in its report to Carl Vinson, Chairman of the House Naval Affairs Committee. "This same lack is unquestionably having an adverse effect upon the procurement of the additional migrant labor that is so badly needed. Because of traffic congestion and delays, thousands of workers are forced to put in 12 or 13 hours a day in order to work 8 hours. The peculiar geographical situation in the bay area probably makes the transportation problem more acute than in any other section of the country."[21]

Related Problems

The problems of transportation, housing, and manpower go hand in hand to a large degree, the subcommittee pointed out. Like many city planners, it wished that wasteful crosshauls could be eliminated by "finding the worker employment in the vicinity of his residence";[22] but it made no proposal for reshuffling workers so as to match men and jobs in the same community. Had it suggested anything of the kind, it probably would have been accused of advocating totalitarian methods on the home front. The subcommittee contented itself with stating that "the Office of Defense Transportation should be given full authority and responsibility for handling all phases of transportation, thereby avoiding the confusion and delays which result from divided authority."[23] In this recommendation the investigating group recognized an important principle of metropolitan transit operations— centralized control.

Only one area-wide need had been adequately met, the subcommittee found. "It is indeed fortunate that the available water supply is plentiful to meet the needs of the vastly increased population in the bay area," its report stated.[24] Within some communities and in some outlying areas the extension of water mains was needed, but otherwise the metropolitan region was not faced with an emergency situation. The related problem of sewage disposal had, however, grown worse. "Some expansions have taken place in the trunk sewers and laterals, but the added population has resulted in increased sewerage, and this has brought about a great problem in the pollution of the inland waters of the area," the subcommittee noted.[25]

In view of the marked shortage of essential facilities for the augmented population of the Bay Area and the alarming lack of necessary manpower, the Congressmen recommended that no further war industries be brought into the area.[26] They had found a bewildering number of federal agencies—the Federal Works Agency, the National Housing Agency, the War Manpower Commission, the War Labor Board, the War Production Board, the War Shipping Administration, the Maritime Commission, the Office of Price Administration, the Food Distribution Administration, the Office of Defense Transportation, the Office of Civilian Defense, the Army, the Navy—all working more or less independently and all experiencing frustrating delays in Washington. To complicate the already aggravated situation in the Bay Area by attempting to expand industrial operations "would be not only foolish but disastrous," the subcommittee members believed.[27] What was clearly needed at once was coördination and an end to red tape, locally and in the national capital. The legislators recommended that the Committee for Congested Production Areas, established by executive order just a few days before they opened hearings in San Francisco, immediately appoint an area representative to bring about teamwork among the federal agencies and promote solutions to the problems brought out at the hearings.

Acting on this recommendation, the Committee for Congested Production Areas did designate a coördinator for the Bay Area and conditions did improve somewhat, although the reports of the area representative continued, month after month, to speak of the urgency of further allocations of critical materials for housing, schools, recreation centers, and other community facilities, and of the need for additional Congressional appropriations. By February, 1944, new schools were completed in Richmond, San Pablo, and Vallejo, and in Napa, Sonoma, and Santa Clara counties. Additional child care centers were opened in South San Francisco, Oakland, Pittsburg, Richmond, and San Pablo. A desperately needed general hospital with 250 beds and a 100-bed nurses' home was nearing completion in Vallejo. A sanitary sewage system was finally in operation at the Chabot Terrace housing project in Vallejo, and there was a new sewer for an area of San Pablo inhabited by approximately six thousand people. In two communities in which the rate of juvenile delinquency had skyrocketed, adolescents themselves were managing new teen-age centers, under adult supervision. In short, some of the physical and social needs that regional offices of many of the federal agencies had struggled almost in vain to get Washington to recognize were at long last being met—but only to a small degree. There was no possibility that the cities and towns most drastically affected by the war migration would be able to provide adequate services while the war lasted. What their situation would be after the war they had no idea—

and this was as great a cause for worry as the shortages of housing and classrooms and nurses and doctors.

Victory in Sight

Up to 1944 the Bay Area had received more than four billion dollars in war supply contracts and was first in the United States in contracts for ships. The civilian population of the area had increased an estimated four hundred and fifty thousand since April, 1940, to say nothing of thousands of military personnel stationed permanently or temporarily in the area. Within the same period more than one hundred thousand housing units, public and private, had been constructed, and half as many more were either under construction or programed. And all this extraordinary expansion, greater than anything the area had ever known in a similarly brief period, had been brought about by a war that was well on the way to being won.

At Teheran in late November and early December, 1943, President Roosevelt and Prime Minster Churchill

The Change of Shift at Kaiser Shipyard No. 2, Richmond. Photograph courtesy of the City of Richmond.

had discussed with Premier Stalin their plans for the opening of a second front in western Europe and had set the date for invasion at the end of May or early June, 1944. In the meantime, Royal Air Force and American bombers were pulverizing German industrial centers; the Russians, having raised the siege of Leningrad in the north, in the south were driving the Nazis from Kiev toward the Polish border; while in the Pacific the American forces, seizing the offensive, were invading the outer defenses of the Japanese Empire in the Gilbert and Marshall Islands. In the Bay Area the peak employment in war industries had been passed in September, 1943; and though production continued at an unprecedented rate, toward the end of 1944 there was already talk of a shift from construction of "Liberty" ships to construction of "Victory" ships. The time had arrived to talk in earnest of postwar planning.

What would become of all the thousands of war workers who had pulled up stakes and come to the Bay Area to build ships? How many of them would go home after the war? Could the peacetime economy of the area possibly provide jobs for those who remained and for returning veterans of the war? What kinds of jobs? Would a tremendous postwar WPA be necessary? Or could private enterprise create most of the new jobs that would be needed?

No one had any glib answers to questions such as these. And everyone remembered the Depression before the war.

CHAPTER SIXTEEN

Postwar Planning

The danger of becoming so completely absorbed in winning the war as to neglect preparations for readjustment to a peacetime economy had been foreseen by President Roosevelt as early as November, 1940, well over a year before the attack on Pearl Harbor. At that time the Chief Executive had requested the National Resources Planning Board to undertake a study of what was then called post-defense planning. This advisory agency, accordingly, had concentrated almost its entire energies on "correlating plans and programs under consideration in many Federal, State, and private organizations for post-war full employment, security, and building America."[1] In particular, it urged state and local governments to plan to assist private industry in the conversion of war plants and the development of new postwar industries; to prepare carefully planned programs, engineering plans, and specifications for needed postwar public works; to enact legislation under which urban redevelopment could be undertaken; and to build up fiscal reserves for postwar work through increased taxation and debt liquidation during the war period.

In the San Francisco Bay Area the national planning agency made its influence felt through the Pacific Southwest regional office in Berkeley, which not only supplied consultants to assist war production centers, such as Richmond and Vallejo, in solving their housing problems but also published detailed analyses of the effect of the war on California and its major metropolitan areas. In a report issued in May, 1943, entitled *After the War—New Jobs in the Pacific Southwest*, the regional office warned of potential postwar employment crises and pointed out that "neither complete economic planning with regimentation of all productive enterprise, nor complete absence of advance planning by both private industry and governmental agencies can be relied upon to bring about readjustments satisfactory to the American people."[2] If, however, both industry and government should accept the necessity for gradual relaxation of wartime controls and should develop plans and programs in their respective fields to expedite immediate postwar reëmployment and to help distribute and sustain employment, then the Pacific Southwest Region (California, Arizona, Nevada, Utah) could create a new peacetime economy in which human and natural resources would be used to greater advantage than ever before.

"The ever widening flow of employment opportunities stemming from technological progress has enabled the Pacific Southwest to absorb huge population increases decade after decade," the report stated. "By continuing to take advantage of new inventions, new methods of production, new types of industrial organization, and new opportunities for trade and services, the Region can shift its expanded labor force from full employment for war to full employment for peace. After victory a new frontier will be awaiting exploitation—an economic frontier opened by technology."[3]

While the regional office foresaw opportunities for postwar expansion of manufacturing, especially among industries producing consumer goods for the greatly increased populations of western metropolitan areas, it stressed the possibilities for new jobs in wholesale and retail businesses and in a wide variety of service enterprises. "Even though the post-war volume of manufactured goods may be greatly in excess of pre-war output, continual streamlining of production should eventually reduce the proportion of workers needed in factories," the regional office observed.[4] It therefore predicted a continuation of a long-term trend toward higher percentages of workers in distribution and service activities; and it discussed at length the number of jobs that could be created through development of better medical care, increased recreation facilities, broader educational opportunities, and more adequate social security.

Public Works Planning

Since the National Resources Planning Board expected no small part of the new service employment to stem from the activities of city and county governments, and since it was interested in having these smaller units of government develop a backlog of public works to provide jobs in the event of a postwar unemployment crisis, it made available a staff member from the Berkeley regional office to assist cities and counties with the programing of public health clinics, branch libraries, parks, roads, and other public facilities to be built after the war. The experience of the depression years, during which state and local governments were faced with the necessity of putting men to work on public improvements but lacked plans for worthwhile projects, had not been forgotten; hence the board's suggestion that cities and counties prepare a list of capital expenditures for public works proposed for construction within the six years immediately after the war met with generally favorable response.

San Mateo County was one of the first counties to request the assistance of a public works analyst from the NRPB regional office. A report entitled *A Planned Program for Public Works*, published in June, 1942, served as a model for other governments in the Bay Area in long-range planning of needed facilities. All county departments were requested to submit projects for necessary capital improvements and to indicate the desirable order of their construction. After analyzing social and economic resources of the county, trends of population growth, and past and prospective revenue and disbursements, a joint committee of the San Mateo County Board of Supervisors and the County Planning Commission assembled the projects submitted into a comprehensive program showing which public works would be undertaken each year for a six-year period. The program did not anticipate a commitment of funds beyond the first year's budget, but it did indicate future requirements for public works and

the probable availability of the funds that would be needed. County officials contemplated that the program would be revised each year in the light of changing conditions and needs, and that, after proper approval, the budget of the first year of the revised program would become the capital budget for the next fiscal year. Thus the county hoped to established a continuing, orderly procedure for construction made necessary by population increases and the wearing out of existing facilities.

Perhaps the greatest advantage of capital improvement programing to the county was that it gave the planning commission an opportunity to consider whether proposed projects were in conformity with long-range plans and to recommend appropriations only for those that would contribute to the planned development of the county. At the same time, the entire procedure imposed upon the planning commission a heavy obligation to prepare a sound general plan for the physical development of the county, which could be used to evaluate the actual need for various proposed projects. In thus encouraging legislative bodies to consider long-term growth and to set up a definite means of translating plans into reality, the National Resources Planning Board contributed materially to the improvement of government. Many cities and counties began preparing reports similar to the one issued by San Mateo County, and ever since then they have been scheduling their public works in an orderly fashion that tends to stabilize tax rates.

Accent on Economic Planning

A Congress which believed that the national planning agency had gone too far in advocating a program of national social security similar to the cradle-to-the-grave Beveridge Plan of England abolished the agency in June, 1943, before it was able to demonstrate ways in which it might be helpful to private enterprise in preparing for the postwar transition. The NRPB, nevertheless, had performed a valuable service for both government and private enterprise by emphasizing the importance of planning for full employment after victory. It served as the inspiration for countless postwar planning committees in individual industries and in manufacturing and trade associations, chambers of commerce, and state and local governmental agencies directly concerned with harbors, airports, and similar facilities vital to commerce. Groups of leading citizens appointed by city and county governments to serve as advisory postwar planning committees studied NRPB reports and pamphlets. Almost all these organizations considered their function to be the creation of postwar employment, either directly or indirectly. Economic planning therefore overshadowed physical plan-

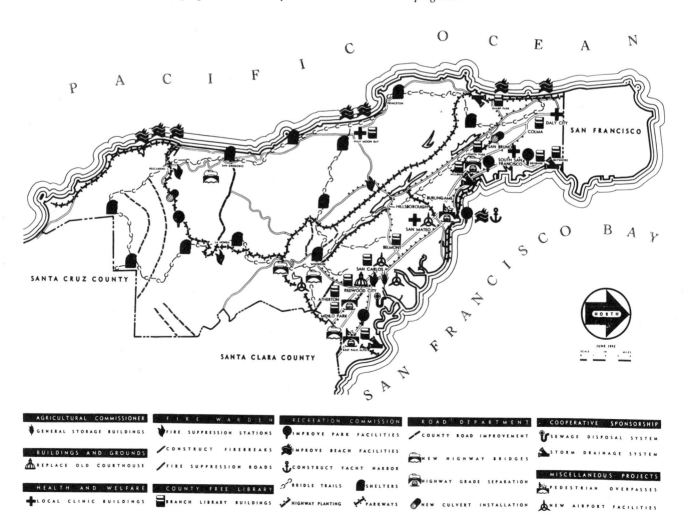

PUBLIC WORKS · DEBT SERVICE · COST OF OPERATING GOVERNMENT

FISCAL YEARS ENDING		
PAST · WAR · PAST	1939	
	1940	
	1941	
WAR	1942	
	1943	
	1944	
PROGRAM	1	
	2	
	3	
	4	
	5	
	6	

$1 MILLION $2 MILLION

EACH SYMBOL REPRESENTS $100,000

Postwar Program of Public Works for San Mateo County, 1941. Above: Financial basis for the program. Below: Improvements included in the program.

PACIFIC OCEAN

SAN FRANCISCO

SAN FRANCISCO BAY

SANTA CRUZ COUNTY

SANTA CLARA COUNTY

NORTH

JUNE 1942

SCALE IN MILES

AGRICULTURAL COMMISSIONER	FIRE WARDEN	RECREATION COMMISSION	ROAD DEPARTMENT	COOPERATIVE SPONSORSHIP
GENERAL STORAGE BUILDINGS	FIRE SUPPRESSION STATIONS	IMPROVE PARK FACILITIES	COUNTY ROAD IMPROVEMENT	SEWAGE DISPOSAL SYSTEM
BUILDINGS AND GROUNDS	CONSTRUCT FIREBREAKS	IMPROVE BEACH FACILITIES		STORM DRAINAGE SYSTEM
REPLACE OLD COURTHOUSE	FIRE SUPPRESSION ROADS	CONSTRUCT YACHT HARBOR	NEW HIGHWAY BRIDGES	MISCELLANEOUS PROJECTS
HEALTH AND WELFARE	COUNTY FREE LIBRARY	BRIDLE TRAILS / SHELTERS	HIGHWAY GRADE SEPARATION	PEDESTRIAN OVERPASSES
LOCAL CLINIC BUILDINGS	BRANCH LIBRARY BUILDINGS	HIGHWAY PLANTING / PARKWAYS	NEW CULVERT INSTALLATION	NEW AIRPORT FACILITIES

ning, and the job-creating potentialities of any proposed project tended to be the measure of its social value. Much that passed for planning was simply industrial promotion unrelated to any considered program for broadening and integrating the state and metropolitan regional economies; and at the lowest level of "planning," chambers of commerce prepared "work pile" plans by gathering information from industries and businesses on how much they would spend for remodeling, repairs, construction, and equipment in the first six months after victory—ignoring the fact that the availability of materials, government controls, and many other factors actually would determine how much remodeling and reëquipping business could undertake.

One consequence of the emphasis on postwar full employment was that the state legislature, never too friendly to the California State Planning Board, abolished it at the same time that Congress did away with the National Resources Planning Board. Even though the state board had operated in the field of economic planning to the extent of collaborating with the Berkeley regional office of the NRPB on economic and industrial surveys of the Los Angeles Area and the San Francisco Bay Area, and even though it had obtained some twenty-eight hundred prospectuses for postwar construction projects from various state agencies that had been asked to study their construction needs for the coming decade, it was accused of being impractical, visionary, and ineffective—the usual charges brought against agencies that must take the long view. A hostile legislature replaced it with a Reconstruction and Reemployment Commission with broad powers "to prevent unemployment, conserve and develop the natural, social and economic resources of the State, promote development of new industries, create new markets, promote the reemployment of discharged service men and readjustment of displaced war workers, and the conversion of industry and commerce from war to peace standards, to provide for postwar readjustment and reconstruction, and to encourage economic and social improvement of the general public."[5]

The New Agency in Action

Under its legislative mandate the new commission could do anything that the State Planning Board had done, but it was obvious that the legislature intended it to stress industrial expansion and the planning of public works. The appointment of a San Francisco businessman, Alexander R. Heron, as director of the agency tended to confirm the impression that it would focus its efforts on stimulating postwar planning by private enterprise and only incidentally would attempt to strengthen physical planning as a function of city and county governments.

The commission sought metropolitan regional coöperation, but of the sort that chambers of commerce and other business groups had sought from time to time in the past fifteen years. This became clear when the state agency held a public hearing on postwar problems of the San Francisco Bay Area in the chamber of the Oakland City Council on August 23 and 24, 1944. Of forty spokesmen who testified before the commission, only a few were public officials, and of these public officials, only three or four were city and county planners. The majority who offered their views on the future of the Bay Area were merchants, industrialists, bankers, executives of utility companies, real-estate developers, and officers of shipping companies, airlines, chambers of commerce, and unions.

The hearing began with a talk by Assemblyman Gardiner Johnson, vice-chairman of the State Assembly Committee on Postwar Rehabilitation, on the distorted labor pattern created by the war and on the threat of postwar unemployment that might "dwarf the last depression."[6] A speaker who followed him presented a survey indicating that three-fourths of the wartime newcomers to the Bay Area hoped to remain after the war. Then came suggestions from various prominent persons for meeting the need for new jobs. They ranged from proposals for old-fashioned industrial ballyhoo, such as Santa Clara County was then indulging in, to proposals for a wide variety of public works, including a new bridge parallel to the San Francisco–Oakland Bay Bridge. State Senator Arthur H. Breed, Jr., vice-chairman of the Senate Postwar Reconstruction Committee, expressed the general sentiment at the hearing when he remarked, "Industry can do the job—but government must step into the gaps."[7] The "gaps," however, appeared to be larger than some might have supposed. They were, indeed, of metropolitan regional dimensions, for the testimony of various speakers brought out the need for solution of the area-wide sewage disposal problem, redevelopment of blighted neighborhoods and areas filled with temporary war housing, development of additional regional parks, provision of schools for all the new residential tracts envisioned after the war, establishment of many new airports, improvement of ports and terminals, reclamation of tidelands, construction of new highways and freeways, and development of an area-wide mass transit system. Clearly, without the action of city and county governments, or of the state and federal governments, on almost every phase of regional physical development, private enterprise could not create a healthy postwar economy in the Bay Area. Area-wide planning of the kind desired by city and county planners was needed, but how was it to be achieved? The hearing in Oakland provided no definite answer to this question. In fact, no one even raised the question.

As Heron and the Reconstruction and Reemployment Commission had hoped, the outcome of the hearing was the appointment of a committee to organize a "San Francisco Bay Region Council," which would stress united effort among Bay Area communities and business firms. Frank N. Belgrano, Jr., president of the Central Bank of Oakland, was named chairman of the committee and R. E. Fisher, vice-president of the Pacific Gas and Electric Company, was selected as vice-chairman. Members of the staff of the state agency were assigned to assist in completing the organization.

A Bay Area Council

The hearing in Oakland had indicated that the Reconstruction and Reemployment Commission was interested primarily in promoting economic development and that it conceived this to be a job for private enterprise, with such public assistance as might be necessary. The group which met in the State Building in San Francisco on December 8, 1944, to form the San Francisco Bay Area Council (then called the Bay Region Council) was therefore composed mainly of businessmen. Mayors of cities and chairmen of county boards of supervisors were decidedly in the minority. No professional planners were present. The organization approved by the gathering was a private organization presumably interested in advancing the well-being of the entire nine-county Bay Area. Heron assured the sixty persons participating in the proceedings that the facilities and staff services of the Reconstruction and Reemployment Commission would be available to the new council "at any time."[8] Funds for the operation of the organization were, however, to be provided by private enterprise.

Bay Area unity was the theme of the organization meeting. R. E. Fisher stressed the importance of avoiding the "mistakes of the past" by enlisting the support of every business, civic, and governmental organization, by "telling a common story to the world," and by giving voice to every community on the bay.[9] Other speakers echoed these sentiments, especially Mayor Roger D. Lapham of San Francisco, who declared that he believed the Bay Area—all nine counties—should be kept in mind at all times, since "it is the Bay Area as a whole that counts."[10] The mayor said that it did not matter whether industry settled on the San Francisco side of the bay or elsewhere in the area, so long as each industry found the most economical place for its own operations. Mayor John F. Slavich of Oakland made a plea for submerging local selfish interests.[11]

Had a new era dawned? Could this new organization serve as the catalytic agent that would change urban jealousies and suspicions into concerted endeavor? Would its membership become sufficiently broad and representative to establish the concept of the multiplicity of cities and counties around the bay as a single great community? Would it work toward some form of metropolitan regional government, particularly to deal with problems clearly of a regional nature? Or would its leaders be satisfied merely with stimulating greater commercial and industrial development?

Until the council had had an opportunity to explore the possibilities for serving the Bay Area, such questions could not be answered. As yet it had only vague objectives and no concrete program. Some of those who took the floor at the initial meeting were anything but vague, however, about certain needs of the area. Significantly, these needs, when considered together, amounted virtually to a program for the physical organization of the nine-county community. R. E. Fisher, for instance, listed seven "major common problems" which he thought deserved the attention of the council.[12] Two of these—the promotion of foreign trade and the correlation of research, information, and advertising—related directly to economic development of the Bay Area; but the other five—increased aviation facilities, transportation in all forms, bridge and highway development, sewage disposal, and public works —had to do with the physical development of the Bay Area. C. D. Lafferty, industrial agent of the Southern Pacific, discussed three main points, two of which— regional highways and the removal of temporary war housing from properties previously available for industrial purposes—were within the sphere of physical planning. E. J. Farina, president of the Contra Costa Development Association, dwelt on the seriousness of intercommunity transportation problems, but without once observing that this was a matter to which city and county planners in the Bay Area already had given considerable study. Mayor Roger D. Lapham, of San Francisco, speaking on public works programs of regional significance, came closer than anyone to advocating area-wide physical planning when he called for regional parks, shoreline improvement in the nine counties, sewage disposal works to end pollution of the bay, a nine-county mass transit system, and unified port development, perhaps under an area-wide authority. Had any professional planners been at the meeting, they might have concluded that the battle for metropolitan regional planning was already half won, because both businessmen and public officials seemed to realize that improving the area physically would aid its economic development. But although the various speakers were talking about elements of a metropolitan regional planning program, not one of them appeared to be aware of that fact. At least, none specifically suggested the need for studying all related physical problems simultaneously and comprehensively, with the objective of producing a general plan for the entire Bay Area. Had any of them done so, many questions might have arisen concerning the advisability of having a private organization develop a plan that could be effectuated only through actions of the governments of the area. Yet the recognition of numerous physical problems of the Bay Area by the participants in the first meeting of the new council showed that there was a good basis for creating understanding of the need for area-wide planning. The failure of the organizing group to invite a single professional planner to the meeting was evidence, however, that the lines of communication between planners and business groups were practically nonexistent.

Pitfalls and Issues

The San Francisco Bay Area Council deserved careful scrutiny as an organization attempting to serve as a unifying force in the nine-county area. Before it lay countless opportunities to make the people of the area aware of the interrelatedness and interdependence of the bay cities and counties. Historically it has been the function of citizen groups to undertake this kind of activity in American metropolitan communities, but the efforts of citizen groups have ever been beset by difficulties. There is always the danger that their aims will be either too narrow, centering on the interests of an oligarchic controlling group, or so broad and nebulous as to result in a futile dissipation of energies. There is the further danger that basic and highly controversial issues will be side-stepped in the interests of maintaining harmony, and that the organization will consequently become ineffective and lose the respect of numerous influential groups. The problem of finances is inescapable and is twofold: the organization must be sustained over a long period, and contributions must be made by a sufficiently representative number of donors to prevent a few large supporters from acquiring a vested interest in it and using it as an instrument for advancing their own policies and programs.

The San Francisco Bay Area Council appeared to have identified two major tasks that demanded consistent, intensive effort, aside from the basic task of furthering acceptance of the nine-county concept. These were the promotion of economic development and, almost as a corollary, the promotion of area-wide physical planning. At first the leaders only vaguely sensed the extent of this second major responsibility and did not seem to realize that some day they would have to make an important decision: either to initiate an unofficial regional planning program of their own or to seek a wholly public solution of the regional planning problem—a problem which poses questions of public policy. Whichever course they chose, they would be grappling with a fundamental question, by no means theirs alone to answer: How should the San Francisco Bay metropolitan community be organized— both physically *and* politically—so as to satisfy the majority of people who live in it?

Preparations for Peace

Nearly five months after the initial meeting of the Bay Area Council the leading diplomats of the nations fighting Germany and Japan gathered at the War Memorial Opera House in San Francisco to draw up the charter of the United Nations.

Many of the delegates attending sessions at the Opera House in San Francisco valued as a souvenir a handsome publication issued by the San Francisco Bay Area Council. Written by Oscar Lewis, *Within the Golden Gate* introduced the distinguished visitors to "a large, varied, and uniquely cosmopolitan community," the seven thousand-square-mile area surrounding the bay.[13] This booklet was the first effort of the new organization to publicize the concept of unity among the nine counties and sixty-six municipalities then comprising the metropolitan region. It came off the press in as hopeful an atmosphere as pervaded the meetings of the diplomats at the Civic Center; but the problem of welding the numerous communities of the Bay Area into something like a metropolitan union promised to be no less formidable than building a world organization from a multiplicity of nations.

The end of the war, now foreseen, did produce unique conditions for growth of the idea of metropolitan coöperation. Nearly every city and county in the Bay Area had an official postwar planning committee at work preparing a report on public improvements to be undertaken after victory. Besides the official groups there were numerous postwar committees active in chambers of commerce and civic organizations. Perhaps at no other time in the history of the Bay Area—not even in the days preceding the opening of the Panama Canal—had so much systematic stocktaking been attempted. Not only were purely local problems identified and projects for solving them suggested; the various groups assessing community needs became aware of the importance to their own city or county of area-wide highway programs, joint sewage disposal projects, and regional parks. Such a scheme as John Reber's San Francisco Bay project, for instance, served

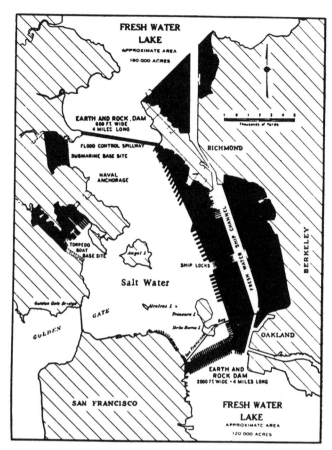

The Reber Plan for Creating Fresh-Water Lakes in San Francisco Bay. Photograph courtesy of John Reber.

to stimulate thinking about future development of the entire bay, even among people who dismissed Reber's proposals as "fantastic" and condemned the Senate of the California Legislature and the San Francisco Board of Supervisors for adopting resolutions recommending governmental study and investigation of the project. Reber's proposal that the south arm of San Francisco Bay and the smaller bays north of Point San Quentin be transformed into fresh-water lakes by construction of earth and rock-fill dikes and that large areas of tidelands be filled for industrial sites, airports, and naval base sites was bold and inclusive enough to provoke responses from communities throughout the Bay Area. Whatever its merits might be, it raised important questions about water supply, national defense, navigation, industrial development, aviation, and regional circulation—questions that were of concern to all the counties and most of the cities. So far as it definitely proposed an area-wide solution of major problems it increased interest in coöperative long-range planning. The Citizens' Postwar Planning Committee appointed by Mayor Lapham of San Francisco

acknowledged that the plan challenged the imagination; but the members refrained from making any recommendation concerning it, because it involved other municipalities as well as the state and federal governments. The very existence of a plan for the entire bay was tonic, for it promised to evoke other plans and it turned the spotlight on the future. The Bay Area found the business of preparing for the postwar period absorbing and in many ways exhilarating.

A City "Down at the Heels"

The Postwar Planning Committee in San Francisco took a critical view of the city and reached the conclusion that San Francisco had "become careless and allowed itself to 'run down at the heels.' " The committee believed that the situation was "far from hopeless," but could become "very serious in a surprisingly short time" if the city did not "correct its deficiencies and take advantage of the opportunities now knocking at its door."[14] Investments recently made by such nationally known firms as R. H. Macy of New York, F. W. Woolworth, Sears Roebuck, Western Crown Cork and Seal, Bullock-Magnin, and Apparel City Corporation (a clothing manufacturing organization promoted by the Reconstruction and Reemployment Commission) impressed the citizen leaders as evidence that business had faith in San Francisco, but they recognized that the city needed to demonstrate more faith in itself. They hoped it would meet the challenge of the future by spending a total of $177,454,000 for public improvements within the next six years and by preparing and following a master plan for the physical development of the city.

Appointed on April 5, 1945, shortly before the United Nations Conference on International Organization, the committee began its work by reviewing a six-year program for planning, land acquisition, and construction issued by the San Francisco City Planning Commission. This program had been formulated by the commission from more than 550 projects submitted by all departments of the city government and by the planning body itself, in much the same way that the San Mateo County "shelf" of postwar public works had been developed in 1942. The official San Francisco program included 277 projects totaling $131,847,294. But the Citizens' Committee put its stamp of approval on many more projects than the planning commission was willing to endorse, and it indicated that they could all be financed through annual budgets, revenue bonds, general bond issues, and funds derived from other sources. In the course of fifteen public hearings the committee had heard from seventy-one citizens, who had spoken either as representatives of organizations or as individuals, and it was convinced that San Franciscans were willing to invest large sums to modernize and augment public facilities.

The committee report submitted to Mayor Lapham on August 20, 1945, six days after the Japanese accepted the demand of the Allies for unconditional surrender, reflected the awareness of civic leaders that San Francisco would have to gird itself for increased competition from other metropolitan centers and from other cities within the Bay Area. Because competition among American cities for the aviation industry already was "becoming very, very keen," the committee recommended an investment of $20,000,000 in the San Francisco Airport.[15] In recognition of the fact that San Francisco had traffic and transit problems of the first magnitude, it approved the expenditure of more than $23,000,000 for street railway rehabilitation, $3,000,000 for a study and plans to relieve "the Market Street problem," $17,544,000 for streets and highways, $3,000,000 for off-street parking facilities, $3,200,000 for a tunnel under Russian Hill, and other large sums for viaducts, freeways, and grade separations.

"Unless means are found to move people freely in and out of the City and within the City limits and to provide adequate off-street parking facilities, our community cannot reach its full development, business cannot expand and there is the danger that business normally done in the City will be forced away," the committee warned.[16] It assigned high priorities to recreation, park, and urban redevelopment projects, indicating that the members perhaps had studied carefully a recent report in which the City Planning Commission had urged "generous provision for local parks, school sites, and playgrounds"[17] as one means of offsetting the movement to suburban areas—a major cause for alarm in the metropolis before the war.

Highly significant was a statement about city planning: "From the outset the Committee recognized the necessity of a Master Plan to guide the future development of the City, and of weighing the many plans for postwar construction in their relation to such a plan. It rejected the idea of approving individual projects as such and instead considered their relative importance to the over-all needs

The Broadway Tunnel Through Russian Hill, San Francisco, 1953. One of the projects included in the postwar planning program formulated with the help of a citizens' advisory committee. Photograph courtesy of San Francisco Department of Public Works.

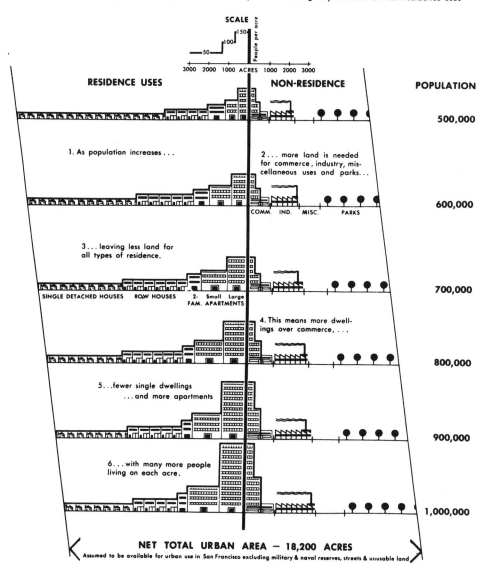

EFFECTS OF VARIOUS ASSUMED POPULATIONS ON THE USES OF LAND

With all available land in urban use, the proportion of dwellings of each type and the densities of
population in each type of dwelling are influenced by the increasing requirements of non-residence uses

*Chart Showing How Increases
in Population Affect the Use of
Land in San Francisco. From a
report of the San Francisco City
Planning Commission, 1945.*

of the City. It believes that the programs of all City Departments should be better interrelated than has been the practice in the past, and that they should be coordinated with the Master Plan. All programs and plans should be subject to constant reexamination and expansion as the needs of a growing city dictate."[18]

Future Uses of the Land

As yet San Francisco really had no master plan, although the planning commission was making progress toward one. In November, 1944, it had issued a report entitled *Present and Future Uses of the Land*, analyzing the distribution of population in the city and the amounts of

land used for every public and private purpose. This report, containing data needed for the preparation of a master plan, presented a fundamental issue for the people of San Francisco to decide:

"The real problem is to find out how many people the city can comfortably house, without so reducing living space as to drive out those whose work requires daily movement to the centers of business or industry. With such a maximum established, the emphasis could be upon constructive measures to increase the attractiveness and stability of neighborhoods, the elimination of substandard development, and the improvement of interurban transportation facilities. Improvements in regional transportation would make the city's cultural, business and industrial facilities more accessible to the population of the surrounding area.

"In this way, the selected maximum would be almost sure to be reached, and would tend to contain a larger proportion of permanent residents, actively identified with the city's true functions. Good homes, good schools and playgrounds, with safe and easy access to places of employment will attract the type of family which is an economic asset. But the pursuit of numbers alone may lead to serious problems of unemployment and relief.

"The decision to be made, therefore, is whether to aim at a somewhat greater population than we now have, with full understanding of the effect upon the average density on residence land, or to aim at a lower average density without loss of population by encouraging the full use of areas now undeveloped. In either case, emphasis will be upon securing better arrangement of land uses, and a more even distribution of population through the establishment of more careful building and zoning regulations, including provisions for control of density in terms of rooms per acre and percentage of site covered.

"At the same time the most congested areas would need to be redeveloped in accordance with modern methods of design. By the use of the latter, densities of population in certain close-in areas might be even higher than at present, but with far better living conditions because of improvements in the plans and in the relationship between building bulk and open spaces."[19]

The idea that a city can establish a population limit and institute policies to attain and not exceed that limit is inherent in all planning and zoning. But seldom have American cities faced the issue of controlling population growth and striving for desirable population densities and a physical environment of generally high quality. Rather, they have accepted a continuing increase in population as inevitable, however unpleasant the attendant crowding might become. Even the suggestion that a ceiling might be set on population growth is generally regarded as contrary to the laws of nature and economics, as basically un-American, or at the very least as totally impractical and unworkable. Yet any city that is serious about making life healthful, safe, convenient, and comfortable for its citizens through city planning must determine limits of population density in various areas and must maintain these limits. That means that unless the city can annex more land for expansion, it must consciously reject growth beyond a certain maximum.

San Francisco, a city with a fixed area, may have doubted in 1940 that it needed to take the trouble to establish a population maximum, for the census returns seemed to suggest that it was standing still. The growth of the city during the war encouraged the belief, however, that it would retain much of the population it had gained during the war and would perhaps slowly make additional gains as the Bay Area attracted more people. In order to determine the maximum population that would be desirable for the city, it would be necessary to analyze its economic prospects realistically and to envision what functions it could continue to perform in its central position among Bay Area communities, because its population prospects would be directly related to the economic activities that it could successfully maintain. The staff of the City Planning Commission, members of the Citizens' Postwar Planning Committee, and many others realized that San Francisco would be affected by the growth of population, industry, and trade in outlying areas and that it would be obliged to rely heavily upon certain administrative, service, cultural, and other functions in which it could excel other cities. What these functions were was not then entirely clear. Without a doubt, though, no other city in the nine counties around the bay would henceforth be so sensitive to regional influences as this one. Its planning problems really could be solved only in relation to those of all the cities and counties in the area. The Postwar Planning Committee failed to say this when it supported the preparation of a master plan; and one of the greatest dangers to the city was that other civic groups also might not recongize that for San Francisco, area-wide planning was practically a matter of economic survival. The metropolis felt that it must assert leadership in a new movement for metropolitan regional planning even though it risked the accusation, heard many times before, that it was seeking to dominate other cities.

A Program for Oakland

Across the bay in Oakland a postwar planning committee appointed by Mayor Slavich on March 2, 1943, submitted "a sound and conservative plan" for the future to the city council in September, 1945. Of sixteen recommendations included in the report, the last, "that the City Planning Commission, in cooperation with the Alameda County Planning Commission, should be the agency to coordinate and develop this entire program," was the most arresting.[20] It was evidence that, over the years, responsible citizens had come to value city planning as the most effective means of insuring a well-organized city, even though Oakland did not yet have a general plan to guide its future growth and development. The Postwar Planning Committee expected a "period of exceptional construction activity" in the years ahead and recommended "that the Oakland City Planning Commission be urged to develop a 'master plan' for residential development throughout the Oakland Area, giving study to ALL factors important to a sound program including future residential developments, industrial areas, downtown business center, retail trade areas, schools, utilities, sewage disposal, storm water disposal, transportation, etc."[21] From the committee's description of "a 'master plan' for residential development" it was apparent that the members actually meant a long-range, comprehensive, general plan for Oakland and its environs. Other suggestions made by the committee were that the Oakland Real Estate Board, the Chamber of Commerce, the Oakland Housing Authority, the Board of Port Commissioners, and the Pacific Gas and Electric Company coöperate in a survey of the housing requirements of the Oakland Area. In all these recommendations the committee recognized the leadership the planning commission could exercise in seeking a high quality of development.

Like other governments in the Bay Area, the Oakland city government had made an inventory of its future needs and had compiled a long list of projects. Since the capital outlay for the 464 improvements submitted by various departments would be $181,219,111, the city contemplated construction over a period of six years or more. The voters already had approved some of the most urgently needed projects, however, at a special bond election on May 8, 1945, and were looking forward to street improvements costing $4,590,000; long-overdue storm and sanitary sewers, $5,311,000; swimming pools and playgrounds, $1,023,000; a hall of justice, $2,707,000; and a new main library and four branches, $1,763,000. Other expenditures foreseen would be for public schools, further port development, expansion of the Oakland Airport, additional parks and playgrounds, streets, and police and fire stations.

The Public Voice in Berkeley

In neighboring Berkeley the postwar report submitted by City Manager Gerrit Vander Ende to the city council in September, 1945, was unusual in that it included recommendations of the Public Administration Service, a Citizens' Postwar Advisory Committee, the Junior Chamber of Commerce, the Berkeley Art Association, and improvement clubs. Already before the council were a long-range recreation plan and a street and highway survey by Ronald Campbell, a planning consultant. From the numerous suggestions received, the city manager selected and recommended to the city council an immediate program totaling $2,690,595—a modest total which reflected the interest of the Citizens' Postwar Advisory Committee in a program that could be "financed by the city" and would not require its officials to "wait with outstretched and suppliant palms for either the federal or state government to dole out subsidies or financial grants."[22] Laudable as might be the committee's desire for civic self-reliance, it had taken an extremely narrow view of community needs and had said nothing about long-range civic development, as suggested in the city council's resolution creating it.

A month later the Berkeley Chamber of Commerce, through its Civic Development Committee, sounded the progressive note that might have been expected from the official committee. Referring to Berkeley as "a patchwork community," the Chamber of Commerce committee called for a comprehensive planning program and asserted that "no major development in a city should be made without study of the relationship of this development to the whole city."[23] It proposed that a committee of citizens be formed to "visualize the Berkeley of 1975" and chart the course for the future in coöperation with the city government and all other agencies. The report indicated that Berkeley, too, was ready for a genuine planning program, as were Oakland, San Francisco, and some other Bay Area cities.

Not by Bread Alone

The postwar problems faced by most cities in the area were as nothing compared with those confronting smaller communities which had suddenly become centers of war production in 1941 and 1942. City officials of Richmond, one of the most drastically affected by the global struggle, estimated that just to provide for the kind of services required by any normal peacetime city with a minimum population of fifty thousand, they would have to spend $7,000,000 for municipal improvements and $2,000,000 for schools. But Richmond was a city of approximately one hundred thousand people, and what if half of them did not depart, now that the war was over and the shipyards were closing down? The bill for new schools, sewers, streets, highways, recreation centers, and other needed public facilities might run as high as $18,000,000 if Richmond continued to hold the new population that it had attracted—and already the tax rate was twice as high as the rate in many cities. How could Richmond raise the money to meet the huge backlog of community needs? And what should it build first?

Other Bay Area cities were frankly surprised by Richmond's answer to these questions. On November 20, 1945, the voters of Richmond approved four to one a $3,850,000 bond issue for construction of a Memorial Civic Center to honor Richmond citizens who had fought and died for their country. Why should a city desperately in need of additional classrooms, places for children to play, sanitary sewers, and new paving on its streets first of all construct a new city hall, main library, hall of justice, and a civic auditorium?

There were two main reasons for the decision to erect a group of public buildings before undertaking other projects. The old city hall was totally inadequate and the various departments of city government were widely scattered in rented quarters, making efficient operation of the municipality almost impossible. But aside from the difficulties experienced daily by city officials and employees, there seemed to be an urgent need to provide some tangible evidence that the motley assortment of people brought together in Richmond under wartime conditions intended to create a new civic life for themselves. Civic leaders as well as city officials believed that a well-designed civic center, with adequate space for expansion of departments as the city grew, would serve as a rallying point for civic pride and would convince industrialists, investors, and other communities that Richmond proposed to move steadily forward in the postwar years rather than lose ground and suffer loss of morale. The investment in the new civic center was the city's way of signifying anew that man does not live by bread alone. After the overwhelming vote in favor of the civic center bonds, Richmond citizens felt confident of their ability to solve many of the other problems that pressed upon them. The election was a turning point in the history of the city, just as the vote for park bonds had been in Oakland in 1907.

The Eastshore Freeway Through the Industrial District of East Oakland. Alameda and Bay Farm Island in the distance. Photograph courtesy of State Division of Highways.

Emergence of a New Problem

The many bond issues approved by voters in Bay Area cities, the extensive lists of public projects to be built in years to come, the plans announced by industrial firms for the conversion and expansion of plants and by commercial establishments for repairs and modernizations all indicated the beginning of a period of intense construction activity and widespread growth in the new and hopeful era of peace. The State Division of Highways was prepared to build, stage by stage, the Bayshore and East Shore freeways planned before the war, giving the nine-county area the first major units of an ultimate super-highway network. Progress in the solution of the problem of bay pollution was foreshadowed by work on plans and specifications for new sewers and sewage treatment plants in San Francisco (for which the voters of that city had approved a $12,000,000 bond issue in November, 1944) and by reports and investigations of sewage disposal under way in Special District No. 1 of the East Bay Municipal Utility District, created by the six East Bay cities of Alameda, Albany, Berkeley, Emeryville, Oakland, and Piedmont about the time the voters of San Francisco took action on their sanitation problem. On the statute books of California was a new Community Redevelopment Act, passed by the state legislature to enable cities to establish redevelopment agencies and make plans for clearing, re-planning, and rebuilding the blighted areas produced by decades of inadequately controlled growth and development. So much activity by private enterprise and by local, county, state, and federal governments seemed assured that the fear of postwar depression began to recede. Not unemployment but the pace of postwar development promised to be the major problem of the Bay Area.

Once wartime restrictions on building materials were relaxed, once construction machinery and skilled labor again were available for building, and once industrialists could start new plants and developers new suburban tracts, would it be possible to fashion the kind of well-ordered cities and towns envisioned in all the postwar planning committee reports that endorsed city planning? None of the cities had general plans; nor did the counties. There was no legal apparatus in the entire Bay Area for coördinating the planning of a multiplicity of cities, counties, special districts, and the state and federal governments. Metropolitan government was totally lacking. The San Francisco Bay Area, at the start of the most gigantic building boom in its history, seemed pathetically ill-equipped to meet the new peacetime conditions. It did have, however, a new awareness of the importance of planning. From the many poor decisions that citizens and public officials alike seemed sure to make, in time would come an appreciation of the value of shaping local policy for physical development in accordance with broad policies suggested by a continuing, long-range planning program for the entire metropolitan region—and perhaps to be carried out, in the main, by some form of metropolitan government.

CHAPTER SEVENTEEN

The Regional Metropolis

Anyone who flew over the San Francisco Bay Area soon after the end of World War II saw large open spaces between the cities on the San Francisco Peninsula, vast prune orchards and truck gardens in the northern Santa Clara Valley, a few small, sleepy towns amid the farms on the eastern side of the bay south of San Leandro, valleys and plains in eastern Contra Costa County still green with apricot orchards and walnut groves, and in the northern counties mile after mile of dairy lands, vineyards, and field crops surrounding historic towns and villages that had grown very slowly for decades.

The Bay Area had increased in population by perhaps half a million between 1940 and the summer of 1945; yet relatively little land on the peripheries of cities had been utilized to accommodate the new population. The war had left its deposits of temporary housing and hastily built private dwellings mostly in or near urban areas adjacent to deep water, where the shipyards and related industrial establishments were. Elsewhere there had been lack of growth, a weathering of the houses, and neglect in the maintenance of city halls, schools, parks, and street surfaces.

By V-J Day there was an enormous pent-up demand for new homes, new industrial plants, schools, and community centers that was like a flood about to break over the levees. Soon the forces of expansion burst in all directions. The cities started spilling over into the fields and orchards on their outskirts. Even if no more people had moved into the Bay Area in the immediate postwar years, tract houses and shopping centers would have spread over thousands of acres. But newcomers poured into the area from every state in the Union, and a new wave of births also swelled the population. The increase in residents between the end of the war and April, 1950, when the census was taken, was almost as great as it had been during the war. And this unpredicted new growth, which brought the increase in population during the decade to 947,014, still further extended the tide of development that had begun to engulf the open spaces.

Industrial Dispersion

For two or three years after the Japanese surrender the dispersion of industry was a subject of even more newspaper editorials than was residential building, since industrial construction was possible, whereas building materials for houses were for a time in short supply. At the end of 1947 the San Francisco Bay Area Council reported that approximately one-third of a billion dollars had been spent on new industrial plants and expansions in the nine-county metropolitan region since January 1, 1945. Many of the new factories were in the smaller cities, such as San Leandro and Hayward in Alameda County and San Jose and Santa Clara in the Santa Clara Valley. The 1947 Census of Manufactures showed that San Francisco had 182 fewer manufacturing establishments than in 1939, whereas Alameda County during the same period had gained more than 200 establishments and Santa Clara County more than 100. Even San Mateo County, a largely residential area that had a reputation for being "cool" to industry, increased the number of its manufacturing firms from 97 to 228, although only 19 of the concerns employed a hundred workers or more. To describe all this industrial development in outlying areas as "decentralization" would be misleading, because many of the new plants were branches of eastern companies that were appearing on the Bay Area scene for the first time. The industrial boom represented expansion of the Bay Area economy even more than it represented some movement of plants from older centers such as San Francisco and Oakland.

The most spectacular of the new plants constructed in Alameda County were the huge, one-story automobile assembly plants and truck and bus body manufacturing

establishments in and about San Leandro. Near major highways and railroads, these industrial facilities covered many acres, provided spacious parking areas for the automobiles of employees, and presented attractive administrative offices and landscaped grounds to the view of passing motorists. The land the establishments occupied had been planted to truck crops as recently as the war years.

By the spring of 1949 the San Jose Chamber of Commerce listed eighty new industries acquired since 1944. Although many of them were in the food-processing category, a rather large number represented a new trend in the county toward industrial diversification. Branch plants of such industrial giants as General Electric Company, International Minerals and Chemical Company,

Industrial Dispersion: Factories and Wholesale Distribution Warehouses near San Leandro. Photograph courtesy of State Division of Highways.

International Business Machines Corporation, Owens-Illinois Glass Company, Owens-Corning Fiberglas Corporation, Pittsburgh–Des Moines Steel Company, and Westinghouse Electric Corporation rose on sites formerly given over to tomatoes or peas or to prunes and apricots.

The conservative agricultural element in Santa Clara County was anything but happy about this industrial invasion. In a foreword to an industrial survey of the county, the San Jose Chamber of Commerce, organizer of the national promotional campaign that had influenced many of these companies to establish western branches, acknowledged that "there were some sincere and intelligent people who looked askance at this industrial development. They had genuine fears that smokestacks would 'encircle the city'; that 'blighted areas' would spring up in industrial sections; that orchards would be torn up 'by the hundreds'; and that by past standards, this accelerated trend in the establishment of new industry might result in an unbalanced, top-heavy economy destined to collapse at some undetermined time in the future."[1]

The fears that orchards would be torn up by the hundreds were indeed well founded; and smokestacks, though they by no means encircled the city, did undeniably contribute to the development of a new problem. The Chamber sought to assure the skeptical that industrial growth was not incompatible with desirable living conditions. Yet it was not long before the Santa Clara County Board of Supervisors found it necessary to designate the entire county an air pollution control district; the skies over the Santa Clara Valley were becoming a dirty gray. In March, 1950, the county health officer, who also served as county air pollution control officer, declared that "smog," the murky atmospheric condition familiar to Los Angeles, was not only a Santa Clara County problem but also a "Bay Area problem."[2] The new factories in San Jose and Santa Clara were producing air pollutants, and, in addition, industrial smoke and fumes from the San Francisco–Oakland area were being wafted into the county. Sooner or later there would have to be area-wide control of the new menace to the human respiratory tract, the health officer asserted.

Acres of Tract Houses

Air photographs of the San Jose–Santa Clara area and air views of Alameda County published in the promotional literature of the Oakland Chamber of Commerce revealed that the march of industry into agricultural areas had been accompanied every step of the way by mass-produced tract houses. San Lorenzo Village, begun by the David D. Bohannon Organization in 1944 in the area south of San Leandro, was a forerunner of the scores of

new "planned communities" of almost identical houses. A whole new town in itself, it housed approximately five thousand people and had its own shopping center, schools, and recreation facilities. In its planning it was, however, superior to many later ventures in large-scale construction of low-cost houses, because the street system at least included service roads paralleling a main highway (which unfortunately sliced through the development) and the interior streets were designed to assure as much safety and convenience as possible.

In many of the other speculative developments built in the immediate postwar years, when returning veterans were taking full advantage of the home-purchasing provisions of legislation enacted during the war, the street layouts were not so carefully planned, and no sites were set aside for needed schools and playgrounds. Some houses faced traffic arteries, and some living-room windows looked toward supermarkets, the handy distribution centers through which the developers assured themselves of long-term returns on the daily expenditures of families in rows and rows of small stucco houses.

In 1949, when columns of the financial pages of newspapers mentioned a "difficult period of change-over from a sellers' to a buyers' market" and a "return to hard-headed competition," the number of building permits issued for family dwelling units in the San Francisco Bay counties exceeded twenty-five thousand. The construction industry seemed immune to the strains being experienced in other segments of the economy. Officials issued permits for nearly fifty-nine hundred units in San Mateo County, for five thousand in Alameda County, for almost as many in Santa Clara County, for thirty-seven hundred in Contra Costa County, for more than a thousand in Marin County, and for more than four thousand in San Francisco, which was fast using up its limited resources of vacant land.

The startling fact about this great volume of building was that a high proportion of it was in unincorporated areas under the jurisdiction of county boards of supervisors, who were suddenly asked to deal with a variety of new problems essentially urban in complexity—problems of police and fire protection, neighborhood and community recreation, library service, sanitation, street lighting, and storm drainage. Most of these were matters that county governments were scarcely equipped to handle. In Alameda County more than two-fifths of the new homes were in unincorporated territory; in Santa Clara County more than one-half were outside the boundaries of municipalities, in Marin County almost two-thirds, and in Contra Costa County more than two-thirds.

In 1950, when the volume of permits issued for family

Tract Houses near the Eastshore Freeway, San Lorenzo. Photograph courtesy of State Division of Highways.

dwellings in the Bay Area rose to more than forty thousand, even larger proportions of new units were constructed in the fringe areas of some counties. In Alameda County, for instance, almost one-half were in unincorporated territory; in Contra Costa County, three-fourths.

"Dingbats" and Future Slums

In one of its publications the United States Bureau of Labor Statistics described the typical house built in the San Francisco–Oakland Metropolitan Area in the summer of 1949. It was a one-story, detached structure, had five rooms and approximately a thousand square feet of floor space, and was of frame construction with wood or stucco exterior. It had one bathroom, a one-car garage, and a fireplace in the living room. Usually it was in a large tract developed by an operative builder.

Only about 15 per cent of all houses had more than eleven hundred square feet of floor space, and very few had more than six rooms. Many were what the building fraternity called "dingbats," indifferently designed, put together with the cheapest of materials, and intended for quick sale on the installment plan, with low down payments. The public often referred to them as "the slums of tomorrow."

In certain unincorporated areas in Alameda and Santa Clara counties, and even in some cities in San Mateo County, the builders of these low-cost houses snapped up

acreage which by any reasonable criterion for the appropriate use of land would have been better adapted to industrial use, since it was near railroads and major highways. Lack of zoning, inappropriate zoning, or changes in zoning ordinances made under pressure from developers and landowners accounted for these ill-advised and detrimental uses of the land. A consulting engineer addressing a committee for the development of light industry in San Mateo County in 1951, after many areas more suitable for industry than for residences had already been covered with tract houses, scored city and county governments "for permitting encroachment of residential development on industrial fringe areas";[3] but by that time his complaints were hardly effective.

The situation in San Mateo County, as in other rapidly developing counties, posed a troublesome long-range problem for planning commissions and civic organizations interested in the economic future of the Bay Area: How could land that would be needed for industry twenty, thirty, or forty years later be maintained as reserve open space? Zoning alone was not the answer, obviously, because city councils and county boards of supervisors sometimes yielded to the pressure for rezoning; and public opinion often supported the landowner who could make more money by selling potential industrial land for residential development.

There was also, for all cities and counties, the still

larger problem, seldom acknowledged, of bringing about a suitable distribution of industrial areas throughout the metropolitan region. How much dispersion or concentration of industry should be encouraged? And to what kind of metropolitan regional distribution of population and economic activities should any pattern of industrial areas relate? In the early 1950's most people concerned with industrial development scarcely asked such questions, and perhaps they are not asking them even today.

Changing Relationships

The census taken in April, 1950, disclosed how much the dispersion of industry and the rapid construction of peas-in-a-pod housing developments in outlying cities and unincorporated areas had altered the prewar distribution of population in the Bay Area. Although San Francisco gained more than 140,000 people and Oakland more than 82,000 in the 1940's, these two central cities together had only 43 per cent of the population of the nine-county metropolitan region in 1950, whereas ten years earlier they had included 54 per cent of the regional total. The proportions of the Bay Area population living in the relatively unindustrialized counties of Marin, Napa, and Sonoma remained approximately the same; but Contra Costa, San Mateo, Santa Clara, and Solano counties all had larger proportions of the regional population than before. Contra Costa County, the fastest growing county in the Bay Area, had had less than 6 per cent of the regional population in 1940, whereas in 1950 it had more than 11 per cent. Its population had increased from a little more than 100,000 to almost 300,000. The populations of both San Mateo and Solano counties had more than doubled—a gain of 123,877 in the former, and of 55,715 in the latter. In Santa Clara County 115,598 new residents represented a two-thirds increase in population.

All nine counties of the Bay Area together included 2,681,322 residents, or almost 55 per cent more than in 1940. More than a third of them had arrived on the scene during the decade.

From time to time in 1950 and 1951, as the Bureau of the Census released statistics on the growth of individual cities and counties, newspapers of the Bay Area showed ingenuous pride in whopping percentage gains. The figures confounded the experts. As recently as November, 1947, the Federal Reserve Bank of San Francisco had ventured an admittedly "hazardous" prediction that "the extraordinary expansion of population experienced in the Twelfth District [seven far western states] between 1940 and 1947 has perhaps come to an end and . . . a much more moderate rate of growth is to be expected in the immediate future."[4] All such judgments were proved erroneous, and although there was general rejoicing over the continuing influx of newcomers and the tidal wave of births, occasionally some writer sounded a sober note. Said the San Francisco *Chronicle* editorially:

"Growth of this sort means nothing less than social upheaval, and it is the responsibility of broad-visioned planning to mitigate the disruptive effects and to capitalize on the beneficial effects of the California trend. It is obvious that we've got to concern ourselves first and incessantly with the problem of increasing our water and power supply. This is the basic anxiety, not alone in Southern California, dependent as it is on the out-of-State resources of the Colorado River, but also of our own community around the Bay Area, and of the Central Valley.

"With water needs go others—the sound location of industries and control of attending atmospheric pollution; the expansion of highway communications; the building of schools to keep pace with the children; the development of . . . community planning.

"These challenges will be met intelligently or unintelligently, depending upon the awareness of them that Californians display. The plain fact is that we're pioneering again, a hundred years after the gold rush, and we've got to invent new patterns for a State that on some future day will be second to none."[5]

New Aqueducts

The Bay Area, like any boom community, was so busy trying to catch up with itself that efforts to anticipate new long-term needs tended to be thwarted by the demands of the immediate present; yet in meeting the needs of the present and of the "middle future," some public agencies and private companies necessarily provided for the demands of the distant future. Among such organizations were utility districts, municipal water departments, and companies supplying the Bay Area with natural gas and electricity.

Long before the end of World War II the cities on the San Francisco Peninsula and in the East Bay had foreseen that they would have to reach out for more water from the distant sources from which they were already drawing the greater proportion of their supplies. Voters in the East Bay Municipal Utility District approved a $12,000,000 bond issue in November, 1946, to finance the construction of a Second Mokelumne Aqueduct; and a year later the voters of San Francisco authorized a $25,000,000 bond issue for expansion of the San Francisco water system, which also supplies water to most of the municipalities on the Peninsula.

The twin aqueduct placed in service in August, 1949,

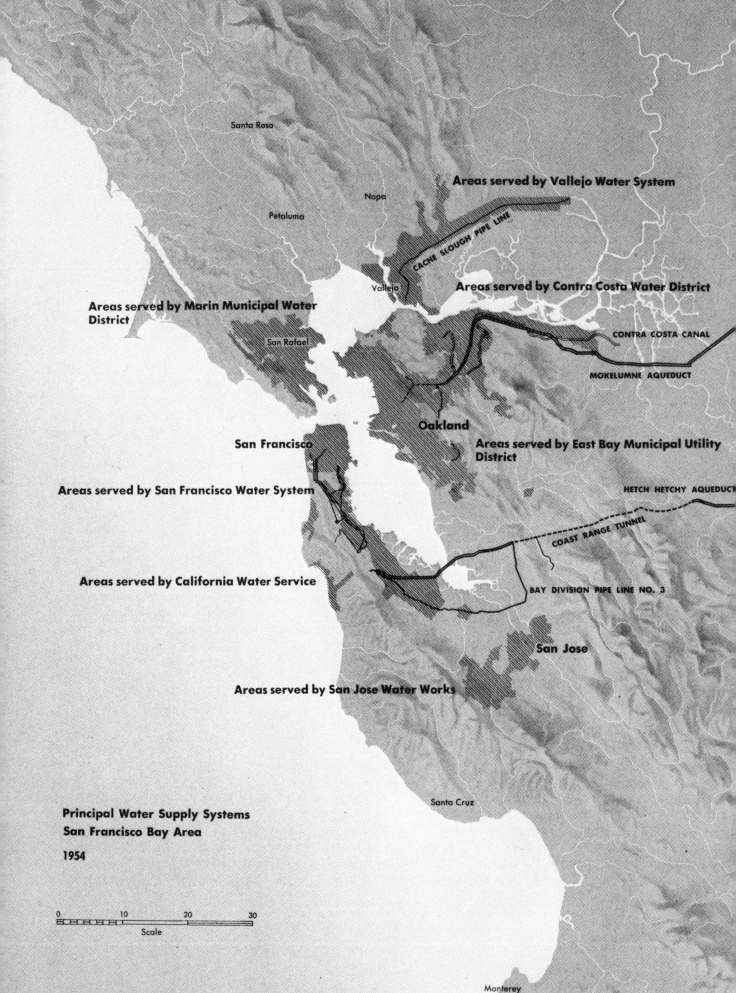

Areas served by Vallejo Water System

CACHE SLOUGH PIPE LINE

Areas served by Contra Costa Water District

CONTRA COSTA CANAL

MOKELUMNE AQUEDUCT

Areas served by Marin Municipal Water District

Areas served by East Bay Municipal Utility District

Oakland

San Francisco

Areas served by San Francisco Water System

HETCH HETCHY AQUEDUCT

COAST RANGE TUNNEL

Areas served by California Water Service

BAY DIVISION PIPE LINE NO. 3

San Jose

Areas served by San Jose Water Works

Santa Rosa

Napa

Petaluma

Vallejo

San Rafael

Santa Cruz

Monterey

**Principal Water Supply Systems
San Francisco Bay Area**

1954

0   10   20   30
Scale

by the East Bay Municipal Utility District assured the East Bay of a daily supply of one hundred million gallons by gravity flow. By operating pumping plants, the district could increase this daily flow through its parallel aqueducts to 210,000,000 gallons, or enough to serve approximately twice the number of people then living in the cities and unincorporated areas within the district.

Although San Francisco had water rights to 400,000,000 gallons daily from the Tuolumne River, it had imported through a single pipe line across the San Joaquin Valley only 60,000,000 gallons daily during the war and had utilized local water supplies in San Mateo, Santa Clara, and Alameda counties for the rest of its requirements of approximately 100,000,000 gallons daily. By 1947 the San Francisco Public Utilities Commission saw the need for building a second pipe line of equal capacity across the valley and for constructing a third Bay Division pipe line, thirty-four miles long, round the southern end of the bay. A further reason for routing the new Bay Division line in an arc round the bay was to avoid the possibility that a submarine disturbance might cut off the total supply from east of the bay. The bond issue of 1947 provided the funds for these and other expansions of the San Francisco system.

Laid in 1949 and 1950, the new Bay Division line had a capacity of 76,000,000 gallons and brought the total capacity for delivery of water from the mountain and Alameda systems to the Peninsula reservoirs up to approximately 190,000,000 gallons daily—more than ample for San Francisco and Peninsula needs for several decades.

In the meantime, in 1948 a drought in California had caused curtailments in the use of power and had threatened San Francisco with a water shortage. In order to fulfill its obligations to the Modesto and Turlock Irrigation districts, the city had had to reduce the water stored in the O'Shaughnessy Reservoir in the Hetch Hetchy Valley to a dangerously low level. The city saw that it no longer enjoyed a safe margin of water and power supply. In fact, engineers had been in the field making surveys and investigations for a dam in the Cherry Valley, some miles northwest of O'Shaugnessy Dam, ever since 1940. In November, 1949, San Francisco voters approved a bond issue of $4,000,000 for constructing the new dam; the federal government, because of flood control aspects of the project, was willing to contribute $9,000,000 toward its costs. From the reservoir formed by the Cherry Valley Dam the city would be able to meet the needs of the two irrigation districts, the water rights of which are protected under the Raker Act, and to save for its own use the waters of O'Shaughnessy Reservoir.

Thus, San Francisco, steadily pursuing the "build-as-needed" policy (by which it avoided paying interest on the staggering bond issues that would have been required to finance a water system built to full capacity in the beginning) moved several steps nearer completion of the multifeatured Hetch Hetchy system.

More Water for More People

Population growth in other parts of the Bay Area created the same kind of uneasiness about water supplies as that felt in the central and more populous areas. In Marin, Solano, and Santa Clara counties millions of dollars went into the development of additional sources of supply, although none of the projects undertaken promised permanent solution of the water problem if population continued to increase in accordance with long-term forecasts.

The Marin Municipal Water District, serving the commuter zone of Marin County from three reservoirs developed between 1887 and 1918, built the Bon Tempe Dam in 1948 and immediately started planning another dam on Lagunitas Creek that would impound more water than all the other reservoirs in the district together. This fifth reservoir, created in 1954 upon completion of the James S. Peters Dam, stored the runoff from a watershed of approximately ten square miles. Other local watersheds remained to be utilized, but by 1957 a state legislature mindful of the rapid growth of California would be appropriating money to plan an aqueduct to bring water from the delta of the Sacramento River to Marin and other North Bay counties.

In Solano County the cities of Vallejo, Benicia, and Fairfield-Suisun had made arrangements during the war to supplement their own inadequate local sources of water supply (mostly ground water) with seven million gallons daily supplied by the East Bay Municipal Utility District through a temporary pipe line across the Carquinez Bridge. Since this arrangement was scheduled to terminate in 1952, the Solano County cities had to find additional water elsewhere. One possibility was to press for immediate construction of the proposed Monticello Dam on Putah Creek by the Bureau of Reclamation; the other was to act quickly and build a pipe line to the delta of the Sacramento–San Joaquin rivers. When controversy over the dam threatened to become prolonged and Navy officials at Mare Island grew alarmed over the risk of being without safe margins of water supply, Vallejo decided to construct a thirty-mile pipe line to Maine Prairie Slough, a tributary of Cache Slough, in the delta. The new line, completed in 1952, can supply 20,000,000 gallons daily and is considered adequate to meet local needs until about 1970.

In Santa Clara County the San Jose Water Works

annually gained so many new customers in its one-hundred-square-mile service area in the northern part of the county that it could no longer depend upon the wells and reservoirs already in use. In 1951 it built the Austrian Dam, a large, earth-fill dam, on Los Gatos Creek in the Santa Cruz Mountains. Upon completion of the new reservoir, the company announced that its sources of supply had a production capacity somewhat greater than the capacity of the first Hetch Hetchy Aqueduct built by San Francisco.

People in the Santa Clara Valley nevertheless engaged in endless discussion about how long the valley could depend exclusively on local supplies of water both for domestic use and for irrigation. Even though the Santa Clara Valley Water Conservation District had built five dams in the late 'thirties to spread stream runoff in percolating beds, so that the badly depleted underground water would be replenished, the recurrence of a dry cycle and heavy pumping during the war had by 1948 reduced the water table below the previous all-time low of 1934. In 1951 the construction of two additional dams, the Leroy Anderson Dam on Coyote Creek two miles east of Morgan Hill and the Lexington Dam on Los Gatos Creek just above the city of Los Gatos, promised to improve the situation temporarily but not to eliminate the long-term prospect of water shortages.

Ironically, the unusually rainy winter of 1951–52, like nothing seen in the past sixty years, suddenly turned Santa Clara County from an area with too little water to one with terrifying surpluses. The Guadalupe, Coyote, Saratoga, Los Gatos, and other creeks draining into San Francisco Bay became furious torrents, overflowing their banks and spreading havoc through new subdivisions and across croplands. Bridges and roads were washed away; silt covered the floors of new tract houses; the buildings of Agnews State Hospital stood feet deep in muddy water; all the residents of the town of Alviso had to be evacuated.

The possibility of all this destruction had been foreseen for many years by the county planning commission, which had warned in 1944 that the county urgently needed a comprehensive plan for disposal of storm water, but no valley-wide drainage study had been authorized. Local districts, self-governing municipalities, county departments, federal agencies, and individuals had all attempted piecemeal, uncoördinated solutions to a highly complex problem that had been getting steadily worse for many years. Land subsidence caused by overdrafts on the underground water storage reservoirs had enlarged the level plain in which storm waters collected during periods of heavy rainfall; the compacting of soils for roadbeds had formed inverted dams that restricted subsurface drainage;

the diking of large areas near the bay to prevent tidal flooding had limited the points at which storm runoff could discharge into the bay; and the building of thousands of impervious roofs, walks, and paved streets in new subdivisions had greatly reduced the land surface capable of absorbing storm runoff.

The county planning commission observed in a report issued after the flood that "the county is little better off today than twenty years ago, excepting for the flood-checking features of the conservation dams and the drainage structures in the Alum Rock–Evergreen area." The county needed a comprehensive plan for the utilization and control of local runoff, but no amount of conservation could solve the long-term problem of an adequate water supply. The commission stated plainly what everyone knew: "An outside source will be needed." Indeed, officials of the Santa Clara Valley Water Conservation District already had applications on file with the State Water Resources Board for water from several outside sources, including the Central Valley Project.

New Sources of Energy

The increasing dependence of the Bay Area on distant sources of water had a parallel in its dependence on sources of energy that were, in some instances, even more remote from the area than the watersheds of the Sierra Nevada. The largest private utility company in the Bay Area, the Pacific Gas and Electric Company, which serves most of northern and central California, reached all the way to the Permian Basin of west Texas and southwestern New Mexico and to the San Juan Basin in the "four corners" area of New Mexico, Colorado, Utah, and Arizona for natural gas to operate its new steam plants and to supply domestic and industrial customers. It also built many new hydroelectric plants, from the McCloud and Pit rivers in the far northern part of the state to the Kings River in the southern canyons of the Sierra Nevada.

More than a little skeptical about predictions of a postwar slump and a population recession in California, the company announced before the end of World War II that it would embark on a ten-year construction program requiring expenditures totaling $1,500,000,000. The program contemplated additional hydroelectric plants in the Sierra, expansion of high-voltage electric transmission lines and distribution lines, steam-generating plants using fuel oil and natural gas, and natural-gas pipe lines hundreds of miles long.

Between 1948 and 1953 the utility company completed seven large hydroelectric plants in the Sierra; yet the entire generating capacity of these new plants did not equal that of either of two huge steam plants constructed in

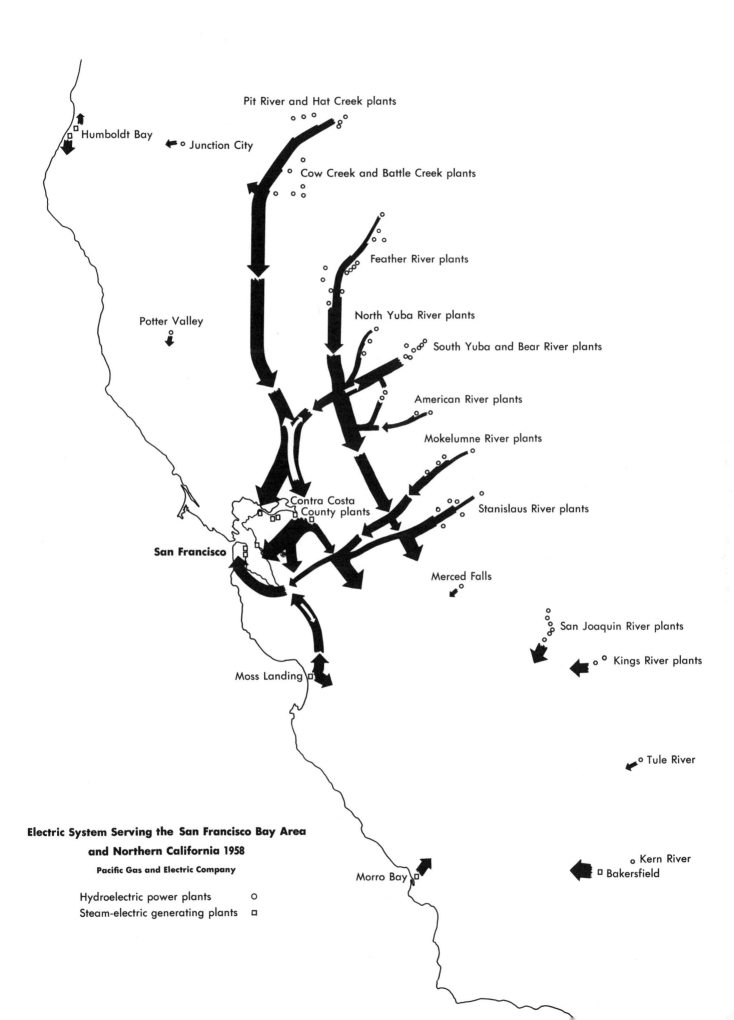

Pit River and Hat Creek plants

Humboldt Bay

← ○ Junction City

Cow Creek and Battle Creek plants

Feather River plants

Potter Valley

North Yuba River plants

South Yuba and Bear River plants

American River plants

Mokelumne River plants

Contra Costa
County plants

Stanislaus River plants

San Francisco

Merced Falls

San Joaquin River plants

Kings River plants

Moss Landing

Tule River

**Electric System Serving the San Francisco Bay Area
and Northern California 1958**

Pacific Gas and Electric Company

Hydroelectric power plants   ○

Steam-electric generating plants   ◻

Kern River

◻ Bakersfield

Morro Bay ◻

Contra Costa County near Pittsburg. One of these has a generating capacity of 575,000 kilowatts, or almost enough to supply two cities the size of San Francisco; the other has a capacity even larger—600,000 kilowatts. A third enormous plant at Moss Landing in Monterey County also supplies some parts of the Bay Area with power. In addition, the company increased the generating capacity of a plant in San Francisco and set to work on other steam plants in Kern, San Luis Obispo, and Humboldt counties.

The importation of natural gas from sources in other states was necessitated by the fact that even before the end of World War II no discoveries of new natural-gas fields of substantial capacity were being made in California. In 1944 the Pacific Gas and Electric Company joined two southern California companies in investigating the possibility of building pipe lines to tap the reserves of the Permian Basin and the San Juan Basin. The southern companies were the first to arrange for the El Paso Natural Gas Company to build a pipe line to make deliveries to them at the California border. In 1948 the Pacific Gas and Electric Company made similar arrangements to take deliveries from the Texas company at Topock on the Arizona-California border. By 1950 the P. G. and E. had constructed its "Super Inch" high-pressure gas transmission line (34 inches in diameter) from Milpitas in Santa Clara County to the junction at Topock with the pipe line of the El Paso Natural Gas Company, a distance of 502 miles.

The initial capacity of the "Super Inch" was 150,000,000 cubic feet daily. As the demand for gas rose sharply, the company again and again enlarged the capacity of the line by installing compressor stations, building "looping" or parallel sections, and enlarging compressor stations, until by 1954 the line was delivering 700,000,000 cubic feet of gas daily—enough to serve the needs of eleven cities the size of Oakland (population approximately 400,000). The greater part of this imported gas was consumed in the San Francisco Bay Area.

Looking ahead, company officials acknowledged that within a few years they would have to parallel the entire line, in order to raise the daily capacity 700,000,000 cubic feet above the 1954 figure.

Flood Tides of Growth

The population growth that compelled these extensive expansions in utilities was especially great during the Korean War; it slowed down during the recession of 1953 and 1954, and from about the summer of 1955 until the summer of 1957 again accelerated while California and the nation surged forward on another wave of prosperity and inflation. As it had all during its history, the Bay Area attracted hordes of newcomers in good years but seemed much less the promised land during economic downturns. The State Department of Finance estimated that the population of the nine bay counties increased more than 140,000 during the fiscal year 1951–52, whereas the estimated increase for the fiscal year 1954–55 was just one-half as much. By 1956–57 the numerical increase was again more than 100,000, of which almost one-half accrued to Santa Clara County, where bulldozers uprooted orchards by the hundreds to make way for tract houses, new industrial plants, and shopping centers surrounded by acres of parking space.

During all these years of economic peaks and setbacks the flood tides of suburban development kept rolling across the once rural landscape on the outskirts of the urban areas. From time to time, restrictions on building materials or "tight money" policies that limited borrowing for home construction retarded their progress, but nothing actually stopped their steady elimination of open spaces. One urban wave swept southward along the bay side of the San Francisco Peninsula into northern Santa Clara County, creating an almost unbroken pattern of low-density development. Other waves surged outward in all directions from the San Jose area. Or perhaps it would be more accurate to say that something like an explosion littered the countryside with subdivisions; for the pattern of urbanization was disorderly and irrational, a testimonial to the failure of city and county governments to say when and where agricultural land could be subdivided for residential use. On the eastern side of the bay another flood of development advanced southward past Hayward into the green acres of Washington Township. And in the San Ramon and Ygnacio valleys of Contra Costa County, east of the Berkeley Hills, still other waves of development displaced walnut groves, apricot orchards, and vineyards. The northern counties experienced to a lesser extent the same kind of "runaway" suburbanization.

The regional metropolis that some people prophesied in the 'twenties and 'thirties took shape with startling rapidity—without benefit of metropolitan regional planning. In 1951 the officials of building departments in cities and counties of the Bay Area issued permits for nearly thirty thousand dwellings, in 1952 for more than thirty-one thousand, in 1953 for almost thirty thousand, in 1954 for approximately forty-one thousand, and in 1955 for more than forty-five thousand. In approximately the same four-year period the California Division of Real Estate approved subdivisions that used up almost eighty square miles of agricultural land; of course a great deal of land had been converted from fields to homesites before then, and a vast amount has been taken over by the ubiquitous "ranch house" since then. If all this land were in one place, say on some coastal plain or in the Central Valley, it would provide space for three or four cities with the area of San Francisco (44.3 square miles). But the regional metropolis that the developers have hastened into being in recent years is strung in relatively narrow strips round the northern and southern arms of the bay, is loosely scattered over some two hundred square miles in the northern Santa Clara Valley, and is strewn haphazardly over eastern Contra Costa County. It is at least eighty miles long from north to south and at its widest point spreads east and west more than forty miles. It has somewhat the form of a thick rubber band, with the bay in the center. Future development will probably extend the metropolis northward and southward.

Desire for Space

The pattern now generally imposed upon the once rural acres reveals the extent to which the dream of home ownership and the desire for space of one's own, even if it be no more than six thousand square feet of land in a "look alike" development, have captured the popular imagination. Many of those who could afford no more than the tract house on its small lot have held the illusion that they were moving from a too-congested urban environment to "the country." With deep nostalgia and romantic notions of success, they have read the tract developer's Sunday advertisements and have overlooked the guile in his query: "Have you ever lived as a country gentleman?" Sometimes the country, with its tree-shaded knolls and its fields of spring wild flowers, has indeed been close by when a family has come into the new "planned community"; but all too often, within a few years the country has receded and the dreamers have awakened fretfully to the reality of an environment that is neither rural nor urban—a vast suburbia of houses constructed from jig-built framing panels and other prefabricated parts. When schools have been overcrowded and recreation centers lacking, when municipal services have been inadequate and taxes high, when monthly payments on the house and on the TV, the car, and the hi-fi set have strained the family budget to the limit, disenchantment has often deepened to despair. But if there is ever a revolt against suburbia, it may take the form of a movement to remodel the suburban scene and way of life rather than a mass migration back to the central city, no matter how handsomely the once blighted city areas may have been redeveloped. Present-day dwellers in the San Francisco Bay Area, as in other large metropolitan regions, are usually only one or two generations removed from the farm and the small town or small city; and the "big city"—the concentrated city of the late nineteenth century and early twentieth century, with its densely built blocks—has never been a place in which they or their parents have felt really at home. The tract development, with all its deficiencies, physical and social, is perhaps a closer approximation of what they want than the older city ever was. Moreover, the urban sprawl, some might say, was almost inevitable, given the automobile and the mass-production techniques of the mid-twentieth century American economy.

This economy, from the time of the Civil War or before, has been generating an awesome capacity to produce. Its corporate enterprise has tended toward giantism and its products toward standardization. Small wonder that urban areas, too, should reflect this bigness and this standardization! For the past four decades they have been shaped by one of the most conspicuous products of this mass-production and mass-distribution economy: the automobile. All suburbia, in the San Francisco Bay Area as elsewhere, depends upon it and could not exist without it. Even if the Bay Area should some day finance and build a mass rapid transit system, large parts of the area would still be dependent upon the automobile.

The freeways that now stretch through the urban belts surrounding the bay and through the valleys filled with tract houses are the expensive progeny of this mechanical invention. In recent years they have been powerful agents of metropolitan growth and dispersion. To be sure, a good deal of tract development preceded the completion of freeways; but every new section of these divided, limited-access superhighways that has been opened to traffic has encouraged further subdivision of farmlands and has, in effect, poured the city out upon the fields.

Since scores of new tracts have been linked to older centers only by freeways, many of these channels of movement have become intolerably congested at morning and evening rush hours. Indeed, some freeways have carried capacity volumes of traffic almost from the day they were completed. Consequently, state highway engineers now emphasize that "it is not realistic to consider that freeways alone will be the answer" to problems of metropolitan transportation. Their plans for additional freeways are predicated on the assumption that rapid transit lines as well as freeways will serve the Bay Area in the future.

In the spring of 1957, state highway engineers reported that they had completed two hundred miles of freeways in the San Francisco Bay Area since World War II. They had plans at the end of 1957 for an additional one hundred miles of freeways and were spending $75,000,000 a year on the construction program in the nine bay coun-

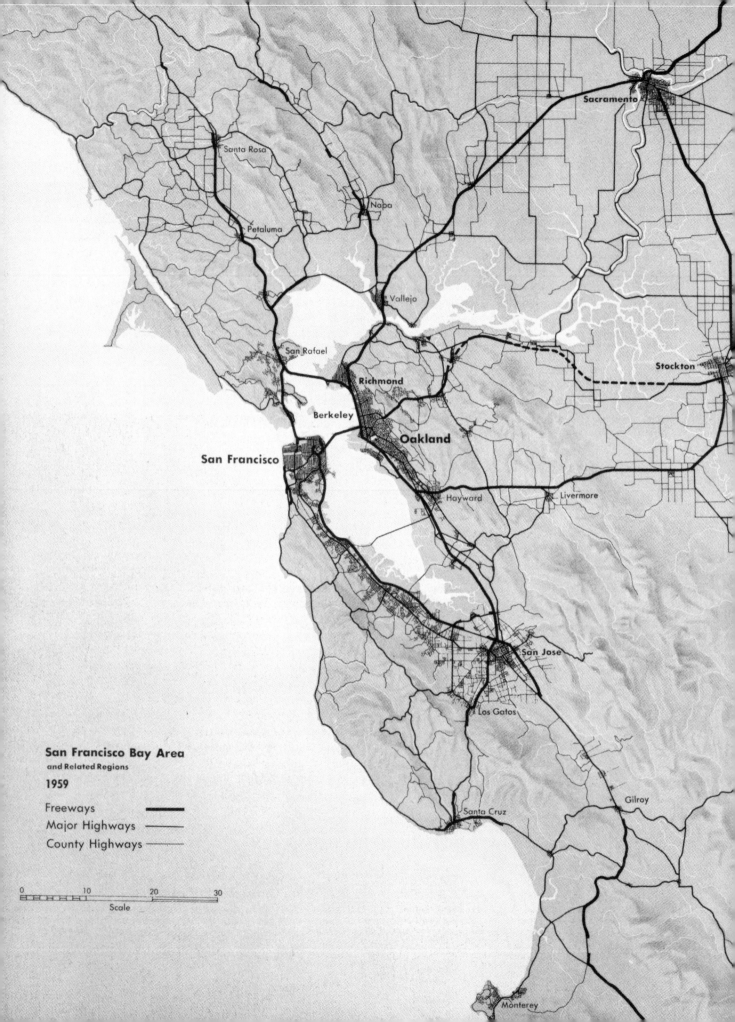

San Francisco Bay Area
and Related Regions

1959

Freeways

Major Highways

County Highways

0   10   20   30
Scale

Santa Rosa

Napa

Petaluma

Vallejo

San Rafael

Richmond

Berkeley

Oakland

San Francisco

Hayward

Livermore

San Jose

Los Gatos

Santa Cruz

Gilroy

Monterey

Sacramento

Stockton

ties, with every expectation that the annual expenditure would increase.

Shopping Centers

A new type of landmark in the outlying areas served by the sweeping freeways is the "regional," or district, shopping center, with its landscaped mall, its department store, specialty shops, and branch bank. The rise of this now-popular retail mecca was foretold by the development of branch stores of San Francisco and Oakland establishments in some of the smaller cities, such as San Mateo, Palo Alto, and San Rafael, even before 1950. The more discerning merchants in the central cities realized at the very beginning of the big suburban expansion that there would be new opportunities to do business in the midst of the tract developments. But the significant change in retail merchandizing in the outlying areas has occurred in the past seven or eight years and has been characterized by the large, planned shopping center.

Like the freeway, the mammoth shopping center is another product of the automobile age; the space allotted to parking is three, four, or five times as great as the floor area of the buildings. Too, the shopping center is peculiarly the symbol of the vast, spread-out tracts, for it consists mostly of one-story structures and reflects, surely much too self-consciously, the "leisurely living" associated with the suburban patio.

One of the first of the new shopping centers, Stonestown, was built not in a typical suburban community but in the Lake Merced Area of San Francisco, near one of

Stonestown Shopping Center, San Francisco. Right: Stonestown Apartments. Upper right: San Francisco State College, with the Park Merced housing project of the Metropolitan Life Insurance Company. Photograph courtesy of State Division of Highways.

the main routes from San Mateo County to the Golden Gate Bridge and Marin County. The developers hoped that it would attract customers not only from near-by neighborhoods but also from residential areas in San Mateo and Marin counties. Opened in 1952, it includes a branch of The Emporium, the largest department store in downtown San Francisco, and branch stores of many other downtown establishments.

Shopping centers similar to Stonestown have since sprung up in Hillsdale near San Mateo, on the extensive grounds of Stanford University near Palo Alto and Menlo Park, on the Stevens Creek Road near the city limits of San Jose and Santa Clara, and at San Leandro, Hayward, El Cerrito, and Walnut Creek. Those at Stanford, El Cerrito, and Walnut Creek have branches of the Emporium-Capwell Company, those at Hillsdale and San Leandro, branches of Macy's. Commercial rivalry, more intense than sound, has given the San Jose–Santa Clara area branch stores of both these retail establishments, in huge shopping centers just across the street from each other.

Besides these several large centers, some of which have sites of fifty or sixty acres and provide parking space for as many as four thousand automobiles, there are many small ones, such as the Boardwalk Shopping Center in Tiburon and the Pala Shopping Center in East San Jose.

Because these new asphalt islands of commerce do solve the retail parking problem, eliminate the conflict between street traffic and pedestrian traffic, bring together at one location a well-selected variety of stores, and offer some of the holiday atmosphere of a fair, they hasten the obsolescence of the older suburban shopping district, with its limited parking facilities and general lack of "glamour." The business districts of Palo Alto and San Jose, for example, have been hurt by the new centers. But these developments have not always been the money-makers that their promoters expected. In time the increase in suburban population may boost the sales of some of those shopping centers that have not yet warranted the faith of investors; but in the meantime, plans for certain additional centers may have been shelved because of the belated realization that a large-scale shopping center must have little or no competition within a trading area inhabited by a hundred thousand to a quarter of a million people. Some of the new centers are simply too close together to be profitable today.

Administrative Offices

The expansion of retail trade in standardized goods in the outlying areas has been accompanied in some places by an increase in professional offices and even by the estab-lishment of administrative offices such as one used to find principally in San Francisco and Oakland. San Mateo, for instance, has attracted a regional office of the General Petroleum Corporation, the West Coast headquarters of the Holly Sugar Corporation, and the headquarters of the Olson steamship company, formerly in San Francisco. A special "professional" zone in Menlo Park includes the editorial offices of Sunset Magazine, which previously were in San Francisco, the offices of several insurance companies, and a Pacific Coast office of the United States Geological Survey. The success of the Menlo Park and San Mateo "executive" and professional zones has been so well publicized, in fact, that it has inspired several other cities to create similar zones in the hope of attracting firms looking for suburban locations.

The site planning and architecture of the establishments in the Menlo Park professional zone explain at a glance why a carefully restricted area in a suburban environment appeals to some companies. Each structure is on a site large enough to provide space for parking the cars of employees, for a variety of game courts, and for terraces and gardens where employees can eat their lunches or take a "breather" in the sunshine. The one- and two-story buildings have a slightly domestic quality and are surrounded by broad lawns, trees, and flowering shrubs. The "decentralized" location has certain kinds of amenities that no metropolitan center can offer.

"Professional and administrative offices may very well become the basic industry of Menlo Park in the future, replacing the harried commuter (who is rapidly becoming less of a predominant figure in Menlo Park)," planning consultants Harold F. Wise and Simon Eisner speculated in their *Master Plan for Menlo Park*, prepared in 1952. "When this day comes, the social, economic, and cultural life of the city and the region will be healthier for it. Living five minutes or less from work will simply mean more time for recreational, educational, and cultural activities; more time to spend with the family; a healthier and more alert citizenry. This certainly should be the aim and end of the economic and social organization of our cities. In the case of Menlo Park, it looks as if an increasingly large number of people will be able to live and work in an environment which will permit the enjoyment of this type of living."[6]

Wise and Eisner had discovered, by means of a sample survey of the residents of Menlo Park made in the summer of 1951, that only 28 per cent of the employed people in the city actually worked in San Francisco. All the others were employed on the Peninsula, and of this group one-half were employed locally, in Menlo Park, Palo Alto, or Redwood City. The survey startled those who had not realized that communities somewhat removed from San Francisco were becoming much less dependent upon it for employment than upon areas close to it.

But the big exodus of top administrative and professional offices from the central cities of the Bay Area that was predicted several years ago has not occurred. A study conducted in 1953 showed that approximately 65 per cent of all firms employing one hundred or more persons and maintaining a single, main administrative office in the Bay Area still had quarters in the central sections of the metropolitan region—central San Francisco, central and northwestern Oakland, Berkeley, and Emeryville.[7] Forty-nine per cent were concentrated in central San Francisco alone, and approximately 17 per cent were clustered within the small "core" known as the financial district. Most of the firms that have shifted their administrative functions from San Francisco to suburban locations have housed them in offices attached to manufacturing plants, warehouses, or transportation terminals. The number of headquarters offices transferred from "the city" to suburban quarters not connected with such facilities is negligible.

The same study did indicate, however, that large firms are selecting suburban locations for certain operations while maintaining their main offices in central areas. Some have established research or accounting offices in the suburbs; others have opened district sales or administrative offices in suburban communities. Only a few have left the sales office in San Francisco or Oakland and moved the regional administrative office to an outlying location.

How many smaller firms have shifted their headquarters from the central cities to suburbia no one knows, for no studies have been made of administrative offices employing fewer than one hundred persons. Whatever the number, these smaller enterprises probably account for a relatively small proportion of the jobs in the territories fifteen to fifty miles from San Francisco and Oakland. The great amount of new employment in these areas is simply the result of metropolitan regional and western growth. Since World War II the school districts in these outlying areas have built hundreds of new schools; private organizations and hospital districts have constructed many new hospitals, and groups of physicians have opened well-equipped clinics; the small cities have expanded their municipal offices and have built new community centers, playgrounds, libraries, and fire stations; and commercial and service enterprises of all sorts have come into being to serve the families in the new tracts and fringe areas. Together with the new manufacturing and wholesale firms in the outlying areas, all these governmental and private establishments employ hundreds of thousands of workers, many of whom live within a few miles of their places of employment.

Problems of Small Cities

Some of the smaller cities struggle desperately to become "balanced" communities, with sufficient industrial and commercial enterprises to provide a high proportion of the jobs needed by their residents. Hayward is an example. In 1952 a high school student who won an annual "Hayward's Future" contest declared that "the men who have moved here with their families and who are still employed in Oakland, Alameda, or even San Francisco do not intend to be commuters forever."[8] But six years later Hayward still was largely a "bedroom" community, 65 per cent of its working people being employed in other cities. Between December, 1952, and May, 1956, its land area had increased, through fifty-nine annexations, from approximately thirty-one hundred acres to more than fifty-seven hundred acres; but almost all the territory annexed had been developed with single-family residences or was committeed to such development. Endeavoring to correct the "imbalance" in the growth of the city, the city council in 1957 succeeded in bringing into the city through further annexations sixteen hundred gross acres of potential industrial property, as well as nine square miles of tideland property belonging to the Leslie Salt Company. The newly annexed areas included several manufacturing plants, and various companies had plans for building factories within the new industrial zones. Hayward thus has hopes of expanding local job opportunities and of shortening, for a greater number of its residents, the long journey to work; but its fiscal situation remains especially trying.

The average new house in the Hayward Area is assessed at $2,500 and returns (if the owner is not a veteran) about $225 a year in taxes for all services provided by the city, the county, the schools, and various special districts; but the cost of educating one elementary school child is in excess of $200 a year. If the schools did not receive substantial amounts of state aid, the governmental units in the Hayward Area would be under even greater financial strain than they are at present.

Cities in many other parts of the Bay Area, especially in San Mateo County, have the same problems as Hayward. Hard pressed to find the tax revenues to build schools and other community facilities and to employ teachers, school nurses, recreation directors, librarians, sanitarians, and engineers, they compete for industries, warehouses, research laboratories, publishing houses, and other establishments that would swell their lean tax rolls.

Although these widespread efforts to cope with skyrocketing local tax rates have contributed to a more general distribution of employment in the Bay Area, they have not necessarily given every community a well-selected group of industries or resulted in the most desirable distribution of industries throughout the metropolitan region. Some municipalities that might have been happier without any industries at all have sought industries; others that had sites and installed utilities to accommodate many new plants perhaps have not enjoyed the industrial development that they should have had.

New Municipalities

Even though many municipalities with few enterprises of high assessed valuation have faced financial difficulties, since World War II several unincorporated residential areas in the bay counties have voted to incorporate. Among them are Campbell, Saratoga, Monte Sereno, Los Altos, Los Altos Hills, and Milpitas in Santa Clara County, Fremont and Union City in Alameda County, and Pacifica and Woodside in San Mateo County. Of these new cities, the three on the eastern side of the bay— Milpitas, Fremont, and Union City, appear to have the best possibilities for balanced development, since all three have large amounts of potential industrial land near freeways and railroads. Union City includes Decoto, Alvarado, and neighboring areas.

Monte Sereno, Los Altos Hills, and Woodside, a socially exclusive community that wished to avoid being annexed to Redwood City or Atherton, seem to be less concerned with the quality of local governmental services than with maintaining a certain detachment. Community identity is a value highly prized by some of the other communities also, but they are concerned with being cities in the true sense of the word rather than municipalized bits of the semiurban fringe area. When the residents of five small but growing towns in Washington Township in Alameda County—Mission San Jose, Niles, Irvington, Centerville, and Warm Springs—considered banding together to form the city of Fremont, they hoped eventually to assure themselves of better services than they could obtain from county government or from overlapping special districts. But the opportunity to transform seventeen thousand acres of farmland and five small towns into a well-planned city, with adequate schools, recreation areas, libraries, police and fire services, and sanitary facilities, was an even greater incentive to incorporation. And the citizens of Fremont soon demonstrated that their goal was a genuine city. Asked by their planning consultant whether they wanted a city that would be mainly a further development of five separate communities or a city that would express its unity through the development of an

important center of governmental, commercial, and cultural activities at approximately the geographic center of the newly incorporated territory, they said they preferred the latter.

The same desire to control development and to pool financial and civic resources for the common good seems to have motivated the formation of Pacifica, on the coastal side of San Mateo County. The communities of Linda Mar, Sharp Park, Edgemar, Westview, Pacific Manor, Rockaway Beach, Fairway Park, Vallemar, and Pedro Point were merely so many subdivisions and towns until they merged in 1957 as a single municipality. Now the twenty thousand people who live within the twelve square miles embraced by Pacifica have the opportunity to create a city that will be more than the sum of many parts, difficult as that will be without the industries and some of the larger service enterprises needed to provide tax revenue.

Like Fremont and Pacifica, most of the other new municipalities are an expression of faith in an urban way of life. Their residents are determined to provide, in areas that are still under development, all those facilities and services associated with urban living. As the cities mature, all parts of the Bay Area suitable for intensive development will offer a reasonably high quality of city-type services; and there will be few areas in which local democratic self-government does not provide the means for improving the immediate physical environment. But the governmental mechanism for guiding the growth and development of the entire Bay Area is still lacking.

A full-circle examination of the San Francisco Bay Area reveals that the former highly centralized metropolitan region developed in the heyday of the steam train and the electric railway has been drastically revised by the state highway engineers who design and build freeways, manufacturers in search of large sites, tract house developers supported by federal mortgage insurance policies, financiers with money to invest in shopping centers, and county assessors who have assessed farmland as potential subdivision acreage and have thereby forced the farmer to sell his holdings. The regional metropolis that now almost encircles the bay still has strong centers in San Francisco and Oakland and older subcenters such as Santa Rosa and San Jose, but elsewhere it is no more than loosely polarized. Even in suburban communities some dispersion of trade and service establishments is taking place in accordance with the trend in the entire Bay Area toward a broader distribution of economic activities. The creation of planned industrial parks and planned shopping centers has not everywhere prevented the scatteration of industries and stores. The strip commercial develop-

The Central Business District of San Francisco. James Lick Skyway in the foreground. Photograph courtesy of State Division of Highways.

ment still flourishes, and industrial zones are perhaps more widespread than might be desirable. In short, the Bay Area is in a transitional stage; its ultimate form is unpredictable until its residents make some important decisions, one of which is whether they wish to depend in the future entirely upon freeways for transportation or are willing to finance and build a regional transit system that might induce the development of fairly concentrated commercial and cultural centers at a limited number of station stops.

The Central Cities

In the meantime, the cities in the geographical center of the Bay Area struggle with problems inherited from the past and with new problems thrust upon them by the enormous growth of the outlying areas. Both San Francisco and Oakland have large blighted areas in which the houses are old and in disrepair and the school sites and recreation areas inadequate by present-day standards. Both cities have central business districts in which the streets are congested and the off-street parking facilities are as yet insufficient to meet peak demands. Reasonably efficient in an earlier period when traffic consisted of horse-drawn vehicles and streetcars in which almost all workers and shoppers rode, these streets at rush hours become clotted with the automobiles pouring out from garages and parking lots. Although San Francisco has sought by various means to improve its municipally owned transit system, private use of the automobile has increased and patronage of the "Muni" has steadily declined. Oakland and its neighbor Berkeley have had their troubles with an ailing privately owned transit system that has been shunned by greater and greater numbers of passengers until its ability to render service has been severely impaired. Freeways built by the state engineers through San Francisco and Oakland have relieved certain streets of much of the traffic that previously used them, but freeways have removed huge amounts of private property from municipal tax rolls and have displaced many businesses and homeowners. More accessible to outlying areas because of these costly arteries, the central cities are better able to serve the entire Bay Area, but not in the same ways that they once did. Their retail and wholesale trade in standardized goods is relatively less important, their trade in specialized goods even more important than heretofore. Their roles as cultural and amusement centers and as centers of finance and administration have been enhanced; but they cannot capitalize fully on the advantages of central location until they clear away blight, modernize their central business districts, improve parking facilities and transit (including regional transit), and offer the beauty and splendor expected in the heart of a regional metropolis as famous as New York and Paris.

San Francisco is burdened with approximately nine square miles of residences that are blighted or threatened with blight—at least one-half the area occupied by residences. Besides these run-down residential sections, the city has several blighted industrial and commercial areas, such as the old wholesale produce district just east of the financial district and certain parts of the area south of Market Street. All represent a continual drain upon the local treasury in the excessive amount of municipal services they require. All present formidable economic problems, and those of the blighted residential areas that have become ghettos of racial minorities present social problems that affect the entire Bay Area. As long as the outer sections of the metropolitan region erect discriminatory barriers against Negroes and other nonwhite families, the difficulties of relocating the tenants of areas slated for redevelopment will increase and the struggle of the city to free itself from blight will be prolonged. The more protracted the efforts of the city to renew itself, the longer it will be in developing the new business and cultural facilities and services needed to serve the whole Bay Area

Shock—and Action

San Francisco was one of the first cities in California to advocate passage of the Community Redevelopment Law enacted by the state legislature in 1945. Its leading citizens had been profoundly shocked by the revelation that the city had made no population gains in the 'thirties, while the suburbs had grown markedly. These citizens had accepted the thesis that if the city was to survive, it would have to clear and rebuild the old, decayed areas and make them even more alluring than the suburbs. Through its department of city planning the city therefore mapped its blighted areas and made a pilot study of the possibilities of redeveloping the Western Addition—two years before Congress passed the Housing Act of 1949, providing for loans and grants to assist cities in clearing blighted areas and preparing such areas for resale or lease to private enterprise.

In 1948 the San Francisco Board of Supervisors officially designated the Western Addition (280 blocks) a blighted area and "activated" a redevelopment agency to undertake a project in the district. The members of the agency realized that redevelopment would be a lengthy process, but they nevertheless entertained some illusory hopes that they would make more rapid progress than they actually did. Evidence of this is their reaction to the acute housing shortage of the postwar period. They viewed it as one of the chief obstacles to their plans for redeveloping the Western Addition, since the law required that before deteriorated buildings could be cleared, the families living in them would have to be relocated. The most urgent course therefore seemed to be to develop new housing elsewhere in the city to house at least some of the families who would be displaced; however, the housing shortage that then appeared so large a hindrance to redevelopment was to lessen before the agency could begin demolishing substandard buildings. Since the members of the agency did not foresee this, they turned their attention to a nearly vacant section of the city known as Diamond Heights, situated almost in the geographical center of the city but long arrested in its development by a pattern of streets wholly inappropriate to the hilly terrain. Indeed, some streets existed only on city maps and had never actually been laid out, because the grades would have been excessive. The staff of the agency and consultant architects began preparing a plan for this blighted area, meanwhile continuing work on plans for redeveloping a number of blocks along Geary Street in the Western Addition.

Plan for Diamond Heights

The plan for the arrested Diamond Heights area envisions a unique new neighborhood housing twenty-three hundred families. The streets in the area are to be properly related to the contours of the land; the residential sections are to include a wide variety of dwelling types: single-family detached houses, step-down apartments on the steeper slopes, tall apartment houses with balconies for each family on the scenic eminences in the area. Ample sites will be provided for schools, playgrounds, shopping centers, and churches.

The tentative plan for Diamond Heights was issued in the fall of 1951 and was revised in March, 1952. In that same month the redevelopment agency published its preliminary plan for the Geary area in the Western Addition. But subsequent events proved that the preparation of plans is the least difficult part of the redevelopment process. "The law's delay" became the bane of the redevelopment program. A test case involving the constitutionality of the California Redevelopment Law moved slowly through the courts and was not adjudicated by the United States Supreme Court until December, 1954, when the high tribunal upheld the California statute by refusing to review a decision in which the Supreme Court of California had approved the law.

Not until January, 1956, did the Housing and Home

Proposed Redevelopment of Diamond Heights, San Francisco. Perspective drawing by Vernon De Mars, A.I.A., for the San Francisco Redevelopment Agency.

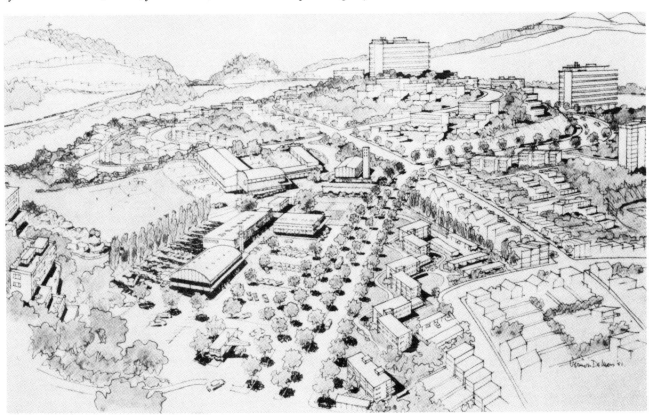

Finance Agency of the federal government approve a loan and a capital grant to assist the San Francisco Redevelopment Agency in redeveloping the 325 acres of Diamond Heights. And not until May, 1956, did the San Francisco Board of Supervisors accept the final plan for redeveloping twenty-eight blocks in the Western Addition, thereby clearing the way for federal financial assistance to the project. At that time the redevelopment agency estimated, perhaps optimistically, that it would take five years to acquire properties in the area, to clear deteriorated structures, and to prepare the land for re-use by private enterprise. Two years later the agency still had not obtained possession of all 604 properties required for the Diamond Heights project, because of condemnation suits. The San Francisco Redevelopment Agency now estimates that it will not be able to sell the land in Diamond Heights to builders until 1961 or to dispose of some of the cleared land in the Geary area until 1960.

The Golden Gateway

Controversy, financial troubles, and delays have marked the progress of another redevelopment project in San Francisco—the Golden Gateway development that would replace the unsanitary wholesale produce market area. In this project many of the issues that beset a central city endeavoring to adjust to metropolitan change have come into focus. Because the Golden Gateway lies directly east of the financial district and will be penetrated by an off-ramp of the Embarcadero Freeway, it is strategically situated to demonstrate ways in which a central city can serve the metropolitan region, and even more than the metropolitan region—the whole West and even lands overseas. Here could be housed an impressive array of administrative offices, financial institutions, export and import companies, and public relations and advertising agencies. Here, too, could be developed elevator apartments for executives and for some of the office workers who now commute long distances to their jobs in downtown San Francisco. Near by, in the vicinity of the Ferry Building, parks and a waterfront recreation area could be created that would be attractive to tourists and visitors, despite the aesthetic blight inflicted on the area by a ponderous elevated freeway. All this the plans prepared by architectural consultants propose; but governmental red tape, lack of coördination among government agencies, and disagreements among public officials, produce firms, and civic groups have plagued the redevelopment scheme. Further, officials of the redevelopment agency discovered, after plans for a twenty-six-block area had been prepared, that eight blocks would have to be eliminated from the first phase of the project so that tower apartments would cover more than half of the total area of the project, in accordance with the federal requirement that slightly more than half of an area not previousuly in residential use be allocated for such use in the future. In the meantime, private capital that might have been used to rebuild the decaying blocks in the produce area has gone into huge new office buildings all around them, to the great alarm of public officials, who fear that the new structures will provide so much additional office space that there will be only a limited market for space in the redevelopment project.

The apprehension of proponents of the Golden Gateway may not be justified, for San Francisco lies at the heart of a metropolitan region that may have eight million or more residents by the end of the century. With far-sighted leadership, the city could become even more important than it is today as a financial, cultural, and tourist center; but that kind of leadership has been lacking, as witness various failures attending the effort to redevelop the produce market area.

In 1955 a plan for simultaneously removing the commission merchants to South Basin and redeveloping the old produce district fell through, chiefly for financial reasons. The redevelopment agency had never asked the city to vote a bond issue to create a redevelopment revolving fund that might have provided the money to buy the South Basin area and to purchase the properties of the market operators, who insisted on being assured fair value for their old quarters before they would commit themselves to move.

In something of a revival of the spirit exhibited in 1904 and 1905 when James D. Phelan and other wealthy men financed the Burnham Plan, a committee headed by J. D. Zellerbach and Charles R. Blyth rescued the Golden Gateway project in 1956 by providing funds to the budget-starved city planning department for the development of site plans. Yet after the plans prepared by the architectural firm of Skidmore, Owings and Merrill had been released in 1957, downtown groups in San Francisco took a stand that threatened to cut off federal financial aid to the project. Real-estate and business associations balked at proposals of the city planning department to limit floor space in downtown office buildings, so that the redevelopment project would be protected from future congestion and from undue competition of high buildings in the surrounding blocks. Only when the federal government insisted upon density controls did they grudgingly accept regulations that were more liberal than those originally proposed by the planning department.

Lack of Leadership

Apologists for the San Francisco redevelopment program cite various reasons for its halting pace: the many plans, public hearings, and approvals required by the California law, bureaucratic deliberateness in Washington, D.C., in the early stages of the program, resistance of property owners, rising costs that have necessitated revisions in plans, and political friction stemming from the fact that the redevelopment agency is a creature of the state rather than a department of the municipal government.

Hindrances imposed by state legislation, cumbersome federal procedures, and inflationary costs are, however, problems which cities throughout the United States also have had to deal with; and in spite of such problems, several cities that were slower than San Francisco in initiating redevelopment programs have already completed some projects. A visiting city planner from Philadelphia pointed out in March, 1959, that San Francisco could have proceeded more rapidly if its elected officials had displayed less "hostility and skepticism toward city planning," if its redevelopment agency had organized a "crash" program, and if more citizens had supported the effort to rid the city of blight.[9]

San Francisco wishes to remain an influential center in a great metropolitan region; yet most of its public officials and many of its business executives display no genuine civic leadership. The office-building boom in the lower Market Street area is evidence of the economic vitality of the city. The construction of new hotels and

Model of Proposed Golden Gateway, Redevelopment Area E, San Francisco. Ferry Building and Embarcadero Freeway in the foreground. Photograph courtesy of Skidmore, Owings and Merrill, Architects, and Kurt Bank, photographer.

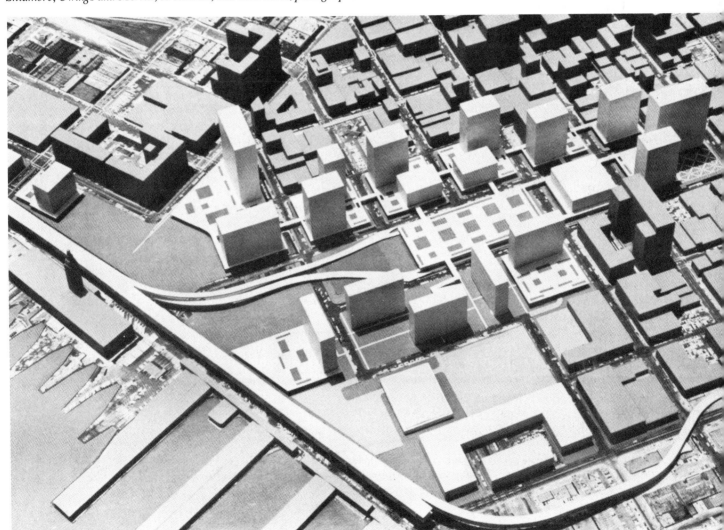

Model of the Crown Zellerbach Corporation Headquarters Office Building, San Francisco. Hertzka & Knowles and Skidmore, Owings & Merrill, Architects. Copyright photograph by Morley Baer.

motels and a host of proposals for better convention facilities, more tourist attractions, and additional parks are evidence that there is an awareness of the increasing importance of San Francisco as a recreation center. But the famed beauty of the city is eroding in some places, and some parts of the central business district are growing cheap and shabby. Market Street west of Powell is a confusion of neon signs and sleazy displays. Oversize billboards blot out the view of the downtown skyline from the James Lick Skyway. South of Market Street new motels wedged in among the warehouses and factories look as out of place as gentlemen in morning coats among workers in overalls. Opportunities to create shopping and hotel-entertainment areas with inviting pedestrian malls, occasional green spaces, and perhaps outdoor sculpture and fountains, such as one sees in some of the suburban shopping centers, go unheeded while inept politicians continue the boast that San Francisco is "the city that knows how." That was what President Taft said more than forty years ago, but it is no longer true. The city flounders in smugness and indecision, ignores the need for a bold, imaginative program to prepare it for a new role in a Bay Area that will have twice the present population in thirty or forty years. San Francisco should scrap the rickety charter that was patched together in 1932 and should provide itself with a form of government adapted to the demands of a new age. Its board of supervisors should increase the budget of the city planning department, to enable it to complete and publish a general plan that the city can follow in reorganizing the uses of land within its boundaries and in conserving its natural and man-made beauties. But little will be gained by completing the plan that has been many years in preparation unless political leaders will utilize it to the full and will seek the advice of the city planners who developed it. San Francisco needs, above all, policy makers who can inspire its citizens to determine their civic goals, to draw up a program for achieving them, and to pursue that program consistently until San Francisco again has stature and a deserved reputation among the cities of America.

Renewal in Oakland

Much slower than San Francisco in attacking the problem of blight, Oakland did not begin to develop any kind of urban renewal program until 1955. A few years earlier the apartment-house interests in the city had taken the lead in defeating a proposal for the construction of additional public housing projects and had created a political climate in which even redevelopment proposals were regarded with suspicion. A Citizens Committee for Urban Renewal appointed in 1954 necessarily proceeded cautiously in its efforts to awaken the community to the need for action. Many residents were unwilling to believe that their own neighborhoods were threatened with blight and to concede that more than one-tenth of the residential area of the city was so seriously deteriorated as to require replanning and a large amount of clearance and rebuilding. The committee went no further at first than to recommend the appointment of an urban renewal coördinator to investigate the possibilities of a rehabilitation program in the Clinton Park area on the east side of Lake Merritt, an old but only partly blighted section.

The investigations of the coördinator, Fred H. Squires, Jr., gradually revealed that if the city wished to undertake a full-scale program of urban renewal it would need both a redevelopment agency to clear slums and a department of urban renewal to enforce housing laws and induce property owners in neighborhoods threatened with blight to improve, repair, and modernize their houses and apartments. The Oakland City Council appointed the members of the redevelopment agency in the fall of 1956, and in February, 1957, established an Urban Renewal Department. Squires became the executive director of both new agencies.

As expected, the city launched its first rehabilitation program in the Clinton Park area. City departments and the board of education spent approximately five hundred thousand dollars in the area on public works and received almost twice as much as that from the federal government, under the liberal provisions of the Housing Act of 1954, for the expansion of an elementary school site and other needed public improvements. Real-estate and financial groups assisted the rehabilitation program by establishing the Oakland Renewal Foundation, Inc., to provide advice and services to property owners that the city was not legally empowered to offer.

In the fall of 1957 the city council further strengthened the renewal effort by enacting a housing code with provisions somewhat more detailed and exacting than those of the State Housing Act previously enforced in Oakland. To administer the new code, the council created a unified department of building and safety.

The decision to undertake a succession of projects that would transform the two hundred and fifty blocks of West Oakland into new industrial zones and attractive residential areas within a decade was perhaps the high point in the municipal effort to lift Oakland from the deadly mediocrity that has characterized it in recent decades. In 1957 the Housing and Home Finance Agency of the federal government allocated $64,000 to the city for planning studies in West Oakland, and at the same time the agency earmarked $1,800,000 as a federal contribution toward the cost of clearing and preparing a first project area of twenty-five blocks for redevelopment by private enterprise.

Oakland faces many controversies as it strives to renew blighted West Oakland. The area is inhabited mainly by low-income Negro families, whom it will be difficult to relocate unless additional public housing projects are developed; yet many interests in Oakland at present oppose any expansion of public housing. The federal government will not approve redevelopment of the area exclusively for Negro occupancy; hence other neighborhoods in Oakland will have to be opened to Negro families who are displaced by other groups. Certain business interests will undoubtedly advocate high land coverage and high population densities in the area, whereas other groups will contend that the city must provide recreation areas and a good deal of open space in the redeveloped neighborhoods and must limit population densities to an average of not more than one hundred persons to the acre in the greater part of the district, as the city planning commission recommends.

Goals for Oakland

The preliminary general plan prepared by Oakland's city planning commission in 1957 and officially adopted by the city council in 1959 suggests public improvements and changes in the physical organization of the city that would enable it to achieve an importance, commercially, industrially, and culturally, far greater than if it sought to serve largely its own residents. The plan seeks to enhance the position of Oakland as part of the regional center by assuring fast, safe, efficient movement between the city and other parts of the Bay Area, by concentrating and intensifying activities within its central business district, by increasing its industrial space by nearly three thousand acres, and by developing city-wide parks, museums, and other cultural facilities that would attract people from many parts of the Bay Area. Significantly, the plan suggests that one of the goals of Oakland should be "to achieve a high standard of beauty in all future development"—a forthright advocacy of quality in civic enterprises that has been almost entirely lacking in city planning reports for several decades.

Oakland city planners foresee an increase in the population of the city from approximately four hundred thousand at present to half a million by 1980. To provide for the social needs of a population of that size, Oakland will need sixty-five neighborhood centers and twenty-two community centers that combine schools, parks, and playgrounds, the general plan states. Each neighborhood center would serve five to six thousand people, each community center twenty to twenty-five thousand people. Eventually more than seven hundred acres will have to be added to the five hundred now occupied by schools in Oakland if the standards proposed for the neighborhood and community centers are to be met.

In suggesting a strengthening of the central business district of Oakland, the planning commission expects no expansion of the area of this East Bay hub, since much of it is not intensively developed. Rather, the commission believes that "concentration will result in efficiency and convenience and can also increase the glamour and excitement characteristic of the downtown areas of big cities."[10] But the professional staff of the commission recognizes that streets in the downtown area must be free from congestion. The general plan realistically proposes a ring of major streets surrounding the central business district which will funnel traffic from freeways and major streets into well-situated parking garages and parking lots. Also, the plan recognizes that without a regional rapid transit system, downtown Oakland can no more hope to function effectively as part of a regional center than can downtown San Francisco. Essential features of the system proposed by the San Francisco Bay Area Rapid Transit Commission in 1956 have been incorporated into the city plan, with slight modifications.

Soon after this carefully prepared plan was issued, the staff of the city planning commission initiated studies of the central business district, to determine what could be done to transform this far from "glamorous" area into the kind of center described in the comprehensive plan. The planners were encouraged in their task by the fact that several tall buildings had risen in downtown Oakland in the past few years, including the First Western Building, a slim structure of blue enameled steel panels. Moreover, just as they began their labors, Henry J. Kaiser signed the final contracts for construction of the twenty-eight-story building on the western shore of Lake Merritt that will be headquarters for his industrial empire. Between the lake and the buildings concentrated near the city hall, the planners envisioned still more skyscrapers, and near the lake some tower apartments to house executives and professional people.

Whether Oakland in time becomes the well-planned and beautiful city that its city planners think it is capable of becoming will depend on the kind of leadership it develops. In the period 1905–1915 Oakland had great civic spirit and accomplished much. Since then it has grown industrially and commercially and has become an important port, but it has achieved little distinction. Except for Lake Merritt and a few sections in the hills, it is an uninspiring city. But it has great potentialities, as the

Kaiser Center, Overlooking Lake Merritt, Oakland. Left: The Central Business District of Oakland. Photograph courtesy of Kaiser Industries Corporation.

preliminary general plan suggests. Moreover, certain developments of recent years indicate the opportunities for civic achievement. The decaying warehouses and commercial buildings that formerly crowded around the foot of Broadway have been replaced by the colorful restaurants of Jack London Square, a waterfront mecca perpetuating the name of a writer who first learned about sailing ships and the romance of distant lands as a roustabout on the docks along the Estuary. An outstanding park department has imaginatively redesigned many of the parks in the city and has brought Oakland fame throughout the nation. If the residents of the city enlarge their perspective to view it as one part of a central complex in a regional metropolis, and if they adopt broad, courageous programs for improving its residential, commercial, and industrial areas, Oakland a quarter of a century hence, or even ten years from now, can enjoy prestige that it has never known.

Regional Problems

Overshadowing the problems faced by individual cities and counties are the still larger problems confronting the entire Bay Area: pollution of the bay and of the skies above the area; decline of transit services throughout the nine bay counties; limited sources of water supply in many of the outer sections where further development should take place; disagreement on methods of reserving land for industrial use; the lack of plans for unified development of the bay; the threatened loss of open spaces that would be suitable for inclusion in a system of metropolitan regional parks or for uses now unforeseen; the possibility of further destruction of the scenic beauties of the area through ill-considered development; the difficulty of coördinating the physical planning being done by cities, counties, special districts, the state and federal governments, and by private enterprise; and the lack of some form of metropolitan government to establish policy on matters affecting the entire area and to carry out physical improvements in accordance with policy decisions.

With the exception of the problem of atmospheric pollution and possibly the problem of reserving open space, these are not new problems. The Regional Plan Association of the 1920's was aware of most of them. The rapid growth and development of the past twenty years has, however, intensified the problems. And at the same time the residents of the Bay Area have begun to realize as they never did before that the problems are interrelated, because life in the present-day metropolitan region is inevitably all of a piece. The same factory that pollutes the bay may also pollute the atmosphere. The wastes that foul the waters of the bay imperil fish, and when fish die sportsmen curse and cannery operators see their livelihood endangered. A subdivision on watershed lands that might have been used for a regional park not only robs a large urban population of needed recreation space, it also creates fiscal problems for the municipality that annexes it if that municipality is already lacking in commercial and industrial establishments of high assessed valuation. The freeway that slices through wooded hills to speed commuters and shoppers on their way funnels problems of congestion into the very heart of the central city. The dump truck that deposits fill on a tideland marsh to create sites for factories deprives cranes and herons of a refuge—and city children of an opportunity to become acquainted with some of nature's creatures. Indeed, the quality of life in any one city or county depends, in ways that are often difficult to comprehend, upon the quality of life in all the other Bay Area communities.

Since World War II, the Bay Area has given greatest attention to the problems of air and water pollution, to the need for safeguarding suitable lands for industry, and to problems of regional circulation, as witness the controversies over the routes of freeways and the arguments over a proposed rapid transit system. Although the approach to each of these problems has been separate, as if each one in no way impinged on the others, a more and more audible chorus just offstage has been asserting that the problems are all aspects of the one big problem of

making the area livable for the millions now here and for the millions expected in the future. Recently some leading businessmen have even emerged from the wings to speak of the need for metropolitan government to deal with all these area-wide problems, whereas only ten years ago some of these gentlemen would have considered all talk of metropolitan government utopian.

Pollution in the Bay

At the end of World War II almost all the cities and sanitary districts in the territory immediately surrounding the bay were defiling its waters. The bay was, in fact, a vast sinkhole, so contaminated along the San Francisco waterfront that Aquatic Park was closed to swimmers, so saturated with polluting materials along the East Bay shore that the tidal mud flats stank, and so poisoned with cannery wastes and human excreta below Dumbarton Strait that ducks inhabiting the tidal marshes could no longer serve as food. But the Bay Area was not unique among California urban regions in having a pollution problem. Every other area that had felt the impact of wartime migration worried about polluted beaches or rivers or underground water. When the State Board of Public Health decided to revoke, as of January 1, 1947, all permits for disposal of raw, untreated sewage into any of the waters of the state, the Bay Area faced the same necessity for action that all other populous areas in California faced.

The central cities in the Bay Area had long been conscious of the problem and had been making plans to construct trunk sewers and large sewage treatment plants. They were the first to act. San Francisco enlarged its Richmond-Sunset Sewage Treatment Plant, which handled about one-third of the sewage of the city, built a huge plant at North Point to serve almost the entire eastern part of the city, and constructed still another plant in the vicinity of Islais Creek to serve the southeastern section of the city. Special District No. 1 of the East Bay Municipal Utility District (serving Alameda, Albany, Berkeley, Emeryville, Oakland, and Piedmont) constructed a single large sewage treatment plant near the eastern end of the San Francisco–Oakland Bay Bridge, with an outfall for the discharge of effluent into the deep waters of the bay.

While these huge treatment plants and trunk line sewers connecting with them were still under construction, the state legislature in 1949 made comprehensive changes in the state laws controlling water pollution. The new legislation authorized nine regional pollution control boards, including one in the Bay Area, and a state board with power to correct conditions should the regional boards fail to do their duty.

In November, 1949, the governor appointed the members of the regional board for the Bay Area. Ten years later the executive officer for this board reported that in the period 1950–1959, cities, sanitary districts, the state and federal governments, and private industries had completed, put into construction, or financed facilities for the treatment of sewage and industrial waste, in the San Francisco Bay Area, costing more than $130,000,000. Only a few small communities had taken no steps to provide adequate treatment of their wastes. Every large community had responded to the proddings of the board, though some had just begun to build the necessary facilities.

But not all residents of the Bay Area were satisfied with the progress report of the regional water pollution control board. Sportsmen, commercial fisheries, and conservationists, especially, accused it of being "soft" on some of the larger industries that discharge noxious waste products into the bay. An official of the State Department of Public Health asserted that the board did not have "enough authority" under the 1949 act to prevent certain types of pollution;[12] and the executive director of the board complained that he was handicapped by the lack of a research program.[13] Critics of the regional board have suggested that its budget and staff be augmented and its powers strengthened.

Air Pollution Control

The vigor with which residents of the more populous sections of the Bay Area have attacked the problem of air pollution contrasts with their apathy toward the problem of reducing pollution of the bay. Rather than allow atmospheric pollution to become as serious as it is in the Los Angeles Area, political and civic leaders in the more heavily industrialized cities and counties of the Bay Area sought authority from the state legislature to establish an air pollution control district embracing the entire metropolitan region. The act introduced by Assemblyman (later Senator) Richard J. Dolwig of San Mateo County at the 1955 session of the legislature permits all nine counties of the Bay Area to join the district, although initially only the six central and southern counties banded together to form a district. Napa, Sonoma, and Solano counties still remain outside the district but may be included later at their own request.

The district opened the first phase of a long-term campaign to control air pollution when its administrator, Benjamin Linsky, announced on October 1, 1956, that in about three months open rubbish fires would be banned throughout the six counties. The chief targets of this prohibition were the city dumps at various points along the shoreline of the bay, all of which sent skyward thick black columns of smoke. Immediately there were protests from many municipalities. Loudest of all were those from the East Bay cities, some of whose mayors and city managers talked as if they had never observed the layers of filthy air that settled over the bay on warm, windless days. Reasonable but firm, the district extended the time during which the cities and operators of private dumps were to make other arrangements for disposing of refuse and garbage. It set October 1, 1957, as the deadline for compliance with its ban; but in the meantime, to show that it intended to use its authority, it appointed a three-man administrative "court" to hear charges against violators.

Most of the municipalities resorted to the fill-and-cover method of getting rid of refuse before the deadline. Forty-six wrecking firms and dump operators in San Francisco resisted through various legal maneuvers, then finally capitulated under threats of prosecution by the district attorney or were forced by court injunctions to cease open-burning operations. On February 4, 1959, when the Superior Court of San Francisco issued a preliminary injunction against one of the most stubborn contenders for the privilege of polluting the air, Control Officer Linsky was able to tell his board of directors, "As far as we know, the last dump fire is out!"[14]

The problem of ending open burning on agricultural land is, however, still under study. Scientists of the University of California are coöperating with the district in an attempt to solve the problem of disposing of fungus-diseased fruit-wood clippings and other farm rubbish otherwise than by burning.

Throughout the early months of 1959 the staff of the district was at work on a second regulation, designed to control emissions from industrial processes, incinerators (other than those used by occupants of one- and two-family dwellings), and heating and power plants. The district also plans to regulate automotive exhausts as soon as automobile manufacturers develop a practicable and satisfactory device for consuming emissions from motor vehicles, now among the chief producers of smog. And by 1963 or 1964 the district hopes to prohibit the use of small incinerators and the burning of rubbish in back yards.

Leaders interested in the eventual establishment of some form of metropolitan government in the Bay Area find the governing board of the air pollution control district an especially provocative example of an area-wide policy-making body. Each of the six counties included in the district is represented by two members: a county supervisor, who serves mainly as a spokesman for unincorporated areas, and a member of one of the city coun-

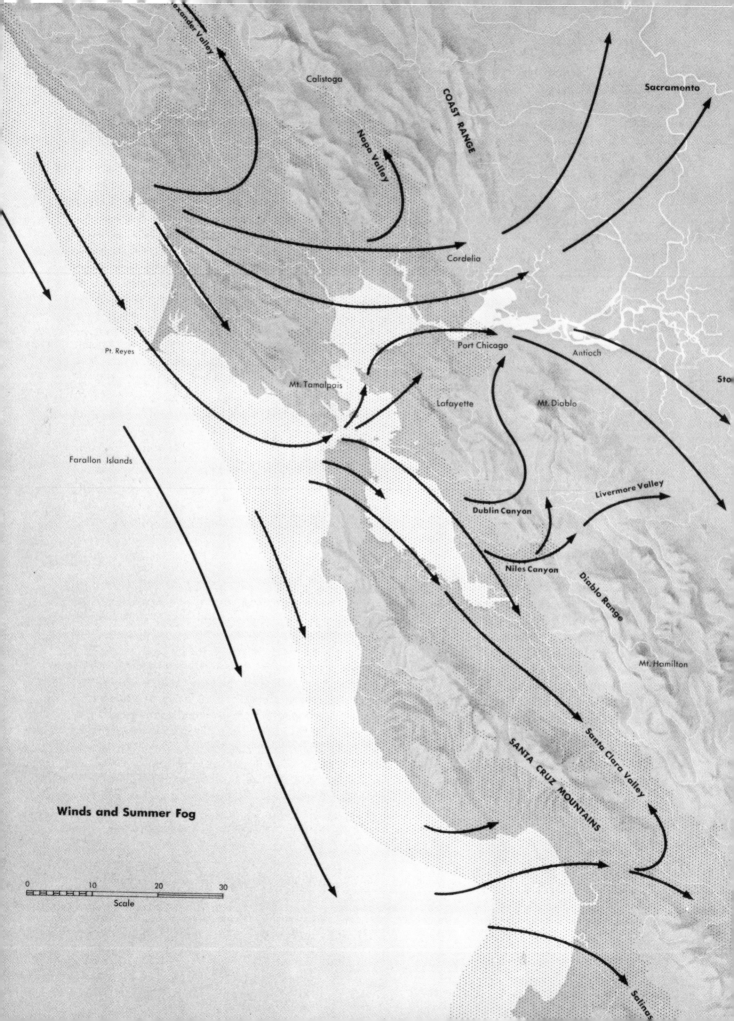

Winds and Summer Fog

Alexander Valley
Calistoga
COAST RANGE
Sacramento
Napa Valley
Cordelia
Port Chicago
Antioch
Sto
Pt. Reyes
Mt. Tamalpais
Lafayette
Mt. Diablo
Farallon Islands
Livermore Valley
Dublin Canyon
Niles Canyon
Diablo Range
Santa Clara Valley
Mt. Hamilton
SANTA CRUZ MOUNTAINS
Salinas

Scale
0   10   20   30

cils in the county, who presumably expresses the urban view on matters of policy. The composition of this board, the proponents of metropolitan government point out, suggests one way of representing cities and counties in any federation that might be created to handle several matters of area-wide concern.

Reservation of Land

Unlike the problems of controlling air pollution and water pollution, which have become the responsibilities of regional boards, the problem of reserving land for various purposes, including land that will be needed for future industrial expansion, remains the concern of city and county governments, with a few significant exceptions. The East Bay Regional Park District is a subregional governmental unit interested in adding to the land reserves available for recreation in the East Bay. The state government, through its Division of Beaches and Parks, likewise has responsibilities for safeguarding shoreline, mountain, and riverbank lands in the Bay Area that would be valuable for recreational use of all Californians. But there is as yet no agency empowered to provide a metropolitan regional recreation system for the entire Bay Area; nor is there any board or district authorized to preserve open space as a necessary regional resource— open space to be used permanently for agriculture, or for future atomic installations, or for industry, or for developments now altogether unforeseen. The swift obliteration of fields and orchards has, however, prompted some city planners and political scientists to suggest that if metropolitan government should be established in the Bay Area, one of the powers that it should have would be that of reserving open space in accordance with a plan for long-term development of the area.

Some of the recent conflicts over the use of land have dramatized the value of long-range, comprehensive planning and the need for effective measures to hold undeveloped land for appropriate uses. A few years ago in Alameda County, for example, industrial realtors and industrial promotion groups became so alarmed over the loss of potential factory sites to tract builders that they demanded that the county government prepare a master or general plan showing the most desirable use of all lands in the county, and especially the open lands subject to intensive development. Specifically, the realtors wanted some "ground rules" established so that there would be no further disputes over the type of development that should be allowed in areas eminently suitable for industry. And they wanted lands designated on the general plan as industrial areas to be zoned accordingly and held for new manufacturing plants and other industrial establishments.

In Santa Clara County, where population is estimated to have increased from 352,000 in 1953 to 620,000 in 1959, agriculturists who were once lukewarm about legal restrictions on the use of land have turned to planning and zoning as means of halting the transformation of farmlands into subdivisions and industrial sites. Beginning in 1953, Santa Clara County pioneered in the establishment of exclusive agricultural zones to protect some of its richest farmlands. By 1958 the county had set aside more than thirty thousand acres in well-defined blocks of land, almost always at the request of agriculturists themselves. As far as possible, this zoning has been based on planning studies showing areas judged to be suitable for long-term preservation as farmland, though undoubtedly much of the effort to save agricultural land in Santa Clara County has been merely expedient—a matter of saving what could be saved after many opportunities for a more orderly pattern of urban and agricultural lands had been lost. Growth has been so rapid and municipal annexations of undeveloped lands have been so numerous and so opportunistic that the county government cannot be said to have established an ideal scheme of greenbelts. It has postponed urbanization in some areas, and it has perhaps salvaged some lands that may make good parks for the city dwellers of the future. If, indeed, some of the acreage now zoned in greenbelts does in time become publicly owned recreation space, later generations will owe a debt of gratitude to the agriculturists, county planners, and county supervisors who protected it from intensive development.

One of the great weaknesses of city and county planning in the San Francisco Bay Area today is that in attempting to satisfy local groups, planning agencies sometimes overlook the long-term needs of the whole metropolitan region. The quality of planning in the Bay Area is in general high, and probably a greater amount of local planning is being done in this metropolitan region than in any other in the United States. Unfortunately, none of the city and county plans made in the past ten years have been based on a detailed and inclusive analysis of regional economic and social trends. Even those plans which are genuinely comprehensive at least for individual political jurisdictions are not necessarily based on the same regional assumptions and population forecasts; they do not recognize the same broad regional goals and do not apply the same general principles and standards. This is because the Bay Area still lacks a metropolitan regional planning agency that could do research on the whole area, make studies of important area-wide problems, stimulate debate on goals for the area, and gradually win acceptance for a set of goals that would represent the desires of a majority of residents, or at least those residents who are vocal and politically active.

The above statement must be modified, however, by pointing out that since 1955 all the city and county planning agencies in the Bay Area have had the benefit of regional studies made by consultants to the San Francisco Bay Area Rapid Transit Commission. In the course of preparing a rapid transit plan for the area, the firm of Parsons, Brinckerhoff, Hall and Macdonald did a vast amount of research on the area and developed an outline regional plan as a basis for proposing routes for a transit system. Data collected by the staff engaged in the transit study have been used by many local planning offices, and some of the city and county plans prepared within the past two or three years have incorporated many of the suggestions in the outline regional plan. But the consultants to the transit commission would themselves be the first to acknowledge that their outline plan is no substitute for the kind of guide for regional development that could be prepared by planners with ample time to determine upon area-wide goals and to investigate the full range of economic and social data that should be studied in developing a comprehensive plan. Moreover, the transit plan, which cannot be considered apart from the outline regional plan on which it is based, will not be submitted to a vote of the people of the Bay Area until November, 1960, and therefore does not yet serve as a general guide reflecting the formally expressed desires of the metropolitan regional community. It is, nevertheless, a milestone in the history of the Bay Area, because it suggests, as nothing else ever has, the importance of reaching agreement on goals for the entire region; and it also stands as a reminder that local plans prepared without reference to some widely approved scheme for regional development are at best piecemeal plans.

Regional Transit

The transit plan proposes far more than a system of transit lines and "feeder" routes served by buses. It proposes a functional and spatial organization of the metropolitan region that might actually be brought about by construction of the system, since the influence of transportation facilities on the "structure" of an urban area probably exceeds that of every other element. Instead of the loosely nucleated regional metropolis that we see today, there might be by 1975 or 1980 a regional metropolis with a hierarchy of well-defined centers: a great center including San Francisco, Oakland, and Berkeley; important subcenters at San Jose and at Concord, in central Contra Costa County; and several district centers, each of which ultimately would serve a population ranging

from one hundred and fifty thousand to three hundred thousand. These district centers, situated approximately twelve miles apart, would be cities in which retail outlets for standardized goods, large business and professional offices offering standardized services, and social and cultural facilities at present appear to be concentrating: Santa Rosa, Petaluma, and Napa in the North Bay; San Rafael and San Mateo in the West Bay; Richmond, Berkeley (in the dual role of district center and part of the metropolitan regional center), and Hayward in the East Bay; Palo Alto and Fremont in the South Bay; and Vallejo and Walnut Creek in a territory designated on the plan as the East Inland Area.

The conception of the metropolitan nerve center as a tri-city complex is an especially striking feature of the plan. Ordinarily, people think of the heart of the Bay Area as downtown San Francisco or as a combination of downtown San Francisco and downtown Oakland; whereas the transit planners would make San Francisco, Oakland, and Berkeley virtually one great hub of activity, unified by swift transit, so that the central business districts of San Francisco and Oakland would be only a few minutes apart by an underwater tube, and the University of California and central Berkeley would be readily accessible from both larger cities.

The plan accepts a dispersion of nighttime or resident population in low-density residential communities, somewhat as at present. It proposes a concentration of employed population during the daytime in large, medium, and small centers, because our economy is characterized by ever-increasing specialization of individuals and firms —and specialization demands that those who serve one another be readily accessible to one another. High-density centers of employment would recognize the interdependence of specialists but would be free from the congestion created by an excessive number of automobiles, since the regional transit system would transport thousands of workers to their jobs swiftly, safely, and economically. The transit system would, in fact, "maximize" opportunities for employment. A worker could change jobs without having to change his residence to avoid an unduly time-consuming or fatiguing journey to work. No matter where he lived, he would have rapid access to any one of a score of centers of employment.

In the largest of these, the tri-city regional center, would be concentrated the major headquarters offices, the top professional offices, the most highly specialized business services, regional wholesaling outlets, the most important educational and cultural institutions, and the specialized retailing activities that serve the entire metropolitan region. Establishments in the subregional and district cen-

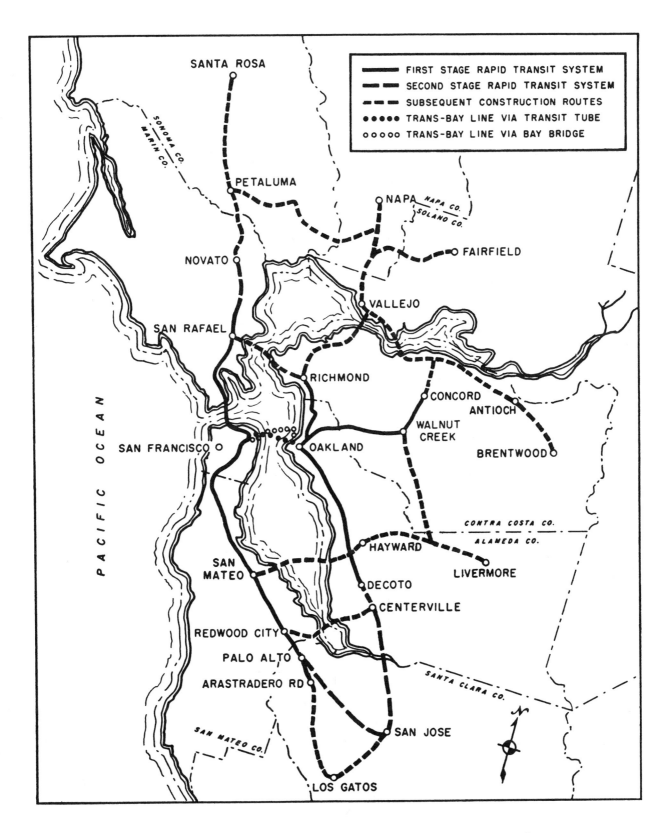

Proposed Interurban Rapid Transit System for the San Francisco Bay Area. Plan prepared by Parsons, Brinckerhoff, Hall and Macdonald, Engineers, New York, for the San Francisco Bay Area Rapid Transit Commission.

ters would provide standardized goods and services and would serve their respective market areas.

The transit planners point out that by linking large and small centers, the projected transit system would serve the greater proportion of workers in the Bay Area, for most of the employment in the area is distributive and service employment, and it tends even now to be concentrated in comparatively small areas. Only approximately one-fifth of the employed persons in the metropolitan region are employed in manufacturing industries, and of these a significant, but unmeasured, number work in San Francisco and Oakland headquarters offices of manufacturing corporations. Furthermore, manufacturing establishments producing light goods and employing large numbers of persons tend to seek locations close to urban centers. Such establishments, then, could also be served by the transit system. The freeways, relieved of much of the traffic that now overloads them, would be adequate in the future to serve the factory districts that form belts along harbors and rail lines, because employment in these areas is relatively low per acre and will undoubtedly continue to fall as automation increases.

In sum, the transit plan envisions a solution of the circulation problems of the Bay Area through the centering of places of employment. The transit system itself would be the chief instrument for bringing about this centering.

Since much of the recent commercial and service development in outlying areas has been predicated upon continuing widespread use of the private automobile and has therefore been somewhat diffuse, would a transit system halt the trend toward loose nucleation and encourage dense clustering of offices, stores, light industries, and similar establishments? Population forecasts leave no doubt that an enormous amount of new development could be directed toward definite centers within the next thirty or forty years; but is this the kind of physical organization of the regional metropolis that the people of the Bay Area want? Do residents of the area understand that they have before them not just a plan for a transit system but a plan for the arrangement of their whole environment?

It is doubtful that more than a very small percentage of Bay Area residents appreciate that they are being asked to make decisions that will in large measure determine how the regional metropolis develops in the future. Discussion of the transit plan has revolved around two questions: Would workers leave their automobiles at home and use a transit system if one were built? What would be the best way to finance construction of the system? Few public officials even mention the influence that the transit system would have on the spatial pattern of economic activities.

Rapid Transit District

Because the rapid transit district formed in the fall of 1957 has preceded a metropolitan regional planning agency and some form of metropolitan government, it perhaps has some of the obligations that either such an agency or such a government would have for explaining and dramatizing the issues inseparable from future Bay Area development. But, unfortunately, the district includes only five of the nine bay counties—San Francisco, Alameda, Contra Costa, Marin, and San Mateo. It cannot reach all the people who must deal with the problems facing the regional metropolis, though it can reach most of them. If it places the problem of transit in the larger perspective in which the consultants to the earlier transit commission viewed it, then the district might well stimulate interest in the establishment of a regional planning agency and its necessary accompaniment, metropolitan regional government, such as Toronto, Canada, has enjoyed since 1953.

Logically, of course, both area-wide planning and metropolitan government should be instituted before so important a determinant of future development as a rapid transit system is financed and constructed. Planners and political scientists would approve such a sequence of events, but history seldom follows the neat patterns conceived by rationalists. Regional planning, talked about in the Bay Area for several decades, is still abstract to most residents. Overloaded freeways, crowded interurban buses, and congested downtown streets are vivid realities, so easily comprehended that anyone who has experienced them has some basis for judging the merits of a proposed rapid transit system estimated to cost $500,000,000 or more in its initial stages and approximately $1,000,000,000 when completed. So again the political leaders and the prominent citizens, with the tacit support of a large number of residents, have taken steps to solve a tangible problem, while the few who realize the need for area-wide planning and metropolitan government still struggle to make these needs equally well understood. One more special district has been added to the multiplicity of governmental units serving the Bay Area, and one more agency that might logically function as an operating branch of metropolitan government has been set up independently. At least, another effort has been made to solve a regional problem on a regional basis. The proponents of metropolitan government can some day ask with insistence: Why not merge all area-wide functions—control of water pollution, control of air pollution, management of regional parks, reservation of open space, operation of regional rapid transit, airports, heliports, and shipping facilities, and perhaps other functions—under one policy-making council or assembly representing all the cities and counties in the Bay Area?

If the board of the rapid transit district, in pursuing its campaign for approval of the proposed system, should directly or indirectly renew interest in the establishment of a metropolitan regional planning agency, it would be performing an invaluable service to the Bay Area. After more than a century the area is still in the early stages of its growth and may double its population well before the year 2000 and quadruple it by the year 2050. The decisions to be made on matters affecting the entire regional metropolis will be countless. Those made in the next twenty years will be especially important, for they will determine for a very long time many of the physical arrangements in the territories surrounding the bay.

Regional Planning

In recent years, planning commissioners and professional city and county planners in the Bay Area have devoted a great deal of time to study of the need for a regional planning agency. In 1952 one hundred and eighty commissioners representing forty-seven local planning bodies recommended the appointment of a study committee "to define and clarify the nature and scope of regional planning in the Bay Area and to recommend the type of agency which could most effectively perform the function of regional planning in the Bay Area . . ."[15] Two years later, the study committee formed at the suggestion of the commissioners issued, through the San Francisco Bay Area Council, the first of two reports on regional planning, *Regional Planning Needs of the San Francisco Bay Area.* The report described familiar problems of the area and pointed out that without a comprehensive, long-term plan for all nine counties, "local planning agencies cannot adequately appraise the probable effects of their plans on their own and other communities and on the area as a whole."[16] The second of the two reports, issued in 1956, presented a proposed statute creating a San Francisco Bay Area regional planning district specifically designed to fit the complex governmental pattern of the area. This report recognized that earlier attempts to form a regional planning commission under the regional planning law of 1937 had failed and that if the Bay Area were to succeed in establishing a regional planning agency, a "fresh start" would be necessary.

The authors of the proposed statute, consultant William A. Doebele, Jr., and a subcommittee composed of Professor T. J. Kent, Jr., and the planning directors of the cities of San Francisco and Oakland and the counties of Alameda and San Mateo favored creation by the state legislature of a regional planning district embracing the entire metropolitan region. To give the governing bodies of cities and counties representation on the board of directors of the district, they provided for a board that would include eighteen city councilmen and county supervisors and eight citizens-at-large. This board, as an advisory body only, "would prepare, adopt, and maintain a regional plan for the physical development of the Bay Area based upon the master plans of the city and county governments of the area and upon studies of region-wide needs," the report on the proposed statute explained.[17] The regional plan, of course, would "serve as a guide for local plans and planning programs and for state and federal agencies and special districts."[18] Like regional planning boards in Detroit, Atlanta, Chicago, Toronto, and other metropolitan communities, the board of the Bay Area planning district would require a professional staff to make regional population, economic, traffic, and land use studies for its own purposes and for the purpose of assisting and strengthening city and county planning programs. The authors of the proposed statute believed, however, that the members of the board would themselves bear a large measure of the responsibility for promoting and encouraging coöperation among city, county, regional, state, and federal agencies and private groups in evolving effective procedures for dealing with regional development problems that concern everyone in the Bay Area.

The proposed statute was introduced in the state legislature in 1957 before planning commissioners and professional planners had had sufficient opportunity to explain it to residents of their localities. In the absence of informed support for the bill, many legislators perhaps failed to appreciate the need for creating a planning district including all the cities and counties in the Bay Area. And they perhaps also did not understand that the Bay Area has governmental, physical, economic, and social problems that are very different from those of other metropolitan regions in California. The bill emerged from the legislative mill as a statute applicable to any metropolitan community in the state, and it provided that any two counties could form a district. Thus Alameda and Contra Costa counties, for example, though constituting only a subregion of the Bay Area, could become a planning district under the legislation approved by the legislature and signed by the governor. The establishment of such a district, however, would contribute little to the solution of area-wide problems. The Bay Area would be as greatly in need as ever of a planning agency capable of dealing with the kinds of regional problems outlined in the first report of the Planning Commissioners' Study Committee.

Planning commissioners and professional planners in the Bay Area realize that an effort of several years may be required to secure enactment of legislation creating a regional planning district embracing the entire metropolitan region. They face no easy task, though, because there is as yet no ground swell in favor of metropolitan regional planning, despite occasional editorials in the daily press pointing out that a regional planning program would facilitate decisions on the location of additional bay crossings, on the development of the bay for shipping and recreation, and on innumerable other matters that have little relation to city and county boundary lines. The augury of eventual success of a regional planning movement is perhaps the increasing frequency with which regional problems come to the attention of local legislative bodies and private groups. Again and again the solution for some local problem appears to depend on solution of a regional problem; and since local political leaders have come to depend more and more on the advice of their planning staffs, the time is probably approaching when they will believe what the professional planners tell them: that decisions on local matters affected by regional considerations can be farsighted only if made with reference to a plan for regional development.

Obstacles to Success

Assuming that a metropolitan regional planning agency could be established in the San Francisco Bay Area in the next five to ten years, there might be one and possibly two great obstacles to its success: (1) the lack of a metropolitan regional council or assembly with responsibility for area-wide functions and (2) the lack of a state planning agency responsible for preparing a general plan for the state that urban regions could use as a guide in matters of population distribution, allocation of state water resources, conservation of agricultural areas, and interregional circulation. Both metropolitan government and state planning are virtually indispensable to satisfactory performance by a metropolitan regional planning agency.

Unless the Bay Area someday establishes a political entity empowered to deal with related area-wide governmental functions, any metropolitan regional planning body it creates probably will be little more effective than a private planning organization. To be sure, some private planning organizations, such as the Regional Plan Association of New York, have made significant contributions to the development of the areas they serve; but no private planning organization, however capably staffed and amply financed, can ever accomplish as much as a public regional planning agency which would submit its recommendations directly to a metropolitan decision-making body capable of carrying them out. The implementation of an area-wide general plan cannot well be left to the voluntary coöperation of cities, counties, and a multiplicity of special districts. Each city or county legislative body would accept or reject proposals of the regional agency according to the way the local political winds were

The Need for Area-Wide Unity as Seen by the San Francisco Chronicle. Courtesy of San Francisco Chronicle.

Progress Demands That the Bay Area Be De-Balkanized

blowing at the moment. Spotty implementation of a regional plan would leave so much to be desired that the results would be little more than failure. Transfer of certain local legislative prerogatives to a metropolitan policy-making body is the only long-term answer to the problem of coördinated development in the nine-county Bay Area. Regional planning recommendations presented to such a body could be carried out with little more difficulty than now attends the approval and financing of a local public works program by a city council in any well-governed municipality today.

But to advocate metropolitan regional government as a necessary corollary of metropolitan regional planning is not to ignore some thorny problems. Local political interests must be convinced that a regional government could deal satisfactorily with numerous matters on which they are now unable to take effective action. The division of responsibility between metropolitan and local governments in the many fields that would require action by both must be clarified. Equitable representation on a metropolitan council must be agreed upon, and the operations of various departments and agencies of metropolitan government must be adequately financed.

The record of attempted coöperation among the cities and counties of the Bay Area raises almost as much doubt as it does hope concerning the possibility of metropolitan government. Did not San Francisco and the East Bay cities fail in their efforts to develop a common water supply? Was not the idea of a great municipality embracing both sides of the bay violently opposed by the East Bay? Has not every proposal for a unified harbor district been rejected? And has not voluntary coöperation among ports of the Bay Area deteriorated in the past year or two? Have not Oakland and San Francisco pursued opposing policies on a southern crossing and on alterations to the Bay Bridge? Yet six of the nine bay counties are included in an air-pollution control district, and five have formed a rapid transit district. The counties that have joined neither district probably will seek to be included as they experience the pressures of additional population growth and industrial expansion. Many of the planning commissions in the Bay Area desire regional planning; and now that leading businessmen are becoming interested in metropolitan government, it is only a matter of time until the politicians who oppose it will find themselves in an untenable position.

We cannot assume that the jealousies, rivalries, and shortsightedness that have plagued this metropolitan region during most of its history will persist forever. Only in the past quarter century has there been much recognition of metropolitan problems, and only since World War II has there been much study of them. As the gaps in our present knowledge of conditions and problems are narrowed through more intensive research, and as information on the findings of authorities in various fields is more widely disseminated and more vigorously discussed, public understanding of the opportunities for coöperative solution of problems will inevitably increase. Universities and colleges in the Bay Area are graduating more and more students who have studied the problems under eminent authorities; and these graduates are taking their places in local governments and in regional offices of the state and federal governments, as well as in private business organizations. State senators and assemblymen, many of whom studied metropolitan problems in the university classroom, are becoming intensely interested in devising political machinery that will effectively meet area-wide needs, as witness the quantity of bills on metropolitan problems introduced at recent sessions of the state legislature. Interest in metropolitanism as a cardinal fact of modern state and national life is cumulative. Rapid population growth and inadequately controlled urban expansion cannot but produce additional crises that will focus attention on the political problems of the metropolitan community. Out of these crises will come, in time, the solutions to problems, perhaps not in the way that political scientists would approve, perhaps not in logical sequence, and almost surely not with the thoroughness that would be desirable. In accordance with the political realities of the moment, there will be compromises that factions of almost equal strength will be obliged to make in the interest of resolving bitter conflicts, and there will be concessions that certain influential citizens or dominant political figures will demand. But the problems sooner or later will be solved, apparently through the creation of various area-wide special districts and boards, and possibly through one or more multipurpose metropolitan authorities, until in the long run, let us hope, there will be a consolidation of area-wide functions under one democratically elected council.

Although the establishment of metropolitan government may be many years in the future, there is good reason to believe that the state legislature may authorize creation of a genuine state planning agency within the next few years. The prospect of an ultimate state population of sixty million or more is frightening and sobering to many state legislators. They are beginning to realize that the future distribution of population in California and the growth of new cities should not result from piecemeal and uncoördinated development of dams, aqueducts, highways, and other large-scale state projects, but rather should come about through planning which carefully examines the consequences of every proposed program of public works and relates the projects of all departments of state government to a state plan for the accommodation of a greatly increased population under desirable conditions. Such a plan is needed not only to guide the activities of state agencies but also to assist local governments and to aid the state in dealing with federal agencies. The activities of the Defense Department, especially, are having a great effect—often a disruptive effect —on the development of many communities in California; yet localities and state agencies usually feel handicapped in dealing with the military because they themselves cannot argue in support of well-conceived plans of their own. The state would be in a better position to come to the assistance of local governments in their dealings with the federal government if it had a comprehensive plan indicating the development that would be appropriate in each important subregion; and the very fact that the state had such a plan might spur localities to work out their own plans with greater thoroughness. Rather than let the state make some of the major decisions about their development for·them, the metropolitan regions might decide to organize for effective bargaining with the state, through metropolitan governments properly served by regional planning agencies. Indeed, the state legislature probably could do more to promote metropolitan government and regional planning by establishing a strong state planning agency than by any other action it could take.

The Way to a Goal

In view of the desirability of establishing metropolitan government and instituting state planning prior to creating a metropolitan regional planning agency, should citizens in the Bay Area who are anxious to bring about coördination of the activities of city and county planning agencies in the area therefore refrain from attempting to promote a regional agency and instead concentrate their efforts on educating the public to the need for metropolitan government and state planning? Ideally, perhaps they should, but the first-things-first approach to governmental problems sometimes produces slim results. The roundabout way to a goal often proves to be the shortest way, since human beings are not strictly rational creatures and are restrained by habits, traditions, emotional ties, and vague fears of the new and unknown from being logical. It is much more likely that the people of the Bay Area would be willing to experiment with metropolitan regional planning *without* metropolitan government and state planning than with either or both of these ultimately necessary developments in government. An official metropolitan regional planning agency could be established

without altering the structure of local government in the Bay Area in any way. Most city hall politicians and county courthouse "gangs" doubtless would find in this situation a persuasive argument for such an agency. Political realists with more knowledge of course would use it as the principal argument against undertaking any metropolitan regional planning at all, since a regional agency unattached to a metropolitan governmental organization would be a kind of parentless body—a waif among official agencies, integrated with neither local government nor state government. But at least such an agency might perform an educational service. Even its failures to induce local governments to coöperate in carrying out area-wide plans would be illuminating. Each debacle on the metropolitan planning front—indeed, there would surely be some—would emphasize the need for devising new governmental machinery for solving area-wide problems. In the more optimistic view, however, a metropolitan regional planning agency might actually accomplish a good deal by defining problems, setting goals, providing reliable population projections and economic analyses, and developing a general plan based on reasonable assumptions concerning future economic, social, and political conditions. If public-spirited citizens and officials throughout the Bay Area would fully support the agency, its influence might far outweigh its ambiguous status among governmental organizations. The agency could be no more effective, though, than the people of the metropolitan community wanted it to be. It might be a dismal failure—and it might be a great success.

Now the question is: Are the residents of the Bay Area ready to take the chance? Although most professional planners and many of the planning commissioners in the Bay Area recognize the need for metropolitan regional planning, most citizens appear to be intent on solving local problems and cannot always see that a local highway location problem is part of an area-wide circulation problem, or that the struggle to increase the local tax base by attracting new industries is related to the whole problem of a unified approach to taxation in the close-knit metropolitan community. Never before in the history of the Bay Area have there been so many citizens' leagues, neighborhood improvements associations, parent-teacher associations, taxpayers associations, and local planning groups attempting to find solutions to problems of rapid and poorly regulated growth, insufficient taxes to support schools and other community services, and inadequate government in unincorporated areas. Few of these suburban organizations seem to realize, however, that the matters with which they are concerned have metropolitan implications and can be properly understood only in relation to a scheme of development for the entire Bay Area.

Is it surprising, though, that many local groups fail to appreciate the metropolitan aspects of local zoning, subdivision regulation, and public improvement programs? In community after community one-fourth, one-third, or even half of the people are newcomers, not only to the locality but also to the Bay Area and to California. They have not lived long enough in this metropolitan region to know its history, to identify their immediate environment with the larger urban complex, or to have gained much insight into the future of the nine-county Bay Area. In the schools the children learn something about their home community and the State of California, but rarely are they introduced to the concept of the metropolitan community, because the teachers themselves usually have not become acquainted with the broader view of the urban area. To counteract the rootlessness, the mobility, and the

limited perspective of residents in suburban communities, especially, Bay Area leaders should undertake a long-term program to develop a new type of citizen—one who is metropolitan in outlook. Civic participation at the local level should be encouraged, but the endeavor to improve the immediate environment must somehow be given a new orientation, so that local effort may contribute to area-wide progress.

A Council of Civic Groups

The many civic groups that have recently sprung up in Bay Area cities and unincorporated areas should first of all be allied in a metropolitan council of civic groups, through which they could become aware, by the exchange of information on their local problems, of the area-wide implications of local struggles. The wider knowledge thus gained could be translated, in time, into material for use

The Encroachment of the City on the Hills: Step One. Photograph courtesy of David Arbegast and Robert Tetlow.

in the public schools throughout the Bay Area. The schools are now presenting a wealth of material on municipal government and urban problems at various grade levels, but they are not emphasizing the metropolitan region as the significant community of our time. Until the metropolitan community is seen as the larger environment in which the family lives and works and plays, there is not too much hope of planning that environment well or governing it properly. The forces of formal and of informal education should be mobilized to advance the welfare of each local community in the Bay Area principally by seeking solutions to problems that are area-wide, because perhaps most so-called local problems are not local at all but metropolitan.

Does the Bay Area have the kind of leadership that can educate citizens to the larger responsibilities of membership in a metropolitan regional community? Before there can be large numbers of citizens with a metropolitan point of view, there first must be an active corps of men and women dedicated to the proposition that urban life in our age requires a new allegiance—to the entire urban area rather than to some part of it. Residents of Maine and Alabama and Wisconsin and Arizona manage to think of themselves first of all as Americans and secondly as residents of a particular commonwealth. It should be possible some day for residents of San Francisco and Oakland and San Jose and Santa Rosa to sublimate pride in a locality to pride in a metropolitan union of cities. But imaginative leaders will have to show the way by rising above home-town sentiments whenever matters of metropolitan regional concern are involved. To date the leaders who can comprehend more than the economic aspects of metropolitan regional development and more than the possibilities of creating an integrated circulation system have been few. These few must now add to their numbers and with their new colleagues must undertake to fashion a truly metropolitan society.

Their first task is the twofold one of organizing a metropolitan council of citizen associations and planning a systematic program of educating the public, intended to reach the schools and every responsible civic group in the Bay Area. From the foundation laid by the educational program—which should be a program making use of every available means of communication—in time should come the popular determination to organize the metropolitan region politically, economically, and physically in a manner clearly in accord with the demands of our mass production, mass consumption, and mass leisure society. That society, making use of more and more technological wonders, has shrunk physical distance and has telescoped time until every part of the metropolitan region is potentially just around the corner from all other parts. The concept of the self-contained city is obsolete. The regional metropolis requires physical integration, economic development coördinated with the physical pattern, and the kind of over-all government that will enable its economic enterprises and social institutions to function efficiently in a vast area, unimpeded by conflicting local ordinances.

The Future Metropolis

Today we see in the Bay Area only the beginnings of the regional metropolis. By the end of the century it will be one continuous urban development around the bay, with extensions into the valleys to the north, south, and east. It will be a world metropolis in every sense of the word, composed of people from all nations, linked by transportation and communication to other world centers, nurtured in its daily life by raw materials, manufactured goods, and cultural exchanges from every corner of the globe. Much that is today old and blighted or new and shoddily built will have disappeared and will have been replaced by better-planned developments. Large areas of the bay will have been reclaimed for waterfront parks, manufacturing sites, residential communities, and additional airports. An area-wide freeway system and an area-wide transit system, perhaps including some aerial services, should by that time have been in operation for two or three decades.

But the danger is that much of the unique charm of the Bay Area may be sacrificed in the development of this world metropolis, by removing scenic hills to reclaim marshlands and tidelands, by bulldozing and blasting huge cuts in wooded slopes in order to construct freeways, and by recklessy permitting residential building in hillcrest and mountainous areas that would be ideal for regional parks. Great and rapid growth, such as this area is now experiencing and probably will experience for decades, imposes herculean responsibilities upon a community. Because the San Francisco Bay Area has been more generously endowed with natural beauty than most of the large urban areas of the world, its residents have an especially weighty stewardship to discharge. Not for ourselves and our own posterity but for the global community should we strive to safeguard the beauties of this magnificent combination of bays and islands, mountains and valleys—and to enhance the heritage received from nature by skillfully wedding the structures and roadways of the evolving regional metropolis to the physical environment. To achieve so lofty a goal we must do no less than perceive new obligations of the individual to society, fashion new laws for controlling individual action in the interest of the entire community, devise a workable system of metropolitan government, and weld into a new creative force the talents of all those concerned with metropolitan regional development—elected officials, businessmen, industrialists, and their employees, members of the professions, and workers in the many governments of the San Francisco Bay Area. Are we equal to the challenge?

The Magnificent Natural Setting of the San Francisco Bay Area, a Heritage to be Safeguarded. Photograph courtesy of Max Yavno.

CHAPTER EIGHTEEN

The Regional Metropolis Twenty-Five Years Later

In the quarter century since the first edition of this book was published, the population of the Bay Area has increased approximately 1,880,000 and is presently estimated at a little more than 5,500,000. This gain is almost as great as the number of people who were living in three important midwestern cities, Milwaukee, Cleveland, and Indianapolis, when the last decennial census was taken. Or it might be said that the population of the nine-county region has been augmented by as many people as the census counted in three of our western states in 1980—Alaska, Hawaii, and Wyoming.

This substantial increase has been accompanied by rapid growth in many outlying areas, by incorporation of seventeen new municipalities, and by losses of population in most of the older cities surrounding San Francisco Bay. Economic expansion (even in certain activities in central cities suffering declines in population) and additional urban development have greatly intensified regional problems and have recurrently precipitated bitter political struggles to solve them. The region has, indeed, frequently taken on some of the aspects of a battleground as groups with widely divergent ideas of "progress" have advocated or opposed suggested regulations, this or that project, or proposals for new governmental agencies.

Underlying most of the conflict has been a widespread appreciation of the unique geographic, climatic, and historical advantages of the area, coupled with a perception on the part of large, well-informed, and highly vocal constituencies of serious threats to the environment from inappropriate development. To a degree unequaled in any of the other large metropolitan regions of the United States in the past

twenty-five years, citizen activists and exceptional political leaders in the Bay Area have fought for legislation and programs to reduce air and water pollution, improve public transportation systems, enlarge recreational preserves, and safeguard such scenic and economic assets as coastlines, waterways (particularly San Francisco Bay), and farmlands.

In the process, there has been a great deal of federal and state participation in areawide affairs, which leadership groups, both official and unofficial, have at times invited or welcomed or barely tolerated or deeply resented. Not many of the resentful groups have objected, however, to enrichment of the regional economy by billions of federal and state dollars allocated for local and regional planning and for new public works. The state legislature, responding to the regional ferment, has from time to time created such special-purpose agencies as the Bay Conservation and Development Commission and the Metropolitan Transportation Commission, to say nothing of several others that were short-lived. But it has not seen fit to give its blessing to the most controversial of all proposals: authorization of a multifunction regional government for the Bay Area.

In some ways the history of the 'sixties and 'seventies is the story of the rise and decline of the movement for regional government. Spawned by the problems that plague metropolitan regions, the Association of Bay Area Governments appeared on the scene early in the 1960's and was impelled almost at once toward the preparation and refinement of the first regional plan ever approved by a majority of municipal and county spokesmen in the area. Certain elements wished to see the association transformed into a statutory regional government, with authority to carry out its comprehensive plan. Many others, including some members of the association itself, desired no such thing; they feared "dictatorship." Lo, their fears dissolved as they beheld proponents divide into opposing factions, unable to agree on fundamental issues: which substantive matters to entrust to a multipurpose agency, and how to constitute the governing board. And so the legislature enacted no statute providing for an areawide government that could exercise several functions. Almost a decade later no attempt is being made to revive interest in forming that type of government. But this historical account runs on too swiftly. To understand why residents of the Bay Area are very advanced in their concern for the quality of life yet still lack some of the means to protect the environment adequately and to create good living conditions throughout the region, one must examine the course of events in the past two and a half decades in more detail.

Regional Growth and New Cities

When the 1960 census was taken, the nine-county region had 3,628,939 residents and had gained more than 957,000 of them through natural increase and in-migration during the 1950's. The 'sixties contributed an even larger addition, amounting to 991,000 and bringing the regional total, in round numbers, to 4,630,000. Though the pace of growth slowed in the 'seventies, owing to high inflation, a staggering boost in the cost of petroleum, and perhaps to the unfavorable "image" (east of the Sierras) of the Bay Area as the home of student rebels and freakish hedonists, the census of 1980 recorded an increase of 551,445, raising the number of residents to 5,182,021. The early years of the present decade have augmented this figure by more than 300,000. Currently the Bay Area is the fifth most populous metropolitan region in the United States and is home to more people than there are in each of forty states.

The most striking growth in the area has occurred in the Santa Clara Valley, in and around San Jose. A city of only a little more than 200,000 residents in 1960, this once small town surrounded by vast prune, apricot, and pear orchards had become by 1980 almost twice as populous as Oakland and was a close second to San Francisco in number of residents—and the orchards had all but disappeared. Indeed, Santa Clara County, of which San Jose is the county seat, had by that year superseded Alameda County as the political jurisdiction having the largest population in the region. By the end of the century, this county at the southern end of San Francisco Bay may have more than 1,500,000 residents, or some 200,000 more than will probably be living in Alameda County.

Perhaps already the largest city in the Bay Area, San Jose has risen to prominence mainly because of the high-technology industries in an area popularly known as Silicon Valley, although the complex actually extends from San Jose to Belmont on the bay side of the San Francisco Peninsula and has even developed offspring in Fremont in southern Alameda County. Stimulated after the Second World War by military contracts awarded to electronics plants, the burgeoning industrial chain grew rapidly in the 1960's when the National Aeronautics and Space Administration established its Ames Laboratory at Moffett Field and the Atomic Energy Commission supported construction of a giant linear accelerator at Stanford University. Microelectronic enterprises, generally identified with the production of computers, proliferated in the late 'sixties and in the 'seventies, then began experiencing Japanese competition as well as environmental, labor, and housing problems. A long-term prediction is, nevertheless, that Silicon Valley, now providing 6 per cent of the employment in the Bay Area, may some day provide an even higher proportion—say, as much as 9 per cent.

Although the skylines of San Francisco and Oakland have risen higher and higher with new office towers, and although employment in their downtown areas has increased, both these central cities have lost residents to rapidly developing territories once considered remote. In the 1970's especially, even smaller cities within the historical commuting belts from which these large centers of employment have attracted workers experienced declines in population. Along the bay shoreline of the San Francisco Peninsula, for instance, no less than a dozen cities had fewer residents in 1980 than in 1970, including such long-established communities as San Bruno, Millbrae, Burlingame, San Mateo, San Carlos, Redwood City, Menlo Park, and Palo Alto. Similarly, on the eastern side of the bay almost every city from San Leandro to Richmond and San Pablo had a lower census count in 1980 than ten years previously. Only the little cities of Emeryville and Albany made small gains. Eight other cities, including Oakland and Berkeley, together lost almost 55,000 residents, or more than were living in the fast-growing city of Walnut Creek in central Contra Costa County in 1980. Even in "marvelous Marin," as the more chauvinistic residents of that county refer to it, four cities within commuting distance of San Francisco lost population: Belvedere, Corte Madera, San Anselmo, and Fairfax.

Opportunities for employment in newly developing areas, the attractions of new housing in these areas, and, sad to say, the desire of some families to live in communities with few minority residents variously influenced the movement to cities on the ocean side of San Mateo County, the northern part of Marin County, the southern part of Alameda County, the central and northeastern sections of Contra Costa County, and the principal valleys of the northern counties of

The San Francisco Skyline of the 1980's as Seen from Diamond Heights. Photograph courtesy of Larry Orman, executive director of People for Open Space.

Sonoma, Napa, and Solano. Cities in most of these areas and in Santa Clara County grew far more, however, by exerting the dynamic pull of new or expanding enterprises than merely by attracting residents from the older urban concentrations. Santa Clara County alone generated 451,000 new jobs in the period from 1960 to 1980, or almost three times as many as Alameda County, which added 158,100, according to the California Department of Employment. And whereas San Francisco provided 85,500 more jobs in the same period, Contra Costa County created an additional 101,100, thereby in great measure accounting for large population increases in several of its cities. In the twenty-year period the population of Concord rose from 36,000 to 103,255, that of Antioch from 17,305 to 42,683, and that of quiet little Martinez from 9,604 to 22,582.

Throughout the nine-county region there were, in areas of rapid development and economic expansion, many small cities that recorded phenomenal rates of growth even in the economically troubled 'seventies. These rates ranged from 70 per cent (Gilroy) to as much as 280 per cent (Suisun City). Vacaville, in Solano County, had a gain of just under 100 per

cent, and Pleasanton, in eastern Alameda County, also almost doubled in population. Morgan Hill, in southern Santa Clara County, and Union City, near the bay shore of Alameda County, both had population increases exceeding 160 per cent.

As in the past, residents of unincorporated areas undergoing bewilderingly fast development took steps to establish community identity more positively by organizing municipal government. Sometimes the chief motivation was dissatisfaction with services offered by county government and a desire to exercise greater control over the uses of land and the location of new industrial and commercial enterprises. In other instances residents were dissatisfied with an increasing number of special service districts and felt that governmental arrangements were becoming unduly complex and uncoordinated. Whatever the reasons for breaking away from the policy-makers at the county seat, community after community, on reaching a certain size or experiencing some crisis in local affairs, voted to form its own government.

Of the numerous municipal incorporations in the past twenty-five years, eight have occurred in central Contra

Costa County and eastern Alameda County, mostly along Interstate Route 680 or on routes connecting with it. Together with such older cities as Walnut Creek, Concord, Martinez, Pittsburg, and Antioch, these new municipalities form a highly balkanized configuration with a population soon expected to aggregate half a million. Incorporated in the 'sixties, Pleasant Hill, Clayton, and Lafayette have taken on most of the aspects of well-established suburbs, as have the newer self-governing communities of Moraga and Orinda. Dublin, Danville, and San Ramon, old towns that grew rapidly in the 'seventies, did not vote to become municipalities until the early 'eighties. The entire group of cities, now struggling with many of the same problems San Jose and northern Santa Clara County faced somewhat earlier, is probably no better able to cope with governmental complexity than some other emerging conurbations in the Bay Area, with the exception of one in Marin County. The several communities composing this urban complex along the bay side of that county are guided by policies clearly set forth in a countywide general plan prepared with their participation as members of a City-County Planning Council established in 1968 under a joint exercise of powers agreement.

To the north, in Sonoma County, a fragmented agglomeration of lesser magnitude than that forming in central Contra Costa County includes two not-so-new municipalities. Rohnert Park and Cotati, incorporated in 1962 and 1963 respectively, lie between Petaluma and Santa Rosa, creating a conspicuous band of cities whose development was mainly responsible for giving Sonoma County the highest rate of growth of any of the Bay Area counties in the 'seventies— 46.3 per cent. According to one forecast, residents of this quartet of municipalities may well number more than a quarter of a million by the end of the century.

In Solano County, the second fastest growing of the nine counties in the Bay Area in the previous decade (38.4 per cent), a similar chain of cities, none newly incorporated but all experiencing rapid population increase, could by the year 2000 constitute yet another rather loosely knit metropolis-in-the-making, with a total population between 225,000 and 250,000. Some observers of the California scene foresee this burgeoning complex on Interstate Route 80 forming the connecting link, some time in the next century, between a much more populous Sacramento metropolitan area and the central and southern parts of the Bay Area, but perhaps just as many others shudder at the thought of a megalopolis extending from the lower Santa Clara Valley to Auburn, on the American River within sight of the Sierra Nevadas.

Incorporations elsewhere in the Bay Area have been somewhat scattered, mostly representing the development of communities on the fringes of older cities or congeries of cities. Half Moon Bay, on the ocean side of San Mateo County, became a municipality in 1959. In January, 1960, Novato, in northeastern Marin County, also elected to establish its own government, and the following year Brisbane, just south of San Francisco, adopted articles of incorporation. Portola Valley, to the west of Menlo Park and Palo Alto, took similar action in 1964, as did Yountville in the Napa Valley and Tiburon in southern Marin County (1965). In 1971 the bayshore development in San Mateo County known as Foster City became still another full-fledged municipality. Twelve years later East Palo Alto, in the same county, voted to incorporate, only to have the validity of a few of the ballots cast in the election challenged in the courts. In the spring of 1985 the issue was before the State Supreme Court. Attorneys representing the town hoped that the high court would validate the initial vote in the community, making another election on incorporation unnecessary. Oddly, the county government had been supporting an unofficial town government in East Palo Alto for some time before the residents went to the polls to vote on incorporation.

In the years ahead additional municipalities may come into being as still more groups of residents determine to take local matters into their own hands and decide to shape development more to their liking. Now numbering ninety-six (counting San Francisco as a city rather than a county), the municipalities of the Bay Area may well exceed one hundred by the end of the century.

A New Regional Association

The problems perplexing cities and counties in the region, as well as in other large urban areas of California, had become so aggravated by the end of the 'fifties that Governor Edmund G. Brown appointed a Commission on Metropolitan Area Problems to study them and recommend needed legislation. The new decade of the 1960's had hardly begun when the members submitted a report proposing that the state legislature enact a statute permitting any metropolitan area to create a single multipurpose regional district governed by a council composed of locally elected officials.

Even before the report of the commission appeared, 120 delegates from fifty-six cities of the Bay Area had met to discuss the formation of a Bay Area Metropolitan Council and had appointed a committee of mayors to suggest the composition and functions of such an organization. Some of the delegates may have been apprehensive about a proposed Golden Gate Authority, patterned after the Port of New York Authority and exercising control over toll bridges, regional airports, and ports. Once established, would such an authority gradually expand and become a threat to city and county governments in the region? Whatever anxiety some city council members and county supervisors may have felt, officials of the State Highway Department even more strongly feared the potentially powerful authority and were already marshaling their forces to kill the legislative bill providing for its creation. But probably a still greater number of delegates to the conference of Bay Area officials disliked the idea of surrendering so much as a degree of power to the sort of multipurpose regional government the governor's commission envisaged, even though council members and supervisors like themselves would serve on the governing board. Well aware of the prevalent antipathy to anything remotely resembling "supergovernment," the committee appointed to draw up a constitution and by-laws for a regional council suggested nothing more than the creation of an advisory group or voluntary discussion forum of elected city and county officials, to be formed by agreements executed under the Joint Exercise of Powers Act of 1921.

The new organization, known as the Association of Bay Area Governments, convened its first general assembly early in 1961, with a charter membership of six counties and fifty-four cities, and in September concluded that it should address itself to such regional matters as water pollution, the development of bay tidelands, an inventory of open space, the desirability of uniform building codes, and the possibility of establishing a governmental data center.

Meanwhile, the state legislature had been considering a proposal to create a San Francisco Bay Area Regional Planning District. Alarmed at the prospect of a state-organized district that might in time become the multipurpose regional government envisaged by the Governor's Commission on Metropolitan Area Problems, the new association declined to support the proposed legislation and itself decided to attempt regional planning, with the help of the planning staffs of member cities and counties. Its first effort, resulting in an inventory of existing plans and the preparation of a single nine-county base map, paved the way for a formal vote of the general assembly, in October, 1962, to undertake the responsibility for advisory regional planning for the Bay Area.

This action, taken four years before the federal government required that applications for various kinds of federal grants be reviewed for conformity with a regional plan, however skeletal, represented a significant shift of purpose on the part of ABAG (as the association was commonly known) and caused some local governments to view its assumption of the regional planning function as a threat to their own autonomy. Indeed, a considerable proportion of local officials serving as members of the general assembly would always be somewhat suspicious of the organization or indifferent to its increasingly ambitious programs. The association was, nevertheless, far in advance of other metropolitan councils of government in assuming responsibility for regional planning in its own area and in applying to the U.S. Housing and Home Finance Agency (later the Department of Housing and Urban Development) for urban planning assistance funds. Many other councils throughout the nation followed its example only when pressured by the federal government.

With an initial grant of $171,000, supplemented by $86,000 in local contributions, the association in 1964 hired a regional planning director and a staff of thirteen and set to work on the formidable task of preparing an areawide plan reflecting regional concern with a wide spectrum of developmental problems. The organization was even ahead of the federal government in proposing a study of housing needs as an element of its land use planning program, although it did not actually create a regional housing task force until 1971, when minority groups accused it of dilatory actions.

Like all regional organizations of local government officials, ABAG was influenced from the outset not only by the momentum of events in the national capital and in Sacramento but also by the skillfully voiced demands of civic and special-interest groups. Among these were the Bay Area Council, representing powerful industrial and commercial firms, the Save San Francisco Bay Association, Citizens for Regional Recreation and Parks (later renamed People for Open Space), and a coalition of the Leagues of Women Voters. All these and other citizen groups were banded together for a time in the Bay Area Congress of Civic Organizations, for which the Bay Area Council served as a central secretariat beginning in 1963. Singly, as well as in unison, the members focused public attention on the interrelatedness of certain metropolitan issues and the urgency of solving critical problems through governmental action.

For many years the Bay Area Council had been particularly interested in transportation issues, and in 1962 it had been a force in convincing voters in San Francisco, Alameda, and Contra Costa counties to approve a bond issue of $792,000,000 for construction of a tricounty rapid transit system (BART) based on the areawide plan prepared in the previous decade. (Unfortunately, in that same year San Mateo and Marin counties withdrew from the five-county district established by the Legislature in 1957. Since Santa Clara County had initially been excluded from the district, owing to the opposition of taxpayer associations, agriculturists, and manufacturers in that county, the elimination of two additional counties of the Bay Area as much as ended hope that a fixed-rail system serving the greater part of the area would ever be built. Real-estate interests in San Mateo County feared that downtown San Francisco would be the chief beneficiary of the system, and the directors of the transit district had been obliged to ask Marin County to withdraw when they themselves could not resolve a dispute with the Golden Gate Bridge and Highway District over the feasibility of running trains across a second deck on the bridge.) Having successfully championed the development of a much reduced rapid transit system, the Bay Area Council in 1963 supported establishment by the legislature of a temporary Bay Area Transportation Study Commission, presumably to concentrate on relating transit and highway planning to detailed consideration of regional airports and bridges. ABAG soon entered into a joint planning effort with this short-term commission, nineteen of whose forty-one members were representatives of cities and counties and of ABAG itself.

Citizens for Regional Recreation and Parks, founded by Dorothy Erskine in 1958 and composed of individuals and groups interested in preserving open space and increasing public recreation areas, had in 1960 made a rough inventory of publicly owned, relatively permanent open space in the Bay Area that was incorporated into the California Public Outdoor Recreation Plan. Having broadened its sights, the organization a few years later was among the first to urge the Association of Bay Area Governments to develop a long-range, comprehensive regional land use plan, one element of which would be a plan for parks and agricultural greenbelts. To make sure that the regional planning program would proceed, the citizen group even assisted the ABAG staff in preparing an application for federal planning assistance funds. And once the general planning program was under way, the group presented the planning staff with a wealth of information, gathered from its constituent organizations and others, regarding areas that would be valuable additions to regional recreation resources or suitable as permanent agricultural lands, watersheds, marshlands, and community boundaries such as those already established by parks and reservoirs in the East Bay and on the San Francisco Peninsula.

This information was incorporated in ABAG's preliminary regional plan of 1966, in an open space element that many regarded as the outstanding feature of the plan. Even at that time the plan contemplated the reservation of 2,000,000 acres as permanent open space, in effect a regional greenbelt similar to the London greenbelt that had finally been established in the 1950's after sixty years of civic and legislative effort.

The Struggle to Save the Bay

While ABAG was instituting its planning program, agents of the National Park Service were busy purchasing properties to be included in a unique 53,000-acre preserve in Marin County, the Point Reyes National Seashore, which Congress had created in 1962. Controversy had marked the campaign to protect this geologically and ecologically unusual landscape, and ABAG had endorsed the congressional

measure despite the opposition of the Marin County Board of Supervisors. The interest aroused in safeguarding historic Drakes Bay and the unspoiled lands in the vicinity undoubtedly aided in focusing attention on another part of the natural heritage of the region that was also threatened by urban development—San Francisco Bay itself. Residents who had long taken the bay for granted as a priceless scenic asset, a great harbor, and an aquatic paradise for fishermen, duck hunters, marine biologists, and sailboat owners suddenly discovered, in response to alarms raised by the Save San Francisco Bay Association, that many local officials, developers, attorneys, banks, title insurance companies, large corporations, and state legislators regarded the huge estuarial system as preeminently desirable real estate.

Although the State of California still owned the greater part of the submerged lands of Suisun and San Pablo bays, it was in possession of less than half of San Francisco Bay proper. Prior to 1880 the state government had sold thousands of acres of tidelands and submerged areas into private ownership, and in the years before the opening of the Panama Canal the legislature had granted huge sections of the bay to cities, stipulating that the submerged acres might be leased for long periods but not sold. Now the public learned that Oakland, Berkeley, Richmond, San Rafael, and several other cities with bay waterfronts were contemplating filling in and permitting development on enormous areas of open, shallow water and tidal marshes. The master plan of San Mateo County indicated that as many as twenty-three square miles of bay tidelands might be transformed into residential, commercial, and industrial properties. The Save San Francisco Bay Association dramatized the dismaying possibilities by distributing leaflets with maps showing the great bay almost obliterated, its waters reduced to mere rivers flowing from the Sacramento–San Joaquin Delta and from Alviso at the southern end of the bay to the Golden Gate through miles of man-made, urbanized flatlands.

The leaflets reminded conservationists of a U.S. Department of Commerce report known as "The 2020 Plan," which was based on studies, carried out by the U.S. Army Corps of Engineers in the late 1950's, of long-range development trends in the Bay Area. Prepared to assist federal agencies and others responsible for making decisions about large-scale projects, the so-called plan made no pretense of advocating anything other than acceptance of presumably beneficial trends. It forecast a population of 14,400,000 in the Bay Area in the year 2020 and assumed that most of San Francisco Bay would have to be "reclaimed" to accommodate the teeming millions. The map depicting the shrunken bay represented the ultimate in nonplanning and was highly effective in mobilizing thousands of citizens to crusade against further destruction of a great body of water.

Convinced that strong measures were needed to halt piecemeal filling of the bay and the use of shoreline areas as garbage and refuse dumps, the leaders of the Save San Francisco Bay Association—Katherine Kerr, Sylvia McLaughlin, and Esther Gulick—urged the Institute of Governmental Studies at the University of California, Berkeley, to undertake a study illuminating the public interest in the bay and proposing some solution to the formidable environmental and political problems at issue. The institute engaged this writer to prepare a detailed report, which was released in the fall of 1963 and suggested that the state legislature create a bay conservation and development commission to make and carry out a comprehensive plan for the entire body of water.

"The mistakes of past generations," the report stated, "must not be allowed to deny present and future generations their rightful heritage: a superb bay used primarily *as a bay,* for navigation, production of minerals and fisheries, and for recreation and scenic enjoyment. Above all, the bay development agency must be able to destroy forever the notion that the bay is a potential source of new living space."[1]

Cautiously, the legislature created a study commission to consider what should be done about the bay, and when it too recommended the establishment of a special-purpose agency to exercise stewardship over the bay, the lawmakers in 1965 adopted the McAteer-Petris Act creating the temporary Bay Conservation and Development Commission (BCDC). The members were given until 1969 to formulate a plan for the bay and submit it to the decision-makers in Sacramento, together with a report suggesting whether a special-purpose agency regulating the bay should have other powers as well. Meanwhile, the commission was authorized to approve or deny all proposals for filling or dredging the bay. It was further enjoined to require public access to the bay in any developments it did permit.

The legislative injunction to consider additional functions for a permanent regional agency reflected keen interest among political and civic leaders of the Bay Area in the increasingly urgent problem of finding a unified approach to matters of areawide concern. In 1965, in the same legislative session that witnessed the creation of the Bay Conservation and Development Commission, the lawmakers also created a closely related agency, the San Francisco Bay–Delta Water Quality Control Program, with a mandate to study ways of avoiding large-scale pollution of the waters of the bay and delta by pesticides and fertilizers carried down by the Sacramento and San Joaquin rivers. It is significant that this agency and still another created two years earlier, the previously mentioned temporary Bay Area Transportation Study Commission, were directed, like BCDC, to recommend some permanent disposition of their responsibilities

in a long-term organization, preferably multipurpose. The issue of general-purpose regional government was therefore very much on the minds of most elected officials and prominent business and civic leaders who were at all concerned about regional problems.

Even the general assembly of the Association of Bay Area Governments, which had been divided on the question of whether there should be some statutory form of regional government, adopted a recommendation in 1966 supporting legislative creation of such a government. The members, or at least a majority of them, were looking ahead to the completion of their general plan of the Bay Area in 1970 and hoped that the association itself might be given authority to carry it out. In fact, in the fiscal year 1967–1968 the association, the Bay Conservation and Development Commission, the Bay Transportation Study, and the Bay-Delta Study together would be spending approximately $6,000,000 on their planning programs, to say nothing of amounts being spent by cities, counties, subregional agencies, and state and federal agencies for their own planning programs. Even though serious efforts necessarily had to be made to harmonize planning programs, it was obvious to almost everyone who thought about it that without some central agency legislatively designated to guide planning for the metropolitan region, a great deal of the money being spent on planning, and on projects based thereon, would be poorly spent and would bring less than satisfactory results. But the thorny issue of how a regional government with areawide planning responsibilities should be constituted had only begun to cause dissension among the proponents of limited areawide government—and it was this issue that would engender bitter animosities and bedevil the movement for metropolitan government.

When the Bay Conservation and Development Commission submitted its comprehensive plan for the bay to the state legislature in 1969, together with its report on long-term governmental regulation of the bay, it recommended that, preferably, BCDC should be transformed into a limited regional government concerned with several areawide problems of overriding importance. At the very least it should have permanent jurisdiction over development along the immediate shoreline of the bay and over filling and dredging in the bay itself. The Bay Area Transportation Study and the Bay-Delta Study agencies likewise favored regional multipurpose government. But another proposal for such government almost eclipsed the urgency of determining the fate of BCDC and embroiled the legislature in torrid argument.

Assemblyman William Bagley of Marin County introduced a Regional Home Rule Agency bill (AB 1846) providing for the conversion of the Association of Bay Area Governments into the proposed agency and for the assignment to it of the functions of BCDC and the temporary transportation and Bay-Delta agencies, as well as any additional functions that might desirably be entrusted to it in the future. Inasmuch as the bill called for a governing board composed entirely of locally elected officials, it could not have been more objectionable to the conservationists who were crusading to save the bay. In their eyes the member governments of the association had been guilty of permitting indiscriminate filling of the bay and the desecration of its shores. Nor were the protectionists in favor of another bill (AB 711) seeking to establish a limited, multipurpose regional agency but providing for a governing board elected by the voters by districts. Equally controversial as the bill introduced by Assemblyman Bagley, it appeared to offer no immediate prospect of a permanent governmental instrumentality empowered to carry on the work of the temporary Bay Conservation and Development Commission, even though the author, Assemblyman John Knox of Richmond, was wholly convinced of the need for long-term planning and control of the bay. The Save San Francisco Bay Association and its allies insisted on an agency concerned only with the bay, and that is what the legislature granted them at the very close of the session when it enacted the Knox-Petris bill giving a permanent, state-supported BCDC the sole function of regulating the bay in accordance with its carefully prepared, comprehensive plan.

Neither Bagley's bill nor the Knox bill providing for regional government survived the legislative debates. Thus the lawmakers, upon adjournment, left unsettled the burning issue of whether a regional governing board should consist exclusively of representatives of local governments or of persons chosen directly by the voters, or of some combination of both. As for the Association of Bay Area Governments, it suffered loss of prestige by failing to become a regional home-rule agency but did not surrender hope of eventually being empowered to carry out a plan for the nine-county metropolitan region. It was by then an organization representing eighty-two cities and eight counties; its annual budget was more than $1,375,000; and as an areawide advisory agency reviewing applications for federal grants, it was making recommendations each year on requests for some $200,000,000 of financial aid to build a wide range of local projects. Resilient in the face of setbacks, the association seized the opportunity, when the legislature terminated the Bay Area Transportation Study Commission, to sign an agreement with the State Business and Transportation Agency creating a regional transportation planning committee—a committee destined to be short-lived.

The Bay Conservation and Development Commission, the victor in the legislative wars, was soon making tough decisions to prohibit multi-million-dollar commercial projects on new fill on the San Francisco waterfront and to ban inappropriate development elsewhere. But it found that it needed additional authority to give more teeth to its regulatory powers. Strengthened by other legislative acts a few years later, BCDC was able to halt illegal filling without going to court, to order the removal of unauthorized fill, to require the destruction of dikes and the return of certain areas to marshland, and to maintain policies forcing cities and industries to initiate secondary treatment of effluent discharged into the waters of the bay.

In the ten-year period from 1974 to 1983 the commission reviewed and acted on applications for permits for 232 large projects, valued in all at more than $1,860,000,000 and affecting almost 500 acres of bayshore lands. A few applications were denied, but most were approved on the condition that the developers provide public access to the bay and agree to increase the surface area of the bay as much as possible in designing their projects. In one five-year period, for instance, the agency sanctioned 76 acres of new fill but through mitigation measures arranged for the creation of more than 400 acres of new bay, thereby achieving a net gain of 351 acres. For the ten-year period mentioned, the gain in open water was 625 acres. Public access to the bay was assured along twenty-nine miles of shoreline.

Like other governmental organizations with several gubernatorial appointees, the Bay Conservation and Development Commission is, however, not proof against political bending and perhaps cannot be depended on to carry out its legislative mandate consistently.

In the meantime, toxic pollution of the bay has increased alarmingly, owing to discharges from storm sewers, oil refineries and other industries, and to irrigation waste water laden with pesticides and fertilizers. The situation concerns not only the State Regional Water Quality Control Board but also other state agencies and the federal government. At issue, moreover, is a question of statewide importance: how much more fresh water can be diverted from rivers flowing into the bay without jeopardizing survival of the bay as a great estuarial system? All these problems constitute a crisis even more serious than the earlier one of a bay being reduced in size by indiscriminate filling.

A City-Centered Regional Plan

In 1970, the year after BCDC became a permanent agency, the Association of Bay Area Governments approved and published its long-awaited regional plan, designed to guide the growth and development of the nine-county region for the next twenty years. The plan was based on forecasts that the population of the Bay Area would be approximately 6,200,000 by 1980 and 7,500,000 by 1990—forecasts not anticipating much slower growth in the 'seventies and 'eighties than in previous decades, as can be seen by the fact that the regional population has not yet increased to the figure projected for 1980 by the regional planning staff and a citizen advisory committee.

Of paramount interest was the evidence of a dramatically changed perspective on the part of the locally elected officials who had been making decisions to guide the professional staff in the preparation of the plan. Instead of setting a goal of retaining only 2,000,000 acres in open space, the plan targeted 3,400,000 acres, of a total of 4,500,000 acres in the Bay Area, to be kept permanently free of urban encroachment. It suggested that rather than permitting new developments to sprawl in all directions, overrunning agricultural lands at the rate of 13,000 acres annually (an area half the size of San Francisco), efforts should be made to center growth compactly in existing central cities and in a number of outlying cities and small towns. Concentration not only would conserve valuable agricultural and recreational resources but also would lessen the cost of installing streets, sewers, and other essential facilities and would reduce time spent in daily travel.

The plan of course embodied compromises made at the insistence of various local governments, and it had not yet been refined to the degree desired by the highly competent planning staff. Still, the document presented more of a consensus than might have been thought possible a few years earlier. That the general assembly of ABAG chose to *approve* it unanimously, after much debate, but not to *adopt* it indicated that some city council members and county supervisors feared it would somehow restrict local decision-making if unreservedly accepted. It was therefore more a symbol of progress toward regional unity than a plan all communities in the region intended to consider seriously as they made controversial decisions on development proposals. Certainly, there was no rush to alter local plans and local zoning ordinances to conform with the general scheme, though the plan did have some beneficial influence throughout the 1970's.

One chapter of the plan, dealing with the knotty problem of implementation, seemed to adumbrate further battles in the state legislature, and indeed there were many, year after year, while the legislature itself created such other special-purpose agencies as the Metropolitan Transportation Commission (1970) and the Bay Area Sewage Services Agency, successor to the Bay-Delta Study Commission. In these political contests Assemblyman Knox continued to champion some form of regional government, one year seeking to establish an agency with only regional planning duties, in other years proposing to merge one or another or several of the existing special-purpose agencies with ABAG, thereby transforming it into a statutory regional government. But all

efforts to enact a measure creating some form of areawide government failed because the groups Knox sought to please invariably disagree about which matters are unquestionably metropolitan in scope and should be assigned to a multipurpose agency. The factions argued still more violently about the composition of the governing board, even though Knox, striving desperately to quell dissension, amended various bills to provide for a mixed board composed partly of city and county representatives and partly of directly elected citizen members, and even representatives of existing special-purpose agencies.

After 1975 the hardworking assemblyman was no longer willing to endure the annual ordeal. The politically potent Sierra Club had held out adamantly for a wholly elected board. The Save San Francisco Bay Association, always protective toward BCDC, had distrusted Knox for so much as thinking about merging that single-purpose agency with others. The Leagues of Women Voters, having made common cause with the Sierra Club year after year, had at last reluctantly agreed to accept a mixed board—after it was already too late to save any bill providing for regional government in the Bay Area. And at every legislative session, members of the John Birch Society had charged that regional government schemes were hatched in Moscow. As conservative legislators from southern California had watched Knox being caught up in divisive struggles, they had concluded that they themselves would be embroiled in similar clashes in their own districts if they set a precedent by establishing multipurpose metropolitan government in the Bay Area. Their "no" votes killed the much-revised bill embodying the compromises their colleague had pinned his hopes on.

The Association of Bay Area Governments continued for some years to lobby without success for bills that would give it statutory authority in an incremental fashion. The organization was, nevertheless, at the height of its influence about the time Assemblyman Knox announced that he would introduce no more bills providing for regional government. It had a staff of 125 and was reviewing more than one thousand proposed projects, most of which required federal assistance, for conformity with the goals and policies set forth in the 1970–1990 regional plan and its several elements, by then greatly broadened and refined. Thus, without having achieved the aim of becoming a regional planning district or a multipurpose regional government, ABAG was to some extent shaping regional development.

Emphasis on Regional Transit

Among the regional special-purpose agencies that Assemblyman Knox at one time or another proposed to merge with the Association of Bay Area Governments was the Metropolitan Transportation Commission (MTC), which had entered into a joint planning agreement with ABAG under which that organization was providing information about land use to the commission. The statutory agency, the only one of its kind in California, replaced the Bay Area Transportation Study Commission that had gone out of existence in 1969, and its advent marked the demise of the transportation planning committee formed by ABAG and the State Business and Transportation Agency.

Legislators recognized several compelling reasons for establishing the new regional transportation planning organization. Ever since the famous "freeway revolts" in San Francisco right after the Second World War and in the 1950's and 1960's, many people had viewed the highway bureaucracy in Sacramento as distant and insensitive to local social values and environmental concerns, as could be seen in its plans to thrust a freeway through Golden Gate Park and to disrupt residential neighborhoods with other multilane rivers of traffic. In the 1960's Congress had added to the pressure for a responsive regional transportation agency by enacting laws making funds for highways and transit in metropolitan areas available only on condition that a continuing, comprehensive transportation planning process was being carried on. But perhaps not until the Bay Area was anticipating the completion, early in the 'seventies, of the tricounty Bay Area Rapid Transit System (BART) did leaders in the nine-county region and in the legislature fully appreciate the importance of having a permanent organization that would be as much concerned with public transit as with private automobiles and trucks—and with other forms of transportation such as ships, airplanes, and trains. The urgent need, though, was for an agency that could assist the costly new rapid transit system, which might be underutilized unless local and subregional bus and railway lines were coordinated with it and their service areas enlarged. Only some areawide supervisory instrumentality would be adequate to oversee the rerouting and rescheduling necessary and to guide the creation of new collector services and the extension of existing routes to serve territories still lacking transit.

The legislative response to the immediate problem, and to others of even broader scope, was the new commission, positioned between the numerous local jurisdictions in the Bay Area and the state government. The board was composed mainly of representatives of the counties and cities in the area, but it also included official representatives of the Association of Bay Area Governments and the Bay Conservation and Development Commission. Nonvoting members represented the California Department of Transportation and two federal agencies, the Departments of Transportation and of Housing and Urban Development.

The new agency initiated its planning program at a time when only 6 per cent of all trips in the Bay Area were being made by public transportation. For two and a half decades federal housing programs had aided and abetted the development of subdivisions with single-family dwellings on large lots, and state and local highways had contributed to the ceaseless sprawl. The public, consequently, depended almost entirely on the private automobile for the daily journey to and from work, for shopping trips and errands, and for weekend travel. Many freeways and highways had already reached the saturation point at peak hours, and unless greater use of public transit could be stimulated, traffic on some routes would move with almost glacial slowness, frequently coming to a standstill. In preparing a regional transportation plan, the new agency was therefore to give particular attention to mass transit facilities, although the legislation creating the agency stipulated that it should also include in the plan the interstate highway system, freeways and expressways, conventional state highways, and transbay bridges, with the exception of the Golden Gate Bridge. (The bright red span was under the jurisdiction of a recently reorganized bridge and highway district authorized to develop bus and ferry services between San Francisco and the North Bay counties of Marin and Sonoma.) In 1972 the legislature added ports, airports, and private rail carriers to the list of elements to be included in the plan.

Two other parts of the agency's program were especially significant. The commission was to draw up a ten-year schedule of priorities for effectuating each element of the plan, project by project, and was to accompany it with a financial plan indicating the necessary sources of revenue. Ostensibly, the new agency was to be the final arbiter in regional transportation matters, approving some projects and vetoing others, but one section of the California Government Code cast doubt on whether the agency had authority to overrule some proposals of the California Highway Commission. In any event, the powers of the Metropolitan Transportation Commission seemed so awesome that it was greeted with suspicion by almost every political jurisdiction in the area and with outright hostility from the major transit bureaucracies, which immediately formed a defensive association, although some of them had been engaged in disputes with one another for years.

The commission was, however, no governmental tiger, as its decisions concerning the regional transportation plan indicated. The small staff chosen to prepare the plan—in all too short a time, since it was to be completed by June, 1973—at first attempted to make use of data assembled for the automobile-oriented plan of the predecessor Bay Area Transportation Study Commission, then devised a scheme based generally on the city-centered regional plan of ABAG. The staff's plan assumed a partial moratorium on freeway construction and a heavy reliance on rapid transit lines to serve densely populated areas. But to the distress of the young, idealistic, and perhaps somewhat doctrinaire members of the staff, the commissioners showed no disposition to endorse controls on urban expansion, strategies to discourage the use of automobiles, and the proposed curtailment of freeways. With a few exceptions, the commissioners were conservatives who viewed development as desirable (it supposedly enhanced the local tax rolls) and believed that determining how land should be used was the responsibility of local governments. They were undoubtedly also uncomfortably aware of being regarded as adversaries by city and county public works officials, state highway engineers, transit operators, and many community groups. Furthermore, they had as yet no great array of financial incentives to induce cooperation, only some carrots for the transit services: approximately $35,000,000 annually of sales tax revenues, generated by the state Transportation Development Act of 1971, to allocate among jealous, self-aggrandizing transit operators to encourage additional transit development. The commissioners therefore embraced what they called a "framework for planning" rather than the plan formulated by the staff, and what planning they did initially amounted more to political bargaining with various jurisdictions than to foresighted decision-making based on a well-balanced, environmentally sound set of goals and policies.

They angered conservationists and ardent regionalists by approving financing for a good many highway and freeway projects mainly because they were "in the pipeline," or, in other words, still in the planning stage but already having cost thousands of dollars for surveys, engineering studies, and financial calculations. Thus some of the commission's decisions contributed to new waves of low-density development, further loss of open land—and to the difficulty of operating transit services successfully in suburban areas.

Though the majority of commissioners tended to remain indulgent toward local governments, new laws of the mid-1970's broadened their perspective by giving them responsibility for reviewing and approving or disapproving a greater variety of projects, particularly in the field of transit. In 1973 an amendment to the Federal Highway Act authorized the use of highway funds for capital improvements in transit; in 1974 another federal law, the National Mass Transportation Assistance Act, provided substantial sums over a six-year period to subsidize transit operations. In 1974, California voters also approved Proposition 5, making funds in the highway users tax account available for transit research and planning as well as for highway and rail transit construction. By the fiscal year 1976–1977 the commission was screening a large number of projects and overseeing the allocation of more than $200,000,000 from various sources, local, state, and federal.

The beneficiaries of the coordinating, review, and financing services offered by MTC were numerous. Besides the "big three"—BART, the San Francisco Muni system, and AC Transit—they included, early on, a new transit district formed in Santa Clara County in 1972, a district organized in San Mateo County in 1974 (SamTrans), three new transit services in fast-growing Contra Costa County, and other transit operations in some of the North Bay counties.

By 1982 the executive director of the Metropolitan Transportation Commission, Lawrence D. Dahms, was able to report that whereas many urban areas of the United States had experienced losses in transit patronage, in the Bay Area transit ridership had increased 17 per cent in a decade. The ten-year gain could be credited in part to the inauguration of transbay service on BART in 1974 and to the stimulus this tricounty system gave to the establishment of local and subregional transit services, and in considerable measure the increase could be attributed to large infusions of federal, state, and local monies.

Though hundreds of thousands of commuters continue to rely on their automobiles, and though highways and freeways increasingly become choked with traffic at the beginning and end of the day, there have been indications from time to time that the public would readily support transit services if they were more widely available and convenient. In 1972, for instance, the voters of Alameda, Contra Costa, Marin, San Francisco, San Mateo, and Santa Clara counties displayed a certain faith in the potential of the new BART system by decisively rejecting a proposal to build a southern crossing for automobiles and trucks from India Basin in San Francisco to Alameda, veritably a twin of the San Francisco–Oakland Bay Bridge. To be sure, the immense cost of the project was a factor in its defeat, but many of the voters who cast their ballots against the proposed high-level span and its extensive approach systems were expressing their belief that when transbay service was opened by BART no second crossing would be needed. They expected to see BART succeed. Its poor performance for several years (it was plagued by mechanical failures) caused many people to continue using their automobiles for a few years longer, but eventually patronage rose to 200,000 passengers on weekdays—and critics grudgingly acknowledged that the system was "running both ways," carrying large numbers of commuters not only from the East Bay to San Francisco but also from "The City" and the Peninsula to centers in Alameda and Contra Costa counties. It was also attracting intensive development around some outlying stations (Walnut Creek and Concord), as planners of the system had theorized it would. Without it, downtown San Francisco would have suffered much sooner from the "gridlock" now threatening its economic health.

If transit has not yet developed to the extent desirable, it is

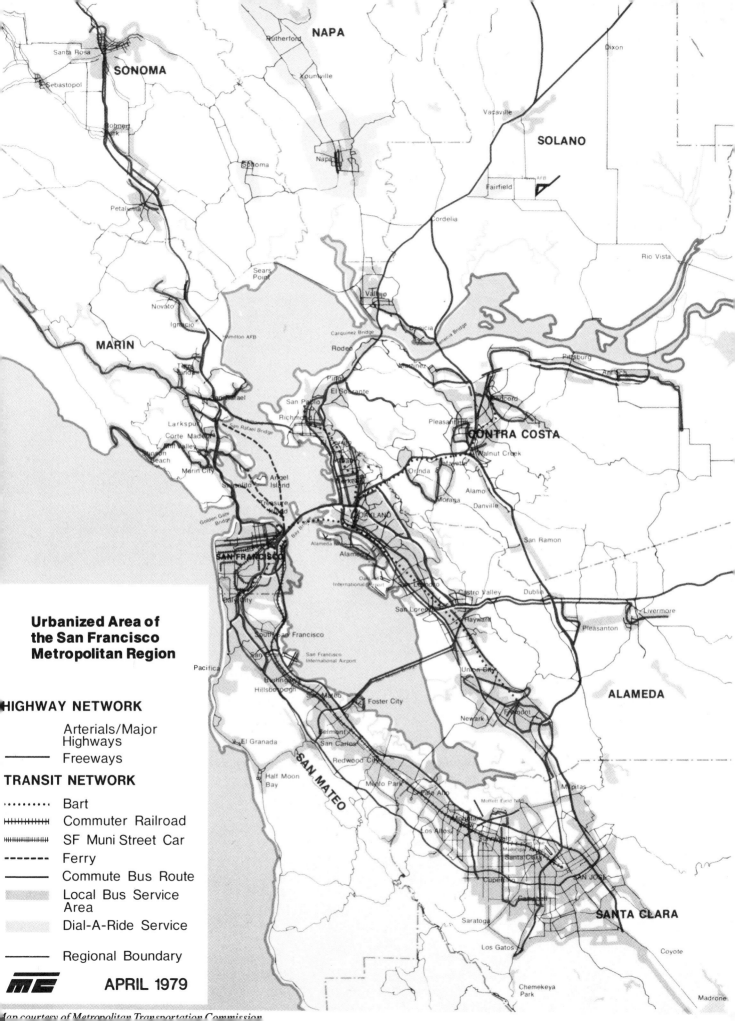

Urbanized Area of the San Francisco Metropolitan Region

HIGHWAY NETWORK

    Arterials/Major Highways

——— Freeways

TRANSIT NETWORK

·········· Bart

+++++++ Commuter Railroad

⊞⊞⊞⊞ SF Muni Street Car

------- Ferry

——— Commute Bus Route

▓▓▓ Local Bus Service Area

░░░ Dial-A-Ride Service

——— Regional Boundary

APRIL 1979

because federal, state, and local monies for transportation are limited, even though they amount to hundreds of millions, and because the costs of extending present systems, especially BART, are enormous, to say nothing about the huge sums needed to add light rail lines in several areas. The ten primary transit operators and the numerous other services in the nine-county region are, however, transporting approximately 1,300,000 passengers daily, and their combined operating budgets exceed half a billion dollars, placing the Bay Area among the metropolitan regions budgeting the most money for transit. A reasonable goal for the region by the end of the century, when the population may be 6,000,000 or more, might be an average of 1,500,000 passengers daily, given the probability that a great many areas can never be adequately served because of the low density of development, but not overlooking the possibility that changes in plans and policies of many cities might result in greater concentrations of population in the years ahead (about which more will be said later).

As an agency concerned, above all, with putting programs into effect, the regional commission has made an especially important contribution by recommending legislation in the national and state capitals to assure the flow of funds to carry out improvements in transit. In this it has been eminently successful, even in a time of reductions in government spending for urban programs. Of the projects it has furthered, several should be mentioned, such as the reconstruction of the San Francisco cable car system, the construction of turnback and storage yards in Daly City to increase the capacity of the BART system, and the upgrading and expansion of bus maintenance facilities for the AC Transit system, which now transports even more passengers—230,000 daily—than the tricounty rapid transit system.

Besides monitoring the performance of transit operators and undertaking programs to better their services, the commission works with businesses and industries to promote the use of transit, van pools, car pools, and bicycles. Of special interest was its advocacy a few years ago of a legislative measure giving permanent status to programs providing door-to-door van, bus, and taxi services for some 400,000 elderly and handicapped persons—the kinds of services the commissioners serving in 1973 did not think possible and dismissed from consideration.

Early in 1984 MTC announced a program for expanding regional transit facilities that evidently was intended to please everyone but actually satisfied very few. The projects included were estimated to cost $2,820,000,000, and even MTC conceded that there was little hope of inducing the federal government to provide the greater part of the money needed for construction. Examination of the "package" of proposed improvements and additions to regional transit

systems revealed, moreover, that only four projects had been fully agreed on and that the commission had merely authorized planning of most of the others. Studies of cost effectiveness, feasibility, and methods of financing could be expected to eliminate some of them. Transit operators and the public therefore wondered just what *would* be added to the transit facilities of the Bay Area in the future.

The four projects about which there was no doubt included a light rail line from the southern part of San Jose through the heart of the city to the Great America Parkway in Santa Clara, a BART rail yard and terminal facility at Colma, new cars and locomotives for the Peninsula commute trains, and a loop track near the Embarcadero Station for the San Francisco Muni Metro system.

Of the other projects listed in the commission's so-called blueprint, several were additions to the BART system that appeared to be based on the original nine-county plan prepared in the 1950's: an extension from Concord to West Pittsburg, another extension from the Bayfair Station in San Leandro to Dublin, and still another from Fremont to Warm Springs, with a light rail line from there to San Jose.

So much controversy swirled around seemingly conflicting proposals to extend BART from Daly City to the vicinity of the San Francisco International Airport in San Mateo County and to build a new terminal for Peninsula commute trains in downtown San Francisco that even after the commission approved both projects, many people still expected that only one would eventually be constructed, but they were uncertain which one it would be.

Proposals to acquire abandoned railroad rights-of-way in Marin County, the San Ramon Valley, and Concord and to reserve millions for unspecified rail projects in Santa Clara County brought charges from persons who support ABAG's city-centered plan for the Bay Area that MTC was encouraging urbanization to the very edges of the metropolitan region.

In sum, the expensive public works program put forth by MTC reinforced the impression that political considerations influence the decisions of the commissioners far more than any firm concept of desirable metropolitan development. The agency does not guide local and regional growth through its decisions; it tends to authorize transit services after growth has taken place.

As for air terminals and ports, MTC admittedly has done little besides including some long-term proposals in its regional transportation plan of 1980 and in revisions made since then. Many years before the agency was created, the status of the ports in the Bay Area had begun to change, owing chiefly to the dynamic expansion of the Port of Oakland to handle container ships. Since 1962, when the first container ship tied up at a terminal near the eastern approach

Seventh Street Public Container Terminal of the Port of Oakland. Photograph courtesy of
the Board of Port Commissioners, Port of Oakland.

to the San Francisco–Oakland Bay Bridge, the East Bay port has become the largest container port on the West Coast, with cargo-handling space of 535 acres and an investment of more than $200,000,000 in berths, container cranes, storage areas, and other facilities at its outer harbor, Seventh Street complex, and at its middle and inner harbors. The port now handles from 80 to 85 per cent of all container cargo and general cargo moving through the Golden Gate, whereas the Port of San Francisco, having none of the advantages of proximity to transcontinental rail lines, has steadily declined in importance. The Port of Richmond, though serving an increasing number of vessels, remains relatively small.

Of fifty companies whose ships call at the Port of Oakland, thirty-eight serve trade areas in the Far East, southeast Asia, Micronesia, Australia, and New Zealand. To expand this flourishing trade with countries of the Pacific and to maintain dominance as a container port against highly competitive rivals in southern California, the Pacific Northwest, and on the Gulf Coast, the port commissioners are making plans to enlarge terminal capacity. Among other things, the port must be able to accommodate in greater numbers a new class of container vessel that has recently entered world trade. These new ships measure as much as 860 feet in length and require a draft of thirty-eight feet or more. Certain channels will have to be dredged to a depth of forty-five feet if the ships are to avoid delays when the tide is low. The commissioners also look forward to increasing the port's trade with the less developed countries of Asia, Africa, Latin America, and the Middle East by offering facilities for combination carriers transporting new, smaller containers and general cargo.

The Oakland International Airport, situated on the bay front opposite the San Francisco International Airport, is under the direction of the Port of Oakland and has handled a rapidly increasing volume of air freight in recent years, as well as a steadily increasing amount of passenger traffic. A new passenger terminal is under construction, and plans have been drawn for a new air cargo building. The airports of Oakland and San Jose, both serving about equal numbers of passengers, cannot, however, compare in importance with the San Francisco International Airport, which handles approximately 80 per cent of all passenger traffic in the Bay Area, not to mention a large amount of air cargo.

Movements to Protect the Coast

The environmental movement that had supported the creation of the Bay Conservation and Development Commission—and had indirectly led to the establishment of the Metropolitan Transportation Commission—embraced new goals as soon as San Francisco Bay seemed assured of protection. In a little less than three years, from about the spring of 1970 until the fall of 1972, an initially rather uncoordinated effort of groups in San Francisco, Marin County, and elsewhere in the Bay Area coalesced into a concerted drive to persuade Congress to include areas on both sides of the entrance to San Francisco Bay in a great new federal preserve. The proponents, banded together as People for a Golden Gate National Recreation Area, exulted with their legislative hero, Representative Philip Burton, when President Nixon signed an act on October 28, 1972, safeguarding for the public some 25,000 acres of previously unprotected land and water—a magnificent recreational resource including miles of beaches, open space, and old forts in San Francisco, the headlands overlooking the Golden Gate, and rugged hills and coastal valleys in Marin County as far north as Mt. Tamalpais State Park. Together with that park, the watershed lands of the Marin Municipal Water District, and the Point Reyes National Seashore, the new recreation area formed an almost continuous greenbelt of 120,000 acres, all of it readily accessible to thousands of urban residents.

In 1984 a historically important area of 1,100 acres, Sweeney Ridge in San Mateo County, was added to the national recreation preserve, several years after the obdurate and unpopular former Secretary of the Interior, James Watt, had refused to act on the congressional authorization to purchase it. From this wild expanse south of Pacifica a group of Spanish explorers first viewed the waters of San Francisco Bay, then considerably more extensive than today.

Significant as the creation of the Golden Gate National Recreation Area was, it represented the attainment of a goal of lesser magnitude than another achieved almost at the same time. In the month following the signing of the act instituting the national preserve, conservationists celebrated the approval, by 55 per cent of the voters taking part in a California general election, of Proposition 20, otherwise known as the California Coastal Zone Conservation Act. The initiative established a coastal planning and regulatory commission and six subsidiary regional commissions modeled somewhat after the Bay Conservation and Development Commission, which had so impressed Janet Adams and other liberal activists on the San Francisco Peninsula that they had concluded a similar agency was needed to prevent further deterioration and destruction of the entire coast of California, extending 1,100 miles from the Mexican border to Oregon. These citizens were in the forefront of the movement to pattern the coastal commissions after BCDC, and later they formed the Coastal Alliance to monitor the performances of the new agencies and to defend the provisions of the coastal law, in much the same way that the Save San Francisco Bay Association closely watched the activities of the bay commission and fended off attacks on the legislation empowering it. If significant evidence were needed that the new coastal agency and its subsidiaries were politically descended from the Bay Conservation and Development Commission, what could be more convincing than the selection of Melvin Lane and Joseph Bodovitz, chairman and executive director, respectively, of the bay commission, to serve in the same capacities on the main coastal commission?

Congress, to be sure, had provided an incentive for states on the Atlantic and Pacific to protect their coasts. It had passed, earlier in 1972, the Coastal Zone Management Act, making federal loans and grants available to state and local governments for planning and regulation of coastal areas. And some would say that the passage in 1969 of the National Environmental Policy Act and the subsequent creation of the Environmental Protection Agency also contributed to the various movements in California and the Bay Area for preserving the natural beauty of the coast. But the Bay Area long before that had come to a zealous appreciation of the nation's more perishable assets and was already in the forefront of national movements to halt exploitation of scenic wonders. It was perhaps to be expected that a campaign to stop misuse of the coast and coastal waters would originate here, where success had crowned efforts to protect San Francisco Bay and its shores. The people of California needed only to be made vividly aware that coastal fields and open spaces were being overrun by new developments, that coastal forests were being carelessly logged and their streams silted by erosion, that coastal waters were being rapidly depleted of marine life by overfishing and the dumping of poisonous wastes, and that the estuaries and marshlands serving as the "nursery grounds" for many species of fish and wildlife were being dredged and filled as heedlessly as the wetlands around San Francisco Bay had been. If not all voters responded to the call to protect what remained of priceless resources, at least a substantial majority did, and the supervisory coastal commission and its six regional affiliates soon set to work developing plans for a coastal zone "extending seaward to the outer limit of the state . . . and inland to the highest elevation of the nearest coastal mountain range" (except in the three southernmost counties, where different provisions of law applied).[2]

Of the six regional commissions, two were responsible for planning coastal areas lying within Bay Area counties. A North Central Coast Regional Commission planned for the coastal zones of Sonoma, Marin, and San Francisco counties, while a Central Coast Regional Commission had jurisdiction over the coastal zone of San Mateo County, as well as over the coastlines of Santa Cruz and Monterey counties. These two regional organizations and the four others, guided by the state commission, had until December 31, 1975, to prepare a plan including every mile of the state's lengthy oceanfront. Meanwhile, every development proposal within a permit area 1,000 yards landward from the mean high-tide line had by law to be submitted to the appropriate regional commission for approval; if a proposal was rejected, the applicant could appeal to the state commission. All the commissions were thus obliged to spend much of their time reviewing requests for permits, yet the state plan, composed of regional components related to comprehensive goals established by the supervisory commission, was completed on time.

In a letter to the governor, the legislature, and the people of California, Chairman Lane of the state commission revealed that all the commissions together had acted on 16,000 permits, granting a high percentage but requiring "conditions to insure appropriate density of development, protection of ocean views, and, of great importance, increased public access to the oceanfront in appropriate areas."[3] In essence, the letter stated some of the principal objectives of the plan for the coast. The plan sought particularly to preserve agriculture on much of the San Mateo coast, to limit second-home developments on the Sonoma coast, to prohibit large commercial structures such as high-

rise hotels and shopping centers, to insure that coastal roads would be designed as recreational routes, and to ban unsightly billboards (existing billboards were to be removed within ten years).

Terminated at the end of 1976, the original coastal act was replaced the next year by a new one continuing the state commission indefinitely and permitting the regional commissions to operate until June 30, 1979. But in 1978 the legislature again extended the life of the regional commissions until midyear 1981—with the approval of most of the groups that previously had vigorously fought coastal planning and management. Thereafter the fifteen counties and sixty-eight cities along the coast took over planning and regulation within their jurisdictions once the state commission had approved their local coastal plans. Cities and counties remained, however, subject to the overview of the state commission, which could aid them in a consultant capacity or could veto proposed developments deemed incompatible with the intent of the coastal act and the overall plan, which in the meantime had been further detailed and adjusted to local situations.

New Regional and County Parks

The regionally and nationally important movements to protect San Francisco Bay, the California coast, the headlands of the Golden Gate, and the Point Reyes Peninsula have had subregional counterparts throughout the past twenty-five years, all aimed at preserving for public use nearby hill, mountain, and shoreline areas more suitable for recreation than for other kinds of development. In the East Bay, on the San Francisco Peninsula, and in Marin County, particularly, these local efforts have succeeded in greatly augmenting the number of unspoiled areas available for picnicking, hiking, horseback riding, boating, swimming, nature study, and, in certain places, organized sports.

The East Bay Regional Park District, serving all but a few relatively small areas in the counties of Alameda and Contra Costa, already had acquired and developed many recreational preserves before 1970, when residents in the district formed a "Citizens Committee for More Parklands" and planned a campaign to increase the tax resources of the jurisdiction. With the aid of the ever-constructive Assemblyman John Knox, the committee persuaded the state legislature to increase the property tax rate of the district significantly, providing substantial revenues for the acquisition of new parklands, as well as considerable monies for development and maintenance for a period of ten years. Sensibly, the directors of the district then engaged a planning organization headed by Stewart Udall, former Secretary of the Interior, to prepare a master plan to guide them in acquiring, developing, and operating additional regional

Open Space on the San Francisco Peninsula: An Element of the Regional Greenbelt Envisaged as a Goal of Bay Area Conservationists. Photograph courtesy of Air-Photo Company, Inc., and People for Open Space.

parks. Large committees of citizens and public officials, thousands of interested residents of the district, and the state legislative delegation from the East Bay contributed to the planning process.

Using the plan submitted by Udall and his associates at the end of 1973, the board of the district in the next five years purchased, acquired by gift, or leased for long terms some 20,000 acres suitable for recreational purposes, bringing the district's total parklands to 50,000 acres in the two counties. Thirteen in number, the new regional parks included six in Alameda County and seven in Contra Costa County. Among them were several shoreline areas on San Francisco Bay, acreage in the foothills of Mt. Diablo, an area on Mission Peak Ridge in southern Alameda County, and old quarries along Alameda Creek. Through its shoreline acquisitions, the district provided access to twenty-six miles of land fronting on San Francisco Bay. Almost 500 miles of trails wound through its parks.

A similar push to save foothill and bay lands for the use and enjoyment of the public got under way in 1972 when voters in northwestern Santa Clara County approved an initiative measure creating an independent special agency known at first as the Midpeninsula Regional Park District. Four years later voters in southern San Mateo County by the same means joined this district, bringing within its enlarged boundaries cities from San Carlos to Los Gatos. On the west the district embraced scenic lands along Skyline Boulevard, on the east the shores of San Francisco Bay.

By the end of 1983 the district (which in the meantime had changed its name to the Midpeninsula Regional Open Space District) had under its jurisdiction approximately 15,000 acres in Santa Clara and San Mateo counties. Several of its twenty preserves are along Skyline Boulevard, though a few, such as the Duveneck Windmill Pasture Area of 430 acres and the Fremont Older Preserve of 734 acres, are on the fringes of urban areas. Nine of the holdings include more than 500 acres each, and one, encompassing the entire upper Stevens Creek watershed in Santa Clara County, comprises 2,634 acres. Together with city-owned and county parks, the district's preserves in one area form a greenbelt nine miles long from north to south, offering urban residents all the variety of wooded canyons, grassy slopes with scattered native oaks and madrones, and secluded meadows in former ranchos.

So widespread was the desire for additional natural recreation areas in the early 'seventies that the electorates of both San Mateo and Santa Clara counties were willing to increase their taxes for the acquisition of more parklands by their county governments. The voters in San Mateo County adopted a "Charter for Parks" establishing a countywide special tax for park purposes. Voters in Santa Clara County passed measures in 1972 and 1978 providing more than $45,000,000 for park acquisitions in the ten-year period from 1972 to 1982. State and federal grants and funds from a 1964 park bond issue increased the total spent for approximately 23,000 acres of additional parklands to $52,376,000.

The largest of the parks purchased by Santa Clara County was the J. D. Grant Park of 9,529 acres, near Mt. Hamilton in the Diablo Range on the east side of the Santa Clara Valley. History buffs were especially pleased by the acquisition of the famous Almaden quicksilver mines, now included in a park of 3,750 acres in the Santa Cruz Mountains. Numerous properties bought over a period of nine years formed the Sanborn Skyline Park of 3,154 acres, in the same range. The county park department and the Santa Clara Valley Water District together purchased additional parcels around several reservoirs previously developed by the district, and the park department then acquired the right of perpetual access for public park and recreational purposes to lands belonging to the district. These water-oriented areas are popular among people who enjoy boating and water sports.

The San Mateo County Park Department also expanded its facilities by adding many more mountain areas relatively close to cities. Among the properties that came into its possession was the greater part of San Bruno Mountain, acquired partly by purchase and partly by gift. Although building is occurring on the lower slopes of this geographic landmark, the top, which is something of a botanical paradise to the initiate, remains accessible to the public.

In 1972 the voters of Marin County approved a measure creating a Countywide Open Space District and authorizing an increase in property taxes to enable the new district to purchase acreage in the greenbelt of ridges between the farmlands in the central part of the county and the band of cities in the eastern part. Some of the lands acquired by the district also serve as natural buffers between cities. Significantly, the new governmental agency was an outgrowth of the countywide planning process, mentioned earlier, in which the cities and the county together developed a long-range general plan. One of the purposes of the plan was to serve as a basis for zoning the central area of the county for agriculture and removing the threat of urbanization.

Sonoma County established a regional park department in 1967 and began developing a park system based on a long-range recreation plan approved in 1964. Of 6,000 acres proposed for purchase, 2,600 acres had been acquired by the late 'seventies, but county planners were pointing out that the county had a long way to go to complete a system initially intended to include thirty-two parks.

The Department of Parks and Recreation of the state, benefiting from five park bond issues passed between 1964 and 1980, has added greatly to the recreation resources of this especially scenic coastal county. It has acquired three parks of more than 4,000 acres each, another of 3,140 acres, and still another of 2,326 acres, as well as several smaller areas.

The programs of all local park departments and of such subregional agencies as the Midpeninsula Regional Open Space District and the East Bay Regional Park District suffered serious setbacks when the voters approved Proposition 13 in June, 1978, after the state legislature itself had wrangled throughout its regular session over tax-reduction bills and had belatedly decided to place on the ballot a proposition a good deal less drastic, and far less appealing to the public, than the state constitutional amendment sponsored by tax-cutters Howard Jarvis and Paul Gann. The midpeninsula agency immediately lost 35 per cent of its tax revenues. Even with the small increases that have been permitted annually since the passage of Proposition 13, the district now has only half as much for acquisition and development as it had prior to passage of the Jarvis-Gann initiative. The East Bay Regional Park District was forced to bring its land acquisition program almost to a halt. Previously more than 80 per cent of the district's revenues had come from property taxes; in 1979 and 1980 less than 60 per cent derived from that source, and the board of directors looked to the state legislature for "rescue funds." The cities of California lost $800,000,000 in tax revenues and eliminated more than 3,000 positions, including some employees in park and recreation departments. The net effect of tax reduction—apparently not foreseen by many voters—was swiftly to curtail the expansion of park systems, except for occasional gifts of land, for which there was little or no money for development and maintenance.

Local governments and park districts have attempted to meet severe decreases in tax revenues by a variety of stringent measures. Besides laying off workers, they have limited staff activities, canceled some training programs, imposed fees and user charges (or increased those already in effect), and reduced the number of hours parks are open to the public. In a time of restricted state revenues and cutbacks in federal grants for park development, no resumption of the remarkable acquisition programs of the 'seventies can be expected.

Efforts to Preserve Farmlands

Throughout the period with which this chapter is concerned, campaigns to protect scenic and recreational resources have been paralleled by efforts to conserve farmlands by slowing down or limiting urban sprawl, or by establishing agencies to preserve agricultural lands. The state legislature has enacted several statutes designed to discourage haphazard urbanization and safeguard fertile soils, and cities and counties have also adopted local measures to prevent the encroachment of subdivisions on good agricultural lands.

One of the outcomes of the Governor's Commission on Metropolitan Area Problems in the early 1960's was legislation creating in each of the fifty-eight counties of the state a Local Agency Formation Commission, in the hope that such agencies would be able to maintain "the physical and economic integrity of agricultural preserves" and promote the orderly development of local governments, including special districts providing various types of urban services—sewers, water lines, police and fire protection—to areas on the fringes of cities. Unfortunately, rapid growth in the 1950's and the first few years of the 'sixties had already checkered many fine agricultural areas with subdivisions before the new commissions came into being. This was particularly true of the northern Santa Clara Valley. Some commissions thus were obliged to deal with conditions not amenable to much improvement, and hardly any of these fledgling agencies were really equipped to perform their functions adequately. They were directed to review and approve or disapprove proposals for the incorporation of cities, the consolidation of two or more cities, the annexation of territory to cities, and the formation, expansion, merger, or dissolution of special districts. To discharge their legislative mandates well, they needed to be, in effect, planning commissions, taking a comprehensive view of the county and determining which areas should be urbanized and which should remain as productive agricultural lands. Yet these agencies had no technical staffs and were dependent on county planning departments for assistance in making decisions about staging urban development and extending or limiting the service areas of special districts. Not until 1971 did the legislature even require them to make or obtain the kinds of studies essential in formulating policies and determining "spheres of influence" of municipalities and special districts.

Lacking guidance from a supervisory state board, the commissions have interpreted their mandates in various ways and in general have not been notably successful in stemming the outward thrust of cities and the loss of farmlands. By the time the commission in Santa Clara County got around to drawing lines around cities to indicate areas needed for development both within five years and in a second stage of ten years, so much subdividing and building had taken place in the northern part of the county that the commission was doing little more than establishing boundaries between cities. In Contra Costa County, in contrast, the local agency formation commission endeavored to draw "sphere of influence" lines rather tightly around cities, showing areas to which growth would be confined for ten years at the most. Within the relatively small geographic area of each sphere no attempt was made to achieve a concentric growth pattern, stage by stage. Small-scale, leapfrog development resulted, pushing growth in some places to the edges of city "spheres" and creating pressures for expansion. In Solano County, which even today has more than 170,000 acres in intensive production, the county planning department has been sharply critical of the local agency formation commission for including within city spheres of influence highly productive agricultural lands "not currently designated for development on local general plans, [thereby] creating uncertainty in the timing and direction of future urban development."[4] The commission's policies, the department observed in a report issued in December, 1980, "may encourage speculation and premature conversion or commitment of agricultural lands to urban uses and disrupt the local farming economy."[5]

Another measure that has fallen short of holding the line against untimely urbanization is the Williamson Act, passed by the legislature in 1965. Under this act farmers may contract with the county to keep their lands in production for at least ten years in return for taxation of the land as an agricultural preserve, instead of as potential urban land, subject to higher assessed valuation and higher taxation. Although some 2,200 square miles of farmland were under contract in Bay Area counties at the end of 1980, the law does not require farmers to renew contracts when they expire. If a farmer's holdings are within the sphere of influence of a city or special district and some developer offers a high price for the land at the expiration of the farmer's contract, the temptation to sell out is almost irresistible.

The alternative to governmental efforts to protect farmlands from the threat of urbanization may be the privately organized agricultural land trust. With the assistance of the Trust for Public Land, dairy ranchers and conservation groups in the western part of Marin County incorporated the Marin Agricultural Land Trust in July, 1980, and set about investigating the possibility of acquiring the development rights over farmlands or purchasing properties outright and then selling or leasing them to the former owners with restrictions on development. Early in 1983 the Marin County Board of Supervisors, who also serve as directors of the Marin County Open Space District, voted to allow 10 per cent of the district's acquisition funds to go to the land trust for the purchase of agricultural easements in western Marin. The action had the strong support of county residents.

Four other Bay Area counties (Santa Clara, Contra Costa, San Mateo, and Sonoma) make some use of open space easements—without having induced many farmers to turn over development rights to the county government for a limited period or permanently.

Since the Second World War county governments in the Bay Area and elsewhere in California have used, with varying degrees of success, a regulatory method of giving some protection to farmlands: zoning that establishes the minimum size of parcel considered appropriate to the scale of agricultural production in particular areas. Zones with minimum parcels of forty, sixty, eighty, one hundred, or one hundred sixty acres have served well in a number of instances to encourage the continuation of agricultural production. But zones permitting parcels as small as two-tenths of an acre, as in some parts of Napa County, or zones establishing minimum sizes of one and a half, two, or five acres, favor the creation of "ranchettes" and weekend homes and hardly retard urbanization. In the late 'sixties Napa County, which has a unique combination of soil and climatic conditions that make it ideal for viniculture, was the scene of an intensive struggle to retain reasonably large minimum parcels in the best wine-producing areas. Still later, in 1980, concerned residents of the county responded to the threat of more and more small-parcel developments by submitting a "slow growth" initiative to the voters. The measure, overwhelmingly approved, limits the number of new housing units permitted in unincorporated territory to 118 annually, in accordance with a formula restricting the population growth rate to approximately that of the nine-county Bay Area yearly.

Since zoning in unincorporated areas can be changed at any time by vote of the county supervisors, it is not a reliable instrument for preventing farmlands from being parceled into smaller holdings, as numerous rezonings on the fringes of urban areas have shown.

Seeking more dependable means of conserving agricultural lands, the group known originally as Citizens for Regional Recreation and Parks and later as People for Open Space (POS) recommended in 1968 that the legislature create a regional open space agency as part of a regional government. If no such government were authorized, POS at least hoped for an independent commission similar to the Bay Conservation and Development Commission. As an initial step toward the establishment of such an agency, the citizen organization proposed a study commission that might later become a special-purpose agency or a department of a multifunction regional government.

A grant from the Ford Foundation had enabled the civic group to make a study showing that the proposal contained in the preliminary regional plan of the Association of Bay Area Governments for a large amount of permanent open space was economically sound and financially practicable. When the legislature reacted coolly to the proposal for an open space agency, POS in 1970 recommended enactment of a bill creating a study commission, only to see the bill killed in the Senate Finance Committee. Still another effort in 1971 for authorization of an environmental agency concerned not only with open space but also with air and water quality and preservation of the bay failed in the state Senate after passing the Assembly. Some members of POS then attempted to work with ABAG in an advisory capacity, investigating other ways to carry out the greenbelt plan embodied in the association's regional plan. But the conservationists found, not altogether to their surprise, that some local governments were unenthusiastic about an areawide greenbelt, especially if it were to be protected by another regional governmental agency.

More determined than ever to overcome the opposition, POS between 1974 and 1978 took steps to become a more influential organization and to arm itself with detailed information about agricultural lands in the Bay Area. It broadened its membership, engaged a small, full-time professional staff, and applied to a foundation for funds to mount a Greenbelt Action Program. Undaunted by being turned down, the organization then approached another foundation and was able to obtain a grant for a two-year study of crop and grazing lands throughout the region. This new endeavor also included investigation of all possible methods of protecting farmlands.

The report on the study, published in the fall of 1980 under the title *Endangered Harvest: The Future of Bay Area Farmlands,* was hailed as the first really extensive presentation of agricultural problems and issues facing the people of the Bay Area. Its appearance signaled the start of yet another campaign in Sacramento, this time for a bill to establish a Bay Area Agricultural Lands Conservation Commission. Many civic groups supported the proposal, and newspapers of wide circulation published editorials commending it. Individual legislators also endorsed it. Still, the general legislative response was negative: saving farmlands would hem in urban areas and lead to a shortage of housing.

To counter this persistent assertion, the leaders of People

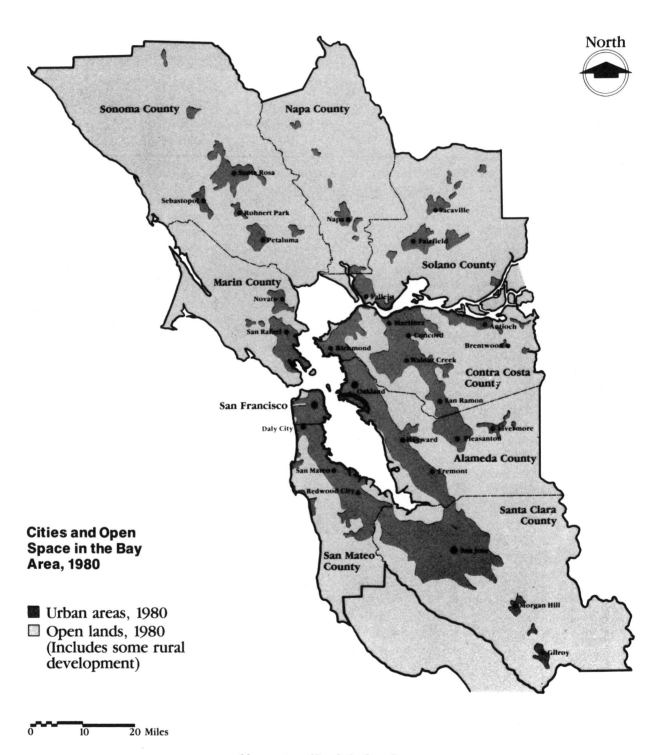

North

**Cities and Open
Space in the Bay
Area, 1980**

■ Urban areas, 1980
□ Open lands, 1980
(Includes some rural
development)

0   10   20 Miles

Map courtesy of People for Open Space.

Sonoma County

Napa County

Santa Rosa
Sebastopol
Rohnert Park
Petaluma

Napa

Vacaville

Fairfield

Solano County

Marin County
Novato
San Rafael

Vallejo

Martinez
Concord
Richmond
Walnut Creek

Antioch

Brentwood

Contra Costa
County

Oakland
San Ramon

San Francisco

Daly City

Livermore
Hayward
Pleasanton

Alameda County

San Mateo
Redwood City

Fremont

Santa Clara
County

San Mateo
County

San Jose

Morgan Hill

Gilroy

for Open Space decided on a further study, supplementing the one already made. In the fall of 1983, *Room Enough: Housing and Open Space in the Bay Area* came off the press. Its dissemination marked the beginning of what will probably be a prolonged effort to convince Doubting Thomases that the objective of saving farmlands and other elements of a regional greenbelt is not in conflict with the aim of providing living space for additional hundreds of thousands of residents. *Room Enough* pointed out that 580,000 units (90 per cent of the new homes expected to be needed in the next twenty years) could be built on lands within existing cities and on 123,000 acres already designated for residential use on the fringes of urban areas in the metropolitan region. The publication urged "infilling" in cities: using vacant land more effectively, building more housing along major streets and in business districts, adding second units in existing houses and on lots containing one single-family home, and constructing housing on land formerly used for industry. To convince readers of the practicality of these suggestions, the authors of the booklet illustrated it with photographs showing examples of buildings erected in a dozen or more cities, counties, and special districts of the Bay Area in accordance with measures permitting more compact development.

Controversy over establishing permanent limits on urban expansion by creating a greenbelt can be foreseen in county after county and in almost every outlying city of the metropolitan area. Although POS has posed the issue regionally, its members realize that farmland is not, like San Francisco Bay, so highly visible to all that piecemeal destruction can be readily observed, made the subject of regional protest, and quickly stopped. The organization has adopted a strategy of supporting the efforts of local groups to carry out county greenbelt plans. The effectiveness of this approach was demonstrated in the spring of 1984 when POS helped an "orderly growth" committee in Solano County design an initiative measure requiring the county board of supervisors to abide by the county general plan adopted in 1980 and direct development toward the seven incorporated communities of the county. The initiative, passed with a majority of fewer than 300 votes, immediately blocked the development of a proposed new town on 1,000 acres of grassland near Vacaville and clouded the future of a housing project near Fairfield. Although the measure forbids the supervisors to rezone farmlands and open space in unincorporated areas without holding a countywide election, it does not prevent municipalities from annexing agricultural land on their borders. The struggle to save open space in Solano County is, therefore, not over, but the victory of the conservationists at the polls has stimulated groups in other Bay Area counties to campaign for local plans, policies, laws, and official actions that may cumulatively result in the achievement of a regional greenbelt.

Perhaps an even more difficult task for POS will be persuading citizens and city council members in some communities to change their minds about allowing second units in single-family neighborhoods and encouraging people to build residential units on commercial thoroughfares. As the distinguished city planners who participate in the activities of POS know, for many years the American planning profession preached its own special brand of orthodoxy, upholding the single-family neighborhood as sacrosanct and anathematizing the area with "mixed use." They should not be surprised to discover that citizens far and wide also embraced the professional articles of faith and now tend to resist revisionism, as can be seen in a bulletin of the Northeast Berkeley Association that reacted to a recently enacted state measure permitting the conversion of single-family homes into two apartments: "We already have serious problems. Further increasing density by adding second units will aggravate these problems."[6] The bulletin foreshadows the heated debates that will attend efforts to adopt some of the infilling strategies advocated by People for Open Space.

Although not enacted with any intent to limit the encroachment of new housing developments on outlying farmlands, growth-management measures adopted by thirty-five or more cities in the Bay Area have had the effect of slowing down and reining in urban expansion and, consequently, of prolonging the economic life of a goodly amount of acreage planted to field crops and orchards. The primary purpose of these local laws has been to reduce the costs of servicing residential areas on the fringes. One of the strongest of these ordinances aimed at curtailing peripheral subdivisions was enacted by Petaluma in 1978. It established a "residential development control system" limiting housing starts to 500 units annually, exclusive of individually built homes and apartments of fewer than five units. Citizens who supported adoption of the measure were concerned not only with preventing too rapid extension of the city but also with maintaining continuity of development and a certain community character. Some feared, however, that a policy of slow growth, unless carefully and responsibly managed, might become exclusionary and result in higher housing costs. Their misgivings were reflected in special provisions requiring developers to include some housing for families with low to moderate incomes. Unfortunately, though, President Nixon severely cut back federal housing programs soon after the ordinance was enacted, making it difficult if not impossible for developers to comply with provisions of the ordinance aimed at creating housing for families of limited means.

Considered drastic and revolutionary at the time it was added to the municipal code, the Petaluma ordinance was attacked as unconstitutional. Eventually the case reached the United States Supreme Court, which upheld the measure by refusing to reverse a lower court decision in favor of the city. Since then the Petaluma ordinance has served as a model for other cities facing the fact that it usually costs far more to provide police and fire protection, sewers, water lines, and other municipal services to new residential areas than these areas return in taxes. Even the nearby municipality of Rohnert Park, which had shown distaste for most forms of control, later followed Petaluma's example by adopting an ordinance imposing strict limits on the number of new homes permitted each year.

The passage of Proposition 13 soon after Petaluma embraced restrictions on residential construction made municipalities more cautious than ever about extending their service areas, because revenues from taxes on property plummeted. Besides increasing business license fees and various user charges, most cities raised development fees and other exactions related to new construction, thereby adding to the cost of bringing new residential areas on the market. Developers reasoned that they had no choice but to build for a more affluent and numerically smaller segment of the public. Not all growth-control ordinances enacted after Petaluma's was found to be constitutional have included requirements that developers provide some low-cost housing, and the cities that do obligate developers to build some inexpensive units have rarely been able to obtain as many units as desired. Growth-control systems, together with diminished local governmental revenues, have thus denied all but a few families with low incomes the opportunity to own new homes—not that developers, even before the 'seventies and 'eighties, had been able to build low-cost units for such families. The Bay Area, like other metropolitan regions, had failed for decades to provide an adequate supply of new housing, particularly units within the reach of those on the lower rungs of the economic ladder. Except for a relatively small percentage of families eligible for subsidized public housing (most of which is in the older central cities), households in the lower income brackets expected to live in the aging and more run-down sections of urban areas.

In recent years inflation and high interest rates have further excluded the lower middle-income groups from the market for new housing. In Contra Costa County, for instance, hardly any of the homes built in the past decade have been within the means of blue-collar workers, the elderly living on small fixed incomes, and minorities. The county is deficient in what has come to be known as "affordable" housing, as are other counties in the region.

In sum, municipal retrenchment, reductions in federal housing assistance programs, the high cost of borrowing money, and cutbacks in state programs have all retarded the onslaught on the green acres of the countryside but have not

permanently deflected it. A huge new office complex has arisen in the San Ramon Valley, large new industrial plants have won approval in Rohnert Park and in the Coyote Valley south of San Jose, and an industrial park of several thousand acres has been proposed for Vacaville. Each of these developments has triggered, or will trigger, plans for new residential projects, almost all to serve upper-middle-income and high-income families. The principals in the new enterprises assume that they will find the kinds of workers they need in suburbia, but the assumption may turn out to be a gross miscalculation. If it should be incorrect, and if workers must be drawn from the older cities of the Bay Area or from other peripheral cities, the strain on trafficways and on the daily lives of the suburban workers will be intensified by long and costly commutes. Further, the social imbalance between the older cities and the newer ones will become all the greater.

Regional Growth in the Future

No one can fail to be impressed by the vigor with which conservationists, many political leaders, most members of the city planning profession, and thousands of concerned citizens throughout the Bay Area have challenged some of the frontier values and attitudes of this country in the past twenty-five years. No longer is growth considered unquestionably desirable. Today these are some of the queries put to city councils, county boards of supervisors, and officials of special districts, and to chambers of commerce, industrial groups, and trade associations: Which kinds of growth should be encouraged? Which discouraged? Where should growth take place, and where should it be prohibited? And, indeed, how much growth should be permitted?

In a dynamic, ever-changing society, increasing in scientific knowledge and technological capability and continually developing new enterprises, there can be no immutable answers to any of these questions. But certainly such questions must be asked more frequently and more insistently in the years ahead, with the hope that time and experience will yield answers that appear reasonable to greater and greater numbers of people. For it has become clear that the United States, and especially the Bay Area, is in the midst of an ethical revolution, struggling to elevate quality above quantity, to foster wise, long-term use of resources rather than hasty, greedy exploitation, and to honor those who are protective of nature and the most inspired works of man instead of those who achieve wealth and position by endangering or destroying the common heritage.

No stronger evidence of a new moral climate can be cited than the California Environmental Quality Act, placed on the statute books in 1970 and in effect since January, 1971. The author of this law was that champion of worthy causes,

Assemblyman John Knox, chairman of the Assembly Committee on Local Government. In words reflecting the fervor of the environmental movement of the 1960's, the act declares that it is the policy of the state to "develop and maintain a high-quality environment now and in the future, and take all action necessary to protect, rehabilitate, and enhance the environmental quality of the state."[7] A subsection of the statute is more specific, stating that the people of California are to be provided with "clean air and water, enjoyment of aesthetic, natural, scenic, and historic environmental qualities, and freedom from excessive noise."[8] To achieve these and other desirable objectives, the act directs "all state agencies, boards, and commissions" to prepare, or obtain under contract, "an environmental impact report on any project they propose to carry out or approve which may have a significant effect on the environment," particularly adverse or irreversible effects that might lead to a project being abandoned altogether or substantially altered in design, or replaced by some alternative.[9] Among other things, "the growth-inducing impact" of any proposed project must be set forth.[10]

The act directed the state Office of Planning and Research to develop guidelines for public agencies to use in preparing environmental impact reports, commonly known as EIRs. Together with the act itself, these regulations and procedural directives constitute the chief means of implementing the policies embodied in the legislation.

Like all measures treating significant and complex subjects, the Environmental Quality Act has been amended many times in the light of experience, and further statements of legislative intent and policy, additional definitions, and numerous clarifications have been added. Similarly, the guidelines have been expanded to explain changes in the law and to institute necessary new procedures.

A court decision in an important case arising in 1972 held that the act applied not only to all departments of state government but also to counties, cities, regional agencies, public districts, redevelopment agencies, and all other political subdivisions of the state. Further, private projects for which public agencies issue permits require environmental impact reports, and cities preparing plans for particular areas, such as a central business district, must subject their own plans to the intensive analysis set forth in the state guidelines.

A study made in 1979 revealed that about 7 per cent of proposed projects were abandoned because of unfavorable environmental impact reports. Many others were probably never even initiated because of fear that they might not meet the test of an EIR. Of adverse environmental effects identified by the study, more than three-fifths proved to be amenable to mitigation.

Housing developments of various kinds far outnumber other proposed projects, such as industrial and commercial projects and public works, that require EIRs. Cities and counties concerned with the potential impact of residential growth on natural resources and urban service systems therefore have come to view the impact report as a welcome device for addressing problems related to growth on a project-by-project basis. Developments that would increase traffic congestion, degrade native habitat, produce excessive noise, overload public services, or increase the consumption of energy either are turned down or returned to the drawing board for suggested changes. Projects that would cause air and water pollution, produce heavy runoff and increase erosion, result in loss of open space, impair views and vistas, greatly change the character of a neighborhood, or disturb sites of archeological value also run the risk of being rejected or held up until they have been redesigned to correct their worst deficiencies.

Developers of course complain of the paperwork and costly delays occasioned by the application of the Environmental Quality Act and its guidelines to their projects, especially when EIRs cite matters not particularly relevant to their proposals. City planners note, however, that some impact reports prepared by consultants are not sufficiently broad and do not take into account the effects of a proposed project on an entire region rather than just on the immediate vicinity.

In the 1983 session of the state legislature, development and construction interests sought to weaken the standards by which proposed projects are judged and to impose huge bonds and attorneys' fees on citizens seeking to enforce the Environmental Quality Act, which is the only environmental law of California necessitating citizen initiative before the courts—no public agency is charged with its enforcement. The Planning and Conservation League of California and other citizens' organizations, aided by strong positions taken by the attorney general, repelled major attacks on the statute, but they expect renewed efforts to reduce its effectiveness. It seems unlikely, though, that citizens familiar with the beneficial provisions of the act will permit it to be emasculated. They might even succeed, as one legal scholar has suggested, in inducing the legislature to add to the law an authorization for the courts to exercise their independent judgment, for instance when reviewing an agency's determination that some reasonable alternative to a proposed project is "infeasible" and that the project should be given the green light even though it might affect the environment harmfully in some respects.

Although environmental impact reports and public hearings on proposals do not invariably prevent the construction

Significant Additions to the Cultural Facilities of the Bay Area:
Above, The Oakland Museum, 1969. Kevin Roche & John Dinkeloo, architects; Dan Kiley and Geraldine Knight Scott, landscape architects. Photograph courtesy of The Oakland Museum.
Below, Berkeley Repertory Theatre, 1980. Eugene F. Angell, AIA–Lockwood & Associates, architects. Photograph by George P. Post.

Above, Louise M. Davies Symphony Hall, San Francisco, 1980. Skidmore, Owings & Merrill, architects. Photograph courtesy of San Francisco Symphony Association.
Below, The Concord Pavilion, 1975. Frank O. Gehry, architect; Christopher Jaffe, acoustician. Photograph courtesy of Concord Department of Leisure Services.

of undesirable buildings or the development of subdivisions in areas where there ought not to be any, the requirements of the Environmental Quality Act represent a salutary broadening of the whole planning process, making public officials as well as developers more socially responsible and more considerate of the sensibilities of the community. Indeed, public officials risk the censure of the courts if they disregard important findings in an EIR. Early in 1984 a unanimous State Court of Appeals harshly criticized the City Planning Commission and Board of Permit Appeals of San Francisco for failing to follow state guidelines in estimating the effect of four proposed high-rise buildings on an already densely built section of the downtown area. Specifically, the court found that officials had not heeded the testimony of Richard Sklar, former manager of public utilities, who pointed out that the quartet of buildings "would cause such an overload on the present [Muni] system that it would be 'near cattle car status.'"[11]

The California Environmental Quality Act and local growth-control ordinances suggest a host of intriguing questions. If a city has the constitutional right to limit its growth to a certain number of new dwelling units annually, does it have the right to declare, at some point, that it does not wish to add any more peripheral developments at all? Will a case eventually come before the United States Supreme Court in which attorneys for some city in the Bay Area contend that growth beyond the existing developed area and the existing level of economic activities would be inimical to the health, welfare, and safety of the residents, and perhaps injurious to the entire surrounding subregion? Will a majority of the justices hold that the city may indeed henceforth restrict construction to a limited amount of infilling and may issue business licenses for no more enterprises than are considered necessary to assure the viability of the local economy?

These very questions may outrage many persons, yet they arise logically from the premises on which growth-management laws and the California Environmental Quality Act are based. If a court, in a decision citing that act, takes city commissions severely to task for ignoring warnings that more tall buildings will strain the capacity of the local transit system beyond all human comfort and convenience, is it not implying that there are limits to the amount of office space and employment that an area—in this instance, downtown San Francisco—can accommodate without adversely affecting the mental and physical health of commuters and residents alike?

A proposition to curtail the number of tall buildings erected in downtown San Francisco lost at the polls in 1983, and now still more multistory structures are going up in this center to which access can be gained only by transit systems, bridges, and freeways that are already above capacity at peak hours. In fact, the proponents of further growth talk of adding office space for 90,000 to 100,000 more workers in this congested area by the end of the century or soon thereafter. But the same city planning department that was judicially criticized for ignoring findings of an earlier environmental impact report later prepared a cautionary report on a downtown plan proposed by city officials, pointing out that expansion providing for an additional 90,000 workers would result in intolerably overcrowded streets and sidewalks, an enormous strain on public transportation, the destruction of more than eighty architecturally significant buildings, a large increase in the consumption of energy, and a steady rise in crime. If city officials do not adopt a plan setting sensible limits on downtown growth, how long will it be before another court, in another case involving an environmental impact report on a proposed huge building or group of buildings, holds—even without specific legislative authorization to use its independent judgment—that the effect on the populace would be utterly detrimental and that growth of the core area must be brought to a halt? Will the decision be appealed all the way to the United States Supreme Court? And will attorneys acting as friends of the court argue that every city has a responsibility to determine limits beyond which it does not intend to grow, including a limit on growth in its central business district?

In preparing its city-centered regional plan, the Association of Bay Area Governments did not address the issue of just how large each of the centers of employment in the nine-county area eventually should be. It did not suggest, for instance, that San Francisco by 1990 perhaps should permit no more office buildings in its central business district and that efforts should be made to encourage the growth of downtown areas of Oakland, or Fremont, or Walnut Creek. Nor did the association even hint that there may be a maximum desirable population for the whole Bay Area. Yet in view of the megalopolitan growth of the world's largest metropolitan areas, it is not academic to ask just how populous the residents of the Bay Area would like it to become. Is it some day to be an agglomeration as huge as New York (15,600,000), or Mexico City (now 15,000,000 and heading toward 26,000,000 by the year 2000), or Shanghai (11,800,000), or Tokyo-Yokohama (17,100,000)? At what point should growth be directed to other regions of California? Which ones?

In a metropolitan region experiencing slower growth than in previous decades and not expecting to have a population of 6,000,000 or more until the end of the century, megalopolitanism may seem remote, yet symptoms of this metropolitan disease are already appearing, not only in downtown San Francisco but also in Silicon Valley in Santa Clara County. Moreover, these early indications of unhealthy growth concern not just the communities immediately affected, but also other parts of the Bay Area such as San Mateo County, Marin County, and the East Bay—every subregion from which people travel daily under stressful conditions to work in congested surroundings.

Unfortunately, the Bay Area is ill-equipped to deal with problems of growth. Such regional agencies as it has—an air quality management district, a water quality control board, BCDC, MTC, and the tricounty Bay Area Rapid Transit District—operate independently, though they do attempt to cooperate with one another and have, in addition, informal or formal relations with the voluntary and advisory Association of Bay Area Governments. With the possible exceptions of BCDC and BART, these agencies are, however, not highly visible. Most people are uninformed about their activities. When the Association of Bay Area Governments held a meeting of its general assembly in the spring of 1984 to vote on increasing the dues of its city and county members, the largest newspaper in the region failed to report on the organization's effort to recover from drastic reductions of its budget and programs in the years following the passage of Proposition 13. Nor are important actions of other regional organizations always reported. If for no other reason than to make all Bay Area communities well aware of areawide plans and programs affecting their welfare, a conspicuous multipurpose regional government such as that sought in the 1970's would be desirable. But there are more cogent reasons for establishing that type of government. It would be able to coordinate areawide functions, and it would be able to state issues of regional growth in a manner guaranteed to provoke widespread discussion and perhaps foresighted action. No organization presently operating in the Bay Area can do either of these things.

The limited environmental gains of the past two or three decades may well be eroded if the metropolitan region continues to have no other mechanisms for regulating growth than a multiplicity of local governments, special districts, and areawide, single-function agencies, each relatively independent and lacking the kind of guidance a well-financed and ably staffed regional government with a long-term regional planning program could offer. The Association of Bay Area Governments, even in the mid-1970's when it was at the height of its influence, was not able to earn the kind of respect and attention such a multipurpose government could command. The state and federal governments, moreover, would be much more inclined to give ear to regional requests and needs if the Bay Area could speak with one voice

on matters of the utmost importance, as the Metropolitan Transportation Commission has shown, in its own field, by obtaining funds from Sacramento and Washington to subsidize transit operations.

Inasmuch as this metropolitan region is but one part of a large state in which population is increasing and great changes in agriculture, industry, and services are continually occurring, it should be in a position to demand that the state itself make plans to manage growth. In the administration of Governor Jerry Brown a very limited attempt at statewide research and planning was made, but not since then has there been any effort to look ahead in a circumspect fashion and consider how population should be distributed in the future, where new jobs should be created, and how the financial and administrative resources of state government might be utilized to bring about a reasonably satisfactory statewide pattern of urban areas, farmlands, forests, mineral-producing areas, and scenic preserves. The Los Angeles area already exhibits many of the insalubrious characteristics of a megalopolis. The Bay Area is in danger of developing similarly in the next century unless steps are taken in the remaining years of this one to control growth more effectively.

If there is resistance from other areas of the state to any suggestion of state planning, as there might well be, then the Bay Area should be prepared to make the most of such locational and economic advantages as it has, depending mainly on its own human resources and its ties with other states, the federal government, and with other nations. A reasonable amount of growth can be accommodated, and apparently will not come so rapidly that it cannot be skillfully managed, if there is the will to guide it regionally. In fact, a certain amount of growth may clearly present the need for regional planning as a function of regional government. For twenty-five years or more the great challenge to the people of the Bay Area has been to move beyond separate areawide agencies and a voluntary council of governments to some coherent way of addressing regional issues and problems, which become increasingly interrelated and suggestive of coordinated resolution. The urgent question is: does the metropolitan region have leaders who fully understand its needs and opportunities and can head a sustained drive to attain the two most important goals of the California Environmental Quality Act—a decent home and a suitable living environment for every resident? Never did the times cry out so loudly for far-sighted men and women to take command.

Notes

NOTES TO CHAPTER 1 (PAGES 1–22)

Heritage

[1] Fr. Francisco Palóu, *Relación histórica de la vida . . . Junípero Serra*, pp. 88–89, translated and quoted by Fr. Zephyrin Engelhardt in *Missions and Missionaries of California*, II, 55.

[2] H. E. Bolton, *Fray Juan Crespi, Missionary Explorer on the Pacific Coast, 1769–1774*, p. 229.

[3] Letter of José Francisco de Ortega to Fr. Francisco Palóu, Feb. 2, 1770, quoted by George Davidson, in "The Discovery of San Francisco Bay," *Transactions and Proceedings of the Geographical Society of the Pacific*, IV, Ser. II, p. 76.

[4] Quoted by C. E. Chapman in *A History of California, The Spanish Period*, pp. 229–230.

[5] Quoted by Neal Harlow in *The Maps of San Francisco Bay*, p. 7.

[6] Quoted by H. E. Bolton in *Font's Complete Diary*, p. 341.

[7] Quoted *ibid.*, p. 346.

[8] George Vancouver, *A Voyage of Discovery to the North Pacific Ocean, and Round the World*, III, 32.

[9] *Ibid.*, p. 34.

[10] *Ibid.*, p. 40.

[11] Quoted by William Halley in *The Centennial Year Book of Alameda County, California*, p. 73.

[12] Nicholas "Cheyenne" Dawson, *Overland to California in '41 and '49, and Texas in '51*, p. 33.

[13] *Ibid.*, pp. 29–30.

[14] *Ibid.*, p. 33.

NOTES TO CHAPTER 2 (PAGES 23–38)

Mother of Cities

[1] San Francisco *California Star*, Jan. 23, 1847, p. 3.

[2] W. T. Sherman, *Memoirs of General William T. Sherman*, I, 33.

[3] Quoted by J. W. Caughey in *Gold is the Cornerstone*, p. 42.

[4] H. H. Bancroft, *History of California*, VI, 159.

[5] Frank Soulé and others, *The Annals of San Francisco*, p. 243.

[6] Quoted by C. G. Murphy in *The People of the Pueblo: The Story of Sonoma*, p. 152.

[7] Quoted *ibid.*, p. 151.

[8] Sherman, *op. cit.*, I, 74.

[9] California, *Journal of the Legislature, 1850*, pp. 498–502.

[10] Munro-Fraser, *History of Alameda County, California*, p. 65.

[11] *Golden Era* (San Francisco), July 31, 1853, p. 2.

[12] Soulé and others, *op. cit.*, p. 482.

[13] *Golden Era*, July 17, 1853, p. 2.

[14] *Ibid.*, July 3, 1853, p. 4.

[15] Bancroft, *op. cit.*, VI, 778.

[16] Soulé and others, *op. cit.*, pp. 489–490.

NOTES TO CHAPTER 3 (PAGES 39–56)

The Plow, the Iron Horse, and New Towns

[1] Quoted by Marguerite Hunt and Harry Lawrence Gunn in *History of Solano County . . . and Napa County, California*, p. 240.

[2] William Halley, *The Centennial Year Book of Alameda County, California*, p. 125.

[3] J. P. Young, *San Francisco: A History of the Pacific Coast Metropolis*, I, 311.

[4] This line later was used exclusively for local service.

[5] *Map of Holly Oak Park, Part of Suscol Rancho, Napa County*, 1869.

[6] F. M. Stanger, *History of San Mateo County, California*, p. 158.

[7] Oakland *Daily News*, Feb. 8, 1869.

[8] J. Ross Browne, *Letter from the Hon. J. Ross Browne . . . in Relation to the Proposed Town Site of Lower Berkeley and the Value of Property and Growth of Population in and Around Oakland*, p. 19.

[9] F. L. Olmsted, *Preliminary Report in Regard to a Plan of Public Pleasure Grounds for the City of San Francisco*, p. 11.

[10] "Opinion of Mr. Justice Field . . .," U. S. Circuit Court, *Opinions . . . City of San Francisco vs. The United States*, p. 9.

11 *Ibid.*, p. 10.

12 Letter, Frederick Law Olmsted (San Francisco) to Calvert Vaux (New York), Sept. 28, 1865. MS, Library of Congress.

13 Olmsted, *Preliminary Report*, p. 12.

14 *Ibid.*, p. 8.

15 *Ibid.*, p. 30.

16 San Francisco Board of Park Commissioners, *The Development of Golden Gate Park*, p. 8.

17 F. L. Olmsted, *Berkeley Neighborhood: Report upon a Projected Improvement of the Estate of the College of California at Berkeley, near Oakland*, p. 23.

18 S. H. Willey, *A History of the College of California*, p. 2.

19 *Ibid.*

20 *Ibid.*, p. 3.

21 *California Constitution* (1849), Art. IX, sec. 4.

22 Willey, *op. cit.*, p. 36.

23 Olmsted, *Berkeley Neighborhood*, p. 23.

24 *Ibid.*, p. 24.

NOTES TO CHAPTER 4 (PAGES 57–70)

Urban Rivalries

1 Quoted by J. S. Hitteel in *The Prospects of Vallejo*, p. 42.

2 Quoted *ibid.*, pp. 60–61.

3 Quoted by J. Ross Browne in *Letter . . . in Relation to . . . the Growth of Population in and Around Oakland*, p. 36.

4 San Francisco *Daily Morning Call*, Oct. 6, 1871, as quoted by Hittell, *op. cit.*, p. 54.

5 Oakland Daily Transcript, *Information Concerning the Terminus of the Railroad System of the Pacific Coast*, p. 31.

6 Quoted by William Halley in *The Centennial Year Book of Alameda County, California*, p. 348.

7 All estimates cited are by H. H. Bancroft, *History of California*, VII, 696–697.

8 A. C. Loosley, "Foreign-born Population of California, 1848–1920," p. 23.

9 B. J. Arnold, *Report on . . . Transportation Facilities in San Francisco*, p. 422.

10 Oakland *News*, June 12, 1873.

NOTES TO CHAPTER 5 (PAGES 71–94)

The Heyday of Enterprise

1 San Francisco *Chronicle*, Jan. 1, 1891, p. 13.

2 *Ibid.*, p. 15.

3 H. H. Bancroft, *History of California*, VII, 743.

4 California Crop and Livestock Reporting Service, *California Field Crops Statistics 1866–1946*, p. 14.

5 San Francisco *Morning Call*, Jan. 5, 1891.

6 *Municipal Reports for the Fiscal Year 1884–85* (San Francisco, 1885), p. 168.

7 *Ibid.*

8 *Ibid.*, p. 207.

9 *Ibid.*, p. 178.

10 R. A. Walker, *The Planning Function in Urban Government*, pp. 55–56.

11 San Francisco *Chronicle*, June 25, 1887, p. 6.

12 L. G. Hughes, "Housing in San Francisco, 1835–1938," p. 95.

13 San Francisco *Chronicle*, Jan. 1, 1891, p. 29.

14 Quoted *ibid.*, p. 26.

15 San Francisco *Chronicle*, June 26, 1887, p. 8.

16 *Ibid.*

17 Quoted by D. E. Wood in *History of Palo Alto*, p. 43.

18 Oakland *Daily Evening Tribune*, Jan. 2, 1891, p. 8.

19 D. W. Smythe, "An Economic History of Local and Interurban Transportation in the East Bay Cities," p. 86.

20 San Francisco Morning Call, *Fettered Commerce—How the Pacific Mail and the Railroads Have Bled San Francisco* (1892), p. 5.

21 *Ibid.*, pp. 6–7.

22 *Ibid.*, p. 7.

23 *Ibid.*, p. 12.

24 Quoted by J. P. Young in *San Francisco: A History of the Pacific Coast Metropolis*, II, 657.

25 A. S. Macdonald, "The Beginnings of Richmond," *Bank News*, October, 1916, p. 3.

26 Richmond *Independent*, Dec. 20, 1939.

27 San Francisco *Examiner*, Sunday Magazine, Dec. 30, 1900, p. 4.

NOTES TO CHAPTER 6 (PAGES 95–108)

The Burnham Plan for San Francisco

1 F. M. Todd, *The Story of the Exposition*, I, 35–37.

2 San Francisco *Bulletin*, Jan. 4, 1904, p. 1.

3 *Ibid.*

4 *The Wasp* (San Francisco), June 3, 1904.

5 San Francisco *Bulletin*, Jan. 7, 1904.

6 *Ibid.*

7 San Francisco *Call*, Jan. 13, 1904.

8 San Francisco *Bulletin*, Jan. 14, 1904.

9 Untitled brochure of the Association for the Improvement and Adornment of San Francisco, 1904.

10 San Francisco *Bulletin*, May 5, 1904.

11 San Francisco *Chronicle*, May 7, 1904.

12 Charles Moore, *Daniel H. Burnham, Architect, Planner of Cities*, II, 57, 173.

13 D. H. Burnham and E. H. Bennett, *Report on a Plan for San Francisco*, p. 35. Hereafter cited as Burnham *Plan*.

14 *Ibid.*

15 *Ibid.*

16 *Ibid.*, p. 39.

17 San Francisco City Planning Commission, *Transportation Section of the Master Plan of the City and County of San Francisco*, par. 37.

18 Burnham *Plan*, p. 44.

19 *Ibid.*, p. 144.

20 *Ibid.*, p. 114.

21 *Ibid.*, p. 145.

22 *Ibid.*, pp. 158, 167.

23 *Ibid.*, p. 180.

24 *Ibid.*, p. 179.

25 San Francisco *Chronicle*, Sept. 28, 1905, p. 9.

26 *Ibid.*, p. 9.

27 Herbert Croly, "The Promised City of San Francisco," *Architectural Record*, June, 1906, as quoted in Oakland *Enquirer*, June 13, 1906, p. 4.

NOTES TO CHAPTER 7 (PAGES 109–122)

The New San Francisco

1 San Francisco *Bulletin*, April 25, 1906, p. 4.

2 *Ibid.*, April 23, 1906, p. 2.

3 *Ibid.*, April 21, 1906, p. 1.

4 Quoted by F. W. Aitken and Edward Hilton in *A History of the Earthquake and Fire in San Francisco*, p. 179.

5 "The Tenement House Question in California," *Transactions of the Commonwealth Club of California*, October, 1906, pp. 85–86, as quoted by Lillian G. Hughes in "Housing in San Francisco 1835–1938," p. 110.

6 Langley Porter, "Report of the President," in San Francisco Housing Association, *First Report*, p. 6.

7 Charles Moore, *Daniel H. Burnham, Architect, Planner of Cities*, I, 141.

8 San Francisco *Chronicle*, April 29, 1906, p. 3.

9 *Ibid.*

10 *Ibid.*, p. 6.

11 San Francisco *Bulletin*, May 3, 1906, p. 3.

12 San Francisco *Chronicle*, May 4, 1906, p. 5.

13 San Francisco *Bulletin*, May 5, 1906, p. 4.

14 *Ibid.*, p. 4.

15 San Francisco *Chronicle*, May 22, 1906, p. 3.

16 *Ibid.*

17 San Francisco *Bulletin*, May 22, 1906, p. 4.

18 *Ibid.*, May 26, 1906, p. 4.

19 San Francisco *Chronicle*, May 23, 1906, p. 6.

20 *Ibid.*, June 6, 1906, p. 14.

21 San Francisco *Bulletin*, May 24, 1906, p. 4.

22 *Ibid.*, May 29, 1906, p. 6.

23 Oakland *Enquirer*, June 6, 1906, p. 4.

24 San Francisco *Chronicle*, May 27, 1906, p. 18.

25 *Ibid.*, June 6, 1906, p. 1.

26 *Ibid.*, June 7, 1906, p. 1.

27 San Francisco *Bulletin*, June 14, 1906.

28 *Ibid.*

29 Oakland *Enquirer*, July 25, 1906, p. 4.

30 *Ibid.*, Sept. 5, 1906, p. 4.

31 *The Nation*, June 3, 1909, as quoted by Robert Glass Cleland in *California in Our Time (1900–1940)*, p. 23.

32 Rufus Steele, *The City That Is*, p. 37.

33 Aitken and Hilton, *op. cit.*, p. 260.

34 Steele, *op. cit.*, p. 46.

35 San Francisco *Bulletin*, April 14, 1909.

36 *Ibid.*

37 Telegram, D. H. Burnham to Willis Polk, from Chicago, April 22, 1909, in Phelan Scrapbook, "Adornment Association 1908 to 1911," Bancroft Library, University of California.

38 "Address of Thomas Magee before the Merchants' Association, May 27, 1909," MS in Phelan Scrapbook.

39 San Francisco *Bulletin*, June 1, 1909.

40 San Francisco *Chronicle*, June 22, 1909.

41 San Francisco *Bulletin*, June 28, 1909.

42 W. H. Irwin, *The City That Was*, pp. 7 and 47.

NOTES TO CHAPTER 8 (PAGES 123–132)

Oakland: The End of the Village Tradition

1 Oakland *Tribune*, April 27, 1906, p. 9.

2 Oakland *Times*, July 18, 1906, p. 1.

3 *Ibid.*, July 27, 1906, p. 2.

4 Oakland *Enquirer*, July 28, 1906, p. 4.

5 *Ibid.*, Aug. 4, 1906, p. 4.

6 *Ibid.*, Sept. 14, 1906, p. 4.

7 *Ibid.*, Sept. 21, 1906, p. 4.

8 *Ibid.*, Sept. 25, 1906, p. 4.

9 *Ibid.*

10 C. M. Robinson, *A Plan of Civic Improvement for the City of Oakland, California*, p. 3.

11 *Ibid.*, pp. 4 and 8.

12 *Ibid.*, p. 5.

13 *Ibid.*, pp. 6–7.

14 *Ibid.*, p. 6.

15 *Ibid.*, p. 9.

16 *Ibid.*

17 Werner Hegemann, *Report on a City Plan for the Municipalities of Oakland and Berkeley*, p. 132.

18 Robinson, *op. cit.*, p. 12.

19 *Ibid.*, p. 14.

20 *Ibid.*, pp. 14–17.

21 *Ibid.*, pp. 17–20.

22 Oakland *Enquirer*, June 12, 1906, p. 9.

23 *Ibid.*, June 9, 1906, p. 3.

24 *Ibid.*, Aug. 10, 1906, p. 6.

25 *Ibid.*, Jan. 10, 1907, p. 6.

26 *Ibid.*

27 Oakland *Tribune*, Jan. 15, 1907, p. 6.

28 *Ibid.*

29 Oakland *Enquirer*, Jan. 15, 1907, p. 4.

NOTES TO CHAPTER 9 (PAGES 133–148)

The Greater San Francisco Movement

1 San Francisco *Chronicle*, April 30, 1910, p. 6.

2 F. M. Todd, *The Story of the Exposition*, I, 97–98.

3 *Souvenir of Golden Gate Park—Rehabilitation Edition of the Golden Gate Park News*, p. 7.

4 Quoted in *Wheel Clicks*, Peninsular issue, Vol. V, No. 1 (July, 1944), p. 4.

5 San Francisco *Chronicle*, April 19, 1910, p. 6.

6 *Ibid.*, June 11, 1910, p. 11.

7 William L. Gerstle, "President's Annual Report," *Sixty-first Annual Report of the Chamber of Commerce of San Francisco*, pp. 17–18.

8 San Francisco Chamber of Commerce *Journal*, Vol. I, No. 9 (July, 1912), p. 11.

9 Oakland Chamber of Commerce *Bulletin*, Vol. I, No. 10 (October, 1910), p. 2; Vol. II, No. 10 (October, 1911), p. 3; Vol. II, No. 12 (December, 1911), p. 1.

10 *Ibid.*, Vol. I, No. 5 (May, 1910), p. 4.

11 *Ibid.*, Vol. I, No. 6 (June, 1910), p. 3.

12 Quoted in Oakland *Tribune*, Centennial Edition, May 1, 1952, p. 4-X.

13 Oakland Chamber of Commerce *Bulletin*, Vol. II, No. 4 (April, 1911), p. 5.

14 *Ibid.*, Vol. II, No. 9 (September, 1911), p. 3; Vol. V, No. 4 (April, 1914), p. 3.

15 Oakland *Tribune*, Aug. 18, 1910, p. 6.

16 *Report on Richmond Harbor Project*, p. 35.

17 Quoted in Oakland Chamber of Commerce *Bulletin*, Vol. I, No. 9 (September, 1910), p. 2.

18 Oakland Chamber of Commerce *Bulletin*, Vol. II, No. 8 (August, 1911), p. 1.

19 John R. Freeman, *On the Proposed Use of . . . Hetch Hetchy, Eleanor and Cherry Valleys . . . as Reservoirs . . . for the Water Supply of San Francisco, California, and Neighboring Cities*, p. 162.

20 *Ibid.*, p. 144.

21 *Ibid.*, p. 9.

22 *Ibid.*, p. 77.

23 *Ibid.*

24 *Ibid.*, pp. 112–127.

25 *Ibid.*, p. 165.

26 *Ibid.*, p. 163.

27 *Ibid.*, p. 166.

28 *Ibid.*

29 The quotations from the three newspapers were printed in Oakland Chamber of Commerce *Bulletin*, Vol. III, No. 8 (August, 1912), p. 1.

30 Quoted *ibid.*

31 Oakland *Tribune*, Nov. 1, 1912, p. 8.

32 *Ibid.*

33 Oakland Chamber of Commerce *Bulletin*, Vol. III, No. 10 (October, 1912), p. 1.

34 Oakland *Tribune*, Nov. 1, 1912, p. 1.

35 *Ibid.*, Nov. 9, 1912, p. 1.

36 *Ibid.*, Nov. 7, 1912, p. 1.

37 San Francisco *Chronicle*, Nov. 7, 1912, p. 6.

38 *Ibid.*

39 Oakland *Enquirer*, June 27, 1906, p. 4.

40 B. J. Arnold, *Report on the Improvement and Development of the Transportation Facilities of San Francisco*, p. 4.

41 *Ibid.*, pp. 5–6.

42 *Ibid.*

NOTES TO CHAPTER 10 (PAGES 149–168)

The Panama Canal: Stimulus to Planning

1 Oakland *Tribune*, Jan. 23, 1913, p. 12.

2 *Ibid.*, p. 8.

3 San Francisco Chamber of Commerce *Journal*, February, 1913, p. 8.

4 *Ibid.*

5 *Transactions of the Commonwealth Club of California*, VII (December, 1912), 539–540.

6 *Biennial Report of the Board of State Harbor Commissioners for the Fiscal Years Commencing July 1, 1910 and Ending June 30, 1912*, as quoted by Werner Hegemann in *Report on a City Plan for the Municipalities of Oakland & Berkeley*, p. 22.

7 *Ibid.*

8 Letter, Col. T. H. Rees to Werner Hegemann, *ibid.*, p. 35.

9 W. W. Ferrier, *Berkeley, California*, p. 315.

10 Oakland *Tribune*, May 6, 1914, p. 2.

11 San Francisco *Call*, July 29, 1911.

12 *San Francisco Municipal Reports for the Fiscal Years 1915–16*, p. 979.

13 Christopher Tunnard, *The City of Man*, p. 326.

14 F. M. Todd, *The Story of the Exposition*, II, 315.

15 B. R. Maybeck, *Palace of Fine Arts and Lagoon, Panama-Pacific International Exposition, 1915*, p. 9.

16 Oakland *Tribune*, Oct. 13, 1913, pp. 11–12.

17 Duncan McDuffie, "City Planning in Berkeley," *Berkeley Civic Bulletin*, March 15, 1916, p. 108.

18 Berkeley *Gazette*, Oct. 14, 1913, p. 1.

19 Hegemann, *op. cit.*, p. 19.

20 *Ibid.*, p. 16.

21 *Ibid.*, p. 36.

22 *Ibid.*, p. 22.

23 California Senate Fact-finding Committee, *Ports of the San Francisco Bay Area*, pp. 381–382.

24 Hegemann, *op. cit.*, p. 155.

25 *Ibid.*, p. 156.

26 C. H. Cheney, "How California Communities Can Profit by Active City Planning," *Pacific Municipalities*, XXVIII (January, 1914), 31.

27 Duncan McDuffie, *op. cit.*, p. 113.

28 *Transactions of the Commonwealth Club*, XI (January, 1917), 638.

29 M. M. O'Shaughnessy, "The Hetch Hetchy Water and Power Project, the Municipal Railway, and Other Notable Civic Improvements of San Francisco," p. 18.

30 "Recent Municipal Activities in San Francisco," *Pacific Municipalities*, XXIX (October, 1915), 439.

31 *San Francisco Municipal Reports for the Fiscal Year 1916–17*, p. 822.

NOTES TO CHAPTER 11 (PAGES 169–187)

Seeds of Metropolitan Regionalism

1 E. L. Finley, ed., *History of Sonoma County, California*, p. 424.

2 Stephen Child, *A Plan for the Development of Alum Rock Park (Reservation) at San Jose, California*, p. 13.

3 *Ibid.*, p. 17.

4 *Transactions of the Commonwealth Club*, XVII (1922), 162.

5 *Ibid.*, XVII, 171.

6 *Ibid.*, XVII, 173–175.

7 *Ibid.*, XVII, 127.

8 *Ibid.*, XVII, 141.

9 *Ibid.*, XVII, 132.

10 *Ibid.*, XVII, 134.

11 *Ibid.*, XVIII (1923), 270–271.

12 *Ibid.*, XVIII, 277.

13 *Ibid.*, XVIII, 277–278.

14 J. C. Bollens, *The Problem of Government in the San Francisco Bay Region*, p. 73.

15 *Ibid.*, p. 92.

16 Los Angeles County ordinance, quoted by J. C. Stephens in "The Development of County Planning in California," p. 18.

17 R. V. N. Black "A Report in Recommendation of a Regional Plan for the San Francisco Bay District by the Regional Plan Sub-Committee of the Commonwealth Club of California" (Feb. 29, 1924), MS in the possession of Mr. Black, p. 2.

18 *Ibid.*, pp. 4–5.

19 *Ibid.*, p. 4.

20 *Ibid.*, p. 5.

NOTES TO CHAPTER 12 (PAGES 188–201)

Fred Dohrmann and the Regional Plan Association

1 Letter, Fred Dohrmann to James D. Phelan, San Francisco, May 13, 1925, copy in files of Regional Plan Association, Bancroft Library, University of California. Hereafter cited as files of Regional Plan Association.

2 MS in files of Regional Plan Association.

3 Berkeley *Daily Gazette*, March 13, 1925.

4 F. R. Dohrmann, "Cooperation for Regional Planning," MS in files of Regional Plan Association.

5 *Transactions of the Commonwealth Club*, XX (1925), 436.

6 Letter, Fred Dohrmann to Homer R. Spence, San Francisco, Jan. 30, 1926, copy in files of Regional Plan Association.

7 Harland Bartholomew, *The San Francisco Bay Region*, p. 10.

8 *Ibid.*, p. 30.

9 *Ibid.*, p. 11.

10 *Ibid.*, p. 12.

11 *Ibid.*, p. 11.

12 *Ibid.*, p. 12.

13 *Ibid.*, p. 18.

14 *Ibid.*, p. 30.

15 Letter, Fred Dohrmann to Marshal Hale, Nov. 20, 1925, copy in files of Regional Plan Association.

16 Letter, Fred Dohrmann to Robert I. Bentley, Dec. 12, 1925, copy in files of Regional Plan Association.

17 Letter in files of Regional Plan Association.

18 Statement made to the author by Guy Wilfrid Hayler.

19 C. H. Lee, "The Future Development of the Metropolitan Area Surrounding San Francisco Bay," *Bulletin of the Seismological Society of America*, XVI (June, 1926), 81.

20 *Ibid.*, p. 103.

21 *Ibid.*, pp. 104–105.

22 G. W. Hayler, *The San Francisco Bay Region of the Future*, p. 8.

23 *Ibid.*, p. 7.

24 Fred Dohrmann, "Regional Planning of the San Francisco Bay Counties," MS in files of Regional Plan Association.

25 *Ibid.*

26 Stephen Child, "A Planning Federation for the Bay Region," MS in files of Regional Plan Association, p. 14.

27 *Ibid.*, pp. 2–3.

28 *Ibid.*, p. 6.

29 *Ibid.*, p. 9.

30 *Ibid.*, p. 12.

31 *Ibid.*, p. 12.

32 *Ibid.*, p. 14.

33 Statement made to the author by G. W. Hayler.

34 *California Statutes*, 1927, chap. 874, sec. 5.

35 Letter, Fred Dohrmann to Russell Wolden, 1928, copy in files of Regional Plan Association.

36 Memorandum in files of Regional Plan Association.

NOTES TO CHAPTER 13 (PAGES 202–223)

Prosperity and Projects

1 W. W. Ferrier, *Berkeley, California*, p. 331.

2 *Transactions of the Commonwealth Club*, XXIV (1929), 469.

3 *California Real Estate Magazine*, VII (February, 1927), 50.

4 F. C. Merritt, *History of Alameda County, California*, II, 583.

5 Quoted by Hale Champion in "How Nine Men Finally Got Bay Bridge Started," San Francisco *Chronicle*, March 23, 1953, p. 1.

6 Quoted *ibid.*

7 Quoted *ibid.*

8 San Jose *Mercury-Herald*, Dec. 4, 1929, p. 1.

9 California Senate Fact-finding Committee, *Ports of the San Francisco Bay Area*, p. 253.

10 San Francisco Board of Supervisors Airport Committee, *San Francisco Airport: A Report* (1931), p. 9.

11 *Ibid.*, p. 13.

12 *Ibid.*, pp. 16–17.

13 *San Francisco Business*, Aug. 5, 1931.

NOTES TO CHAPTER 14 (PAGES 224–243)

Progress in Troubled Times

1 California State Planning Board, *An Economic and Industrial Survey of the San Francisco Bay Area*, p. xxxi.

2 San Francisco Bay Area Chambers of Commerce, *Serving Pacific Markets*, p. 5.

3 *San Francisco Business*, June 3, 1931.

4 *Ibid.*

5 *Ibid.*

6 San Francisco *Chronicle*, May 26, 1932, p. 24.

7 *Ibid.*, Aug. 19, 1932, p. 12.

8 Albert Raeburn, "The East Bay Regional Park District," p. 9.

9 Quoted by R. G. Martin in "Water Conservation in the Santa Clara Valley," pp. 58-59.

10 Quoted *ibid.*, p. 65.

11 *California Public Record*, XVII, Sept. 9, 1935, p. 1.

12 Tomaschke-Elliott, Inc., *The Effect of Bridge Construction on Population Movement*, p. 34.

13 San Francisco Examiner, *How Will the Bridges Affect San Francisco Business? A Forecast . . .*, p. 3.

14 *Ibid.*

15 *Report of the San Francisco Public Utilities Commission, Fiscal Year 1935–1936*, p. 143.

16 *California Highways and Public Works*, November, 1936, p. 1.

17 *Ibid.*, p. 5.

18 *Ibid.*, p. 2.

19 San Francisco *Chronicle*, May 28, 1937, p. 1.

20 *Report of the San Francisco Public Utilities Commission, Year 1936–1937*, pp. 151–152.

21 Miller McClintock, *Report on San Francisco City-wide Traffic Survey*, p. 110.

22 *Ibid.*, p. 251.

23 *Ibid.*, p. 254.

24 East Bay Cities Sewage Disposal Survey, *Report upon the Collection, Treatment and Disposal of Sewage and Industrial Wastes of the East Bay Cities*, p. 8.

25 *Ibid.*, p. 9.

26 *Ibid.*, p. 6.

27 Yerba Buena Exposition Association, *A Site for the 1938 Exposition*, p. 6.

28 Advisory Planning Committee to Bridge Celebration Founding Committee, *Report to J. W. Mailliard, Jr., Chairman, Bridge Celebration Founding Committee*.

29 *Transactions of the Commonwealth Club*, XXVI, 355.

30 Miller McClintock, *op. cit.*, 30.

NOTES TO CHAPTER 15 (PAGES 244–257)

Crisis in an Arsenal of Democracy

1 O. W. Campbell, "Regional Defense Problems," in California State Planning Board, *San Francisco Bay Regional Planning District —Proceedings of Hearing, March 28, 1941*, p. 34.

2 Letter, Samuel C. May, Chairman of California State Planning Board, to city and county officials of the San Francisco Bay Area, Feb. 18, 1941.

3 California State Planning Board, *op. cit.*, pp. 54–55.

4 Remarks of James N. Long, *ibid.*, p. 57.

5 Remarks of Will Weston, *ibid.*, p. 51.

6 Remarks of P. Victor Peterson, *ibid.*, pp. 63–64.

7 Remarks of L. Deming Tilton, *ibid.*, p. 56.

8 California State Planning Board, *A Proposal for the Formation of a Temporary Regional Planning Organization for the San Francisco Bay Area*, p. 1.

9 *Ibid.*, p. 5.

10 *Investigation of Congested Areas*, Part 3, Hearings, House Sub-

committee on Naval Affairs, 78th Cong., 1st sess. (Washington, 1943), p. 899.

[11] *Ibid.*, p. 858.

[12] *Ibid.*, p. 867.

[13] Testimony of W. P. Cooper, *ibid.*, p. 890.

[14] Housing Authority of the County of Marin, *Fighters on the Home Front: First Annual Report.*

[15] Catherine Bauer, "Outline of War Housing," *Task* (no date), p. 6.

[16] *Investigation of Congested Areas*, p. 661.

[17] *Ibid.*, p. 765.

[18] *Ibid.*, p. 804.

[19] *Ibid.*, p. 1006.

[20] *Ibid.*, p. 804.

[21] *Report on the San Francisco Bay Area*, House Subcommittee of the Naval Affairs Committee Appointed to Investigate Congestion in Critical War Production Areas, p. 810.

[22] *Ibid.*

[23] *Ibid.*, p. 811.

[24] *Ibid.*, p. 809.

[25] *Ibid.*

[26] *Ibid.*, p. 818.

[27] *Ibid.*

NOTES TO CHAPTER 16 (PAGES 258–270)

Postwar Planning

[1] National Resources Planning Board, *Post-War Plan and Program*, p. 1.

[2] National Resources Planning Board, Pacific Southwest Regional Office, *After the War—New Jobs in the Pacific Southwest*, p. 18.

[3] *Ibid.*, pp. 3–4.

[4] *Ibid.*, p. 37.

[5] California statute as quoted by California Housing and Planning Association in "New Commission Aids Postwar Readjustment," *Agenda*, II (October, 1943), 10.

[6] California State Reconstruction and Reemployment Commission, *The Bay Region Takes Stock*, p. 2.

[7] *Ibid.*, p. 16.

[8] *Ibid.*, p. 20.

[9] San Francisco Bay Region Council, Minutes of the first meeting, p. 7.

[10] *Ibid.*, p. 4.

[11] *Ibid.*, p. 6.

[12] *Ibid.*, p. 2.

[13] Oscar Lewis, *Within the Golden Gate*, p. 2.

[14] Citizens' Postwar Planning Committee, *Report . . . to Mayor Roger D. Lapham*, p. 4.

[15] *Ibid.*, p. 23.

[16] *Ibid.*, pp. 6–7.

[17] San Francisco City Planning Commission, *Present and Future Uses of the Land*, p. 53.

[18] Citizens' Postwar Planning Committee, *op. cit.*, p. 3.

[19] San Francisco City Planning Commission, *op. cit.*, pp. 53–54.

[20] Oakland Postwar Planning Committee, *Oakland's Formula for the Future*, p. 48.

[21] *Ibid.*, p. 46.

[22] *Recommendations of the Citizens' Postwar Advisory Committee* (Berkeley), p. 1.

[23] Berkeley Chamber of Commerce, *A Report to Berkeleyans*, p. 2.

NOTES TO CHAPTER 17 (PAGES 271–309)

The Regional Metropolis

[1] Industrial Survey Associates, *Santa Clara County: Its Prospects of Prosperity*, p. 4.

[2] Palo Alto *Times*, March 3, 1950, p. 13.

[3] *Ibid.*, May 9, 1951.

[4] "Outlook for Future Growth," *Monthly Review of the Federal Reserve Bank of San Francisco*, November, 1947, as quoted in San Francisco Bay Area Council, *San Francisco Bay Area: Its People, Prospects, and Problems*, advance review edition, pp. f–g.

[5] San Francisco *Chronicle*, July 25, 1950, p. 16.

[6] H. F. Wise and Simon Eisner, *Master Plan for Menlo Park*, p. 27.

[7] D. F. Foley, *The Suburbanization of Administrative Offices in the San Francisco Bay Area*, p. 4.

[8] Quoted in Hayward City Planning Commission, *Hayward Prepares a Master Plan for Future Development*, p. 16.

[9] Aaron Levine, *The Urban Renewal of San Francisco*, San Francisco Planning and Housing Association and the Blyth-Zellerbach Committee, March, 1959.

[10] Oakland City Planning Commission, *Preliminary General Plan* (Oakland, 1958).

[11] San Francisco *Chronicle*, Jan. 12, 1958, p. 2.

[12] *Ibid.*, Jan. 13, 1958, p. 2.

[13] *Ibid.*, Nov. 6, 1957, and Jan. 12, 1958.

[14] Bay Area Air Pollution Control District *Air Currents*, Vol. 1, No. 1 (April, 1959), p. 4.

[15] San Francisco Bay Area Council, Planning Directors' Committee, *A Regional Planning Agency for the San Francisco Bay Area*, p. ii.

[16] V. B. Stanbery, *Regional Planning Needs of the San Francisco Bay Area*, p. 29.

[17] San Francisco Bay Area Council, *A Regional Planning Agency*, p. v.

[18] *Ibid.*

NOTES TO CHAPTER 18 (PAGES 310–337)

The Regional Metropolis Twenty-Five Years Later

[1] Mel Scott, *The Future of San Francisco Bay*, p. 107.

[2] California Coastal Zone Conservation Act of 1972, chap. 2, sec. 27100.

[3] Melvin B. Lane, "Letter to Governor Edmund G. Brown, Jr., the Members of the California Legislature and the People of California," Dec. 1, 1975, in Coastal Zone Conservation Commissions, *California Coastal Plan*, p. iv.

[4] Solano County Planning Department, *Solano County Land Use and Circulation Element: A Part of the Solano County General Plan*, p. 27.

[5] *Ibid.*, p. 28.

[6] North East Berkeley Association, *NEBA News*, December, 1983, p. 1.

[7] *California Statutes*, 1979, chap. 947, sec. 21001 (a).

[8] *Ibid.*, sec. 21001 (b).

[9] *California Statutes*, 1976, chap. 1312, sec. 21100.

[10] *Ibid.*, sec. 21100 (g).

[11] San Francisco *Chronicle*, Jan. 25, 1984, p. 18.

Bibliography

MANUSCRIPTS

Bowman, Jacob N. "The O'Farrell Swing." MS in author's possession.
———— "The Roads of Provincial California." MS, Bancroft Library, University of California, 1946.
Bowman, Jacob N., and George Whiting Hendry. "The Spanish and Mexican Adobe and Other Buildings in the Nine San Francisco Bay Counties, 1776 to about 1850." 7 vols. MS, Bancroft Library, University of California, 1945.
Burgess, Sherwood Denn. "Early History of the Oakland Water Supply, 1850–1876." Unpublished M.A. thesis, University of California, 1948.
Burns, Thomas P. "Centennial of the City of San Francisco, 1835–1935." MS, Bancroft Library, University of California, 1935.
Houston, Mary Ruth. "The Early History of Berkeley, California." Unpublished M.A. thesis, University of California, 1925.
Hughes, Lillian Gobar. "Housing in San Francisco, 1835–1938." Unpublished M.A. thesis, University of California, 1940.
Kesseli, Thelma Dorothy. "The Railroad as an Agency of Settlement in California, 1870–1890." Unpublished M.A. thesis, University of California, 1948.
Key, Leon Goodwin. "The History of the Policies in Disposing of the Public Lands in California, 1769–1900." Unpublished M.A. thesis, University of California, 1930.
King, Margaret Goddard. "The Growth of San Francisco, Illustrated by Shifts in the Density of Population." Unpublished M.A. thesis, University of California, 1928.
Klein, Julius. "The Development of Manufacturing Industry in California up to 1870." Unpublished M.A. thesis, University of California, 1908.
Loosley, Allyn Campbell. "Foreign-born Population of California, 1848–1920." Unpublished M.A. thesis, University of California, 1927.
Martin, Richard G. "Water Conservation in the Santa Clara Valley." Unpublished M.A. thesis, University of California, 1950.

Maverick, Lewis Adams. "Activity in Real Estate in Alameda County, California, 1853 to 1930." Unpublished Ph.D. dissertation, University of California, 1931.
Miller, Louis Richard. "The History of the San Francisco and San Jose Railroad." Unpublished M.A. thesis, University of California, 1948.
Nickell, Sadie F. "Economic History of California, 1850–1870." Unpublished M.A. thesis, University of California, 1926.
Phelan, James Duval. Scrapbook. Bancroft Library, University of California.
Raeburn, Albert. "The East Bay Regional Park District." Unpublished M.A. thesis, University of California, 1943.
Rinne, Rose Marie Shiely. "The San Francisco–Oakland Bay Bridge: Its History and Economic Development." Unpublished M.A. thesis, University of California, 1936.
Smythe, Dallas Walker. "An Economic History of Local and Inter-Urban Transportation in the East Bay Cities, with Particular Reference to the Properties Developed by F. M. Smith." Unpublished Ph.D. dissertation, University of California, 1937.
Solovsky, Ruth Mary McGinty. "Spanish and Mexican Ranchos in the San Francisco Bay Region: San Antonio, San Pablo, and San Leandro." Unpublished M.A. thesis, University of California, 1921.
Stephens, James Charles. "The Development of County Planning in California." Unpublished M.A. thesis, University of California, 1938.
Teese, Edith. "Waterfront Developments in the San Pablo and Richmond, California, Region to 1917." Unpublished M.A. thesis, University of California, 1947.
Voget, Margarette Lamberta. "The Waterfront of San Francisco, 1863–1930: A History of Its Administration by the State of California." Unpublished Ph.D. dissertation, University of California, 1943.
Williams, R. L. "Eighty Years of Subdivision Design: An Historical Evaluation of Land Planning in San Mateo County, California." Unpublished M.C.P. thesis, University of California, 1951.

Woodruff, Jacqueline McCart. "History of Benicia, 1846–1880." Unpublished M.A. thesis, University of California, 1943.
In addition to the foregoing manuscripts, letters from the following persons to the author have been used in the preparation of this book: Glenn A. Harris, City Engineer of Vallejo, August 12, 1954. William R. Seeger, Assistant General Manager, Marin Municipal Water District, January 8 and 26, 1954. Robert R. Gros, Manager, Advertising and Publicity Department, Pacific Gas and Electric Company, November 3, 1954.

PUBLIC AND SEMIPUBLIC DOCUMENTS

Association of Bay Area Governments. *The Emergence of a Regional Concept, 1910–1976.* Berkeley, 1976.
——— Letter of Revan A. F. Tranter, Executive Director, to President Grote and Members of the Executive Board, December 1, 1977. Mimeo.
——— *Summary of the Findings of ABAG's "Projections '83."* Berkeley, 1983. Mimeo.
Bartholomew, Harland. *The San Francisco Bay Region: A Statement Concerning the Nature and Importance of a Plan for Future Growth.* [San Francisco, 1925?] Cover title: Preliminary Report on Regional Plan Problems of San Francisco Bay Counties. (Submitted to the Regional Plan Association of the San Francisco Bay Counties, September, 1925.)
Bay Area Real Estate Report. San Francisco, 1949–1957. (Published by the Bay Area Real Estate Research Committee, an affiliate of the San Francisco Bay Area Council.)
Berkeley. Chamber of Commerce. *A Report to Berkeleyans: Major Post War Problems That Face the City of Berkeley, as Viewed by Berkeley Business Men.* Berkeley, 1945.
——— Citizens' Postwar Advisory Committee. *Recommendations.* Berkeley, 1946.
California. Assembly, Committee on Rules. *California Local Government and the CEQA, 1979.* Report submitted by Small and Knust, Inc. Sacramento, 1980.
——— Coastal Zone Conservation Commissions. *California Coastal Plan.* San Francisco, 1975.
——— Department of Finance. Division of Budgets and Accounts, Financial Research Section. *Estimated Population of California, 1950–1954, with Projections to 1955.* Sacramento, 1954.
——— Department of Health. *Status of Sewage Disposal in the San Francisco Bay Area.* Berkeley, 1948. (Mimeographed.)
——— Department of Industrial Relations. *Monthly Estimates of Employment in California.* San Francisco, February and May, 1943.
——— Department of Natural Resources, Division of Mines. *Geologic Guidebook of the San Francisco Bay Counties . . .* Prepared under the Direction of Olaf P. Jenkins. San Francisco, 1951. (Bulletin 154.)
——— Highway Advisory Committee. *Report of a Study of the State Highway System of California.* Sacramento, 1925.
——— Metropolitan Transportation Commission. *A History of the Key Decisions in the Development of Bay Area Rapid Transit— BART Impact Program.* Prepared by McDonald & Smart, Inc., under contract with the Metropolitan Transportation Commission for the U.S. Departments of Transportation and of Housing and Urban Development. Berkeley, 1975.
——— ——— *Annual Report, 1976–1977.* Berkeley, 1977.
——— ——— *Annual Report, 1977–1978.* Berkeley, 1978.
——— ——— *Annual Report, 1981–1982.* Berkeley, 1982.
——— ——— *Five Years of Progress, 1970–1975.* Berkeley, 1975.
——— ——— *Third Annual Report to the Bay Area Congressional Delegation.* Berkeley, 1982.
——— ——— *Fourth Annual Report to the Bay Area Congressional Delegation.* Berkeley, 1983.
——— Office of Planning and Research. *CEQA: The California Environmental Quality Act: Law and Guidelines, as Amended, January 1, 1981.* Sacramento, 1981.
——— Railroad Commission. *Report . . . July 1, 1917, to June 30, 1918.* Sacramento, 1918.
——— ——— *Report . . , July 1, 1921, to June 30, 1922.* Sacramento, 1923.
——— San Francisco Bay Area Rapid Transit Commission. *Preliminary Report.* [Sacramento, 1953.]
——— Secretary of State. *California Blue Book, 1950.* Sacramento, 1950.
——— Senate, Fact-finding Committee on San Francisco Bay Ports. *Ports of the San Francisco Bay Area—Their Commerce, Facilities, Problems, and Progress.* Sacramento, 1951.
——— ——— Interim Committee on San Francisco Bay Area Metropolitan Rapid Transit Problems. *Mass Rapid Transit, Answer to Traffic Congestion in the San Francisco Bay Area.* [San Francisco.] 1953.
——— ——— Interim Committee on State and Local Taxation. *Report.* Sacramento, 1953.
——— State Park Commission. *Report of State Park Survey of California.* Prepared by Frederick Law Olmsted (the younger). Sacramento, 1929.
——— State Planning Board. *An Economic and Industrial Survey of the San Francisco Bay Area.* By Robert D. Calkins and Walter E. Hoadley, Jr. Sacramento, 1941.
——— ——— *A Proposal for the Formation of a Temporary Regional Planning Organization for the San Francisco Bay Area.* Sacramento, December 8, 1941. (Mimeographed.)
——— ——— *San Francisco Bay Regional Planning District—Proceedings of Hearing, March 28, 1941.* Sacramento, 1941.
——— State Reconstruction and Reemployment Commission. *The Bay Region Takes Stock: An Account of the Public Hearing on Postwar Problems of the San Francisco Bay Region, August 23 and 24, 1944.* [San Francisco, 1944.] (Pamphlet No. 3.)
——— ——— *Richmond, California; A City Earns the Purple Heart.* Sacramento, 1944. (Pamphlet No. 2.)
——— State and Regional Water Pollution Control Boards. *Water Pollution Control: Progress Report for 1950 Through 1952.* Sacramento, 1952.
——— *Statutes,* 1849, 1927, 1937.
California Association of Local Agency Formation Commissions. *CALAFCO Newsletter,* XI (January, 1984).
California Conference on City Planning. *Procedure for Zoning or Districting of Cities.* By Charles Henry Cheney. Bulletin No. 2. San Francisco, 1917.
California Crop and Livestock Reporting Service. *California Field Crops Statistics 1866–1946.* Prepared by Lowell M. Clarke and George A. Scott. Sacramento [1947].
East Bay Cities Sewage Disposal Survey. *Report upon the Collection, Treatment and Distribution of Sewage and Industrial Wastes of the East Bay Cities of California.* To the Mayor and Council representing the City of Berkeley as the sponsoring agent for

the seven cooperating cities . . . by the Board of Consulting Engineers: Charles Gilman Hyde, Harold Farnsworth Gray, A. M. Rawn. [Berkeley], 1941.

East Bay Municipal Utility District. *Engineering Board of Review Report on Sewage Disposal for the District* [Special District No. 1]. By Samuel A. Greeley, Clyde C. Kennedy, and N. T. Veatch. Oakland, 1946.

—— "Future Water Requirements of the San Francisco Bay Region." Oakland, 1947. (Unpublished technical report.)

—— *The Story of Water* . . . Oakland, [1931?].

—— *Water: Where It Comes From . . . How It Reaches Your Faucet.* Oakland, n.d.

East Bay Regional Park District. *The East Bay Log: 1979–1980 Biennial Report.* Special edition. Oakland, 1980.

Hayward. Planning Commission. *Hayward Prepares a Master Plan for Future Development.* Hayward, 1953.

Industrial Survey Associates. *Santa Clara County: Its Prospects of Prosperity. Digest of a Report for the Santa Clara County Industrial Survey Advisory Council and the San Jose Chamber of Commerce.* San Francisco, 1948.

Joint Subaqueous Tunnel Commission. *Report on a Proposed Additional Tube.* Oakland, 1940.

League of Women Voters of California. *Protecting the California Environment: A Citizen's Guide.* San Francisco, 1980.

Marin County. Housing Authority. *Fighters on the Home Front: First Annual Report.* San Rafael, 1943.

McClintock, Miller. *Report on San Francisco Citywide Traffic Survey.* Prepared for the Department of Public Works. San Francisco: [Pisani Printing and Publishing Co.] 1937. (W.P.A. Project 6108–5863.)

Menlo Park. *Master Plan for Menlo Park, California.* By Harold F. Wise and Simon Eisner. Menlo Park, 1952.

Midpeninsula Regional Open Space District. *Your Open Space Preserves.* Los Altos, n.d.

—— *Openspace,* No. 10 (Summer, 1983). Los Altos, 1983.

Oakland. Board of Port Commissioners. *Port of Oakland.* Oakland, 1983.

—— —— *Oakland's North Airport.* Oakland, 1982.

—— Chamber of Commerce. *How to Win the Markets of the New West.* Oakland, 1948.

—— City Planning Commission. *Annual Report for the Fiscal Year Ending June 30, 1944.* Oakland, 1944.

—— —— *Shoreline Development: A Part of the Master Plan.* Oakland, 1951.

—— Park Commission. *The Park System of Oakland, California.* [Oakland, 1910.]

—— Postwar Planning Committee. *Oakland's Formula for the Future.* Oakland, 1945.

Olmsted Brothers and Ansel F. Hall. *Report on Proposed Park Reservations for East Bay Cities* (California). *Prepared for the Bureau of Public Administration, University of California, in Consultation with the East Bay Regional Park Association.* [Berkeley], 1930.

People for Open Space. *Room Enough: Housing and Open Space in the Bay Area.* San Francisco, 1983.

—— *Annual Report.* San Francisco, 1983.

Richmond. City Council. *Postwar Richmond, California . . . 1945–1949.* [Richmond], 1949.

—— —— *Report to the City Council of Richmond on the Port of Richmond.* By Main and Company. San Francisco, 1950.

—— —— *Report on Richmond Harbor Project, with Supplementary Report on Tunnel and Roadway. To the Council of the City of Richmond.* San Francisco: Haviland & Tibbets, 1912.

San Francisco. Board of Park Commissioners. *The Development of Golden Gate Park* . . . San Francisco, 1886. (Report of William Hammond Hall, Consulting Engineer, is on pp. 7–20.)

—— Board of Supervisors. *General Ordinances* . . . San Francisco, 1907. Ordinance No. 31 (New Series).

—— —— *Municipal Reports for the Fiscal Years 1884–85, 1905–1906, 1906–1907, 1915–16.*

—— —— Airport Committee. *San Francisco Airport: A Report.* San Francisco, 1931.

—— Chamber of Commerce. *San Francisco Tackles Its Housing Problem.* San Francisco, 1943.

—— —— *Sixty-first Annual Report.* San Francisco, 1911. ("President's Annual Report," by William L. Gerstle, is on pp. 17–18.)

—— Citizens' Postwar Planning Committee. *Report to Mayor Roger D. Lapham.* San Francisco, 1945.

—— City Planning Commission. *The Case for the Southern Crossing.* San Francisco, 1949.

—— —— *History of Public Transit in San Francisco, 1850–1948.* San Francisco, 1948.

—— —— *Present and Future Uses of the Land.* San Francisco, 1944.

—— —— *Transportation Section of the Master Plan of the City and County of San Francisco.* San Francisco, 1951.

—— —— *Western Addition District Redevelopment Study.* San Francisco, 1947.

—— Department of City Planning. *The Population of San Francisco, 1900–1950: A Half Century of Change.* San Francisco, 1954.

—— Housing Authority. *Fifth Annual Report.* San Francisco, 1943.

—— Mayor. *Annual Message to the Board of Supervisors of the City and County of San Francisco.* By Roger D. Lapham. San Francisco, 1946.

San Francisco. Public Utilities Commission. *Report, Fiscal Year 1935–1936.* Also: *Report, Fiscal Year 1936–1937.*

—— —— *San Francisco Water and Power.* San Francisco, 1949.

San Francisco Bay Area Chambers of Commerce. *Serving Pacific Markets from the Center: A Study of the Basic Factors Affecting Successful Manufacturing and Distribution on the Pacific Coast.* Prepared by the chambers of commerce of communities surrounding San Francisco Bay, under the general supervision of McCann-Erickson, Inc. (San Francisco? 1931.) Cover title: San Francisco–Oakland Metropolitan Area: An Industrial Study.

San Francisco Bay Area Council. *The Bay Area '70 Census Series.* San Francisco, n.d.

—— *The Bay Area Census Series No. 3.* San Francisco, n.d.

—— *San Francisco Bay Area: Its People, Prospects and Problems.* San Francisco, 1947.

—— *San Francisco Bay Area: A Year of Action—1947.* San Francisco, 1948.

—— Planning Directors' Committee. *A Regional Planning Agency for the San Francisco Bay Area; a Report and Statutory Proposal.* Prepared under the supervision of the Regional Planning

Subcommittee of the Bay Area Planning Directors' Committee. [Berkeley? 1956.]

San Francisco Bay Regional Development Council. *Minutes of Meeting at the Claremont Hotel, April 11, 1942.*

San Francisco Housing Association. *First Report.* San Francisco, 1911. (Langley Porter, "Report of the President" is pp. 6–10.)

San Jose. Chamber of Commerce. *Distinguished Neighbors.* San Jose, 1949.

San Jose Water Works. *What's Back of the Faucet.* San Jose, 1953.

San Mateo County. Planning Commission. *Industrial Survey of San Mateo County.* Redwood City, 1953. (Prepared for the Urban Land Institute.)

———— ———— *A Planned Program for Public Works.* Redwood City, 1942.

Santa Clara County. Planning Commission. *Flood Problems in Santa Clara County.* San Jose, 1952. (Monograph No. 3.)

———— ———— *General Plan.* San Jose, 1982.

Scott, Mel. *The Future of San Francisco Bay.* Institute of Governmental Studies, University of California, Berkeley, 1963.

Tomaschke-Elliott, Inc. *The Effect of Bridge Construction on Population Movement: A Study of Eastern Cities.* Prepared for the Residential Development Committee of the Oakland Chamber of Commerce. [Oakland,] 1934.

U. S. Bureau of Public Roads. *Report of a Study of the California Highway System.* Washington, 1922.

———— Circuit Court. *Opinions and Decrees . . . for the Northern District of California in the Case of the City of San Francisco vs. The United States: The Pueblo Case.* San Francisco, 1865. ("Opinion of Mr. Justice Field . . . Confirming the Claim of the City of San Francisco for Four Leagues of Pueblo Lands, Filed October 31st, 1864," is on pp. 4–13.)

———— Congress. House. Subcommittee of Naval Affairs Committee. Investigation of Congested Areas, Pt. 3: San Francisco, Calif., Area. Hearings, 78th Cong., 1st sess., pursuant to H. Res. 30. Washington, 1943.

———— ———— ———— *Report on the San Francisco Bay Area by the Subcommittee Appointed to Investigate Congestion in Critical War-Production Areas.* [Washington, 1943.]

———— Executive Office of the President. Committee for Congested Production Areas. *San Francisco Bay Area, California.* San Francisco, 1944.

———— National Resources Planning Board. *Pacific Southwest Region—Industrial Development.* Washington, 1942.

———— ———— *Post-War Plan and Program.* Washington, 1943.

———— ———— *Post-War Planning.* Washington, 1942.

———— ———— Pacific Southwest Regional Office. *After the War—New Jobs in the Pacific Southwest.* Berkeley, 1943. (Mimeographed.)

University of California Conference on City and Regional Planning. *Proceedings of the Second Annual . . . Conference on City and Regional Planning.* Berkeley, 1954. (Norman Kennedy, "A Coordinated Attack on the Urban Transportation Problem" is on pp. 17–22.)

BOOKS

Aitken, Frank W., and Edward Hilton. *A History of the Earthquake and Fire in San Francisco: An Account of the Disaster of April 18, 1906, and Its Immediate Results.* San Francisco: Edward Hilton Co., 1906.

Altrocchi, Julia Cooley. *The Spectacular San Franciscans.* New York: Dutton, 1949.

Arbuckle, Clyde, and Roscoe D. Wyatt. *Historic Names, Persons, and Places in Santa Clara County.* San Jose: Chamber of Commerce, 1948.

Arnold, Bion J. *Report on the Improvement and Development of Transportation Facilities in San Francisco.* San Francisco: Hicks-Judd Co., 1913.

Baker, Joseph E. (ed.). *Past and Present of Alameda County, California.* 2 vols. Chicago: S. J. Clarke Publishing Co., 1914.

Bancroft, Hubert Howe. *History of California.* 7 vols. San Francisco, 1884–1890. (*Works*, Vols. XVIII–XXIV.)

Bartholomew, Harland. *The San Francisco Bay Region: A Statement Concerning the Nature and Importance of a Plan for Future Growth . . . to the Regional Plan Association.* (San Francisco: Regional Plan Association of the San Francisco Bay Counties, 1925.)

Bartholomew, Harland, and Associates. *A Major Street Plan for Oakland.* Oakland: Major Highway and Traffic Committee of One Hundred, 1927.

The Bay of San Francisco, the Metropolis of the Pacific Coast, and Its Suburban Cities: A History. 2 vols. Chicago: Lewis Publishing Co., 1892.

Bean, Walton. *Boss Ruef's San Francisco: The Story of the Union Labor Party, Big Business, and the Graft Prosecution.* Berkeley and Los Angeles: University of California Press, 1952.

Black, James B. *California: "Stored with Many Blessings Fit for the Use of Man."* New York: American Branch, Newcomen Society of England, 1949.

Beckman, Roy C. *The Romance of Oakland.* Oakland: Landis & Kelsey, 1932.

Blow, Ben. *California Highways: A Descriptive Record of Road Development by the State and by Such Counties As Have Paved Highways.* San Francisco: Ben Blow, 1920.

Bollens, John C. *The Problem of Government in the San Francisco Bay Region.* Berkeley: Bureau of Public Administration, University of California, 1948. (Processed.)

Bolton, Herbert Eugene. *Outpost of Empire: The Story of the Founding of San Francisco.* New York: Knopf, 1931.

Bolton, Herbert Eugene (ed.). *Font's Complete Diary: A Chronicle of the Founding of San Francisco.* Berkeley: University of California Press, 1931.

———— *Fray Juan Crespi, Missionary Explorer on the Pacific Coast, 1769–1774.* Berkeley: University of California Press, 1927.

Browne, J. Ross. *Letter from the Hon. J. Ross Browne, Late U. S. Minister to China, in Relation to the Proposed Town Site of Lower Berkeley and the Value of Property and Growth of Population in and Around Oakland.* San Francisco, 1870.

Burnham, Daniel Hudson, and Edward H. Bennett. *Report on a Plan for San Francisco.* Edited by Edward F. O'Day. Presented to the Mayor and Board of Supervisors by the Association for the Improvement and Adornment of San Francisco. San Francisco: Published by the City, 1905.

California Promotion Committee. *Sixth Annual Report.* San Francisco, 1908.

Caughey, John Walton. *Gold is the Cornerstone.* Berkeley and Los Angeles: University of California Press, 1948.

Chapman, Charles E. *A History of California: The Spanish Period.* New York: Macmillan, 1939.

Child, Stephen. *A Plan for the Development of Alum Rock Park (Reservation) at San Jose, California.* San Francisco, 1916.

Cleland, Robert Glass. *California in Our Time (1900–1940)*. New York: Knopf, 1947.

—— *From Wilderness to Empire: A History of California, 1542–1900*. New York: Knopf, 1947.

Cleland, Robert Glass, and Osgood Hardy. *March of Industry*. ("California Series.") Los Angeles: Powell Publishing Co., 1929.

Country Club of Washington Township. *History of Washington Township*. 2d ed. [Niles, Calif.] 1950.

Coy, Owen C. *California County Boundaries: A Study of the Division of the State into Counties and the Subsequent Changes in Their Boundaries*. Berkeley: California Historical Survey Commission, 1923.

Cummings, G. A., and E. S. Pladwell. *Oakland: A History*. Oakland: Grant D. Miller Mortuaries, 1942.

Daggett, Stuart. *Chapters on the History of the Southern Pacific*. New York: Ronald Press, 1922.

Davidson, George. *The Discovery of San Francisco Bay . . .* San Francisco, 1907. Transactions and Proceedings of the Geographical Society of the Pacific, Vol. IV, Ser. II. San Francisco, 1907.

Davis, William Heath. *Seventy-five Years in California*. San Francisco: John Howell, 1929.

Dawson, Nicholas "Cheyenne." *Overland to California in '41 and '49, and Texas in '51*. San Francisco: Grabhorn, 1933.

De Roos, Robert. *The Thirsty Land: The Story of the Central Valley Project*. Stanford: Stanford University Press, 1948.

Eldredge, Zoeth Skinner. *The Beginnings of San Francisco*. 2 vols. San Francisco: Published by the author, 1912.

—— *The March of Portola and the Log of the San Carlos*. San Francisco: California Promotion Committee, 1909.

Elliott, Orrin Leslie. *Stanford University: The First Twenty-five Years*. Stanford: Stanford University Press, 1937.

Engelhardt, Fr. Zephyrin. *The Missions and Missionaries of California*. Vol. II, Upper California, Part I, General History. San Francisco: James H. Barry, 1912.

Ferrier, William Warren. *Berkeley, California: The Story of the Evolution of a Hamlet into a City of Culture and Commerce*. Berkeley: Published by the author, 1933.

Finley, Ernest Latimer (ed.). *History of Sonoma County, California, Its People and Its Resources*. Santa Rosa: Press Democrat Publishing Co., 1937.

Freeman, John R. *On the Proposed Use of a Portion of the Hetch Hetchy, Eleanor and Cherry Valleys Within and near to the Boundaries of the Stanislaus U. S. National Forest Reserve and the Yosemite National Park as Reservoirs for Impounding Tuolumne River Flood Waters and Appurtenant Works for the Water Supply of San Francisco, California, and Neighboring Cities*. San Francisco: Published by Authority of the Board of Supervisors, 1912.

Giffen, Guy, and Helen Giffen. *The Story of Golden Gate Park*. San Francisco: Published by the authors, 1949.

Goodwin, Cardinal. *The Establishment of State Government in California, 1846–1850*. New York: Macmillan, 1914.

Gregory, Thomas J., and others. *History of Sonoma County, California . . .* Los Angeles: Historic Record Company, 1911.

Hall, Frederick. *The History of San Jose and Surroundings*. San Francisco, 1871.

Halley, William. *The Centennial Year Book of Alameda County, California*. Oakland, 1876.

Harlow, Neal. *The Maps of San Francisco Bay from the Spanish Discovery in 1769 to the American Occupation*. San Francisco: Book Club of California, 1950.

Hayler, Guy Wilfrid. *The San Francisco Bay Region of the Future: What the Great Regional Plan Means*. San Francisco, 1926. (Reprinted from the *Daily Commercial News Annual*, 1926.)

Heath, Erle. *Seventy-five Years of Progress: Historical Sketch of the Southern Pacific*. San Francisco: Southern Pacific Bureau of News, 1945.

Hegemann, Werner. *Report on a City Plan for the Municipalities of Oakland and Berkeley. . . .* [Oakland], 1915.

Hinkel, Edgar J., and William E. McCann (eds.). *Oakland 1852–1938: Some Phases of the Social, Political and Economic History of Oakland, California*. 2 vols. Oakland: Oakland Public Library, 1939. (A Works Progress Administration project.) (Mimeographed.)

Hittell, John Shertzer. *The Prospects of Vallejo; or, Evidences That Vallejo Will Become a Great City: A Re-Publication of a Series of Articles First Printed in the Vallejo* Evening Chronicle, *from March to July, 1871*. Vallejo, 1871.

Holterhoff, G., Jr. *Historical Review of the Atchison, Topeka and Santa Fe Railway Company (with Particular Reference to California Lines) as Furnished to the Railroad Commission of the State of California in Compliance with Its General Order No. 38*. Los Angeles, 1914.

Hulaniski, F. J. (ed.). *The History of Contra Costa County, California*. Berkeley: Elms Publishing Co., 1917.

Hunt, Marguerite, and Harry Lawrence Gunn. *History of Solano County . . . and Napa County, California . . .* Chicago: S. J. Clarke Publishing Co., 1926.

Hunt, Rockwell D., and Nellie van de Grift Sanchez. *A Short History of California*. New York: Thomas Y. Crowell, 1929.

Irwin, William Henry. *The City That Was: A Requiem of Old San Francisco*. New York: B. W. Huebsch, 1906.

James, William F., and George H. McMurray. *History of San Jose, California, Narrative and Biographical*. San Jose: A. H. Cawston, 1938.

Jennings, Rufus P. *Statement of Rufus P. Jennings, Executive Officer of the California Promotion Committee, at a Meeting Held April 4, 1905*. San Francisco: California Promotion Committee, 1905.

Langley, Henry G. (comp.). *The San Francisco Directory for the Year Commencing September, 1862*. San Francisco, 1862.

Langsdorff, G. H. von. *Voyages and Travels in Various Parts of the World During the Years 1803, 1804, 1805, 1806, and 1807*. London, 1813.

Lewis, Oscar. *Within the Golden Gate*. San Francisco: San Francisco Bay Area Council, 1945.

McEntire, Davis, and others. *The Population of California: A Report of a Research Study Made by Authorization of the Board of Governors of the Commonwealth Club of California*. San Francisco: Commonwealth Club of California, 1946.

McKittrick, Myrtle M. *Vallejo, Son of California*. Portland, Oregon: Binfords & Mort, 1944.

Marshall, James. *Santa Fe, the Railroad That Built an Empire*. New York: Random House, 1945.

Maybeck, Bernard R. *Palace of Fine Arts and Lagoon, Panama-Pacific International Exposition, 1915*. San Francisco: Paul Elder, 1915.

Merritt, Frank Clinton. *History of Alameda County, California . . .* 2 vols. Chicago: S. J. Clarke Publishing Co., 1928.

Moore, Charles. *Daniel H. Burnham, Architect, Planner of Cities*.

2 vols. Boston: Houghton Mifflin, 1921.

Mount Gregory Water and Mining Company. *Water Supply for San Francisco, Oakland, Vallejo, Sacramento, and Other Places.* Oakland, 1874.

Munro-Fraser. *History of Alameda County, California* . . . Oakland: M. W. Wood, 1883.

────── *History of Contra Costa County, California* . . . San Francisco: W. A. Slocum & Co., 1882.

────── *History of Marin County, California* . . . San Francisco: Alley, Bowen & Co., 1880.

────── *History of Santa Clara County, California* . . . San Francisco: Alley, Bowen & Co., 1881.

────── *History of Sonoma County* . . . San Francisco: Alley, Bowen & Co., 1880.

Murphy, Celeste G. *The People of the Pueblo: The Story of Sonoma.* Sonoma: W. L. and C. G. Murphy, 1937.

Oakland Daily Transcript. *Information Concerning the Terminus of the Railroad System of the Pacific Coast.* Oakland, 1871.

Ogden, Adele. *The California Sea Otter Trade, 1784–1848.* Berkeley and Los Angeles: University of California Press, 1941.

Olmsted, Frederick Law. *Berkeley Neighborhood: Report upon a Projected Improvement of the Estate of the College of California at Berkeley, near Oakland.* New York, 1866.

────── *Preliminary Report in Regard to a Plan of Public Pleasure Grounds for the City of San Francisco.* New York, 1866.

O'Shaughnessy, Michael M. *Hetch-Hetchy—Its Origin and History.* San Francisco: M. M. O'Shaughnessy, 1934.

Pacific Gas and Electric Company. *Pacific Gas and Electric Company—History, Facilities, Service.* San Francisco, 1936.

Palmer, Lyman L. *History of Napa and Lake Counties, California* . . . San Francisco: Slocum, Bowen & Co., 1881.

Palóu, Francisco. *Palóu's Life of Fray Junípero Serra.* Translated and annotated by Maynard J. Geiger, O.F.M. Washington, D.C.: Academy of American Franciscan History, 1955.

Peralta Associates and Vernon J. Sappers. *From Shore to Shore: The Key Route.* Oakland: Peralta Associates, 1948.

Purcell, Mae Fisher. *History of Contra Costa County, California.* Berkeley: Gillick Press, 1940.

Quiett, Glenn Chesney. *They Built the West: An Epic of Rails and Cities.* New York: Appleton-Century, 1934.

Reed, Albert S. *The San Francisco Conflagration of April, 1906.* New York: National Board of Fire Underwriters, 1906.

Robinson, Charles Mulford. *A Plan of Civic Improvement for the City of Oakland, California.* Oakland: Oakland Enquirer Publishing Co., 1906.

Robinson, W. W. *Land in California.* Berkeley and Los Angeles: University of California Press, 1948.

San Francisco Morning Call. *Fettered Commerce—How the Pacific Mail and the Railroads Have Bled San Francisco. A Series of Articles Reprinted from the San Francisco Morning Call.* San Francisco, 1892.

San Francisco Theatre Research [W.P.A.] Project. Edited by Lawrence Estevan. *The History of Opera in San Francisco.* Monograph XVIII, Pt. II. [First Series.] San Francisco, 1938.

San Francisco Water Company. *Reports of Engineers and Others on a Permanent Supply of Pure Fresh Water to the City of San Francisco.* San Francisco, 1872.

Santa Clara County and Its Resources: A Souvenir of the San Jose Mercury. San Jose, 1895.

Sherman, William T. *Memoirs of General William T. Sherman.* 2 vols. New York, 1875.

Shugg, Roger W., and H. A. DeWeerd. *World War II: A Concise History.* Washington: The Infantry Journal, 1946.

Soulé, Frank, John H. Gihon, and James Nisbet. *The Annals of San Francisco* . . . New York, 1855.

Souvenir of Golden Gate Park: Rehabilitation Edition of the Golden Gate Park News. San Francisco: Golden Gate Park News Company, 1907.

Stanger, Frank M. *History of San Mateo County, California.* San Mateo: Arthur H. Cawston, 1938.

Steele, Rufus. *The City That Is: The Story of the Rebuilding of San Francisco in Three Years.* San Francisco: A. M. Robertson, 1909.

Thompson, Frank R. *Electric Transportation.* Scranton, Pa.: International Textbook Co., 1940.

Todd, Frank Morton. *The Story of the Exposition . . . Official History of the International Celebration Held at San Francisco in 1915* . . . 5 vols. New York and London: Putnam, 1921.

Tunnard, Christopher. *The City of Man.* New York: Scribner, 1953.

Vancouver, George. *A Voyage of Discovery to the North Pacific Ocean and Round the World . . . in the Years 1790, 1791, 1792, 1793, 1794, and 1795 . . .* 6 vols. London, 1801.

Vigness, Paul G. *Alameda Community Book.* Alameda: A. H. Cawston, 1952.

Wagner, H. Howe. *Mount Tamalpais State Park, Marin County.* California Historical Survey Series—Historic Landmarks, Monuments and State Parks. Edited by Clark Wing. [Sacramento, 1941.] (W.P.A. Project 665-08-3-147, sponsored by State of California Department of Natural Resources, Division of Parks.)

Walker, Robert A. *The Planning Function in Urban Government.* 2d ed. Chicago: University of Chicago Press, 1950.

Wheat, Carl I. *The Maps of the California Gold Region, 1848–1857: A Biblio-Cartography of an Important Decade.* San Francisco: Grabhorn, 1942.

Whitnah, Joseph C. *A History of Richmond, California.* Richmond: Richmond Chamber of Commerce, 1944.

Willey, Samuel H. *A History of the College of California.* San Francisco, 1887.

Winn, W. B. *Souvenir of Marin County, California.* San Rafael, 1893.

Winther, Oscar Osburn. *The Story of San Jose, California's First Pueblo, 1777–1869.* San Francisco: California Historical Society, 1935.

Wood, Dallas E. *History of Palo Alto.* Palo Alto: Arthur H. Cawston, 1939.

Writers Program of the Work Projects Administration in Northern California. *Berkeley: The First Seventy-five Years.* Berkeley: Gillick Press, 1941.

Young, John P. *San Francisco: A History of the Pacific Coast Metropolis.* 2 vols. San Francisco and Chicago: S. J. Clarke Publishing Co., 1912.

ARTICLES

Bauer, Catherine. "Outline of War Housing," *Task*, 1943 [?].

Bowman, Jacob N. "Weights and Measures of Provincial California," *California Historical Society Quarterly*, XXX (December, 1951), 315–338.

Bradley, La Verne. "San Francisco: Gibraltar of the West Coast,"

National Geographic Magazine, LXXXIII (March, 1943), 279–308.

Cheney, Charles Henry. "How California Communities Can Profit by Active City Planning," *Pacific Municipalities,* XXVIII (January, 1914), 31–35.

Douglas, J. R. "The City-Planning Movement in Berkeley," *Berkeley Civic Bulletin,* Aug. 22, 1916, pp. 2–5.

Greene, B. D. M. "Legal Aspect of the Zone Ordinance," *Berkeley Civic Bulletin,* Aug. 22, 1916, pp. 5 and 9.

Heizer, Robert F. "Indians of the San Francisco Bay Area," in *Geologic Guidebook of the San Francisco Bay Counties,* California Department of Natural Resources, Division of Mines, Bulletin 154, pp. 39–56. San Francisco, 1951.

Jenkins, Dorothy G. "Opening of the Golden Gate," in *Geologic Guidebook of the San Francisco Bay Counties,* California Department of Natural Resources, Division of Mines, Bulletin 154, pp. 11–29. San Francisco, 1951.

Lee, Charles H. "The Future Development of the Metropolitan Area Surrounding San Francisco Bay," *Bulletin of the Seismological Society of America,* XVI (June, 1926), 81–132.

Louderback, George D. "Geologic History of San Francisco Bay," in *Geologic Guidebook of the San Francisco Bay Counties,* California Department of Natural Resources, Division of Mines, Bulletin 154, pp. 75–92. San Francisco, 1951.

Luten, Daniel. "Progress Against Growth," *Sierra Club Bulletin,* June, 1972, pp. 22–24.

Macdonald, A. S. "The Beginnings of Richmond," *Bank News,* October, 1916, pp. 1–3. (Publication of First National Bank and Richmond Savings Bank, Richmond, Calif.)

McDuffie, Duncan. "City Planning in Berkeley," *Berkeley Civic Bulletin,* March 15, 1916, p. 108.

"Oakland's Municipal Airport," *Western City,* May, 1930, pp. 25–27.

Perkstein, Joel T. "Substantive Enforcement of the California EQA," *California Law Review,* Vol. 69 (January, 1981), pp. 112–188.

Phelan, James D. "Historical Sketch of San Francisco," in Daniel H. Burnham and Edward H. Bennett, *Report on a Plan for San Francisco,* ed. Edward F. O'Day. San Francisco, 1905.

Planning and Conservation League. 1983 Annual Report, "CEQA Under Attack," *California Today,* Vol. 14 (January/February, 1984), pp. 1, 4.

San Francisco Downtown Association. "Bay Area Gets Huge Defense Orders," *The Downtowner,* Nov. 20, 1940, p. [2].

——— "Bay Area Shipbuilding," *The Downtowner,* Dec. 26, 1940, p. [4].

Skeggs, John H. "The Bayshore Highway Dedication," *California Highways and Public Works,* November, 1929, pp. 9–10, 26.

Upton, M. G. "The Plan of San Francisco," *Overland Monthly,* II (February, 1869), 131–137.

NEWSPAPERS AND PERIODICALS

Benicia *Herald,* 1909, 1910, 1912.

Berkeley *Daily Gazette,* 1913, 1952.

California Real Estate Magazine, VII (February–December, 1927).

Commonwealth Club of California, *Transactions,* Vol. VII (1912), IX (1915), XI (1917), XII (1918), XVI (1921), XVII (1922), XVIII (1923), XIX (1924), XX (1925), XXIV (1929), XXVI (1931).

Contra Costa Gazette, 1913, 1914.

The Golden Era (San Francisco) June 5–October 9, 1853.

Oakland Chamber of Commerce *Bulletin.* Vols. I (1910), II (1911), III (1912), V (1914).

Oakland *Enquirer,* 1906, 1907.

Oakland *Times,* 1906.

Oakland *Tribune,* 1906, 1907, 1910, 1912, 1913, 1914.

Palo Alto *Times,* 1949, 1950, 1951.

Richmond *Independent,* 1928, 1939, 1954; Civic Center edition, Sept. 15, 1959.

San Francisco *Bulletin,* 1906, 1909, 1912.

San Francisco Business, June 3, Aug. 5, 1931.

San Francisco *Call,* 1909, 1911, 1915.

San Francisco Chamber of Commerce *Journal,* I, Nos. 8, 9 (June, July, 1912).

San Francisco *Chronicle,* 1906, 1909, 1910, 1912, 1913, 1924, 1932, 1937, 1942, 1943, 1949–1958.

San Francisco *Chronicle.* "Special Report: Contra Costapolis." Series of articles appearing January 9–12, 1984.

San Francisco *Examiner,* 1909, 1924.

San Jose *Herald,* 1912, 1913.

San Jose *Mercury-Herald,* 1917, 1920, 1929.

Sausalito *News,* Souvenir edition, Feb. 27, 1941. Article: "Farewell to Northwestern Pacific Railroad Interurban Train-Ferry Service."

Vallejo *Times-Herald,* Sept. 16, 1954.

MAPS

Map of the City of Benicia Founded by Mariano G. Vallejo, Thomas O. Larkin & Robert Semple, 1847. Surveyed and drawn by Benjamin W. Barlow. San Francisco: Britton & Rey, [185–?]

Map of Holly Oak Park, Part of Suscol Rancho, Napa County. San Francisco: Britton & Rey, 1869. (Lots to be sold at auction by Maurice Dore & Co.)

Index